THE PHOTIAN SCHISM

HISTORY AND LEGEND

THE PHOTIAN SCHISM

HISTORY AND LEGEND

BY

FRANCIS DVORNIK

D.D., D.-ès-Lettres (Sorbonne), Hon. D.Lit. (London)
Corresponding Fellow of the British Academy

Associate of the Royal Academy of Belgium, Hon. Member of
the Royal Academy of Rumania, Member of the Czech
Academy and of the Slavonic Institute, Professor
in Charles IV University

CAMBRIDGE
AT THE UNIVERSITY PRESS
1948

Printed in Great Britain at the University Press, Cambridge
(Brooke Crutchley, University Printer)
and published by the Cambridge University Press
(Cambridge, and Bentley House, London)

Agents for U.S.A., Canada, and India: Macmillan

CONTENTS

vii

CONTENTS

ix

CONTENTS

PREFACE

The personality of the Patriarch Photius has attracted the attention of almost all Church historians ever since the Reformation, and their verdict has in most cases been unfavourable. This traditional view was confirmed by the researches of J. Hergenröther in the second half of the nineteenth century, and it was generally agreed that his judgement was based on sound historical evidence. When in 1895 the French Jesuit A. Lapôtre ventured to propose a few exonerating circumstances to mitigate the indictment, his voice failed to carry weight and his plea was rejected by many as being too daring. However, the great advances in Byzantine studies in the first decades of the twentieth century tended to modify this unfavourable opinion, though not to any considerable extent. Even that great and critical Byzantinist, J. B. Bury, after making a promising start towards a revision of the conventional estimate of the Patriarch, was unable to dispose of the formidable array of arguments advanced by the Western historians against him. The same may be said about the French Church historian E. Amann, though he was on the whole on the right way to a solution.

Ever since I began to study the many problems arising from the chequered history of the ninth century in East and West, especially the lives and works of the Slavonic apostles SS. Constantine-Cyril and Methodius, I gradually realized that the history of the unfortunate Patriarch required to be rewritten and that the documents on which his condemnation was based demanded thorough revision. As soon as I had completed my study of the two Greek founders of Slavonic letters I proceeded to examine the Collection of anti-Photian documents and pamphlets. Being the work of contemporary writers, and undoubtedly authentic, they had been used as an incontrovertible *dossier* against Photius. The first result of my researches was the discovery that the sources on which the history of the second schism was based were valueless, and that whatever had been written about a second rupture between Photius and Rome was not only inaccurate, but pure mystification (*Byzantion*, vol. VIII, 1933). This finding was confirmed to a certain extent by V. Grumel, who, in a study published in the *Revue des Sciences Philosophiques et Théologiques* (vol. XII, 1933), came independently to a similar conclusion.

But other problems remained unsolved, one of them being the oecumenicity of the Ignatian synod (869–70) in Western medieval tradition. Moreover, it would have been impossible to reassess Photius' character and career unless it were first made clear how the primitive Photian tradition came to be forgotten in the West and obscured in the East. This tradition was easily reconstructed when once the trustworthiness of the Photian Collection had been seriously challenged. I accordingly began to trace in detail the development of what may be called the Photian Legend in the Middle Ages.

As the results of my researches clashed with conventional opinion, I made a point of communicating them to the specialists in Byzantine history at the last two international congresses of Byzantine studies at Sofia in 1934 and at Rome in 1936. In 1938 I summarized some of my researches in a lecture at the Royal Academy of Brussels, and Professor H. Grégoire, of the University of Brussels, who had been kept informed of the progress of my work, did the same at the Academy of Athens. Furthermore, in order to afford experts and Church authorities every opportunity to check my arguments I published the main results of my inquiry in various periodicals. The present work embodies those studies, with the addition of more evidence and the necessary historical setting.

It had been my original intention to publish in a separate volume some relevant documents, chiefly bearing on the Latin and Greek conciliar tradition; but present difficulties interfered with the project and forced me to limit myself to short quotations from the most important manuscript sources. The same reasons prevented me from completing my researches in the manuscript departments of important European libraries. I particularly regret that a prolonged stay in Rome, where I intended to consult some specialists and complete my study of Greek and Latin manuscripts in the Vatican Library, as had been planned in 1939, was made impossible by political events. I trust, however, that the evidence I was able to gather before 1939, incomplete as it is in some details, is amply sufficient to substantiate my statements.

I am therefore well aware of the deficiencies in the present work, but the times have been hard on writers, and in order not to tax the reader's patience I have restricted myself to such facts as I deemed essential. If the narrative be considered too long at times, historians who know the difficulty of eradicating century-old legends will recognize the necessity of elaborating certain points that may seem obvious to others.

This book was originally written in French, and my first intention was to publish it in the *Corpus Bruxellense*, as was announced in *Byzantion* (vol. XIV, 1939) by Professor H. Grégoire. He took the MS.

to Paris a week before the invasion of Belgium and I brought it safely to London, where it was rewritten in English.

The work was completed under trying circumstances, and I should like to express my gratitude to all who helped me to bring my researches to a satisfactory conclusion. I am grateful to my colleagues of the Charles IV University, who granted me special leave in June 1938 to prosecute my research work. When after the occupation of my country I declined to return to my post, losing both salary and government grant, I found hospitality at St George's Cathedral House, then administered by my friend Father J. J. Farrell, with the kind permission of His Grace the Archbishop P. Amigo; and again in 1940, after the collapse of France.

The French Government also offered me in 1939, for the purpose of facilitating my research work, the post of Chargé des Recherches, and the professors of the Collège de France elected me, on the advice of Professor André Mazon and G. Millet, to the Schlumberger Lectureship for 1940. The École des Hautes Études, on the suggestion of Charles Diehl and G. Millet, invited me to lecture on Early Christian and Byzantine History and Literature.

In preparing the English text of my work I was greatly assisted by the Rev. A. Gille, who also kindly undertook the compilation of the index. I am indebted to the Syndics of the Cambridge University Press, who agreed to publish my work in spite of the difficulties that hamper the publishing of scholarly books in these days, and I have been happy in the aid that I have received from Mr S. C. Roberts, who personally undertook to revise the manuscript in the matter of language and style.

In the course of my researches I received encouragement and valuable advice from several competent scholars, especially from Professor H. Grégoire, from the Bollandists P. Peeters and the late H. Delehaye. I am especially grateful to Professor Norman H. Baynes, who read the manuscript and gave me invaluable advice on many matters. I was most courteously treated in all the libraries where I worked, particularly in the MSS. Department of the Bibliothèque Nationale in Paris, at the Vatican, in Brussels, Prague and in Vienna. I must specially thank the Superintendents and Staff of the Reading Room at the British Museum, where the greater part of this book was written.

I am dedicating this work to the memory of my illustrious teacher, Professor Charles Diehl, who took a personal interest in the progress of my researches, encouraged me never to be deterred by the difficulty of finding and telling the whole historical truth, and gave invaluable advice on many details. He accepted the dedication shortly before his death. It is my tribute to the memory of a great teacher, a distinguished Byzantine scholar and a trusted friend, who towards the close of his life offered his students and admirers a noble example in bearing the greatest misfortune that could befall a scholar—blindness—with Christian fortitude and patience.

F. DVORNIK

LONDON, VINCENT HOUSE

August 15, 1947

Part I. *History*

CHAPTER I

POLITICAL PARTIES, RELIGIOUS PROBLEMS AND OPENING CONFLICT

Introduction: Photius' case—Political and religious parties in Byzantium—Extremists and Moderates in Irene's and Nicephorus' reigns—Moderate policy of Methodius and the Studite Schism—Was Ignatius appointed or elected?—When and why Gregory Asbestas, leader of the Moderates, was condemned by Ignatius—Gregory's appeal to Rome and the Holy See's attitude—Extremist and Moderate intrigues.

FEW names in the history of Christianity have inspired feelings so conflicting as that of the Greek Patriarch Photius. Saint and hero in the eyes of the Christian East, he is branded by the Christian West as the man who unbolted the safeguards of unity and let loose the disruptive forces of dissent and schism. Whilst the East invokes his name as one that carries weight with God, the West still quotes it as the symbol of pride and lust for ecclesiastical domination; hailed by all who ever claimed a larger share for nationalism in the life of the Church and a closer association between man and God, it is reprobated by others as the badge of disruption and an element destructive of Christian universality.

Photius is stated to have inspired Luther, Calvin, Melanchthon and other famous reformers in launching their campaigns against the Papacy and its authority; and yet, Orthodoxy disowned their main doctrines for being at variance with the tradition of the early Eastern Fathers, and to these Photius was the last living witness. For centuries he has stood as a sign of contradiction, a symbol of disunion, a challenge that still keeps apart the Western and Eastern fragments of Christendom.

But his influence and personality are not confined to the religious field, for since the Renaissance philosophers and philologists have venerated him as the genius who among others was instrumental in transmitting to later generations through the Byzantine period classical Greek and Hellenistic culture. A man of his stature deserves a study and the significance of his memory to the living minds of East and West makes such a study all the more timely and urgent.

The very discordance of the contradictory estimates of the character and activities of this enigmatic Greek would call for a revision of the judgement of history for, despite centuries of tradition, championship and abuse, both views cannot be right, however sincere they claim to be. It is then the historian's duty to reopen the case, reduce the jarring verdicts to their just proportions, confront the witnesses, and if there has been miscarriage of justice, to rehabilitate the defendant in the eyes of posterity.

But before proceeding with the case, it will be necessary to state it, give a rough outline of the background of Photius' life, and summarize the judgements pronounced so far on his activities and character. Only then can we call in the witnesses and examine their statements.

Photius' name stands at the very centre of the history of the ninth century, one of the most brilliant periods in Byzantine records, when Byzantium stood at the close of a transformation inaugurated at the beginning of the eighth century by the Isaurian dynasty and characterized by the influx of oriental ideas. Of this transformation, iconoclasm was the most notorious symptom. The final restoration of ikon worship, which took place in 843, embodied the vigorous reaction of the Greek spirit against the invasion of novelties and the reaction achieved its object: the two elements that had been at variance for over a century, the Eastern and the Hellenic, at length brought together into common action the two main and equally important factors of Byzantine civilization. From that moment onward, their harmonious combination led to the happiest results: Byzantium knew a renaissance that spread from the intellectual to the political arena, and national sentiment sufficiently asserted itself to claim preponderance in Byzantium's relations with other powers—the Mussulman and Latin worlds.

Of this intellectual renaissance, the central figure was incontestably the Patriarch Photius. The extent of his learning amazed his contemporaries and commanded the respect of his bitterest enemies. He was the scion of a noble Byzantine family of ancient Greek stock and related to the Macedonian dynasty. His father, who had suffered persecution for his fidelity to the cult of images, was held in great veneration among the faithful. A favourite at the imperial court, Photius commanded, if not the love, certainly the esteem of many rival personalities—the Empress Theodora, the Logothete Theoktistos, and the young Emperor's uncle Bardas; and it was his scholarly reputation that raised to such a high standard the institute of learning in Constantinople which was equivalent to a University. His literary *salon*, where classical literature, the Byzantines' favourite study, supplied the most popular topics of debate, attracted everybody of note in the Byzantine intellectual world.

But Photius lived in too stormy a period to confine his activities to the literary field. Years of theological controversy had created an explosive atmosphere and driven sensitive minds to the borders of religious fanaticism, while the persecutions of the iconoclastic period had bitten deep into the Church's soul. Memories were still fresh; the victors were still jubilant over the turn of events in their favour and the defeated iconoclasts bitter about their collapse and hoping against hope for better days. Two Patriarchs had already been dealing with a situation of the utmost delicacy, St Methodius (843–7) and St Ignatius, both remarkable men, who knew by experience what it meant to suffer for one's beliefs. St Methodius was not very successful in steering clear of the shallows; a new schism arose out of the radical elements which claimed the monks of the monastery of Studion as their leaders, and the saintly Patriarch died without the satisfaction of healing the rift. His successor, the Patriarch Ignatius, whose personality appealed more to the radical monks, succeeded in healing the schism, but not without provoking a strong reaction among ideological opponents. Political intrigues stirred up dissension between the party of the Empress and that of her brother Bardas in league with the young Emperor Michael III and brought the Patriarch with his followers into sharp conflict with the government (858).

At this juncture, Photius, who at the time held the important office of President of the Imperial Chancellery, was selected to succeed Ignatius. Photius, following the example of his uncle Tarasius (784–806), who had similarly relinquished the same duties in the imperial service to devote his energies to the government of the Church, accepted the appointment. This opened the chapter in Eastern Church history which was to assume such disproportionate importance and is still read by many as the blackest in the annals of Christendom.

Photius' patriarchal activities met with strong opposition and his enemies had the advantage of painting him in such malevolent colours that they left him with a name blackened for centuries. In the picture painted by his enemies, he was unscrupulous and so covetous of patriarchal honours that he conspired with the government of Michael III and Bardas to overthrow Theodora; he offered himself as a tool for the riddance of the Patriarch Ignatius, whose sole fault had been to castigate

Bardas for immoral conduct. When Ignatius refused to abdicate, Photius seized his throne and let loose upon the unfortunate Ignatius and his followers a merciless persecution.

Blinded (so it is alleged) by pride and lust for power, Photius tried to obtain recognition from Nicholas I by misrepresenting the circumstances of his installation in Constantinople, but the Pope, duly informed by Ignatius' envoys of the true state of things, refused to recognize a Patriarch who had raised himself to the dignity in total disregard of canonical precedent. Photius, without taking any notice of the sentence, summoned a synod of the Eastern Church, deposed the Pope and created the 'first great Schism'. Not until the pious Emperor Basil I had murdered the iniquitous Emperor Michael III, whose reign was execrated by the whole of Byzantium, did Photius receive his punishment; then he was dethroned and solemnly condemned by the Eighth Oecumenical Council (869–70), that favourite source in the medieval canonical legislation of the West. But Photius insinuated himself once more into the Emperor's favour and, after Ignatius' death, reoccupied the patriarchal throne; to make sure this time of papal approval, he deceived the Pope, who was willing on certain conditions to show leniency, by falsifying his letters and also those sent by the Pope to the Emperor and the Fathers of a Council summoned to examine his case. He bribed the legates sent by the Pope and tampered with the Acts of the Council. When John VIII learned that he had been hoodwinked by the astute Greek, he forthwith excommunicated him. Hence arose the second schism, which was to last till the end of the ninth century and to cast its shadow over the tenth; finally there came the great rupture of 1054 between East and West, the rift that has withstood all attempts at healing and has been such a disaster to Christendom.

This was the kind of picture which many of the contemporary sources drew of Photius' ecclesiastical career and it is the picture that has generally been accepted as authentic in the West. So overwhelmingly did the evidence produced by those witnesses strike the imagination that even the easterners were impressed, and had it not been for the tradition of their Church which from the earliest beginning had venerated the memory of 'the saintly Patriarch' and uncompromisingly disowned the Eighth Council that had condemned him, they might have accepted the conclusions which the Western Church historians drew from documents whose authenticity seemed to be beyond dispute.

Such is the position which faces every student of this fascinating and intricate period of Byzantine and ecclesiastical history. Amid facts and valuations so perplexing, how is one to judge a man who is venerated as a saint by some, while others class him among the reprobates? It will thus be our task to unravel amongst those contradictory estimates what can be established as historical truth and to find out whether a legend did not grow round this great figure to mystify the Christian world and belittle a prelate who deserved a better memory. To this end, we cannot rest content with an examination of contemporary documents. We must follow up the tradition which, right through the Middle Ages down to modern times, has grown round the name of Photius in West and East; we must analyse the elements which in successive periods helped to obscure the facts as revealed by contemporary writings and to create the legend.

One problem directly concerns the history and legend of Photius. It is a serious matter that there should be a discrepancy in the computation of the first Oecumenical Councils which define the principles of the Christian faith, the Eastern Churches counting only seven Councils where the West numbers eight. The explanation will be found, once the Photian case has been settled, when we turn to a class of documents which historians have so far neglected, the Collections of Western canon law drawn up between the tenth and twelfth centuries, most of which are still unpublished.

The Photian case is not merely a matter of Byzantine interest. It concerns the history of Christianity and of the world, as the appraisement of Photius and his work lies at the core of the controversies that separate the Eastern and the Western Churches. We must therefore proceed warily and make sure of each step before we can fix the responsibility of circumstances and men concerned in the birth and growth of the Photian legend.

Anybody who takes the trouble to read the writings of Photius' chief opponents, especially of the abbot Theognostos, the archbishops Stylianos and Metrophanes, the author of the *Vita Ignatii*, believed to be Nicetas of Paphlagonia, and the remarks of the anonymous author of the anti-Photian Collection, will be struck by the virulence of their tone, obviously inspired by hate, and unaccountable on the current assumption of purely religious fervour. Its political bias is only too evident under its thin camouflage of religious and moral considerations. These writings show all the characteristics of politico-religious pamphleteering and are the unmistakable product of the existence in Byzantium in Photius' days of two powerful hostile clans which were competing for supreme control over Church and State.[1] The existence of these two currents of opinion and temperament can no longer be denied. The whole of Byzantium was towards the end of the eighth century split into two great parties, whose constant rivalry enlivened their politics as well as their religion; each aspired to monopolize the management of the Church and the Empire.

This same antagonism was likewise a leading factor in the conflict between Ignatius and Photius and provides the key to the inner meaning of the fateful clash within the Byzantine Church and of the rupture between Eastern and Western Christendom at the period. But if we try to examine the original meaning of this division in Byzantine society, we are driven to the conclusion that the reason for its existence will not be found at this particular stage. Not even the iconoclastic interval could be selected as a possible starting-point of this evolution, since similar symptoms are discovered at earlier stages, when Byzantium was rent by clashes between orthodox and heretics. Party spirit runs through the whole skein of Byzantine history like a thread which should be followed up to the very dawn of the Empire, if one wishes to get at its true meaning and its many implications. It would steer us back to some venerable institutions of old Rome which were transferred to Byzantium, where in a Hellenistic atmosphere impregnated by Christian ideas they took shapes which citizens of the Roman Republic would never have recognized. We should then find that Byzantine partisanship grew out of the Old Roman Circus parties of the Blues, the Greens, the Reds and the Whites.

But such a study would lead us too far astray.[2] The part played by the Blues and the Greens in particular in Byzantine history from its earliest years till the reign of Heraclius is not yet fully known and many problems still await a solution; yet one thing is certain, the religious evolution of Byzantium and of the whole East is inseparably bound up

[1] This fact has forcibly caught my attention ever since I started inquiring into the history of the ninth century; and on one occasion I labelled the two rival parties, strange as it may sound to some ears, as respectively Liberals or Moderates on the one hand, Reactionaries, Radicals and Die-hards on the other. Cf. my lecture 'De Sancto Cyrillo et Methodio in Luce Historiae Byzantinae', read in 1927 at the Fifth Congress for Church Union (*Acta V. Conventus Unionistici Velehradensis* (Olomouc, 1927), pp. 149 seq.).

[2] I have summed up all that is known of the Byzantine partisanship that grew out of the Old Roman Circus parties in a short study, where the bibliography that matters will also be found—'The Circus Parties in Byzantium, their Evolution and Suppression', published in *Byzantina-Metabyzantina*, Symposium in honour of Prof. H. Grégoire and E. Honigmann (New York, 1946), vol. I, pp. 119–33.

with the rivalry between the foremost Circus parties of the Greens and the Blues. They grew to be a factor of paramount importance in the political and religious life of the Empire.

The part they played in the theological discussions on the doctrine of the Blessed Trinity and on the nature of the Divine Saviour finds its explanation in the peculiar character of Eastern Church organization and mentality. Eastern Christianity was erected on a national basis,[1] which gave the average faithful active participation in the divine service and Church life and facilities to give their opinion on even the subtlest points of theology. Popular organizations such as the Blues and the Greens thus offered themselves as rallying centres for champions of doctrines true or false to help them in their respective activities.[2] Be it enough to observe here that in nearly every encounter they ranged themselves on opposite sides as a matter of course, the Greens mostly favouring the heretical tenets and the Blues championing Orthodoxy. This division was strongly marked in the Monophysite conflicts.[3]

It was Heraclius who put an end to activities that so often placed the Empire in the greatest peril. But even after his administrative reforms, the two currents—one more liberal and moderate, the other more conservative and reactionary—continued to run side by side. We can trace them in the history of the struggle for and against image worship. In the policy of the Emperors of the Isaurian dynasty who favoured iconoclasm and in the resistance offered by the orthodox there were

---

[1] Cf. my booklet, *National Churches and the Church Universal* (London, 1944), pp. 5–18.

[2] An interesting instance of Christian influence on the evolution of Byzantine political institutions. It is paralleled by a similar influence on the Byzantine senate which acquired more rights than it enjoyed in imperial Rome. This was due to the growing prestige of the Oecumenical Councils, which had been modelled on the Roman Senate. Cf. the author's study, 'De Potestate Civili in Conciliis Oecumenicis, Acta VI Congressus pro Unione Ecclesiarum', in *Academia Velehradensis* (Olomouc, 1930), vol. X. An English translation of the lecture appeared in the review *The Christian East* (1932), vol. XIV, pp. 95–108. A masterly *exposé* of Byzantine political institutions will be found in N. Baynes' book, *The Byzantine Empire* (London, 1925), especially on pp. 5 sq., 114 sq. Cf. also J. B. Bury's *The Constitution of the Later Roman Empire* (Cambridge, 1910).

[3] See the short account of the parties' attitude in religious matters in my study, 'Circus Parties in Byzantium', loc. cit., and in G. Manojlović's study, re-edited with additions and corrections in a French translation by H. Grégoire under the title 'Le Peuple de Constantinople', in *Byzantion* (1936), vol. XI, pp. 655–65. A more detailed study is found in Gerazim Yared's 'Otzuivui sovremennikov o sv. Fotiye Patr. Konst. v svyazi s istoriyeu politicheskikh Partii v imperii', *Khristyanskoe Chtenie* (1872–3). This work has been overlooked by all those who have dealt with the problem.

features that recalled the conflict between the Monophysites and the champions of the traditional creed of the two natures in Christ.

Leaving aside the many problems[1] that still remain unsolved, we shall make it our task to show how, after the liquidation of iconoclasm, the old Byzantine spirit emerged again in another form, in the struggle between the partisans of 'oeconomia', the liberal policy of compromise in matters not concerning the fundamentals of the faith, and the intransigent ultra-conservatives, who held that Church prescriptions should be carried out in all circumstances and with the utmost rigour.

This new antagonism flared up immediately after the restoration of image worship by the Empress Irene. Fully aware that too rigid an application of ecclesiastical rules would only exasperate the iconoclasts returning to Orthodoxy and wreck the chances of a restoration, she selected and appointed to the patriarchal office Tarasius (784), a layman and a Moderate, President of the Imperial Chancellery, an expert in public affairs and unrivalled in the art of negotiating with recalcitrant opponents.

The Moderates also won the day at the Council of Nicaea (787), which, after defining image worship and condemning iconoclasm, allowed the iconoclastic bishops who abjured their heresy to continue to exercise their episcopal functions. Some intransigent monks, however, protested against the concession and advocated stronger measures against the former iconoclasts. No sooner was this trouble settled than another cropped up under the leadership of St Theodore of the monastery of Studios, he and his followers alleging that the punishment meted out by Tarasius to the simoniacal bishops was inadequate.[2]

These incidents only illustrate the new ferment that was stirring both

---

[1] Some of these problems have been outlined by G. Ostrogorskii, *Studien zur Geschichte des Byzant. Bilderstreites* (Breslau, 1929), pp. 23 seq. Cf. also F. Dölger's review of Ostrogorskii's book in *Göttinger Gelehrte Anzeigen* (1929), vol. 191, pp. 352–72 and J. B. Bury, *A History of the Later Roman Empire from Arcadius to Irene* (London, 1889), vol. II, pp. 429 seq. For the history of iconoclasm see E. J. Martin, *A History of the Iconoclastic Controversy* (London, 1932). I have summarized the history of Byzantine civilization, of which iconoclasm was a consequence, and of the Hellenic reaction in my study, 'Quomodo incrementum influxus Orientalis in Imperio Byzantino s. VII–IX dissensionem inter Ecclesiam Romanam et Orientalem promoverit', *Acta Conventus Pragensis pro Studiis Orientalibus a.* 1929 *celebrati* (Olomucii, 1930), pp. 159–72. There I emphasize the role of the European provinces in the restoration of Orthodoxy and at the Council of 787.

[2] For further details, consult J. Hergenröther, *Photius* (Regensburg, 1867), vol. I, pp. 250 seq.

laity and clergy and throwing Byzantine society into rival camps—the Extremists and the Moderates. The Extremists were generally to be found among the monks, chiefly the reformed monks of the monastery of Studion, and their spiritual clients, the devout, the traditionalists and the ultra-conservatives, elements which in virtue of the norms that will prevail as long as there exist rich and poor, must necessarily preponderate among the leisured and bourgeois classes. The Moderates, on the other hand, belonged to classes more in touch with the humdrum of daily life and were for this reason more inclined to compromise. They also numbered many well-wishers among the secular clergy, who were in closer contact with the world than cloistered monks, and among higher clergy, who were conscious of heavier responsibilities. Intellectual circles were all the more in sympathy with the latter tendency as the Extremists persisted in their obstinate prejudices against all profane knowledge. Finally, iconoclasts who had returned to Orthodoxy with more or less sincerity, could not but support the Moderates in their own interest.

Its framework thus recast, the Byzantine population found itself back to the old politico-religious factions of Greens and Blues; and the way questions of ecclesiastical policy which roused the new party spirit were being exploited by both sides for political purposes only deepened the similarity. When in 790 Irene had to hand over the government to her son Constantine VI, who had come of age, the first thing he did was to divorce Mary, whom his mother had forced on him as a wife, and to wed the court lady Theodota. For fear the impetuous young Emperor should turn iconoclast if pressed too hard, the Patriarch limited his intervention to a protest against this violation of a Church law, and refrained from taking any ecclesiastical proceedings against abbot Joseph, who had blessed the union.

The Extremists, led by abbot Plato and his nephew Theodore, disagreed and insisted on a strict application of ecclesiastical measures against the imperial delinquent. But some of them went further and took action. When Constantine recalled his mother to share in the government, the Logothete Stauracius, her trusted confidant, was the first to realize the value of the Extremists' party for furthering Irene's ambition to rule alone. He was aware of her popularity among the traditionalists who first and foremost venerated in her the pious restorer of image worship. Constantine was hopelessly compromised in their estimation as a result of his divorce and second marriage. This left that party as the mainstay for Irene and Stauracius to count upon, for the success of their plot for removing Constantine from government. Visionaries, always so plentiful among enthusiastic devotees, undertook to lend the plan a religious consecration and declared in their 'prophecies' that Irene, notwithstanding Constantine's coming of age,[1] had been elected by God to carry on the regency; and trusting in such backing, she felt herself in a position to undermine her son's influence and hold the reins of government alone. What greatly assisted the Extremists in their venture was Constantine VI's evident incapacity, his peculiar treatment[2] of the Armeniac Theme, once so loyal to him under Irene's first regency, and his failure to rally the opposition party to his defence. By his mother's orders, his eyes were gouged out (797) in the very room in which she gave him birth, and Constantine VI sank back into dark oblivion to meditate upon his past mistakes. The Extremists had won the day, but not for long.

A counter-plot by the patriots who considered that the Empire would never be safe as long as a woman sat on the throne of the Roman autocrats ended in the proclamation of Nicephorus as Emperor (October 802)[3] and deprived the Extremists of their political and religious ascendancy in State affairs. They then relieved their disappointment by heaping insults on the Patriarch Tarasius for the part he had played, probably with a light heart, at the coronation ceremony of the new Emperor. After Tarasius' death, they vainly tried to put forward their own candidate for the office, Plato apparently proposing his nephew Theodore,[4] but the Emperor was on the Moderate side and selected Nicephorus, a lay monk and once President of the Imperial Chancellery. The Extremists treated the appointment as irregular, and lost all restraint when the two Nicephori rehabilitated abbot Joseph, who had been placed under discipline after the fall of Constantine VI.

The Emperor's moderate policy, without ceasing to favour image worship, did not display any particular fervour against iconoclasm. This was enough to prompt some impatient zealots to use weapons other than spiritual against a regime they judged to be mischievous. One plot by the partisans of Irene against Nicephorus immediately after his

---

[1] Theophanes (Bonn), vol. I, p. 719; (de Boor), vol. I, p. 464.

[2] Theophanes (Bonn), vol. I, pp. 721–6; (de Boor), vol. I, pp. 465–8.

[3] For further details, consult J. B. Bury, *A History of the Eastern Roman Empire, from the fall of Irene to the accession of Basil I* (London, 1912), pp. 1–8.

[4] For details, see my book, *Les Slaves, Byzance et Rome au IXe siècle* (Paris, 1926), pp. 125 seq.

ascent to the throne is reported by two Syriac writers.[1] This was followed later by another plot in which, according to the chronicler Theophanes,[2] many 'saintly bishops and monks, including the synkellos, the sakellarios and the chartophylax of the great Church, all men eminent and worthy of every consideration', were implicated. Both plots were evidently engineered by the Extremists, a curious illustration of what lengths the fanatics of this party were ready to go to in support of their opinions.

The Extremists also had their share in blackening Nicephorus' reputation by branding him as a hypocrite, a miscreant and a tyrant, and by picturing his government as extremely disastrous for the Empire. In such colours did Theophanes hand down Nicephorus' testimonials to posterity in his chronicle, and it was only recently that historical criticism began retouching the Emperor's portrait.[3] Nicephorus was indeed a capable administrator, an efficient financier and no mean statesman. He was, it is true, no expert in military science, but his sad end was no justification for the treatment he received at the hands of our pious Theophanes.[4] If it be remembered that this writer did not belong to the die-hards of the Extremist party; that, as the son of a civil servant who was at least familiar with current affairs, he made no secret of his friendly feelings for the Patriarchs Tarasius and Nicephorus, and that he did not invariably approve the radicalism of St Theodore of the monastery of Studion,[5] one can easily imagine what others must have thought of Nicephorus.

It is well to remember the treatment he received at the hands of the Extremists, as we shall find that a similar fate befell the Emperor Michael III and his uncle Bardas who had so much to do with Photius' elevation to the patriarchal throne. One should also bear in mind that the Extremists' tactics were anything but ideal for dealing with a heresy

---

[1] *Gregorii Abulpharagii Chronicon Syriacum* (ed. Bruns and Kirsch; Leipzig, 1789), vol. II, p. 137; Michael Syrus, *Chronicon* (ed. J. B. Chabot; Paris, 1905–6), vol. III, pp. 12 seq.

[2] Theophanes (Bonn), vol. I, pp. 750 sq.; (de Boor), vol. I, p. 483.

[3] Cf. Bury, *A History of the Eastern Roman Empire* . . ., pp. 8 seq.

[4] Not all contemporaries agreed with Theophanes' opinion on the unfortunate Emperor. The monk Theosterikos, author of the Life of St Nicetas of Medikeion, calls him 'very pious and a friend to poor and monks', *A.S.* 3 April, t. I, p. 261.

[5] Theodore even classes him in one of his letters among the 'moechians', *P.G.* vol. 99, II, ep. 31, col. 1204. In one place he uses an even harsher word. Theophanes (Bonn), vol. I, p. 775; (de Boor), vol. I, pp. 497–8. Cf. Bury, *A History of the Eastern Roman Empire* . . ., pp. 38, 181; Gelzer, 'Das Verhältnis von Staat und Kirche in Byzanz', *Ausgew. Kleine Schriften* (Leipzig, 1907), p. 111.

such as iconoclasm. This is what happened. When Nicephorus perished in the Bulgarian campaign and his son Stauracius was dying of wounds received in battle (811), the Extremists had the satisfaction of finding in Michael I, Stauracius' brother-in-law, an emperor after their own hearts. The Studites were recalled from exile to take an active share in the councils of State, the unfortunate abbot Joseph was again suspended and the most drastic measures were enforced against the iconoclasts. But the monks' inexperience only precipitated the military disaster in Bulgaria and their radicalism provoked the iconoclastic reaction under Leo V (813–20).

Common danger brought the two parties again together, when the Patriarch Nicephorus and the abbot Theodore, the representatives of the clashing tendencies, made peace in exile. Nevertheless, the mistakes committed by the Extremists in the reign of Michael I so strengthened the position of the iconoclastic party that Byzantium had to wait another thirty years for the restoration of image worship. Neither Michael II (820–9) nor Theophilus (829–42) was impressed by the arguments of the image worshippers. Their turn came under Theophilus' widow, the Empress Theodora.

The final restoration of image worship by Theodora in 843 opened a new phase in the growth of the two parties and the split that had featured the first restoration in the time of Irene occurred again. The prestige of the die-hards of the Extremist party, the monks, had risen considerably after the persecution they had suffered under the iconoclastic emperors; but by the same token, the former iconoclasts of a milder type than their last Patriarch John the Grammarian, had swelled the ranks of the Moderates and the partisans of 'oeconomia'. Among them were many scholars, or at least men of culture, the product of the reign of the last iconoclastic Emperor Theophilus, who with the aid of John the Grammarian and Leo the Philosopher had liberally encouraged the cultivation of sciences and letters.

The interest which the last iconoclastic emperors evinced in the renaissance of classical studies deserves emphasis, for it explains among other things why the die-hards, the monks especially, professed to be the determined foes of such studies,[1] which they considered pagan—not merely as reviving the writings and doctrines of the Greek pagan

---

[1] About the monks' opposition, often violent, to classical studies, see what I wrote in my book, *Les Légendes de Constantin et de Méthode vues de Byzance*, Byzantino-Slavica, Supplementa (Prague, 1933), pp. 27–31.

philosophers, but because they were patronized by the iconoclasts, who in their eyes were little better than pagans. It also explains why they so frankly detested the intellectuals of the Moderate party, frequently going so far as to suspect the orthodoxy of their former allies in the fight against iconoclasm.

By her personal inclinations, the Empress Theodora felt drawn towards the Extremists, though she was intelligent enough to see that the interests of the dynasty called for discretion. One is surprised to learn from the accounts of the chroniclers that she all but opposed the official restoration of image worship, and that none but the arguments of Theoktistos and of his relative, Magister Sergius,[1] finally succeeded in convincing her. At first, the government of her Minister Theoktistos encouraged liberal views: the new Patriarch was selected, not from the Extremists, though they had presented their own candidates—Athanasius of Saccudion, Naukratios of the monastery of Studion, archbishop Katasambas of Nicomedia and the metropolitan of Cyzicus—but from the partisans of a more liberal policy.[2] This was Methodius, a Sicilian monk, reputed not only for his zeal for image worship, but also for his learning, his friendship with the Emperor Theophilus, as well as for his liberal views. Theoktistos carried on his master's programme in other fields with equal vigour, and the present writer has elsewhere explained his share in the reorganization of higher education in Byzantium.[3] His was the nomination of Leo the Philosopher and of Photius as professors at the University of Constantinople;[4] his, too, the promotion of Photius to the presidentship of the Imperial Chancellery and the appointment of Constantine the Philosopher as University professor. These men belonged to the circle of intellectuals who formed the backbone of the Moderate party.

Anxious to preserve peace in the Church and to forestall the possibility of a revival of heresy, Methodius studiously avoided appointing partisans of Extremist views to any vacant see and chose the candidates exclusively from among the partisans of the Moderate party. And recent experience justified his policy.

It was only to be expected that Methodius' policy would provoke criticism. The Extremists found it unjust to the men who had suffered

[1] Consult with reference to this personality the important and discerning study by H. Grégoire, 'Études sur le IXe siècle', *Byzantion* (1933), vol. VIII, pp. 517 seq.
[2] See my book, *Les Slaves, Byzance et Rome au IXe siècle*, pp. 128 seq.
[3] *Les Légendes de Constantin et de Méthode*, pp. 39 seq.
[4] If we may so designate the Constantinople High School.

most for the faith and resented it as a compromise. Witness the story told by Genesios[1] and the Continuator of Theophanes,[2] who stated that Methodius had been accused by his enemies of indecent assault on a woman, alleged to be the mother of Metrophanes, the future arch-bishop of Smyrna. And the story goes that Methodius gave an ocular demonstration before an amazed crowd of his innocence, or rather of his physical inability to commit such a crime.

The story has a strong legendary flavour, though there may be some truth at the bottom of it. The implication of Metrophanes' mother is characteristic. Metrophanes, as will be seen later, was no admirer of Methodius and was subsequently to join the partisans of Ignatius. This raises the suspicion that the campaign against Methodius originated from the circle that bred the enemies of Photius. The anecdote also shows that the Extremists did not shrink from vulgar calumny.[3] This for further reference.

The monastery of Studion was another hot-bed of rebellion against Methodius. Since the time of Plato and Theodore, the Studites had been the foremost champions of rigidity. To fill vacancies and to stabilize his Church policy, the Patriarch admitted to ordination candidates who failed to satisfy all the requirements of canon law, directly they gave evidence of their orthodoxy during the iconoclastic persecution, pro-vided they did not belong to the die-hard and rigorist wing. Of this irregularity the Studites duly made capital, and posing as the champions of Church canons, they turned on the Patriarch and severely criticized his procedure. The conflict ended in tragedy and landed the Byzantine Church in a grave internal schism. Exasperated by this ceaseless and malevolent bickering, St Methodius felt driven to excommunicate the more radical elements of the Extremist party—Studites, partisans and all. I have on two different occasions recalled the facts of this conflict.[4] Methodius apparently had the whole-hearted backing of the Olympian monks, the hermits and the hesychasts, who were jealous of their

---

[1] (Bonn), pp. 83 seq.   [2] (Bonn), pp. 157 seq.

[3] Cf. F. Hirsch, *Byzantinische Studien* (Leipzig, 1876), p. 154; and J. B. Bury, *A History of the Eastern Roman Empire...*, p. 151.

[4] *Les Slaves, Byzance et Rome au IXe siècle*, pp. 128 seq.; *Les Légendes de Constantin et de Méthode*, pp. 123 seq. Attention is called to a notice on this schism which may be read in the anti-Photianist collection (Mansi, vol. XVI, col. 444): ἐὰν ἐπὶ τοῦ ἁγιωτάτου Μεθοδίου, διὰ τὸ παραβῆναι ἐν ἰδιόχειρον, τινὲς καθηρέθησαν· οὐ μόνον οὗτοι, ἀλλὰ καὶ οἱ συλλειτουργήσαντες τούτου· πόσῳ μᾶλλον οἱ νῦν ἐπίορκοι οὐχ ἅπαξ, ἀλλὰ πολλάκις, οἳ δὲ καθ᾿ ἑαυτῶν αὐτοὶ καὶ ψῆφον ἐπήνεγκαν, ἀναθεματίσαντες ἑαυτούς, εἰ παραβαῖεν. This reference to the schism under Methodius is characteristic and has escaped the historians' attention.

reformed confrères of the monastery of Studion. The wording of the sentence of excommunication may well warrant the inference that by their opposition and by overstepping the rights accorded to humble monks to criticize the regularly established hierarchy,[1] the Studites made themselves responsible for regrettable dissensions within the Church. They had no doubt grounds for irritation: this was their second rebuff since the restoration of Orthodoxy, which they had so gallantly defended, but it was important to underline the incident, were it but to demonstrate to what lengths the over-zealous members of the Extremist party were ready to go.[2]

The quarrel must have lasted till the death of Methodius, and it is just possible that the Patriarch made the first move towards reconciliation; at any rate, we find in the fragment of his will quoted by John Chilas at the end of the thirteenth century[3] one reference to the Studites, when the Patriarch wrote: 'Receive to communion with honour those willing to do penance, provided they disown with anathema their father's [St Theodore Studite's] writings against the saintly Patriarchs Tarasius and Nicephorus; those who with sincere hearts return to the Church, fully reinstate them in the dignity of the priestly order.' These words suggest that the Patriarch was only too anxious for a reconciliation, but that it never took place, since he left instructions on the way to deal with excommunicated and repentant monks. On the other hand, the biographer of St Methodius mentions the incident as though the parties had come to terms before his hero's death.[4] According to this account, Methodius would have granted pardon on his death-bed to those who had offended him personally and have imposed penances on those who had rebelled against patriarchal authority; but the reference is not clear enough to invalidate the statement in the first document, though

---

[1] St Methodius reminded the Studites of the place occupied in the Church by the humble monk: 'Narratio de Beatis Patriarchis Tarasio et Nicephoro', *P.G.* vol. 99, col. 1853.

[2] Cf. Th. Uspenski, *Ocherki po istorii Viz. obrazovannosti* (St Petersburg, 1892), pp. 84 seq.; von Dobschütz, 'Methodios und die Studiten', in *Byzant. Zeitschrift* (1909), vol. XVIII. V. Grumel returned to the subject in 'La Politique Religieuse du Patriarche St Méthode', in *Échos d'Orient* (1935), vol. XXXIV, pp. 385–401, where he makes it clear that Methodius agreed with the Studites on the attitude adopted towards repentant iconoclasts, by admitting only those who had been ordained by Tarasius and Nicephorus. I accept his conclusions all the more readily, as they substantially confirm what I wrote in my two works already quoted, concerning Methodius' 'oeconomia' policy.

[3] Pitra, *Juris Ecclesiastici Graecorum Historia et Monumenta* (Rome, 1864–8), vol. II, p. 362.

[4] *P.G.* vol. 100, cols. 1257, 1260.

one can sympathize with the biographer's desire to place his hero in the best possible light and earn for him the goodwill of monastic circles—so particular and sensitive on this point—to which he probably belonged himself. Again, he was writing at the time the incident was definitely closed, when it was only to be expected that he should not wish to insist on an occurrence which the admirers of Methodius, and chiefly the Studites, always a powerful element in the Church, were only too glad to forget. One only regrets not to be able to collate this biographer's account with what a fellow-countryman of Methodius, Gregory Asbestas,[1] wrote on this incident. The fact that the Life of Methodius by the bishop of Syracuse was probably destroyed later by the Ignatians would suggest that it contained information particularly unpalatable to the enemies of Methodius.

The incident we have just related was more momentous than it has been till recently realized, for the Studite schism, whose rise and growth remained so long unsuspected,[2] was to cast its deep shadows over the religious evolution of the whole subsequent period. It is extremely difficult to find a key to the vicissitudes through which the Byzantine Church had to struggle after the death of Methodius. The position, anyhow, seems to have been critical. When some of the monks passed over to the schism, the government took alarm; and though it had approved the deceased Patriarch's religious tactics, it was none the less taken by surprise at the Studites' attitude. It had never occurred to the government that the opposition would prove so obstinate, nor that the Patriarch would put so much energy into the defence of his authority. The Empress Theodora, whose personal inclinations lay with the extremist monks, must have felt particularly sorry, in view of this pious woman's touching efforts with certain eminent members of the party to rehabilitate her husband's memory.[3] So anxious was she to prevent the heroes of her faith, whom she held in the highest esteem, from condemning the memory of one she had loved so dearly, that she did not even shrink from a pious lie, when she asserted that her husband

[1] According to a marginal note in the Vatican MS. (Leo Allatius, Diatriba de Methodiis, P.G. vol. 100, cols. 1233–4), Gregory wrote a Life of St Methodius. This biography must have disappeared, since no copy of it has been found.

[2] Hergenröther, Photius (Regensburg, 1867), vol. I, pp. 354 seq., is very brief and hazy on this point, though he admits some connection between these troubles and the Photian imbroglio.

[3] Cf. Bury, A History of the Eastern Roman Empire..., p. 149; Dvornik, Les Slaves, Byzance et Rome au IXe siècle, p. 127.

had repented on his death-bed. If Methodius showed a desire to settle this business amicably, he probably did so to meet the Empress' wishes and it is not unthinkable that the monks, even after the incident, tried their utmost to curry favour with Theodora, encouraged, no doubt, by the gradual recasting of the political groups in Byzantium. In the first years of the regency, Bardas, the Empress' brother, had been completely left out in the cold. Since, relegated to his villa, he cannot have been content with the pleasures the countryside had to offer, it is from this period of inactivity that we should date his interest in learning. As a reigning Empress' brother and conscious of his ability, it must have galled him to be asked to yield his rightful place to Theoktistos, an eunuch! As Bardas made many friends among the intellectuals and made no secret of his progress in liberal circles, Theoktistos, suspecting a possible rival, must have been only too glad to welcome the Extremists' overtures, which, moreover, came from a quarter where the pious Theodora—that second Irene—enjoyed enormous prestige.

The choice of the new Patriarch gave the two parties a chance to measure their strength, and the struggle seems to have been a bitter one. Nicetas himself[1] mentions several candidates who had been eliminated for various reasons, and among them Genesios names two sons of the former iconoclastic Emperor Leo V, Basil and Gregory.[2] Outstanding among them all was the archbishop of Syracuse, Gregory Asbestas, Methodius' countryman and leader of the partisans of his religious policy, of whose activities under Methodius and after the latter's death we shall learn more presently.

Under the circumstances, one can understand that the government had to intervene for fear a clash between the two opinions should, on the pretext of the new Patriarch's appointment, make irreparable mischief in Church and State. Probably prompted by her Minister Theoktistos, the Empress decided on the choice of a monk, Ignatius, the son of the late Emperor Michael I. But how was the appointment made? Did Theodora first summon a synod or did she dispense with the canonical routine? There is no direct evidence for or against either election or nomination, but contemporary sources may guide us to an answer.

Nicetas, in mentioning the consent of the episcopacy, insinuates that the Empress played a leading part in Ignatius' elevation;[3] and it is significant that he is silent about a canonical election in accordance with

---

[1] Vita Ignatii, *P.G.* vol. 105, cols. 500 seq.   [2] Genesios (Bonn), p. 99.
[3] Vita Ignatii, *P.G.* vol. 105, col. 501.

Byzantine tradition, knowing full well that the attacks of Ignatius' opponents had fastened on this particular grievance.[1] He also affirms that Ignatius had been recommended to Theodora by St Joannikios, the famous ascete of Mount Olympus and a keen supporter of Methodius. There is no truth in this statement, since Joannikios died on 4 November 846,[2] after the Patriarch Methodius had visited him on 1 November of the same year;[3] so that no one at that moment could have foreseen Methodius' death, and Theodora could not possibly have given thought to his successor's appointment. Nicetas only meant to show by this deliberate fabrication how groundless were the criticisms of Ignatius' adversaries about his alleged hostility to Methodius' religious policy.

We learn nothing more definite from other sources.[4] Everything then points to the fact that in her anxiety to avoid aggravating existing troubles, the Empress did without the usual procedure and omitted to convoke the synod that should have selected the candidates for presentation to government; and after consultation with a few influential bishops, without any further ado, she appointed as Patriarch Ignatius. The irregularity of this procedure was later to be cast up against Ignatius, but exceptional circumstances—a schism within the Byzantine Church—may be enough to explain why Theodora deemed herself justified in dispensing with a few formalities.

Ignatius' accession to the patriarchal throne had all the semblance of a victory for the Extremists, but as he had not been involved directly in the differences that set Methodius and the Studites by the ears, the followers of Methodius could not refuse him obedience. That is how the whole episcopate agreed to the elevation, as was evidenced by the readiness with which Gregory Asbestas and his friends paid their homage at the Patriarch's enthronement. But the new prelate's behaviour towards Gregory Asbestas also proves that Methodius' successor was in agreement with the Extremists' game. According to Nicetas,[5] Ignatius bluntly signified to Gregory that since his case had not been cleared up, he (Ignatius) did not wish to see him at the ceremony. Thereupon, the fiery Sicilian made a scene, flung down the candle he

---

[1] See infra, p. 81.　　　　[2] A.S. Nov. t. II, p. 318.

[3] Loc. cit.; in the biography written by Sabas, p. 382; the one written by Peter, p. 432.

[4] The other writers are also very brief on the subject of Ignatius' nomination and wander off into vague generalities; for instance, the Contin. of Theophanes (Bonn), p. 193; Pseudo-Simeon (Bonn), p. 657. Zonaras (Bonn), vol. II, p. 403 (lib. XVI, 4), however, attributes the appointment of Ignatius directly to Theodora.

[5] Vita Ignatii, P.G. vol. 105, col. 512.

was holding and exclaimed that instead of being blessed with a pastor, the Church had been handed over to a wolf. He then swept out, followed by a number of ecclesiastics, chief of whom were Peter, bishop of Sardis, and Eulampius, bishop of Apamea.

The incident was ominous. Nicetas himself, though he defends Ignatius, acknowledges that his conduct raised many criticisms, and once for all prevented Ignatius, had he so desired, acting as intermediary between the two parties at loggerheads in Byzantium. Henceforth he would be classed for good, with no alternative left but to follow die-hard tactics and rely exclusively on the Extremists' favour.

It is generally supposed that Ignatius took action against Gregory immediately after the incident and this with energy, since his patriarchal authority was at stake. He convoked, it is stated, a local synod, which duly judged, excommunicated and suspended Gregory with all his partisans. It is also imagined that the ground for this condemnation was the complaint Ignatius made against Asbestas at the time of his consecration. Meanwhile Gregory appealed to Pope Leo IV. The Holy See's attitude has generally been regarded as somewhat strange, since the case was left to drag on throughout the whole of Ignatius' first patriarchate, only to be settled—so it is believed—by Leo's successor, Benedict III.

Let us now examine how far an opinion so generally accepted is exact. Asbestas' appeal to Rome, together with other circumstances, is known to us from a letter addressed by Leo IV to the Patriarch and, according to this document, Ignatius' performance seemed to the Pope[1] to have been contrary to custom as observed by his predecessors on the throne of Constantinople, who in similar cases invariably first applied to Rome for advice. By convoking a synod and condemning the said bishops without the approval of the Church of Rome, Ignatius had exceeded his powers. Unfortunately, the letter bears no date. It was certainly dispatched before 855, the year of Leo's death; but as Benedict III, his successor, had to deal with the case, the letter must have been written towards the end of Leo's pontificate. Jaffé dates it 853, and this calls for a few remarks.

We owe it to the famous canonical Collection called *Britannica*, in the possession of the British Museum,[2] that the extract from the letter in

---

[1] Ph. Jaffé-P. Ewald, *Regesta Pontificum Romanorum* (Lipsiae, 1885–8), vol. I, no. 2629; *M.G.H.* Ep. v, p. 589.

[2] On this Collection see pp. 296, 303 seq., 324 seq.

question has been preserved (Add. MS. no. 8873, ff. 162, 162 a). By mischance, the copyist has omitted to follow the chronological order. He has also copied as mall fragment from another letter addressed by Leo IV to Ignatius, in which the Pope refused to accept the pallium sent by the Patriarch. The Church of Rome, 'magistra et caput omnium ecclesiarum', cannot accept the pallium from another Church, since it is hers to distribute it 'per totam Europam ad quod delegatum est'. The refusal is courteous, the Pope apologizing twice, but the tone of the letter is none the less firm. Now Jaffé also dates this letter about 853.[1] It may be questioned whether it bears any reference to Gregory Asbestas' case and whether it may be thus dated.

It rather looks at first sight as though this fragment had been extracted from the Pope's reply to the Patriarch's synodical letter, since it used to be on such occasions that mutual presents were sent. It should therefore be dated 848 or 849, even 850. There exists but scant information on the dispatch of synodical letters, which perhaps were not always sent immediately after a Patriarch's accession. P. Ewald[2] also is of opinion that the letter relating to the pallium had been dispatched previous to the letter concerning Gregory Asbestas, and he surmises that the copyist contented himself with copying a few fragments from the register of the last five years of Leo IV (850–5), a hypothesis which seems well founded. If such be the case, the condemnation of Gregory Asbestas and his friends could not have taken place till some time after Ignatius' accession. Though 853 might be retained, 854 seems the likelier date; for one cannot admit such a protracted interval between the appeal to Leo IV and the second move with Benedict III.

It is clear from the foregoing that the writer of the letter knew only of one synodical condemnation of Gregory and his friends, though its exact date cannot be given, since the letter in question bears no date. Owing to the traffic difficulties between the two cities, we are left to

---

[1] *Regesta*, no. 2647, MS. f. 170 a; *M.G.H.* Ep. v, p. 607.

[2] 'Die Papstbriefe der Britischen Sammlung', in *Neues Archiv* (1890), vol. v, p. 396. Cf. the two letters, ibid. pp. 379, 392. We must take into account the traffic difficulties between Rome and Constantinople (see pp. 139, 171). Ignatius became Patriarch in June 847. As he had first to settle the Studite Schism and as the disagreement with Asbestas had caused a stir in the ecclesiastical circles of Byzantium, it took some time for the situation to return to normal. Traffic between the two cities being suspended from October till March, he could scarcely have sent a legate to Rome before the spring or the summer of 848. Normally, the Pope would have answered his letter only in 849. Any delay in the dispatch of legates by either the Patriarch or the Pope would have deferred the papal reply till 850.

guess that the synod had taken place the year previous to the dispatch of the Pope's letter in 852 or 853. It also follows that the charges brought in 847 against Gregory must have been pretty feeble for his condemnation to be held over for five years and one may reasonably wonder if Ignatius was not somewhat rash in provoking the painful scene at St Sophia on his enthronement day. But this incident had nothing to do with Asbestas' condemnation and the true motive must be sought elsewhere.

Let us see now if the conclusions derived from Leo IV's letters find confirmation in other sources that bear on Asbestas' case. It is alleged by Pseudo-Simeon[1] that Asbestas committed a breach of canon law by consecrating the priest Zacharias to the bishopric of Taormina. It should, however, be remembered that this same priest, again according to the same quotation from Pseudo-Simeon, had been sent to Rome by his fellow-countryman Methodius and was the Patriarch's trusted confidant. There would then have been no difficulty for Asbestas in obtaining a dispensation in favour of one whom the Patriarch held in such high esteem. Pseudo-Simeon's allegation is therefore suspect. This same writer further pretends that the bishop of Syracuse had been suspended by Methodius on the ground of this same ordination, a statement which is patently false and puts the witness out of court.

The most important document on the Greek side is the letter of Stylianos of Neocaesarea to Stephen V. After stating that the Devil had prompted Asbestas and his two companions to alienate the faithful from Ignatius, Stylianos writes:

The Patriarch tried to save them from falling a prey to the unclean spirit by their severance from the Church of God: he repeatedly summoned them before a synod, treated them kindly, but could not save them; and eventually deposed and anathematized them. They however sent messengers and letters to the most holy Pope of Rome at that time, the blessed Leo, and asked him for protection, as though they had been the victims of injustice. The Pope wrote to Ignatius, asking him to send a representative to the older Rome so that he might learn from him how matters stood with those schismatics. Without unnecessary delay, the Patriarch sent the monk and confessor Lazarus with letters, as he was well acquainted with the affair. Lazarus told the Pope everything; and the Pope judged and condemned them as schismatics as Ignatius had done. When the blessed Pope Leo died, they again molested Benedict, the Pope of Rome, and his successor with the same

---

[1] (Bonn), p. 671.

complaints. But after careful examination, the most holy Benedict pronounced against them the same sentence as Ignatius.

Stylianos then goes on to state that the condemned schismatics used the influence of Photius—then a high functionary at court and also a schismatic—on Bardas, the Emperor's uncle, who resented the Patriarch's accusation of incest. After charging the Patriarch Ignatius with many crimes, they forcibly deprived him of his throne. The Emperor then expelled him and placed Photius on the patriarchal throne. He was the schismatics' candidate for the honour.

Stylianos' statement only confirms my inference from the Pope's letter, i.e. that there was only one condemnation of Asbestas and his friends, and that this had nothing to do with the St Sophia incident. Stylianos postulates a long interval between the incident and the actual condemnation, when the Patriarch tried to make up for the bad impression the incident had caused and to treat Asbestas and his followers with every kindness. This reveals a sympathetic side of the Patriarch's character: he was certainly not as stubborn and as touchy about his dignity as most historians have pictured him, but ready to acknowledge his mistakes and to mend matters. We may further conclude from Stylianos' account that the true ground for the condemnation was the Asbestas party's systematic opposition to the Patriarch's ecclesiastical policy.

Nicetas in his 'biography' of Ignatius[1] is not as accurate as Stylianos. He attributes all Ignatius' misfortunes to Asbestas, 'who is stated to have been some time ago bishop of Syracuse and to have been summoned to Byzantium over some accusations and to have already been condemned by the Roman Church for acting uncanonically'. He then relates the notorious incident 'for which act committed at the beginning [of his career], however justifiable, many have blamed the Patriarch'. 'Throughout the eleven years of his first patriarchate, Ignatius was unable, for all his kindness in word and deed, to appease his [Asbestas'] malevolence. He used to call on influential people, reviling him [Ignatius] everywhere and ridiculing him in sheer malice, refusing even to call the holy man a Christian. This accursed one!'

Though silent about the date, Nicetas agrees that the synodical condemnation did not happen immediately after Ignatius' accession. He also confirms Stylianos' statement that Ignatius tried to pacify Asbestas by kindness. But he is more explicit about the nature of Asbestas'

---

[1] Mansi, vol. XVI, col. 232; *P.G.* vol. 105, col. 512.

anti-Ignatian bias: calling upon the aristocracy to ridicule and revile Ignatius points to a deliberate campaign against his religious policy.

Our third informant is Anastasius the Librarian. He had his information from the Ignatians, when he was in Constantinople in 870. He first states[1] that the accession of Ignatius provoked discontent among some bishops, one of whom was Gregory of Syracuse, for the following reason: 'Because he declared with due restraint and in accordance with the canons that he could not receive them—owing to a judgement pronounced on them over some well known and public transgression in their priestly life—before this judgement were reversed. For this reason and for their failure to make due satisfaction, they were justly condemned later (postmodum) by himself and by a synod.'

The words, though lacking Stylianos' precision, indicate at least that the synodal condemnation by Ignatius took place after he had been Patriarch for some time. Unlike Stylianos, Anastasius generalizes and includes Gregory's associates in the condemnation which, according to him, had been pronounced before Ignatius' patriarchate. This statement is suspect, and the way Anastasius refers to the opposition of Gregory's party to Ignatius' accession only intensifies our suspicion. We know that Gregory and his friends accepted Ignatius, since they were present at the ceremony of his enthronement, and that it was Ignatius who objected to the presence of Gregory. This calls for caution and his statement on a previous condemnation of Gregory and his friends for some unnamed transgression may be questioned. As he was not well acquainted with the circumstances and had got his information from the Ignatians, the words possibly convey his own reading of their feelings. A Roman mind, trained on juridical lines and unfamiliar with the motives that stirred the partisanship of the Greeks, could not have read the events or sifted his information in any other way: the bishops must have been guilty of some serious breach of canon law, for which they were condemned by the Church authorities before Ignatius' accession. But such premises are worthless.

Further in his statement, Anastasius is more exact on the sort of trouble Gregory and his group were making. He blunders of course in selecting Photius as the main opponent, but that was the Roman way of looking at it. The Ignatians' hostility to Photius was not understandable to a Roman, unless Photius was identified with Gregory and his schismatic circle. As to the nature of the opposition, Ignatius was blamed for dishonouring St Methodius' memory and on that ground

[1] Mansi, vol. XVI, cols. 2, 3.

was called a parricide. As Anastasius emphatically denies the accusation, since Ignatius paid due homage to his predecessor's memory and celebrated the anniversary of his death, he can only mean that Ignatius was criticized by Asbestas' group for deviating from his predecessor's conciliatory policy or the policy of 'oeconomia'. This was the old antagonism between the partisans of rigorous measures in ecclesiastical policy and the champions of more conciliatory tactics, wherever the essentials of doctrine were not involved. It was the story all over again of the breach between Theodore of the monastery of Studion and the Patriarch Nicephorus in the divorce and marriage affair of Constantine VI and of the clash between the Studites and Methodius which led to the Studite schism. Under Ignatius, the rigorists took possession of the patriarcheion, but were crossed by the champions of Methodius. Foremost among these were Asbestas and his two friends. The result was another schism ending in a synodical condemnation of Asbestas and his party, most probably in 853.

Since there is no evidence of any serious canonical lapse (in this case Ignatius was to pass sentence immediately after his installation at the patriarcheion), we must assume that he merely objected to the policy of oeconomia as practised by Methodius and championed by Asbestas. Already under Methodius, the rigorists must have fastened their criticisms on Gregory who as Methodius' countryman (both were Sicilians) had great influence on him. He probably had also had a hand in the condemnation of the Studites. They therefore naturally looked upon him as their worst enemy and were responsible for the accusations mentioned by Stylianos.

Ignatius knew all this. But the new Patriarch had not had time to examine the Studite case and the accusations. He could not reconcile the Studites to the Church till after his enthronement. Hence, to avoid any appearance of partiality, he ordered Asbestas, the man responsible for the condemnation of the Studites by Methodius, to keep away from the ceremony of enthronement. Asbestas of course resented this as a slight on the memory of Methodius and as favouritism for the men he had condemned. This would best explain the St Sophia incident.

We are also told that Gregory and his friends appealed from the synodical condemnation to Pope Leo IV. This must have happened in 853, or better, in 854. Let us now examine the attitude of the Roman See. Stylianos' assertion that Leo, after hearing Ignatius' envoy Lazarus, confirmed the Patriarch's sentence and that his successor Benedict did the same, is flatly contradicted by Pope Nicholas I, who stated in his letter to Michael III:[1]

But my predecessors of blessed memory Leo and Benedict refused in accordance with the rules of the Apostolic See to listen to one party to the prejudice of the other, for it is not the mediator for one side only. That is why his [Gregory's] deposition has in the meantime remained invalid for lack of sanction from the Holy See. And although the same Gregory admitted through the delegate of his party called Zachary that the Apostolic See had in no way consented to his deposition, he never thanked....

The statement is clear. Further in the letter, the same Pope adds that if Gregory and his friends had committed against Ignatius, in the reigns of Leo IV and Benedict III, the same offence as they perpetrated by deposing him and crowning Photius, and had thus taxed the patience and clemency of the Holy See, those two Pontiffs would to a certainty have unhesitatingly condemned them.[2] This can only mean that Nicholas was quite aware that those two Pontiffs had condemned neither Gregory nor his companions. Besides, according to the *Liber Pontificalis*,[3] Lazarus did not reach Rome till after the death of Leo IV which occurred on 17 July 855. In that case, Leo could neither hear him nor consider Ignatius' sentence.

The letter sent to Ignatius, probably in 854, severely rebukes the Patriarch for abusing his powers in condemning bishops without consulting the Holy See; and we must presume that it also contained an invitation to send representatives to Rome to answer the charges made by bishop Zachary, Asbestas' envoy. The copyist of the *Britannica* quotes from the papal letter only the passage on the rights of the Roman See, but omits the Pope's request for the dispatch of a special envoy. There is nothing in the letter to indicate any move on the part of Ignatius before the summons from the Papal Chancellery.[4] It is difficult to state with any precision when Lazarus arrived in Rome. It may have been in the second half of 855, or in 856. The *Liber Pontificalis*, it is true, mentions Lazarus' arrival at the end of the sketch of Benedict's life; but this is not conclusive, since the writer prefaces his account of

---

[1] *M.G.H.* Ep. VI, p. 500; cf. ibid. p. 527.
[2] Ibid. pp. 501, 528; cf. also p. 511.
[3] Ed. L. Duchesne (Paris, 1886, 1892), vol. II, pp. 147, 150.
[4] The wording 'vos autem praedictorum, ut fertis, virorum' does not imply that the Pope is here hinting at a letter sent by the Patriarch. The meaning is: 'you, however, who pretend to be the successor of those men [Patriarchs of Constantinople] mentioned before.'

Lazarus' visit with the non-committal 'huius [Benedicti] temporibus Michael...imperator...misit...'.

The letters sent in 865 and 866 by Nicholas I, the successor of Benedict III, to Michael III give us information about the answer to Leo IV's request brought by Lazarus. It is to the effect that the Patriarch sent to the Roman Pontiff the Acts of the synod which condemned Asbestas' group, and from these Acts Nicholas learnt that the Patriarch had not attended that synod.[1] But Ignatius' absence was quite in order. The Gregorian party's attacks being personal and aimed at the Patriarch's religious policy, he preferred to stay away to allow the bishops perfect freedom to discuss him. It did the saintly man credit and was moreover true to custom in Constantinople. We shall presently see that neither did Photius attend the sessions of the synod of 861, which examined Ignatius' case.

According to the same document, the Acts were endorsed with a letter from Theodora on behalf of the Emperor Michael III. It was the imperial decree confirming the decision of the synod. The Patriarch, in his letter, requested the Pope to confirm by his authority the synod's sentence and his own.[2] The document illustrates the procedure followed whenever an appeal from the Patriarch's decision was lodged in the papal court. As Nicholas I states in his letter to Photius written in 866, Zachary, when appealing in the name of the bishops condemned by a synodical and patriarchal sentence, quoted in his support the canon of Sardica which gave everyone such a right.[3]

How did Benedict III (855–8) deal with Gregory's case? The writer of Benedict's *Vita* in the *Liber Pontificalis* was deeply impressed by the presents which Theodora sent to the Pope: and yet, the Pope did not confirm Ignatius' sentence. This we learn on the authority of Nicholas' letter to Michael III, written in 866 and quoted above; and it gives the lie to Stylianos' statement. The document relating to the case which Nicholas I found in the Archives in Benedict's file must have been so favourable to Gregory and his friends as to prove embarrassing to

---

[1] *M.G.H.* Ep. VI, p. 478: 'Ecce enim scripta vestra missa ad antecessorem nostrum, quae penes nos recondita servantur, quosdam partis Gregorii Syracusani congregatis episcopis etiam absente fratre nostro Ignatio vos anathematizasse testantur.' [2] *M.G.H.* Ep. VI, p. 500.

[3] *M.G.H.* Ep. VI, p. 537: 'Zacharius, qui se pretendebat episcopum, ex parte Syracusani Gregorii et collegarum eius apostolicam sedem adiit eorum deposcens renovari iudicium, hos se in appellatione canones [i.e. canon 3 of the Council of Sardica, Mansi, vol. III, col. 23] et eos, a quibus missus extiterat, fuisse secutus aiebat.'

Nicholas, and he is obviously at pains to explain his predecessors' attitude.[1]

The Acts of the fourth session of the Council of 869–70 supply some more detailed information on the intervention of Pope Benedict III.[2] After the Fathers had listened to the Photianist bishops Zachary and Theophilus, the Patrician Baanes, who was in the chair and directed the debate, declared: 'We never called for Zachary's case, for he admitted yesterday that he had been ordered by Pope Benedict not to perform any pontifical function until he appeared again and went to Rome, with all those who had fallen away from the saintly Patriarch Ignatius, for his trial: this he never did and he never went there.' These words make it clear that Benedict III never confirmed Ignatius' verdict; he only reminded Zachary that he and his friends should suspend their ministry as long as judgement remained pending. The same is hinted at by Pope Nicholas I in chapters I, II and III of the decrees of the Roman synod concerning the Photian case;[3] so that the observation made by Benedict III was quite in order, for whoever is condemned in the first instance is naturally expected to abstain from any functions whilst his case is under consideration in a higher court. Zachary duly notified Gregory Asbestas of this injunction, as is evidenced in the 'Libellus' written by Theognostos and presented to Nicholas I.[4]

But the passage quoted above also shows that Benedict's verdict was not final. The Pope evidently was not satisfied with Ignatius' reasons for such a grave decision against bishops. But he did not annul the Patriarch's sentence, apparently waiting for further information. Both parties were then summoned to appear again before his tribunal.

Benedict III's action has surprised many a historian.[5] Being in possession of the Acts of the synod and in a position to gather the necessary information from the monk Lazarus, having moreover free

---

[1] *M.G.H.* Ep. VI, pp. 500, 501.   [2] Mansi, vol. XVI, col. 74.

[3] *M.G.H.* Ep. VI, p. 519: 'A Gregorio, Syracusano dudum episcopo a synodo damnato et ab apostolica sede vincto.' P. 521: 'Gregorius...a decessore meo sanctae memoriae papa Benedicto obligatus.' And further down: 'A decessore vere sanctae memoriae Benedicto papa obligatis hominibus.' Cf. the circular letter to the oriental bishops, ibid. pp. 557, 558, 559.   [4] Mansi, vol. XVI, col. 300.

[5] Cardinal Hergenröther conjectures for instance (*Photius*, vol. I, p. 361) that the Holy See's dilatory attitude to the Asbestas case only encouraged his partisans to intensify their attacks on Ignatius and that as a result Theodora convoked the synod which Ignatius did not attend. This second synod would have excommunicated Gregory's schismatic party and sent the monk Lazarus to take the Acts to Rome. This speculation is unwarranted. We have seen that there is evidence only of one synod, that of 853, and that it was the only one to pass sentence on Asbestas.

access to the defendant's file, since Zachary must have stayed in Rome waiting for the arrival of the Patriarch's envoy, he considered it premature to decide the case. Instead, he gave the instructions we know.

It is clear from the documents that there was no final verdict and that the affair must have dragged on from 856 till 858, a long time in a matter considered to be so urgent. Before trying to find out what happened to cause the delay, let us first examine the Acts of the synod of 861 summoned to judge Ignatius, and where his attitude to Asbestas was explained.

An extract from the Acts of this synod has been preserved in the famous canonical Collection of Cardinal Deusdedit and the problems raised by this Collection will be discussed presently.[1] The story of Gregory's condemnation and of the Pontiff's intervention could have been reconstructed in the light of these Acts, but since their authenticity has been questioned, we preferred first to examine the information supplied by documents whose authenticity is undisputed. In any case, the evidence of the Acts is exactly identical with that of other sources. In these we find that in the course of the first session the legates of Pope Nicholas I—Radoald, bishop of Porto, and Zachary, bishop of Agnani —addressed Ignatius in the following words:[2] 'There is this against

---

[1] See below, pp. 297–308.

[2] Wolf von Glanvell, *Die Kanonensammlung des Kardinals Deusdedit* (Paderborn, 1905), p. 604. Owing to its importance we give here the text in full, though its Latin would have broken Cicero's heart: 'Hoc malum tibi est, quia cum accusatoris est Romae, scripsit tibi Benedictus Papa, ut responderes. Tu neque per te ipsum neque per alium dignatus es respondere. Venimus ergo perscrutari causam tuam juxta traditionem sanctorum patrum et canonum.... Cum irate reclamavit Romae Zacharias episcopus et Benedictus papa misit tibi epistolam, ut imperator [imperando, ut?] condicto mitteres apocrisiarios ad apostolicam sedem et rursum veniet idem Zacharias episcopus cum aliis quibusdam, ut utriusque partis in conspectu papae ventilaretur negotium; et hic quidem venit, tu vero nequaquam misisti. Ignatius dixit: Et quo mense recepi epistolam papae? Responderunt: Nescimus. Ignatius dixit: Julio mense recepi epistolam; post VIIII aut X dies eiectus sum et quando habui mittere?... Nosti [loc. cit. pp. 607–8] quod tempore Benedicti papae venerunt episcopi Romam reclamantes contra te multa et gravia et misit apostolicus epistolam tibi, ut de parte tua mitteres aliquos, et non fecisti. Ignatius dixit: Quod videtis, contigit mihi: ideo non potui mittere.... Dixit Ignatius: non iudicor, quia iudices missi non estis a magno iudice papa Romano. Item non misit iste Lazarum Romanum [Romam] ut dispositionem [depositionem?] quam injuste fecerat confirmaret? In illo iudicem recepit Romanam ecclesiam et modo non recepit.... Quare non recipis nos, cum miseris ad Benedictum papam requirens Romanum iudicium?...Ego veni Romam et reclamavi apud sanctitatem papae, quod Ignatius sine electione intravit in ecclesiam et ejecit episcopum Syracusanum et alios duos fecit pro eo. Synodus dixit: Omnes novimus, quoniam sine causa eiecit episcopos istos Ignatius et alios fecit in locis eorum.'

you, that as you were accused in Rome, Pope Benedict wrote to you expecting an answer; yet you did not deign to reply either personally or by proxy. So we have come to examine your case according to the tradition of the holy Fathers and the Canons.' Later they said: 'As bishop Zachary had lodged an indignant complaint at Rome, and Pope Benedict sent you a letter requesting you to send at once your representatives to the Apostolic See, and as the same bishop Zachary with some others again would come so that both parties should explain themselves in the presence of the Pope, he did come, but you sent nobody.' Ignatius: 'Which month did I receive the Pope's letter?' They answered: 'We do not know.' Ignatius said: 'I received the letter in the month of July and I was expelled nine or ten days later: where was the time to answer?' During the third session the apocrisiaries declared: 'You know that at the time of Pope Benedict bishops came to Rome with many and grave complaints against you and the Apostolic See sent you a letter asking you to send your representatives and you did not comply.' Ignatius said: 'You see what happened to me; so, I could not send them.' The protospathar John then pointed out: 'Ignatius has said: "I am not being judged, for you have not been sent as judges by the great judge, the Pope of Rome." And yet, did he not send Lazarus to Rome on a similar occasion to ask for confirmation of a deposition which he had unjustly ordered? He accepted the Roman Church as the judge then, but does not do so now!' Then the apocrisiaries: 'Why do you not receive us, since you wrote to Pope Benedict asking for a Roman judgement?' Lastly, bishop Zachary declared at the fourth session: 'I went to Rome and complained to the Holy Father that Ignatius had entered the Church without an election, ejected the Bishop of Syracuse and replaced him by two others.' The synod said: 'We all know that Ignatius deposed those bishops without any reason and put others in their place.'

The comparison of these documents is significant, since they all complement each other. Whatever is said on the subject by the Acts of the synod of 861, whose extracts have survived only in Latin in the canonical Collection of the eleventh century, is confirmed from other sources. This is important, for the Acts supply on the Ignatian case other details which we shall have occasion to examine. All one can say at present is that these are important witnesses it seems difficult to set aside.

One thing seems certain: invited by Benedict III to send representatives to Rome to explain matters, Ignatius did not comply. By his own declaration, he received a letter with the injunction in July 858, nine or ten days before his expulsion from the patriarcheion. This letter must have been sent from Rome in the early spring of 858. Even assuming that Lazarus arrived in Rome only in 856, it seems hardly possible that the Pope should have waited till 858 to ask Ignatius for additional information. Even if the Pope wished to put off the decision, the aggrieved bishops were not likely to be so patient.

We read in the extract from the Acts that Zachary went to Rome. This was first stated by the papal legates at the first session and repeated by Ignatius' accusers at the third:[1] 'The apocrisiaries addressed Ignatius' accusers: "Some of your men went to Rome to complain against Ignatius." The accusers said: "Yes, and at the time they were poor and harassed men. But he, with his influence and power, why did he not send [any]? You know how Zachary did go."' Both apocrisiaries and complainants here seemed to have in mind, not the first, but a second journey of Zachary to Rome. The extract is not clear, but the context in both passages seems to suggest it.

But there is a passage in a letter of Hadrian II, also written to Ignatius in 869, stating that Ignatius failed to comply with the Pope's request, not in 858, before his ejection, but much earlier. The Pope writes:[2] 'Among the false charges made against you, your enemies have tried to incriminate you, saying that, as though scorning Pope Benedict of venerable memory, you had contemptuously refused, like Dioscorus mentioned above, to receive his letter.' If there is any substance in this statement, it cannot refer to the letter which Ignatius received some days before his fall. There was no necessity then for Ignatius' enemies to spread rumours of a refusal to receive papal letters, since at that time his position was already seriously undermined. But there was point in the accusation, if made in 856 or in 857. It follows that Ignatius ignored the Pope's request then, and that only Zachary returned to Rome in 857. But as the Pope could not pass sentence in the defendant's absence, he reiterated his request in the spring of 858. To this of course Ignatius could not reply, since he was expelled from his office. He was only referring to this second letter in his defence at the synod, and wisely ignored the first. His tactics were legally correct, since none could tell how he would have dealt with the second letter, if given freedom of action. In any case, the Pope overlooked Ignatius' disobedience to the first summons and merely repeated his citation.

There is one difficulty. How are we to reconcile the statement con-

[1] W. von Glanvell, loc. cit. p. 607.   [2] *M.G.H.* Ep. v, p. 753.

tained in the Acts of the synod of 861 to the effect that Zachary went to Rome for the second time, with the Patrician Baanes' denial at the fourth session of the Council of 869–70 that Zachary ever went to Rome 'for his trial'? But the contradiction is only apparent. Baanes referred to the actual trial and so far was right, as Zachary and his friends never went to Rome for it. Whilst their case was pending before the court of appeal, they omitted, after Ignatius' expulsion, to press for a decision in Rome and contented themselves, as we shall see presently, with the satisfaction which the synod of 861 gave them. The undertaking they had signed in Rome, as stated by the papal legates in the same passage, that they would 'in all things follow the judgement of the Holy Roman Church', did not trouble them.

One more detail that might explain Ignatius' omission to send explanations to Benedict III. According to a statement made by Zachary at the synod of 861, the aggrieved bishops, besides complaining in their appeal to Rome of their unfair deposition, also questioned the legitimacy of Ignatius' office on the ground that instead of being elected by a local synod and confirmed by the Emperor, he had straightaway been appointed Patriarch by the Empress Theodora, then the Regent, in contravention of local canonical custom. It appears that it was this particular charge which the Pope wished especially to investigate, since Lazarus, the Patriarch's first envoy, could neither deny the fact nor give any satisfactory explanation. One can understand the Patriarch's dismay and that of his followers on learning that both his verdict and the legitimacy of his office had been taken exception to. Rome's intention even to consider such a charge must have looked to many Ignatians like taking sides with the Patriarch's enemies, and this at a time when, after the elimination of the Empress's Minister Theoktistos, Theodora's power seemed to slip into the hands of the Gregorian party. Little wonder that Ignatius felt reluctant to submit to such an inquiry. This frame of mind would be more consistent with the attitude he adopted at the synod of 861, as we shall see in the next chapter.

The facts as explained allow us to draw a few conclusions. First of all, the incident under discussion was far more serious than has generally been supposed, although the Holy See's hesitation, and chiefly Pope Benedict's attitude, would lead one to think that the reasons for Gregory's and the two bishops' deposition were trivial and open to discussion. It is also important to underline the fact that Gregory's co-defendants appealed to Rome as to a higher court, on the strength, as explained, of the canons of the Sardican synod. Let us also note that Gregory's faction, for all its anti-papal reputation, actually chose to fight Ignatius by spreading the rumour that he had refused to acknowledge the Pope's letter. These facts cast a curious light on the mentality of the Byzantines in the ninth century and on their respect for the See of Rome. To be noted also is that Ignatius, at least at that time, was not sufficiently aware of the importance of that See and its claims on the universal Church, as was evidenced by his first official contact with the Pope. Ignorance of usage on similar occasions in presenting the Pope among other things with a pallium and drawing on himself a categorical refusal illustrates Ignatius' simplicity, though the way he dealt with Asbestas' appeal to Rome proves that he protected none the less jealously the rights of the Patriarchs of the second Rome and did not like the Roman See's intervention in the affairs of his patriarchate. Nevertheless, he did not deny the rights of that See, though it is also true to say that he could not have done so without provoking his enemies' legitimate criticism for disregarding the canons of Sardica.

So far, we have only considered the ecclesiastical aspect of the conflict. There is not much information to give us a glimpse of what took place behind the scenes. Gregory's associates were apparently not very numerous, for the synod of 853 only prosecuted those who had been loudest in their criticisms of the Patriarch's policy; but few as they were, they raised many sympathies among the clergy and other quarters.

The intellectuals, who usually ranged themselves on the Moderate side, were naturally partial to Gregory. Remember that Ignatius, as even Anastasius the Librarian acknowledges in his preface to the Acts of the Eighth Council,[1] treated profane learning with the utmost contempt, sharing in this respect the feelings of the die-hard monks and zealots in painful contrast to the long line of men of learning who had sat on the patriarchal throne of Byzantium. The names of the Patriarchs Tarasius, Nicephorus, John the Grammarian and Methodius had set a high tradition; and it was only human that the intellectuals should closely watch the Patriarch's doings and feel supercilious. But the radical elements of the liberal party did not stop there and went even so far as to sneer publicly at the Patriarch's ignorance in matters philosophical and theological. Anastasius tells us in the preface quoted that Photius, then professor at the University of Constantinople, later, president of the Imperial Chancellery and future Patriarch, was one of those who ridiculed poor Ignatius. He is even supposed to have concocted a sham

[1] Mansi, vol. XVI, col. 6: 'Qui scilicet viros exterioris sapientiae repulisset.'

32

heretical doctrine on the two souls, and explained to his intimate friend Constantine the Philosopher, future apostle of the Slavs, who upbraided him for it, that he only wanted to see what the Patriarch, ignorant of syllogisms and contemptuous of philosophy, was going to do about it, were a heresy suddenly to burst at his feet.

This anecdote sounds suspect. Even Hergenröther[1] refused to take it literally, and attributed the heresy in question to some of Photius' students deliberately exaggerating certain of their master's sayings in order to bait the unlettered Patriarch. But the Acts find nothing to say about it. As the Eighth Council voted a canon—the tenth in the Greek summary and the eleventh in the translation by Anastasius[2]—which condemned a similar heresy, it must have been preached in Byzantium by somebody, but its author was certainly not Photius, nor one of his students. The Fathers of the Eighth Council, who collected whatever they could lay hands upon in order to convict Photius, would certainly not have overlooked a heresy propagated either by him or by one of his students. The condemnatory canon mentions neither, and Photius' bitterest enemies, bishop Stylianos, Theognostos and Nicetas, knew nothing about it. Only one single writer, Simeon Magister,[3] fathers the heresy on Photius, with this important difference between him and Anastasius, that according to Simeon, Photius, as a Patriarch, openly preached the said doctrine from the ambo of St Sophia. But his story betrays signs of fantastic romancing and should be classed with the mendacious fabrications scattered over Byzantium by Photius' worst enemies, bent on rousing the populace against him. It is not the only fairy tale in Simeon's collection. There is, besides him, the compiler of the anti-Photian Collection,[4] to be discussed later, who also attributes to Photius the doctrine of the two souls, but we shall find that this writer does not always deserve the credit he claims.

As regards Anastasius, he picked up his anecdote in Constantinople, in ultra-Ignatian circles, which he frequented at the time. In his letter to Gauderich of Velletri,[5] a letter intended to preface his translation of Constantine's work on the recovery of St Clement's relics, he confesses having had in Constantinople interviews with Metrophanes of Smyrna, one of the most devoted partisans of Ignatius and who happened to be an exile in Cherson at the time of the alleged recovery of the relics;[6]

---

[1] *Photius*, vol. III, pp. 444–6.   [2] Mansi, vol. XVI, cols. 404, 166.
[3] (Bonn), p. 673.   [4] Mansi, vol. XVI, col. 456.   [5] *M.G.H.* Ep. VII, p. 437.
[6] Consult on this subject my book, *Les Légendes de Constantin et de Méthode*, pp. 190–7.

and it had been Anastasius' intention to collect in the Byzantine capital all the information he could about his friend Constantine. The Ignatians, aware of the Roman librarian's interests and of the prestige this young Greek scholar commanded in Rome, naturally endeavoured to associate the reputation of such a notability with their own cause; but being unable to present Anastasius with more forcible evidence of Constantine's friendliness to their cause, they forged the story of a quarrel between the two friends, a tale which Anastasius faithfully copied, but most certainly did not gather from Constantine. The latter's alleged reply is too obviously inspired by the Ignatians' hatred for Photius to have come from Constantine's own lips, for he was, on the Ignatians' own showing, his best friend; for he attributes to Photius nothing less than hatred for Ignatius and greed, i.e. the very character traits which the Ignatians fastened on him to bolster up the belief that he desired at all costs to take possession of the patriarchal throne. Anastasius was then no longer in a position to verify their statements, since Constantine had died in Rome in 869,[1] perhaps even before Anastasius had left for Byzantium. It is only right to add that Photius' writings do not permit one to suppose that he was the author of the doctrine of the two souls: whatever he wrote on the existence of the human soul was perfectly orthodox,[2] and the sceptical comments on this anecdote by E. Amann are more than justified.[3] From all this we may gather one thing, that the intellectuals were in sympathy with Gregory's party and that its radical elements ridiculed Ignatius' ignorance.

These people seem to have indulged in other exaggerations in their campaign against Ignatius. Canon XVI of the Eighth Council[4] severely forbids parodies of the sacred liturgy, as organized by 'certain laymen of senatorial rank in the reign of the late Emperor' (Michael III). Nicetas also mentions these parodies;[5] and the Continuator of Theophanes describes them very picturesquely, often in a manner scarcely

---

[1] Cf. Laehr, 'Briefe und Prologe des Bibl. Anastasius', in *Neues Archiv*, vol. XLVII, p. 429.

[2] See for instance Photius' homilies, Aristarchos, Φωτίου λόγοι καὶ ὁμιλίαι (Constantinople, 1900), vol. I, pp. 339 seq., 358 (hom. ΜΓ), p. 423 (hom. ΜΕ); *P.G.* vol. 102, cols. 85 seq., 101, 156; Aristarchos, loc. cit. vol. II, pp. 81, 130 (hom. ΜΘ). See also Photius' sayings which Aristarchos takes for the Patriarch's lectures on philosophy, ibid. vol. I, pp. 62, 63, 90–5, 110–13, 218, 220.

[3] E. Amann, 'Photius', *Dictionnaire de Théologie Catholique*, vol. XII, col. 1560: 'Quant à l'histoire racontée par Anastase sur l'hérésie des deux âmes, ballon d'essai lancé par Photius pour démontrer l'incapacité théologique d'Ignace, on aimerait à en avoir de plus sérieux garants.'

[4] Mansi, vol. XVI, col. 169.   [5] *P.G.* vol. 105, col. 528.

dignified. According to him, their author was no less a man than Michael III himself.[1] But he should be read with caution, since his work was intended to glorify Basil, founder of the new dynasty and murderer of Michael III. All the writings issuing from the Constantine Porphyrogennetos circle were directed to the one object of painting Michael III in the most unfavourable colours so that his murder by Basil might emerge as a just retribution by Providence and a meritorious deed. Whatever therefore Theophanes' Continuator has to say on the point that interests us originates from a legend invented in Byzantium to the detriment of Michael III at the instigation of the Ignatians and Basil's panegyrists.

But whilst refusing to take literally what the Ignatian writers tell us about Michael in this matter, one can hardly deny the fact that Michael was actually an active party to these travesties. The spathars, when cross-questioned on the subject by the legates in the course of the ninth session of the Council of 869–70,[2] definitely confessed that they had been forced by the young Emperor to take part in these parodies. It is surprising to note that after such a charge the legates should have let off the late Emperor so lightly. Whether they wished to spare Basil's feelings, who in deference to his young friend probably attended this kind of entertainment, or whether Michael was only indirectly responsible for it, is not clear: in any case, the same passage of the Acts seems to prove that these spectacles were pointedly aimed at Ignatius and his party and that directly Photius became Patriarch they stopped. The legates failed to make Photius liable for these incidents, though not for want of trying.

And yet, the mere fact that Michael III should have been directly mixed up with these incidents by writers of a later period points to another finding: the fellowship uniting young Michael and his uncle Bardas with Gregory's followers. Here we come up against the political side of the wrangle. We have seen already that the condemnation of Asbestas and his friends had been confirmed by Theodora, to whose government Pope Nicholas attributed a leading initiative in convoking the synod that indicted Gregory, so that by 853, the time when the breach between Gregory and Ignatius occurred, people in Byzantium had taken their stand and chosen their sides on the political platform. Theodora and Theoktistos counted on the Extremists and supported Ignatius to the utmost: Bardas with Michael relied on the Moderates; whereas the attitude of the Roman See in the clash between Ignatius

[1] (Bonn), pp. 244–7. [2] Mansi, vol. XVI, cols. 153–5.

and the bishop of Syracuse no doubt enhanced the Moderate party's prestige.

The political rivalry that smouldered between Theoktistos and Bardas exploded in 856, the year of the young Michael's coming of age. We cannot but remember what happened under Irene, when her son attained his majority. It would have been an easy matter for Bardas, by recalling the past, to convince his young nephew of Theoktistos' ambition to become a second Stauracius and to eliminate the young Emperor from government once for all. Theodora was no Irene; but the idea of handing over the reins of government to her son did not appeal to her and still less to Theoktistos. Both knew perfectly well that the transfer would lead to a complete change of political orientation, for Bardas, the patron of the Moderates, was holding himself ready in the background.

A decision according to Byzantine usage was therefore imperative: either the one or the other leader of the rival forces had to disappear. Theoktistos would not have hesitated, at a pinch, to get rid of Bardas by force, but Bardas happened to be more wide-awake and less scrupulous than his rival; and so, at the beginning of 856, with the complicity of Michael,[1] he assassinated Theoktistos. Deprived of his support, Theodora found it impossible to hold her own against the Moderate party and its leaders, Bardas and the young Emperor Michael. But the Extremists refused to disarm, remaining hopeful so long as Theodora succeeded in staying at the imperial palace. They therefore concentrated all their venom on Bardas, the man to be removed at all cost. For the purpose of discrediting him in the eyes of the public, rumours were set going about his immoral conduct and his incest with his daughter-in-law;[2] and taking advantage of Ignatius' honesty and zeal, the Extremists planned to cause a breach between the highest religious authority and the political powers. Given Byzantine mentality, the coup was astute and well aimed; for, with Bardas and Michael disgraced in public estimation, it would have been an easy matter to undermine their influence in the imperial palace and restore Theodora and her Extremists to power.

Their machinations were partly successful: Ignatius allowed himself to be won over and the congregation at St Sophia had the thrill of witnessing a sensational scene, when the Patriarch refused communion to the man who then represented in Byzantium supreme political power.

[1] For details, cf. Bury, *A History of the Eastern Roman Empire...*, pp. 157 seq.
[2] On these rumours and Ignatius' line of conduct consult my book, *Les Légendes de Constantin et de Méthode*, pp. 139 seq.

The new regime had little reputation left; but on the face of it, Ignatius seems to have carried his zeal too far. There is a simple and natural explanation for Bardas' affection for his daughter-in-law: after losing a son he loved dearly, he transferred his paternal affection to the son's wife, who in her bereavement needed it. Such cases are fairly common. All the chroniclers who mention the accusation, including Nicetas the Paphlagonian, Ignatius' 'biographer', only refer to rumours current in Byzantium and reported to the Patriarch;[1] and they would have spoken in different terms had there been any serious evidence of Bardas' immorality. St Tarasius, St Nicephorus and St Methodius would in similar circumstances have acted with greater circumspection than did St Ignatius. It is not here suggested that Ignatius was in any way implicated in this political plot; for we are more and more convinced that he was a saintly man and fully deserved the honours which the two Churches have paid him on the altars for centuries; and the study of contemporary documents only confirms this conviction. The fanatics of the Extremist party merely took advantage of his simplicity, his lack of discretion and his inexperience in politico-religious matters, and that was all there was to it.

To cut short all further intrigues and deprive his enemies once for all of all hope of return to power with the assistance of Theodora and her daughters, Bardas decided to render his sister and his nieces harmless by sending them to a convent. He acted, it must be admitted, with great leniency, for Byzantium was used to worse scenes and a repetition of the tragedy that befell Constantine VI and his sons and cost them their lives would not have perturbed its equanimity so very deeply.

Ignatius was asked to bless the Empress' veil, a request which to Bardas' way of thinking was meant to give him the chance to prove his innocence in the political plots of the Extremist party. But this was asking too much. It was not so much his religious temperament and his rectitude that caused him to demur, but the fact that he owed the Empress everything: she had selected him for the patriarchal dignity and he meant to remain loyal. He refused. In his refusal the government found evidence of the Patriarch's complicity with the enemies of the new political regime and felt all the more irritated as the fanatics exploited his attitude against Bardas, Michael and their partisans, and

[1] Consult my book (loc. cit.), where I quote Bury's judgement on Ignatius' conduct. It is interesting to note that Yared's conclusions (loc. cit., 1872, vol. II, pp. 556 seq.) on this incident were thus confirmed by Bury.

went so far as to organize a conspiracy. Simeon Magister,[1] unfavourable as he was to Photius and openly in sympathy with Ignatius and Theodora, and the Continuator of George the Monk[2] both mention a murderous assault on Bardas. It was engineered by the imperial protostrator and it appeared that the ex-Empress was implicated. It was, however, discovered in time and the conspirators were beheaded in the Hippodrome. Meanwhile the position grew more serious, as the failure of this first attempt did not entirely discourage or dishearten the opposition. Gebeon, one of the fanatics, tried his chances by asserting that he was the Empress' son; not unsuccessfully, for Theodora's partisans began to rally round him, when he was caught and cruelly done to death. Ignatius, already under serious suspicion and closely watched by the imperial police, made a slip: maybe out of pity, or because the culprit's pose as a monk brought him under the Patriarch's jurisdiction, he undertook the man's defence. This only made suspicions worse and Ignatius was arraigned for high treason and banished to the Isle of Terebinthos.[3] This must have happened, according to his own statement before the synod, at the end of July 857.

[1] (Bonn), p. 658.   [2] (Bonn), p. 823.

[3] For details, cf. Bury, *A History of the Eastern Roman Empire...*, pp. 188 seq. Even the biographer of St Theodora states that the Empress numbered many partisans among the senators, which may suggest that the conflict was rather of a political nature (Vita S. Theodorae, ed. Regel, *Analecta Byzantino-Russica*, Petropoli, 1891, p. 15).

CHAPTER II

IGNATIUS' RESIGNATION AND PHOTIUS' CANONICAL ELECTION

Nicetas' testimony—Ignatius' abdication confirmed by the Extremists' reports—Photius' canonical election—Asbestas and Photius' consecration—Extremists' revolt and its motives—Photius' reaction—Repercussions of these conflicts among the episcopacy and the monastic world.

BARDAS and his partisans finding it impossible to leave on the patriarchal throne a man who to all appearances was under the influence of an opposition party that made no secret of its sympathies for the fallen regime, the question arose of ways and means for getting rid of him: Was it to be straightforward deposition, which was in contravention of canon law and therefore liable to aggravate the difficulty— or resignation? The latter alternative carried the day.

Did Ignatius then actually resign? The documents we possess on this issue contradict each other. The main Ignatian documents deny it and this version has commanded general acceptance. But there are other sources which support the view that Ignatius actually did resign. As the issue is of capital importance in the history of Photius and his first schism, it calls for a thorough examination.[1]

Of all the contemporary accounts of the events that followed the internment of Ignatius on the Isle of Terebinthos, only one so far has been generally considered reliable, that by Nicetas the Paphlagonian,[2] author of a pamphlet commonly assumed to be the genuine biography of St Ignatius. That several Byzantine chroniclers such as the successors of Theophanes and George the Monk depended for their information on Nicetas' so-called biography[3] only tended to establish his reliability.

After relating the events that preceded Ignatius' internment, Nicetas dwells on the repeated efforts made by the government to extract Ignatius' resignation: a deputation of prelates is said to have approached him and induced him to resign in view of the difficulties of the time.[4]

---

[1] Cf. my study, 'Le Premier Schisme de Photios', in *Bulletin de l'Institut Archéol. Bulgare* (Sofia, 1935), vol. IX, pp. 312–25, which I summarize here with the addition of some new evidence.

[2] Vita Ignatii, *P.G.* vol. 105, cols. 505 seq.

[3] See Part II, ch. 5, pp. 391, 401 of this book, where I give the reasons why these writers followed Nicetas' account.   [4] Loc. cit. col. 505.

On their request being refused, a second deputation of bishops, reinforced by a number of patricians, senators and high functionaries of the Empire, went to Terebinthos. Exhortations, threats, nay, the use of force, if we are to credit Nicetas, proved all in vain. A lengthy description of the fatal effects which a government of miscreants may have on the destinies of the Church, with the additional remark that Providence permits such trials to test His own, is rather startling at this particular place and suggests that the author intends by this digression to slur over something unpleasant. He then passes immediately to the nomination of Photius, who, at the instigation of Asbestas,[1] was busy exerting his energies against Ignatius to the length even of threatening his life. Two months after his appointment, the new Patriarch withdrew the pledge he had given the bishops, who had acknowledged him only on condition that Ignatius should be well treated.[2] Photius then began persecuting his predecessor and his predecessor's partisans. Nicetas tells of Ignatius' deportations, of the renewed efforts to wring from him an abdication and of his excommunication by Photius. Then follows the account of the embassy charged with informing the Pope of Ignatius' resignation, of the convocation of the Council of 861 which stripped Ignatius of his patriarchal dignity on grounds of an uncanonical election,[3] and lastly, of renewed persecution. It was then that his tormentors succeeded in forcing Ignatius to sign a scrap of paper on which Photius is supposed to have subsequently scribbled with his own hand a forged confession of the irregularity of Ignatius' election.

Such is the tale which has commanded general credit. But the affair is not so simple. Nicetas' account leaves open many gaps, and although he seems to record the historical sequence of events with some precision, he omits to mention a number of facts which he must have known, but which did not tally with his preconceived notions.

One point is particularly striking: whilst on several occasions flatly denying Ignatius' resignation (his insistence suggests that at the time of his writing many people affirmed the reverse), Nicetas does not pretend that the Emperor deposed Ignatius; he simply states that the Emperor appointed Photius as the Patriarch. Yet, such a procedure was not in keeping with tradition in a State, where in different circumstances, juridical forms at least had been consistently observed. No action was taken in the appointment of a new Patriarch, until the see had first been declared vacant: any other method might have implied that there

---

[1] Loc. cit. col. 509.
[2] Loc. cit. col. 513.
[3] Loc. cit. col. 517.

were two Patriarchs at the head of the Church. And yet, Nicetas' special pleading in favour of Ignatius would have been much enhanced, had the author been able to record an unjust deposition.[1] His silence seems fairly significant.

In order to get at the truth, which in Nicetas' story can sometimes be read between the lines, one should collate it with other accounts, some of them coming from Ignatian circles. Now we happen to possess the evidence of five valuable contemporary documents, two of them, the Acts of the Eighth Council and the Life of St Euthymios, being in a class apart, and the three others—the statements of bishop Stylianos of Neocaesarea, of the monk Theognostos and of Metrophanes, metropolitan of Smyrna, all partisans of Ignatius. To these three Ignatian records may be added what Anastasius the Librarian states about events in Byzantium at the time of Photius' elevation to the patriarchal throne and the account given by the anonymous author of the anti-Photian Collection.

The Acts of the Council of 869 are the first source to mention Ignatius' abdication. In the sixth session, Elias, representing the Patriarch of Jerusalem, said:[2]

...Inquiring into all the facts, we have ascertained that when Ignatius, the saintly Patriarch, was in exile, he suffered violence and that a rumour was falsely and unjustly spread of his having resigned the throne of Constantinople. To this we must add, as the Church of the Romans has repeatedly maintained, that we do not believe that any resignation was ever tendered; and if it was tendered, we cannot accept it, since it was wrongly forced on him by violence and against his will, as is easily perceived. This much is therefore certain, that whoever lives in exile and under duress cannot be held to renounce a throne as it ought to be renounced, for he did not expect to live; he expected death at any moment and daily prepared to suffer the worst.

The Greek summary of the Acts is more laconic, though more explicit than the translation by Anastasius: 'The deed of abdication signed by the Patriarch Ignatius in exile is null and void and must be considered vitiated by the fact that it was forcibly extorted....'[3]

Other evidence comes from the same session of the Council, namely, the cross-examination of the Photianist Eulampius by the Emperor

[1] Carefully note that by insisting on the efforts made by the government to induce Ignatius to resign, Nicetas implicitly denies the belief so generally accepted that Ignatius' internment in Terebinthos was equivalent to a deposition. Had a sentence of deposition been passed, why those efforts on the part of the government to compel the Patriarch to abdicate?

[2] Mansi, vol. XVI, col. 85.   [3] Ibid. col. 345.

Basil:[1] 'Eulampius: And yet, kind sir, the Lord Ignatius did resign. The Emperor...: Who deposed him? Eulampius: The Emperor deposed him. The Emperor...: And where was he when he resigned? Eulampius: Abroad, in his island. The Emperor...: No doubt, he sent a messenger to the Emperor to inform him of his intention to resign....Give us the name of that messenger.' But just when we expect to hear particulars of Ignatius' resignation, the dialogue is cut short by the Holy See's legate Marinus refusing to listen any further to people who have already been condemned by Rome. In the Greek summary of the Acts, this passage is also given in abbreviated form, but in clearer terms:[2] 'But meanwhile the lord Ignatius resigned. The Emperor said: When he had been forcibly dethroned, sent into exile and asked to resign in that state, how could his resignation be valid and not extorted?' It should be observed here that this official document directly contradicts the evidence of Nicetas.

In another document, the Life of St Euthymios, a contemporary work, we read:[3]

He [Ignatius] governed the Church for ten long years; but being persistently harassed by the imperial rulers and openly and deliberately persecuted, he at last gave up this hopeless struggle against men who suffered from an incurable disease and breathed nothing but malevolence. He therefore relinquished the patriarchal throne and the direction of the Church, a decision in which he yielded partly to his own preference and partly to external pressure. After handing in to the Church his act of resignation, he withdrew to his monastery, being persuaded that this would be preferable. The Government's evil dispositions being what they were, he elected to devote himself to meditation and quiet commune with God rather than draw disaster on himself and his flock. When the rumour spread that the archbishop had been expelled from his ecclesiastical see against his will and that for this reason people refused to enter into communion with the new Patriarch, the holy father Nicholas himself, for fear of entering into communion with the same, left his monastery. All this happened under the new Patriarch, a shining light of orthodoxy and of all the virtues, namely, the blessed Photius, who as suggested by his name, illuminated the whole world with the plenitude of his wisdom. From his infancy he had been consecrated to Christ and in defence of His icons had faced confiscation and exile. From the outset, he was a true associate of his father in all his struggles and virtuous practices.

---

[1] Mansi, vol. XVI, col. 88.   [2] Ibid. col. 349.

[3] L. Petit, 'Vie et Office de St Euthyme le Jeune', in *Revue de l'Orient Chrétien* (1903), vol. VIII, pp. 178, 179. See my book, *Les Légendes de Constantin et de Méthode*, pp. 143, 144.

Hence his life was made wonderful and his death agreeable to God and confirmed by miracles.

The Life of Euthymios flatly contradicts Nicetas' statement, but its evidence has seldom been taken seriously. Hergenröther[1] mentions the extract from the sixth session of the Acts of the Council but attaches no importance to it, and those who gave it some credit only understood it in the light of Nicetas' story regarding Ignatius' extorted signature at the bottom of the confession forged by Photius. As the Life of St Euthymios the Younger was published only in 1903, little use could be made of it and its statements could not be seriously collated with the evidence of Nicetas.

Let us now examine the evidence coming from other Ignatian witnesses. First of all, it is surprising that Stylianos, in his letter to Pope Stephen V,[2] Theognostos[3] and Anastasius[4] in their accounts, also addressed to the Pope, were studiously silent on the events intervening in Byzantium between the Patriarch Ignatius' internment on the Island of Terebinthos and Photius' election. And yet, both Stylianos and Theognostos must have known that it had been Photius' wish that his accession to the patriarchal throne should have every semblance of legitimacy, since the Emperor alleged in the letter which endorsed Photius' synodical letter to the Pope that Ignatius had abdicated on grounds of old age and unsettled conditions. Logically, one would have expected them all to concentrate their main attack on Photius by making the Pope understand that both the Emperor and Photius were simply shameless liars. It is therefore strange that all the accounts, which were intended to inform Rome of the actual state of things, should be so reticent about events preceding Photius' accession.

Fortunately, another document, being that written by Metrophanes, Metropolitan of Smyrna, is more expressive. This document was not meant for the Pope, but purported to send information to a high Byzantine official, Manuel, Logothete of the Course, about Photius' downfall at the Council of 869. Addressed to a Byzantine who knew all about the happenings in Constantinople at the time, it is more explicit and helps to fill the gaps we noted elsewhere. This is how the Metropolitan describes the events:[5]

Photius...like an adulterer, seized the throne of Constantinople during Ignatius' lifetime. Without having been elected to the dignity by the bishops'

---

[1] *Photius*, vol. II, p. 102.   [2] Mansi, vol. XVI, cols. 425–46.
[3] Ibid. cols. 296–302.   [4] Ibid. cols. 3 seq.   [5] Ibid. col. 416.

votes in accordance with law and usage, he was summarily installed by the Caesar. This is the reason why the bishops unanimously disowned him, nominated their own three candidates and for a long time stood by their decision. Eventually, they were outwitted and all gave in, except five, including myself. When we realized that all the bishops were corrupt, we considered that we should demand that he should sign an official declaration in which he professed to be a son of the Church in Christ and bound himself to remain in communion with our very saintly Patriarch. We preferred doing this rather than disobey our Patriarch, who had expressed a desire that we should elect as Patriarch one belonging to our Church in Christ. It was then that he signed in our presence a declaration affirming his wish to regard Ignatius as a Patriarch above suspicion and guiltless of the charges made against him;[1] that he would never say a word against him nor allow anyone else to do so. On those conditions we accepted Photius, though under protest and pressure from those in authority. But he soon broke the word he had signed and deposed Ignatius. Thereupon the whole body of the bishops of Constantinople met and anathematized Photius, declaring him dethroned by the Father, the Son and the Holy Spirit. So unanimous were the bishops at that moment that they turned the anathema against themselves, in case any one of them should ever acknowledge Photius. And as they went on holding meetings for forty days in the church of St Irene, he retaliated by summoning, with the assistance of Bardas, a synod in the church of the Holy Apostles and again deposing and anathematizing Ignatius. It was then we personally upbraided him for his crime, with the result that we were subjected to violence, arrested without a warning and imprisoned for days in the evil-smelling jail of the Numeroi. Ignatius was imprisoned with us and put in irons; others were locked up in the Pretorium prison. Then we were set free and banished, the Patriarch to Mytilene, others elsewhere, whilst Photius sent to Old Rome four metropolitans of his own party, to explain his case to his own advantage and to Ignatius' detriment. But the godly Pontiff, although there was none present on our behalf to plead our cause—our enemies would not allow it—summoned a council of the Western bishops, condemned Photius on the strength of his own letters and treated him like a layman.

Metrophanes then goes on to the dispatch of the pontifical legates to Constantinople.

This text is important, since it concerns events that followed Ignatius' internment and was addressed, not to the Pope, but to a local official. It is the account by an eye-witness, obliged against his will to tell the truth in exact proportion to the reader's capacity to verify for himself the information supplied. That truth is very simple and fairly easy to reconstruct.

[1] This is my translation of the word ἀκαταιτίατος.

Ignatius was deported to the Isle of Terebinthos for the simple reason that the government suspected him of being in league with the Extremists who were bent on the overthrow of the existing regime. This suspicion, despite the lack of unimpeachable evidence, seemed to be well founded. The Patriarch's uncompromising attitude towards Bardas and Michael had been cleverly exploited by the opponents of the regime to foment a revolt, which had gravely compromised him in the eyes of the government. This clash between the civil and ecclesiastical powers having placed the Church of Constantinople in a very precarious position, Ignatius was pressed to resign on grounds of old age and public unrest; and among the bishops who made this attempt there were not only prelates in sympathy with the Moderate party, but others, not a few, who up to that time had supported Ignatius and made no secret of countenancing the opinions of the Extremist section. This much can be read between the lines in Nicetas the Paphlagonian's account,[1] in which the writer expresses indignation that among the delegation there should be found bishops who once had sworn and confirmed in writing that they would rather deny the Trinity than allow their legitimate pastor to be condemned by any other than a canonical sentence. We may here observe that Nicetas slightly exaggerates. It does, however, clearly emerge from his words that the Byzantine higher clergy gradually came to acknowledge, almost unanimously, that in the circumstances it would be advisable in the interests of the Church for the Patriarch to abdicate. It was the application of the famous principle of 'oeconomia'. Faced with the insistence by bishops and high imperial officials, among whom he noted many friends who certainly did not credit the calumnies levelled against him, the Patriarch ended by giving in and even went so far as to invite his most faithful partisans to elect another Patriarch. They were the five bishops mentioned by Metrophanes, including himself. They also finally acquiesced for fear of 'disobeying our Patriarch, who had expressed a desire that we should elect as Patriarch one belonging to our Church in Christ'.[2] Since Ignatius could not invite his own partisans to elect another Patriarch, unless he had previously given his resignation, Metrophanes, an Ignatian, confirms the statement in Photianist sources relating to Ignatius' resignation.

[1] *P.G.* vol. 105, col. 505.
[2] This enigmatic passage puzzled me already at the time I wrote *Les Légendes de Constantin et de Méthode* (see p. 140). Not satisfied with the solution proposed, I have gone over the same ground again.

Now let us test this conclusion in the light of the statement by another writer, an extreme Ignatian and the compiler of the anti-Photianist Collection. This contains all the documents against Photius and served the extreme Ignatians as an armoury in their struggle against the Photianists. After recording how many times the Photianists had dishonoured their signatures and thereby fouled the cross which according to usage preceded their names, the author proceeds:

They did so for the first time, when the Caesar Bardas tried to dethrone Ignatius, who to anticipate an ignominious expulsion decided to resign of his own free will.[1] But the bishops agreed among themselves that if Bardas ever tried to use force, they would rather die than tolerate such a thing. They thus prevented Ignatius carrying out his intention.[2] But when later Bardas forcibly ejected him, the bishops made common cause with him [i.e. Bardas] and thereby fell under the anathema they had decreed against themselves. Later again, when Photius had forced his way in, the bishops asked him to pledge his word in writing and undertake always to honour Ignatius and do him no harm. Photius then signed a document to that effect. But he violated his pledge, ignominiously summoned a synod and anathematized Ignatius, and induced some bishops who had supported Ignatius to join in the anathema: they had defended him at the outset, but violating their crosses, turned against him.

It is obvious that this document goes even further than the witnesses quoted previously, for it shows that Ignatius wished to resign at the beginning, i.e. at the first clash with the new government. No sooner had Bardas interned Ignatius at Terebinthos, than the latter's followers, probably realizing that things were beginning to look dangerous, went back on their previous intentions and advised Ignatius to resign, taking the precaution to ask Photius for guarantees. The account makes it evident how misleading it was to interpret events exclusively in the light of Ignatius' 'biography'.

Another witness from the Ignatian camp, the monk Theognostos, confirms the accuracy of this interpretation. He is, as we have said, silent about the events following Ignatius' internment, but when he describes in Ignatius' name his trial by the synod of 861, he makes a slip and allows the truth to leak out. This is what he puts into Ignatius' mouth:[3]

I asked leave to greet the legates Rhodoald and Zachary, and leave being granted, I bowed to them and asked what they desired. They answered: We

---

[1] Mansi, vol. XVI, col. 441: ἑκὼν ὑποχωρῆσαι ἐβούλετο.

[2] καὶ οὕτως ἐπέσχον τῆς ὁρμῆς τὸν Ἰγνάτιον.

[3] Mansi, vol. XVI, col. 297; P.G. vol. 105, cols. 857, 860.

are the legates of the Roman Pope Nicholas I and we were sent to try your case. I asked them again if they had not brought me any letter from His Holiness. They answered: No, since they had not been sent to a Patriarch, but to a man condemned by a local synod. We are ready, they said, to do whatever the canonical decrees lay down. Then, said I, first dismiss the adulterer. If you cannot do that, you are no true judges. They replied by pointing to the Emperor: He wants it so. Then those around the Emperor turned to me and invited me, by suasion and threats, to resign.[1] But they failed to convince me. Then they turned to the metropolitans, insulting and incriminating them in many ways, saying that surely[2] they had already accepted my resignation.[3] Why then did they again claim me as their Patriarch? To this the metropolitans replied: At that time,[4] having to choose between two evils—the Emperor's anger and the people's revolt—we chose the lesser. To-day, you who are near the Emperor, return the throne to the Patriarch and leave us alone. Then the imperial officials began again to exhort me, insisting on my resigning of my own accord, so as to enable the adulterer to rule the Church in perfect peace. As I refused to be persuaded, they dispersed that day.

Theognostos' words are sufficiently clear. This keen partisan of Ignatius unconsciously confirms what the Ignatians persisted in denying, i.e. that Ignatius had spontaneously resigned and that his resignation had been acknowledged to be valid even by his own supporters. Later, yielding to a 'popular revolt', that is, to the pressure of the radicals of their own party, they again proclaimed Ignatius their Patriarch. Government adherents then endeavoured to obtain from the latter a new spontaneous declaration, confirming his abdication. Although Theognostos asserts that this new pressure was put on during the synod of 861, we may surmise, all the more justifiably as we find it suggested by Nicetas, that these attempts were made even before the synod of 859.

This passage from Theognostos has been misinterpreted to this day, the fault lying mainly with Raderus who edited the document. So convinced was he that Ignatius had been unfairly deposed that he translated the word *apotaxis* by 'depositio', which is of course incorrect, and all the more inexplicable as he had shortly before translated it by 'abdicatio'. Hergenröther accepted this translation[5] and lent his weight to another instance of how prejudice can twist an argument.[6]

---

[1] τὴν ἀπόταξιν ἐзήτουν.   [2] τάχα used ironically.   [3] τὴν ἀπόταξιν ἐμήν.
[4] τότε.   [5] *Photius*, vol. I, p. 424.
[6] Theognostos seems to convey fairly clearly that there were then two parties in Byzantium. He calls the members of the party in opposition to his own not only οἱ περὶ τὸν βασιλέα, which might just as well refer to the imperial officials, but also οἱ βασιλικοί. Reading between the lines, one can find confirmation in another

Having examined all the important accounts of Ignatius' attitude after his internment, we may then conclude with confidence that Ignatius was not deposed by force, but that he abdicated to forestall worse complications. His abdication was made at the request of the new regime, it is true, but it was acknowledged as valid and canonical by all the members of the higher clergy gathered in Constantinople, including Ignatius' staunchest supporters. Ignatius himself invited his followers to accept the situation and to proceed to elect the new Patriarch.

The foregoing records have given us a clear picture of how the election of the new Patriarch came about. It remains to complete them with information from elsewhere. From the evidence produced, we may already infer that the government wanted a man whose loyalty was above suspicion, and it betrayed an inclination to nominate one straight away. It hinted at the name of Photius as that of the most likely candidate. But the bishops, chiefly Ignatius' partisans, insisted on the observation of canon law, i.e. on the bishops meeting synodically and presenting three candidates of their choice to the Emperor. Satisfaction had to be given and the synod was summoned. But before the synod could proceed with the election, it was called upon to settle another matter. We must remember that at the time of the synod meeting Gregory Asbestas' group was still under a ban. The position needed rectifying, since the Moderates had after all had the best of the fight and Gregory was still the leader of the party's ecclesiastical members. The position forcibly recalled that of the Studites at the death of the Patriarch Methodius, though Asbestas and his friends could claim that the highest court of appeal, the See of Rome, had not confirmed the Patriarch's verdict. Their suit was then pending. Ignatius gone, they were now in a position to ask the synod, which represented the Church of Constantinople during the vacancy of the patriarchal See, to do the right thing by annulling the sentence passed on them; and the synod felt all the more disposed to give them that satisfaction, as it saw no other way of restoring peace within the Byzantine Church. The new government took a personal interest in the affair and the synod rehabilitated Gregory and his friends.[1]

passage of Theognostos, that the whole episcopate had acknowledged Photius as the rightful Patriarch; in the character of Ignatius he writes (Mansi, vol. xvi, col. 300): 'And even when he [Photius] had induced the metropolitan to rally to him, they asked him for a document signed with his own hand concerning my person.'

[1] These two facts may be inferred from the letter by Pope Nicholas I to Michael III, *M.G.H.* Ep. vi, pp. 498–9: 'Porro si dicitis Gregorium ab imperio vestro et ab antistitibus fuisse receptum, percontari libet... quibus hoc documentis, quibus

It appears that the bishops deposed by Ignatius gave the Fathers of the synod, who represented the Church of Constantinople, some sort of satisfaction before being definitely absolved. So much, at least, emerges from the defence by Zachary of Chalcedon, who spoke in the course of the sixth session of the Council of 869–70.[1] Zachary refuted the opponents' charge that Photius had been ordained by deposed bishops: 'For they were not deposed for actual misdeeds, but for their attitude of resistance to the Church. United again and disowning their conduct, they show themselves worthy of being received.' This statement by the counsel for the defence must have been based on fact. It seems probable, if not certain, that the synod must have asked Gregory for some declaration to conciliate Ignatius' partisans, whose votes were indispensable for annulling Ignatius' sentence. This rehabilitation had been laid down as a necessary requisite by the victorious party prior to the Patriarch's election. We must remember that the Studites, who had been excommunicated by Methodius, had been readmitted to the Church by the Patriarch Ignatius and not by a synod, since the Empress Theodora had appointed Ignatius without the formality of a synod. Michael III and the Regent Bardas first meant to follow Theodora's precedent, and if the new Patriarch had been appointed by the Emperor in the same informal way, Asbestas' group would have been taken back into the Church by the Patriarch just as the Studites had been. But as Michael and Bardas acceded to the clergy's demand for the customary procedure and the holding of a synod, Asbestas and his followers only stood to gain by having their reconciliation confirmed by a synod attended by both parties.

The synod then dealt with the new Patriarch's election. With the two camps face to face, the discussions, according to Metrophanes, were heated. The Moderates probably had their own candidates in readiness, with Asbestas presumably foremost among them, as the leader of the ecclesiastical wing. But his opposition to Ignatius had been too conspicuous for his election to make for peace. The Ignatians had their own candidates as a matter of course.

For fear of a schism, it was then agreed to eliminate all the bishops, whether Ignatians or anti-Ignatians, and to look for a capable candidate among the higher officials. This tradition had for a time proved popular

canonibus jubentibus agi rite potest.... Jam vero si dicitis: Non ego absolvi, sed a pontificibus, ut solverentur, postulavi, e contra illi multo magis a vobis postulare debuerunt, ut, si eum velletis absolvi, legitima ecclesiastici tenoris absolutio proveniret.' [1] Mansi, vol. xvi, col. 87.

in Byzantium, when troubles were many, and the practice had been resorted to with excellent results, as in the case of Tarasius and Nicephorus. So the synod presented to the government, besides an Ignatian and an anti-Ignatian, a neutral candidate, the protoasekretis Photius, the very man whom the Emperor and Bardas had had in mind from the beginning. The choice, besides giving the government some satisfaction, rallied all the bishops present, except five, of whom Metrophanes, and no doubt Stylianos, were the most refractory.

Why did most of the Ignatian bishops rally to Photius? First, because he was a new man: though a sympathizer with the Moderate party, he evidently was not numbered among its most outspoken members. His orthodoxy was above suspicion, since he had been persecuted by the iconoclasts; he was moreover related to Theodora, whose government[1] the Ignatian bishops still remembered, so that he gave reasonable hopes of not being too zealous in the service of the new regime. On the other hand, he was also related to Bardas, which was a recommendation with the government. But it should be remembered that Photius owed his promotion to Theoktistos, the Logothete, who first appointed him professor at the University of Constantinople, then President of the Imperial Chancellery; this was his best recommendation to the Extremists who favoured the regime of Theoktistos and Theodora.

We now come to Photius' consecration. This matter is of importance, as Photius' opponents particularly objected at a later stage of the Photian controversy to some features of the ceremony.

The new Patriarch's consecration was a hurried affair, for he received all the degrees of the priesthood within the space of a week, a procedure that was of course against the rules of canon law, but under such exceptional circumstances the Byzantines considered themselves exempt from habitual practice. Nor was it an isolated case in Byzantium. Had not the consecrations of the Patriarchs Paul III in 687, Tarasius in 784, and Nicephorus in 806, all laymen at the time of their elections, been conferred in total disregard of canonical rules? By a curious coincidence, all these Patriarchs had, like Photius, occupied the position of imperial

---

[1] It would be more obvious still why Theodora's partisans decided to acknowledge Photius, were Rosseikin's hypothesis on the degree of relationship between Photius and Theodora proved. Rosseikin, *Pervoe Patriarshestvo Patriarkha Fotiya* (Sergiev Posad, 1915), pp. 32–3, asserts against Bury ('The Relationship of Photius to the Empress Theodora', in *Engl. Hist. Rev.* (1890), pp. 252–8) that Theodora had given away her sister Irene in marriage to Photius' brother Sergius.

protoasekretis or President of the Imperial Chancellery. Then again, negotiations before and at the time of the synod seem to have lasted longer than had been expected;[1] Christmas was near, and for the liturgical ceremonies to be celebrated with the usual solemnity the presence of the Patriarch was considered indispensable. When it is remembered what an important place the liturgy held in Byzantine life and at court, one may admit the plea for telescoping the new Patriarch's consecration.

Protracted negotiations must have taken place about who should consecrate the new Patriarch and eventually it was decided that bishops of both parties should share in the function. The Moderates delegated their leader, Gregory Asbestas, in satisfaction for what he had suffered at the hands of Ignatius, and two other consecrators (a consecration must be performed by three bishops)[2] were selected from among those bishops who did not belong to the party of the bishop of Syracuse. So much can be gathered from the speech of the synkellos Elias, who represented the Patriarch of Jerusalem at the sixth session of the Eighth Council:[3] 'We should not condemn those bishops who are convicted of having consecrated Photius, as they were forced to do so under imperial pressure.... But he alone who had been previously deposed and anathematized both by the Patriarch Ignatius and by the Apostolic Church of Rome, Gregory of Syracuse, is condemned and deposed.' The context makes it clear that Elias was not thinking of the election, but of the consecration of Photius, and he would have altered his terms, had the two other consecrators been friends of the Syracusan, for instance, Peter of Sardes and Eulampius of Apamea.[4]

---

[1] As Nicetas (Vita Ignatii, Mansi, vol. XVI, col. 261, P.G. vol. 105, col. 541) states that Ignatius was reinstated in his dignity by Basil I on 23 November, the same day as he was expelled, it seems that this must stand for the date of Ignatius' resignation. This would be the only way of reconciling Ignatius' declaration that he was expelled at the end of July from the patriarcheion with Nicetas' dating.

[2] See I. Habert, Archieraticon. Liber Pontificalis Ecclesiae Graecae (Paris, 1643), pp. 80–4: 'De numero pontificum qui Episcopum apud Graecos legitime ac rite ordinaturi sint.'   [3] Mansi, vol. XVI, cols. 85–6.

[4] Hergenröther, Photius, vol. I, p. 380, was not unaware of this passage and his scepticism regarding its importance seems unjustified. The Greek Acts (Mansi, vol. XVI, col. 348), in summarizing Elias' speech, are still more emphatic than the Latin Acts. It is true that Zachary, bishop of Chalcedon, in pleading for Photius at the same session, only mentions Gregory as Photius' consecrator (ibid. col. 87). According to the Greek Acts (ibid. col. 348), he even seems to insinuate that all the consecrators belonged to Gregory's party. Metrophanes, however, states in his reply to the defence (ibid. col. 90): 'Promoventes eum et consecrantes violenter et coacti ac inviti, atque sine proposito ac voluntate in illius et promotionem et consecrationem ex imperatoris necessitate ac tyrannide impulsi sunt et secuti.' Clear,

How then are we to reconcile the above with the tradition of the Byzantine Church giving the titulary of Heraclea the exclusive right of consecrating and enthroning a new Patriarch?[1] It is not necessary to assume that the privilege was suspended in Photius' case. First, we do not know the names of the two other consecrators and the titulary of Heraclea may have been one of them. It is also possible that the two functions of consecration and enthronement were held separately and that the latter was performed by the titulary of Heraclea.[2] Cases were many in Byzantine Church history of new patriarchs being transferred from other sees to Constantinople and needing only enthronization by the metropolitan of Heraclea.[3]

The fact that bishops of the Ignatian party took part in Photius' consecration is generally omitted by the Ignatians, who at a later stage mainly objected to Gregory Asbestas' participation. They[4] even inferred from it that as an intimate friend of Gregory, Photius had been excommunicated with him by Ignatius. But since Gregory's share in the consecration was rather in the nature of a concession to his party, it need not have been evidence of any friendship between the two men concerned. If on the other hand Photius had been excommunicated for his friendship with Gregory, what about Constantine-Cyril, venerated as a saint by the two Churches, whom Anastasius called Photius' 'amicus fortissimus'? It is true that Photius later adopted Gregory's ecclesiastical policy, but then Ignatius also adopted the ecclesiastical policy of the Studites who had been excommunicated by Methodius and no harm was done. All one can say about Photius' association with Asbestas is that he was a favourite with the majority of the intellectuals of Constantinople who patronized the Moderate party and that Gregory was the leader of its ecclesiastical section.

The documents under discussion seem to suggest that the govern-

---

too, are the Greek Acts, which differentiate between Gregory and the other consecrators (ibid. cols. 352, 353). The attestation of these two opponents of Photius is significant.

[1] On this right, cf. Nicephorus Gregoras (Bonn), vol. I, pp. 164, 165, and Codinus, *De Officiis* (Bonn), ch. xx, p. 104.

[2] Cf. Yared, op. cit. (1872), vol. II, p. 56, and Ivantsov-Platonov, *Sv. Patriarkh Fotii* (St Petersburg, 1892), p. 62 (notes).

[3] For instance, Germanus, Metropolitan of Cyzicus (715), Constantine, of Sylaeon (754), Anthony, of Perge-Sylaeon (821).

[4] Metrophanes, Mansi, vol. xvi, cols. 415, 420. Cf. Nicetas, *P.G.* vol. 105, col. 512; Anastasius, Stylianos, Mansi, vol. xvi, cols. 3, 428. Pope Nicholas I (*M.G.H.* Ep. vi, p. 519, ch. 1 of the synodal decision of 863) was also impressed by the same conclusion. Cf. Hergenröther, *Photius*, vol. I, pp. 362 seq.

ment of Michael and Bardas keenly wished to see the end of all the troubles caused by the party spirit in the ecclesiastical field: it insisted on reconciliation and on the recognition of the elected Patriarch by the body of the Byzantine episcopacy. The opponents of Photius, as we have seen, had eventually dwindled to five;[1] and in compliance with the government's wishes, Photius was successful in securing their recognition of his patriarchal authority by signing a compromise on the treatment of Ignatius. Its details will be discussed presently. When Photius had for the sake of the Church's peace signed the agreement, each of the five bishops received a copy of the document.

Thus it seemed that Photius' elevation to the patriarchal throne, after the recent trying events, meant a return to peace and unity in the Church of Constantinople; and such was the conviction at the time which Photius expressed in a letter to the Patriarch of Antioch,[2] in recalling the grave danger of schism that had threatened the Church: his election, so he wrote, had brought back peace at last. The same impression seems to have prevailed among the Byzantine public, who felt that peace had been saved and that party wrangles would be a thing of the past. Even Nicetas states, though with a touch of irony, that once consecrated, Photius immediately announced to the people the restoration of peace.[3] This consummation was due to Ignatius' wisdom in resigning and thus sacrificing his personal interests to those of the Church and to the new Patriarch's conciliatory spirit and readiness to make concessions.

Peace, unfortunately, was not to last. Two months after Photius' advent according to Nicetas,[4] forty days according to Metrophanes,[5] the fight

[1] Their names were probably listed among Ignatius' partisans by Nicholas I in his letter dispatched to Michael on 28 September 865. The Pope enumerates the bishops who were expected to come to Rome to plead Ignatius' cause (*M.G.H.* Ep. VI, p. 482): 'Antonius Cyzicus, Basilius Thessalonicae, Constantinus Larissae, Theodorus Syracusanorum, Metrophanes Smyrnae, Paulus Ponti Heracliae.' Stylianos of Neocaesarea was certainly one of them. We cannot therefore exactly say who the five bishops referred to were.

[2] J. Valetta, *Photii Epistolae* (London, 1864), vol. I, pp. 145, 146.

[3] *P.G.* vol. 105, col. 512. S. Aristarchos, *Photii Orationes et Homiliae* (Constantinople, 1900), vol. I, pp. 149–60, even wrote after his own method the homily which Photius is supposed to have delivered on 25 December 858.

[4] Loc. cit. col. 513.

[5] Loc. cit. col. 416. This is how to my way of thinking the words ἐπὶ ἡμέρας τεσσαράκοντα should be interpreted. It is difficult to admit, as does Hergenröther, *Photius*, vol. I, p. 382, that the synod lasted forty days. It is, however, possible that the church of St Irene was staffed by an extremist clergy and that the Ignatians used it as their headquarters during the forty days or two months preceding the final rupture.

between the two parties was resumed with greater virulence than ever. As we have seen, Ignatian sources make Photius responsible for the resumption of the struggle by breaking his pledge to the Ignatian bishops and letting loose another persecution against Ignatius and his friends. Nicetas is particularly wrathful in his account of this persecution. To verify any such information coming from an anti-Photian environment, we have only four letters addressed to Bardas by the Patriarch at the outset of his tenure [1] and written in the throes of excitement. There Photius makes the government directly responsible for the excesses committed, intercedes on behalf of some of their victims, the secretary Christodulos and the chartophylax Blasius, and even threatens Bardas with his resignation, should this persecution persist. Thus, again, the Ignatian and Photianist documents contradict each other. To get at the truth, we must find out the motives for a resumption of hostilities.

In this particular matter, we must take as a basis of our inquiry Metrophanes' account, as it is more circumstantial than that of Nicetas. According to him, the new conflict was provoked by the Ignatians. They gathered in the church of St Irene, proclaimed Ignatius the legitimate Patriarch and forthwith excommunicated Photius. Since Metrophanes and other Ignatian sources accused Photius of breaking his promises to the Ignatians, the sense of the compromise signed at the request of the recalcitrant bishops should yield the principal motive of the rupture.

Metrophanes' account gives us the main stipulations of the compromise: Photius was to regard 'Ignatius as a Patriarch above suspicion and guiltless of the charges made against him; he would never say a word against him or allow anyone else to do so'. Theognostos, impersonating Ignatius in his *Libellus* to Nicholas I quoted previously, makes Ignatius say:[2] 'And even when he [Photius] had induced the metropolitans to rally to him, they asked him for a document signed with his own hand concerning my person. In this document he asserted in writing and under oath his determination to undertake nothing but what I should approve, as though I were his own father.' Nicetas[3] completes the terms by stating that Photius undertook 'to leave to Ignatius his patriarchal dignity, to do everything in accordance with his wishes and not to place any obstacles in his way'. The implication then was that Ignatius had to be treated as the former Patriarch, living

[1] *P.G.* vol. 102, cols. 617 seq.
[2] Mansi, vol. XVI, col. 300.
[3] *P.G.* vol. 105, col. 513.

with full episcopal honours in honourable retirement and that all accusations of political intrigue should cease. Such appears to have been the only possible meaning of the terms that could have been acceptable to Photius.

But Nicetas suggests that at least some Ignatians read into the terms much more than they conveyed. 'To do everything in accordance with his wishes' implied that the new Patriarch was in all things to follow the line of policy laid down by his predecessor who would thus virtually remain in office. The new Patriarch would secure recognition only on condition that he was one of 'our Church in Christ': these words which Metrophanes put into the mouth of Ignatius struck the exact note of the radical Ignatians' feeling.

Such a reading Photius considered to be utterly inadmissible. The crisis which ended in Ignatius' resignation and Photius' election was therefore ultimately provoked by the Extremists. For the purpose of removing Michael III from the throne and reinstating Theodora, they misused Ignatius' prestige in the Church. To follow Ignatius' policy was, as they understood it, to follow their own policy. This was asking too much. Photius, as the Patriarch, owed loyalty to the existing government, the same ground on which Ignatius had refused to bless Theodora's and her daughter's veils. Anastasius the Librarian, who knew the circumstances of the refusal, explained it in these terms:[1] 'The Patriarch refused, because the two Empresses had not yet freely embraced that vocation, and chiefly because he had sworn never to countenance any intrigue against them, an oath customary under every Emperor or Empress.' And if one may say so, what was sauce for Ignatius was also sauce for Photius, who likewise had sworn allegiance to the government that had confirmed his election.

It is easy to follow the steps that led to the conflict between the Patriarch and the Extremists. When Photius forbade ecclesiastics to meddle in politics and to take part in demonstrations hostile to the regime, the radical Extremists at once denounced the measure as a breach of the compromise. Disappointed in their expectations and seeing the chances of Theodora's return to power vanishing, they reminded Photius of his promise and of the meaning they attributed to it. To their way of thinking, Ignatius would automatically return as their Patriarch, should the compromise which Photius had signed not be observed. Were Photius ever to make it clear that Ignatius was no longer the Patriarch, he would be instantly accused of violating his

[1] Mansi, vol. XVI, col. 3.

promise, and of robbing Ignatius of the honours due to him. Here the Ignatians made good use of the signed document of which they had the copies. Let him move another step, and they would break away from him and transfer their allegiance to Ignatius as the one legitimate Patriarch. This, as has already been said, did actually happen, when the Extremists, assembled in the church of St Irene, issued their manifesto.

It may be that the initiative came, not from the five bishops, but from the more radical elements which disapproved of their ecclesiastical leaders' acceptance of the compromise, and were spoiling for a fight. They would have found it only too easy to convince the bishops that the pledge had been broken and that there was every legitimate reason for a rupture. We shall see later that the Ignatians numbered in their ranks fanatics who were more radical than Stylianos himself.

What was Photius' reaction to this outburst? The sources at our disposal do not agree, but according to Nicetas:[1]

Scarcely two months had elapsed since his ordination, when he broke his pledge. He began by imprisoning those of the Church rulers who had been friendly to Ignatius and whom he succeeded in getting hold of, and condemned them to heavy penalties and sanctions; then he overwhelmed them with promises of presents and honours in return for the signed document, trying by every possible means to encompass Ignatius' ruin. Baffled in this, he suggested to the unscrupulous Bardas and through Bardas to the light-headed Michael to send agents to inquire into Ignatius' activities, as though he had been secretly conspiring against the Emperor. A cruel and brutal band of prefects and soldiers immediately left for Terebinthos to make inquiries and to harass Ignatius' friends with a variety of vexations. When at the end of their search they had found no plausible pretext for proceeding against him, they took to methods of open tyranny.

Ignatius was deported to the Isle of Hiera and there locked up in a stable; thence he was sent to Prometon, with only two servants to help him, and subjected to ill treatment by Leo Lalacon, a Domestic of the *Scholae*. Again according to Nicetas, the purpose of all these molestations was to wring from him his abdication from the patriarchal throne. Afterwards he was incarcerated in the Numeroi jail, to be deported, in the first days of August, to the Isle of Mitylene. His friends and intimates were no better treated, and the chartophylax Blasius had his tongue cut out. During Ignatius' stay in Mitylene, Photius summoned a synod in the church of the Twelve Apostles, where he had him deposed and condemned.

[1] *P.G.* vol. 105, col. 513.

Stylianos, in his letter to Pope Stephen V, is not as explicit as Nicetas. After stating that the new Patriarch had rallied many followers by threats and bribes, he says:[1]

Besides this, he pledged his word in his own hand that he would not raise any further objection to Ignatius or to the priests ordained by him; yet, shortly after, he violated his own signature and summoned a synod, or rather a meeting of brigands, in the noble church of the Holy Apostles, where this adulterer deposed and anathematized the Patriarch Ignatius.

This is a very vague indictment; but Metrophanes, in the passage quoted previously, is more definite. After a reference to the synod held in the church of St Irene, he says:[2]

Photius retaliated by summoning, with the assistance of Bardas, a synod in the church of the Holy Apostles, again deposing and anathematizing Ignatius. It was then that we personally upbraided him for his crime,...with the result that we were subjected to violence, arrested without a warning and imprisoned for days in the evil-smelling jail of the Numeroi....

Another Ignatian document, the so-called *Synodicon Vetus*, published by J. Pappe[3] and giving, with an anti-Photian bias, an account of the synods that met in Constantinople in those days, describes Photius' reaction as follows:

Thus, when Photius had occupied the throne in contravention of the holy and godly canons, he gave himself no rest until he had provoked the Emperor's anger, inflicted untold miseries on Ignatius and finally relegated the innocent man to Mytilene. He then summoned a conventicle [synedrion] of reprobates in the Church of Our Lady in Blachernae and unjustly deposed Ignatius, who was present at the synod. Those who refused to yield to his evil suggestions [pravis nutibus] and to communicate with him, he subjected to endless trials [infinitis malis affecit] and banished to places of his own choice.

All these documents agree in two particulars: they refer to a violent persecution of the Ignatian clergy and to a synod summoned by Photius in answer to the meeting in the church of St Irene; but whereas Nicetas seems to place the convocation of the Photian synod after the persecution, probably in the month of August when Ignatius was in Mytilene, Metrophanes of Smyrna seems to place it immediately after the meeting

---

[1] Mansi, vol. XVI, col. 428.   [2] Ibid. col. 416.
[3] In J. A. Fabricius and G. C. Harles, *Bibliotheca Graeca* (Hamburg, 1809), vol. XII, p. 417.

in St Irene's. The *Synodicon Vetus* on the other hand, speaks of a synod that met in the church of Our Lady in Blachernae. On this basis we must reconstruct the facts. Reconstruction is important, since it is the only means of getting at the meaning behind the conflict and of weighing the Patriarch's responsibility for the persecution which, according to all accounts, followed those incidents.[1]

Fortunately, we are able to quote another interesting document which throws some light on the events in Constantinople after the revolt of the Ignatians. Its author is not a contemporary, but his account carries weight, since it expresses the Byzantine tradition and the opinion of those Byzantines who were not directly interested in the incidents and were in a better position to pass judgement through the mellowing perspective of time. We find the account, not in a historical writing, but in the work of a Greek canonist of the twelfth century, and for that reason it failed to attract general attention. Zonaras, in explaining, and commenting on, the canons voted by the 'first and second Synod of Constantinople', the synods of 859 and 861, writes as follows:[2]

This synod is thus designated: the holy and great first and second synod of Constantinople assembled in the venerable church of the Holy and most glorious Apostles. Those who read this inscription may wonder why this synod is called first and second. In this connection, we learn that it met in the above-mentioned church of the Holy Apostles [in 859], that a discussion arose between the orthodox and their opponents and that when the orthodox had clearly won their point, all that had been said had to be put in writing. [We further learn] that the heretics objected to the decisions being put on record lest it should emphasize their defeat and their ejection from the community of the faithful, and that this was the reason why they fomented a revolt, which ended in fighting and bloodshed. That is how the first assembly suspended its deliberations and its meetings and how some time later [in 861] another synod was summoned in the same church to discuss the same subjects, and placed on record all the previous decisions on dogmatic matters. That is the reason why this synod, though it was, in fact, one, received the name of 'first and second', the Fathers having met twice.

Zonaras thus confirms the report by Metrophanes of Smyrna who, as already stated, wrote it for the benefit of one who knew the facts, and so was not at liberty to distort them at will. From these reports

[1] Anastasius the Librarian also mentions the incidents in his introduction to the Acts of the Ignatian Council of 869–70, but his report is too short to supply any new information (Mansi, vol. XVI, col. 4).

[2] J. Zonaras, 'Commentaria in Canones...', *P.G.* vol. 137, cols. 1004 seq.

it appears that to put an end to agitation Photius countered the move on the part of the extremist clergy in a strictly canonical way by convoking a synod in the church of the Holy Apostles, where it was declared that Ignatius, having resigned his see, was no longer Patriarch and that the new nomination by the Extremists was null and void. In the event of Ignatius accepting the nomination, he was declared to be *ipso facto* deposed and excommunicated. Furthermore, in order to anticipate any future disturbance, some canons were formulated to suppress abuses that were to a great extent responsible for encouraging the turbulent elements inside the Church. But to prevent the implementing of the synodical decisions, the opposition went to great lengths and by resort to violence succeeded in wrecking every possible canonical settlement.

Metrophanes confirms Zonaras' reference to the uproar at the meeting: 'It was then that we personally upbraided him [Photius] for his crime in stripping Ignatius of his patriarchal dignity, with the result that we were subjected to violence....' He unwittingly discloses the fact that the Ignatian clergy attended the synod summoned by the Patriarch in the church of the Holy Apostles; that it was therefore a genuine synod convoked for the purposes of putting an end to agitation and countering the *pronunciamento* of the church of St Irene. The canonical character of the synod is also confirmed by Zonaras' account of the first meeting of the 'first and second synod'.

Zonaras' and Metrophanes' statements therefore corroborate each other. Metrophanes places his own arrest and imprisonment, and the persecution of his friends after his intervention, at the synod in the church of the Holy Apostles; and this again is confirmed by Zonaras who speaks of a rising of the 'heretics', one that ended in bloodshed, to avert their defeat at the synod. But it is difficult to admit that this rising was provoked by purely religious considerations; and since the monks and the bishops who disagreed with Photius and with the decisions of the synod did not carry swords, somebody else must have taken advantage of the incident to do some fishing on his own in troubled waters. If we remember the incidents that accompanied the change of regime in Byzantium after the dethronement of Theodora, we shall appreciate the implications of Zonaras' words and form a shrewd guess at who saw his opportunity for the overthrow of the new regime. Apart from this, we must also admit that the new government was fully entitled to take energetic measures for the maintenance of public order and it is evident that the accusations levelled by the Ignatians at Photius which make him responsible for the heavy punishments inflicted on some dangerous agitators among the Extremists completely miss the mark. The Patriarch had no police under his orders and wielded no executive power: the government alone could deal with such disturbances of the peace.

The truth is that Photius did not see eye to eye with the government in the severity with which it stamped out the revolt. In one of his letters addressed to Bardas, probably the first written after the outbreak, he bitterly complained of the government's brutality in bringing the offenders to book.[1] There is a short passage in this letter hinting that the true reason for the new rift among the Byzantine clergy was his loyalty to the new regime and that the rebels had committed grave offences against the existing laws. 'We should have much preferred', he writes to Bardas, 'to find in you the man who punishes the offenders rather than the author of such outrages.' The Patriarch further complains that half of his jurisdiction is gone—a clear reference to the refractory bishops' meeting at St Irene's—and adds, as a thinly veiled threat of resignation, that he would rather lose the whole of it. On another occasion, he pleads for the secretary Christodulos, probably one of the leaders of the revolt, who claimed right of sanctuary, and for the chartophylax Blasius, who had had his tongue cut out.[2]

Even Nicetas, who naturally made Photius responsible for all the repression, indirectly admits that the main reason for this new quarrel was political—Photius' refusal to turn against the new government; for by his allegation that Photius had instigated Bardas to inquire into Ignatius' alleged conspiracy against the Emperor, Nicetas was clearly reverting to the old political antagonism between Moderates and Extremists. But the government was not going to allow itself to be dictated to by these hot-heads and having once discovered the true motive of the opposition, took, as was only to be expected, the necessary measures to make an end of it.[3]

[1] *P.G.* vol. 102, col. 620.
[2] On the nature of the 'glossotomia', cf. Bury, *A History of the Later Roman Empire from Arcadius to Irene*, vol. II, p. 329. Attention should also be drawn to the fact that the Byzantines never looked upon confinement and restriction of movement as a severe punishment. Isolation and the contemplative life exercised on them a special attraction inherited from oriental mentality. But they possessed a detailed catalogue of corporal punishments and mutilations which they knew how to inflict with exceptional skill. See in this connection Zachariae von Lingenthal, *Geschichte des Griechischen-Römischen Rechtes* (Berlin, 1892), 3rd ed. pp. xi, 331 seq.
[3] Nicetas' statement to the effect that the interpretation put on the compromise signed by Photius served as the main pretext for the opposition party's aggression is also confirmed by Pseudo-Simeon, who, in his *Chronicle* (Bonn, p. 671), states that

But Nicetas also tells us another thing: the very fact that not Ignatius, but men who claimed to be his followers, were the first to be proceeded against implies that the rupture could not be laid to the charge of the old Patriarch; and, moreover, the rigorous inquiry conducted by the imperial police proved his innocence. This detail has its importance in showing once more that Ignatius was not personally responsible and— at least at the outbreak of the dispute—had no thought of resuming the functions which he had handed over for the peace of the Church, but that once again the radical elements of the Extremist party had taken advantage of his *naïveté* and prestige to raise their banner against Photius and the government he supported.

Nicetas' account also affords a good illustration of the way the government reacted: in order to prevent the fanatics seizing the person of Ignatius and making further capital of his influence over the masses, Bardas placed him under the special surveillance of the police and had him frequently transferred from place to place, so as to impede communications between him and the leaders of the malcontents.

To put a final stop to any further agitation, it would have been best to obtain from Ignatius a formal attestation that he no longer considered himself to be the Patriarch. Nicetas' reference to Ignatius' refusal to abdicate shows that the government and Photius must have vainly tried to secure it.

Why did Ignatius not sign this declaration demanded from him, when it would have so effectively contributed to the general appeasement? Because the methods employed by Bardas were anything but conducive to the results intended. Ignatius must have been particularly sensitive to the ill treatment meted out to his friends. Probably, some of his trusted partisans may have eluded the watchfulness of the police and succeeded in communicating with him, to convince him that if the government harassed his friends unreasonably, it would take advantage of his declaration to treat them even worse. Besides, Ignatius had only to say that he had already made his abdication and deemed it unnecessary to repeat it.

Lastly, Nicetas informs us that the agitation engineered by the opponents of the government and of Photius lasted a long time. According to him, Photius summoned his synod after Ignatius had been banished to Mytilene, and this, according to the same author, happened

Photius, after fraudulently obtaining from the leader of the opposition the copy of the document in question, tore it up, saying: 'Neither you nor Ignatius do I acknowledge as bishops.'

in August. In view of what has been said previously, the Extremist clergy refused obedience to Photius some forty days or two months after Photius' consecration, i.e. in February 859, and Photius' synod must have met at the end of February or in March. The revolt mentioned by Zonaras must have broken out in March, or, if we accept Zonaras' suggestion that the deliberations of the synod were considerably advanced, perhaps a month later. Nicetas' account of the incidents is not quite reliable, and this need not surprise anyone familiar with his method, but there may be some truth in his statement that another ecclesiastical meeting was held in Byzantium in August. Once the revolt had been suppressed and the agitation put down, it is only natural to suppose that Photius imposed ecclesiastical sanctions on the prelates and clergy responsible for the trouble and that judgement was given at a different meeting.

We are quite entitled to surmise that Nicetas omits all reference to the convocation of the synod at the church of the Holy Apostles which was to answer canonically the challenge of the Extremists. It is more than probable that this new synod was held, not in the church of the Holy Apostles, but in Blachernae, as the *Synodicon Vetus* has it, and that Ignatius was summoned in person before this synod, since the same document states that Ignatius' deposition was proclaimed in the former Patriarch's presence. A renewed declaration of the decisions taken at the council that met at the church of the Holy Apostles being made in Blachernae in the presence of Ignatius would have been quite a normal procedure. This second meeting was not as large as a synod and took no new decisions; hence it is not listed among the synods that met at this period, and only the *Synodicon Vetus* and Nicetas have recalled its existence. The canonical decisions taken at the synod which met in the church of the Holy Apostles in the spring of 859 were, as we shall see presently, reconsidered and made public only in 861.

Nicetas then adds that the synod anathematized Ignatius, but this is probably an over-statement, as the synod had no sufficient grounds for going to that length, if it is true, as his biographer testifies, that the inquiry set up against Ignatius had produced no incriminating results. Theognostos does not mention an anathema in his *Libellus*,[1] but it should be observed that neither the one nor the other dared affirm that the sentence was confirmed by the synod of 861, of which more will be said later. We must conclude then that Ignatius was simply deposed at the synod held in Blachernae mentioned by the *Synodicon*

[1] Mansi, vol. XVI, col. 300; *P.G.* vol. 105, col. 861.

Vetus, or rather declared to have no right to the patriarchal See, in spite of his 'promotion' by the Extremists.

It is unfortunately impossible to obtain an adequate idea of the importance of the revolt, the documents in our possession being in this respect extremely vague. In any case, it does not seem that the Byzantine episcopacy joined it in a body. Theognostos, in his *Libellus* written in 861, poses as the mouthpiece of ten Metropolitans and fifteen bishops; but Pope Nicholas, in his letter to Michael III already quoted, only names six Metropolitans. It is hard to say whether the number quoted by Theognostos is exact: as we have seen, Theognostos often exaggerates and his information is not always so reliable as has been thought. Is he exaggerating in this case?

What is certain is that shortly after the revolt, and probably after the synod of August 859, the opposition leaders, all members of the higher clergy, were replaced by safer prelates. But we happen to know very few of these leading Ignatians: Theodore of Syracuse, who had to hand over his see to Gregory Asbestas, Basil of Chalcedon to Zachary, Anthony of Cyzicus to Amphilochus. Peter of Miletus, once deposed by Methodius, was moreover reinstated and appointed archbishop of Sardes in Lydia. The other changes mentioned by Hergenröther [1] were introduced only later. This, however, is not all. We know that at the opening of the first session of the Council of 869–70 the prelates who had remained loyal to Ignatius numbered only twelve,[2] a figure nearer the one quoted by Theognostos; but not even this computation can be considered accurate, as we must allow for the death of some Ignatian bishops, perhaps for the absence of others due to illness. Aristarchos, who collected all the information relative to the changes effected in the Byzantine episcopacy during Photius' first patriarchate,[3] reached the approximate figure of thirty-five prelates deposed or replaced, though these transfers cannot all be dated from the beginning of the patriarchate or otherwise accounted for with any certainty. Therefore, the figure quoted by Theognostos should not be discarded *a priori*, though it may be observed that it is not very impressive compared with the hundreds of prelates who submitted to Photius. After all, the rebels amounted to but a small minority of the Byzantine episcopacy.

It is readily admitted on the other hand that the monastic world all

---

[1] *Photius*, vol. I, p. 403.
[2] Mansi, vol. XVI, col. 18; Hergenröther, *Photius*, vol. II, p. 76.
[3] Loc. cit. vol. I, pp. ιγ, ιδ, λξ.

but unanimously refused allegiance to the new Patriarch; unfortunately, Ignatian sources, chiefly Theognostos, only refer vaguely to a 'multitude' of monks who remained loyal to Ignatius. What Hergenröther[1] has written, and what I personally have said about this opposition,[2] needs supplementing.

The monastery of Studion seems to have been the most important storm centre: its abbot Nicholas flatly refused to hold communion with Photius and went into exile, though the fact that five abbots in succession carried on after him the administration of this important community suggests that not all the Studites adopted the same attitude. The Life of St Evaristus contains an interesting report of the repercussion the troubles we are studying had in the monastic world in general and in the monastery of Studion in particular. The author of this Life[3] tells us why and how Nicholas left the monastery he had governed. His extremely discreet account is worth reproducing in full:[4]

> ...A certain change and misunderstanding had come over the Church, but I would rather not give the reasons and circumstances. The result at all events was that Nicholas, probably feeling the weight of his charge and responsibilities, or perhaps considering it inconvenient to enter into communion with the pastor, addressed to his disciples a spiritual and salutary exhortation to show his hearers the road that leads to good spiritual pastures; and having carefully and paternally advised them to violate none of their promises to God, to live and show themselves worthy of the monastic state, and bravely to endure earthly trials in view of the consolation that awaits us, he left the monastery, followed by those who openly conformed their conduct to that of their pastor.... They split up into many groups, just numerous enough to make true the Lord's promise that He would be with those gathered in His name (Matt. xviii. 20), and thus scattered to various places in various lands....

Among the monks who left the monastery of Studion with Nicholas we find Evaristus and Paphnucius. They were received by a certain Samuel, a pious citizen, who offered them the hospitality of his home. Later, Evaristus was requested by abbot Nicholas, who had fallen ill, to join him in Hexamilium, presumably in Cherson of Thrace, and he subsequently accompanied him to see the Emperor Michael III, apparently for another effort at reconciliation between the Studites, Photius and the government. Initiated by government, this venture came to

[1] Loc. cit. vol. I, pp. 392 seq.
[2] *Les Légendes de Constantin et de Méthode*, pp. 135–47.
[3] C. Van de Vorst, 'La Vie de Saint Évariste, Higoumène à Constantinople', in *Analecta Bollandiana* (1923), vol. XLI, pp. 288–325. [4] Loc. cit. pp. 306–7.

nothing, owing, no doubt—though the biographer has nothing definite to say about it—to Nicholas' unyielding attitude. After the interview with the Emperor, Nicholas betook himself to Samuel, and on hearing where he was, the old Studites promptly flocked to the pious citizen's house and put their host to the trouble of founding a new monastery for their benefit, the Kokorobion. Such an influx of monks soon attracted the government's attention: Nicholas was arrested, taken back to the monastery of Studion and there placed under the watchful care of some monks known to be loyal to the regime. The Kokorobion monastery, however, continued to exist and to thrive under the direction of St Evaristus.

The anonymous biographer, part of whose work is summarized above, was not far from the events he described, since the only surviving MS. of his work dates from the tenth century and the author treats of his hero as of a contemporary. This being so, his punctilious discretion in speaking of the quarrel that had arisen in the Church, in which he refers neither to Photius nor to Ignatius by name, is somehow curious. Though his hero was an Ignatian, no sign of hatred for the new Patriarch or Michael III escaped him. Now, according to him, the monks who refused obedience to Photius were not persecuted in the least; they found easy sanctuary with pious laymen, and even succeeded in opening a monastery in Constantinople. Nicholas of the monastery of Studion alone was the object of some governmental severity, though the Emperor in person attempted to overcome his resistance. In short, this evidence in no way corroborates the dark picture conjured up elsewhere with vague hints at a dreadful persecution.

We know the names of some other abbots who remained loyal to Ignatius: Joseph, Euthymios, Nicetas of Chrysopolis and Dositheus of Osion Dion, not to mention the famous Theognostos, abbot of the Monastery of the Source (Pege). Although they were certainly not the only abbots to refuse submission to Photius' authority,[1] the Ignatians'

---

[1] The community of St Anne in Bithynia seems likewise to have remained faithful to Ignatius, as we learn from a manuscript of the Meteora, No. 591 (Νίκου Α. Βέες, "Ἔκδοσις παλαιογραφικῶν καὶ τεχνικῶν ἐρευνῶν ἐν ταῖς μόναις τῶν Μετεώρων κατὰ τὰ ἔτη 1908 καὶ 1909. Edited by the Athens Byzantine Society, 1910, pp. 24, 25, 69). The MS. contains the homilies of St Chrysostom on the Gospel of St Matthew. According to a copyist's note, it was written by the monk Eustathios in 861–2: "Ἔγραφε δὲ καὶ ἐτελειώθη ἡ ἱερὰ καὶ σωτηριώδης αὕτη βίβλος ἐν τῷ ΣΤΟ (861–2) ἔτη, ἐν τῇ ἑνδεκάτῃ ἰνδικτίονι, ἐν τῇ μόνῃ τῆς ἁγίας Ἄννης τῆς διακειμένης ἀπὸ τῶν τῆς Βιθυνίας μερῶν ἐν τῇ ἐνορίᾳ τῆς Κίου, ἐπὶ τῆς ἐξορίας τοῦ ἁγιωτάτου πατριάρχου Ἰγνατίου. Cf. Nicos A. Bees, 'Un manuscrit des Météoris de l'an 861–2', in *Revue des Études Grecques* (1913), t. XXVI, pp. 53–74.

remarkable discretion on the subject is worth noting, as it was by no means their habit to be reticent in emphasizing their Patriarch's popularity. That is why it is difficult to take literally what Anastasius the Librarian tells us of the happenings at Mount Olympus in Asia Minor, where the monks' cells are stated to have been burned to the ground.[1] Olympus lost none of its importance in the second half of the ninth century and the beginning of the tenth. Another hagiographical composition written in the first years of the tenth century and already quoted, the Life of St Euthymios, corrects to some extent the account by Anastasius. It is stated there that on refusing to enter into communion with Photius,[2] Nicholas, the abbot of the Pissidion, left his monastery: which evidently proves that the majority of the monks of this important community had acknowledged Photius as their legitimate Patriarch. Euthymios also left after the abbot's departure, but not for the reason given by the hagiographer for Nicholas' exit:

Fond of peace and solitude, Euthymios...saw there a good opportunity to hasten to the mountains of Athos. Not having received so far the holy habit of a monk...he was sad, disconsolate and broken-hearted, mainly because his holy pastor John had gone to rest in the Lord, and also because Nicholas had left the monastery. Distressed for all these reasons, he received a divine inspiration telling him to go and see the ascetic Theodore and receive at long last the habit from his hands; for Theodore also lived on the heights of Olympus, shedding the light of his virtues like a torch on all those who dwelt around. To him therefore he went...[and] he was considered worthy of receiving the sacred and salutary monastic habit. The saint then...after a stay of fifteen long years at Mount Olympus, left with the blessed and godly Theosteriktos for Athos. Soon after Theosteriktos left to settle once more at Olympus, where he invited St Euthymios to join him in 863, this saint being in search of his old master, who also had a desire to settle in Athos.[3]

All this only shows that the holy mountain continued to thrive in spite of religious conflicts; that the monks were in no way disturbed in their pious exercises and went about freely; lastly and not least, that contacts between Olympus and Athos, the new centre of Byzantine monas-

---

[1] Mansi, vol. XVI, col. 5.

[2] I made in this connection a mistranslation in my previous work *Les Légendes de Constantin et de Méthode*, p. 144. Read 'pour ne pas entrer en communion (avec Photius)' instead of 'pour rester en communion'. This is the Greek text: πολλῶν δὲ διὰ τοῦτο τῆς τοῦ νέου πατριάρχου κοινωνίας ἀποκλινάντων, καὶ ὁ...

[3] Loc. cit. pp. 182, 186.

ticism, seem to have been frequent and friendly. How then are we to explain the anti-Photianist accounts of the so-called persecution of monks?

The answer, it seems, is to be found in the canons of the synod of 861, known by the name of 'first-second'.[1] Of these seventeen canons, the first seven deal with various problems raised at the time by Eastern monasticism. The first forbids the transformation of private houses into monasteries without episcopal authorization; a house thus transformed will no longer be considered as the founder's property; he will lose the right to rule the new institution, or to appoint anyone to this function. The second canon forbids the consecration as a monk of anyone who refuses to place himself under the direction of an abbot legitimately established; it will no longer be lawful to impose the monastic habit on those who intend to go on living in their own private houses, without a care for monastic discipline. The third canon reminds the abbot of his duties towards the monks under his care. The fourth is particularly important; it censures those monks who leave their monasteries without permission or take up residence in lay people's houses: such a practice was permissible in times of heresy, says the canon, referring no doubt to iconoclasm, but can no longer be tolerated at the present time, when heresy has been uprooted; the bishop alone has the right to transfer monks for reasons of piety from one monastery to another. The fifth canon insists on the necessity of giving every candidate for the monastic order the opportunity to break himself in to monastic duties for the space of three years. The sixth forbids the monks to own property; they must dispose of their goods before entering the monastery. The seventh forbids bishops to found private monasteries and to endow them with revenue from the *mensa episcopalis*.

All these canons were prompted by abuses that had been rife since before the iconoclastic days. It is generally known that for economic or other reasons the first iconoclastic emperors endeavoured to limit the number of monasteries; and that their decrees aimed at the suppression of the practice, then prevailing among rich Byzantines, of converting their houses into monasteries, where they went on living as they did before, and of disposing of their wealth in total disregard of

[1] Mansi, vol. XVI, cols. 536–48. Cf. on the evolution of Byzantine monasticism at this period Sokolov, *Sostoyanie Monashestva v Viz. Tserkvi s polov. IX do nachala XIII v.* (Kazan, 1894) (especially pp. 60 seq. on Ignatian and Photian monks). The study by W. Nissen, *Die Regelung des Klosterwesens im Rhomäerreiche bis zum Ende des 9. Jhts* (Hamburg, 1897) (Programm Nr 759 der Gelehrtenschule des Johanneums), is written on more general lines.

canonical prescriptions.[1] These measures chiefly hit the well-to-do classes and naturally were not welcomed by monks who lived on the generosity of the rich. Now it was chiefly to these regulations that the iconoclastic emperors owed their reputation of being persecutors of the monks. After the final restoration of Orthodoxy, the monks recovered all their former prestige; Irene and the pious Theodora patronized them and their influence went on increasing under Ignatius' patriarchate; but the old abuses which the iconoclastic emperors had fought crept stealthily back, as evidenced by the seven canons summarized above.

Such a situation was, however, fraught with danger. Iconoclasm was not suppressed by Theodora till 843, and it would have been unwise to afford the more or less sincere converts from iconoclasm new opportunities for criticism or to panegyrize Constantine V for fighting such abuses whilst the memory of his military fame was still fresh. The iconoclastic reaction under Leo V, Michael II and Theophilus served as a grim reminder that too zealous a championship of monasticism, such as was displayed by Michael I, could do Orthodoxy more harm than good. The Patriarch Methodius had learnt his lesson and practised moderation in his religious policy. Ignatius thought otherwise, but the new government under Michael III and Bardas was alive to the risk of giving an easy rein to the Extremists. Photius also saw the danger and was only too keen on removing all grounds for criticism. His first endeavour was to restore order in the monastic world and the canons discussed above, though some of them had already been voted at the synod of 859, show the drift of his policy and clarify the position in the first decades after the suppression of iconoclasm.

Under the circumstances, it is not surprising that Photius' cautious attitude should be so little appreciated by certain zealots and that the radical monks should suspect another attack on monasticism. Hence the agitation against Photius raised by some of them and the stigma of persecution attached to his name. Wild statements by some of his bitterest enemies created the impression that the whole monastic world had risen in arms against him and have since imposed upon the historians' credulity.

This consideration throws light on the character and the passions of

---

[1] It is not true to say that the iconoclastic emperors were the sworn enemies of monastic life, as it has been generally alleged. I, among others, have found evidence of the existence of an iconoclastic monastery in Asia Minor, as shown in the Life of St Gregory Decapolites, which I published in my book, *La Vie de St Grégoire le Décapolite et les Slaves Macédoniens au IXe siècle* (Paris, 1926), pp. 40 seq., 48 seq.

the two currents of opinion prevailing in Byzantium and shows in which quarters the new ecclesiastical and secular regime met with its worst opposition. Next to the Extremist monks and a few bishops who shared their opinions, came the wealthy zealots who looked askance at the changes in the imperial palace and in the patriarcheion and their attendant reforms. These had, in the opinion of many of them, an iconoclastic flavour. Indeed, the iconoclastic emperors, chiefly Constantine V, had tried to bring about by authoritarian methods exactly what Photius and his supporters were trying to achieve by canonical means. The Moderates were as sincere in their orthodoxy as any, and as keen on preventing a possible iconoclastic revival, but their efforts were liable to be misunderstood.[1]

[1] This chapter was nearing completion, when I came across V. Grumel's study, 'La Genèse du Schisme Photien', in *Studi Bizantini e Neo-Ellenici* (1939), vol. V (Atti del V Congresso Internazionale di Studi Bizantini), pp. 177–85, but it failed to make me alter a single word in the chapter. It is possible to take the wrong turn in trying to shift the responsibility for the revolt from the retired Patriarch's radical supporters to Ignatius himself. One finds it difficult to understand this persistence in presenting Ignatius as a headstrong monk, intractable and deaf to reasonable arguments. Nor was Ignatius 'un drôle de saint'. Contrary to what has been asserted, and as we shall see in the course of this work, Ignatius did acknowledge Photius' ordination, ordained though he had been by Asbestas. Again, Photius' own ordination by Asbestas was the condition laid down by the victorious party as a compensation for the concessions made by Photius to the radical bishops.

CHAPTER III

THE SYNOD OF 861

Photius' and Michael's letters to Nicholas—Was the Pope in communion with
Photius' envoys?—Negotiations between the legates, the Emperor and the Patriarch
before the synod—The Acts of the synod and accounts by Nicetas and Theognostos—Did Ignatius appeal to Rome?—Legates' attitude during the synod.

THE assumption that iconoclasm came to an abrupt end in 843 and left
no traces was shown in the previous chapter to be at odds with the facts.
As we have seen, when Photius ascended the patriarchal throne the
heresy had not yet been completely liquidated. It is certainly surprising
to learn from a homily which Photius delivered at St Sophia in 867[1]
at the inauguration of an ikon of the Virgin, that the picture was one
of the first to be restored in the Church since the official suppression
of iconoclasm, though twenty-four years had elapsed since the restoration of Orthodoxy. It therefore looks as though the authorities, for
fear of provoking reactions among the penitent iconoclasts, acted with
some caution.

All this must be kept in mind in considering the Emperor Michael's
initiative in 860. Taking advantage of the dispatch of the synodal letter
by the new Patriarch to Pope Nicholas I,[2] Michael III, after recalling
the latest events that had occurred in the Church of Constantinople,
invited the Pope to send legates to Byzantium, where he was planning
to hold a Council, for a second elucidation of the Catholic doctrine
concerning images.

Surprise has often been expressed that Photius should not have issued
his encyclical letter sooner;[3] but it is only fair to remember that the
synod summoned to put an end to the Ignatians' opposition only met
in August 859, i.e. eight months after Photius' election. It was natural
that no apocrisiaries should be sent to Rome in the autumn of the same
year, probably to save them a journey during an inconvenient season
and chiefly a winter stay in Rome. Communications between Italy and
Greece were also, so it seems, suspended from the end of October till

---

[1] (Aristarchos), loc. cit. vol. II, pp. 294 seq. Cf. my study 'Lettre à
M. H. Grégoire à propos de Michel III' in Byzantion (1935), vol. X, pp. 5–9.

[2] P.G. vol. 102, cols. 585–93.

[3] Cf. Hergenröther, Photius, vol. I, p. 406.

spring.[1] It would in any case have been considered preferable to send them in the spring of 860 so that the papal legates should start for Constantinople at a time better suited for journeys of that length. The Byzantine delegates then reached Rome in summer and left again with the legates at the end of September, reaching Constantinople probably before Christmas and completing a most difficult journey before the bad season set in.

It has also been thought strange that Photius should have omitted to mention in his letter the synod that was to be summoned in Constantinople;[2] but there was good justification for the omission. To convoke and direct a General Council was, according to Byzantine law, solely the Emperor's concern, a privilege that had been his since the time of Constantine the Great: Patriarchs—even of Rome—had no business to meddle.[3] Photius, once President of the Imperial Chancellery, evidently knew and respected court usage and imperial privileges; hence he confined himself in his letter to Nicholas I[4] to the formulae in common use in synodal letters,[5] mainly insisting on the importance of the episcopal dignity to which, in spite of himself and all but against his will, he had been raised after his predecessor's resignation, and adding his profession of faith.

The letters were taken to Rome by a distinguished delegation, headed by the Protospathar Arsaber, a relative of the Emperor and of Photius, and including the metropolitan Methodius of Gangra, the bishops Samuel of Colossus, Theophilus of Amorion, and Zachary of Taormina, who, having represented Gregory Asbestas' group in his appeal to Rome, was familiar with the journey and with the Eternal City. According to custom, the delegation took numerous presents, which Anastasius the Librarian, author of the Life of Nicholas I, enumerates with a certain relish in the *Liber Pontificalis*.[6] The pallium was not among them, a sign that Photius knew the Pope's feelings better than Ignatius.

---

[1] Cf. J. Haller, *Das Papsttum* (Stuttgart, 1934), vol. I, p. 500. Idem, *Nikolaus I. und Pseudo-Isidor* (Stuttgart, 1936), p. 30.

[2] Hergenröther, *Photius*, vol. I, p. 413.

[3] I dealt with this problem in my study, *De Potestate Civili in Conciliis Oecumenicis*, quoted on p. 7.

[4] Cf. Hergenröther, *Photius*, vol. I, pp. 407–11 (translation and analysis of the letter).

[5] Cf. synodal letter by the Patriarch Nicephorus to Leo III, *P.G.* vol. 100, cols. 169–200. Also, the formulary published by I. Habert, *Archieraticon. Liber Pont. Eccl. Graecae* (Paris, 1643), pp. 557–9.

[6] Ed. L. Duchesne, loc. cit. vol. II, p. 154.

As regards the Pope's attitude towards the Emperor's and the new Patriarch's envoys, Baronius[1] and Hergenröther[2] assert that, suspecting something irregular in Photius' elevation, Nicholas I refused to receive them to communion with the Roman bishops; this rests on a declaration made by the papal legate Marinus at the fourth session of the Council of 869–70,[3] and has generally found favour with historians.

Let us recall the fact that according to the minutes of that session the bishops Theophilus and Zachary stated that Nicholas I had received them to communion when they were in Rome: 'We have said and we repeat that we were received by Pope Nicholas as bishops, that we co-celebrated with him and that we were treated as such.' The Pope, they said, had thereby acknowledged Photius as Patriarch. The Acts suggest that the claim of the two bishops was accepted by many people and that the papal legates agreed to both being heard by the Council. There they repeated their assertion on several occasions and even offered to produce the witnesses—presumably the officials and servants who had accompanied them to Rome—provided the Emperor promised they would suffer no harm. Lastly they quoted the evidence of Marinus, one of the papal legates, who had been present at their reception, but the latter emphatically declared:

I was sub-deacon of the Roman Church at that time, consecrated by the saintly Roman Pope Leo, and had ministered in the Roman Church from the age of twelve and when these men came to Rome with Arsabir I was ministering in the Roman Church of Mary, the Blessed Mother of God, called 'Praesepis'. It was there that the very saintly pope Nicholas met them to examine their Libellus and to tender the oath; and he did not receive them to communion as bishops. If they deny this, let them prove that he did receive them to communion as bishops.[4]

One finds it difficult to admit that either Marinus or the two bishops would have been daring enough to tell a bare-faced lie in the presence of the assembly; but the letter in which the Pope reserves to himself the right to give a final decision on Ignatius' case whenever his legates should have concluded their inquiry, enables us to reconcile two assertions so obviously contradictory.

The Pope could not refuse to receive the ambassadors of the Emperor and of the Patriarch without reasons grave enough to justify the affront; and Marinus admits that Nicholas I had actually received them. Strictly

---

[1] *Annales Ecclesiastici*, ad a. 859, n. 60.
[2] *Photius*, vol. I, p. 414.
[3] Mansi, vol. XVI, cols. 53–74, 328–40.
[4] Ibid. col. 58.

speaking, and allowing for a generous dose of mental reservation, he could pretend that the Pope had not granted the delegates communion with his bishops, since the validity of their reception had been made conditional on the Pope's final decision, which was to be given after the report of the board of inquiry and eventually did turn out to be unfavourable to Photius. But he would have been splitting hairs, and it seems inadmissible that a papal legate's usual veracity should have failed him to such an extent. But Anastasius, the translator of the Acts, fortunately comes to our rescue. This is what he writes about the embassy in his Life of Nicholas I preserved in the *Liber Pontificalis*:[1]

In his [Nicholas'] days Michael, son of the Emperor Theophilus, Emperor of the city of Constantinople, sent for the love of the Apostles gifts to the Blessed Apostle Peter through the good offices of the bishops called Methodius the Metropolitan, bishop Samuel and two others who had been deposed from their episcopal office, Zachary and another called Theophilus, together with a lay imperial official called Arsavir, protospathar....[2]

Observe that here Anastasius discriminates between the two bishops Methodius and Samuel and the two others who had been suspended, Zachary and Theophilus. Zachary himself acknowledged, as pointed out in the minutes of the same session of the Council, that he had been suspended by Ignatius at the same time as Gregory Asbestas, and he stated to the imperial commission that Pope Benedict III had ordered him to abstain from the exercise of ecclesiastical functions, as long as his case awaited trial by the Holy See.[3] It is clear, then, that the legate Marinus, in his reply, referred only to Zachary and Theophilus, the only partisans of Photius then present before the Fathers of the Council.

This clears the puzzle. Nicholas I must have officially received the Byzantine delegation at the church of St Mary Major, after the bishops had taken the oath prescribed by the protocol of the Roman Chancellery. Rumours that had reached him concerning events in Constantinople[4] did not authorize him to withhold the traditional honours, though they prompted him to look into the facts more closely. He probably also noticed that the cases of Ignatius and of the Asbestas group had not yet been tried by the Holy See and that the decree of the synod of Constantinople of 858 rehabilitating Gregory and his friends had, as far as he was concerned, and in his own conception of papal rights, the same

---

[1] Ed. Duchesne, loc. cit. vol. II, p. 154.
[2] Follows the list of presents.   [3] See p. 27.
[4] The Pope refers to them in his letter to Michael III, *M.G.H.* Ep. VI, p. 490. Cf. p. 108.

legal value as Photius' election, and no more. He therefore reminded Theophilus and Zachary of his predecessor Benedict III's injunction, of which he must have found a record in the archives, and consequently refused the two bishops communion with the Western bishops. Thus are explained and reconciled the two contradictory assertions, and we may conclude that Nicholas received the Byzantine embassy with due honour and admitted the four Eastern bishops—at least at the beginning —to communion with the Roman clergy.

To return then to Anastasius' text after the enumeration of the presents brought to the Pope by the Byzantine ambassadors:

When they had presented the Pontiff with many other gifts, they at once read out the ambassadorial message they had been ordered to deliver, namely, that being made Emperor of the Greeks, he [Michael III] asked through his envoys that legates of the Apostolic See be sent to Constantinople to deal with the destroyers of the sacred images. In reality, he only had in mind the case of the Patriarch Ignatius and of Photius, the usurper of the Church of Constantinople, with a jealous and cunning desire to have this holy man Ignatius condemned by a sentence of the Apostolic See, as he later succeeded in doing and then to place the neophyte Photius at the head of the Church. Presently, the Supreme Pontiff, still ignorant of the Emperor's evil designs, sent thither two bishops, Radoald and Zachary, ordering them to settle in synod whatever the issue of the sacred images should suggest and also solemnly to inquire into the case of the Patriarch Ignatius and of Photius, but only to inquire and then to report to him.

This text is really suggestive: Michael III had not asked the Pope for a re-trial of the cases of Ignatius and Photius by the synod he intended to summon: in the Emperor's mind, the sole purpose of that synod was to define again the Catholic doctrine on images and once again to condemn iconoclasm. It is therefore clear that both the Emperor and Photius considered Ignatius' case to have been definitely closed since the synods (of the Holy Apostles and of Blachernae) in 859.

Another contemporary document, coming from a quarter hostile to Photius, confirms this conclusion—the *Synodicon Vetus*,[1] whose author writes: 'After all this, Photius sent to the Roman Pope Nicholas, of blessed memory, a delegation declaring that Ignatius had abdicated of his own free will and owing to his physical weakness, and urgently requesting the dispatch of legates for the purpose of a final condemnation of the iconoclastic heresy, yet all the time busy preparing underhand

[1] J. A. Fabricius, B. D. J. Pappe, loc. cit. vol. XII, pp. 417, 418. Cf. p. 57.

the condemnation of Ignatius.' The texts of Anastasius and the *Synodicon* are not unrelated, which shows to what extent Anastasius, whilst staying in Constantinople, had come under the influence of the Ignatians: none but the Ignatians ever alleged that the condemnation of iconoclasm was only a pretext for the convocation of a Council and for the condemnation of Ignatius. But, by their statements, they thus unwittingly bore witness to the fact that the Byzantine embassy had not asked for a re-trial of the old Patriarch.

The replies by Nicholas I to the letters of Michael III and Photius throw light on the Pope's feelings towards the imperial intentions. In his letter to the Emperor,[1] after commending Michael's interest in the Church, the Pope expresses surprise that Ignatius should have been deposed by a synod 'sine Romani consulto pontificis'. To him, the trial of Ignatius seemed unfair, the witnesses quoted in the imperial letter being incompetent, their evidence unconvincing and Ignatius not having pleaded guilty. As, moreover, a layman had been elected in disregard of canonical interdictions, Nicholas concluded by refusing to acknowledge Photius' nomination to the patriarchate before the results of the inquiry made by the legates in Constantinople should reach him. The Pope then lays down the procedure of the inquiry. The passage is important enough for the interpretation of the Acts of the Council of 861 to be reproduced in full:

In order that fairness be observed in all things, we wish, O merciful Augustus, that Ignatius who, as you have informed me through your letters, has spontaneously and of his own free will relinquished the government of the above-mentioned See and has been deposed in the presence of the General Council of the people by Your Highness, should appear before our legates and the General Council in accordance with your imperial custom so that they may inquire why he abandoned the flock entrusted to him and why he made so little of, and treated with such contempt, the wishes of our predecessors and holy Pontiffs, Leo IV and Benedict. For this purpose the legates will make a careful inquiry into his deposition and his censure, with a view to discovering whether the canons have been observed or not; then, when the matter has been reported to us, we shall direct by our apostolic authority what is to be done, so that your Church, daily shaken by these anxieties, may henceforth remain inviolate and unhurt.

The Pope then outlines the Catholic doctrine on images; requests the Emperor to return to the Roman patriarchate the jurisdiction of Illyricum, the patrimonies of Calabria and Sicily, and the right to

[1] *M.G.H.* Ep. VI, pp. 433–9.

consecrate the bishops of Syracuse, concluding with a recommendation in favour of the papal legates.

The Pope's reply to Photius' synodical letter is brief, firm in its tenor, but friendly in tone. After expressing satisfaction at the new Patriarch's orthodox profession of faith, the Pope nevertheless blames him for having been ordained in contravention of canonical rules forbidding laymen's hurried elevation to the episcopal dignity, adding, however, that should his legates' findings in Constantinople be favourable, he 'will embrace the Patriarch of so eminent a city in brotherly love'. The reply, be it observed, makes no reference to Ignatius' case.

We may therefore conclude from this correspondence that Ignatius' re-trial was ordered, neither by Photius nor by the Emperor, but by the Pope himself. Contrary to the wishes of the Byzantines, who looked upon the incident as closed, the Council and the legates were to examine Ignatius' conduct, the Pope reserving the final decision to himself personally.

Constantinople had not expected such a solution. Unfortunately, as we possess no information on the negotiations carried on before the opening of the Council between the legates and the ecclesiastical and civil authorities of Byzantium, we can only guess what was discussed between them. We are also ill-documented on certain discussions at the Council itself: for instance, we know absolutely nothing about the meetings devoted to the dogmatic question. The conciliar decisions about the monks, previously discussed,[1] suggest that much of the discussion was devoted to the problem of Byzantine monasticism, a problem that had raised controversies at the outset of iconoclasm and of which we still know very little.

As the Acts of the Council of 861 were destroyed by the Fathers of the Ignatian Council of 869–70, we only possess a few summaries of the meetings that dealt with Ignatius. Nicetas, Theognostos, Anastasius and Stylianos have left us minutes of varying accuracy; but fortunately we possess an extract[2] from the Acts, based, as we shall show presently, on the text brought to Constantinople by the papal legates Radoald and Zachary, or more exactly, by the imperial ambassador Leo. This extract having proved reliable on another occasion,[3] we can try, without neglecting other documents already mentioned, to reconstruct the facts in the light of this additional document.

[1] See p. 67.   [2] Wolf von Glanvell, loc. cit. pp. 603–10.
[3] See pp. 28 seq.

On their arrival in Constantinople, the legates insisted on the Pope's instructions being carried out to the very letter; and on seeing that the Roman Pontiff wished to introduce something contrary to their plans and the traditions of their Church, the Emperor and Photius made some opposition: in their view, as Ignatius had resigned in conformity with canonical rules, and had been deposed by a synod to make it evident to all that he had ceased being a Patriarch, and as his successor had been elected in accordance with the laws of the Byzantine Church, there could be no question of going back upon past decisions. And yet the Pope's request could not be disregarded; though no one had asked him for a decision in the matter, his authority had to be respected, for fear of creating new difficulties at the very moment when it was hoped to end them once for all. So, a compromise acceptable to both parties had to be found.

At first the outlook was not promising. It is generally held that strong pressure was brought to bear on the legates and that they were refused all intercourse with Ignatius and his partisans. In support of these allegations, a passage is quoted from the letter of Nicholas I to Photius, dated 18 March 862.[1] But this text does not specifically show that the legates were prevented from communicating with the partisans of the fallen Patriarch; they were rather kept away from intercourse with the Greeks in general.[2] Let it be stated at once that the legates' reports, after their return to Rome, need cautious handling, for when they had lost all hope of bringing the Pope round to their own views, they were only too evidently in search of good excuses in defence of the attitude they had adopted in Byzantium.

And yet, one cannot, with Theognostos,[3] exactly blame them for having accepted presents from Photius. Handed over by officials sent to greet them at Rhoedestus on the way to Constantinople, these presents

---

[1] *M.G.H.* Ep. VI, p. 451: 'De missis siquidem nostris, quos petitos in servitio beati Petri principis apostolorum pro utilitate sanctae Constantinopolitanae ecclesiae contra depositores imaginum vel alias necessitates ingruentes necnon et pro causa solum modo depositionis saepefati viri Ignatii inquirenda illas in partes direximus, silendum non est. Qui, cum iis, sicut dicunt, per centum dierum spatia *omnium nisi suorum alloquendi facultas fuisset denegata*, ut apostolicae sedis missi non digne suscepti sunt, neque, ut decuerat, retenti. Quod non pro alia gestum putamus re, nisi ut inquirendi locum de depositione praefati viri non invenirent.... Quibus secundum horum relationem longa exilia et diuturnas pediculorum comestiones, si in tali intentione persisterent, quidam minantes quod illis a nobis injunctum fuit clam vobis cum sequacibus vestris resistentibus perficere minime potuerunt...'

[2] It is, however, a fact that the Ignatians were prevented handing a memorial to the legates. See p. 79.

[3] Mansi, vol. XVI, col. 297.

were not bribes, but were simply a matter of diplomatic amenity. The same custom may be observed in the reception in 869 of the legates sent by Hadrian II to condemn Photius. As reported by Anastasius,[1] the representatives of Nicholas I were met at Thessalonica by a high imperial official, then at Selymbria by Theognostos and the Proto-spathar Sisinnius, who brought 'forty horses from the imperial stables and all the silver cutlery from the imperial table'. The presents mentioned by Theognostos and consisting of clothes may be assumed to be tokens of the court's anxiety to protect the legates against the rigours of the winter after a journey that had lasted longer than was expected.[2]

But even if there be nothing to prove the use of pressure to dissuade the legates from re-trying Ignatius in accordance with the Pope's instructions, negotiations before the convocation of the synod were, we must admit, unconscionably long. The legates arrived in Byzantium certainly before Christmas, but judging from the allocution delivered at the third session, the synod was convoked only shortly before Easter. The Emperor and the Patriarch eventually yielded to the Roman legates' request that the inquiry into Ignatius' case should be placed first on the Council's agenda. The minutes of the Acts[3] will tell us that they consented to the re-trial only on condition that the legates should give judgement in Constantinople without first referring the case to the Pope. They naturally argued that a final verdict would promote the pacification of the Church and was well worth a concession.

The Emperor personally presided at the first session, when Paul, metropolitan of Caesarea in Cappadocia, opened the debate: 'There is no question of going over Ignatius' case again, since he was deposed for flagrant offences', said the bishop, but he added: 'In order, however, to honour the Holy Roman Church and the Holy Father Nicholas in the person of his representatives, we are willing to allow a second examination of the problems that concern him.' 'The sentence against Ignatius', said the spokesman of the Byzantine Church, 'was passed by a synod. As far as our Church is concerned, the case is therefore closed and has not to be considered again. But to do homage to St Peter and to the Holy Oecumenical Father Nicholas, we all agree to his case being reconsidered and tried again.'

It appears that Ignatius, who had been taken to Constantinople,

---

[1] *Liber Pontificalis* (ed. Duchesne), vol. II, p. 180.
[2] J. Haller, *Nikolaus I und Pseudo-Isidor*, p. 23.
[3] Wolf von Glanvell, loc. cit. pp. 603–10.

tried to hand in a memorial at the opening of the synod, for Theognostos, in his *Libellus*, writes in the name of Ignatius:[1] 'We presented to the bishops through the good offices of the priest Laurentius and the two Stephens, one of whom was a sub-deacon and the other a layman, a memorial in the form of a letter, adjuring them to place it in the hands of your Holiness; but they did not do so.' Now this passage has been wrongly interpreted. It has been the fashion to infer that after the Council of 859 the fallen Patriarch tried to lodge with the Pope a complaint against Photius, the three persons named having sworn to transmit the document but broken their oath. This interpretation, which is accepted by Hergenröther,[2] is completely mistaken and was prompted by the Latin translation of Raderus—another instance of his unreliability. Theognostos' account shows that the three persons concerned discharged certain duties at the Council and were also responsible for preparing the necessary documents for the trial. Ignatius, or rather, some of his partisans—perhaps Theognostos himself, as he is the only one to mention the incident—tried to approach them and through their intermediary to send to the bishops and the papal legates a memorial of the Ignatian party. Theognostos naturally presents the incident in such a way as to create in the mind of the Pope the impression that Ignatius had appealed to the Holy See before the Council. Further on, Theognostos writes in Ignatius' name: 'When we were invited to appear before a tribunal worthy of Caiphas, we implored them to let us be judged by Your Holiness, but none would listen to us.' Had Theognostos, after this outburst, omitted to mention the three persons already identified, it would have been harder to detect his motive, but he showed his hand too clearly.

It seems, indeed, evident from the context that Ignatius never made any such declaration. Theognostos only interprets in that sense the attempt to present a memorial to the legates and through them to the bishops of the synod and to the Pope. We repeat that the memorial, on the face of it, had been drawn up not by Ignatius, but by Theognostos and his friends; and it failed to reach its destination—the legates, the Fathers of the Council and the Pope—because the secretaries of the synod, the priest Laurentius and the two Stephens,

---

[1] Mansi, vol. XVI, col. 296. This is the Greek text: αἱ δὲ παρ' ἡμῶν δοθεῖσαι τοῖς ἐπισκόποις ἔγγραφοι πίστεις, ἤγουν ἐπιστολαί, διὰ τοῦ πρεσβυτέρου Λαυρεντίου καὶ τῶν δύο Στεφάνων, τοῦ τε ὑποδιακόνου καὶ τοῦ λαϊκοῦ, οὓς καὶ ἐνωρκώσαμεν τοῖς χερσὶ τῆς σῆς ἁγιότητος αὐτὰς ἀποδοθῆναι, ἄπρατοι μεμνήκασιν.

[2] *Photius*, vol. I, p. 422: 'dieselben die ihm ihr eidliches Versprechen, seine frühere Klagschrift nach Rom zu bringen, gebrochen hatten.'

refused to oblige Theognostos and his friends by acting as their messengers.

If we are to believe Theognostos and Nicetas,[1] Ignatius would have asked the Council in what apparel he was to appear before his judges: in a monk's garb, being condemned, or in pontificals, being merely accused. The choice being left to him, Ignatius left the Posis palace, where he had taken up his residence, to go to the church of the Apostles, where the Council was holding its sittings; he made the journey 'in great pomp', clad in pontificals and surrounded by an endless *cortège* of his partisans. On reaching the church of St Gregory of Nazianzus, the procession was stopped by the Patrician John Coxes, who in the Emperor's name ordered Ignatius to present himself alone and in monastic garb. The three secretaries of the Council then angrily upbraided him for having put on 'the sacred stole'.

It is easy to surmise from this story what really happened. Quick to seize their opportunity for a noisy anti-government display, the Extremists made Ignatius don his patriarchal robes and mobilized all available forces to escort the Patriarch to the Council. One can imagine this *cortège* parading through the streets of Constantinople and raising a riot, but is it surprising that the imperial police should have stepped in? Ignatius' appearance in episcopal regalia might have been overlooked, but who would have tolerated such an exhibition and given the Extremists the chance to use the occasion for making trouble among the populace? In any case this incident proves what an important concession to the Pope Ignatius' re-trial really was, in view of its political and religious implications.

The details just mentioned are not of course reported in the extract from the Acts already referred to; nor does one find there any confirmation for Theognostos' statements on the Emperor's attitude towards Ignatius before the Council. One can understand, however, that Michael was not profuse in his praise for the old Patriarch's behaviour, and Theognostos makes it sufficiently clear that the unexpected Ignatian demonstration had created a certain sensation in Byzantium by reason of its anti-government sting. The extract from the first session of the Council also lends colour to another statement by Theognostos to the effect that Ignatius, after greeting the legates, demanded the return of his see, for we read that Ignatius, fully conscious of his dignity, insisted on his being the Patriarch, successor of the Apostles St John and St Andrew, implying thereby that Constantinople was an apostolic see

[1] Mansi, vol. XVI, col. 296; *P.G.* vol. 105, col. 517.

on a level with Rome, and he worded his request to the legates in a most resolute manner: 'If you are genuine judges, you must return my see. That is how you should judge.'

The minutes of the first session summarize the main charges brought against Ignatius, mainly his failure to reply to a request from Pope Benedict III to send to Rome information concerning the Asbestas case. Ignatius explained that he had been dethroned only a few days after receipt of the papal letter,[1] and therefore had not had the time to reply. This charge must have come from the legates, as it was mainly their business to see that the Holy See's authority was respected.

The second charge was formulated by the Protospathar John: 'It is a custom with us, as it is also with you, I believe, that after a Patriarch's death, the Emperor summons all the bishops, priests, abbots and deacons, saying: Go and choose the successor God will suggest to you and bring me your decision. They thereupon withdraw to deliberate. They then announce to the Emperor the candidate they have elected and the Emperor gives his consent to the consecration. That is how they receive him.' In other words, John raised the issue of Ignatius' elevation and argued from the fact that he had not been elected by a synod, but simply nominated by the Empress Theodora. To this Ignatius replied: 'My lord and father Tarasius himself was raised [to the throne] by a woman.' The Emperor here interjected: 'You should not say that he was raised by a woman, but that the lord Methodius and the lord Tarasius were appointed under a woman's rule', the Emperor hereby confirming the fact that the Patriarchs Methodius and Tarasius had been canonically elected.

All this is omitted by the monk Theognostos, who instead inserts the passage already quoted and dilates[2] on the renewed efforts by imperial officials to induce Ignatius to abdicate again; there is nothing to justify the repudiation of this passage, since the mere omission of the incident from the Acts is not enough to invalidate it. A formal declaration by Ignatius would have simplified matters considerably, making the re-trial claimed by Nicholas no longer necessary, and gracefully extricating the Emperor and the Patriarch from an entanglement that was both unpleasant and liable to impede the future development of the Byzantine Church. However that may be, Ignatius' attitude made it clear that he had gone back on his abdication and had therefore come under the control of the Extremists.

[1] See p. 29.   [2] P. 80.

The second session of the Council received from Theognostos but scant notice, the abbot being content to recall Ignatius' refusal to appear before the Council, to which he had again been summoned by Laurentius and the two Stephens, members of the Board. The ex-Patriarch is alleged to have declared that he could not acknowledge as judges men in collusion with the intruder Photius, who ate with him and accepted his rich presents: 'I do not accept that sort of judge. I appeal to the Pope: to his judgement I will willingly submit.'

The minutes of this second session, brief as they are, contain several important particulars. Ignatius' contumacy, for one thing, is confirmed. After taking cognizance of the fact at the opening of the meeting, the legates reassert their intention to revise Ignatius' trial as representatives of the Pope and on the strength of the decisions of Sardica, which give the bishop of Rome the right to re-try any bishop. To this the bishop of Laodicea replied in the name of the Byzantine Church: 'Our own Church only rejoices at this; she neither opposes nor deplores it.' He then expressed regret that Ignatius should have scorned the legates' two invitations. Apocrisiaries proposed to send him a third summons, after which, should he persist in his contumacy, proceedings would be taken against him in accordance with canonical law. Amphilochus, bishop of Cyzicus, suggested that the third summons should be served that very day, as had been done in the case of Dioscorus at the Council of Chalcedon; but the legates expressed the wish to follow Roman, and not Byzantine procedure. The summons was worded deferentially, but firmly: it contained a protest against Ignatius' request to see the legates taking the preliminary oath: Ignatius forgets, they said, that he is dealing with the representatives of the Roman See. It appears that certain bishops registered surprise at the courtesy shown by the legates to the ex-Patriarch, whose pretensions must have been offensive to them; but the papal legates replied that they had indeed no intention of trying Ignatius for any offences that were merely personal, but for the transgressions he had committed against the Church. Their gentleness was not relished by the Fathers, since the bishop of Laodicea declared: 'Our Church has different customs from yours; but our saintly Emperor submits to your will.' The apocrisiaries then cut short further criticism by this emphatic declaration: 'We have no wish to follow our own customs in this trial, but the canonical authority and the constitution of the Roman Church.' It would be superfluous to stress further the importance of this session as a witness to Byzantine feelings at that time on the supremacy of the See of Rome. One can only regret that it has been ignored to this day, shifted into the background by Theo-gnostos' doubtful account.

The third session, which was held after Easter, again saw the Emperor in the chair, assisted by Bardas. After the first formalities of the protocol and notice having been given of Ignatius' refusal to appear, the ex-Patriarch was introduced to the assembly, having come under police escort by order of the Emperor. Ignatius persisted in repudiating the legates' competence and opened the debate by a startling declaration: 'Ego non appellavi Romam, nec appello. Quid vultis judicare?' He then asked whether the legates had brought a pontifical letter addressed to him, and the legates answered No. There followed an interesting and lively skirmish. To a question by Ignatius asking who were the judges, the legates replied: 'It is we and the Holy Synod who are the judges', and on his retorting: 'If you had brought me a letter, I would have acknowledged you', the Emperor intervened urging him to accept and acknowledge the judges accredited by his Imperial Majesty and by the whole Church. The Protospathar John then reminded Ignatius that his refusal was at variance with his own attitude towards Benedict III, to whom he had sent the monk Lazarus with a request to ratify the sentence passed on Asbestas. But in vain did the legates, the Emperor and Bardas insist: all their protestations that they willingly acknowledged the legates as legitimate judges only drew from him ironical retorts on their ability to bring about a change in his position.

The final sentence was passed at the fourth session. The case of Asbestas and his group came up first for settlement, and when Zachary, the principal witness, had reviewed the facts again, the legates annulled the judgement given by Ignatius. Next came the question of the legitimacy of Ignatius' elevation to patriarchal honours, and evidence was called to prove that he had not been canonically elected. The legates, on the strength of St Sylvester's prescription, insisted on the sworn evidence of seventy-two witnesses; and though the oriental Church was usually content with ten even in the case of a bishop's trial,[1] the synod deferred to their wishes. But another difficulty arose. Most of the competent witnesses were either patricians or senators, and contrary to usage in Byzantine law, the legates wished them to take the oath. Thus the special consent was required of Bardas, who in the Emperor's name authorized the high officials mentioned to take the oath; this Ignatius himself was called upon to administer. The legates then ratified the

---

[1] Cf. Hergenröther, *Photius*, vol. I, p. 426, n. 38, on the different practices in the two Churches.

sentence of deposition and the sub-deacon Procopius divested the ex-Patriarch of the insignia of his dignity.

Theognostos inserts between the two last sessions a passage of which no trace can be found in the Acts. According to his version, Ignatius, harking back to the past, claimed that the text be read of the decision by Innocent, ordering that John Chrysostom, before being judged, should be restored to his See; as also the fourth canon of the Council of Sardica, forbidding the appointment of a successor to a bishop on whom sentence had been passed, but not yet ratified by Rome. Ignatius is also alleged to have protested against the procedure of his summons before the Council and against the selection of witnesses:

Who are those people? Who can believe them? What canon lays it down that the Emperor should produce witnesses? And if I am not archbishop, you yourself are not the Emperor, these are not bishops, and no more is the adulterer [Photius], for you have all been created such by my hands and my unworthy prayers. Had the adulterer belonged to the Church, I would willingly have come to an understanding with him, but since he is an outsider, how could I make him a pastor of Christ's sheep? And there are many things against it: first, the fact that he is numbered among the damned and the excommunicated, a penalty imposed on them [Asbestas' friends] not only by me, but also by the other Patriarchs, nay, even by your own authority. For the unworthy Zachary notified to them that they had no power to exercise any liturgical functions, to communicate or to ordain, until they were released from the ban: but they did exactly the reverse. The second reason is that he was a State official and a layman, being made a pastor before he was a sheep. On top of all this, he was ordained by one who had been deposed and excommunicated.

Theognostos then makes Ignatius repeat how Photius had broken the promise he made to the bishops to respect him, and snatched the signed document from their hands, adding that Ignatius was again urged to resign and that the Metropolitan of Ancyra, who took the ex-Patriarch's defence too energetically, was struck with a sword 'by the barbarian'.[1] Other friends of Ignatius were similarly ill-treated, so

---

[1] Raderus (Mansi, vol. XVI, col. 299) translates the word βάρβαρος by 'nefario ipso parricida', meaning Photius. The translation is worse than inaccurate. But Theognostos also runs riot in his statements; for instance, when in another place he described the ill-treatment received by the Metropolitan of Cyzicus at the meeting. The man who mishandled him must have been an official or a member of the constabulary. Photius, of course, carried no sword and was only present at the last session, if at all; yet it is none other than Photius whom Theognostos tries to incriminate as the author of the ill-treatment he reports.

it is alleged, and after ten days Ignatius was at last tried and condemned.

Is it really true that all this occurred at the last session but one? It is hard to say. We are inclined to believe that Theognostos rather dramatizes his own ideas about the trial, his own arguments and those of his friends on the Council's methods of procedure. But he forgets that his first two arguments, had they ever been actually used, would have received short shrift at the hands of the Fathers; for Ignatius had not observed the fourth canon of the Sardica Council when he appointed a successor to Gregory before his case had come up for trial in Rome. As to Pope Innocent's decision, the Fathers could have answered that the cases of Ignatius and of John Chrysostom were not on all fours: Ignatius had actually resigned and was not deposed until ecclesiastics in revolt against his successor had recalled him to the patriarchal throne again; also because, being requested to put a stop to this agitation, he declined to do so, thereby tacitly agreeing to his second nomination.

The canonist who drew up the extract from the Acts of the synod would probably have been far too interested in that controversy not to record it in his text, had it ever taken place.[1] It looks therefore—to repeat it once more—as though Theognostos had been summarizing various incidents bearing on Ignatius' case, but not strictly relevant to the debates of the Council.

Such seems to be the most probable reconstruction of the principal phases of the Council of 861; but it must be remembered that what was said in the course of the second period of the debates on dogmatic and disciplinary problems still remains a secret.

One point of exceptional interest remains to be cleared up: did Ignatius, after deposition by legates and Council, appeal to the Pope? Theognostos affirms it, since it is in Ignatius' own name that he addresses his *Libellus* to the Pope; but we have seen how, in order to make us believe that his hero had appealed to Rome immediately after the synods of 859, he confused his own arguments; furthermore, the Acts of the synod emphatically contradict his statements, since the ex-Patriarch exclaimed at the third session: 'Ego non appellavi Romam, nec appello.' If then Theognostos intended to deceive us with that first appeal, who is going to believe his allegations on a 'second' appeal?

---

[1] See pp. 303 seq., 324 seq. on the character and the purpose of the Collection that has preserved this valuable document.

First, it should be made clear that Ignatius does not seem to have been an expert at canon law. His *faux pas* at the beginning of his tenure in sending a pallium to the Pope already proves it; and his overt opposition in Asbestas' case to the fourth canon of the Council of Sardica confirms it. We also note that he did not seem to take the appeal addressed to Rome by Asbestas very seriously; that at the Council of 861 he persistently refused to acknowledge the legates' competence and addressed them in terms bordering on arrogance; that he did not appear before the Fathers till well after the third summons served on him by the representatives of Rome, and then, apparently, only because he was compelled by the imperial police. And yet, there was no justification for his refusal, even when he learned that the legates had received no powers from the Pope to pass a final sentence, since both the inquiry and the examination in the presence of the Emperor and of the Fathers had been ordered by the Pope. This persistent disregard of canonical rules by the pious ascetic, and especially his attitude towards the legates, do not seem to lend support to the theory of an appeal to the Holy See.

Is it not then surprising that after refusing to appear before the Council and to answer the legates' cross-examination, Ignatius seems tamely to have submitted to their verdict? Yet the extract from the minutes of the last session indicates that the witnesses took the oath administered by him and that he offered no resistance when the sentence of degradation[1] was being carried out. Nor do we find the slightest hint to justify the supposition that Ignatius appealed to the Pope from the legates' sentence. All this is, we must confess, not thoroughly convincing, since we cannot refer to the Acts in full, but only to an extract.

Fortunately, we can quote witnesses to belie Theognostos' statements. First, Metrophanes, speaking of the monk's mediation with the Pope in the Eternal City, credits him alone with the initiative: 'Then the monk and archimandrite, Theognostos, driven by his zeal, disguised himself as a layman and secretly left for Rome to inform the Holy Father of what had taken place in connection with Ignatius.'[2] Nicetas,[3] Ignatius' keenest champion, says nothing about Theognostos' attempt but attributes to Nicholas alone the responsibility for the legates' condemnation.

---

[1] Cf. the description of this scene in Nicetas Paphlago, *P.G.* vol. 105, col. 520.
[2] Mansi, vol. XVI, col. 429. Once more Raderus blunders in his translation: Ζήλῳ κινηθείς = 'rei indignitate commotus'. It shows that his zeal often clouded his Greek.   [3] Loc. cit. col. 525.

Now let us see how Ignatius reacted after his condemnation. According to Nicetas,[1] he was placed under very strict surveillance, but the account of the sufferings he is alleged to have endured at the hands of his gaolers is undoubtedly exaggerated. The same writer then states that the ex-Patriarch signed a declaration acknowledging that he had not been canonically elected and that he had set up 'a tyrannical regime', two confessions corresponding to the main charges against him at the Council of 861, i.e. his nomination by Theodora and his condemnation of the Asbestas group. According to Nicetas' report, Ignatius was handed a blank sheet of paper and Theodore, one of the gaolers, took hold of the old man's hand and scrawled the sign of the cross, Photius subsequently writing out the declaration. But what truth is there in this tale? Is Nicetas merely trying to disguise the fact, so unpalatable to extremist Ignatians, of the ex-Patriarch's final submission to the Council's decision, in consideration of which Ignatius was allowed to live at the Posis palace, once his mother's property? Later, Nicetas tells us that Photius suggested to the Emperor to have Ignatius summoned to the church of the Apostles, there to listen to the public reading of his own declaration and to be anathematized. It was even proposed to blind him and to cut off one of his hands; his residence, so it is stated, was surrounded on Whit Sunday by a cordon of police, and Ignatius, seeing his life threatened, fled disguised as a servant and accompanied by his disciple Cyprian. This is just another story to be taken with caution, for the 'hagiographer' is certainly not saying everything. Considering the Ignatian radicals' obstinacy in refusing to accept the ex-Patriarch's spontaneous submission and in accusing Photius of forgery, would it not rather have occurred to the authorities to make Ignatius repeat his declaration before the Fathers of the Council? Fearing lest it should foil all their plans, the anti-Photianists perhaps advised Ignatius to fly and escape from the threat of losing his eyes. The fugitive hid in the Isles of Propontis until the August earthquake shook his shelter,[2] a shock that mollified the authorities towards Ignatius: alarmed by the divine punishment which their cruel persecution had called down on their heads, they decreed—according to Nicetas—that Ignatius could now return to Constantinople in peace, without any

---

[1] Loc. cit. cols. 521–5.

[2] It was at that time that Ignatius consecrated an altar on one of the islands (Nicetas, *P.G.* vol. 105, cols. 529 seq.). According to Nicetas, the altar was deconsecrated by Photius' envoy to signify that Ignatius had lost all jurisdiction by deposition and had acted *ultra vires*.

further fear of retaliation. The ex-Patriarch then left his hiding place and presented himself to the patrician Petronas, who took him to Bardas. 'Deeply affected by the man's virtue,' says Nicetas, 'Bardas let him return to his monastery, a free and innocent man.'[1]

Does Ignatius' panegyrist not bear out the fact that Bardas and the government were convinced in the end of Ignatius' innocence in his over-zealous partisans' recent intrigues? Would they not have acted differently, if the ex-Patriarch had legally appealed to Rome? Would his withdrawal to a monastery not have spelled danger? And would Bardas have been so lenient, if Ignatius had persisted in his opposition? All these questions, in my view, can only be answered in the negative, all the probabilities converging on the one conclusion, that Ignatius finally submitted to his fate and did not appeal to Rome.[2]

There only remains to explain, and form an estimate on, the legates' conduct in the proceedings of the Council. It seems absolutely certain that by passing sentence on Ignatius in the Pope's name they exceeded the limits of their powers, since the Pope, as we have seen, had in so many words reserved the right to himself. On the other hand, the criticism often raised that they overstepped their mandate by summoning Ignatius before the Council is unjustifiable, since the inquiry by the Fathers had been ordered by Nicholas I. The Emperor Michael, in his reply to the Pope, also corroborates the fact that the legates were quite conscious of exceeding the limits set to their activities by Nicholas, as it was with the greatest reluctance that they were induced to go beyond their warrant.[3]

Photius' enemies have pretended that violence and corruption account for the result; but why should the Byzantine government have resorted

---

[1] Nicetas, *P.G.* vol. 105, col. 525. At one place in his 'biography' of Ignatius Nicetas reveals the true culprit in all the persecutions against Ignatius, namely, Bardas, not Photius. In relating a dream Bardas had before dying, he represents St Peter inviting Ignatius to point out the man responsible for all his misfortunes and the ex-Patriarch singled out Bardas (ibid. col. 536). Here Nicetas unwittingly tells the truth and by the same token shows that all the unpleasant measures taken against Ignatius had politics as their inspiration.

[2] This is confirmed by Nicetas' report that Bardas examined, and found no truth in, the statement made by the impostor Eustratius to the effect that he had received from Ignatius a letter addressed by him to the Pope who had refused to receive it, whilst sending a friendly letter to Photius. Nicetas (*P.G.* vol. 105, cols. 528 seq.) pretended that the two letters had been forged by Photius; yet he admitted that Bardas looked into the allegation and found no truth in it.

[3] *M.G.H.* Ep. VI, p. 514 (letter from Nicholas to Michael, 13 November 866).

to force, when it was its obvious wish to bring the legates round to its own designs by persuasion? As to the reproach of corruption, one needs to be cautious: Radoald and Zachary were very capable bishops, whom the Pope used to honour with particularly delicate missions; and to think that the Pontiff numbered among his trusted agents men accessible to venality would be casting an unwarranted slur on the Roman clergy and on the pontifical court of that period. Even when he came to disapprove his legates' conduct, Nicholas never went so far as to accuse them of being open to arguments so alien to morality. Motives for their attitude should be looked for elsewhere.

The legates were intelligent enough to realize that conditions in Byzantium were somewhat different from what was thought in Rome; that the anti-Photianist opposition was not so formidable and that its members were not as harmless and innocent as they claimed to be. They could not but be aware of the immense significance of a Patriarch of Constantinople being condemned and deposed by the representatives of the Holy See. Whatever we may think of their statesmanship, one thing is certain: Radoald and Zachary were excellent canonists,[1] and knew enough about the religious policy of Nicholas I to anticipate that the negotiations, of which they were the instruments, would meet their master's deepest desire, and that the Pope, who had succeeded in imposing his authority on the Western bishops and had stifled the dreams of independence of the Frankish Church, the most powerful Church in the West, would appraise their initiative at its true value. They also knew that the Pope never liked to leave important decisions to his representatives, and that in the particular instance of Ignatius he had jealously reserved the verdict to himself. This was why they withstood so long the request of the Emperor, who consented to the resumption of the Council meetings only on condition that the issue should be definitely settled on the spot. Their reluctance displeased him; and they knew it; and they were made to understand that if they refused to yield he would drop all idea of a Council, in which case Nicholas would have lost his chance of having a say in Ignatius' case. Faced with this alternative, which seemed to them fundamental, they decided to go ahead, expert canonists as they were, and to exchange the humble part of inquirers for the role of judges. Thanks to them, the Church of Constantinople fully and freely, one may say for the first time, acknowledged the Roman Pontiff's right to try a Byzantine Patriarch. Two

[1] Cf. E. Perels, *Papst Nikolaus I und Anastasius Bibliothecarius* (Berlin, 1920), pp. 209 seq.

other instances of this exercise of supremacy can be found back in the sixth century,[1] although the circumstances were entirely different: Pope Agapet's intervention against the Patriarch Anthimius (535) was prompted not by disciplinary, but by dogmatic motives, the defendant having lent his support to the Emperor Zeno's *Henotikon*; while the liquidation by Pope Hormisdas of Acacius' schism (519) centred mainly on a doctrinal issue. In the case of Ignatius and the Council of 861, the issue was purely disciplinary, in no way touching on doctrine, and the Byzantine Church, by allowing Ignatius to be tried by the Pope's representatives, granted to the See of Rome more than a mere right of appeal, since, as we have seen, the ex-Patriarch had lodged no appeal with the Holy See.

Such an achievement was worth a few concessions, and Radoald and Zachary made them in the hope that the Pope would be only too thankful for it. Obviously, Nicholas' letter to the Emperor could not be read at the Council meeting in its original form and it was modified, the passage relating to the reservation of the final verdict being suppressed. A similar incident had occurred at the Seventh Council: having been sent to Constantinople by Hadrian I merely to inquire into the necessity for, and the convocation procedure of, an oecumenical council (the decision of summoning or not summoning it having been reserved to the Pope),[2] the legates eventually decided to take part, as papal representatives, in the Council summoned by Irene, and as the Pope's letters could not be read as they stood to the Fathers, their terms were altered to suit the occasion, without any results unpleasant to the legates. In the light of this precedent, coupled with the fact that Radoald and Zachary brought to the Pope the submission of the Byzantine Church to his judgement, the legates' 'perversion' should be much less of an unpardonable sin.[3]

---

[1] Cf. Caspar, *Geschichte des Papsttums* (Tübingen, 1933), vol. II, pp. 153 seq., 221 seq. J. Haller, *Das Papsttum* (Stuttgart, 1934), vol. I, pp. 232 seq., 245 seq.

[2] See the letter from Hadrian I to Constantine and Irene, in Baronius, *Annales Ecclesiastici, a.* 785, para. 37. Jaffé-Ewald, nos. 2448, 2449. Cf. J. Haller, *Das Papsttum*, pp. 5 seq.

[3] Cf. J. Haller, *Nikolaus I und Pseudo-Isidor* (Stuttgart, 1936), pp. 27 seq.

CHAPTER IV

NICHOLAS, PHOTIUS AND BORIS

Radoald and Zachary return to Rome—Nicholas' policy and letters to the Emperor and the Patriarch—Theognostos and the Roman Synod of 863—Byzantine reaction in Bulgaria and its development in Rome—Nicholas' fatal reply—Was the breach permanent?—Reaction in Byzantium—Boris' *volte-face*; his influence on the growth of the conflict—The Byzantine Synod of 867—Did Photius challenge the Roman primacy?

ON reaching Rome, the legates explained to the Pope the reasons why they had taken it upon themselves to exceed their mandate, and the Pope could not but see the important advantage the Holy See had secured over the most powerful patriarchate in the East. Everything points to the fact that, at least on principle, he approved all that the legates had done in Constantinople. This is proved by the way he dealt with them; for Radoald of Porto was actually entrusted towards the end of November 862 with an important mission to the Frankish court.[1] The Pope would certainly not have sent Radoald on this new embassy, had he not been pleased with his last mission to Constantinople. As for Zachary, he quietly and honourably resumed his duties at the pontifical court.

In one particular matter, however, the mission of Radoald and Zachary had failed completely. The Pope had commissioned them to claim the return of the patrimonies of Sicily and Calabria and of Illyricum to the direct jurisdiction of the Roman See. In this the legates were unable to give the Pope any satisfaction, nor did the proposals seem to have come up for discussion at the Council. None the less, the fact that the Byzantine Church and the Emperor had accepted the papal legates' verdict suggested that the prestige of the See of Rome was very considerable in Byzantium. Was there then no hope that the Byzantines would ever yield on this particular point? But the Pope still possessed, should the need ever arise, a powerful weapon at his disposal. If it was true that the Patriarch Ignatius had been tried and condemned by the legates in the Pope's name, it was no less true that the new Patriarch had not yet been officially acknowledged by the See of Rome as the legitimate successor.

---

[1] *M.G.H.* Ep. VI, pp. 268–70. The letter is dated 23 November 862.

The letter sent to the Pope by Photius after the Council seemed to raise and encourage such hopes, for it was couched in very deferential terms, as though Photius had been aware that the Pope had not yet fully entered into communion with him. Hence the efforts in his letter to meet all the objections which the Pope had previously raised against the legitimacy of his elevation. After repeating what he had said in his previous letter, he insisted that he had been forced to accept a dignity which in no way appealed to him; he also tried to justify his rapid promotion from the laity to the patriarchate, since the Church of Constantinople, he said, had not accepted the canon of Sardica quoted by the Pope in his letter to Michael III,[1] prohibiting such rapid rise of laymen to ecclesiastical dignities.[2] But to meet the Pope's wishes, Photius had a canon voted by the Fathers of the last synod putting an end in the Church of Constantinople to a practice at variance with Roman usage; he went on to quote several instances to the Pope of the canonical prescriptions being disregarded and ended by requesting him not to listen to calumnies from people reaching Rome from Constantinople without any letters of recommendation from the ecclesiastical authorities.[3]

The contents of this letter seemed to the Pope to be encouraging, for

---

[1] *M.G.H.* Ep. VI, pp. 435 seq.

[2] Hergenröther, *Photius*, vol. I, pp. 445, 541 holds that this assertion by Photius is 'eine offenbare Lüge'. Rosseikin, *Pervoe Patriarshestvo Patriarkha Fotiya*, pp. 156 seq. tries to reconcile the Pope's and the Patriarch's contradictory statements. But the matter seems quite simple. Photius was justified in saying that the Church of Constantinople had not accepted the Pope's decretals quoted in Nicholas' letter to Michael; and as to the canons of Sardica, Photius never pretended that his Church did not know them. All he implied was the tenth canon, quoted by the Pope, which, although contained in the canonical Collections with the other canons of Sardica (cf. V. Beneshevich, 'Joannis Scholastici Synagoga L titulorum', in *Abh. bayr. Akad., Phil.-Hist. Kl.*, 1937, p. 48), had not been carried into practice by the Church of Constantinople, as evidenced by the appointments of Tarasius and Nicephorus. It was to remedy this defect that Photius had had a special canon voted. Cf. on this point J. Langen, *Geschichte der Römischen Kirche* (Bonn, 1893), vol. III, p. 19: 'Es ist nicht auffallend, dass Nikolaus dem Konzil von Sardica eine solche Bedeutung einräumt, da man im Abendlande seine Kanones mit denen des nicänischen bald verbunden hatte, und es oft genug für oekumenisch erklärte. Thatsächlich aber war es nur ein abendländisches Generalkonzil gewesen, und seine Kanones im Orient nicht recipiert. Die Decretalen der Päpste waren aber im Orient nur zum Theil bekannt, und galten nur insoweit, als ihr Inhalt sich an den anerkannten Glaubensquellen, Schrift, Tradition und oekumenische Koncilien bewährte. Die römische und orientalische Anschauung trafen hier gleich hart auf einander.'

[3] *P.G.* vol. 102, cols. 593–617. See the analysis of this letter in Hergenröther, *Photius*, vol. I, pp. 439–60 and in Rosseikin, loc. cit. pp. 151–71.

he saw clearly that the new Patriarch was very keen on recognition by the See of Rome as the legitimate incumbent. This was important, making it worth his while to look about for a counterpoise equivalent in the scales of pontifical politics to the Patriarch's desire, and there was no better test than the return of Illyricum to the direct jurisdiction of the Holy See. There was in Photius' letter a passage which seemed to justify the attempt.[1] There the Patriarch stated that he would have been only too willing to meet the Pope's demands, had the Emperor not vetoed some of the concessions, so that the Patriarch and the legates had to give way for fear of worse risks. In these words Photius evidently hinted at the Pope's demand that Illyricum should become Roman again, and the Pope naturally concluded that the Patriarch had on principle no objection to the request.

The Pope immediately proceeded to action. Leo, the imperial ambassador, had reached Rome after the legates; he was armed with a letter from the Emperor and with the Acts of the Council and was charged to supply the Pope with full information. But as pourparlers with the imperial ambassador dragged on, it gradually dawned on the Pope that an important concession such as he was scheming could hardly be extracted from the Emperor; all that the Pope's tenacity achieved was to make Leo miss the last boat to Constantinople and to force him to spend the winter in Rome, but without making the slightest impression on his firm determination to obey his master's instructions. No arrangement that could please Nicholas was in sight.

Anyone familiar with Nicholas' ecclesiastical policy will understand why the Pope was so anxious to reach a satisfactory solution of his problem. The stake was first of all a young and vigorous nation which occupied a part of ancient Illyricum—the Bulgarians.[2] They were still pagans, but their conversion to Christianity was only a matter of time. Had Nicholas' plans succeeded, the papacy would have registered a twofold success: first it would have secured, through the medium of the Bulgarians, won over to Roman Christianity and occupying, so to speak, the very threshold of Constantinople, an indirect influence over the Byzantine Church; and second, the Roman missionaries would then have been in a favourable position to elbow out of those countries the

---

[1] *P.G.* vol. 102, col. 613.

[2] For further details, see my study on Illyricum in my book, *Les Légendes de Constantin et de Méthode*, pp. 248–83.

Frankish missionaries, whose activities extended to the whole periphery of the Frankish Empire as far as Croatia and Bulgaria to the south and Pannonia, Moravia and Bohemia to the east and north-east. For it was not in the interest of the papacy, as conceived by Nicholas, that the Frankish Church should grow too powerful and extend its direct influence over these new nations. Such was the reason, as I have explained in a previous work, why Nicholas was so keenly interested in the young nations that sprang up round the Frankish Empire, and this policy, which inspired the acts of the pontificate of this great Pope, will help us to understand better Nicholas' dealings with Photius and his rival Ignatius.

The firmness with which the imperial ambassador Leo met the Pope's overtures in this matter should, however, have made Nicholas realize that he was treading on dangerous ground. It was not only the Franks and the papacy, but the Byzantines as well who had their hearts set on Bulgaria, with this difference, that whereas the Bulgarian problem was for the Franks and for Rome only a matter of prestige, it was for the Byzantines a matter of life and death, for Byzantium could not possibly permit another power, whether political or cultural, to settle at its very doors.

His failure with Leo did not damp Nicholas' hopes, and he tried his counterpoise theory in the expectation that the desire of Photius to obtain the Pope's acknowledgement would be keen enough to justify the cost. The ambassador left with two letters, dated 18 March 862, addressed to the Emperor and to Photius, both containing the Pope's refusal to acquiesce in the new conditions in Byzantium, and pleading the Roman primacy, which obliged him to ensure the observation of canonical laws throughout the Church. In both letters Nicholas refutes the arguments of the Emperor and Photius in support of a layman's promotion to ecclesiastical dignities even in cases of urgent necessity and protests against the reading of his letters to the Fathers in a bowdlerized version. In his letter to Photius, the Pope complains that his legates had not been treated with courtesy and insists repeatedly that they had no right to pass sentence on Ignatius.

The tone of his letter to Michael is very courteous, as though the Pope were trying to give the Emperor the impression that he had no wish to sever relations with him; but Nicholas makes it clearer in his letter to Photius that his verdict should not be considered as final. After expressing doubts concerning the truth of Photius' statement that he had felt no inclination to accept the patriarchal dignity,[1] the Pope proceeds:

We do not number Ignatius among the deposed, and as long as we are not in a position to ascertain, in all truth, his offence and his guilt, we refuse to pass sentence of condemnation; for we must beware lest an innocent man be condemned on false pretences. As the Roman Church maintains him in his dignity, if no accusation against him is substantiated, so also she refuses to admit you to patriarchal honours, as you have come by them in reckless defiance of the traditions of the Fathers; nor will she consent to your retaining your priestly functions unless and until the Patriarch Ignatius be justly condemned.

Now it is easy to read between the lines of this letter that the Pope left open the possibility of his confirming the sentence passed on Ignatius by his legates, since all he maintains is that the evidence produced in support of the condemnation did not seem to him adequate. He does not, of course, mention the price Byzantium would have to pay for a new revision of this sorry business; but Leo had stayed in Rome long enough to fathom the secrets of Nicholas' policy; and he had opportunities enough, during those long winter months, of sounding the Pope's canonists and officials to acquaint his imperial master and Photius with what lay behind an apparently definite refusal. And in order to lend his words more weight and a more menacing significance, Nicholas at the same time announced his decision to the Patriarchs of Alexandria, Antioch and Jerusalem.[2]

But if the Pope imagined that these dignitaries would ever be able to influence Michael and Photius and induce them to yield to the See of Rome, he made a great mistake. Those poor oriental Patriarchs were far too dependent on imperial good will and bounty ever to indulge in

---

[1] *M.G.H.* Ep. VI, p. 450. Hergenröther, *Photius*, vol. I, p. 441 goes too far in casting doubts on the sincerity of the Patriarch's statement that he had accepted the patriarchate against his will: he calls it 'die alte Lüge'. And yet, it is one of the most moving passages in the letter (*P.G.* vol. 102, col. 597). Scholars who have a love for learning and know how to be absorbed in its deepest secrets, will read with emotion what the old professor of the Byzantine 'University' has to say about his studies and his students. They alone will understand the feelings of regret and bitterness Photius experienced, when harking back to those peaceful years of study which he had to give up for ever. Instead of an idyllic life, devoted to study and teaching, he finds himself swallowed up in public life and dragged into political party conflicts for which he professed nothing but contempt. Did Hergenröther never experience the feelings of a scholar wrested from his studies by occupations that have nothing to offer in common with scholarship?

[2] *M.G.H.* Ep. VI, pp. 440–2.

activities that might inconvenience their more fortunate and more powerful confrère of the Imperial City; and if the Pope entrusted those letters to Leo's diplomatic bag he gave evidence of greater *naïveté* still. It is not likely that the successor of St Peter's refusal to acknowledge Ignatius' successor ever reached those Eastern Patriarchs' ears.

In vain did Nicholas await a reply to his demand: Michael and Photius remained dumb, which, to put it frankly, was the only possible thing for them to do. Unable to pay the price the Pope expected for a new revision of the Photian and Ignatian cases, their most discreet policy was to wait till the Pope changed his mind rather than start a quarrel which would have gravely compromised the good relations between the two Churches.

But the Pope kept on hoping that his letters would produce the desired effect on the Byzantines, whilst the legates Radoald and Zachary continued to enjoy his favours. Radoald received, on his mission to the Frankish court, new instructions from the Pope as late as the month of April, 863: but the imperial embassy did not make its appearance. Instead of the ambassadors, other people came to Rome, namely, the so-called champions of Ignatius, the principal mischief-makers in all the troubles that had divided the Byzantine Church. The most prominent among them were the abbot Theognostos and his followers, all trying to draw the Pope to their side. Though none of them had letters of recommendation from the Patriarch of Constantinople, Nicholas gladly welcomed all these refugees, listening to their complaints and their views on the position. Theognostos came forward as Ignatius' spokesman, though I have already said that the ex-Patriarch had not appealed to the Pope and had given no one a mandate to act in his name; but being one of the Ignatian leaders, Theognostos considered himself entitled to do so.

It is hard to say when Theognostos arrived in Rome; only one thing is certain: it was after the ambassador Leo's departure. It would be interesting to know whether it was in the course of the year 862 or at the beginning of 863, but notwithstanding the vigilance of the imperial police, he certainly did his utmost to be in Rome at the earliest possible date.

If Theognostos arrived in Rome in 862, it is important to observe that he failed to induce the Pope to adopt his point of view, for it must in that case have taken him a full year to decide on the resolute step in favour of Ignatius, which he actually took, as we know, at the Roman synod of 863.

The exact date of this meeting is not given in the Pope's letter about the synod.[1] As it is said there that after first meeting in the church of St Peter the assembly transferred its sittings to the church of the Saviour, 'propter frigidiorem locum', it has been assumed that the synod took place in the spring of that year, Baronius and Hergenröther dating it in the month of April. Yet the text seems rather to indicate that the venue of the meeting was altered on account, not of the cold, but of the heat. Hence J. Haller[2] is right in dating the convocation of the synod in the month of August, a time of the year when the heat in Rome is wellnigh intolerable.

The timing is important, for it proves that Nicholas waited till the last possible moment for the arrival of an embassy from Constantinople armed with full powers to negotiate the Photius affair and the restitution of Illyricum to the Roman See. Balked in his expectations, he then made up his mind to intensify the pressure, and the month of August was the most appropriate for the move. Assuming that sea communications between Italy and Byzantium would be practically suspended by the end of October, there was no likelihood of an imperial embassy arriving at such a late date in Rome: the envoys would have had little time for their negotiations and a winter stay in Rome was not particularly attractive. No embassy would be sent from Byzantium at that time of the year to find itself marooned in Rome till the reopening of sea traffic, i.e. till the month of March of the following year. On the other hand, if the Pope wished to dispatch the decision of the synod to Constantinople, he had little time to waste to enable his messengers to set out before the bad season started.

Of what took place at this synod we are well informed by the letter Nicholas sent on 13 November 866 to the the Eastern Patriarchs.[3] First were read the Acts of the Byzantine Council of 861 together with the letters of Michael and Photius. Then the legates' procedure in Constantinople was examined. Zachary, questioned by the synod, confessed that he had exceeded his powers by holding communion with Photius

---

[1] *M.G.H.* Ep. VI, p. 517: 'Tunc convocato multarum provinciarum Occidentalium regionum sanctissimorum episcoporum coetu et collecta sancta synodo in ecclesia Dei, in qua beatus Petrus apostolorum princeps redolet et virtutibus emicat, deinde propter frigidiorem locum in ecclesia Salvatoris, quae ab auctore appellatur Constantiniana' (Church of the Lateran).

[2] Loc. cit. pp. 32 seq.

[3] *M.G.H.* Ep. VI, chiefly pp. 517–23.

and deposing Ignatius; and for his pains was deprived of his episcopal dignity and excommunicated. The synod then voted six canons. The first declared that Photius, having been ordained by a bishop who was 'tied' by the Holy See on account of his misdeeds against Ignatius, was stripped of all ecclesiastical dignity. He was also blamed for trying to bribe the papal legates. The second canon declared Gregory Asbestas to be deposed and excommunicated; and the clergy ordained by Photius were disqualified from all ecclesiastical functions (canon III). Canon IV restored in very solemn terms the patriarchal dignity to Ignatius. Bishops and clergy who had been victimized for their loyalty to Ignatius were to be immediately reinstated in their honours and functions (canon V). The last canon ratified the condemnation of John the Grammarian, the last leader of iconoclasm and its sectaries.

If we now compare these new decisions issued by Nicholas with the contents of his letters to Michael, Photius and the Eastern Patriarchs in 862, we note, indeed, an immense 'progress' in the Pope's mental attitude towards Photius; and it is also easy to guess who was responsible for this 'progress': none, of course, but Theognostos and his friends: and the Pope himself confessed as much, when he mentioned in the same letters the rumours brought to Rome by people coming from Constantinople.[1]

Let us specify the points in which Theognostos influenced the Pope. First in importance was Gregory Asbestas' association with the Photian affair. Until then Nicholas had known little about him, or at any rate attached little importance to his case, since he mentions him nowhere. The legates' decision annulling the condemnation of Gregory and his group had not been, up to that date, particularly questioned by the Pope, the only objection he raised being against the sentence on Ignatius and Photius. Yet, at the Roman synod, Asbestas' case held the floor, no doubt as a result of the intervention of Theognostos and his friends.

A careful scrutiny of the Acts of the Roman synod discloses first of all the fact that the relations between Photius and the Asbestas group supplied the main grievances against Photius, who was blamed, for instance, for having communicated with 'schismatics', i.e. with Asbestas' friends, even before his ordination, a detail of which the Pope had been completely unaware before Theognostos' arrival in Rome. Photius was

---

[1] Loc. cit. p. 517: 'Sed procedente tempore murmur multorum ab illis partibus Romam venientium, quin immo persecutiones a fautoribus Photii commotas fugientium, sensim eosdem coepit episcopos muneribus fuisse corruptos diffamare et, quod communicassent Photio et deposuissent Ignatium, divulgare.'

also indicted for having been ordained by a deposed bishop and for having sentenced Ignatius with the assistance of deposed and anathematized bishops—again Asbestas' group—and of bishops 'without a see', this last designation implying, no doubt, that the Pope—again at the instigation of Theognostos—did not acknowledge the promotions among the clergy made by Photius. Until the synod, the Pope had apparently no knowledge of any promise made by Photius to some Ignatian bishops or of his dealings with the outgoing Patriarch; yet, in the first canon of the Roman synod, the violation of this promise was listed among the main crimes laid at the 'intruder's' door. The Pope also gave credence to Theognostos' account of the 'persecutions' against the Ignatians. The fact that for the very first time he blamed his legates for having communicated with Photius[1] could only be due to reports carried by the Ignatian refugees to Rome, informing the Pope of particulars he did not know before, or rather, to which he had attached no importance.

For the first time, too, the Pope honoured Photius with the 'uncomplimentary designations' so dear to the Ignatians: the new Patriarch is now called a 'rapax et scelestus adulter', 'adulter et pervasor' (canon I of the synod), 'neophytus et Constantinopolitanae sedis invasor' (canon III), and 'adulter, prevaricator, pervasor' (canon IV), titles one can find on nearly every page of Ignatius' *Life*, as written by Nicetas-David, and of the anti-Photianist Collection, of which mention will be made later.

Why, then, did Nicholas lend so much credit to the reports of Theognostos and his like? For we must remember that the Pope could easily control their statements by consulting either the Acts of the synod of 861, or the archives of his predecessors Leo IV and Benedict III (both Popes rather unfavourable to Ignatius), containing the documents of the Asbestas case and of his trial under Ignatius, or the letters of the Emperor and Photius; yet the Pope so disregarded these documents that he even indirectly accused the Emperor of telling lies. The Emperor had stated in his correspondence that Ignatius had resigned, and the Roman synod emphatically states in its fourth canon: 'Qui primo quidem imperiali violentia ac terrore trono privatus est.' Nicholas even preferred to disown his own legates who until then had been his trusted agents. How is such extraordinary conduct to be explained?

We must remember what has been previously said about Nicholas'

---

[1] Loc. cit. p. 515: 'Denique et cum Photio adultero, ecclesiae invasore atque neophyto, quod sibi multipliciter prohibitum fuerat, inter sacrosancta mysteria communicaverunt.'

policy: it did not take Theognostos and his associates long in Rome to discover the Pope's dominant thoughts and the motives of his quarrel with the Emperor. Theognostos found the target to aim at and proceeded with methodical cunning. He first gave Nicholas a complete assurance of the Ignatians' profound attachment to the Roman See: for did not their leader Ignatius appeal to the Pope's judgement immediately after the synod of 859?—a statement it was difficult for the Romans to verify, since Photianist evidence, the only one at their disposal, said nothing about it. So, why not believe it? Again, one thing seemed certain: Ignatius had commissioned Theognostos to appeal to Rome after his condemnation in 861: Theognostos said so; his *Libellus* containing the appeal was written in the ex-Patriarch's name and the document was replete with expressions of extreme deference to Rome. How was the Pope to verify the pious monk's statement?

There was also a sentimental side to the affair: the round of sufferings endured by Ignatius, after the vivid, picturesque and passionate account by his faithful supporters, must have moved to tears a Pope of Nicholas' temperament, a saintly man who had ever been the champion of the rights, not only of the Church, but of all the oppressed; who had undertaken the energetic defence of Theutberga, the repudiated wife of Lothar II, one of the finest gestures to the credit of a successor of St Peter. Nicholas always loved to step into the breach in defence of bishops against powerful Metropolitans, as was the case with Rothad of Soissons and Wulfad of Bourges. Nothing fired his sense of justice and touched his heart so much as the report that somebody was being unjustly treated;[1] and here the evidence of unjust persecution was glaring in the very city of Rome, where Theognostos and his co-sufferers had taken refuge from 'imperial fury'; such pious and virtuous folk, too, who edified all the Romans with their fervent practices. One can well imagine with what zeal they played up to the crowd, conscious that there was no better way to the heart of the pious Pontiff and his faithful and naïve flock. And the obstinate silence of the Emperor and Photius bore out the version given by Theognostos of events in Byzantium.

There remained still another consideration which, more than any other, must have confirmed Nicholas in his last decision. For all their protestations of submission to Rome, the Emperor and Photius refused the request that seemed to Nicholas so fair, the return of Illyricum to the Roman jurisdiction. But after all, the Patriarch's position in Byzan-

[1] Cf. Perels' opinion on Nicholas (loc. cit. p. 178): 'Ein moralischer Untergrund ist in den Motiven seines Handelns gar nicht zu verkennen....'

tium did not seem so strong as it looked, judging from the legates' account. Theognostos airily spoke of innumerable crowds of pious monks and bishops, who refused to accept Photius as their legitimate Patriarch. Photius had, therefore, come up against an opposition, which in Theognostos' opinion was very serious and seemed to have a more decided lean to Rome than Photius had. Then why not back it up, all the more so as justice demanded it?

Again, there were good prospects that, once restored to his see by the Pope, Ignatius would show himself more grateful to the papacy than his rival, and in this respect Theognostos had no doubt given the Pope more definite assurances, calculated to dispose of his lingering hesitation.

Of this we find corroboration in a letter from Pope John VIII to Boris-Michael, written at the end of 874 or at the beginning of 875, where the Pope exhorts the Khagan to throw up his obedience to the Byzantine Patriarch and make his submission to the Roman See. This is what he says about Ignatius:[1]

> For it was on this condition that Ignatius was acquitted by our predecessors, that if he undertook anything against apostolic rights in connection with Bulgaria, which not even Photius ever dared to attempt, he would, despite his acquittal, remain under the sentence of his previous condemnation. Therefore, either he stands acquitted, if he respects the rights of the Apostolic See on the Bulgarian question, or, if he does not, he falls back under the previous ban.

This passage surprised M. P. Kehr, who published it, but the only possible explanation is that the words reflect the negotiations between Nicholas and Theognostos before Ignatius' reinstatement.

Another circumstance deserves our attention: whereas the Pope paints his legates' doings in Constantinople in the darkest colours, one is surprised to find that the punishment meted out to Zachary of Anagni did not fit the 'misdeeds' deplored by the Pope. Zachary, it is true, was deposed and dispossessed of his diocese, but the Pope gave him as a reward the disposal of the rich and important monastery of St Gregory the Great.[2] Nor was his diocese handed to another titular. After his

---

[1] *M.G.H.* Ep. VII, pp. 294 seq.: 'Sub ea enim conditione Ignatius a nostris predecessoribus solutus est, ut, si per Bulgariam, quod neque Photius ille temptaverat, aliquid contra jura apostolica temptavisset, sub pristinae damnationis suae sententia nichilominus permaneret. Aut ergo in Bulgariam contra institutionem sedis apostolicae nil temptans vere solutus est, aut, si temptaverit, pristinis utique laqueis inretitus est.' Cf. chapter VI, pp. 159 seq.

[2] Joannis Diaconi Vita Gregorii M. IV, ch. 93, *P.L.* vol. 75, col. 236.

rehabilitation,[1] Zachary quietly resumed his office and his title, as though there had been a private understanding between him and the Pope. Besides, Zachary had honestly told the truth, when he confessed to the synod that he had exceeded his powers in Constantinople.[2]

Radoald did not fare as well as Zachary, for he refused to appear before the Pope and must have been condemned for contumacy by a synod held in Rome on 1 November 864, as reported in a letter from the Pope to the Western Patriarchs and bishops.[3] Radoald was threatened with anathema, should he ever attempt to make contact with Photius.

It seems then that, according to the Pope's account, Radoald had refused to fall in with the new trend of pontifical policy towards the oriental Church, and maintained that his own way with Photius in Constantinople had been justified and that the Pope was wrong in altering his attitude.

That is how we believe Nicholas' abrupt *volte-face* with regard to Photius may be explained, the Illyricum problem and Theognostos' plausible reports operating as the main levers. But even this decision by the Pope, despite its severity, was not to be the last word; his verdict was reversible, if only the defendants would yield to reason and give the Pope satisfaction on matters on which he felt so keenly.[4]

But in this respect the Pope was mistaken. As he was waiting for the Emperor's reply and preparing his attack on the Patriarch, things went on in Byzantium very much as before: the die-hard Ignatians' opposition was broken and paralysed; the Emperor's power was steadily expanding, and Byzantium, under the rule of its young Emperor and of the remarkable statesman Bardas, had recovered its pristine influence. By 860–1 the Empire's political and religious prestige had penetrated as far as the Khazars, and by 862–3 to the Moravians.[5] Yet the ambassador Leo's report and Nicholas' letter revealed to Bardas and Michael the danger that threatened the Empire from Bulgarian quarters, and this report, together with Nicholas' claims, accelerated the encirclement

---

[1] See p. 202.

[2] Cf. the passage in the Pope's letter, *M.G.H.* Ep. VI, p. 517.

[3] Loc. cit. pp. 561, 562. Cf. Haller, loc. cit. p. 29.

[4] Cf. what J. Haller says on this matter, loc. cit. pp. 31 seq. He explains the relations between Byzantium and Rome at that time with remarkable insight and clearness, though he unwarrantably underestimates Theognostos' share in the change of pontifical politics.

[5] For further details, cf. my book, *Les Légendes de Constantin et de Méthode*, pp. 148–209, 226–31.

manœuvre which Byzantium had been planning round Bulgaria. It was then that the embassy sent by Rastislav (862), the Moravian prince, proposing an alliance against the Bulgarians, came in the nick of time. At the very moment when the Pope signed the Acts of the Roman synod, Byzantine ambassadors and missionaries, Constantine and Methodius, were presenting their credentials to Rastislav in his fortress on the banks of the Morava; and when, towards the middle of 864, the Pope was wishing King Louis the German every success in his campaign against Rastislav with promises of prayers for the conversion of Bulgaria, which he hoped to be imminent,[1] the Bulgarians' fate had already been sealed. In the spring of the same year, the Byzantines, in concert with their Moravian allies, had unexpectedly invaded Bulgarian territory, whilst their fleet made a demonstration on the Bulgarian coast. Boris promptly capitulated, threw up all his schemes for an alliance with the Franks and promised to accept baptism. The Pope's prayers were therefore realized; but alas, it was not the Frank and Roman missionaries, but the Greeks, who had been chosen as God's instruments.

We do not know when the Pope heard for the first time of the disaster that upset all his plans and knocked the bottom out of his Illyrican schemes, and it is difficult to say whether he clung to his hopes, after realizing the facts. We should have known more about this, if we possessed the letter which the Pope addressed in the summer of 865 to Michael III, but which never reached him. Nicholas mentions this letter in his reply to one from the Emperor, which he did not receive till the end of the summer in 865. It was written, he says, with all the love a father can have for his son,[2] and all the courtesy a Pope must have for an Emperor. It is a pity that the original here summarized was not preserved by the Pontifical Chancellery, but the mere fact that the Pope wished to write to Michael even before he had received his reply proves at least that the Pope was waiting and hoping for an answer from Constantinople, long overdue, until the summer of 865. The Photian incident was therefore not considered definitely closed, as far as he was concerned, notwithstanding the new Patriarch's condemnation by the Roman synod.

Michael's reply, so eagerly awaited, was brought by the Protospathar Michael towards the end of the summer of 865, at the time when the Bulgarian incident seemed to be closed for good and Boris had received baptism. It may be that the Emperor had watched and chosen his

[1] Letter to Solomon, bishop of Constance, *M.G.H.* Ep. VI, p. 293.
[2] *M.G.H.* Ep. VI, p. 454.

moment, but his reply to the Pope has unfortunately been lost, though its main lines can be restored from Nicholas' answer.

The Emperor must have written in the tone of one who was sure of his advantage. He first blames the Pope for failing to appreciate at its true value the concession he and the Byzantine Church had made to the Roman See by allowing Ignatius to be tried by his legates. No instance of such concession[1] had ever been heard of since the Sixth Oecumenical Council. Then the Emperor protests against the Pope's request for a revision of Ignatius' trial. He had never asked the Pope to send his legates to try Ignatius, whose case had been settled by a local synod of the Byzantine Church long before the legates arrived and could not be reconsidered.[2] As the incident did not touch on orthodox doctrine[3] and was a purely disciplinary affair, which the Byzantine Church could perfectly well settle for itself, it was no concern of the Roman See. What the Emperor did ask for was the dispatch of legates for a second condemnation of iconoclasm, knowing that iconoclastic ideas were also spreading in the West: but not even for this was the presence of the Roman legates essential, since that heresy had already been condemned by the Council of Nicaea.[4] But the Emperor knew the man who had supplied the Pope with such one-sided information and incited him against Photius, i.e. none other than Theognostos and the other refugee monks in Rome, where they also intrigued against his Imperial Majesty. The Pope should repatriate these culprits to Constantinople, and should he refuse to comply with this demand, the Emperor would feel obliged to use more forcible methods to help him to change his mind.[5]

Judging from some bitter remarks made by the Pope,[6] the letter apparently was written in an arrogant tone, though Nicholas seems to have exaggerated and been too sensitive on certain points. He took

[1] Loc. cit. p. 457.

[2] Loc. cit. p. 460: 'Ceterum dicitis non ideo ad nos misisse vos, ut secundum iudicium Ignatius sustineret....Dicentes vero, quod synodice fuerit condemnatus....' P. 476: '...noluisse vos, ut a missis nostris Ignatius iudicaretur, eo quod fuerit iam iudicatus et condemnatus.'

[3] Loc. cit. p. 469: 'Sed dicitis fortasse non fuisse in causa Ignatii sedem apostolicam convocare necesse, quia non hunc ullus hereseos error involverat....'

[4] Loc. cit. p. 472: 'Quod autem scripsistis vos idcirco quosdam nostrorum adesse voluisse, quoniam dicebamur cum expugnatoribus sacrarum imaginum concertare....Quamvis dixeritis non nostri eguisse vos ad expugnandos hereticos pro eo, quod iam fuerit huiusmodi heresis in Nicea secundo convocata synodo... subversa.'

[5] Loc. cit. p. 479.

[6] For instance, loc. cit. p. 454: 'epistola...quae tota blasphemia, tota erat iniuriis plena'; p. 455: '...vos ab iniuriis scribentes', etc.

offence at the Emperor calling Rome an 'old town', when Michael seems to have used the epithet 'The old Rome' to distinguish Rome from Byzantium 'The new Rome'.[1] The Pope, however, had good reason to protest against the Emperor calling Latin a barbarian and Scythic language.[2] This is the first time that we see Greek patriotism at odds with Roman and Latin nationalism.

It used to be said that Michael's reply had been written by Photius,[3] but there is nothing to prove it, nor does Nicholas seem to have thought so; and some statements by the Pope into which a hint at Photius was read are not convincing.[4] All these fancies are based on the notion, still prevalent, of the Royal and Imperial Chancelleries of the Latin Middle Ages, when all the work of composition and editing of documents was done by bishops and clergy. But what was true of the Latin West is not applicable to the Byzantine Empire. Byzantium had no need for bishops to compose its imperial letters, for the Empire boasted an excellent bureaucratic tradition. Functionaries were laymen, learned and well versed in whatever was expected from efficient State officials.[5] Photius had certainly trained his subordinates well at the time he was directing the Imperial Chancellery and he had, no doubt, a worthy successor to take over his functions.

The Pope was dangerously ill when he received this letter from Michael III, and not in a fit state to word the reply himself.[6] The lengthy answer which the imperial ambassador was handed at the last minute at Ostia, just before the departure of his boat for Constantinople, and dated 28 September, must have been drawn up by the president of the Pontifical Chancellery, Anastasius the Librarian, the Pope contenting himself with giving him the general outline.[7] The letter was destined to be one of the most important documents in the evolution of the papacy. From the eleventh century onward, it has been exploited to

---

[1] Loc. cit. p. 474: 'Urbs, quam vos quidem inveteratam, sed Honorius pius imperator aeternam vocat....ἡ πρεσβυτέρα, ἡ νεωτέρα Ῥώμη.

[2] Loc. cit. p. 459: 'In tantam vero furoris habundantiam prorupistis, ut linguae Latinae iniuriam irrogaretis, hanc in epistola vestra barbaram et Scythicam appellantes....'

[3] Hergenröther, *Photius*, vol. I, p. 553.

[4] For instance, *M.G.H.* Ep. VI, p. 473: 'non enim nos ex pio corde vel ore vestro tam profana tamque perversa processisse putavimus....'

[5] Cf. A. Andreades, 'Le recrutement des fonctionnaires et les Universités dans l'Empire Byzantin', in *Mélanges de Droit dédiés à M. G. Cornil* (Paris, 1926), pp. 17–40. F. Dvornik, *Les Légendes de Constantin et de Méthode*, pp. 25–33, 39–45.

[6] Loc. cit. p. 474.   [7] Cf. Perels, loc. cit. p. 307.

the utmost by the canonists of the Gregorian and post-Gregorian periods. Not only did the great canonists of the time, like Anselm of Lucca, Deusdedit and Ivo of Chartres, bolster up their doctrine on the Roman papacy with extracts from this letter, but it is also quoted in all the other canonical collections of minor rank which are more or less dependent on the larger Collections mentioned before.[1] Gratian, the leading canonist of the Middle Ages, copied twenty-four extracts from the letter in his *Decretum*.

Such extensive quotation has greatly contributed to Nicholas' popularity among the theorists of pontifical jurisprudence. But it is often imagined that Nicholas made a striking innovation by formulating in his letter theories which had not been current in the Church or at the pontifical Curia.[2] This is an exaggeration. Perels[3] has demonstrated that Nicholas, in defining the Popes' supreme power, often quotes the words of Pope Gelasius I without mentioning his name; and he also made his own the theories of Leo I. Nor should one exaggerate the influence of Pseudo-Isidore's Collection on the evolution of Nicholas' ideology, though this Collection was, apparently, already known in Rome under Leo IV or Benedict III.[4]

This is not the place to analyse all the ideas of pontifical primacy[5] contained in this letter. All one can do is to point out items of special importance in the later development of the relations between Nicholas I and Byzantium.

In the first part of his letter Nicholas refutes Michael's statements concerning Ignatius' condemnation. The Emperor, in the Pope's

[1] See E. Perels' excellent study, 'Die Briefe Papst Nikolaus I. Die kanonische Überlieferung', in *Neues Archiv* (1914), vol. XXXIX, pp. 45–153. Cf. what is said on pp. 292 seq.

[2] Cf. A. Hauck, *Der Gedanke der päpstlichen Weltherrschaft bis auf Bonifaz VIII* (Leipzig, 1904), pp. 14 seq. H. Böhmer, 'Nikolaus I,' *Realenzyklopädie für prot. Theologie* (3rd ed., Leipzig, 1904), p. 69: 'Nikolaus hat die mittelalterliche Papstidee geschaffen....' But this honour rather belongs to Gelasius I.

[3] *Papst Nikolaus I*, pp. 153 seq., 170 seq. Cf. J. Haller, loc. cit. p. 77. Remember Leo IV's refusal of the pallium sent to him by Ignatius as a present.

[4] Cf. A. Hauck, *Kirchengeschichte Deutschlands* (Leipzig, 1900), vol. II, p. 542.

[5] See specialized studies by A. Thiel, *De Nicolao I papa commentationes duae historico-canonicae* (Brunsbergae, 1859). F. Rocquain, *La Papauté au Moyen Age* (Paris, 1881), pp. 1–74. J. Roy, 'Principes du pape Nicolas I sur les rapports des deux puissances', in *Études d'Histoire du M.A. dédiées à G. Monod* (Paris, 1896), pp. 95–105. A. Hauck, *Kirchengeschichte Deutschlands*, pp. 533 seq. H. Lämmer, *Papst Nikolaus I und die byzantinische Staatskirche* (Berlin, 1857). A. Greinacher, *Die Anschauung des Papstes Nikolaus I über das Verhältnis von Staat und Kirche* (Berlin, 1909). (Abhandlungen zur mittelalterlichen und neueren Geschichte, vol. x.)

opinion, failed to respect the privileges of the See of Rome and spoke of St Peter's successor in a most outrageous manner. Since the Sixth Council until recent days, most of the Byzantine Emperors had been heretics.[1] The Greeks were in the habit of tampering with pontifical documents, for they did so at the Council of 787 and again in 861. It is outrageous for an Emperor to order a Pope to send his legates to a Council. Not even Michael, though he claimed the right, dared to exercise it; on the contrary, he invited the Pope to send his legates to the Council, as is easily judged from the letter he sent to the Pope at the time. It was really regrettable that Michael should not have imitated his predecessors' deference.[2] Then, why did he claim the title of Roman Emperor, if Latin, the Romans' tongue, was no better to him than a barbarian language?

With regard to Ignatius' condemnation by a synod of Constantinople, the Emperor must admit that until then no Patriarch had ever been deposed or condemned without the consent of the Roman See. It is absurd to contend that the synod of 861 which ratified the condemnation had the same number of Fathers as the great Council of Nicaea: Ignatius' condemnation was, none the less, unfair. The Emperor had no right to convoke that Council and stand by, whilst a pious Patriarch was being disgraced; such a Patriarch could not be tried by his own subordinates, or by schismatics and laymen, but only by a higher court, i.e. by the Pope. Besides, without his consent, no Council is valid.

In the second part of his letter, the Pope defines with firmness, clarity and precision the traditional and inalienable rights of the Holy See.[3] These rights, he says, were given by Christ Himself to St Peter, who handed them down to his successors. Rome alone can boast of having seen living and dying within its walls St Peter and St Paul, founders of its glory. After Rome, Alexandria and Antioch had the closest contact with the two Apostles, whereas Constantinople had to import some relics (of St Andrew, Luke and Timothy in 356) to give itself a semblance of apostolic tradition.[4]

These privileges give the Pope power 'super omnem terram, id est, super omnem ecclesiam', therefore even the right of watching over the Church of Constantinople; and that is why the Pope took an interest

---

[1] Loc. cit. pp. 456, 457. [2] Loc. cit. pp. 457–9.
[3] Cf. chiefly the impressive passage, loc. cit. pp. 474 seq.: 'praesertim cum ecclesiae Romanae privilegia...ecclesiam Dei'; p. 484: 'non itaque inimicitiae... nequaquam permittunt.' [4] Loc. cit. p. 475.

in Ignatius' case, reserved its decision to his own judgement and never gave his legates leave to pass sentence on the Patriarch.

As regards Theognostos and his associates, the Pope refuses to send them back to Constantinople, since they only tell the truth, and their reports are borne out by other monks coming from the East. The Pope has the right to summon any cleric to his court in Rome.[1]

At the end of his letter, the Pope states that he wishes nevertheless to offer a concession to the Emperor and declares his readiness to revise the case of Ignatius and Photius, but only in Rome: the two rivals must appear before the Pope or at least send their representatives to him. He even specifies which Ignatian bishops he wishes to see in Rome to plead their Patriarch's case before his court. The Emperor must send his representatives too. All this, he insists, is a great concession. The Holy See's verdict can be altered by none but the Pope himself, but Nicholas assures the Emperor that he wants to be an equitable judge,[2] and only refuses to reconsider the condemnation of Asbestas and his party.

It must be confessed that the conclusion of this letter comes as a shock, for the firmness of Nicholas' tone throughout his letter on the privileges of his See and the violence of his language addressed to the Greeks and even to the Emperor lead one to expect a different solution to Ignatius' case. The Pope was apparently seriously disposed to reconsider his verdict against Photius and to leave open the possibility of his rehabilitation; but to help the Ignatians to become reconciled to the fact, he suggests to the Emperor between the lines that he should make up his mind and sacrifice Asbestas and his confederates: their being held responsible for all the trouble would open an avenue to a compromise between the two parties.

Whatever motives led the Pope to such a proposal, it does not seem that he was still nursing hopes of recovering Bulgaria.[3] Realist as he was, he could not but see that all his hopes for the return of eastern Illyricum had vanished, directly Byzantium had laid its hands on the Bulgarians; but of course, when he dispatched his letter, Nicholas could not anticipate what was to happen in Bulgaria some months later.

It is not here that we shall discover the motive of Nicholas' decision. The vigour of the Emperor's reply brought home to Nicholas that he

---

[1] Loc. cit. p. 478: 'Jus habemus non solum monachos, verum etiam quoslibet clericos de quacumque diocesi...ad nos convocare.'

[2] Loc. cit. pp. 480–4.

[3] That is what J. Haller says, loc. cit. pp. 79 seq., though he is not so well inspired here as in his reading of the first phase in the conflict.

had gone too far: after losing Illyricum, he was now busy wasting the finest achievement Radoald and Zachary had brought from Constantinople—the recognition by the Byzantine Church of the Roman supremacy, a loss he realized to be more serious and deplorable than the first. One can trace Nicholas' fear and worry in the terms, often violent, or at least unconventional, which he uses in addressing the Byzantine Emperor. It is then that he feverishly casts about for props to his argumentation in support of the inalienable rights of the Papacy over the whole Church and in justification of his previous refusal to acknowledge Photius without any further ado. As long as these rights and privileges are admitted, a revision of the sentence passed may be expected on the strength of those very same privileges.[1]

Notwithstanding its lofty and confident tone, Nicholas' letter marks therefore a regression in pontifical politics, though the retreat is heavily screened by an imposing mass of arguments in support of Rome's privileges and by fresh attacks on imperial pretensions:[2] but it is a retreat for all that. This letter therefore did not convey a threat or a warning of a complete rupture between Rome and Byzantium; far from it: the Pope took it to be the first step towards an honourable and peaceful liquidation of the whole dispute.

It is difficult to say what effect it produced in Byzantium. The Byzantines' first impression must have been that the Pope was spoiling his own case. By allowing his legates to sit in judgement over an Eastern Patriarch, the Byzantine Church was offering him an unique concession that did full justice to his claims. But the Pope overlooked this, and instead of taking advantage of such an admission, went hunting for arguments in support of his primacy in Western documents which to Easterners must have sounded strange, if not suspicious. Asbestas and his followers, who themselves had appealed to the Pope against the verdict of their own Patriarch, were ready to go to any length in their recognition of the Pope's privilege: yet, here was the Pope deciding

---

[1] Loc. cit. p. 481: 'Ergo de iudicio Romani praesulis non retractando, quia nec mos exigit, quod diximus comprobato, non negamus eiusdem sedis sententiam posse in melius commutari, cum aut sibi subreptum aliquid fuerit aut ipsa pro consideratione aetatum vel temporum seu gravium necessitatum dispensatorie quiddam ordinare decreverit, quoniam et egregium apostolum Paulum quaedam fecisse dispensatorie legimus, quae postea reprobasse dinoscitur.'

[2] It would be interesting to know what was formulated in this letter by the Pope, and what by Anastasius. Not without good reason does the Pope (loc. cit. p. 474) complain that he was so ill that he was unable even to attend to the composition of this letter. Cf. J. Haller, loc. cit. p. 76.

against them by claiming against Photius the same rights as his predecessors had claimed against Ignatius. For they had not forgotten
what Leo IV had written to Ignatius,[1] when the Pope took him severely
to task for condemning Asbestas without the Roman See's consent, in
violation of previous observance.

Another bone of contention must have been the Pope's assertion
that no synod could be summoned without the Pope's consent, and
worse still, that Councils were no concern of the Emperor's. Nicholas
simply ignored the Byzantine 'doctrine' on Councils as it had evolved
in the East since the days of Constantine the Great. For indeed all the
first oecumenical Councils had been convoked by the Emperors; they
presided at the meetings and it was their exclusive right to do so. It was
actually their practice to order bishops and patriarchs to attend the
Councils, their representatives being present at all discussions, even those
of a disciplinary character; but they had no right to vote, this being
strictly reserved to the bishops, though they afterwards confirmed the
decisions and made them legal throughout the empire.[2]

Nicholas' views on the Councils, as explained in his letter, represented in fact the last stage in the development of the conciliar theory
in the West. Yet, even in Byzantium, a slow approach towards the
curtailment of imperial power in the Councils was in progress, and the
Seventh Oecumenical Council held its meetings under the chairmanship,
not of the Emperor or his lay representative, but of Tarasius. Even the
Council of 879–80 did not have the Emperor, but Photius in the chair,
the Patriarch on similar occasions exercising the functions of the Em-

[1] The following is the text of the letter (*M.G.H.* Ep. v, p. 589): 'Ex quo
unigenitus Dei filius sanctam in se fundavit ecclesiam caputque universorum
apostolicis institucionibus sacerdotum perfecit, cuiuscumque contradictionis liti-
giique contentio vestrae oriebatur vel accidebat ecclesiae, Romano vestri predeces-
sores pontifici ingenti eam studio procacique celeritate innotescere procurabant;
et postmodum eius roborati consensu lucifluo consilio cuncta, quae necessitas
provocabat, beatifico moderamine peragebant. Vos autem, predictorum ut fertis
virorum [successores], sine conscientia nostra congregatis episcopis depositionem
perpetrastis, quod absentibus nostris legatis vel litteris nullo debuistis explere
modo....' Cf. also Leo's second letter to Ignatius about the pallium (loc. cit.
p. 607). Though some of the Pope's claims as formulated in his letter to Michael
were already familiar to the Byzantines and had proved acceptable, others raised
criticism at the court and the patriarcheion, for instance, the claim to judge all major
cases in first and second instance. This seemed an unprecedented innovation to the
Byzantines, however willing they were to admit the principle of appeal to the Pope's
supreme court even in disciplinary matters.

[2] For further details see my study, *De Potestate Civili in Conciliis Oecumenicis*...,
already quoted.

peror, a fact that was significant for its liability to prejudice the Emperor's rights in the future development of the conciliar notion in Byzantium.

Now, this evolution was far more rapid in Rome; it was facilitated by the fact of the Emperor's residing elsewhere, and the road lay open to a rapid advance towards the complete elimination of all lay influence in ecclesiastical assemblies. Further, it should be emphasized that Nicholas now laid down this principle for the first time in precise and unmistakable terms. Given the position in Byzantium, one can understand that his theory of Councils must have sounded too advanced for Michael's taste, as he could not help seeing there a serious limitation of his imperial powers.

Lastly, the Pope's views on the patriarchates of Alexandria and Antioch must have been particularly offensive to the Byzantines: he places Byzantium fourth after the patriarchates of Rome, Alexandria and Antioch, an allocation that seems to have been popular at the Roman Curia in those days. Even in his letter to Boris-Michael, prince of Bulgaria,[1] the Pope bluntly stated that the Patriarch of Constantinople had in reality no right to call himself a Patriarch, since his see was not of apostolic origin. Perhaps Photius admitted that after all the Pope was right in denying the apostolic origin of Constantinople, as his historical knowledge must have been deeper than that of his contemporaries; but in his days the belief was generally current and popular in Byzantium. We have heard Ignatius himself proudly boasting before the papal legates that he occupied the see of St Andrew the Apostle.[2] But why stress this claim in a letter purporting to inaugurate the resumption of negotiations between Byzantium and Rome?

There is in the Pope's letter a hint that the Emperor had formulated in his missive the Byzantine definition of the Roman Primacy as known to the Byzantines of the ninth century. The passage makes one regret the loss of the Emperor Michael's letter and it is a pity that the Pope neglected to report the Emperor's words with accuracy. These are the Pope's words:[3] 'Sed dicitis fortasse non fuisse in causa Ignatii sedem apostolicam convocare necesse, quia non hunc ullus hereseos error involverat.' Does the Emperor here admit the necessity for the Pope's

[1] See p. 114.
[2] Cf. F. Dölger about this legend in his recent study, 'Rom in der Gedankenwelt der Byzantiner', in *Zeitschrift für Kirchengeschichte* (1937), vol. LVI, pp. 1–42. It seems safe to say that, as demonstrated by the Ignatian case, the legend was not mainly invented and spread by Photius, as this learned author seems to think. I shall shortly have occasion to return to these problems.
[3] *M.G.H.* Ep. VI, p. 469.

co-operation in all matters of doctrinal definition, though defending at the same time the Byzantine Church's right to settle its own internal problems of ecclesiastical discipline alone, without recourse to the Holy See?[1] Again, observe that the Byzantine Church, whilst jealously safeguarding its right to settle its own domestic affairs, admitted nevertheless the right of appeal to the Roman court, as was proved to the hilt in Asbestas' case and in the Acts of the synod of 861. I note only facts, leaving on one side the question whether this notion of the primacy is correct or not.

Despite all this, even this letter would have failed to provoke in Byzantium any move particularly unpleasant to Rome, had events not abruptly taken a new turn: and the *deus ex machina* which brought about this sudden change was no other than the Prince of the Bulgarians, recently converted to Christianity. It is not often in history that one sees a barbarian, barely converted, wield such an influence on the fate of the Church.

But the Khagan Boris-Michael is an interesting figure. He seems to have been deeply impressed by the liturgy of his baptism, a ceremony conducted by the Patriarch himself, and he would have loved to grace his court with the same liturgical splendour. The one to impress him most was the Patriarch himself and he found it difficult to admit that he would ever be a genuine Christian prince, unless he also had his own Patriarch. Application for one to the Byzantines was refused as a matter of course, Photius sending him instead a long and beautiful letter to explain how a Christian prince should behave in his private and public life.[2] Of course, Photius would not hear of a Bulgarian Patriarch; but the desire was very characteristic of Boris, though it would be difficult to say how much of it was due to sheer *naïveté*, and how much to statesmanlike instinct. At any rate, it was in the best interest of the young Bulgarian State to remain independent of Byzantium, even in religious matters, as long as possible.

Then it was that the Khagan remembered what the Frankish priests had promised him, when they preached on his territory, and their preaching certainly did not remain unproductive. There was, besides,

[1] The word 'fortasse' no doubt means that the Pope is not quoting the Emperor's words literally. In the preceding sentences, he enumerates the Patriarchs who were deposed with the Pope's collaboration, but all of them were heretics. The Pope may also have intended to forestall an objection which the Emperor might make. In any case, Nicholas seems to have caught the correct drift of the Emperor's thoughts and words.   [2] *P.G.* vol. 102, cols. 665 seq.

a Frankophile party at the Khagan's court, as he had fostered the closest relations with the Franks, and this party worked against the Greek missionaries. It prevailed in the end, and the Khagan made up his mind to try his luck with the Franks again, addressing not only Louis the German, but also Nicholas I.

The Bulgarian embassy, headed by Peter, a relation of the Khagan's, John and Martin,[1] reached Rome in August 866.[2] It appears that all that Boris asked the Pope for was a Patriarch;[3] but he also addressed to him a considerable number of questions and asked advice on matters of exceptional importance. He did not apply to the Pope for missionaries, as he expected them from Louis the German.

Nicholas was elated at the good news, never expecting such a sudden turn in what he had given up as hopeless. Rome spoke of a miracle, and one can understand the feeling, remembering how keen Nicholas had been on the recovery of Illyricum.

The Pope decided to make the utmost of the godsend. The new Bulgarian Church must be founded by Rome and be directly under Roman jurisdiction, without the intermediary of the Frankish Church: so he decided to send to Boris two bishops—Paul of Populonia and Formosus of Porto—with missionaries 'ad praedicandam gentem illam', as the *Liber Pontificalis* has it. He also took trouble over a detailed and careful reply to all the questions.

We know what vogue these answers had among the medieval canonists, who loved to quote them under the heading 'Nicolai responsa ad consulta Bulgarorum'. The letter is, indeed, a masterpiece of pastoral wisdom and one of the finest documents of the history of the Papacy. I cannot analyse it here in detail: all I can do is to point out certain particulars showing what care the Pope took to immunize the new Church against Greek influence.

He insists, for instance, on the first place in the Church being occupied by the Roman See, Constantinople being shifted back to the fourth

---

[1] *M.G.H.* Ep. VII, p. 154 (letter of 8 June 879 from John VIII to Michael).

[2] *Liber Pontificalis* (ed. Duchesne), vol. II, p. 164: 'Tunc ad hunc apostolicum et vere praesulem orthodoxum legatos suos mense augusto, indictione XIIII, destinavit, donaque non parva tam sanctis locis quam eidem summo pontifici contulit, suggerens eius apostolatui quid se facere salubrius oporteret, vel quid erga reliquum Vulgaricum adhuc baptismo sacro carentem populum, ut fidei sacramenta perficeret, agi deberet. Quod beatissimus audiens papa, magna repletus laeticia, laudes Christo reddidit amplas et cum omni sibi divinitus commissa ecclesia gratulans, infinita preconia Deo nostro qui novissimis his temporibus tantum fecit miraculum devota mente, supplici quoque voce resolvit.'

[3] Ch. 72 of Nicholas' reply. *M.G.H.* Ep. VI, p. 592.

place (chapter 92), as has already been stated. A number of Greek customs are condemned.[1] When the Bulgarians asked for a code of civil law, it seems that the Pope, instead of the Justinian code, sent them the Collection of Lombard laws.[2]

The papal embassy was received in Bulgaria with extreme satisfaction; and Boris was delighted every time the Pope's gracious letter was read out to him. All his doubts were cleared and all the problems he had raised were solved: he was pleased that his Bulgars—men and women— could go on wearing breeches, without the fear of committing a mortal sin; he could henceforth take his bath on Wednesdays and Fridays and go to communion wearing his belt. But why could he not dispense with the horse's tail, which served his army as a banner, since the Pope promised him victory over all his enemies, if his Boyars would hoist the cross as an ensign? Though, after all, he might as well do without a Patriarch, if it came to that, and be content with an archbishop, since the Pope had told him that it came more or less to the same thing. He was especially pleased to hear that the Patriarch of Constantinople, who had impressed him so deeply, was only a sham Patriarch, not in the same class as the Patriarchs of Rome, Alexandria and Antioch.

There was among these replies one which was certainly not welcomed by the Boyars, who would have liked to keep their old practice and continue to live each with several wives; but unfortunately, the Pope severely reprobated this custom (chapter 51), proving in this no more lenient than Photius. It was aggravating, but one could not get everything; and there was still hope that the missionaries would not show themselves too difficult in this respect.

Making the most of the good impression they had made on Boris and acting in the spirit of the instructions they carried with them from the Pope, the legates prevailed on the Khagan to dismiss the Frankish missionaries on their arrival, with bishop Ermenrich of Passau at their head.[3] And yet, Louis the German had prepared this mission so carefully, to the extent even of soliciting his brother Charles for assistance in sending sacred vessels for the use of the missionaries.

Hearing what had happened, the Emperor Louis II asked the Pope to let him have the presents which Boris had made to the Pope, including

[1] Ch. 6 concerns bathing on Wednesdays and Fridays; ch. 54, prayers with hands crossed over the chest; ch. 55, communion; ch. 57, eunuchs; ch. 77, sortes biblicae; ch. 94, the chrism.

[2] M. Conrat, 'Römisches Recht bei Papst Nikolaus I', in *Neues Archiv*, vol. XXXVI, pp. 724 seq. Cf. Perels, loc. cit. p. 162.

[3] *Annales Bertiniani*, *M.G.H.* Ss. vol. I, p. 474.

the armour which the Khagan had worn the day he crushed the pagan rebellion: a strange request, but Louis II probably assumed that by receiving Latin Christianity Bulgaria would henceforth be part of the Western Empire of which he was the sovereign; and not to disappoint him, the Pope sent him some of the presents.[1]

So everything was going well. Boris was so pleased with the new missionaries that, pulling his hair, he took a solemn oath ever to remain the faithful servant of St Peter,[2] and Nicholas' hopes seemed at last to be realized.

This unexpected success encouraged the Pope once more to try his luck in Byzantium. The Emperor's reply had not yet reached him, and the Bulgarian checkmate having provided the Pope with a new weapon, Nicholas decided to increase the pressure. To the legates to be sent to Boris he added bishop Donatus, the priest Leo and the deacon Marinus, who were to accompany them to the Khagan's court and cross over to Byzantium via Bulgaria, carrying letters to Michael III, Photius, Bardas, the Empress Theodora, the Emperor's wife, Eudocia, some senators and the clergy of Constantinople. Their presence in Bulgaria certainly enhanced the prestige of the papal embassy; they stayed there for some time and set out for Byzantium in the spring of 867.[3]

The letter addressed to Michael[4] was couched in a much calmer tone than the letter sent in 865; and though the Pope mostly repeated what he had said previously, his treatment was more consistent and systematic. After recalling the story of the Photius case, the Pope mainly protests against the expedient of tampering with the letter carried by the legates to the Council of 861 and refuses to ratify the condemnation of Ignatius, who could be judged by none but a higher court, i.e. by the Pope. The same holds for Gregory Asbestas. The synod was not competent to annul the sentence passed by Ignatius, which could only be

---

[1] *Liber Pontificalis* (ed. Duchesne), vol. II, p. 167; Annales Bertiniani, loc. cit.; J. Haller, *Nikolaus I und Pseudo-Isidor*, p. 81.

[2] Cf. Anastasius, Mansi, vol. XVI, col. 11; cf. also my book, *Les Légendes de Constantin et de Méthode*, p. 281.

[3] It is not necessary to suppose with J. Haller (loc. cit. p. 84) that the Bulgarian embassy had left Rome long before the legates bound for Byzantium. The fact that Byzantium knew about the happenings in Bulgaria at the moment the legates had reached the frontier proves nothing. The Byzantines may have heard of them, if the legates tarried for some time at the Khagan's court. In his letter of 23 October 867, addressed to Hincmar (*M.G.H.* Ep. VI, p. 603), the Pope clearly states that the two embassies had left Rome at the same time.

[4] *M.G.H.* Ep. VI, pp. 488–512. Cf. the analysis given by Hergenröther, *Photius*, vol. I, pp. 618 seq.

done either by the Patriarch or by the Pope. Photius must first make up for the damage he has done. By ordaining him, Asbestas could only give him a share in his own condemnation; but Ignatius must be reinstated by the Emperor, who therein should follow his predecessors' example; else, the Pope will summon a Western Council and have the calumniating letter the Emperor had sent him condemned.

However, the Pope concludes by repeating that he is always ready to grant the Emperor the concession offered in his last letter; for Ignatius' trial can still be revised, the Pope even refusing to justify every one of Ignatius' acts. If he has offended, he deserves blame. This time, to forestall any fraud, the Pope has entrusted his legates with copies of all his previous letters.

The letter is firm and resolute in tone, but much less violent than that of 865, and suggests that the Pope had more to do with this letter than on the previous occasion.

Nicholas' letter, therefore, leaves a door open to prospects of mutual understanding. His other letters, besides being mostly a repetition of the reasoning developed in the letter to Michael, yet let the readers guess that what the Pope really wished from his heart was not so much a revision of the trial as the downfall, pure and simple, of Photius. For instance, in his letter to Photius,[1] the Pope no longer mentions any concession; he merely summons the 'intruder' to give place to Ignatius, or forfeit his right to absolution till his death.

The letters designed for the bishops[2] often repeat word for word what the Pope said in his letter to Michael, but they also are silent on the concession. All the other letters[3] betray the Pope's secret wish for Photius' downfall. Their peremptory tone is no doubt stiffened by his recent success in Bulgaria, whereas the legates have naturally received detailed instructions to work in Byzantium for the 'intruder's' overthrow.

But they were on the alert in Byzantium and the legates could scarcely be under any illusion about the difficulty of their mission. When the papal envoys presented themselves at the frontier of the Empire, they were received by an official called Theodore. The reception could not have been warm, and even the Bulgars who had escorted the legates to the frontier got a taste of the Byzantines' anger.[4] Theodore must have

---

[1] *M.G.H.* Ep. VI, pp. 533–40.   [2] Loc. cit. pp. 512 seq., 553 seq.
[3] Loc. cit. pp. 540 seq.
[4] *Liber Pontificalis*, vol. II, p. 165. Cf. Nicholas' letter to Hincmar, *M.G.H.* Ep. VI, p. 603.

questioned the legates on the purpose of their mission and noticed their heavy dossier of letters addressed to important people. It all looked suspicious and a special messenger was dispatched to Byzantium to ask for further instructions, whilst the legates were left waiting forty days for the reply. They do not seem to have carried away pleasant memories of this adventure.[1]

In Constantinople, people must have been quite aware of what was going on in Bulgaria well before the messenger's arrival. The news of Boris' defection created consternation at the imperial palace and at the patriarcheion, for there was no disguising the fact that it meant a serious political setback. Boris must have quickly recovered from his defeat in 864 to rush back so soon to his former allies, the Franks. It was, moreover, difficult to counter Boris' move with a military demonstration, as in 864, the Khagan having taken good care to provide for his security on the Byzantine border and to have his Boyars at their posts guarding the roads and the defiles. And the moment for his change of front had been well chosen: whilst he was carrying out his plans, the Byzantine army was away on an expedition to Crete,[2] and Caesar Bardas, the principal designer of the encirclement policy of 864, had been assassinated by his rival Basil on 21 April. The authorities had their hands full for the moment, and the season did not favour expeditions.

Yet such things could hardly be tolerated: if war was out of the question and diplomacy had lost its efficacy, there remained some expedients of a religious nature that could be tried. The Greek missionaries who had been asked to leave Bulgaria, had made complaints about certain 'suspicious' doctrines which their Frankish rivals were disseminating over Bulgaria. The Franks, for instance, allowed the Bulgars to take milk and cheese in Lent. This was dreadful! And they were all but Manichaeans, since they forbade priests to marry, those heretics affecting a particular aversion from marriage. Then the Franks limited priestly powers by holding that confirmation could not be administered to children by ordinary priests, the function being strictly reserved to bishops. What was more serious still, the Franks taught that the Holy Ghost proceeded not from the Father only, but also from the

[1] It is not impossible that Pope Stephen V, speaking in his letter to Basil (see p. 221) of Marinus' imprisonment whilst on a papal mission, is really referring to this frontier incident, though the Pope makes Basil responsible for the imprisonment, a confusion on the part of the Pope that cannot be ruled out.

[2] Cf. H. Grégoire, 'Études sur le IXe siècle', in *Byzantion* (1933), vol. VIII, pp. 524 seq. on this expedition.

Son: this was rank heresy, and such abominations deserved condemnation by a synod.

The synod was duly summoned,[1] but whether before or immediately after the arrival of the messenger conveying the news that the legates stood waiting at the frontier is not known. One thing is certain, that the messenger had time to take back to the legates the decisions of this synod, very severely condemning all these 'false' doctrines. The legates were invited to sign them and to acknowledge Photius as the legitimate Patriarch,[2] being permitted on no other conditions to prosecute their journey. Unable, of course, to accept them, the legates had no choice but to withdraw to Bulgarian territory with all the letters they had brought from Rome, none of which reached its addressee. Thus vanished the Pope's last hopes of undermining Photius' position in Byzantium through his embassy.

The Byzantines had prepared their plans with great care. Had the legates signed the synodal decrees and acknowledged Photius, they would automatically have wrecked the Latin mission to Bulgaria; or should this manœuvre fail, there was always the possibility of trying the effect of the condemnation on Boris and awaiting the result. That this attempt was actually made[3] we learn from the Pope's letter to Hincmar: an imperial letter, signed by Michael and his new associate Basil, informed the Khagan of the condemnation. But Boris was still under the spell which Nicholas' letter had woven round his primitive soul: no, the Latins could not be so wicked. Moreover, he had by his side the bishop of Porto, who certainly was as good a psychologist as the Greek missionaries, and doubts that might have been raised in Boris' mind were soon laid. The Khagan even handed over the letter to the legates about to return to Rome, happy to be thus of service to the Pope. The legates also happened to pick up in Bulgaria some pamphlets which the Greek missionaries had tried before their expulsion to disseminate among some half-civilized Boyars.[4] The Pope carefully

---

[1] This is an obvious inference from Photius' encyclical letter to the Eastern Patriarchs (*P.G.* vol. 102, col. 732).

[2] The fact is confirmed in Nicholas' letter to Hincmar, *M.G.H.* Ep. VI, p. 604: 'a missis nostris contra omnem regulam et praeter omnem consuetudinem libellum fidei, si se ab illis recipere vellent, exigere moliebantur, in quo tam ista capitula quam ea tenentes anathematizarent, necnon et epistolas canonicas ab his ei, quem suum oeconomicon patriarcham appellant, dandas improbe requirebant.' Hergenröther, *Photius*, vol. I, pp. 641, 656 seq.

[3] Loc. cit. p. 603.

[4] That is how I understand the Pope's words (loc. cit. p. 603): 'accipientibus ...nobis et perscrutantibus eandem *cum aliis scriptis* epistolam...'

scrutinized these documents and felt hurt. They blamed the Latins for offering on Easter Sunday, with the Eucharist, a lamb which they placed on the altar after the Jewish fashion; also, for their priests' habit of shaving, for making chrism with water and for raising deacons to the episcopacy without first conferring on them the priesthood.

One could afford to smile at these childish accusations and rivalries, if the consequences of such wrangles had not been so disastrous to the whole of Christendom. All these details may seem to us petty and insignificant to-day, but they should be read in the setting of the two documents—Photius' encyclical letter to the Eastern bishops and Nicholas' letter to Hincmar. The irate and violent tone of the Patriarch's letter reveals the soreness of the wound the Pope had inflicted on the Byzantines' national pride: to their way of thinking, vital interests of the Empire were involved in the question, and no compromise was possible. So severely hurt and threatened did they feel that they lost their heads and were ready to make every attempt to recover lost ground.

The Pope was no less alarmed: it seems as if he had never realized before how vital to the Byzantines the Bulgarian problem was, and never understood the Greek reaction to his success in Bulgaria. But he really did take fright, fearing a rupture between Rome and Byzantium that was more than dangerous, one that might easily shift to dogmatic issues. This is why he gave such a cry of alarm in his letters and tried to mobilize all the spiritual forces in his Church before the great blow that he feared should fall.

The threatened repercussion from Constantinople was stupendous, but Nicholas apparently never heard what Photius was really planning against him. There is in his letter to Hincmar a reference to a message which the Byzantines had sent to the Patriarchs of Alexandria and Jerusalem,[1] but as the Pope stated its object to be Photius' recognition by the Eastern Patriarchs, he could not have meant Photius' famous encyclical, though he must have heard some vague rumours on what Photius was plotting.

This notorious encyclical announced the convocation of a synod of the Oriental Church for no other object than to put increased pressure on Boris: as the decisions of a local Council had failed to produce the desired effect, perhaps those of a General Council would have a better

[1] Loc. cit. p. 608.

119

chance, the more so as the Council was also to condemn Nicholas' line of conduct.

In this document Photius stated that the Council would first proceed to condemn the 'false' doctrines of the Frankish missionaries; and as regards Nicholas' policy, he pointed out that he had received a number of letters from Western bishops complaining about the Pope. The Italian bishops even sent him a synodal letter requesting him to defend them against Nicholas' tyranny: and many monks coming from Rome (Photius names the monks Basil, Zosimus and Metrophanes) confirmed the complaints and implored the Patriarch to intervene in the interests of the Church. Lastly, the third object of the Council was to be (again according to the encyclical) the solemn recognition of the second Council of Nicaea as an Oecumenical Council.

It is quite possible that Photius did receive letters taking exception to Nicholas' rule, and was no doubt the recipient of protests from the archbishops of Cologne and Trier, two prelates who were the foremost critics of the Pope's 'tyrannical' regime.[1] There was also between Byzantium and the Greek monasteries of Rome a fairly close contact, as I have shown in another work;[2] and the Greek monks of those houses may very well have kept the Patriarch posted on all that happened in the West, particularly in Rome. Photius appears also to have been in touch with another dangerous opponent of Nicholas, John, archbishop of Ravenna, for we possess a letter sent to John by Photius, after his reinstatement on the patriarchal throne, either at the end of 878 or at the beginning of 879. It is a peculiar document,[3] which reads as though the Ravenna titular had raised hopes that Photius' campaign against the person of Pope Nicholas might find some support in the West; but when Photius decided to strike, John failed to back him up as expected, and his hesitation may have had a good deal to do with Photius' downfall after Basil had come to power.

As, with regard to Radoald, it was stated that the Pope himself was afraid to see this prelate's open contact with Photius after his condemnation, we are inclined to believe that Photius' information on the discontent over Nicholas' severity was based on fact.

The Council met in Constantinople in the summer of 867, but little

---

[1] Cf. Bury, *A History of the Eastern Roman Empire*, p. 201.

[2] *Les Légendes de Constantin et de Méthode*, pp. 286 seq.

[3] Papadopoulos-Kerameus, *Ss. Patris Photii...epistolae XLV* (Petropoli, 1896), p. 6. Cf. V. Grumel, *Les Regestes des Actes du Patriarchat de Constantinople*, vol. II (Istanbul, 1936), p. 102.

of what occurred there has reached us, the meagre information we happen to possess coming exclusively from anti-Photianist sources.[1] Only the following facts can be inferred with certainty: the Council really did take place, though some Ignatians tried to deny its occurrence; many Fathers took part in it; Pope Nicholas was judged and condemned; lastly, Louis II was acclaimed Emperor at the closing meeting of the Council, in the presence and with the consent of Michael III and Basil.[2]

Did their acclamation imply that the Fathers had charged Louis II with the execution of the sentence passed on Nicholas, and was the recognition of his imperial title a reward for the services expected of him? It is difficult to prove that any negotiations to this effect had been carried on between the two courts before the meeting of the Council. It is not impossible, as a certain contact could be made unofficially, though we know absolutely nothing about an exchange of embassies between the two Empires. They had, indeed, common interests in Southern Italy and the Mediterranean. The Byzantines could not help seeing that relations between the Pope and Louis had not always been cordial and the Byzantine court possibly had under consideration a pact with Louis, promising him military aid against the Arabs on condition that he should carry out the decisions of the Council of Constantinople and depose Nicholas. But these are mere conjectures, except for a strong presumption in their favour, since Basil, after Michael's assassination, carried on his friendly policy with Louis II. More would have been known about the negotiations, had we been in possession of the letter from Photius to Louis' wife, Engelberta, and the letter from Michael to Louis, which the metropolitan of Chalcedon, Zachary, had been asked to transmit.[3]

One thing seems certain, that Photius tried to enlist Western aid, the services of Louis II and of part of the episcopacy against Nicholas. Now, putting on one side all other considerations and concentrating on this simple fact, I ask: can it be seriously admitted that the Patriarch,

---

[1] *Liber Pontificalis* (ed. Duchesne), vol. II, pp. 178 seq.; Anastasius the Librarian (Mansi, vol. XVI, col. 5); the Acts of the Eighth Council (Mansi, vol. XVI, sessions VII, VIII, IX); Metrophanes of Smyrna (ibid. col. 417); Nicetas-David, Vita Ignatii (*P.G.* vol. 105, col. 537); the Roman synod of Hadrian II (Mansi, vol. XVI, cols. 125, 128). Cf. Hergenröther, *Photius*, vol. I, pp. 649 seq.; Ivantsov-Platonov, *Sv. Patriarkh Fotti*, pp. 108 seq.; Bury, loc. cit. pp. 201 seq.

[2] Nicetas, loc. cit., col. 537. Metrophanes, loc. cit., col. 417.

[3] Cf. what J. Haller says (*Nikolaus I und Pseudo-Isidor*, pp. 94 seq.) about the relations between Nicholas and Louis II about the year 867.

wishing as he did to secure the assistance of the Latin episcopacy, expected to enlist its support by attacking the whole Western Church and the venerable customs to which those bishops and the Emperor were loyally attached? No, fairness and consistency drive us to the conclusion that the Council of 867 was not aimed at the Western Church as such. The anathemas and condemnations hurled by the Eastern Fathers against some Western customs were only directed against the Roman missionaries of Bulgaria for the purpose of impressing Boris and his Boyars; in fact, Photius' encyclical, I insist, only mentioned the 'so-called' bishops preaching in Bulgaria.

These condemnations were meant to be the Eastern Church's reply to the attacks the Latin missionaries in Bulgaria permitted themselves upon some century-old customs of the Orientals, attacks and counter-attacks being both understandable in a country where two rival rites were practised side by side. But it is worth repeating that the Byzantine Government needed a conciliar decree to make any impression on Boris.[1]

Besides, Photius had no reason whatsoever for falling out with Nicholas over the *Filioque*, to take only one instance. In 860 he had, in his enthronement letter to the Pope, professed his faith in the procession of the Holy Ghost from the Father only,[2] and the Pope, instead of rebuking him for his profession, declared in his letter of 18 March 862[3] that the faith of Photius was perfectly orthodox. Photius could then suppose, or at least pretend, that in this respect the Pope did not essentially differ from the Greeks. We shall presently see that Photius took another declaration of the same kind, that of John VIII, very seriously,[4] and that in Byzantium the origin of that doctrine was often attributed to Formosus, bishop of Porto, of all men, the leader of the Latin mission to Bulgaria.[5]

It should also be observed that such accounts of the Council as have come down to us nowhere mention any condemnation of the Western Church on the ground of any false doctrine she might have been teaching

---

[1] Cf. Rosseikin, loc. cit. pp. 424 seq.

[2] *P.G.* vol. 102, col. 589: οὕτω γὰρ καὶ τῆς χρονικῆς ἐννοίας ὁμοτίμως ἡ Τριὰς ὑπεριδρυθήσεται, καὶ τῆς αὐτῆς οὐσίας τῷ Πατρί, ἐξ οὗπερ ὁ μὲν ἀρρεύστως καὶ ἀρρήτως γεγέννηται, τὸ δὴ ἐκπεπόρευται, θεολογικῶς ὑμνολογηθήσεται.

[3] *M.G.H.* Ep. VI, p. 440: 'Unde directionis vestrae sumptis apicibus laetificati sumus, quia vos catholicum in eis cognovimus. Nam ibi prudentiae vestrae utilitatem intelleximus ideoque multas gratias Deo omnipotenti retulimus, quia vestrum scire de catholico fonte manare experti sumus.'

[4] See p. 196.   [5] See pp. 253, 456 (late treatises on schism).

and that the Fathers of the Eighth Council reproved this synod for nothing but the condemnation of Nicholas.

The opinion that the Council of 867 meant a declaration of war between the two Churches and a rupture between the Latins and the Greeks is due to Pope Nicholas' letter to Hincmar, for it was he who attached to the Bulgarian incident the significance attributed to it since. It was only natural that the Pontiff should be looking for allies against Photius and that he should try to incense against him the Frankish episcopate more than any other, for there was real danger threatening from that quarter. The Byzantines were certainly aware of the fact that the Roman missionaries had ousted those of the Franks from Bulgaria, a circumstance that may have induced Byzantines and Franks to join hands in their opposition to Nicholas. To forestall such a danger, the Pope had to gain the confidence of the Franks, chiefly Hincmar, by asserting that the interest of the whole Church was at stake: hence Nicholas generalizes the accusations made by Photius against the Bulgarian missionaries, giving the impression that they had been made against the whole Latin Church, and therefore against the Franks as well.

At bottom Nicholas was right, for the customs spread by the Latin missionaries in Bulgaria were customs dear to the Latins which the Franks, who were exceptionally keen on singing the *Filioque* in their creed, also understood. Flattered at having been singled out by the Pope to mobilize the Frankish Church, Hincmar did his utmost, and the writings, composed at his suggestion,[1] against the Greek denunciations, substantially helped in spreading the opinion throughout the West that Photius had indicted the whole Latin Church. Incidentally, the Pope, at the moment of writing to Hincmar, could have no knowledge of the Council summoned by Photius.

It is generally assumed, too, that the Council of 867 was up in arms, not only against the Pope personally, but rather against the very notion of the Roman primacy: Photius is alleged to have proclaimed the downfall of Rome from the government of the Universal Church and to have behaved generally as though he were the supreme head of the Church.

[1] See p. 280. J. Haller, loc. cit. p. 93, disagrees with Perels, loc. cit. p. 167, by minimizing the Pope's appeal: 'Eher könnte man darin, dass weder von den lothringischen noch von den westfränkischen Bischöfen eine Gesammterklärung entsprechend der von Worms erfolgte, ein Zeichen von Unlust sehen, die durch den angesammelten Verdruss über die Regierungsweise des Papstes leicht zu erklären wäre.'

There is in Nicholas' letter to Hincmar a passage which seems to confirm the assumption:[1]

No wonder that they should pretend such things, since they even maintain and boast that when the Emperors moved from the Roman city to Constantinople, the primacy of the Roman See was also transferred to the Church of Constantinople and that the privileges of the Roman Church changed hands together with the royal honours, so much so that the usurper of that same Church Photius calls himself in his writings archbishop and universal patriarch.

It does not seem that the words can bear this interpretation. First of all, when writing this letter on 23 October 867, the Pope knew nothing yet about the Council referred to: the synod must have terminated its sittings towards the end of August of the same year, for we learn that after the assassination of Michael III on 24 September 867 the ambassadors, headed by Zachary of Chalcedon, taking the Acts of the synod to Louis II, were overtaken by a messenger from Basil and called back. They cannot have been far from the capital, since they had left Constantinople in the first days of September, after the closing of the Council. It was not till about 24 September that the Council's decisions could be dispatched to Bulgaria; but at that moment the papal legates were already back in Rome, having left Bulgaria long before the convocation of the said Council. As a matter of fact, Hincmar's envoys, who reached Rome in the month of August, found the Pope appalled by the news just received about the stand taken by the Greeks.[2] It is therefore evident that the Pope could not, in the document under consideration, refer to the Council of 867.

Nor can it be that Nicholas quoted the passage from one of Michael's or Photius' letters addressed to him, for I have studied the Pope's replies to these letters without discovering a single reference to any

---

[1] *M.G.H.* Ep. VI, p. 605: 'Sed quid mirum, si haec isti praetendunt, cum etiam glorientur atque perhibeant, quando de Romana urbe imperatores Constantinopolim sunt translati, tunc et primatum Romanae sedis ad Constantinopolitanam ecclesiam transmigrasse et cum dignitatibus regiis etiam ecclesiae Romanae privilegia translata fuisse, ita ut eiusdem invasor ecclesiae Photius etiam ipse se in scriptis suis archepiscopum atque universalem patriarcham appellet.' Cf. Hergenröther, *Photius*, vol. I, pp. 656 seq.

[2] Hincmari Annales, a. 867, *M.G.H.* Ss. vol. I, p. 475: 'Hincmari clerici mense Augusto Romam venientes, Nicolaum papam iam valde infirmatum et in contentione quam contra orientales episcopos habebat, magnopere laborantem invenerunt; qua propter usque ad mensem Octobrium ibidem sunt immorati. Nicolaus...et alteram epistolam ei [Hincmari] misit innotescens...Graecorum imperatores, sed et orientales episcopos, calumniari sanctam Romanam ecclesiam......'

such statement by either Photius or Michael, though Nicholas never left one Greek stricture unanswered.

The fact is that Nicholas only interprets in this sense the title of oecumenical Patriarch which Photius, Ignatius and all their predecessors had claimed ever since John the Faster. Nicholas could only refer to canon 28 of the Council of Chalcedon, and the interpretation of this canon which the Pope fathers on the Greeks seems somewhat far-fetched, since before Nicholas no Greek had ever read into it such a radical meaning.

Yet I would not presume to accuse Nicholas of having gone too far[1] and of consciously intending to throw oil on the fire, for it is quite possible that the Greek missionaries in Bulgaria had actually defended that theory to prove to the Bulgarians that the see of Constantinople was superior to that of Rome, and it is certain that discussions about the pre-eminence of those two sees were at that time in full swing in Bulgaria. After all, Nicholas himself had belittled the importance of the see of Constantinople in the Church, by placing its Patriarch after those of Rome, Alexandria and Antioch, contrary to common usage as agreed to by the Roman Church: which only shows that both the rival parties in Bulgaria were apt to exaggerate.

Cardinal Hergenröther,[2] however, is inclined to think that Photius actually did proclaim such a doctrine, and attributes to him, though not without some hesitation, a writing against the primacy, which was published by Beveridge[3] among the canonical letters of Alexios Aristenos. One reads there that the Romans could not base their pretensions to the primacy on the fact that St Peter lived and died in Rome: Jerusalem, too, had at its head a great apostle, the 'brother' of the Lord; Peter, before settling in Rome, had been bishop of Antioch and the Apostle Andrew had founded Constantinople.

Then again, the rock on which Our Lord had built His Church (Matt. xvi. 18) was not the person of the Apostle Peter, but his faith.[4]

[1] As A. Pichler seems to have done in *Geschichte der kirchlichen Trennung* (München, 1864), vol. I, p. 186. On the other hand, Pichler is right here as against Hergenröther, loc. cit. vol. I, p. 656.

[2] Loc. cit. vol. I, pp. 662 seq.; vol. III, pp. 170 seq.

[3] *Synodicon*, loc. cit. t. II, at the end of the first part; G. Rhalles and M. Potles, Σύνταγμα τῶν ἱερῶν κανόνων (Athens, 1854), t. V, pp. 409 seq.

[4] Photius, Ad Amphilochium, q. 194, *P.G.* vol. 101, col. 933 interprets the passage in a similar sense: διὸ καὶ μισθὸν τῷ Πέτρῳ τῆς ὀρθῆς ὁμολογίας, τάς τε κλεῖς τῆς Βασιλείας ἐνεχείρισε, καὶ ἐπὶ τῇ αὐτοῦ ὁμολογίᾳ ἐστηρίχθαι τὴν Ἐκκλησίαν. He is, however, not so emphatic and prejudiced as the author of the treatise. Anyhow, Nicholas I could not take offence at Photius' interpretation of Matt. xvi. 18,

The Roman primacy is of pagan origin, having been founded by Aurelianus; and no Council ever confirmed the primacy as claimed by the Popes: the Synod of Sardica cannot be appealed to in support of the primacy. The Popes often, though unsuccessfully, rose against other bishops, whereas the Byzantine Patriarchs frequently deposed their predecessors.

Hergenröther [1] enumerates the following reasons for ascribing this treatise to Photius: two manuscripts of the Vatican Library call Photius the author of the treatise (Cod. Vat. 829 and 1150); the ideas expressed in the treatise are those of Photius; even the style and some expressions recall the Patriarch's writings, in particular, his *Synagogai*.

None of these reasons is valid. That two late manuscripts should attribute the treatise to Photius proves nothing, since other manuscripts do not make such ascription. Nothing was easier than to append to an anonymous treatise the name of Photius at a time when it was associated with anti-Latin polemics more than any other. The same happened to the treatise against the Franks, which certainly was not by Photius.

Hergenröther admits himself that the leading ideas of this treatise were familiar to the Greek mentality of the twelfth century. Then why not place it in that period? It was not till after 1054, chiefly during the Crusades of the twelfth century, that animosity between Rome and Byzantium rose to sufficient heat for such arguments to have originated in Byzantium. [2]

since he himself had explained the words in the same way, as appears from his letter of 18 March 862 to the Eastern bishops (*M.G.H.* Ep. VI, p. 447): 'When Our Lord and Redeemer had given to Bl. Peter, Prince of the Apostles, the power to bind and to loose in heaven and on earth and to close the gates of the heavenly kingdom, He deigned to erect His Holy Church on the solidity of the faith [supra soliditatem fidei suam sanctam dignatus est stabilire Ecclesiam], according to His authentic words, as He said: Verily, I say unto thee, thou art Peter....' A similar reading is found in the prayer of the Roman Mass on the Vigil of SS. Peter and Paul: 'Praesta quaesumus omnipotens Deus ut nullis nos permittas perturbationibus concuti, quos in apostolicae confessionis petra solidasti....'

[1] Loc. cit. vol. III, p. 171.

[2] By comparing, for instance, the meaning given by the author of the treatise to Matt. xvi. 18 with that given by Photius, one can see how fast animosity against everything Roman had grown by the time the treatise was published. A new edition of the treatise has since been issued by M. Gordillo ('Photius et Primatus Romanus') in *Orientalia Christiana Periodica* (1940), vol. VI, pp. 5–39. Additional details will be found there on the controversy concerning Photius' authorship of the treatise. M. Gordillo produces decisive evidence against Hergenröther's assumption and attributes the treatise to an anonymous writer belonging to the first decades of the thirteenth century.

There remains to prove that the ideas expressed in the treatise tally with those of Photius: but there is not a trace of them to be found in any of the Patriarch's writings. Nicholas' references to Greek attacks against the primacy are far too vague, as already stated, to justify the inference that Michael or Photius put forward such ideas as square with those of the treatise; and had Hergenröther known about the Acts of the Council of 861, he would perhaps have been less emphatic in his conjecture. The notions set forth in these Acts are poles apart from those advocated in the treatise, making it difficult to presume such 'progress' among the Byzantines of the period, particularly in Photius, within such a short span of time, unless one be determined to make him a spineless character, always ready to deceive the public and tell lies according to the needs of the moment—an assumption that would be anything but fair.[1]

What then are we to think of Photius' letter to the Khagan? In enumerating the Patriarchs who had attended the seven general councils, Photius every time lists the Patriarch of Constantinople first, before even the Patriarch of Rome:[2] does this not suggest that Photius assumed the superiority of the see of Constantinople over all the other patriarchal sees? No; the bearing of this passage should not be exaggerated, for at this place Photius underlines the greatness and importance of the see of Constantinople only to impress Boris. The Byzantines knew perfectly well that Boris was always leaning towards Rome and the Franks. Making too much of the Roman patriarchate would only have jeopardized Photius' own work in Bulgaria, and the scrupulous, naïve and cunning Khagan might have thought it preferable to get his missionaries from a bishop who was superior to the Patriarch of Constantinople.[3] It is well to remember that Nicholas followed exactly the same tactics in Bulgaria towards his rival in Constantinople.

---

[1] Cf. Th. Kurganov, 'K izsledovaniyu o Patr. Fotiye' (*Khrist. Chtenie*, 1895), t. I, p. 198. He finds it, however, strange that the treatise in question should place the Council of Nicaea under Sylvester and Julius, as Photius did in his letter to Michael-Boris. But this coincidence proves nothing and cannot be quoted in support of the authorship of the treatise by Photius. Such attributions seem to have been common in Byzantium in the ninth century. Even the *Synodicon Vetus*, published by Fabricius-Harles (loc. cit. vol. XII, p. 370) and representing Ignatian opinion, makes the same assertion. An anonymous treatise on the Councils, preserved in the Paris-Graec. 3041, fols. 131, 132, said the same as Photius not only about the First Council, but also about the Fifth.

[2] *P.G.* vol. 102, cols. 632 seq.

[3] In his letter to Ashod, King of Armenia, Photius, speaking of the Council of Chalcedon, places the See of Rome at the head of the list. A. Finck, 'Esnik

Attention should also be called to the allocution by Pope Hadrian II to the thirty bishops of the Roman synod of 869, after reading the report by his experts, charged with the examination of the Acts of the Council of 867. This is what he said about this Council:[1]

After that, Photius raised his face to heaven, but his tongue came down to earth as he opened his evil-smelling mouth against divine providence which miraculously set up the primacy of the Blessed Peter, Prince of the Apostles and against the Apostolic See of the key-bearer of the same heavenly kingdom, whilst he poured out the poison of his viperish tongue against the highest dignity and power on earth. In other words, not fearing to slander the life of my blessed predecessor Pope Nicholas, nor sparing us who are his unworthy servant, not to say follower, and thinking he could curse both of us and heap blasphemies on us as far as lay in his power, he tried to trump up charges undoubtedly false and pile up incredible pythonic dreams and arguments. Yet, you all certainly know what our father was like, how great and how eminent, as you remember the qualities of his character and the triumphs of his virtues.

The first portion of this extract suggests that Photius had actually reprobated the Roman primacy as such and his choice of terms points that way, but when the Pope proceeds to substantiate his assertion, he finds no argument to produce but Photius' criticisms of the life and actions of Nicholas: *Vitam scilicet decessoris mei beatae recordationis papae Nicolai lacessere nullo modo metuens...*, after which Hadrian lavishes high praise on Nicholas' activities in answer to Michael and Photius.

Gjandschezian, Der Brief des Photios an Aschot und dessen Antwort', in *Zeitschrift für armenische Philologie* (1904), vol. II, p. 2: 'Denn Rom ehrt zuerst so das vierte Konzil, wie die drei Konzilien, die diesem vorgegangen sind. Mit solcher gleichen Verehrung nimmt auch der grosse [Patriarchen] Stuhl von Alexandrien und der Stuhl von Jerusalem [es] an und tragen keine Feindschaft wegen dieses heiligen Konzils. So auch die Konzilien, die diesem d. h. dem vierten gefolgt sind, [nämlich] das fünfte, sechste und siebente.' See the Armenian text in *Palestinskii Sbornik* (1892), vol. XI (Papadopoulos-Kerameus), pp. 210 seq.

[1] Mansi, vol. XVI, col. 123: 'Post haec vero posuit Photius in coelum os suum, et lingua eius transiit super terram, dum videlicet contra divinam ordinationem, coelitus in beati Petri principis apostolorum primatu dispositam, putridi gurgitis guttur aperuit, ac adversus eiusdem regni caelestis clavigeri apostolicam sedem, et praecipuam et summam dignitatem et potestatem, linguam suam more serpentis exacuit; vitam scilicet decessoris mei beatae recordationis papae Nicolai lacessere nullo modo metuens, nec nobis, qui eius vix digni famuli, ut non dicam sequaces, exstitimus, parcere utcumque consentiens, sed utrosque maledictis impetere, quantum in se fuit, et blasphemis inficere verbis existimans, falsitatis praestigia fingere conatus; et nescio quae Pythonica est somnia vel argumenta, compilando procul dubio, commentatus. Et certe quis ille pater noster, vel quantus aut qualis exstiterit, omnes, qui morum eius insignia, vel virtutum trophaea recolitis, plenius agnovistis....'

It is evident, then, that the Pope found in the Acts of the Council of 867 nothing but personal criticisms of Nicholas and his doings: but this is not the same as denying the Roman primacy as such any more than criticizing the conduct of Alexander VI—if we may draw the comparison without prejudice to the saintly memory of a great Pope of the stature of Nicholas—could ever be regarded as taking exception to the Roman primacy.

Photius' manner in criticizing certain acts of Nicholas was perhaps unconventional and offensive; but then, it is also difficult, it must be confessed, to draw a hard and fast line between the Pope's person and the high position he occupies in the Church. One can understand why Hadrian was shocked by Photius' outburst; nevertheless, the distinction between the two notions still holds good.

To summarize what has been said about the whole incident, one can maintain that the significance of the Photian encyclical and of the synod of 867 has too often been overrated by both historians and theologians; in this they merely followed Baronius,[1] who was the first to stretch Photius' words to an attack on the Western Church and on the rights of the bishop of Rome in the Church.

Contrary to what we are made to believe, Photius spoke of the Pope, until the Council of 867, as little as possible. I have already pointed out his efforts to obtain Nicholas' recognition and his deliberate silence after Nicholas' reiterated refusal. It must be admitted that till 867 Photius' attitude was perfectly dignified. Nor is it true to state that Photius had been planning his attack on the Pope ever since 864 and had sent his agents to Italy to gather materials for the Council that was to proclaim Nicholas' downfall. Hergenröther[2] could produce no evidence for this assertion. Knowing the reasons for Nicholas' refusal; knowing that his enemies' intrigues had done their work in Rome; unable to oblige the Pope with what was expected in exchange for his recognition or to agree with his point of view, Photius remained content with keeping an obstinate but respectful silence from 861 till 867.

This was the only attitude he could adopt without prejudicing his own rights and the peace of Christendom. The information that reached him from time to time from Western countries bore out his conviction that silence and time would be the best means of breaking down Nicholas' opposition. Photius had no difficulty in discovering that

[1] *Annales Ecclesiastici...*, an. 867, chs. LXVII seq. Cf. Norden, *Das Papsttum und Byzanz* (Berlin, 1903), p. 9. [2] Loc. cit. pp. 551 seq.

Nicholas had his antagonists among his own subordinates; and the prelates concerned volunteered the information, knowing well that the Patriarch of Constantinople also came in for some of Nicholas' resentment: Radoald, who in 864 had made common cause with Günther and Theotgand, had certainly informed the bishops of what had taken place in Constantinople in 861 and demonstrated to them that his own point of view with regard to Photius was right whereas Nicholas' policy was a blunder. Photius was, moreover, the only man who could have openly withstood Nicholas, without fear for his own safety.

And yet, Photius was not spoiling for a fight of this sort; nor would he have moved a finger even in 867, had the Bulgar incident not completely altered the position. His letter to John of Ravenna suggests that the last overtures made to him from the West had come that very year: it was this appeal and the Roman offensive in Bulgaria that had such a decisive effect on his change of attitude. Photius, however, exaggerated the importance and the extent of the opposition to Nicholas in the West just as much as Nicholas overrated the prestige his See commanded in the East.

These considerations may explain Photius' conduct, though no reasons are adequate to excuse his last move, which proved so disastrous. By daring to pass judgement on a Pope, Photius committed a deed till then unheard of in history, one that endangered the unity of Christendom, for which there could be neither excuse nor justification. Rightly or wrongly, his action set a precedent invoked or imitated by all those who later were to break the unity of the Church.

Photius' desperate move was moreover premature, inconsiderate and thoughtless; he was wrong in abandoning his attitude of patient procrastination, when Providence was busy settling things for the best. Nicholas died on 13 November, without hearing of the sentence passed on him by the Orientals. A letter from Anastasius the Librarian to Ado of Vienna, written on 14 December 867,[1] tells us that dissatisfaction with Nicholas' policy was at the time widespread in Rome; and Anastasius, his chief collaborator, feared for the future of the great Pope's work. The opinions of his successor Hadrian II not being known yet, Anastasius expressed his anxiety lest the new Pope should side with his predecessor's enemies and reverse his whole policy.[2]

[1] *M.G.H.* Ep. VII, pp. 400 seq.

[2] For further details cf. Lapôtre, 'Hadrien II et les Fausses Décrétales', in *Revue des Questions historiques* (1880), vol. XXVII, pp. 377–431, chiefly pp. 383–402. Also, for signs of apprehension cf. the *Liber Pontificalis*, vol. II, pp. 173 seq. Cf. Langen, *Geschichte d. Röm. Kirche*, pp. 117 seq. J. Haller, loc. cit. pp. 95 seq.

But a change seemed to be preparing even in the Papacy's oriental policy. Zachary of Anagni, who for his feelings towards Photius had fallen foul of Nicholas, returned to favour under Hadrian and, together with some other bishops who had been dismissed by Nicholas, received holy communion from the Pope's hands on the very day of Hadrian's consecration.[1] The Greek monks who were refugees in Rome seemed to scent danger and ceased to come to the meal which Nicholas had daily provided for them at the Lateran. As they fought shy of Hadrian, the Pope deemed it advisable to make the first step to ease the tension and offered them a banquet on 20 February 868,[2] when he gave the refugees tokens of exceptional friendship, condescending even to eat with them and pour out the wine with his own hands. In his toast, he gave them the assurance that they had nothing to fear from him and that he had no intention of introducing any radical changes into his predecessor's oriental policy. Theognostos must have breathed again, as anxious concern for his work had given him more than one bad night in Rome. His urgent and oft-repeated pleas to Hadrian[3] had therefore borne some fruit, though he did not have it all his own way.

It goes without saying that nothing at that moment was known of the changes in Byzantium and the Council of 867. On reading these reports, one gathers the clear impression that one move from Photius for an amicable settlement of this business would at that moment have produced the best impression and might have altered the whole course of pontifical policy.

---

[1] *Liber Pontificalis*, vol. II, p. 175.

[2] Ibid., p. 176: 'A cuius videlicet sanctissimi Hadriani papae collegio cum per dies aliquot quidam Graecorum et aliarum gentium servorum Dei per id tempus Romae morantium se clanculo suspendissent, sexta feria Septuagesime idem summus antistes secundum consuetudinem refectionis gratia solito pluris numeri convocavit. Quorum omnium manibus per semet humiliter aquam fudit, cibos apposuit, pocula ministravit et, quod nullum pontificum ante se fecisse noverat...cum illis discubuit.' Cf. my book *Les Légendes de Constantin et de Méthode*, p. 289.

[3] Hadrian mentions this in his letter to Ignatius (*M.G.H.* Ep. VI, p. 749).

CHAPTER V

PHOTIUS' DOWNFALL AND THE COUNCIL OF 869–70

Michael's regime, Basil and the Extremists—Did Photius resign?—Basil's embassy to Rome—Hadrian II's reaction—The Council of 869–70—The Emperor and the legates' uncompromising attitude—The Bulgarian incident—Was Ignatius' recognition by the Pope conditional?

IT was impossible for such a move on the part of Photius to be made, for when Hadrian took possession of the Lateran patriarcheion it was two months since Photius had vacated the patriarcheion of St Sophia. Basil had murdered Michael III on 24 September 867,[1] and the new Emperor decided to turn to Rome and to make a complete reversal of his predecessor's religious policy. Photius had to yield place to Ignatius.

What were the reasons for this *coup d'état*? And why did the Emperor alter the Empire's policy towards Rome so radically? How did this change of front bring about at the same time Photius' downfall? Ignatian sources and histories of Constantine Porphyrogennetos' school paint the regime of Michael III in the very darkest colours in contrast to Basil as the one man who saved the Empire from disaster. In their version, Michael's murder was hailed with a sigh of relief and Photius' downfall as a well-deserved punishment administered by Providence and welcomed by the whole Church of Constantinople. This point of view has until quite recently prevailed among the majority of historians.

And yet, recent discoveries on the reign of Michael III prove that the traditional view of his reign and the regime of Bardas was wrong. To judge only from some stories told by the Continuator of Theophanes and the Pseudo-Simeon, the Emperor and his uncle must have found sympathetic support, especially among the lower and the middle classes.

Michael loved to move among ordinary people to such an extent that those two writers were deeply shocked by his contempt for imperial propriety.[2] For instance, the Emperor thought nothing of holding children of the poor over the baptismal font, of visiting them in their miserable hovels;[3] and he loved sports and games at the Hippodrome,

---

[1] For details, cf. Bury, loc. cit. pp. 177 seq.
[2] Theoph. Cont. (Bonn), pp. 199 seq.; Pseudo-Simeon (Bonn), pp. 660 seq.
[3] Theoph. Cont. (Bonn), pp. 172–3. Cf. Manasses, versus 5066, p. 216.

always so popular in Byzantium.[1] The anonymous author of the *Patria Constantinopoleos* tells a beautiful story[2] about Michael giving justice to a poor woman against the powerful official Nicephorus, and it was not the only edifying story circulating at the time in the poor quarters of Byzantium. The jaundiced descriptions by writers hostile to his memory reveal the very characteristics that must have made Michael popular among the masses. Compare their portraiture of Michael III with that found in a homily delivered in 867 in St Sophia by Photius:[3] A great Emperor, victorious and brave; a wise administrator; popular; knowing how to address the people and to put his wealth to good use; full of piety and care for the churches; a real 'father of the country'. This picture, so different from the caricatures left by the panegyrists of the dynasty founded by his murderer, Basil I, certainly comes nearer the truth, as recent discoveries have amply shown.

As H. Grégoire[4] has been able to prove, Michael was a gifted statesman whose reign reached the high-water mark of Byzantine military

[1] Theoph. Cont. (Bonn), p. 198; Pseudo-Simeon (Bonn), p. 681. It should, however, be observed that the imperial Hippodrome of S. Mammas used to be closed to the public during the races in which Michael III took an active part. None but high State officials were invited (cf. Bury, loc. cit. p. 162). Therefore annalists exaggerate in saying that Michael thereby lowered imperial dignity.

[2] Th. Preger, *Scriptores Originum Constantinopolitarum* (Teubner, Leipzig, 1907), vol. II (*Patria Constantinopoleos*, vol. III, p. 27), pp. 233 seq. Theophanes' Continuator (Bonn), p. 208 and Cedrenus (Bonn), p. 1056, state that Bardas liked to dispense justice in the Hippodrome. Cf. A. Vogt, *Basile Ier* (Paris, 1908), p. 34. It is matter of common knowledge to every student of Byzantine history that George Cedrenus, who lived at the end of the eleventh and the beginning of the twelfth century, did not produce an original work but copied, for the period 811–1057, the work of Skylitzes, who lived in the second half of the eleventh century and wrote a chronicle extending from the reign of Michael I to that of Nicephorus Botaneiates (811–1079). Skylitzes' work was, however, never published and has so far been known only through Cedrenus' transcription. To simplify matters, I have preferred to quote this historical source as Cedrenus' work. Cf. Krumbacher, *Geschichte der Byzantinischen Literatur* (München, 1897), pp. 365–9.

[3] S. Aristarchos, *Photii Orat. et Hom.* vol. II, pp. 314–17. Cf. my note, 'Lettre à M. H. Grégoire à propos de Michel III...', in *Byzantion* (1935), vol. X, pp. 6–8.

[4] H. Grégoire, 'Inscriptions historiques Byzantines', in *Byzantion* (1927–8), vol. IV, pp. 437–48 ('Ancyre et les Arabes sous Michel l'Ivrogne', idem, 'Michel III et Basile le Macédonien dans l'Inscription d'Ancyre', ibid. (1929–30), vol. V, pp. 327–40; idem, 'Études sur le IXe siècle', ibid. (1933), vol. VIII, pp. 515–50). Cf. my *Les Légendes de Constantin et de Méthode*, pp. 85–112, on the Arab mission. Cf. also M. N. Adontz, 'L'Age et l'Origine de l'Empereur Basile I', in *Byzantion* (1933), vol. VIII, pp. 475–513; (1934), vol. IX, pp. 223–60; idem, 'La Portée historique de l'Oraison funèbre de Basile I', ibid. vol. VIII, pp. 501–13. The old thesis is defended in A. Vogt's study, 'La Jeunesse de Léon VI Le Sage', in *Revue Historique* (1934), vol. CLXXIV, pp. 389–428.

power against the Arabs: by defeating them in 863, he and his gallant uncle Bardas substantially enhanced the prestige of Byzantium. Little wonder then that Michael stood high in public veneration and long did his name live in popular 'tragedies'. Even Michael's morals have benefited by the findings. He was no paragon of virtue, it is true. He loved drink and good cheer; he was jovial and had a weakness for coarse jokes. But he was not drunk every day and if in his younger days he permitted himself in the company of his boon companions some irreverent travesties of the liturgy, he was not for that reason either cynical or impious. He founded two churches, both dedicated to Our Lady,[1] and richly endowed the church of St Sophia. The Continuator of Theophanes, no friend of Michael's, enumerates the rich presents the Emperor made to the principal churches of Constantinople and makes no secret of his admiration for the splendour of the gifts.[2] Photius in a homily praised the Emperor's lavish generosity and expressed the hope to see more such marks of imperial favour lavished on the great church.[3]

Even Michael's attitude towards his mother Theodora was not as heartless as we have been made to believe. Her dethronement, as we have seen, was dictated by political interests. She was not sent to a convent immediately after her fall: not until after the fruitless endeavour by supporters of the old regime to overthrow Bardas did her brother and her son decide to resort to this expedient. She must have been subsequently set free again, for in 863 she took her share in the triumph of her son and of Bardas, when the populace that day hailed 'the emperor together with the august empresses who share the purple'.[4] Pope Nicholas knew that Theodora held an important position at the court, for in 866 he wrote to her as to one who might wield a salutary influence on Michael, and Theognostos had certainly kept the Pope informed about the circumstances at the Byzantine court. As he left Byzantium probably at the beginning of 862, Theodora's reinstatement should be dated from 861, the year when the intrigues of the Ignatians and of Theodora's old supporters were definitely foiled.

Henceforth Michael and his mother must have been on friendly

---

[1] The τῶν ὁδηγῶν and the καραβίτξιν. See *Patria Constantinopoleos*, vol. III, p. 277; (ed. Th. Preger), loc. cit. vol. II, p. 233. Bardas founded the church of S. Demetrius (ibid. p. 295). Cf. G. Yared, loc. cit. (1872), vol. II, pp. 561–4.

[2] Theoph. Cont. (Bonn), pp. 210 seq.

[3] S. Aristarchos, Φωτίου λόγοι καὶ ὁμιλίαι (Constantinople, 1900), vol. II, pp. 294, 300 seq. Cf. my 'Lettre à M. H. Grégoire...', p. 5.

[4] Const. Porph., *De Ceremoniis* (Bonn), vol. I, p. 333: σὺν ταῖς τιμίαις αὐγούσ-ταις ἐν τῇ πορφύρᾳ. Cf. Bury, loc. cit. pp. 169, 284.

terms, for we learn from the same sources as those which refer to Michael's murder[1] that Theodora had invited her son to a dinner on 25 September 867 and that Michael sent his protovestiarios Rentakios out to hunt to provide his mother with venison for the banquet. After learning of her son's tragic death, Theodora went with her daughters to view the body and bathe it in her tears, a touching demonstration clearly attesting that Michael had after all not been such an undutiful son to his mother.

Chroniclers' gossip on the marriage à trois between Michael, Basil and Eudocia was given the lie in the funeral oration which Leo VI delivered in memory of his father Basil.[2] So none need be shocked at the fact that Photius gave his support to Michael. Corruption at the Byzantine court was not so bad as some would have it;[3] and besides, if Photius is to be blamed for having been associated from his youth in the life of the Byzantine court, it should be remembered that the Patriarch Tarasius, for instance, should share in the same censure; but this did not prevent the Church from honouring him with canonization. Even the most judicious scholars admit to-day that Michael III was not the 'triste sire' who richly deserved the title of 'Drunkard' bestowed on him by posterity.[4] As I have stated already, there was in Michael's case the same blackening of character as in that of the Emperor Nicephorus, and in both instances the defamation came from the same quarter—the Extremists. There is, therefore, no justification whatever for pretending that dissatisfaction with Michael's regime was widespread and that Basil's ascent to the throne was hailed with a sense of relief. Far from this being the case, Michael's murder alienated several classes of the Byzantine population.

What then were the reasons for Basil's *coup d'état*? The main and possibly the only reason was extremely commonplace: Basil's insensate desire to become Emperor. The same ambition that had led him to commit the previous murder, that of Bardas, this time prompted him to assassinate his greatest benefactor and friend Michael, his only excuse being the fear lest Michael, who was beginning to suspect a rival, should steal a march upon him.

[1] Pseudo-Simeon (Bonn), pp. 684 seq.; Georg. Cont. (Bonn), pp. 836 seq.

[2] A. Vogt, I. Hausherr, 'L'Oraison funèbre de Basile I', in *Orientalia Christiana* (Rome, 1932), vol. XXVI; Adontz, 'La Portée historique de l'Oraison funèbre de Basile I', in *Byzantion* (1933), vol. VIII, pp. 501–13.

[3] For instance, Hergenröther, loc. cit. vol. I, pp. 336 seq.

[4] Cf. F. Dölger, *Byz. Zeitschrift* (1936), vol. XXXVI, on the subject of my 'Lettre à M. H. Grégoire...', in *Byzantion*, vol. X, pp. 5–9.

For all these reasons, it is only too evident that Basil, once Emperor, could no longer count on the support of the party that had stood behind Bardas and Michael, and was forcibly driven to turn to the party which in Michael's reign formed the opposition—the Extremists; and the favours of this party were his, on condition that he should adopt its religious policy. Basil had no choice but to close the bargain. Photius' downfall and Ignatius' reinstatement thereupon followed as a matter of course, for it was only among the Extremists that Basil could find people ready to condone, or if need be to countenance, his crime.

But Basil's leaning to the Extremists was of older date. As Caesar Bardas had been the Moderates' principal mainstay, his murder not only made Basil a favourite with the Extremists, as was only to be expected, but greatly facilitated matters for him; for after the Caesar's assassination, in which the Emperor had played a regrettable part, Bardas' friends lost interest in the Emperor, who had not the same commanding personality as his uncle Bardas, and the Moderates' position deteriorated. From that moment the Extremists must have been on the alert. Basil probably also made contact with their leaders before carrying out his scheme, and though the blow must have been struck sooner than anticipated, the revolution seems to have been carefully planned.[1] This brings us once more to the eternal rivalry between the two political parties, mutually jealous and ever greedy of supremacy in Church and State.

It only remains to examine the circumstances of Photius' dethronement. Here we are faced with two different versions: the one handed down by the Continuator of George the Monk[2] presents Photius as in direct and irreconcilable opposition to Basil, going so far even as to refuse Basil holy communion and to call him a robber and a parricide. The other version is embodied in the account by Anastasius and reads: 'Basilius Photio sacro ministerio post depositionem irregulariter abutenti *throno Constantinopolitano cedere persuadet.*'[3]

Which of these two versions comes nearer the truth? At a first glance, one would be inclined to adopt the Continuator's version, which

---

[1] Adontz, 'L'Age et l'Origine de l'Empereur Basile I', in *Byzantion* (1934), vol. IX, p. 232 is of the same opinion. Basil also initiated into his plot two bodies of military under the command of his two accomplices, his brother Marianus and Artavasdes.

[2] (Bonn), p. 841. Also, cf. Leo Gram. (Bonn), pp. 254 seq.; Pseudo-Simeon (Bonn), pp. 688 seq.

[3] Mansi, vol. XVI, col. 6.

Hergenröther[1] naturally discards for reasons that are not valid; for he finds it strange that a man who approved Bardas' murder could in less than no time turn virtuous enough to protest against Michael's murder. And yet, Photius' reply to the imperial account of what had taken place in the course of the expedition to Crete[2] could not justify the conclusion that Photius approved the murder of Bardas. Naturally enough, he accepts the official explanation supplied by the Emperor, or rather by Basil, to the effect that Bardas had been plotting against the Emperor; but in his letter to Michael one can find more than one sentence indicative of the Patriarch's true feelings. What he regretted most was that Bardas had been killed without being given time to repent.[3] Equally sincere was his request, repeated in a second letter, urging Michael to return to Constantinople soon, there being serious fear of trouble from the loyal partisans of Bardas.

But plausible as such a line of argument is, we cannot give this version unreserved credit. In the first place, it recalls too much the story of Ignatius' refusal to give holy communion to Bardas, as though one of Photius' admirers had concocted the parallel story in order that his hero should not be outdone by Ignatius. Then again, why should Basil have courted the affront and risked his prestige among the population of the city, when there was no need for it? He must have known Photius' feelings and could not but expect a rebuff; and he was cunning enough to realize that any overtures to Photius would have lost him the good will of the Extremists, whose support he had to solicit above all things.

For all these reasons Anastasius' version seems preferable; it is brief and truthful. It was the obvious thing for Basil to do—to invite Photius to resign—since he had to reinstate on the patriarchal throne Ignatius, the very candidate of the political party with whose assistance he intended to govern. The procedure was also canonical and true to Byzantine tradition: Photius' resignation was sent in soon after the coup d'état, probably the day after,[4] and Ignatius' installation took place only on 3 November, the anniversary of his first enthronement.

---

[1] *Photius*, vol. III, pp. 13 seq. Cf. vol. II, pp. 588 seq.

[2] *P.G.* vol. 102, cols. 717 seq.

[3] Cf. Bury, loc. cit. pp. 172 seq., and Rosseykin, loc. cit. pp. 341–4.

[4] The crowning of Basil by Photius mentioned in the Patriarch's letter to the Emperor (*P.G.* vol. 102, col. 765) did not take place after Michael's murder. Photius merely recalls the ceremony as it was narrated by the Continuator of George the Monk (Bonn, p. 832) and which took place when Michael proclaimed Basil co-Emperor. Basil, after Michael's murder, did not have himself crowned again, but simply went on ruling alone.

After ascending the throne, Basil found himself in a somewhat delicate position: as he had announced a change of policy, he had to try to be on good terms with Rome; but, on the other hand, he had badly committed himself in the eyes of the Romans by attending with Michael the Council that had indicted Nicholas, the same Pope, so it was then believed in Constantinople, who was still in occupation of the See of Rome. Under the circumstances, one can understand that Basil should try to doctor whatever might in this respect have placed him in an unfavourable light: so he hurriedly recalled the ambassadors, who were on their way to Italy, carrying the Acts of that Council to Louis II; ordered, as soon as he was in power, a search to be made in the Patriarch's palace,[1] and confiscated the copy of the Acts found among the Patriarch's papers, a document it was wise to secure before it could be used against him.

Similar motives may have prompted Basil to inform the Pope at the earliest possible date of the recent change in Byzantium and to despatch the spathar Euthymios to Rome with a letter. As the envoy did not arrive till the beginning of the summer of 868, the Pope's reply to this letter being dated August of the same year, Euthymios cannot have left Byzantium till the spring of 868, at the opening of sea traffic. Basil, however, summarized the facts in his second letter to the Pope; it is preserved in the Acts of the Eighth Council.[2]

When Theognostos got to know of its contents, he had every reason to rejoice, for the very terms used by the Emperor made it evident that the Extremists had gained the upper hand in Byzantium. Theognostos could hardly have expected such a sudden and complete turn, and all those in Rome who had trembled for the future of Nicholas' work breathed a sigh of relief. The news brought to Rome by Euthymios created the same sensation as Boris' embassy in 866: the 'Nicholaites' had scored; the great Pope's Oriental policy had been marvellously justified by the Byzantines themselves. And there was none left in Rome to criticize it. Whatever, then, Nicholas had said or written about Photius must be absolutely true, since here was the Emperor himself to confirm it. None in Rome, of course, knew anything about the conflict between the two political currents, and Theognostos was not going to enlighten the Romans in the matter; so the sudden change was soon explained à la romaine and the whole of Nicholas' work benefited by the explanation. This circumstance probably stiffened Hadrian's deter-

[1] Nicetas, Vita Ignatii, *P.G.* vol. 105, col. 540.
[2] Mansi, vol. XVI, cols. 46, 47.

mination to pursue in all things and as far as possible his predecessor's policy,[1] thus leaving Anastasius henceforth to sleep more peacefully. The *émigré* Theognostos in one day rose to celebrity for the important services he would be able to render in Byzantium in the interests of the Papacy.

The Pope immediately made a call on his services and sent Theognostos to Constantinople with the ambassador. They carried two letters.[2] The missive to Basil expressed the Pope's deep satisfaction on hearing that the Emperor had decided to carry out Nicholas' verdict in the two cases of Ignatius and Photius; also, his hope that Basil would bring the incident to a satisfactory conclusion; and ended by warmly recommending Theognostos. This recommendation is couched in warmer terms still in the letter to Ignatius, who is asked to send Theognostos back to Rome with the apocrisiaries. But the Pope is surprised that the Patriarch should not have notified his advent to the throne sooner. However, he will never diverge from what Nicholas of blessed memory has decided against Photius and in favour of Ignatius.

Euthymios and Theognostos, who should have reached Constantinople before winter, apparently were not there by 11 December, the day the Emperor sent a second letter to the Pope, telling him of his fears concerning his first ambassador, and wondering if his letter had reached the Pope, as the writer had been waiting in vain for a reply. The letter does not, however, indicate the year of its dispatch, though it was later given the date of 11 December 867.[3] But this date is in no way admissible, for, even if Basil had sent Euthymios to Rome by the end of September 867, there was no reason for him to be surprised at not getting an answer before 11 December of the same year. If the date 11 December must be kept, then it should belong to 868, not 867.

But there is one objection against this assumption. If sea traffic between Byzantium and Rome was closed in winter, the date indicated in the letter must be a mistake, unless it be assumed that the Emperor deliberately exposed his ambassadors, owing to the importance of their mission, to the dangers of a sea journey in winter. Some particulars seem to point that way. In his reply to this second embassy, Hadrian dwells with emphasis on the dangers which the ambassadors had had

[1] Lapôtre, 'Hadrien II et les Fausses Décrétales', in *Revue des Questions historiques* (1880), t. XXVII, pp. 383 seq.

[2] *M.G.H.* Ep. VI, pp. 747–50.

[3] Last, by F. Dölger, *Regesten der Kaiserurkunden* (München, 1924), vol. I, p. 58. The author omits to mention the letter committed by the Emperor to the care of Euthymios.

to face, dangers as bad as those St Paul ran on his travels.[1] These words
are only intelligible, if the journey was undertaken in winter. Even the
ship that carried Photius' delegates was wrecked, and Peter, bishop of
Sardes, drowned.[2] The sources relating the incident pointedly mention
that the ship Peter had chosen was brand-new, a sign that special pre-
cautions had been taken to minimize the risk the ambassadors were to
run on their sea-crossing. All this is easily explained, if the journey
took place at the season particularly dangerous for navigation, i.e. in
winter. It also appears that the delegation travelled overland to the
Adriatic coast to mitigate the danger; and the ship mentioned was
wrecked, according to Nicetas, in the Dalmatian Bay.

On the other hand, it would seem most unlikely that the voyage
should have lasted from December 867 till December 868. Moreover,
the delegation did not include Theognostos, who went to Constantinople with Basil's envoy Euthymios, a sure indication that the abbot
was not yet in Rome when the Emperor dictated his letter. That was
11 December 868. Be it also remembered that the Pope had asked
Ignatius to include Theognostos among the envoys.

If our surmise is correct, the imperial embassy reached Rome towards
the end of winter in 869, perhaps at the end of February or the beginning
of March. The composition of the embassy clearly revealed the Emperor's intentions: not only did he send his spathar Basil, but also a
representative of Ignatius—John of Silaeon—and one of Photius—
Peter of Sardes; in other words, Basil completely accepted the terms of
Nicholas, as laid down in his last letter to Michael, and remitted the
whole case to the Pope's court in Rome. He did not omit to point out
in his letter that he had carried out the Pope's wish expressed on the
same occasion and had restored Ignatius to his throne. The fate of the
Photian bishops is left entirely to the Pope's discretion: all that was
asked for was magnanimity in the verdict,[3] which a special pontifical
delegation should communicate to the Church of Constantinople. In
asking for the Pope's decision in the Photian bishops' case, Ignatius
specially recommends to his clemency Paul, archbishop of Caesarea in
Cappadocia, a repentant Photianist.

[1] *M.G.H.* Ep. VI, p. 758: 'Qui tanta, postquam illinc profecti sunt, offendicula,
ut didicimus, pertulerunt, ut nullum properantes pene periculorum, quae Paulus in
epistolis suis dinumerat, evasisse videantur. Quapropter dignis sunt vicissitudinibus
a tua pietate remunerandi, qui pro ecclesia Christi proque iniunctae sibi a majestate
tua legationis consummatione tot ac talia subire promptissime consenserunt.'
[2] Mansi, vol. XVI, col. 7; *Liber Pontificalis*, vol. II, p. 178; Nicetas, Vita Ignatii,
P.G. vol. 105, col. 544. [3] Mansi, vol. XVI, cols. 46, 47.

The *Liber Pontificalis*[1] gives us a detailed account of the reception given to the Greek embassy in the church of St Mary Major, where the ambassadors presented the Acts of the Council of 867 with expressions of horror at their contents and characteristically Greek gesticulations, the spathar Basil roundly accusing Photius of having forged the Emperor's signature at the foot of the Acts: Michael signed in a fit of drunkenness. The ambassadors were unable to ascertain whether Euthymios and Theognostos had reached Constantinople and it was feared that disaster had overtaken them. The Romans must have been surprised to learn that the ambassadors knew nothing about their fate.

It was thus not until early spring in 869 that details of the Eastern synod of 867 reached Rome, when fortunately the outgoing Patriarch's daring deed had lost its sting, since Constantinople had on its own initiative disowned and condemned it. One could therefore afford to be shocked in perfect comfort.

The Pope had the Acts examined by a commission of experts, but the imperial ambassadors urged Hadrian to expedite the examination and his own decision.[2] There was good reason for haste, as Basil was growing impatient at the pace of the negotiations, which had dragged on for eighteen months. Preparations for the Council in Constantinople had started before the ambassadors embarked for Rome and the delegates of the Patriarchates of Jerusalem and Antioch were waiting impatiently for the arrival of the Roman delegates.[3]

The synod at last took place in the first days of June,[4] as the Pope's letters, which the apocrisiaries had to take to Constantinople, bear the date 10 June 869. Bishop Peter, the counsel for the Photian party's defence, having perished on his way, there was no one to plead for the defendants, and though the Pope repeatedly urged the monk Methodius, the only survivor of Peter's party, to undertake Photius' defence, the monk, whether he felt unable to undertake the task, or because he knew the verdict to be a foregone conclusion, declined to do so. Then the Pope decided to continue the proceedings and to pronounce judgement without giving the defendants a hearing.

---

[1] Loc. cit. vol. II, pp. 178 seq.

[2] Stated by the Pope in his letter to Basil, *M.G.H.* Ep. VI, p. 758. In the same letter Hadrian explains the delay by the number of important items of business he had to settle before the convocation of the synod.

[3] Cf. their declaration at the first session of the Eighth Council (Mansi, vol. XVI, col. 25). The Roman legates failing to arrive, they wished to leave.

[4] Cf. Jaffé-Ewald, *Regesta*, p. 370. Lapôtre, 'Hadrien II et les Fausses Décrétales', loc. cit. p. 384.

The Acts of the Roman synod are to be found in the Acts of the Eighth Council, as they were read during the seventh session.[1] The allocution which the Pope addressed to the assembly bears out what has been said about Hadrian's irresolution in following his predecessor's policy in every detail, as the Pope made desperate efforts to make the Nicholaites, whose confidence had received an extra fillip from the new turn in Ignatius' case, forgive and forget his fumbling in the first days of his reign, by lavishing lengthy praise on Nicholas' achievements and charging Photius with having, by his challenge to Nicholas, personally challenged him (Hadrian), since Nicholas' policy was equally his.[2]

The Pope's allocution shows that Hadrian had completely veered round to the point of view of Theognostos and his associates, then still in Rome, in Ignatius' case. The Fathers' opinion was expressed by Gauderich of Velletri, whose proposals were adopted and improved upon by the Pope and read out by his spokesman, the deacon Marinus. Formosus then assured the Pope that the synod agreed to everything he would judge it necessary to decide. In the third allocution, which was read by the deacon Peter, Hadrian very severely took Photius to task for daring to judge a Pope: 'Romanum pontificem de omnium ecclesiarum praesulibus judicasse legimus, de eo vero quemquam judicasse non legimus.' When the synod had endorsed the condemnation and interceded for those bishops who had been misled by Photius, the Pope passed sentence:

Photius' conventicle must be put on a par with the Ephesus act of brigandage; his decrees are valueless; his Acts, as well as all the documents written by him and the Emperor Michael against the Church of Rome, must be burned; even the councils summoned by Photius against Ignatius are condemned. The third canon renewed in the most virulent terms the anathemas hurled by Nicholas against Photius; and should the 'intruding' Patriarch repent he will be admitted to lay communion only. The fourth canon was aimed at the signatories of the conventicle of 867, who were promised lay communion if they repented. Lastly, the fifth canon threatened with excommunication all those who

---

[1] Mansi, vol. XVI, cols. 122–31, 372–80.
[2] Cf. the passage quoted on p. 128. That is how I explain the Pope's words. Ch. J. Hefele (Hefele-Leclercq, *Histoire des Conciles*, IV, 1, p. 471) and Hergenröther (loc. cit. vol. II, p. 37) offer opinions on this passage that are unacceptable; for how could Photius have possibly spread rumours to the effect that Hadrian's opinions differed from his predecessor's? Photius could not know of Hadrian's election till the end of December 868, after the arrival of Euthymios and Theognostos; and who else could have reported such rumours to the Pope?

should refuse to hand over the condemned writings. The synod was brought to an end with a solemn bonfire, when the Acts of the Council of 867, brought by the imperial ambassadors, were burned in front of the church of St Peter, where the synod had met, and the volumes burned so fiercely under pouring rain that all the onlookers pronounced it a miracle.[1]

In his letter to Ignatius, which the legates were to convey to Constantinople with copies of all the letters written by Nicholas on the Photian incident, the Pope, among other things, communicated the sentence passed against the defendants. Photius, Gregory of Syracuse and those who had been consecrated by the ex-Patriarch are deposed, with the sole exception of Paul of Caesarea; the clergy ordained by Ignatius, who subsequently followed Photius, may obtain pardon, if they sign the 'Libellus satisfactionis' which the legates will present to them; absolution for the signatories of the Acts of the Council of 867 is reserved to the Holy See; Ignatius is also called upon to justify himself against his enemies' accusation that he refused to receive the letter of Benedict III, by having the pontifical decrees signed by all the members of the Council shortly to be summoned in Constantinople; the Acts of the Roman synod are to be kept in the patriarchal archives.

In his letter to Basil, Hadrian repeats his decisions, with special emphasis on the fact that, owing to the Emperor's intervention, he had exercised special clemency in his judgement; the Emperor is requested to summon a great council to carry out the Pontiff's sentence under the presidentship of his legates; the Acts of Photius' conventicle must be solemnly burned there; lastly, the Emperor is asked to send back to Rome the Greek monks who with Photius had intrigued against Pope Nicholas in Constantinople; and the Pope concludes by recommending his legates, bishops Donatus and Stephen and Deacon Marinus, to Basil's favour.

In comparing the contents of the letters from Basil and Ignatius to Hadrian with the decisions of the synod of St Peter's, and the Pope's answers to those letters, one notes that the Pope had gone far beyond the Emperor's intentions. Basil had naturally wished to comply with Nicholas' desire to reserve to himself the final verdict in the case, in the presence of the two parties in Rome, believing that this was the best way to curry favour with Rome and to screen his murder behind the authority of the supreme See. He needed the support of this high moral patronage to strengthen his regime in Byzantium. But it was not in his

[1] *Liber Pontificalis*, vol. II, p. 179.

best interest to exasperate the Photianists by excessive severity and stiffen their opposition to the new conditions. Being clever enough to see that the ecclesiastical wing of the moderate or liberal party, which had identified itself with the Photian loyalists, was a power to conjure with, he only sought the Pope's assistance in bringing about an honourable liquidation of the whole business, the very reason why he so urgently insisted with the Pope on the exercise of clemency towards the Photianists. His ambassador must have been instructed in the same sense, for he actually tried to obtain a mitigation of the sentence against Ignatius' enemies.

In this respect, the Emperor's attempt proved a failure, and the Pope in no way made things easier for him. His sentence was stiff and far too severe. Evidently, the Pope failed to understand Basil's wishes in the matter; he only saw things in the light in which Nicholas had seen them, and took advantage of the Photian case to convince the Nicholaites, always ready to criticize some of his first acts, that he really was a faithful follower of his great predecessor.

On learning of Hadrian's decision, Basil must have regretted his ignorance of the change in the See of Rome at the moment he dictated his letters. If Euthymios had arrived from Rome sooner, if Basil had known of Nicholas' death, he would very probably have dealt with the new Pope differently, and as Hadrian was not so deeply committed in the case, he would have found it easier to induce the Pope to make concessions.

The discrepancy between Basil's intentions and the Pope's decisions came for the first time to the surface at the legates' audience at court. In his speech on that occasion, the Emperor wished the legates every success in their mission for the restoration of peace and unity in the Church of Constantinople in the spirit of Nicholas' decrees; and the legates replied that such indeed was their mission. They insisted, however, that they could admit no one to the synod, unless he first signed the 'Libellus' which they had brought from Rome and which had been drawn up after a formulary preserved in the Vatican archives. Amazed at this declaration, the Emperor and the Patriarch replied: *Quia novum hoc et inauditum de libello proferendo asseritis, necesse est ut tenoris illius formam videamus.*[1]

The 'Libellus' in question was a formula neither new nor unknown in the East, having been drawn up after Pope Hormisdas' *Regula Fidei,*[2]

---

[1] *Liber Pontificalis*, vol. II, pp. 180, 181.
[2] Mansi, vol. VIII, cols. 407, 408.

a document which the Eastern bishops had been asked to sign on their abjuration of Acacius' schism; only, it had been slightly enlarged by Hadrian's Chancellery, who, for the anathemas hurled at the heretics mentioned in the *Regula*, had substituted a long and vehement condemnation of Photius and his adherents, with, naturally, additional emphasis on the primacy of the Roman See.

Thus the 'Libellus', though its contents were not particularly objectionable, was not a document likely to be very welcome to the Byzantines. However, Basil accepted it; but what angered him was the way the 'Libellus' was forced on them and made a *sine qua non* condition for admission to the Council.

Under the circumstances, there was in fact no reason left for convoking a council, since judgement had already been passed. This did not square with the intentions of Basil, who would have liked the Council to try the case anew and the legates to give their verdict in the name of the Council and of the Pope. He had a feeling that the legates' procedure would only complicate matters and upset all his plans.

The Council opened on 5 October with fairly disheartening prospects. This time, the legates would hear of no compromise between their instructions and the Emperor's real intentions: the Pope's orders were to be carried out literally. But the legates must have been painfully surprised at the meagre attendance at the first session of only twelve bishops, prelates who had always remained faithful to Ignatius, a clear indication that Rome had been labouring under a misconception of the numerical and moral importance of the Ignatian party; and had the true position among the Byzantine clergy after 861 been better known, Rome would have modified her proceedings against the Photianists. The man really responsible for the misunderstanding was none other than Theognostos with his Extremist monks, then refugees in Rome.

Difficulties grew worse. The reading of the 'Libellus' at the first session, when the number of prelates consenting to sign the document was anything but imposing, seems to have created something of a sensation among the audience.[1] At the second session, only ten more bishops[2] came forward to sign; and at the third session, the metropolitans Theodoulos of Ancyra and Nicephorus of Nicaea, though seemingly not unfavourable to Ignatius, refused to sign, arguing that they had vowed never to sign any documents of that nature, because such signatures had

[1] Mansi, vol. XVI, col. 30: 'Et post completionem libelli *silentio facto*, surgens Bahanes...dixit....'   [2] Ibid. col. 41.

been so badly abused of late.[1] At the fourth session, thirty-six bishops came forward, with the addition of only one at each of the following sessions. At the ninth session, the number rose to sixty-six, and at the last to 103, no great achievement after all. Even Anastasius, the translator of the Acts, registered surprise.[2] There was no explaining away the fact by arguing that the prelates only dribbled in after the invitation to come, for we know that Basil had been long in preparing the Council and had certainly taken every precaution to secure an attendance. Nor should we forget that nearly two years had elapsed since Ignatius' reinstatement, leaving his supporters plenty of time to prepare the Council and to canvass for friends among the Photian clergy. They had apparently not been very successful in that quarter.

The true reasons for the failure can be read between the lines of Anastasius' report. They were the strength of the Photian party, the bishops' loyalty, and the wooden rigidity of the procedure in Council. For one thing, the clergy ordained by Photius had nothing to gain by transferring their allegiance to Ignatius, as all they were promised was lay communion, and those ordained by Methodius and Ignatius, who returned to the new Patriarch, were given long and fairly humiliating penances. One has but to imagine oneself in their place: they knew much more about the whole business than the apostolic delegates and the Roman See; they knew all its details, all the intrigues of the opposition party as well as the true motives behind the hatred it heaped on their leader; and they deeply resented the fact that the Roman See and its representatives, completely ignoring issues that had nothing to do with religion and ecclesiastical discipline, had straight away condemned their master and themselves, without even giving them a hearing. Under the circumstances, the See of Rome only stood to lose part of a prestige which they and their master had willingly acknowledged.

The legates were not aware of the dreadful dilemma into which they were driving the consciences of the majority of the Byzantine clergy, and in fear of the fate of Zachary and Radoald and wishing to carry out the Pope's orders literally, they refrained from a closer examination of the case. Obviously, things were far too complicated for anyone who had not followed them at close quarters and lived in the thick of them. In Rome, numerous facts, apparently beyond dispute, besides Basil's own approval, seemed to warrant and vindicate the sentence that had been pronounced, but what Roman of those days could have been familiar with all the intricacies of the case?

[1] Mansi, vol. XVI, col. 45. [2] Ibid. col. 190.

Even the Ignatians attending the Council seemed to be aware of this and took exception to the legates' procedure; for they must have felt the solidity of their opponents' position, and so realized that the clear-cut and categorical sentence passed by Rome in their favour could only recoil on their own position in the eyes of the Byzantine public. They were after all given nothing to do in the Council, since the issue had been decided in advance in Rome and all they were asked to do was to sign the decree, a treatment humiliating for the Byzantines, which could and did make people say that Constantinople had been enslaved by Rome. One can just imagine the lively commentaries on the first seven conciliar sessions of the month of October that set all the presbyteries agog in those long winter evenings. The 'Libellus' signed by the Ignatian bishops was evidence enough. It also makes one understand how at the end of the Council some prelates approached the Patriarch and the Emperor to represent to them that the 'Libellus' would survive as a standing token of the Byzantine Church's subjection to Rome, and why the Emperor attempted to seize the signed copies locked up in the legates' safe. Anastasius congratulated himself on inducing the Emperor to have the said documents, after being stolen by the legates' servants on Basil's own orders—so Anastasius avers—restored to them.[1]

Basil saw, of course, the difficulties in which Ignatius and his party had been placed, and, although unable to act in opposition to the Pope, whose judgement he had asked and obtained, he tried at least to minimize the deplorable impression such a peremptory prejudgement had produced in Byzantium. Attentive reading of the Acts of the Council reveals that Basil had planned more than one unpleasant surprise for the legates.

At the first session, Baanes, a high official, who presided over the conciliar debates, first called upon the legates, to their utter amazement, to present their credentials to the assembly. Here is their reply: 'So far we have never come upon the practice at General Councils for representatives of older Rome to be asked by anybody for their credentials.' ('Hoc nos usque nunc non invenimus in universali synodo factum, ut vicarii senioris Romae a quolibet perpendantur, utrum talem existimationem habeant.') Not until they had been assured that no offence against the honour of the Roman See had been intended did the legates cool down—a precaution to avoid a repetition of the story of Zachary and Radoald! At the same session, Baanes asked the Pope's representatives why Photius had been condemned without being given a hearing,[2]

[1] Loc. cit. col. 29.   [2] Loc. cit. col. 34.

whereupon the legates felt themselves obliged to give a lengthy answer and summarize the story of the embassies sent to Rome by Michael and Photius. Even representatives of the Eastern sees had to be called to order on the same issue.

Basil's intentions are not difficult to detect behind this procedure: the Emperor wished to give the assembly at least a semblance of an impartial court and expected the Pope's sentence to be pronounced again, after a minute examination. Having no wish to exasperate the Photianists, he persistently emphasized his readiness to find a compromise acceptable to all, as was made clear in the inaugural address which he sent to the Fathers and had read out by the secretary Theodore. The same was repeated in other addresses, for instance, at the sixth and seventh sessions.[1] At the fourth session, Baanes gave expression to the Emperor's wish in almost brutal terms: The Emperor will not sign the Acts, if Photius and his associates are refused a hearing.[2]

Hence it was that the Emperor ignored the Pope's order to have the Council presided over by his legates, a privilege the Emperor, as in other oecumenical councils, reserved to himself or to his representative, the Patrician Baanes, and forced the legates to accept. At the fourth session, the legates were asked to re-examine the case of the Photian bishops Theophilus and Zachary, a particularly unpalatable request, as the bishops soon confounded the legates by producing Marinus' evidence to the effect that the Pope had held communion with them in 860.[3] The Emperor also imposed on the legates the obligation of giving Photius and all the bishops who supported him a hearing (fifth, sixth and seventh sessions). Among all those who attended, the fourth session created a most awkward impression.

The legates, of course, upheld their own point of view as best they could, seizing every opportunity to insist that they had not come to

[1] Mansi, vol. XVI, cols. 18, 19, chiefly 93: 'Unum solum nobis desiderium, et ad praefatos iudices, postquam illos vidimus supplicatio fuit, ne quemquam permitterent deperire, vel ab ecclesia Dei quemquam si fieri potest projici...quos non proprie tantum, sed et communiter hodie, omnibus videntibus, deprecamur, manum iis qui compassione opus habent porrigere, et unam ecclesiam celebrantium festivitatem perficere.' Cf. also cols. 99, 100.

[2] Loc. cit. col. 55: 'Si vultis ergo a nobis...in fine sanctae et universalis huius synodi exigere proprias subscriptiones per me indignum servum sanctorum imperatorum nostrorum, cuncti fratres mei et compatricii dicunt sanctissimo domino nostro patriarchae et sanctissimis vicariis...nisi audierimus et ab ipso Photio in conspectu nostro stante, et ab episcopis eius...ut in conspectu obstruantur ora ipsorum ex canonicis et synodicis praeceptionibus, non scribet manus nostra litteram in synodo ista.' Cf. Vogt, Basile Ier (Paris, 1908), pp. 22 seq.

[3] Cf. Mansi, vol. XVI, cols. 77, 88, 97, 98, 100. See pp. 72 seq.

listen to the arguments of the ex-Patriarch and his associates, but to pronounce the sentence passed in advance in Rome by Nicholas and Hadrian.[1] Their words were plain and always the same: Do you acknowledge Rome's judgement? Will you sign the 'Libellus', yes or no? They interrupted Baanes and even Basil, as they cross-questioned Eulampius. At the seventh session, when the iconoclast Crithinos came up for trial, the legates asked, not for the reading of the decisions of the Seventh Council against the iconoclasts, but only for Nicholas' decree on images.

As matters stood, the Emperor's efforts were doomed to failure. Photius had, to the legates' exasperation, kept an unbroken and dignified silence. Zachary tried to plead for Photius and his cause at the sixth session, and Metrophanes replied, but when Zachary rose to answer Metrophanes, the legates cut him short: A truce to words and to procrastination! Submit, or else you will be committed to eternal fire and flames.[2]

After that, it need surprise no one that at the seventh session Photius and Asbestas should have urged the legates to do penance.[3] From their point of view, the legates' procedure was nothing but an exhibition of partiality and unfairness. The Photian bishops, who were quick in detecting the incompatibility between the Emperor's and the legates' standpoints, summed up the debates of the seventh session in these words: 'Quid volumus dicere? Si dixerimus justitias nostras, non fient.' By interrupting during the debate between these bishops and Baanes, the legates only provided their words with the corroboration they needed. They stopped the debate and ordered the reading of the whole dossier containing the sentence against Photius and its confirmation by Nicholas and Hadrian. In their opinion, the incident was closed, and there was no going back on the judgement. And that is how the trial of Photius and his followers was concluded. On his refusal to sign his own condemnation, Photius was, on a proposal by the legates, excommunicated.[4]

---

[1] Photius hit off the legates' state of mind in his letter to Theodosius (*P.G.* vol. 102, col. 893). There he quotes the legates as saying: ἡμεῖς οὔτε κρίνειν συνήλθομεν, οὔτε κρίνομεν ὑμᾶς· ἤδη γὰρ κατεκρίναμεν· καὶ δέον στέργειν τὴν κατάκρισιν…. This letter, the letter that precedes it in the Hergenröther-Migne edition and is addressed to the same person, Photius' letter to Michael the Protospathar and two letters to Michael of Mytilene, give a good idea of what Photius thought of the council summoned against him (loc. cit., cols. 889–92, 948, 860).

[2] Mansi, vol. XVI, cols. 87–92.   [3] Loc. cit. col. 98.

[4] Nicetas (loc. cit. col. 545) states that the bishops signed with pens dipped into Our Lord's Blood. This anecdote seemed 'too tall' even to Hergenröther, loc. cit. vol. II, p. 109.

The legates' intransigence in the literal execution of their mandate was equally conspicuous at the ninth session, when the officials guilty of deposing Ignatius at the Council of 861 came up for trial.[1] As only thirteen out of seventy-two State functionaries concerned answered the summons, the legates insisted that the other officials should also be put on trial, when Baanes interposed with the request that Ignatius should be given power to absolve them, whenever they should apply for absolution. The protocol of this session made it abundantly clear that the government had no wish to go to extremes, for fear of exasperating the State service and of swelling the ranks of the opposition. It should be added that Ignatius understood and promptly rallied to the proposal.

Strangely enough, the legates even failed to carry their point with the Fathers in a matter that interested them most. As they tried to gain their point in every detail of the decisions of Nicholas and Hadrian, the Fathers just yielded to their claims as far as these tallied with their own point of view, but they refused to vote for a canon designed to stress those two Popes' ideas on the primacy. There is, in the speeches, a startling repetition of the doctrine on the pentarchy, i.e. the five Patriarchs' rule over the Universal Church;[2] and the definitions voted by the assembly show a certain tendency to place the five Patriarchs on the same footing, or at least to hold them as equally important.[3] Even canon XXI, which condemned Photius' indictment of Nicholas, was certainly not worded after the legates' wishes, for the Fathers contrived to insert after the Pope's name the names of the other Patriarchs, which undoubtedly emasculated the canon for the purposes of the Holy See. The insertion is not so alarming as it looks at first sight, but it has its importance.[4]

---

[1] Loc. cit. cols. 150 seq.

[2] Cf. the discourse by Elias of Jerusalem, Mansi, vol. XVI, cols. 82, 341, of Metrophanes of Smyrna, ibid. cols. 82, 344; of Basil, ibid. cols. 86–9, 95, 356; of Baanes, ibid. cols. 99, 360, 140, 141; also, what Hergenröther (loc. cit. vol. II, pp. 132–49) says on this doctrine from a theological point of view. We may also quote, for instance, Baanes' declaration made at the eighth session (loc. cit. col. 140), which sounds very characteristic: 'Posuit Deus ecclesiam suam in quinque patriarchiis, et definivit in evangeliis suis, ut numquam aliquando penitus decidat, eo quod capita ecclesiae sint: etenim illud quod Christus: Et portae inferi non praevalebunt adversus eam...hoc demonstrat....'

[3] Chiefly canon XVII. Cf. also canons XVIII, XIX, XX. Vide Hergenröther, loc. cit. vol. II, p. 139.

[4] A similar tendency is shown in the writings of the Greek summarist of the Acts, who also belonged to the Ignatians' extreme wing. In summing up the *Libellus*, he omits whatever in the original Latin is too glaringly in favour of the Roman primacy; also, the scriptural argument (Matt. xvi. 16–17) in favour of the same (Mansi, vol. XVI, col. 316). Cf. Hergenröther, loc. cit. vol. II, pp. 64–8 on other

What is the explanation of such undisguised resistance? One might be tempted to say that in putting such stress on the orders received from Rome and in opposing on principle any new investigation of the trial, the legates had given offence to the Fathers, who instinctively retaliated by taking exception to the Roman thesis for its being presented, to their way of thinking, in a manner too blunt for their consumption.[1] One feels somewhat embarrassed in comparing the results secured in Constantinople by Radoald and Zachary in 861 with those registered by the legates in 869–70, for the declarations by the Fathers of the Council of 861 are far more pro-Roman than those made in the Ignatian Council. It only goes to prove that, with a spirit of conciliation and a better regard for the feelings of the Byzantine Church, it was possible to obtain far more from the Greeks than by peremptorily laying down the law.[2]

At the very moment when the legates saw success within their grasp, another defeat awaited them, for a Bulgarian embassy reached Constantinople in February, just in time to attend the last session of the

abbreviations less pertinent to our subject; also, what he says about the two versions of the canons that were voted (pp. 68 seq.). I shall presently, pp. 271 seq., discuss the author of the summary.

[1] Animosity against the West was so bitter in Byzantium that even Louis II's embassy had to bear the brunt of it, and the ambassadors feared for their own safety. Cf. on this matter *M.G.H. Ss.* vol. III, p. 526.

[2] Hergenröther, loc. cit. vol. II, pp. 47–63, dwells at length on Photius' recognition by the Eastern Patriarchs and on their representatives at the Ignatian Council. Those representing the patriarchates of Antioch, Alexandria and Jerusalem may have been armed with the full necessary powers. As to their assertion that their respective Churches had never recognized Photius, that is another question altogether. The letters of the Patriarch of Jerusalem, Theodosius, and of the Patriarch of Alexandria, Michael, say nothing about Photius (Mansi, vol. XVI, cols. 25–7, 145–7), these Patriarchs being unaware of what had happened in Constantinople. How then could they possibly have refused Photius their recognition? As the latter had been in correspondence with the titular of the See of Antioch, Eustathios (*P.G.* vol. 102, cols. 821–3), and had sent his enthronement letter to all the Patriarchs, there was no reason why they should have refused to acknowledge him; and as their living depended on the Byzantine Emperors' favour, such a refusal was not within their power. The same motive influenced the representatives of Jerusalem and Antioch at the synod of 869 and prompted them to say what they knew would please Basil. Moreover, when they realized the true position, they drew up the letter (Mansi, vol. XVI, cols. 30–3) anent the incident, which condemned Photius, in Constantinople. With regard to the representatives of the same patriarchates, who attended the Council of 867 and were tried during the eighth session of the Ignatian Council, one gathers the impression that this Council was not dealing with the same persons as were in Constantinople in 867. What the imperialists had to say about this council should be treated with caution, as it was in Basil's interest not to make too much of what happened at this synod. It was as easy for Michael to provide himself with representatives of those patriarchates in 867 as it was for Basil in 869. Neither Michael nor Photius had therefore any real need to resort to fraud.

Council[1] in its official capacity. Its arrival on such an occasion was the crowning achievement of Byzantine diplomacy in Bulgaria, for the ambassadors had come to ask the Council for a decision upon which patriarchate their country belonged to. We know that Boris was a very scrupulous man—at least in certain matters—who loved to make a show of his anxiety to keep clear of every possible ecclesiastical transgression. This step, however, was taken not only to relieve the conscience of a good Christian, but because Boris was angry with Rome for refusing to pander to his fads and give him an archbishop of his own choice.[2]

A passage in the *Liber Pontificalis*,[3] where we find a detailed account of the incident, may also hint at some family difficulties which worried Boris at the time and were possibly due to his son Vladimir. In fact, when Boris handed over the government to Vladimir and retired, Vladimir inaugurated a pagan revival and had to be replaced by Simeon. It is possible, even likely, that Boris was afraid of Byzantium taking advantage of his son's ambition, to overthrow him. At any rate, the Byzantines missed no opportunity to sever Boris from Rome. Here again, one realizes how thoughtless was Photius' move against Nicholas, after the latter had ousted the Greeks from Bulgaria; it was a time when not everything was lost, and Photius had but to watch his chance and let the imperial agents do their work. It is also possible that Boris' move had been planned by Photius and Michael in good time and that the decisions of the Council of 867 against the Latin missionaries had, after all, made some impression on the scrupulous and astute Khagan.

The Byzantines knew how to strike while the iron was hot: a conference was immediately summoned, in which the representatives of all the patriarchates, including the Bulgarian envoys, took part under the chairmanship of the Emperor, to discuss this important item of business. Anastasius[4] has recorded this meeting in detail, though he had not been invited to attend it, a slight for which he never forgave

---

[1] Mansi, vol. XVI, col. 158.

[2] Cf. my book, *Les Slaves, Byzance et Rome au IXe siècle*, pp. 193 seq.

[3] P. 185: 'Vulgarorum rex expectationum moras diutius ferre non valens, quanta esse quam a Graecorum imperatore, quoniam natorum thororum [suorum?] occasione alterna regna sibi alternatim rapere machinabantur abductus, eundem Petrum quem a Roma sine desiderii sui effectu sero receperat, cum aliis e latere suo Constantinopolim...emisit....' The passage is very faulty. Cf. L. Duchesne, ibid. p. 190: 'The biographer apparently meant that this prince, impatient of all these delays, threatened with a family feud, deemed it inadvisable to make an enemy of the Greek Emperor, by resisting his demands.'

[4] *Liber Pontificalis*, vol. II, pp. 182–5; Mansi, vol. XVI, cols. 10–13.

Basil. The legates vehemently protested against the procedure, arguing that the Council had been closed and that they had no mandate to discuss such matters. To their great chagrin, they were not invited to the discussions; the issue had to be decided at one sitting and the representatives of the Eastern Patriarchs were to arbitrate in the matter.

The enormity of it did not escape the legates. They had seen in the course of the Council how subservient to the imperial will those same representatives had always been, and they were glad at the time, as it served their own interests; but in this case, they had a good idea of what those legates would decide under the circumstances. Basil had set his trap with care. But what irritated the legates more than anything was that the Greeks and the Orientals should presume to pontificate in a business that concerned only the Holy See, against the very principles which Hadrian had formulated and which they were commissioned to uphold in Constantinople. No wonder they exclaimed with some heat: 'The Holy Apostolic See has not chosen you to sit in judgement over it, because you are its subjects, nor has it commissioned us, since the whole Church is under its sole jurisdiction.'

In vain did they protest: the Oriental legates decided that Bulgaria belonged to the Byzantine patriarchate.[1] It was then that the Roman representatives produced a letter from Pope Hadrian, in which he forbade Ignatius to attempt anything in Bulgaria against Rome. Ignatius did not even trouble to read it.[2]

On this letter the *Liber Pontificalis* is intensely interesting. The document has been lost; and as in the other letters, which the legates had brought to Constantinople, there is no reference to the Bulgarian

[1] The decision was not as unfair to Rome as the legates pretended. Canonically, the Byzantine claim was legitimate, since Bulgaria included only a small portion of Macedonia which had been under Roman jurisdiction, and included a great part of Thrace which had always been under the jurisdiction of Constantinople.

[2] *Liber Pontificalis*, vol. II, p. 184: '...teque reum, patriarcham Ignatium, auctoritate sanctorum apostolorum principum, coram Deo suisque angelis omnibusque presentibus contestamur, ut secundum hanc epistolam sanctissimi restitutoris tui domini Hadriani summi pontificis, quam tibi ecce offerimus, industria tua ab omni Vulgariae ordinatione immune nullum tuorum illuc mittendo custodias; ne sancta sedes apostolica, quae tibi tua restituit, per te sua perdere videatur. Quin potius si, quod non credimus, iustam te habere querimoniam estimas, sanctae Romanae ecclesiae restitutrici tuae solemniter suggerere non omittas. Tunc patriarcha Ignatius apostolicam epistolam suscipiens, licet magnopere monitus eam legere distulisse respondit: Absit a me ut ego his praesentibus contra decorem sedis apostolicae implicer, qui nec ita iuveniliter ago ut mihi subripi valeat, nec ita seniliter deliro, ut quod in aliis reprehendere debeo ipse admittam. Hoc fine locutio ista finita est.'

affair, it must be supposed that the Pope had written another letter in which he forbade Ignatius to trespass on Bulgaria, and which the legates were not to produce, unless the interests of the Roman See in Bulgaria should be in peril.

The *Liber Pontificalis* also gives in the same place some interesting particulars on the way the Latin missionaries were ousted from Bulgaria. Boris took things very seriously, and only wished piously to carry out the decisions of a very holy oecumenical council; he thereupon invited the Latin priests to quit his territory. And yet, Boris had been exceedingly generous to Grimoald, the leader of the Roman mission, for Anastasius, the writer of this portion of the *Liber Pontificalis*, saw the bishop arrive in Rome. 'Romam ditissimus remeavit', he writes about him with ill-disguised envy and regret, never having had such good fortune himself. His feelings happened to be shared by other confederates of his, so much so that Grimoald was suspected of having been too lenient to Boris. Possibly, the bishop of Bomarzo, seeing that his mission was a complete failure as far as Rome was concerned, chose at least to make a profit out of it for his personal benefit. It would of course have been absurd to pose as a hero, and to be unceremoniously pushed over the frontier by the Bulgarian police.

Grimoald may have arrived in Rome before the legates, who had been captured by the Narentine pirates and set free only in December 870; and Anastasius, who must have been in Rome at the beginning of the summer of the same year,[1] may have seen them arrive. The Pope duly protested against the violation of his rights in a letter written in November 871, and asked the Emperor to order Ignatius to recall from Bulgaria the bishops he had sent there.[2]

But this letter to the Emperor appears to have been preceded by another addressed to Ignatius, for we find in the anti-Photian Collection, as an addition to the Greek summary of the Acts of the Eighth Council, a fragment of a letter from Hadrian to the Patriarch.[3] In this fragment, the Pope refers to a letter from Ignatius: 'You wrote to us', he writes, 'that our priests were ignominiously and shamefully expelled from Bulgarian territory and how even the bishops were dismissed in disgrace....' All this, the Pope continues, happened without the Roman See being consulted.

If you object that we ourselves had previously forbidden priests of the diocese of Constantinople to celebrate the liturgy in the above-mentioned

---

[1] Cf. my book, *Les Légendes de Constantin et de Méthode*, p. 269.
[2] *M.G.H.* Ep. VI, p. 760.   [3] Mansi, vol. XVI, col. 413; *M.G.H.* Ep. VI, p. 762.

territory, we are not going to deny it; for they were in communion with Photius and were priests of his ordination. These we forbade to exercise any priestly functions and still do so, not only on Bulgarian territory, but throughout the Church. Knowing this, you should not have interfered in Bulgaria.

The Pope then adds that, on information, Ignatius committed other breaches of ecclesiastical law; for instance, he raised some laymen to the diaconate without the canonical intervals, a thing forbidden even by the last Council, as it was by such transgressions that Photius had set out on the road of injustice.

This letter is all that remains of the correspondence exchanged between the Pope and the Patriarch after the Council on Bulgaria. On hearing from Grimoald, Anastasius and the legates what had happened in Bulgaria and Constantinople, Hadrian must have addressed a letter to Ignatius, severely rebuking him for what he had done, to which Ignatius replied that not he but the Emperor was responsible. Besides, Rome had done the same by expelling Greek priests from Bulgaria. The fragment above mentioned is an extract from the letter by Hadrian in reply to Ignatius.

We are thus able also to explain why the Pope wrote to the Emperor on this matter so late. The letter to Basil previously mentioned was meant to put pressure on Ignatius, but proved to be a failure, for the Emperor was evidently keener than the Patriarch on the Greek priests staying in Bulgaria.

To return now to the letter which the legates handed to the Patriarch after the representatives of the Eastern Patriarchs had voted against the Roman interests in Bulgaria, we must examine whether our explanation was exact. This is important, because if we are right, Ignatius' recognition by Hadrian was conditional on his behaviour in Bulgaria. Luckily some letters written by Hadrian's successor, John VIII, give us more detailed information.

Among the remnants of John VIII's register preserved by the *Britannica* we find an extract from a letter of John to Boris, which was dispatched between December 872 and May 873:[1]

If Greek perfidy does not refrain from trespassing on your territory, which naturally belongs to our diocese, as ancient documents testify, know that we shall once more punish the Patriarch Ignatius, who recovered his throne by

---

[1] *M.G.H.* Ep. VII, p. 277.

our favour, with anathema and deposition for temerity and defiance. As regards the Greek bishops and priests who are there, we shall not only depose, but excommunicate them, as most of them are said to be of Photius' ordination, his associates and followers....

In a letter, dated about the same period, to Domagoï, a Croat prince, John VIII writes that Ignatius had already been several times excommunicated owing to his encroachments on Bulgaria:[1]

We remind you how, acting through the person of Ignatius, the perfidious Greeks did not fear to take possession of the country of the Bulgarians, who belong to our jurisdiction and are now again under our authority. Repeatedly excommunicated, Ignatius not only did not desist, but even sent there some schismatic with the title of archbishop.

More important for our investigation is the letter dispatched by John VIII to Michael-Boris towards the end of 874 or at the beginning of 875, in which, after reminding Michael that the Church of Rome was founded by Christ on the rock of Peter and that therefore the decisions of that Church were the decisions of the Founder, the Pope exclaims:[2]

Ignatius was absolved by our predecessors on this condition that should he ever violate apostolic rights in connection with Bulgaria, which not even Photius ever attempted to do, he would despite his acquittal remain under sentence of his previous condemnation none the less. Therefore, he either stands acquitted if he respects the rights of the Apostolic See, or if he does not, he falls back under the previous ban.

The implication of this letter is that Pope Hadrian had acknowledged Ignatius as the legitimate Patriarch on condition that he should undertake nothing contrary to Roman interests in Bulgaria; that, should he be daring enough to do so, he would be severed from communion with Rome, and therefore be excommunicated. In no other sense could these words of John VIII be explained. We therefore have here indisputable evidence that the Bulgarian issue played a leading part in all dealings with Photius by Nicholas, since his successor makes his recognition of Ignatius conditional on the latter's attitude towards Roman interests in Bulgaria. This condition was laid down in the letter which the legates handed to Ignatius at the time of the conference that met after the Ignatian Council to settle Bulgaria's fate; and the legates were

[1] *M.G.H.* Ep. VII, p. 278. [2] Ibid. p. 294.

not to produce the letter except in the urgent case of Roman interests being actually at stake.

This helps us to explain the enigmatic passage in the Pope's letter to Domagoï, referring to Ignatius as having been repeatedly excommunicated as a result of these offences. If Ignatius' recognition by Hadrian had been made to depend on his attitude towards Bulgaria, and if the Patriarch had been threatened with excommunication if ever he dared to trespass on Roman rights in Bulgaria, then John could treat Ignatius as excommunicated, as soon as it became clear that Ignatius had failed to observe the condition.[1]

Yet, on the other hand, because John VIII did not wish to close the door upon a possible settlement, he put off passing public sentence on Ignatius as long as there remained the least hope of the Patriarch acknowledging his fault. He must therefore have twice appealed to him before the last summons, the only one attested by a papal letter. It is worded in very resolute terms: Ignatius will be excommunicated, if he does not recall the Greek priests from Bulgaria within thirty days.[2] In another letter to the Greek clergy of the same country, the Pope confirmed the sentence of excommunication once pronounced against them by Hadrian.[3] But should the bishops and priests not quit Bulgarian territory within a month, they would all be suspended and excommunicated.

The sorry experience which Hadrian's successor, John VIII, had with

[1] Regarding the identity of the bishop consecrated by Ignatius for Bulgaria, consult the penetrating study by H. Grégoire, 'Une Inscription datée au Nom du Roi Boris-Michel de Bulgarie', in *Byzantion* (1939), vol. XIV, pp. 227–34, in which he published an important inscription of Cerven (near Roustchouk) which he discovered in the Sofia Museum. The inscription is of 5 October 870. It mentions not only Boris-Michael, by giving him the Byzantinized title τοῦ εὐκλειοῦς καὶ φιλοχρίστου ἄρχοντος, but also a bishop of Bulgaria, Nicholas, probably the first bishop of that country. Unfortunately, we know nothing definite about the number of bishops sent to Bulgaria by Ignatius.

[2] *M.G.H.* Ep. VII, pp. 62, 63: 'secundo iam sedis apostolicae litteris probaris admonitus et per missos eius contestatoriis conventus hortatibus.... Unde merito post primam et secundam comminitionem a nostrae te debueramus communionis contubernio sequestrare...sed quia sedis apostolicae moderatione utentes spiritu lenitatis...ecce tertio canonice per missos et syllabas commonemus et hortamur et protestamur.' Among the extracts from the register of John VIII is found a fragment of a letter from John VIII to the Emperor (ibid. p. 296), in which the Pope complains of Ignatius' encroachment in Bulgaria, and states that he had summoned Ignatius to Rome to justify himself against the charges. This letter has been lost. It all shows that not all the correspondence between John VIII and Ignatius has come down to us.

[3] Ibid. pp. 66 seq.

Ignatius completed the failure of the pontifical mission to Constantinople in 869–70. They scored a victory, it is true, but only a Pyrrhic victory. They were able to present the Pope with the 'Libelli' signed by a hundred or more bishops; it had cost them and Anastasius much trouble to preserve these, and whatever else they carried with them had been seized by the Narentine pirates; but they escaped with their lives and their belated and inglorious entry into Rome faithfully symbolized the advantage they claimed to have secured in Constantinople.

CHAPTER VI

PHOTIUS' REHABILITATION AND THE SYNOD OF
879–80

Ignatius' difficulties—Basil's change of policy and his reconciliation with the Moderates and Photius—Ignatius and Photius on friendly terms—John VIII, Basil and Photius—Papal letters analysed—*Pourparlers* with the legates in Byzantium—The 'Greek edition' of the pontifical letters—The first five sessions of the Council—Authenticity of the sixth and seventh sessions—John VIII's alleged letter on the *Filioque*—The legates and the primacy.

BUT this was not all by any means. The judgement against Photius and the clergy, so solemnly delivered by the legates and the Council, could not be upheld for very long. The Ignatian Council had in no way eased the tension in Byzantium, for the Photian clergy remained loyal to their leader and left Ignatius to face the very difficult problem of providing for the spiritual needs of the faithful. Difficulties must have been so overwhelming, that the Emperor considered it necessary once again to apply to the Pope for a certain mitigation of the sentence passed on the Photian clergy. In a letter, dispatched towards the middle of 871 and transmitted by Theognostos,[1] Basil asked the Pope in Ignatius' name for a dispensation in favour of the chartophylax Paul and bishop Theodore, whose services were particularly valuable. Later he again applied for more lenient treatment in favour of the many Readers ordained by Photius and his bishops, a similar request being addressed to the Pope by Ignatius.

The choice of Theognostos for this embassy made it evident enough that both the Emperor and the Patriarch were keen on a more satisfactory solution of the whole business; but though Theognostos did everything in his power—Hadrian himself vouched for it[2]—to induce the Pope to come to terms, Hadrian, in a letter dated 10 November 871, refused to go back on Nicholas' decisions and his own. It is safe to say that Ignatius' attitude in the Bulgarian imbroglio had something to do with the Pope's point-blank refusal, but nothing is heard again of a second attempt on the part of the Emperor and the Patriarch. We unfortunately possess no definite information on the way the Gordian knot was cut in Byzantium, but a compromise was apparently reached, though not on the lines of the Ignatian Council's decisions.

---

[1] Mansi, vol. XVI, cols. 203, 204.   [2] *M.G.H.* Ep. VI, p. 761.

In fact, Hadrian soon expressed surprise that Ignatius should fail to observe the prescriptions of his own Council by abruptly raising laymen to ecclesiastical honours;[1] which only shows that Ignatius was merely trying his utmost to find a sufficient number of ecclesiastics to meet the needs of public worship; he was, in fact, very much in the position in which Methodius once found himself and getting out of it as best he could.

But John VIII had worse to lay to Ignatius' charge. In a letter to Boris, written between December 872 and May 873,[2] John VIII alleges that the Greek clergy sent to Bulgaria by Ignatius were most of them, as rumour had it, of the Photian ordination, a startling statement for the Pope to make, as we know that these clergy had been suspended by the decisions of Nicholas, Hadrian and the Ignatian Council. Was the Pope's information correct?

It seems, on the face of it, very unlikely; but a letter from Photius, probably written in the first days of his exile, shows that a certain collaboration between the Photian clergy and Ignatius in the Bulgarian incident had really taken place. Addressing his loyal friend, the monk Arsenius,[3] Photius expresses satisfaction that the young Bulgars who desired to join monastic life had been confided to his care. Be it noted incidentally that Ignatius admitted the validity of Photius' ordinations, since he asked the Pope for dispensations in favour of some priests who had been ordained by the ex-Patriarch.

In this connection, it is significant that Ignatius did not share the radical opinions of Photius' bitterest enemies, who treated the Patriarch as a layman and considered his ordinations as null and void: in this case, it would not have been impossible for Ignatius to let a portion of that clergy work in Bulgaria. Bulgarian needs were urgent, and where was Ignatius to find priests in sufficient numbers to meet all the requirements? As the Bulgarian mission was of the utmost importance to both Church and State, it was the Photian clergy's duty to support Ignatius in this particular work. Nor should we forget that the very first Greek missionaries to work in Bulgaria actually were priests ordained by Photius, and pastoral wisdom prompted the use in this enterprise of men who knew the work and were acquainted with the Bulgars.[4]

[1] *M.G.H.* Ep. VI, p. 762.   [2] See pp. 155 seq.
[3] *P.G.* vol. 102, cols. 904, 905.
[4] John VIII, in his letter addressed to Basil in 874 or 875 (*M.G.H.* Ep. VII, p. 296), also blames Patriarch Ignatius for transgressions other than that of sending Greek clergy to Bulgaria. Maybe he is referring to his negligence in carrying out the decisions of the Ignatian Council in the matter of the Photian clergy.

If all this information proves correct, we find here new evidence of the pontifical legates' failure at the Ignatian Council and of the miscarriage of Pope Hadrian's Oriental policy. The Pope's, and chiefly the legates' wooden methods in Constantinople exasperated not only the Emperor but even the Patriarch and the more reasonable of his friends.

We can now examine how the last traces of the legates' 'achievement' were obliterated and how Photius was reconciled with Basil and Ignatius. The successive stages of this development can easily be followed in the exile's correspondence. Photius had been fairly harshly treated, at least in the first days of his banishment, for in his letter to the Emperor he details a long catalogue of sufferings he underwent in his retreat. But what he felt most was the loss of his library.[1] In another letter to Arsenius, Photius bitterly complains that there is no longer any justice in this world.[2] But, he goes on, Arsenius must not despair, despite the trials that beset them, for it is Providence who sends us sufferings.[3] The letter is exceptionally touching for its beautiful thoughts on suffering and trust in Providence, Photius concluding by urging his correspondent frequently to invoke the Blessed Virgin, who understands their tragedy, is full of compassion and will know how to relieve their burden. The letters to the exiled bishops also contain an eloquent passage on suffering.[4]

Some other letters by the ex-Patriarch throw light on some of the material difficulties that worried the deposed bishops, and Photius recounts them in his letter to the spathar Nicetas. Left without any resources, the bishops had to borrow money from usurers, live on their friends' bounty, and for the rest submit to extreme want. Photius recommends to his correspondent the metropolitans of Cyzicus and Laodicea, whose needs were particularly urgent;[5] John of Heraclea, Euschemon of Caesarea, George of Nicomedia and Michael of Mytilene were also the objects of exceptionally harsh treatment;[6] and the Patrician John is requested to help a friend of Photius whose life is in danger.[7]

---

[1] *P.G.* vol. 102, cols. 765–72.   [2] Loc. cit. col. 901.

[3] Loc. cit. cols. 897–900.

[4] Loc. cit. cols. 764, 765. Cf. 'Ad Amphilochium', qu. 172, *P.G.* vol. 101, cols. 869–73, a fine passage on Providence and suffering.

[5] Loc. cit. cols. 981, 984.   [6] Loc. cit. cols. 821, 836, 860, 861.

[7] Loc. cit. col. 961. Cf. what Hergenröther, loc. cit. vol. II, pp. 207–28, 241–58, has to say about the correspondence of Photius in exile. Even he has to confess that pages of exceptional beauty and words from the heart are to be found in this correspondence.

Photius' correspondence shows that the ex-Patriarch had kept a host of friends among the higher officials, who had succeeded in keeping in office under the new government, the danger of 'apostasy' in these circles naturally being greater, as material considerations tempted many functionaries to join the party actually in power. In several letters, Photius endeavours to stimulate the loyalty of his lay friends.[1]

The clergy, with few exceptions, remained loyal to Photius, which made it appropriate to speak of two Churches within the Empire, as in some places the Photian bishops had remained at their posts. In his letter to the monk Arsenius, Photius speaks of a schism within the Church;[2] and to the exiled bishops, of 'his Church'.[3] Gregory Asbestas is urged to go on organizing the Church; he must ordain new ministers for the altar, open new churches and administer the sacraments;[4] Photius continues to rule his Church, answers questions put by his followers and distributes advice. The monks, faithful to Photius, continue to recognize him as Patriarch and ask for counsel. The Metropolitan Zachary of Antioch in Pisidia asks Photius how to carry out the decrees regarding the length of the novitiate and Photius in reply mentions persecution as sufficient ground for relaxing some prescriptions: the bishop must follow his conscience.[5]

One realizes how the position must have embarrassed the Emperor: it was not what he had intended. The Roman See's assistance which he had deemed indispensable to prop up his regime had not come up to expectation, since the legates had refused every compromise. It also appears that Basil did not get such a warm reception from the army, which remembered the victories won over the Arabs by Bardas and Michael too well to idolize their murderer. This would explain Basil's negotiations with the Emir of Syria and the encomiums lavished on the pacific regime inaugurated by Basil in the propaganda writings on the new reign. Not being quite sure of the bulk of the army, Basil could not afford to run any risks in military adventures.

The complete failure of the pacification of the Byzantine Church seriously aggravated the position, and the radicalism of the die-hards

---

[1] Cf. letters to the stratege of Hellas, the Patrician Michael, the Logothete Leo, the spathar John, who all had prevaricated, and to the lawyer Constantine (loc. cit. cols. 944, 949, 941, 933, 935, 945, 960, 961).

[2] Loc. cit. col. 900.

[3] Loc. cit. cols. 757 seq.   [4] Loc. cit. cols. 832, 833.

[5] Loc. cit. cols. 841-5. Cf. Hergenröther, loc. cit. pp. 207 seq. on the organization of the Photian Church.

of the reactionary party must have seemed ill-advised and dangerous, whereas the Photian clergy's steadfastness revealed the Moderate party's enormous strength.

It was going to be extremely difficult to govern, if this party persisted in its opposition. But Photius had from the first adopted an extremely shrewd policy, when he and his bishops seized every opportunity to pledge their loyalty to the Emperor, making it difficult for Basil to deal severely with the bulk of a clergy that was friendly to the dynasty and would never dream of overthrowing the new regime. In this the Moderates were wise not to imitate the tactics of their rivals, when they were turned out of office by Bardas and Michael.

The manœuvre was to be completely successful. In reply to Photius' letter, written in exile, Basil ameliorated the ex-Patriarch's treatment, as attested by a second letter from Photius to the Emperor.[1] The concession was exploited by Basil's agents who jumped to the conclusion that Photius was ready to come to a compromise with the opposite party, no doubt to its benefit, as appears from a letter from Photius to Gregory, deacon and chartophylax of Amasia,[2] for he mentions there idle rumours of peace shortly to bring together the two parties, and calculated to deceive and mislead the simple and the righteous. In another letter, addressed to Leo and Gaton, imperial asekretis, Photius also states that the rumours about Basil's total change of feelings towards him are premature and unfounded.[3] But Photius was not going to act in a hurry, and the spathar and drungary Helias is urged to be very cautious in his efforts in favour of Photius;[4] the same advice is given to Theodore of Laodicea.[5] Photius, indeed, knew the position and the Emperor's character too well: confident of final victory, conscious of his rights and knowing that time was on his side, he was in no need to hurry; and that is why he denounced in his letter to his bishops[6] the man who put it about that the ex-Patriarch had forgotten past happenings and was only anxious for reconciliation.[7] This talk, which at the time was all over Byzantium, at any rate pointed in the direction of Basil's efforts from the first to discover a compromise.

Photius' calculation proved correct, and reconciliation with Basil

---

[1] *P.G.* vol. 102, col. 772.   [2] Loc. cit. cols. 872, 873.
[3] Loc. cit. col. 968. Cf. Hergenröther, *Photius*, vol. II, p. 249.
[4] Loc. cit. col. 965.
[5] Loc. cit. cols. 845. Cf. letter to the bishops in exile, cols. 741 seq.
[6] Loc. cit. cols. 741 seq.   [7] Loc. cit. cols. 744 seq.

could not be far off. We have no accurate information on the date of
the suspension of hostilities, which in any case could not be later than
873. The Emperor received Hadrian's reply in the negative to the request
made at the beginning of 872, and this letter must have been instrumental in Basil's 'conversion'. In the spring of 871 Basil sent to Louis II[1]
the notorious letter in which he forbade him the use of the imperial
title, which, if it did not imply a complete break with the West, meant
at least that the Emperor thought himself strong enough to do without
its friendship. Hadrian's refusal completed the severance, the main
reason why the Emperor had to deal gently with the Pope having
vanished. Henceforth, i.e. after 872, it became more imperative for
Basil to find his allies among the Moderates, since, unlike the Extremists,
they had lost none of their power. Photius' recall from exile was the
first step in this direction.

We are, of course, not going to look for the true reasons of Basil's
change of feelings for Photius in the gossip of Nicetas, the so-called
biographer of Ignatius, or that of Simeon Magister.[2] A learned study
by an Armenian scholar[3] has thrown light on Basil's famous genealogy,
Photius' alleged forgery, to which he owed the recovery of the Emperor's favour. But the story seems to be a replica of a similar 'discovery'
made for the benefit of the Emperor Theophilus and designed to explain
the origin of Theophilus' regard for the future restorer of image-worship,
the Patriarch Methodius. Photius was naturally interested in the history
of Basil's family, since he himself, like Basil, had Armenian blood in
his veins: Photius' mother, Irene, was in fact Arsaber's (Arsavir)[4]
sister. But the forging of the fabulous genealogy of Basil by Photius
had nothing to do with this reconciliation. The real reason was different.
Basil, no longer in need of pandering to the Extremists in deference to
Rome, and disappointed at the meagre results of his policy in favour
of that party, altered his line of action, and transferred his friendship
to the Moderate side, whose ideology, if we may use the word, appealed
more to him than that of the Extremists. Photius then became his
intimate friend; Basil entrusted to him the education of his children and
gave him an apartment in the imperial palace. Photius must also have

[1] See bibliography in F. Dölger's *Regesten der Kaiserurkunden*, vol. I, no. 487.
Cf. also W. Henze, 'Über den Brief Kaiser Ludwigs II an Kaiser Basilius I', in
Neues Archiv (1910), vol. XXXV, pp. 661–76.
[2] *P.G.* vol. 105, cols. 565 seq.; (Bonn), pp. 689 seq.
[3] M. N. Adontz, 'L'Age et l'Origine de l'Empereur Basile I', in *Byzantion*,
vol. IX, pp. 232–59.
[4] Theoph. Cont. (Bonn), p. 175.

resumed his lectures at the Magnaura University, for it was there that the Emperor had reserved his rooms.[1]

Photius' peace with the Emperor must have raised heartburnings among some of his followers, for we find a reference to this in the ex-Patriarch's correspondence with the monk Nicephorus, when Photius announced to him a certain improvement in his condition and invited his correspondent to come and see him. As Nicephorus hesitated and expressed misgivings about the change, Photius sent him a long letter to assure him that his feelings had not altered, and only after this explanation did Nicephorus understand.[2]

Other friends of the ex-Patriarch urged Photius not to rest content with the compromise offered by the Emperor, but to take advantage of his change of mind to overthrow Ignatius. This Photius mentioned in his speech at the second session of the Council of 879–80,[3] and there was justification for the statement. It was only to be expected that the radical wing of the Moderate party should find the compromise unsatisfactory: they demanded complete vindication; but Photius was too intelligent to tempt fortune. He knew how to pause after a first successful round for fear of risking the game by any extravagant claims; he knew that the interests of the Empire and the Church stood more to gain by a reconciliation between the two parties than by open hostilities. It is also likely that the Emperor gave the Moderates to understand that he looked upon Photius as the legitimate successor of Ignatius in the event of the latter's death.

In the same speech, Photius stated that the Emperor had decided on this step by himself and of his own accord, a statement that disposed of all the stories in circulation in Byzantium on the motives of Basil's change of mind, though a slight exaggeration on the part of Photius, stressing Basil's contribution to his own reinstatement, may be admitted. But it is only right to observe that Photius could not have made such an assertion to an audience that must have known the true position, if he had been unable to substantiate it. Time and the State's altered circumstances had been on Photius' side. Nor did the Moderates remain idle; and they certainly knew how to turn the Extremists' failure to their own profit.

---

[1] Theoph. Cont. (Vita Basilii) (Bonn), pp. 276, 277. We recall a similar case with Leo the Philosopher, who after his dismissal from the see of Thessalonica was appointed to lecture at this High School.

[2] See letters of Photius, *P.G.* vol. 102, cols. 905–17.

[3] Mansi, vol. XVII, col. 424.

An echo of this change of front can be found in the correspondence between Photius and Baanes, an official who, it will be remembered, had made himself prominent at the Ignatian Council. In a letter addressed to him in the first days of the prelate's exile,[1] Photius complained that Baanes had refused leave for medical attendance in his recent illness. Baanes may have been carrying out instructions too literally; but directly he became aware of the changing mood at court in favour of Photius, he sent him a letter to assure him of his secret friendship, somewhat reminiscent of the feelings of Joseph of Arimathea for Our Lord. Conscious of his stock being high at the Imperial Exchange, Photius in reply[2] advised Baanes to display his friendship in open daylight, as Joseph did after Our Lord's death. Baanes' adaptability afforded a suggestive illustration of the mentality of Byzantine officials, who switched their sympathies and antipathies as the wind blew from the imperial palace. It also explains why Emperors could afford to alter their political programmes without fear of boycott from the imperial bureaucracy.

Photius had the same experience. Abrupt as the change in his favour had been, to the surprise even of the Extremists' leaders, they could hardly blame the Emperor, since Ignatius was still installed in the patriarcheion. Basil's variation was therefore put down to Photius' intrigues. The stories about the fabulous genealogy invented by Photius, the intervention of Theodore Santabarenos and the sprinkling of the imperial bed with water specially treated to act on the Emperor's feelings, were concocted only after the event, as explanations of the startling change.

Did the exiled bishops benefit by it? It is difficult to say how far Basil meant to go. It certainly did not suit his plans to provoke any violent reaction among the Extremists, who had backed him in the first critical days of his reign—a reaction that was a dead certainty, had Basil ventured too far in his condescension to Photius and his party. For these reasons, all the proceedings taken against the bishops by the Ignatian Council could not have been cancelled by the Emperor at that particular moment. Photius also stated in the speech already quoted that he had laid down as a condition for consenting to his reinstatement on the patriarchal throne after Ignatius' death that all the exiled bishops should be recalled and reinstated in their functions. Therefore, not all the bishops were set free at the same time as Photius, though their conditions must have been bettered.

[1] *P.G.* vol. 102, cols. 952, 953.   [2] Loc. cit. col. 949.

As regards the number of exiles, it is hard to state anything definite; but the Emperor had apparently only selected the more zealous and dangerous of Photius' supporters for banishment,[1] the others being merely deposed; though, wherever the Moderate party was felt to be too influential, the Photian bishops seem to have been maintained in their functions. None dared to touch them.

Peace with Basil did not necessarily imply peace with Ignatius, although Photius emphatically stated on the same occasion that he made friends with his rival after his return to the imperial palace. These were his words:

As long as Blessed Ignatius was alive—and we call him Blessed, having made friends with him in his lifetime, a friendship God preserve me from ever denying—as long as he was alive, we say, we refused at all cost to take possession of his throne, though many urged us, or tried to force us, to do so. There were other things more important than this—the captivity, the persecution, the banishment of our brothers and fellow-ministers. However, we refused to resume possession [of the see], as all here present well know.... Instead, we tried every avenue to the restoration and growth of peace. We both fell on our knees, asked each other's pardon and forgave each other for any mutual offence we might have given. Later, when he fell ill and asked to see us, we visited him, not once or twice, but frequently, doing everything we could to relieve his suffering; and if words could convey any consolation, this consolation we have given him too. Thus did he gather sufficient conviction of our good intentions to recommend to our special care his most intimate friends, that we should take responsibility for their safety and security. None of his friends will ever blame him for lack of devotion....

Ignatian sources flatly deny the fact of the two rivals' reconciliation. Nicetas[2] asserts that Photius, once back in the Emperor's favour, unceasingly and secretly worked against Ignatius with the assistance of Theodore Santabarenos, and tried every move to recover his see. Photius also, according to Nicetas, approached Ignatius to claim reinstatement in his episcopal functions; but the Patriarch, in obedience to canonical prescriptions, refused to hear of it; for whoever had been condemned by a synod cannot be rehabilitated but by another synod of a higher authority. Disregarding, however, all canonical laws, Photius comported himself like a bishop and a Patriarch, setting up

[1] S. Aristarchos, loc. cit. vol. I, p. ξα', enumerates twenty-four Photian bishops replaced by Ignatian bishops after Photius' dismissal.
[2] P.G. vol. 105, cols. 568, 569.

exarchs and presiding at ordinations. He did everything he could to harm the Church and hurt the Patriarch; gained the confidence of the Emperor and of the court and, driven by his mad ambition, forced an entry into the church of St Sophia three days after Ignatius' death to get possession of the patriarchal throne; then he turned against the friends and intimates of Ignatius, sending them into exile and to prison.

Stylianos [1] also records that Photius, once restored to Basil's favour by Theodore Santabarenos' incantations, ordained priests in Ignatius' lifetime. Once, he even invaded the church of St Sophia, accompanied by friends and soldiers, whilst the sacred mysteries were being celebrated, and the priests busy officiating fled before concluding the service. Photius and Santabarenos, with the Emperor's support, went on intriguing against Ignatius. Stylianos so describes Ignatius' death as to give the impression that it was the result of these intrigues; after which Photius took possession of the patriarchal throne and promoted Santabarenos over the heads of the other bishops.

To turn now to the third source—the compiler of the anti-Photian Collection—let us hear what he has to say about the relations between the two prelates: [2]

Some people would have it that Photius expressed regrets to Ignatius for what he had done to him and that the latter replied: God forgive you for what you have done to me: but what you have committed against the Church, God will not forgive you, unless you stop injuring her and cease to exercise the priestly functions. As for me, I will write to the Patriarchs, and if they absolve you from your ban, I, too, will dispense you.

But Photius himself, with the Emperor's complicity, prevented Ignatius writing to the Patriarchs, knowing well that it was impossible for him to be absolved and allowed to carry out his priestly functions. Since then, he never ceased raising enmities against the Patriarch. Even when installed in the Magnaura of the palace, he conducted ordinations, and severely punished or banished any who dared to protest. He also prevailed on the Emperor to forbid his magistrates to proceed with Ignatius' burial, if he should meet with a miserable death, as a result of these intrigues. Three days after the end, Photius entered the church with noisy display; and as the priests, who were busy celebrating the sacred mysteries, saw him, they fled, leaving the sacred vessels standing.

What is one to think of these different and contradictory accounts? The Ignatian reports themselves give one to understand that *pourparlers*

---

[1] Mansi, vol. XVI, cols. 429, 432, 433.   [2] Ibid. cols. 452, 453.

in view of a reconciliation did take place between Photius and Ignatius, but that possibly Ignatius first wished to comply with the decisions of the Council of 869–70 and actually intended to apply for dispensation in favour of Photius. But to such a procedure Photius could not agree, since he looked upon the decisions of that Council as utterly unjust and valueless. Here the Emperor may have intervened and concurred with Photius. So much of the report from Ignatian sources may thus correspond to fact. Photius may also have taken possession of his see three days after Ignatius' death, and the priests who at that moment stopped their liturgical service were Ignatians belonging to the extreme wing of this party. But it should be noted that Stylianos' account differs from the versions of Nicetas and of the compiler of the anti-Photian Collection: Stylianos, by asserting that this 'irruption' into the church was made by Photius in Ignatius' lifetime, gives evidence of being less conscientious in the presentation of facts than the other Ignatian writers.

As regards the actual fact of reconciliation, there is not the least room for doubt. Photius' own evidence is borne out by another contemporary witness, one who might in a way be called neutral—the Emperor Leo VI, son and successor of Basil. In his funeral oration on his father, and in summarizing the story of the schism and the part played by Basil in its settlement, Leo spoke as follows:[1]

There was raised among the ministers of God an absurd conflict and schism, whose beginning went back to the days before his [Basil's] advent, but by the inscrutable judgement of God, had grown worse, when the most peace-loving of men came to imperial power. Those who should have been for their people the preachers of peace, waged against each other a merciless war; those who should have set the flock an example of charity and union, bred hatred. He who struck hardest was considered the best priest. The whole thing was absurd: pontiffs and priests fighting with priests and pontiffs! The evil seemed to defy every cure, until this man of mighty thought, summoning the full energy of his intelligence, or rather raising it to God and deliberating with Him upon what was to be done, found at last the solution to this great evil and restored concord among the clergy. The whole Church being in exile with its archbishop, he ordered his recall, and all, finding themselves together, shook hands, when these long dissensions ended with the symbol of holy charity, the sacred kiss of peace. And as the ruler of the Church at that time had gone to his abode beyond, the archbishop, recently

[1] A. Vogt, I. Hausherr, 'L'Oraison funèbre de Basil Ier', in *Orientalia Christiana*, vol. XXVII, pp. 62–9.

returned from exile,[1] received the throne and the government of the priestly body. There was then, in accordance with the Gospel, one flock, one pastor: no longer were they divided, one with Cephas, another with Apollo, a third with the Lord knows whom, but all were really in Christ, the first corner-stone that gives unity to the whole construction of the Gospel.[2]

Taking into consideration the circumstance that this document is a solemn speech, a panegyric by a son in memory of his father, and that therefore some exaggerations and inaccuracies must be allowed for, we must admit that at least with regard to the fact of the reconciliation before Ignatius' death, Leo's attestation is fairly clear and it would be difficult to question its cogency. The way Leo recounts the adjustment between the two dignitaries forcibly recalls what Photius said about it in his speech at the Council of 879–80: their pacification was sincere and lasted till Ignatius' death.[3]

When did the reconciliation take place? I am inclined to place it in the year 876, as we possess a letter from John VIII to Basil, dated April 878,[4] which presupposes another letter by the Emperor, sent to Rome in the course of the year 877, to reach its destination probably towards the end of the summer. In it, Basil asked the Pope to send to Constantinople legates for a new pacification of the Byzantine Church; but as the dispatch of legates took some time, one can understand that the Pope did not reply till the spring of the following year, at the first reopening of sea-traffic.

Now the pacification mentioned in Basil's letter and referred to by the Pope could only mean the settlement of the Photian schism, for the Pope wrote:

On hearing, beloved, that the scandals of controversy are still rife in the Church of Constantinople and that many religious are still scattered far and

---

[1] ὁ ἄρτι τῆς ὑπερορίου φυγῆς ἀνεθεὶς ἀρχιερεύς. These words suggest that Photius had been recalled from exile shortly before Ignatius' death, though I have no wish to press their bearing unduly. Leo speaks oratorically, summarizing the facts for rhetorical effect. The date 873 I propose for Photius' recall from exile is not incompatible with this passage in the speech. Besides, Photius and Ignatius made peace later, perhaps in 876.

[2] It was A. Vogt's special merit to discover and publish this document, though the true import of it escaped him. Read what he says about the passage, loc. cit. pp. 18 seq.

[3] Note that in his *Synagogai* Photius calls Ignatius ἁγιώτατος and ὁ ἐν ἁγίοις. This declaration by Photius flatly contradicts Nicetas (*P.G.* vol. 105, col. 572), when he alleges that Photius reordained those of Ignatius' ordination. Photius apparently, as a token of peace, handed them priestly vestments blessed with his own hands. [4] *M.G.H.* Ep. VII, pp. 64 seq.

wide and are treated harshly, we are naturally pained and full of sorrow. What we feel most is that peace, which we thought the many efforts of the Apostolic See had restored, is disturbed there in endless bickering and that a number of men in holy orders who, we hoped, were safe from all oppression, have been subjected to various indignities.

The exiled and persecuted ecclesiastics could be none but the Photianist bishops and priests, since there were no other exiled priests in Byzantium in 877.

It seems then evident, judging from the contents of the pontifical letter, that Basil was anxious to efface the last traces of dissension in the Byzantine Church, and this before Ignatius' death.[1] But the Emperor's attempt had not a chance to succeed, unless Photius and Ignatius concurred in the matter. Peace then may well have been made in 876 and Basil's move in the spring of 877 may have been its first result.

Thus, the Pope's letter indirectly confirms the fact that Photius and Ignatius were at one. They also agreed, with Basil's approval, to settle their differences once for all and prepare a revision of the Council that condemned Photius and his friends. But it was a pity that Ignatius should have died before the final covenant, which he himself had assisted in negotiating, for, had he been alive, the legend depicting Ignatius as an obstinate old man, more reactionary than his supporters, would never have arisen. The description of him by his opponent Photius before the Fathers of the Council of 879–80 totally differs from the portrayal by his so-called biographer Nicetas-David. Ignatius was far more human than would appear from his 'biography', for he knew how to sacrifice his self-love in the interest of the Church over which he ruled. It was not an old man's bodily weakness that made him yield to Photius, as we are asked to believe, but the magnanimity of an ascetic, not well versed in the ways of life, but ready, in the long run, to acknowledge his own shortcomings and to stretch out his hand to an adversary. Had the revision of the decisions of the anti-Photian Council been completed in Ignatius' lifetime, and on Ignatius' initiative, the essentials of the rupture would have been better understood in Rome

---

[1] Hergenröther, *Photius*, vol. II, pp. 289 seq., alleges that this letter was written or dictated by Photius after his restoration, and that he deliberately omitted to mention Ignatius' death. But this allegation is inadmissible. Ignatius died on 23 October 877. It would have been difficult for Basil, given the risks of the voyage, to send legates to Rome in December, as journeys by sea were most unusual at this time of the year. Basil tried the experiment only once (in 869), with anything but encouraging results.

and opinions that had gained general credence since Nicholas and were in reality nothing but Theognostos' tittle-tattle would have been similarly revised.

As things were, it is quite possible that Photius actually exercised patriarchal functions in the last months before Ignatius' death, to which, after peace was made, no objection could be raised, since Ignatius, as stated before, considered Photius' ordinations to be valid. He certainly agreed likewise to Photius' right of succession.[1] As, however, by tradition in the Eastern Church, a sentence passed by a Council could only be reversed by another Council, it was actually arranged to convoke it, as is proved by Basil's request to John VIII concerning the sending of legates.

John VIII acceded to Basil's demand all the more readily, as he had hopes of definitely settling the Bulgarian problem on the same occasion, and throughout his correspondence we can guess the outlines of his scheme. The legates, Paul and Eugene, were to hand a very energetically worded letter to Ignatius,[2] this letter, to which previous reference has been made, to be the third and last summons served on Ignatius to withdraw his priests from Bulgaria; and refusal to obey it would carry the severest sanctions against him.

The document suggests that the Pope felt something in the situation in Constantinople had altered. Basil did not tell everything in his letter, in the hope of coming to an understanding with the legates in Byzantium, the very reason why he asked that the legates should be acquainted with the position, and even proposed to the Pope certain names, among them probably that of Zachary of Anagni.[3] Though we do not know exactly what the Emperor said in his letter, it certainly gave the reader to understand that Photius' conditions had altered for the better and that the Emperor meant to have the ex-Patriarch's position regularized. Was that not the best moment for the Pope to try some pressure on Ignatius?

The pressure may have looked all the more effective, as the Pope— or rather his collaborator Anastasius—had been busy paving a way leading straight in the direction of Photius. A letter from him to Anastasius[4] intimates that the Librarian had got into touch with Photius,

---

[1] Photius would in this way have been a sort of 'coadjutor cum iure successionis'; and as a matter of fact there was after Ignatius' death neither synod nor election of a new Patriarch, Photius automatically taking possession of the throne.

[2] *M.G.H.* Ep. VII, pp. 62, 63.

[3] Ibid. p. 64: 'Quia vero Deo amabiles viros, quos nominatim litteris expetitis, quibusdam incommodis impediti destinare nequimus, misimus Paulum et Eugenium....'

[4] *P.G.* vol. 102, cols. 877, 880. Cf. what I have said in my book, *Les Légendes de Constantin et de Méthode*, pp. 315 seq.

very likely after the latter's recall from banishment; for Anastasius followed the march of events very closely and overlooked nothing that might further his master's interests.

The legates were also to present to Boris a new request definitely to declare for Rome;[1] Greek bishops and priests were to be intimidated with threats of excommunication and degradation, should they refuse to leave Bulgaria within a month.[2] Thus the offensive was well planned. Everything seemed to go in the Pope's favour and fervent wishes saw the legates off on their way to Byzantium. Such was the irony of fate that the last remnants of the so-called success scored by the pontifical legates at the Ignatian Council were to be swept aside by the Greeks themselves on the initiative of Ignatius.

However, things did not get quite as far as this. When the legates passed under the gates of Constantinople, Ignatius was no longer alive, having died on 23 October 877, and Photius, after the agreement between the Emperor, Ignatius and himself, had resumed possession of his throne, leaving the legates to face, to their utter embarrassment, the situation they had least expected. Everybody in Constantinople expected the legates to make immediate contact with the new Patriarch; unfortunately, John VIII had not counted on such a turn of events nor given the legates any instructions to that effect; and Paul and Eugene remembered too vividly what was thought and said in Rome about Photius to deem it advisable to open negotiations with him. The fate of Radoald and Zachary served as a painful reminder and the thought that they might be condemned to share it came as a nightmare to trouble their sleep on the banks of the Bosphorus.

This gave Basil his second unpleasant experience with the Roman legates: it was exactly what he had feared and the very reason why he had hoped to welcome to Byzantium men who like Zachary knew the position. But there was nothing for the moment he could do, except once again to get in touch with John VIII, and that was what Basil and the Patriarch did. Already in April 879, the Pope had heard of the Emperor's intentions through the Primitiarius Gregory,[3] who in 877 was in command of the imperial fleet at Beneventum, and he immediately notified Count Pandenulf of Capua[4] of the imperial embassy's proximate

---

[1] *M.G.H.* Ep. VII, pp. 65, 66.   [2] Loc. cit. pp. 66, 67.
[3] Loc. cit. p. 142. Cf. John's letter to Gregory sent in April 877, ibid. p. 45.
[4] Loc. cit. p. 141. On the dates of these letters, cf. E. Caspar, 'Studien zum Register Johanns VIII', in *Neues Archiv* (1910), vol. XXXVI, p. 153.

arrival, requesting him to have the ambassadors taken to Rome: there they must have arrived in May.[1] They explained the new circumstances in Byzantium and presented letters from the Emperor, the clergy of Constantinople and the Patriarch Photius. The Emperor in his letter asked for recognition of the new Patriarch and for the convocation of a Council to regularize the position in Byzantium; the letter from the clergy of Constantinople made it clear that Photius had been all but unanimously acknowledged.

Thereupon, John VIII summoned a synod of eight bishops, including his most intimate collaborators, for the purpose of sanctioning the results of his *pourparlers* with the ambassadors. These details and what happened at that synod we learn from the letters which the Pope sent to the Emperor, to the clergy of Constantinople and to the leaders of the Ignatian party.[2]

In his letter to Basil, the Pope begins by expressing satisfaction that Basil should submit to the authority of the Roman See an authority confirmed by the Founder of that See, when He said to St Peter, 'Feed my sheep'. He also notes with pleasure that Basil acknowledged this See to be the head of the whole Church. In deference to the Emperor's wishes, although Photius had resumed his see without Rome's consent, the Pope is agreeable to his being the legitimate Patriarch; but Photius should apologize before the synod and make amends for his previous conduct. In the exercise of his powers to bind and loose, the Pope releases Photius and his bishops from the ecclesiastical censures imposed on them. It is the Roman See's right to judge Patriarchs; and as the condition of his recognition by Rome, Photius must no longer exercise any ecclesiastical powers in Bulgaria. The Emperor must honour Photius and give no ear to his detractors. Basil must also receive all the Ignatian bishops returning to Photius, and those who refuse to accept the new state of things are threatened with excommunication.

The letter addressed to the bishops of Constantinople and to the three Eastern Patriarchs, whose letters of assent Photius had forwarded to John VIII, expresses the Pope's great satisfaction to note the unanimity of the episcopacy's feelings towards Photius. The Pope also, in virtue of the authority vested in the successor of St Peter, approves his nomination to the patriarchate; but, as previously Pope Hadrian I had

---

[1] Cf. V. Grumel, 'Qui fut l'Envoyé de Photius auprès de Jean VIII?', in *Échos d'Orient* (1933), vol. XXXII, pp. 439–43. Photius' envoy was Theodore, bishop of Patras.

[2] *M.G.H.* Ep. VII, pp. 166–87.

laid down certain conditions for his recognition of Patriarch Tarasius, who had been raised without the canonical intervals from the lay state to patriarchal dignity, so John VIII considers himself bound to stipulate certain conditions for the recognition of Photius. They are as follows: Photius is forbidden in future to promote in the Byzantine Church any laymen to the episcopacy; he must restore Bulgaria to the Roman See; he must apologize to the Council; he and his bishops must endeavour to induce the Byzantine clergy to accept the new conditions in the Byzantine Church.

In the letter addressed to Photius, the Pope praises his wisdom, humbly confesses that the compliments addressed to himself by Photius are undeserved and expresses satisfaction at the concord established in Constantinople on Photius' appointment. And yet, the Pope should have been informed of the fact. Dismissing this in a few words and happy over the return of peace, he recommends to Photius the utmost condescension towards his adversaries, restores him to his dignity, provided he apologizes before the Council, and adds that the legates have received special instructions contained in a Commonitorium.

This Commonitorium had been sanctioned by the synod and signed by all present; it was also read to the Fathers of the Photian Council at the fourth session.[1] We do not possess the Latin text of this document. As the tenth clause of the Commonitorium orders the legates to proclaim the suppression of the Eighth Council and of the synods held against Photius, it has generally been assumed that this clause was inserted into the document by Photius, an assumption which has rendered the whole contents of the Commonitorium suspect. The fact is that none of the other letters of the Pope makes mention of the suppression of the Ignatian Council, which would justify the general suspicion in which this passage and the whole document are held.

We should, however, draw attention to the Pope's last letter on Photius' recognition, a letter addressed to the principal leaders of the Ignatian opposition, the Patricians John, Leo and Paul and bishops Stylianos of Neocaesarea, John of Silaeon and Metrophanes of Smyrna.[2] After urgently exhorting them to foster peace and union with Photius, the Pope concludes:

Let none of you on turning back find excuses in writings on the subject, since all fetters are unfastened by the divine power which the Church of Christ has received, whenever what is bound is undone by our pastoral

[1] Mansi, vol. XVII, cols. 468–73. Cf. *M.G.H.* Ep. VII, pp. 188 seq.
[2] Loc. cit. pp. 186, 187.

authority; for, as the saintly Pope Gelasius says, there is no tie that cannot be unfastened, except for those who persist in their error. For if you refuse to listen to our apostolic warnings which so many divine attestations have confirmed, and decide to remain obdurate, know that we have instructed our legates to deprive you of all communion with the Church as long as you refuse to return to the unity of the Body of Christ and to your Patriarch.

It is evident that the Pope refers here to the Acts of the Eighth Council: these Acts and documents, which were read before the Fathers, should not serve as a pretext for the die-hard Ignatians to refuse communion with Photius. When pastoral authority looses what is bound, then, in virtue of the divine power the Church of Christ has received, all fetters are undone. To judge from the context, the Pope pointedly refers to the same Acts when he writes: 'Cuncta solvuntur vincula.' Therefore, even the fetters that bound Photius were undone. How then could fetters that were undone keep the force of law that was revoked by supreme authority? The Roman synods of 863 and 869 as well as the Council of 869–70 were summoned solely against Photius and the Patriarch's condemnation was virtually the only topic of their deliberations: if these decisions are declared to be valueless, what is left of the synods? Hence, the version of this clause of the Commonitorium, such as was read before the Photian Council,[1] corresponds roughly to what John VIII intended to convey; and if the passage was altered, in accordance with the compromise arranged with the legates, the alteration must have left its substance untouched. It may be that the original text was worded in terms more abrupt and that instead of three declarations, there was only one, on the synod's annulment. In fact, the last sentence of the text seems to reflect Byzantine mentality; Rome was not so keenly concerned as Constantinople about counting synods.

What mainly leads one to think thatt his passage remained substantially unaltered is the phrase in the Greek text—ἀπὸ τοῦ παρόντος ('from this very moment')—words that stand exactly for the point of view on the Photian affair that had prevailed in Rome since Nicholas. The expression, in fact, conveys the view that these synods had kept their full value till that very moment, because the sentence they had passed on Photius was considered well justified. John VIII, although better

---

[1] Mansi, vol. XVII, col. 472. Θέλομεν ἐνώπιον τῆς ἐνδημούσης συνόδου ἀνακηρυχθῆναι, ἵνα ἡ σύνοδος ἡ γεγονυῖα κατὰ τοῦ προρρηθέντος πατριάρχου Φωτίου ἐν τοῖς καιροῖς τοῦ Ἀδριανοῦ τοῦ ἁγιωτάτου πάπα ἐν τῇ Ῥώμῃ, καὶ ἐν Κωνσταντινουπόλει ἀπὸ τοῦ παρόντος ᾖ ἐξωστρακισμένη καὶ ἄκυρος καὶ ἀβέβαιος, καὶ μὴ συναριθμῆται αὕτη μεθ᾽ ἑτέρας ἁγίας συνόδους.

disposed towards Photius than his predecessors, was still, at least in 879, of their opinion, and that is why, speaking in other places on the Photian business, he still used the words 'absolution', 'dispensation' and 'pardon' to be granted by the Holy See.[1] How could the Photian point of view have been adopted in Rome at that moment and in its completeness, since there had been neither time nor opportunity to know the exact state of affairs in Byzantium? Nicholas' prestige was then still paramount in Rome. It is even surprising that Photius should have made no reference to these words, which, fundamentally, did not accord with his own position.

The Pope had also to mention those synods in the instructions he gave to the legates and to make it clear that they had lost all value, owing to the Ignatians' refusal to acknowledge Photius, and their appeal to the very same synods. It was necessary that his words should be sufficiently precise to obviate every possible pretext on the part of the Ignatian clergy. But the Commonitorium, in the version known to us, is the only document in which the Pope mentions this matter: it therefore cannot substantially differ from the original.

A passage in the letter from John VIII to Basil reveals the Pope's true feelings with regard to the Eighth Council fairly clearly. He writes:[2]

For even the legates of the Apostolic See who were sent to Constantinople by our predecessor, the eminent Pontiff Hadrian, gave their well considered assent to the synod held there 'with the approval of their Pontiff', nor did they wish to remain severed from the *Apostolicus* [the Pope], since the See of St Peter, the key-bearer of the heavenly kingdom, has after due consideration power to absolve prelates from all ties. It is well known that many Patriarchs, Anastasius and Cyril of Alexandria, Flavianus and John of Constantinople and Polychronius of Jerusalem, who were condemned by synods, were promptly acquitted and reinstated by the Apostolic See.

Do these words not imply that even the synod of 869–70 would remain legally valid only so long as the Pope considered it expedient? When a synod loses its legislative value, it may be said to be suppressed. And incidentally, the prelates mentioned by the Pope in the same letter were all men who had been unfairly condemned by synods.

All things considered, this passage of the Commonitorium need no longer be considered suspect; at most can it be said that Photius, in agreement with the legates, only worded more emphatically and pointedly what the Pope actually said.

[1] *M.G.H.* Ep. VII, pp. 170, 171.　　　[2] Loc. cit. p. 171.

With regard to the other chapters of the Commonitorium under discussion, their contents reveal still more unmistakably the style of the Pontifical Chancellery of that period and recall the Commonitorium given by Pope Stephen V in 885[1] to the legates dispatched to Moravia for the settlement of its ecclesiastical problems after Methodius' death. The first part of this Commonitorium, like the document of 879, also deals with questions of protocol. Another analogy is to be found in the Commonitorium which John VIII gave in 873 to Paul, bishop of Ancona, who was sent as ambassador to Louis the German, and to Moravia.[2]

What in my opinion enhances the historical value of this document and corroborates its authority is the fact that other instructions given to the legates correspond nearly word for word with certain passages of the pontifical letters. For instance, chapter v, which concerns the reception of the Ignatian clergy who would consent to submit to Photius, tallies with what the Pope says in his letter to Basil and to Photius.[3] It is true that the Commonitorium draws a distinction between those bishops who had been ordained under the first patriarchate of Ignatius and must be restored to their sees, and those bishops who were ordained under the second patriarchate and are told to take their living from their former dioceses. But this is no proof that this passage was added by Photius and that this chapter of the Commonitorium was altered. We are told how at the second session of the Council the legate Peter understood the pontifical letters that had been read at the meeting: they ordered the Ignatian bishops who accepted Photius to return to their sees. Peter said:[4]

You see, most holy Patriarch, how the most holy Pope wishes all the dispersed bishops to be recalled again and to be treated by your Holiness with mercy and pity: so that those who were ordained first should recover their sees, and those who were ordained later should receive living and upkeep from those same churches until they re-enter into possession of their old or of other sees.

The copyist whose extract from the Acts was used by Deusdedit adopted the same reading, for he writes:[5]

The letter of the most holy Pope John directs that all the scattered bishops should be summoned together and be treated with mercy and compassion;

---

[1] *M.G.H.* Ep. VII, pp. 352 seq.
[2] Loc. cit. pp. 283–5.
[3] *M.G.H.* Ep. VII, pp. 175, 184.
[4] Mansi, vol. XVII, col. 417.
[5] Wolf von Glanvell, loc. cit. pp. 614 seq.

that those who were first ordained be received into their own sees, and those who were ordained later should receive food and clothing from their churches until they recover either the same or other sees.

There is then no reason for assuming that this passage of the Commonitorium was altered by Photius because he did not admit the legitimacy of the second patriarchate of Ignatius.[1]

The excommunication of priests refusing after two summonses to obey the pontifical orders, as threatened in chapter VII, is likewise held out in the Pope's letters. The two following chapters concern the prohibition to raise laymen to episcopal dignity without the intervals, and Bulgaria, but the latter topic is underlined in the Commonitorium where Photius is threatened with severe canonical censures, should he refuse the Pope's request.[2]

Only chapter IV in the Commonitorium has been substantially altered by Photius, for its original text certainly contained the Pope's order, expressed in all his letters, that Photius should apologize to the Council. This order is suppressed and in its stead is found a feeble invitation addressed to Photius to be thankful for what has happened to him and to give due credit to the Roman Church. This is the only portion of the Commonitorium that has been completely altered; but the alteration is connected with another problem that calls for special treatment.

The Commonitorium was to be conveyed to Constantinople by Cardinal Peter, who had been selected by the Pope as the additional member of the delegation that was waiting in Byzantium for further orders. Peter had also to deliver to Paul and Eugene a letter from the Pope expressed in somewhat severe terms. This is the text:[3]

You have acted against our will. After reaching Constantinople and examining the conditions of ecclesiastical peace and unity, you failed to carry out the mission with which we had entrusted you. We should really not entrust you with another, but to show apostolic kindness and mercy we are giving you as an additional member of the second mission, which this time you will have to carry out faithfully, Peter, a pious priest, cardinal and our

[1] Cf. Grumel, 'Lettres de Jean VIII pour le Rétablissement de Photius' in *Échos d'Orient* (1940), vol. XXXIX, p. 153.

[2] Observe a similar passage contained in the Pope's letter to Photius (*M.G.H.* Ep. VII, p. 185), with similar threats of censure, but omitted from the Greek edition of the letter.

[3] Loc. cit. pp. 188–90.

personal friend, so that you may do what is best for the peace and unity of God's Church, in accordance with the instructions of our apostolic authority and the tenour of our Commonitorium, which is divided into chapters. Act with intelligence and judgement and try by faithful loyalty to regain our favour, which you have exasperated by your previous disobedience.

I have quoted the whole of this document, because the letter decisively influenced the legates during the first negotiations that preceded the Council. I stated that the attitude of Paul and Eugene had exasperated the Emperor and the Patriarch, when the legates, for fear of committing themselves, had abstained from all action and waited for further orders. To John VIII this seemed absurd, since it left him without a true and accurate report on the position in Constantinople and compelled him to rely on the accounts by the Emperor and the Patriarch, with presumably a letter from the delegates. Note that the Pope here blames his legates for their lack of initiative in an unexpected emergency and tells them to follow the tenour of his instructions with 'intelligence and judgement'; so that they could not but read into the Pope's recommendations an injunction not to limit themselves to their standing orders but to act on their own responsibility, were they ever to find themselves in a similar position.

When Peter arrived with the Byzantine ambassadors in Constantinople, *pourparlers* between the Patriarch and the legates on the procedure of the coming Council were resumed, and it soon became evident that the points of view of the Pope and of the Patriarch radically differed on one item: the Pope wanted the Patriarch to apologize for his past conduct to the Council, and Photius flatly refused. He and his partisans looked upon the measures taken against them by Nicholas and Hadrian as utterly unfair and canonically unjustifiable. To their way of thinking, the synod of 867 was only an act of self-defence against Nicholas' interference in the domestic life of their Church. If on that occasion they went beyond the limits of self-defence, they had been sufficiently punished by the Council of 869, when, from the Photian point of view, the papal legates also exceeded their powers by condemning Photius and his friends without any preliminary legal examination. Moreover, Photius had made peace with Ignatius before his death. All that the Council about to be held in Constantinople was asked to do was to sanction the position as it had existed since Ignatius' death and to give Photius and his friends due satisfaction.

This placed the legates once more in the quandary which had so puzzled Radoald and Zachary in 861. Like them they could see that in Byzantium things had gone contrary to what was thought in Rome, where Theognostos' reports still remained the only source of information. What was more, they saw that in the opinion of Photius and his friends the Ignatian Council was the main bone of contention, and that there was more to be said for Photius' standpoint than they had thought at first. They were also aware that in view of conditions in Byzantium their mission was doomed to failure, if they persisted in their demand that the obnoxious condition should be fulfilled; in which case, the two Churches would sink back into schism and John VIII would lose his last chance of recovering Bulgaria. For they knew how keen the Papacy was on this item of foreign conquest achieved by Nicholas I. Their master also expected other things from the Emperor, to wit, his military aid against the Arabs. What were they to do? A second recourse to Rome was out of the question, for the Emperor was getting impatient, and besides, the Pope had blamed them for their lack of initiative.

The legates apparently demurred to the Emperor's solicitations for some time; finally, yielding to common sense, they consented to the suppression, on their own authority, of John's condition, but in return asked for the cession of Bulgaria.

The logical consequence of the understanding between the legates and the Patriarch was that the Pope's letters could not be read to the Fathers of the Council as they stood. When writing them, the Pope was, as stated above, under the influence of ideas about Photius that had been current in Rome since Nicholas I. John VIII, like nearly everybody else in Rome, was also convinced that Nicholas' proceedings against Photius were perfectly justified. No doubt, the unpleasant experience he had had with Ignatius in connection with Bulgaria and the fact that the see of Constantinople was in reality vacant at the moment inclined the Pope to condescension towards Photius. He had also heard the imperial envoys' explanations with more sympathy. But all this was not enough to dispose of old prejudices. Not even the intervention by Zachary of Anagni could dissipate all doubts, for since the time of his mission something had happened of which even the new Librarian, successor to Anastasius, was at a loss to afford adequate explanations—the condemnation of Nicholas by the synod of 867. John VIII therefore considered himself quite in order, when he asked Photius for apologies before he would annul the sentences passed by the anti-Photian synods.

But as soon as the legates perceived that the prejudices prevailing in Rome against Photius were not wholly defensible, it became necessary to delete the passages reflecting this prejudice. It was the usual procedure in Byzantium; and similar action had been taken at the Eighth Council, at the synod of 861 and had been tried again without success in 869. As rapid communication with Rome was out of the question, the legates had no option but to take the responsibility on the spot and, after the Council, to justify their action with the Pope as best they could.

Alterations made by the patriarchal chancellery in the pontifical letters were fairly numerous, and as the practice has for centuries raised severe criticism and some embarrassment among historians, let us examine these alterations more closely and emphasize some features which have so far not received the attention they deserve.[1]

In the original pontifical letter to Basil, the Patriarchal Chancellery first paraphrased the introduction, which was too severe, and considerably improved upon the Pope's compliments paid to the wisdom of the Emperor and of his sons. This is not very material; but what is curious is that the Pope's emphasis on the primacy of his See has scarcely been touched. This is what we read in the Greek version:

It was then that, wishing to establish and possess this concord, you have addressed, through your legates and your godly letters, the Holy Roman Church, firmly confident that she would help you in your work and give you energetic support. In this you did not take the initiative but followed and imitated the excellent example of those who ruled the Empire before you. But it is worth asking who taught you to act thus. It was certainly the first Apostle Peter, whom the Lord placed at the head of all the Churches, saying: Feed my sheep. Not only St Peter, but also the sacred synods and constitutions, the sacred and orthodox decrees and declarations by the Fathers, as testified by your saintly and godly letters. You act thus, in order that your faith, already firm and renowned, may shine the more brightly.

The original text is more explicit in its proclamation of the Roman primacy,[2] but the Greek text does sufficient justice to the Pope's leading idea. Is it not surprising that the man who till then had been looked

---

[1] Cf. Mansi, vol. XVI, cols. 396 seq. *M.G.H.* Ep. VII, pp. 166 seq.; Hergenröther, *Photius*, vol. II, pp. 396–416; Hefele-Leclercq, *Histoire des Conciles*, vol. IV, pp. 570 seq.

[2] *M.G.H.* Ep. VII, pp. 167: 'Romanae sedi reverentiam more praedecessorum vestrorum piissimorum imperatorum conservatis et ei cunctam subicitis auctoritatem, ad cuius auctorem, hoc est apostolorum omnium principem, domino loquente praeceptum est: Pasce oves meas. Quam esse vere omnium ecclesiarum caput et beatorum patrum praecipuae regulae et orthodoxorum principum statuta declarant et pietatis vestrae reverentissimi apices adtestantur.'

upon as the bitterest enemy of the primacy should have left such a compromising passage untouched?

Later, the Pope referred to the imperial letter in which Basil asked for recognition of Photius, a request that was duly granted by the Pope, who says in the authentic version:

Knowing that the Patriarch Ignatius has departed this life and having considered all the circumstances mentioned in your letter, we decree that Photius may be forgiven whatever he is known to have done in the past, although he usurped functions that were forbidden him without reference to our See; and we decree this without prejudice to the apostolic statutes or the rules of the holy Fathers: rather do we act on the strength of those rules and their manifold authority....

Then, after quoting canon 2 of the Council of Nicaea, a decree of Gelasius, Leo, Felix and Innocent, John VIII declares that he acknowledges Photius in common with the other Patriarchs and bishops who were consecrated by Methodius and Ignatius, on condition that he should ask pardon before the Council. In virtue of the same supreme power to bind and to loose, given to Peter, the Pope relieves Photius and his clergy of all censures.

This passage could of course not remain in the Greek version of the letter and was thoroughly overhauled: mention of Ignatius, of the Eighth Council and of the apology is suppressed, but curiously enough, even the Greek version, for all its doctoring, has preserved some expressions endorsing the Roman thesis of the primacy, which John VIII appealed to in the original. This is for instance what Photius makes the Pope say: 'As we considered it advisable to pacify the Church of God, we sent our apocrisiaries to carry out your will, although your own piety had already anticipated us, i.e. our legates' arrival, to reinstate that man. But we accept him [none the less], *not by our authority, though we have the power to do so*, but in obedience to the apostolic institutions.' And later on:

After receiving the keys of the Kingdom of Heaven from the first great Pontiff Jesus Christ through the intermediary of the first of the Apostles, Peter, to whom He said: I will give thee the keys of the kingdom of heaven; and whatever thou shalt bind on earth shall be bound in heaven, and whatever thou shalt loose on earth shall be loosed in heaven, this apostolic throne has the power to bind and loose all, and in the words of Jeremiah, to uproot and to plant. For this very reason, we also, by the authority of the Prince of the Apostles, Peter, announce to you with our entire Holy Church, and through you, to your dear confrères and co-ministers, the Patriarchs of Alexandria,

Antioch and Jerusalem, and the other bishops and priests and to the whole Church of Constantinople, that we agree and consent with you, or rather with God, to your request. . . . Accept that man without hesitation. Let no one seek pretexts for refusal in the decisions of the iniquitous synods that met against him; let no one—as many simple people think they can do—appeal to the decrees of our blessed predecessors, Nicholas and Hadrian, for they never credited what was alleged against the very saintly Photius. Let no one use your signatures against him as a pretext to sever communion with him or with you. Everything is over, everything repudiated, everything annulled and whatever was done against him has lost all validity. All these things, we, however unworthy, have handed to the Coryphaeus, to be laid on the shoulders of Jesus Christ, the Lamb of God, who remits the sins of the world. . . . Intensify your love, your faith, your obedience, your reverence in Him and by Him in the Holy Roman Church. Whoever refuses to accept him also refuses to accept—this is evident—either our decrees or those of the Holy Roman Church; and he declares war, not on us, but on the very holy Apostle Peter, or rather on Christ, Son of God, who so honoured and glorified His Apostle as to give him power to bind and to loose.

The words are as clear as those used by the Pope himself. What is more, Photius' words so appealed to the canonists of the post-Gregorian period that they were quoted word for word by Ivo of Chartres,[1] and many canonists who copied them from him, who fully understood their significance and quoted them precisely for the purpose of exalting papal power and of proving that the Pope can annul any sentence—a fact which, unfortunately, has so far not been sufficiently realized.

The other conditions of Photius' reinstatement as laid down by the Pope are translated fairly accurately in the Greek version of the letter. Mention is made of the Pope's prohibition in future to elect Patriarchs from among the laity, with the additional remark that this canonical rule has not always been observed. The order forbidding Greek priests to be sent to Bulgaria is worded in the form of a request; Photius at the same time making the Pope imply that the Greek priests may stay in Bulgaria in anticipation of the compromise that would afford a solution. Photius also suppresses the threat of excommunication uttered in the original letter in the case of disobedience in this particular matter.

The Pope's letter to the Eastern Patriarchs and to the Fathers of the Council is less important than the letter addressed to the Emperor, and the alterations introduced by Photius are less glaring, though even here

---

[1] *P.L.* vol. 161, cols. 56–8. Cf. pp. 302 seq.

the Patriarch has left nearly intact the words by which the Pope means to vindicate his rights. To quote the passage after the Greek version:[1]

...It was then your saintly and solicitous zeal, quoting the Blessed Prince of the Apostles, Peter, that appealed to our love and asked us to embrace the very saintly Patriarch Photius, after his reinstatement in the countries of the Church of Constantinople, and that we should join you in accepting him. This we have done with joy and promptitude, observing what was said in the Gospel to the first pastor, to whom the Lord said: 'I have prayed for you, Peter, that your faith may not fail; and you, once converted, confirm your brethren.' Inspired by these divine words and possessing full power to succour all Christians, as far as we can without incurring blame or damnation —a power whose fame has reached the confines of the world—and following the example of our predecessors, we have acknowledged Photius....Let this very saintly and pious confrère of ours, the Patriarch Photius, not take it ill, if we ask him to do honour before the synod to our grace and favour, or rather, to the heart of the Roman Church. For we have conferred on him our brotherly favour and acknowledged him as the legitimate Patriarch, raised to that dignity according to the canons, and as associate of the Blessed Peter the Apostle. And the whole Roman Church, after the example of our predecessors, has opened her heart to him....For many bishops, who lost, and were expelled from, their sees, recovered them by apostolic intervention....

Obviously, Photius deleted the Pope's order to apologize before the Council, but without tampering with the essentials of the text in reference to the pontifical primacy.

There was no equivalent passage in the original of the papal letter to Photius, who paraphrased the opening lines; made the Pope say that the see in which he was reinstated belonged to him by right; accentuated the reference to the Ignatians who should refuse to acknowledge him; attenuated the Pope's order to apologize before the Council; removed allusions to the Ignatian Council, the threats of papal censures and the order to recall the Greek priests from Bulgaria; and, lastly, put into the Pope's mouth the solemn declaration that the Councils held against him were null and void.[2]

On the whole, therefore, all the alterations concerned the differences of Roman and Byzantine views regarding Photius' case: some amplifications are rhetorical and superfluous; the compliments addressed to Photius and to the Pope are in every case touched up to create an

---

[1] Mansi, vol. XVII, cols. 452 seq.; *M.G.H.* Ep. VII, pp. 177 seq.
[2] Mansi, vol. XVII, cols. 412 seq.; *M.G.H.* Ep. VII, pp. 181 seq.

impression of perfect understanding between Rome and Byzantium and to underline the cordiality of the tone, which, in fact, is evident even in the original. Let this Photian 'impudence' shock people to their hearts' content, as it has done with a vengeance; nevertheless it is clear that in these avalanches of fiery and indignant criticisms, critics have been too excited to notice that Photius nowhere interfered with essential passages expressing John VIII's views on the primacy of the Roman See—a point of capital importance.

It must also be admitted that Photius and his friends could not possibly accept the Roman view of their own affairs: it was that of their enemies, and had been injected into the Romans by Theognostos, Photius' bitterest opponent. This was common knowledge in Byzantium and was well summed up by an unknown Latin cleric who in Gregory VII's reign prepared an extract from the Acts of the Photian Council to document the canonical writers.

I shall have occasion in the first chapter of the second part of this work to deal with those intermediary collections of canon law from which the great canonists of the period derived materials for their modernized canonical collections. Two of the Gregorian and post-Gregorian canonists, Deusdedit[1] and Ivo of Chartres,[2] have preserved in their Collections some extracts from the Photian Council. There we read a curious passage which differs from the corresponding version found in the current edition of the Acts of that Council. Here it is: 'Nullus sanctorum praedecessorum meorum Nicolai et Adriani sententias contra eum causetur. *De ipso enim surreptum est illis.*' (Let none allege against him the sentences passed by my holy predecessors Nicholas and Hadrian, since [what they said] about him was surreptitiously obtained from them.)[3]

Here the author has grasped better than the Acts the idea which inspired the Fathers of the Council by suggesting that Popes Nicholas and Hadrian had been misled on the true state of affairs by a third person (the Fathers had Theognostos in mind), who acted surreptitiously, or

---

[1] W. von Glanvell, loc. cit. p. 614.   [2] *P.L.* vol. 161, col. 57.

[3] It is inadmissible to translate the word 'surripere' by the word 'suppress' (*abroger* in French), as does M. Jugie, 'Schisme Byzantin', in *Dict. de Théol. Cath.* (1939), vol. xiv, col. 1341; 'Les Actes du Synode Photien de Sainte-Sophie', in *Échos d'Orient* (1938), vol. xxxvii, p. 98; *Le Schisme Byzantin* (Paris, 1941), p. 129. Nor is there any reason why the word 'sententiis' should be added after 'surreptum est illis', since the text is perfectly intelligible without the addition. The word 'surripere' always connotes fraud or *dolus*, and none would suppose that in the author's meaning the suppression of the sentences against Photius was obtained by fraud.

by fraud. The Greek original insinuates the same: 'They never credited what was alleged [rather, plotted] against Photius.'[1] Now the author of the extract from the Acts faithfully rendered the thought of Photius and the Byzantines by the words 'surreptum est illis'. This does not mean that Deusdedit and Ivo of Chartres used a version of the Acts which differed in many ways from the version we know. As we shall see in greater detail, both used an extract from the Acts which must have circulated in their days in so-called intermediary Collections of canon law.

Let us remember that what embittered the Photian bishops' feelings against Rome and put their consciences to such a hard test was that the Popes should have so uncritically adopted Theognostos' view of their case. Of this we find reliable information in a speech which Zachary of Chalcedon, one of the persecuted Photian bishops, made at the first session of the Council, when he said at the beginning of his address that the troubles of the Church of Constantinople were due to Ignatius' simplicity.[2] Strange as this appreciation may sound, it faithfully reflects what the Photianists thought about Ignatius. It may even surprise some to hear a Photianist as prominent as Zachary expressing so moderate an opinion about his master's leading opponent.

After a lengthy paean in praise of the address of the Patriarch Photius, too long and rhetorical to suit our modern taste, Zachary went on:[3]

We have restored to the Church what belonged to her and she has recovered her spouse. Whatever was done against him is now treated as insensate and futile; and when this came about, many promptly rallied to the decision, whilst many others did so later. But a few, no friends of the peace of the Church, have yielded to their self-love, and when asked why they had severed themselves from the common body of the Church, were ready to answer in their defence: 'The Roman Church ordered it so.' But they only behaved like church thieves and murderers, who on being charged with their misdeeds, would answer: 'I did it by permission of the Romans.' And that Church [the Roman], which so far has enjoyed peace and to the best of her ability radiated that peace to others, is made—if not truthfully, at least in their mouths—the cause of all the troubles, conflicts and scandals, nay all the evils that have afflicted our Church.

---

[1] See p. 184. Mansi, vol. XVII, col. 401: μηδεὶς...τὰς τῶν πρὸ ἡμῶν μακαρίων ἀρχιερέων, Νικολάου τέ φημι καὶ Ἀδριανοῦ, καταψηφίσεις αἰτιάσθω· οὐ γὰρ ἀπεδείχθησαν παρ' αὐτῶν τὰ κατὰ τοῦ ἁγιωτάτου Φωτίου τυρευθέντα....

[2] Mansi, vol. XVII, col. 384: οὐδὲ πρότερον ἀστασιάστου ταύτης οὔσης τῇ τοῦ κρατοῦντος ἁπλότητι....

[3] Mansi, vol. XVII, cols. 385 seq.

And that is why our very pious Emperor has summoned you [legates] here. You are gathered here to rebut all the imputations and charges which nearly everybody levels at you by making you responsible for the evils that have undeservedly afflicted us. Truth to tell, this synod has been summoned for your sakes;—for you, our brothers and Fathers, for the very Holy Roman Church, for your honour, lest the last remaining schismatics should accuse you of being the authors of all these dissensions and disorders. Now everything is at last satisfactorily settled without any further need for correction, all by the grace of God, by the action of that lover of Christ, our Emperor, by the prayers of our very saintly Patriarch, by the agreement and collaboration between the three Eastern pontifical sees and by the godly prayers and supplication of the very saintly Pope John. You can hear for yourselves that what I say is not only my voice, but that of this numerous synod.

After energetic and reassuring applause from the Fathers, their protestations of loyalty to Photius and their protests against the dissidents, Zachary continued:

In fact, those who have clung to their schismatic errors deserve reprobation; for, apart from other crimes they are committing, they are guilty of a paradox, the very thought of which is revolting to me. What is it? They are trying to enslave the Roman Church, which for centuries has kept her freedom unbroken. How? By saying: 'Nicholas' and Hadrian's decisions we accept; but we repudiate the decisions of the very holy and blessed Pope John. Why? Because those two Popes submitted to our will, whereas this one, instead of obeying our orders, expects us to obey his.' This only means one thing, that they refuse to obey the decrees of the Roman Pontiffs and would force those great and admirable men to obey their own behests; they accept the Roman decrees they have dictated in advance, and reject those that clash with their own prejudices. You may repeat those decrees a thousand times, they may be true to the canons and reflect superior inspiration—those men will in their pride have their own way: could there be greater folly? Hasten then, beloved, and gallantly stand up to liberate the Holy Roman Church from this dreadful barbarian slavery. Wipe away the dishonour and disgrace that cling to you and substitute the glory of working for the universal peace of all the Churches.

Hergenröther chose to be deeply shocked by this *Lügengewebe*;[1] and yet, Zachary's words faithfully reflected the mind and the opinions of the Photian clergy on the part played by the Holy See in this business. The Photian clergy were at the time in an overwhelming majority and

[1] *Photius*, vol. II, p. 468; cf. also M. Jugie, *Le Schisme Byzantin* (Paris, 1941), p. 122.

their opinions deserved respect, unless the Roman Church was ready to risk the prestige she had commanded in the East. The legates could not but see the importance of the issue and the danger that again threatened the peace of the Church; and as Photius was ready to make many concessions to the legates and the legates could ill afford to exasperate the Byzantine clergy by ill-advised rigidity, a compromise was arrived at and the Council could meet.

It has always been a surprise to many that this Council should have been presided over, not by the Emperor, but by Photius; this has led to him being suspected of a desire to occupy the supreme position in the Church, but the suspicion is unfounded. There was a precedent in the Seventh Oecumenical Council, when the conciliar debates were directed by Tarasius. Imperial officials were also present, but unlike Baanes at the Eighth Council, did not participate in the debates. Evidently, Tarasius officiated for the Emperor for the simple reason that at that time the Empire was ruled by Irene, when it would have been inconceivable in Byzantine eyes for an oecumenical council to be directed by a woman. It should also be remembered that as Tarasius, before being a Patriarch, had filled the important post of president of the Imperial Chancellery, he knew the routine; and Photius, before being a Patriarch, had occupied the same post as his uncle. So it was no matter for surprise that the Emperor should appoint him to the chair at the Council in his own name and allow him to exercise the rights hitherto reserved to the Emperor, when he himself could not perform the function.

The reason for the Emperor's absence was also a natural one: Basil had just lost his eldest and favourite son Constantine. The chroniclers who record this painful accident make it clear how deeply Basil must have felt the loss;[1] and as the death must have occurred shortly before the opening of the Council,[2] one can understand that the Emperor, in mourning over the greatest loss of his life, could not appear in public at such an important function.

The outstanding event of the first session occurred at the Church of St Sophia at the beginning of November—the exact date of this session not being given in the Acts—the great speech by Zachary, mentioned before, and the presentation of the legates. The second session,

---

[1] Theoph. Cont., Vita Basilii (Bonn), pp. 345 seq.; Leo Grammaticus, ibid. p. 258; Pseudo-Simeon, ibid. pp. 692 seq.; Georgius Monachus Cont., ibid. p. 844.

[2] Cf. Vogt, Basile Ier, pp. 58, 155, 333.

summoned for 17 November, opened with the reading of the pontifical letters, of course in their revised and corrected version. After the reading of Pope John's letter to Basil, Procopius of Caesarea in Cappadocia expressed the Fathers' satisfaction at Pope John's conciliatory attitude towards Photius and asked the legates to induce the dissidents, few as they were, to rally to the Patriarch. Peter, the Cardinal, then emphatically promised in the legates' name to do whatever was in the apostolicus' (Pope's) delegation's power in that direction, in accordance with the Pontiff's instructions.[1]

After the reading of the Pope's letter to Photius, the Cardinal once more summed up the leading points of the letter with regard to the Ignatian bishops. To this Photius replied that the Emperor had banished no more than two bishops, accused of civil disturbances.[2] One of them moreover had publicly insulted Pope John; but the Patriarch undertook to apply to the Emperor for the recall of these two bishops, so that they might be persuaded by the legates to unite with the Church.

The Cardinal then asked for explanations of the Pope's request on the subject of Bulgaria. In reply, Photius stated that since his accession to the throne he had refrained from sending the pallium to Bulgaria or making ordinations there, and that he had declared himself ready to make any sacrifice for the sake of peace and unity. He then added these striking words:

We once even went so far as to reply to Pope Nicholas, who claimed some sees and some dioceses as his own, to the following effect: 'What your Holiness claims is only within the powers of the Emperor of the East. Were my great love for God not hampered either by imperial orders or by other canonical considerations—even the clergy under me would agree with me in this—I should be only too ready to hand over on demand not only the sees which you say once belonged to the Roman See, but even those that were never under it, as far as it would be necessary to keep your friendship.'

The Metropolitan of Caesarea in Cappadocia stated that there would be a redistribution of the dioceses under the various patriarchates, once the Emperor had finished subjugating all the peoples to his power. Gregory of Ephesus then rose on a point of order, observing that the Council had not been summoned to solve that question.[3] This discussion is interesting for its revelation of public opinion in Byzantium.

---

[1] Mansi, vol. XVII, col. 409.   [2] Ibid. col. 417.
[3] Ibid. cols. 417, 420.

After all, Photius declared his readiness to accept a compromise: what that compromise was to be, we shall see presently.

The legates then examined the circumstances of Photius' recovery of his see, emphasizing that he became Patriarch for a second time, before the Church of Rome was duly informed. To this Elias, legate of Jerusalem, replied: 'Each of the three patriarchates of the East has always had its own Patriarch, and in this instance nearly all the bishops and priests of Constantinople wanted him [Photius] as their Patriarch: who then was to stop him from returning to his see?' By these words, the Patriarch's legate meant to vindicate the right of the Eastern Church to elect its own Patriarchs and bishops without the intervention of Rome: it was an ancient custom in the Church, and to that extent the Fathers did not accept the Roman claims as put forward by the Pope's legates.

Photius then considered it necessary personally to explain how he became Patriarch again, and emphasized his attitude towards Ignatius.[1] Then the letters from Michael of Alexandria were read; these had been brought by his delegate and addressed to Photius and to the Emperor, and their main contention was that the persons representing his patriarchate at the Eighth Council had no mandate from his see. Moreover, Thomas of Tyre had confessed his sin and sent to the Council a *Libellus Poenitentiae*, which gave the Fathers great satisfaction. Photius thereupon pardoned him. Then followed the reading of the letters sent by the Patriarchs of Jerusalem and Antioch.

The third session[2] began with the reading of the pontifical letter to the Fathers of the Council. The various points contained in the letter were agreed to in the course of the debate. Procopius of Caesarea and Zachary of Chalcedon tried to prove that the order forbidding the elevation of laymen to episcopal honours was not absolute.

Then followed a letter to Basil from the delegate of Theodosius of Jerusalem, who was duly cross-questioned by the legates to make sure that his mandate was genuine. After a solemn protestation by the legates that they had not been bribed into their recognition of Photius, there followed the reading of the Pope's Commonitorium.

On Christmas Eve and in the course of the fourth session, the reading of the letters from the Patriarchs of Antioch and Jerusalem, brought at the last moment by the Metropolitan of Martyropolis, Basil, enabled the Fathers to make it clear that Photius would have become Patriarch even without the consent of the Eastern Patriarchs.[3] This declaration

---

[1] See p. 167.   [2] Mansi, vol. XVII, cols. 449 seq.   [3] Loc. cit. col. 484.

by the bishops of Constantinople, made a second time in the course of the Council, was meant to vindicate their right to elect their own bishops without the intervention of any other power, and their insistence showed how jealously the Church of Constantinople stood on her rights. This part of the session ended with lengthy tributes, paid by Elias of Jerusalem and by the Cardinal, to Photius' address; Photius, they said, was like the sun, illuminating the world and other constellations.

The legates then rose to ask for two Patricians, who till then had refused to recognize Photius, to be admitted to penance. There followed the examination of the principal items of the Pope's letter to the Emperor and of the Commonitorium. The Pope's request about Bulgaria was discussed chiefly by Procopius of Caesarea, Theophilus of Iconium and Nicetas of Smyrna, who concluded that only the Emperor could decide, and that since John and Photius were agreed and loved each other like brothers, there was no point in bringing in the question of a redistribution of dioceses.

The question of the elevation of the laity to episcopal honours met with severer criticisms than in the preceding sessions; but clauses 4 and 5 of the Commonitorium, pronouncing the suppression of the anti-Photian synods and the excommunication of recalcitrant Ignatians, received general approval. On a proposal by the legates, it was decided that the perfect unanimity prevailing among the Fathers of the Council should be symbolized by everyone joining with Photius in the celebration of the sacred mysteries on Christmas Day.[1]

The fifth session, held on 26 January, was particularly important. Photius first proposed that the Council should officially confer on the second synod of Nicaea the title of Seventh Oecumenical Council, and the Cardinal threatened to excommunicate any who should refuse to number that synod among the oecumenical councils. The legates of the other sees concurred.

Then, on the proposal of the apostolic legates, the Council decided to send three bishops to Metrophanes of Smyrna to urge him to declare himself openly for Photius before the Council. After giving an evasive reply and excusing himself on grounds of ill-health from appearing before the Council, Metrophanes was excluded from the Church until such time as he should change his mind.

Metrophanes' case being settled, the Council voted on the first canon, which was proposed by the pontifical legation and worded as follows: This Holy and Oecumenical Synod has decided that the clerics or

[1] Loc. cit. cols. 475–92.

laymen or bishops of Italy, living in Asia, Europe or Libya, and having been suspended, deposed or excommunicated by the very Holy Father John, be regarded as such, i.e. as either deposed, or anathematized or deprived of communion; also, that the clerics, laymen, bishops or priests, of whatever diocese they be, who have been excommunicated, deposed or anathematized by our very Holy Father Photius, be likewise regarded as such by the very Holy Pope John and by the Church subordinated to him, i.e. as subjected to the same punishment, without any prejudice whatsoever to the privileges of the very Holy Roman Church or its bishops, either now or in the future.[1]

When this canon had been adopted by the representatives of the other patriarchates and by the Fathers, a vote was taken on the second canon, on a motion by Photius, forbidding bishops who became monks to resume their former dignity and functions. The third canon voted by the assembly anathematized any layman who, with or without provocation, should strike a bishop, this canon being intended to put an end to abuses that had spread in Constantinople during the recent conflicts between the two parties; of these both Ignatian and Photianist bishops had been victims.

The items on the agenda being exhausted, the legates proposed that the conciliatory decisions should be signed by all present. Paul, bishop of Ancona, signed first in the following terms:

I, Paul, unworthy bishop of the Holy Church of Ancona, legate of the Holy Apostolic See and of my master, Blessed John, the Supreme Pontiff of the Roman, Catholic and Apostolic Church and oecumenical Pope, accept, in accordance with my mandate, order and consent of the very Holy, Apostolic and Oecumenical Pope John, and with the assent of the Church of Constantinople and of the legates of the three other Patriarchs and with the approval of the same Holy and Oecumenical Synod, this venerable Photius, legitimate and canonically elected Patriarch, to his patriarchal dignity, and I am in communion with him in accordance with the tenour and the terms of the Commonitorium. I repudiate and anathematize the synod that was summoned against him in this Holy Church of Constantinople. Whatever, in whatever manner, was done against him at the time of Hadrian, of pious memory, then Roman Pope, I declare abrogated, anathematized and rejected in accordance with the Commonitorium, and that assembly I in no way reckon among the sacred synods. Whoever shall attempt to divide the Holy Church of God and sever himself from his own supreme pastor and oecumenical Patriarch, the saintly Photius, must himself be severed from the Holy Church of God, and until he returns to her, communicates with the Holy and

[1] Ibid. col. 497.

oecumenical Patriarch and submits to the judgement of the Holy See, must remain excommunicated. Moreover, to the holy and oecumenical synod which met for the second time in Nicaea on the subject of the sacred and venerable images, at the time of Hadrian I, Roman Pope of blessed memory, and of Tarasius, the very holy Patriarch of the Church of Constantinople, I give the name of Seventh Council and number it with the six holy synods. Signed with my own hand.

The two other pontifical legates signed in the same way. There followed the signatures of the representatives of the Oriental sees and of the 383 bishops who had attended the Council. Thus concluded the Council's weighty deliberations.

One important, and all but essential, item was still lacking in the Acts of the Council, the Emperor's signature: without it, the conciliar decisions could not become laws of the Empire, obligatory on all citizens. The Emperor had attended none of the conciliar sessions and his officials had attended in fewer numbers than was usual on such occasions; one looks in vain in the Acts for a list of imperial functionaries after the bishops' names. The Emperor and the court were in mourning, and in this the prescriptions of Byzantine ceremonial seem to have been followed to the letter. But as the Emperor's presence at one meeting at least was indispensable, a special session in the Emperor's presence was arranged, opening on 3 March in the triclinium of the imperial palace.

This session, the seventh on the list, was especially remarkable. First, its opening apparently did not coincide with the closing of the court mourning. It is not known exactly when Basil's son died: all we know is that it was towards the end of 879, possibly at the beginning of October, in which case it is likely that the Emperor's and the court's mourning lasted six months, from the beginning of October till the end of March.

Then again, the session took place, not at St Sophia, but in the imperial palace, which on the face of it meant that the Emperor still refused to make his appearance in public. Out of respect for his feelings and his loss, the Fathers went to the imperial palace, but not all were admitted to the session: only the Patriarch, the legates and the eighteen metropolitans and archbishops were present to represent the 383 Fathers of the Council; the others were summoned ten days later to St Sophia, to hear the reading of the protocol of that session and to signify their agreement with what had already been decided.

It has been a matter of general surprise that these two sessions, short as they were, should have been held in a manner apparently so irregular, after the debates on the most important problems had been closed. Following the example of a Greek scholiast, who in a marginal note preserved in some Manuscripts of the fifteenth century cast doubts on the authenticity of the last two sessions,[1] many have thought they were only a fabrication by Photius. But Hergenröther[2] has already pointed out the flaw in this argument. By taking into account the Emperor's mourning for his son Constantine and the Byzantine customs that governed general councils, we have seen many difficulties vanish or yield to simple and straightforward explanations.

On closer examination, the proceedings of these two sessions disclose nothing that might invalidate their authenticity. The canons of the Council had been proposed and voted at the fifth session; but each Council required its *horos* or Symbol of faith, a practice introduced by the first four Councils and followed by all the great oecumenical councils; and apart from the definitions of the first five Councils, the Sixth, the Seventh and even the so-called Eighth Council invariably proclaimed their Symbols.[3] This rule was certainly followed by the Photian Council in 861 and must likewise have been observed by the Council of 879–80.

This time the proclamation of the *horos* was held over till the session that was attended by the Emperor, who presided and proposed the Symbol of the Council of Nicaea and of Constantinople for adoption as the Symbol of faith of the present synod. After a dogmatic introduction, the Symbol was read out by the protonotary Peter, after which the Fathers firmly forbade any alteration, addition or suppression to be made to the Symbol. The Emperor then, together with his sons, signed the Acts of the Council and the Symbol. A short speech of thanks, delivered by the Metropolitan of Ancyra, Daniel, and the usual acclamations brought the session to a close.

The seventh session, with Photius in the chair, met only to report to the Fathers what the delegates of the Council, the legates and the Patriarch had done at the imperial palace. The *horos* was adopted by acclamation, and after the usual compliments addressed to the Emperor and to Photius by the protonotary Peter, the pontifical legates and

---

[1] Mansi, vol. XVII, col. 512.
[2] *Photius*, vol. II, pp. 528–39.
[3] Mansi, vol. XI, cols. 633 seq.; vol. XIII, cols. 376 seq.; vol. XVI, cols. 179–84 (after the vote on the canons of the Council).

Procopius of Caesarea, the synod was formally terminated with a second anathema against any who refused to acknowledge Photius and the customary acclamations.

There was, therefore, nothing to justify any misgivings about the authenticity of these two last sessions of the Photian synod, and they yielded nothing which the pontifical legates could not have signed or which might have given offence to the Romans at the time. Nowhere was the doctrine of the *Filioque* questioned: the only objection was to the addition of the formula to the Symbol. It is well known that the Roman Church in those days still recited the Symbol without the addition. Photius also clearly referred to the sixth session of this Council and to what was said and done there in his letter to the Archbishop of Aquileia,[1] confirming the same in the *Mystagogy*.[2] These two documents, belonging to the period that followed the Council almost immediately, afford all but unimpeachable evidence in favour of the authenticity of these two sessions; and if credit is refused to Photius' word, we have other proofs which completely dispose of the latest attempt to question their authenticity.[3]

[1] *P.G.* vol. 102, col. 820: 'Also at a synod of certain ecclesiastical leaders, holy Pope John's legates, who had been sent to attend it, subscribed, as though Pope John had been present and joined us in professing the true doctrine of the Trinity, to the symbol which is professed and believed at the conclusion of all General Councils in conformity with the word of the Lord, and they confirmed it in the same sense and with the same conviction, in writing and in speech and with their own signature.'

[2] *P.G.* vol. 102, ch. 89, col. 380: 'My own John (he is also mine for other reasons and because he took my defence more vigorously than any)—so my John, so manly in thought and piety, so virile in attacking and castigating every injustice and disloyalty, so strong on sacred and civil law and on the restoration of order, this gracious Pontiff, I say, through his saintly and illustrious legates Paul, Eugene and Peter, prelates and priests of God who came to our synod, accepted the symbol of faith as the Catholic Church of God and his predecessors on the pontifical See of Rome had ever done, subscribed to it through the medium of the minds, the voice and the sacred hands of those worthy and saintly men and signed it. Moreover, his successor, the saintly Hadrian, in sending us his synodical letter according to ancient custom, professed the same faith and taught that the Spirit proceeds from the Father....'

[3] Cf. V. Grumel, 'Le Filioque au Concile Photien de 879–880', in *Échos d'Orient* (1930), vol. XXIX, pp. 257–64; also V. Laurent, 'Le Cas de Photius dans l'Apologétique du Patriarche Jean XI Beccos au Lendemain du Deuxième Concile de Lyon', ibid. pp. 396–415; my book *Les Légendes de Constantin et de Méthode*, pp. 324 seq.; Laurent, 'Les Actes du Synode Photien et Georges le Métochite', in *Échos d'Orient* (1938), vol. XXXVII, pp. 100–6; V. Grumel, 'Le Décret du Synode Photien de 879–880 sur le Symbole de Foi', ibid. pp. 357–72; V. Grumel, *Les Régestes des Actes du Patriarcat de Constantinople*, pp. 106 seq. (cf., however, A. Michel's criticism of the same in *Byz. Zeitschr.* (1938), vol. XXXVIII, pp. 452–9). E. Amann, whose

But we cannot be so emphatic about the authenticity of a letter from John VIII to Photius regarding the addition to the Symbol and which was published by Mansi at the end of the Acts of the Photian Council. In this letter the Pope complains of unfriendly rumours spread in Constantinople about the Church of Rome. Lest these rumours should raise suspicions in Photius' mind, the Pope hastens to assure him that the Symbol has always been recited in Rome without any addition or suppression and that it does not at all contain the 'article' that had caused so many scandals in the Church. He severely condemns all those who dared, 'in their short-sightedness', to insert it and compares them to Judas. He observes, however, that it is not easy to persuade the bishops of the Roman patriarchate to abandon a practice which is, in fact, quite a recent one. The Pope himself refuses to believe in the use of force and thinks it better to proceed cautiously in trying to suppress the usage. It is anyhow false to accuse the Pope of the innovation, and at the end of the letter he requests Photius not to allow himself to be scandalized by the practice and to help the Pope in suppressing it.

Hergenröther, who specifically dealt with this problem, came to the conclusion that the document was a forgery, whose author might be Photius or rather some Greek polemist of the fourteenth century.[1] In agreement with Hergenröther's finding, I have placed the forgery in the fourteenth century and know of no reason for revising this conclusion. But I should draw the reader's attention to some particulars that deserve consideration.

First of all, this document nowhere touches on the doctrine of the

merits in Photian researches I have noted, as also those of Lapôtre, in my book *Les Légendes de Constantin et de Méthode*, pp. 314, 320, 324, expressed in his study on Photius (*Dict. de Théol. Cath.* (1935), vol. XII, cols. 1536–1604), the best and most recent study on the Patriarch, the opinion that the doubts cast on the two last sessions of the Council were not justified (loc. cit., cols. 1589, 1590). I note with satisfaction that M. Jugie is ready to admit the authenticity of the Greek Acts, including the last two sessions: 'Schisme', in *Dict. de Théol. Cath.* (1939), vol. XIV, cols. 1340 seq.; 'Les Actes du Synode Photien', loc. cit. pp. 89–99; *Le Schisme Byzantin* (Paris, 1941), pp. 126–30. On pp. 383 seq. I set forth evidence which proves decisively that the authenticity of the two last sessions can no longer be questioned. I here call attention to the short, but judicious *exposé* of the Photian affair and the main problems connected with it, by E. Amann in vol. VI of *Histoire de l'Église*, edited by A. Fliche and V. Martin ('l'Époque Carolingienne', Paris, 1937, pp. 465–501).

[1] *Photius*, vol. II, pp. 541–51. Cf. M. Jugie, *Theologia Dogmatica Christ. Orient.* (Paris, 1926), vol. I, pp. 247–56, where the author mostly copies the Cardinal's arguments. Cf. also Amann, 'Jean VIII', in *Dict. de Théol. Cath.* vol. VIII, cols. 609–11.

Filioque, as Hergenröther seems ready to admit:[1] all that the author is concerned with is the addition of the *Filioque* to the Symbol. Once this is clearly realized, there is no difficulty in admitting that whatever is said in the document roughly corresponds to fact, barring a few expressions that could never have been written by John VIII: the particular passage in which the writer compares the initiators of the innovation to Judas certainly did not issue from the Pontifical Chancellery. Then again, the fact that the existence of this letter was never referred to either by Photius or by any of the Greek polemists before the fourteenth century is not so extraordinary as might seem at first sight, for the Greeks always preferred to quote conciliar decisions, naturally with papal attestations, in support of doctrines and standards that were common to the whole Church. Granted this mentality, declarations by the legates of John VIII at the sixth session of the Photian Council had in their estimation far greater value than any letter from the Pope.

On the whole, it is not absolutely impossible, but most unlikely, that John VIII should have written to Photius on the addition to the Symbol; and certainly the letter could never have been couched in the terms alleged. Even if the possibility of such a letter be not ruled out, one must admit that it was drawn up in such vague and general terms that it failed even to attract the attention of the Greek polemists, who preferred to quote the legates' declarations at the sixth session of the Photian Council rather than this letter. If not wholly an invention, it was at least, as is well known to-day, thoroughly altered by some polemist of the fourteenth century.

To return once more to the Acts of the Council, it remains to examine the pontifical legates' procedure in the course of the Synod. Western historians have in general been very hard on them and blamed them for grossly departing from pontifical instructions, for adopting the Greek point of view throughout and for being too complimentary, nay servile, to Photius. I have tried to show why the legates had to adopt the Photian view in the settlement of the dispute, for, had they insisted on the Pope's orders being carried out to the letter, their mission would have collapsed completely. A full examination makes it clear that they

---

[1] Ibid. p. 541: 'Er, der Papst, nehme jene Lehre, um derentwillen Spaltung zwischen beiden Kirchen entstanden, nicht nur nicht selbst an....' The original Greek has: περὶ τοῦ ἄρθρου τούτου...ὅτι οὐ μόνον οὐ λέγομεν τοῦτο. The word τὸ ἄρθρον does not mean 'doctrina' but 'articulus', i.e. part of a sentence. Hergenröther's summary is therefore very inaccurate.

honestly tried on every possible occasion to do justice to the Roman views on the pontifical primacy.

For instance, Cardinal Peter, addressing the Fathers, declared at the opening of the first session: 'Like a good father and a good pastor, the holy Pope constantly exhorts and visits you by his letters and his legates; and wishes to see the whole Church united into one flock with one single pastor.' The words did not appeal to John of Heraclea, who retorted that the Byzantine Church had achieved that unity, before the Pope ever made his exhortation.[1]

Without allowing himself to be disconcerted by the interpellation of the Metropolitan of Heraclea, the Cardinal repeated towards the end of the session in more solemn words that the purpose of his legation was to establish peace and union in the Byzantine Church.[2] After that, he presented the gifts the Pope had sent to Photius, including the pallium. What this meant for the Romans, we know; but the Byzantines saw in it only a token of friendship for their Patriarch on the part of the Pope.

At the beginning of the second session, Peter conceded to his inter-pellator of the first session that peace had indeed been restored in the Byzantine Church before the legates' arrival, but added emphatically that the Emperor and the other Patriarchs had never ceased to beg the Pope to set his seal to this peace.[3] To this Procopius of Caesarea retorted again that peace had been restored before the Pope's admonition. But Peter was not to be thwarted and repeated the same statement in nearly the same words; then calmly proceeded to detail the procedure to be followed in dealing with those who refused to acknowledge Photius. After the reading of the Pope's letter to the Byzantine Patriarch, Peter asked several questions regarding the manner of Photius' resumption of office, making it therefore perfectly clear that he wanted to assert himself before the Fathers as judge and arbiter. After the Patriarch had given his own explanations, Peter again rose to declare that the Holy See had restored several Patriarchs and bishops to their sees, and that John only followed their example in restoring Photius to this throne.[4]

When the Fathers had heard Thomas of Tyre's *Libellus Poenitentiae* and pleaded with the Patriarch for the repentant prelate's pardon, the pontifical legates objected that this case would have to be submitted to

---

[1] Mansi, vol. XVII, col. 384.   [2] Ibid. col. 389.
[3] Ibid. cols. 393, 408, 409.
[4] Ibid. col. 428: ἀπέδωκε τῇ ἁγιωσύνῃ ὑμῶν τὸν οἰκεῖον θρόνον.

the Pope personally, since they had no powers to absolve such a grievous sin. On the Fathers and Photius expostulating with them, the legates relented from their rigidity, whereupon the Fathers asked Photius to decide for himself, since he alone was the aggrieved party in the case. Photius then pronounced the absolution of the repentant prelate and the legates at once rallied to his decision.[1]

It has already been stated that the legates had only consented to such alterations in the Commonitorium as were absolutely necessary to effect a compromise. If read with care, the document expresses with sufficient clearness the views held at that time in Rome on papal powers.[2] In the fifth chapter the Pope orders the bishops to acknowledge Photius; in the next chapter, he makes his legates declare that the Roman Pontiff had the care of all the Churches, a principle often reiterated in pontifical documents of the period; in general, the Pope adopts the tone of a master giving orders and these orders are preserved, even after the modifications made by the Patriarchal Chancellery in agreement with the legates.

At the fourth session Peter unequivocally stated that the Pope was the head of all the Churches,[3] and at the fifth session the Cardinal's assertions in the same sense were still more explicit. Whatever has been said to the contrary, the first canon voted by the assembly had been drawn up by the legates, and the clause added to the canon was meant to guarantee the privileges of the Roman Church: those who read into the canon an infringement of the Roman See's powers[4] only wasted their breath, for the Greek canonists[5] read into it exactly the reverse, and their opinion was well worth having. In the course of the debate on methods of procedure with those who might alter their minds and join Photius, the Cardinal said: 'Pope John, oecumenical and apostolic, who received his powers from Peter, Prince of the Apostles, has conferred the same powers of binding and loosing on the very saintly Patriarch Photius.'[6]

The above instances should suffice to show that the legates did not, in the course of the Council, deviate from their duty to the extent it has generally been believed, but remained faithful to the instructions they

---

[1] Mansi, vol. XVII, cols. 440, 441.   [2] Ibid. cols. 468–71.
[3] Ibid. col. 480.
[4] For instance, Hefele-Leclercq, *Histoire des Conciles*, vol. IV, p. 600; cf. Hergenröther, *Photius*, vol. II, p. 506.
[5] Balsamon (ed. Beveridge), *Synodicon*, vol. I, p. 360; Zonaras, ibid. p. 361.
[6] Mansi, vol. XVII, col. 501.

had received on the essential point which the Pope valued most highly—
the primacy of the Roman See.[1] One may be shocked by the extrava-
gance of some of the compliments paid to Photius, but the legates had
sufficient perception to see that they were dealing with a really extraordinary man and that the Patriarch had actually conquered the hearts
of the whole Empire and of the whole Byzantine Church.

[1] Cf. Jugie, *Theologia Dogmatica Christ. Orient.* vol. I, pp. 229–44: 'De iis quae
in actis synodi Photianae primatui Romanae Sedis favent...et in detrimentum
ac irrisionem cedunt.'

CHAPTER VII

THE SECOND SCHISM OF PHOTIUS,
A HISTORICAL MYSTIFICATION

Photius' letters to the Roman bishops—John VIII approves the Acts of the Council—Basis of the compromise concerning Bulgaria—Anti-Photian Collection and the legend of Photius' second condemnation by John VIII—Photius, Marinus I and Hadrian III—Stephen V and Byzantium—Stephen's letters on the Photian incident.

THE legates arrived in Rome with somewhat heavy hearts: it is true, their mission had succeeded, the two Churches were once again at peace, but only at the cost of their disregarding some of the Pope's strictest orders. Would John VIII be satisfied with their explanations? Would he be convinced that Byzantium was not exactly what it was imagined to be in Rome? Would he believe that they could not possibly have acted otherwise? Their predecessors, Radoald and Zachary, had also achieved a signal success in Constantinople in 861, but with what fatal results to themselves! And now their only hope lay in that very same Zachary of Anagni, who had succeeded at the Pontifical Chancellery to the post of Anastasius the Librarian, the man who certainly had had something to do with the revision of Pope John's Oriental policy.

It also appeared that Zachary had had a long talk with Cardinal Peter before the latter's departure for Byzantium and had handed him a letter addressed to Photius, explaining to the Patriarch the true circumstances in Rome and apologizing for his inability to do more for him at the Pope's court: this much at any rate can be inferred from the Patriarch's letter to Zachary which the legates handed to him:[1]

It is told of one of the ancients—I think it was Theodektes—that he had asked a friend for the gift of something he needed at the time; but his friend, instead of giving only what he had been asked for, decided in a free-hearted moment to add something equally desirable. Isidorus—for that was his name —perhaps wanted to make a show of his munificence, but that did not suit his friend, who took the addition as an insult and returned the whole parcel. He did not regard it as a sign of true friendship, that when one modestly

---

[1] We owe the last edition of this letter to A. Papadopoulos-Kerameus, *Photiaca* (St Petersburg, 1897), pp. 6 seq. See ibid. pp. 7 seq. on previous editions. Cf. Hergenröther, *Photius*, vol. II, pp. 556 seq.

asked a friend for less than one's needs, the friend should in fact give a great deal more. But what becomes of the law of friendship, if friends must condemn each other either for excess of gifts or for lack of trust?

For fear the same should happen to us, we have sent you, dearest friend, no more than the proofs of old and true friendship you asked for; and if ever you should need more—but perhaps these very words are a breach of the rules of friendship—you will find us as ready to oblige you as we are now. Though your efforts did not meet with the success they deserved, we welcome the zeal you displayed on our behalf as gratefully as if it had benefited us; for we know that results must be left to the decision of time and are often frustrated by events.

But the law of true friendship knows how to value struggles, zeal and favours, not by their appearances, but by the energy of their mainspring. For you know without my telling you—I would not tell you, if I feared to be suspected of not trusting my friends with the whole truth—that things happened not only differently from, but contrary to, our intentions. As for the rest, we wish you, saintly soul, the best of good fortune and safety from all attacks and threats, from enemies visible and invisible, by the intercession of our Glorious Lady, Mother of God and all the saints. Amen.

Zachary may have cautioned the Patriarch against some particularly dangerous personalities at Rome, whose intrigues might defeat his friends' efforts at the pontifical court. Foremost among these was Marinus, bishop of Cere, the same who played a leading part at the Council of 869–70. Photius had understood his friend, for to disarm Marinus he sent him a letter, offering his friendship. The document which the legates were asked to deliver to Marinus is indicative of Photius' intentions and feelings:[1]

When you presided as a judge in the case that did us such injustice, you were evidently put to a severe test; but you refused to submit to that test, when it pleased God to vindicate us against our aggressors. Had you had the courage to face us, God is our witness that you would have severely condemned not only your first judgement, but also your present hesitation, under the pressure not of revenge, but of the friendship of which you would have been the object. Lest you should mistake these words for empty vapourings, I have sent to your holiness, as first evidence of my vengeance, the particles of the Holy Cross framed in gold. Fare you well, and do not forget that the bonds of true friendship are often forged, not in joy, but in pain, as the words of the Lord, great and divine words, confirm it. I will ask you for a favour—see how far we dare venture—but a favour of which I need not be ashamed, and which if granted will benefit you: should anybody at

---

[1] Loc. cit. p. 5. Cf. Hergenröther, *Photius*, vol. II, pp. 553 seq.

any time hurt or offend your feelings, intentionally or not, for such things do happen among men—take my attitude to you as a pattern for your attitude to the sinner and inflict on him the same punishment as our humility has inflicted on you.

It is difficult to see why, following Hergenröther, we should find in this letter nothing better than 'the Byzantine Patriarch's deeply wounded pride' (den ganzen schwer gekränkten Stolz des byzantinischen Patriarchen). Far from this being the case, the letter is good evidence of Photius' goodwill, with all the dignity to be expected from a Byzantine Patriarch: it is the letter of one who feels at last rehabilitated and sends the good news to those who contributed to his downfall. He does not stoop to flattery to bring an old enemy round to his cause, but is the first to stretch out a friendly hand. It is at once the *beau geste* of a priest and the master-stroke of a shrewd diplomat.

Another close associate of John VIII was the bishop of Velletri, Gauderich, who had been spokesman for the bishops summoned to Rome by Hadrian II before the legates' departure for Constantinople in 869.[1] It was he, too, who in the name of the assembled bishops urged the Pope to take the most drastic steps against Photius and his supporters. But Gauderich also attended the Roman synod of 879 which was called to rehabilitate Photius, and his signature was found at the foot of the Commonitorium.[2] The following is the gist of a letter from Photius to Gauderich:[3]

Those who are joined in bonds of friendship unspoiled by past quarrels and misunderstandings usually take their mutual good feelings for granted, and though afraid of any possible breach, are fairly lenient in cherishing their friendship; but those who become friends after earlier quarrels, especially if the offended party is chivalrous enough to make the first advance, act so as to ease a feeling of shame (which is only right) and find in past regrets an incentive to keep the laws of friendship. That is why those who were the main cause of old scandals try not only to remove similar provocations in the future, but also to let bygones be bygones. We then—and you would say the same, if you looked squarely at the truth—invite you, after the misunderstandings that severed us, to a true friendship in the Holy Spirit. It would be your task to intensify and quicken the flame of divine love, not to extinguish it by inconstancy or foster the bad feelings which uprooted the law of love and banished it from our thoughts and memories. That is why

---

[1] Mansi, vol. XVI, col. 124.
[2] Mansi, vol. XVII, col. 473; *M.G.H.* Ep. VII, p. 189.
[3] *Photiaca*, pp. 5, 6. Cf. Hergenröther, *Photius*, vol. II, pp. 555 seq.

I embrace your holiness in these lines as with the lips of the purest feelings and wish to be bound to you by the bonds of cheerful friendship by the gift I send to you as a symbol of friendly welcome.

It is possible that Photius sent similar letters to others whose names had been submitted to him by the legates; but it is also evident that Photius and the legates took every precaution, a lesson they had gathered from the unpleasant experiences of Radoald and Zachary, and that they did everything in their power to forestall similar surprises on the part of the Pope.

After receiving the legates in the summer of 880, John VIII carefully studied their reports, the Acts of the Council and the letters from the Emperor and the Patriarch. The reply to these letters, dated 13 August of the same year,[1] shows fairly clearly how the Pope reacted to the happenings in Constantinople. As his letter to Photius is extremely important for a true estimate of Photius' case, I translate it from the original and quote it in full:

It has always been the object of our endeavours, labours and wishes that for the maintenance of the orthodox faith and for the peace and welfare of all the Churches of God for whose care we are responsible, we should strive to reunite what is scattered, to preserve what is united and to watch over whatever is wrong or objectionable among the things which the providence of God has committed to us. For this purpose, true to apostolic custom and taking pity on the Church of Constantinople, we have decided that the advantage of one should not be the detriment of another; rather, that every one should be of spontaneous assistance to all.

After summoning our Church, urged by the necessity of the times, we have turned our attention to the Church of Constantinople in the exercise of our apostolic authority and power and instructed our legates to proceed cautiously. We rejoice at her unity of peace and concord and abundantly praise Almighty God and, though we cannot sufficiently thank One who has bestowed so many benefits on His servants, we bless Him and try to give Him unstinted glory. Glory, praise and virtue be to Him by whose majesty and praiseworthy grace crooked things are made straight, evil is mended, obstinacy broken, humility exalted, dissension uprooted, goodness intensified and all scandals thrown aside. Let us therefore not glory in ourselves but in God, rejoice and exult in His mercy who says: 'Have confidence, for I overcame the world'; and elsewhere: 'You can do nothing without Me.' But though we have determined to deal with you in writing and speech with exceptional restraint, it is a wonder to us why so many things that we had

[1] *M.G.H.* Ep. VII, pp. 227, 228.

decided should have been obviously altered, transformed and, we do not know through whose mistake or design, distorted.

Moreover, you have hinted in your letter that at your suggestion only those should ask for mercy who have done ill. We also charitably agree that we should thus deal with those who say they do not know God. Yet we do not wish to exaggerate what has been done, lest we should have to judge according to deserts. So, let such excuses be dropped, for fear they should come under the condemnation: 'It is you who justify yourselves before men, but God knows your hearts; for what is great in the sight of men is abominable in the eyes of God.'

Therefore, let your wonderful prudence, which is reputed to know humility, not take offence that you should have been asked to sue the Church of God for mercy, but rather to humble yourself that you may be exalted and that you may learn to give brotherly affection to one who showed mercy to you; and if you try to increase in devotion and loyalty to the Holy Roman Church and to our insignificant person, we also embrace you as a brother and hold you as the closest friend.

We also approve what has been mercifully done in Constantinople by the synodal decree of your reinstatement and if perchance at the same synod our legates have acted against apostolic instructions, neither do we approve their action nor do we attribute any value to it.

What conclusions emerge from this document? First, we discover that the Pope, before writing this letter, had carefully studied the Acts of the Photian Council and seen with his own eyes the alterations which the patriarchal chancellery had introduced into his own letters: 'Sed cum nos scriptis et verbis misericorditer tecum specialiter agendum esse decrevimus, mirandum valde est, cur multa, quae statueramus, aut aliter habita aut mutata esse noscuntur.' It is, however, important to note that the Pope confines himself to these few words, without insisting on the non-compliance with his orders; he is even loath to point out the culprit responsible for the alterations, and with the utmost discretion fastens the responsibility on Photius, without naming him, 'nescimus cuius studio', and on the legates, 'vel neglectu variata monstrentur'. He is surprised at such daring, but refrains from denouncing the fact.

The same text informs us that Photius had, in the letter delivered by the legates, drawn the Pope's attention to the alterations and explained the reasons for them: the Patriarch chiefly objected to the Pope's command to sue for the Council's mercy. The Pope reproves Photius for his lack of humility. Photius, says the Pope, is not an unbeliever, but a bishop from whom more is asked and expected than from one who has not the faith. Yet, Photius must have explained to the Pope why he looked upon the injunction as impossible, and his reasons must have made a certain impression on the Pope, for after his solemn exhortation to humility, addressed to Photius, John VIII hastens to apologize for having imposed on him such an obligation: 'Igitur laudabilis tua prudentia, quae dicitur humilitatem scire, non moleste ferat, quod ecclesiae Dei miserationem iussa est postulare, quin potius se, ut exaltetur, humiliet.'

Contrary to what has been believed to this day, these words do not in the least convey that Photius had actually asked the Council Fathers' pardon and that the Acts were later tampered with by the Greeks, for in the version extant to-day there is not a trace of such a capitulation by the Patriarch,[1] and the Pope's letters authorize no such assumption.

The sentence in the pontifical letter means on the contrary that the Pope, after reading the legates' report, the Acts and the letters from the Emperor and the Patriarch, realized that he had ventured too far on ground which was not nearly so firm as he had thought, and discovered, as a good strategist, that to cling to his position would risk the fine victory he had scored in Constantinople: so he beat an honourable retreat, screening his strategic move by exhortations to humility addressed to Photius. It is clear that in this sentence the Pope meant not to insist further on such a trifle, for he says to Photius: 'if you persevere in your loyalty and devotion to our Holy Roman Church, we embrace you as a brother and as our dearest relation.' 'Nam et ea', he goes on, 'quae pro causa tuae restitutionis synodali decreto Constantinopoli misericorditer acta sunt, recipimus.'

These last words distinctly imply that the Pope agreed to everything done at the Council of Constantinople for Photius' rehabilitation. Now, what did the Council actually do in the matter? The Patriarch was reinstated without begging the Fathers for mercy; those who refused to acknowledge him were excommunicated and all the synods held against Photius were annulled. This was done 'pro causa Photii restitutionis synodali decreto Constantinopoli', and all this was put down in the synodal decrees: therefore, all this was agreed to by John VIII. No other conclusion is logically tenable.

But the Pope's declaration ends on a sentence that has puzzled the historians: 'Si fortasse nostri legati in eadem sinodo contra apostolicam

---

[1] It was in this sense that I interpreted the letter in question in my book, *Les Légendes de Constantin et de Méthode*, pp. 324 seq., in the light of Father Laurent's researches, 'Le Cas de Photius...', in *Échos d'Orient*, vol. XXIX, pp. 396–415. His conclusions are, however, erroneous. See pp. 180 seq. for my evidence.

preceptionem egerint, nos nec recipimus nec iudicamus alicuius existere firmitatis.' What is the proper interpretation of these words? Taken literally, they would mean that the Pope here withdraws what he has just agreed to in a previous sentence: for the legates did go against the Pope's orders by allowing Photius to be reinstated without the apologies and by tolerating the alterations in the Pope's letters and in the Commonitorium. It was all done 'pro causa Photii restitutionis synodali decreto Constantinopoli'. This would imply a strange contradiction and a procedure at variance with every precedent in pontifical diplomacy.

We must then conclude that the last restriction laid down by the Pope did not refer to the points which John VIII had just agreed to in the same document, those points being, to sum them up again: Photius' reinstatement without apologies, the annulment of the Anti-Photian Councils, the alterations in the pontifical letters and the excommunication of all those who refused to submit to Photius.

In the light of the above, we can only interpret the sentence as a precautionary clause, designed to safeguard the rights of the primacy: if after a close examination of the whole case it should ever become evident that the legates had exceeded their mandate and disobeyed their instructions to a degree incompatible with the rights of the Papacy, the possibility would be left open of shifting the responsibility on to them and declaring the concessions null and void.

On the whole, therefore, the legates came off better with their master than their colleagues of 861; but on one thing John VIII refused to go back: not a single clear hint can be found in this letter to suggest that he looked upon his predecessor's policy to Photius as mistaken. The legates, of course, had arrived at this conclusion consistently with their action at the Council in Constantinople; but John VIII, even supposing that he concluded from their report that the case called for revision, hesitated to venture that length. In this very document, one can discern a trace of the same opinions on Photius' case as the Pope had expressed in his letters to Constantinople before the convocation of the Photian Council and he still persists in looking upon Photius' rehabilitation as an act of gratuitous condescension on the part of the See of Rome. The words 'misericorditer tecum specialiter agendum' and 'quae pro causa tuae restitutionis...misericorditer acta sunt' are clear enough. As was to be expected, the Pope was not as explicit as in his previous letters, and in this respect he did veer round. At the same time, it would have been awkward, if not impossible, for John VIII to unsay and set aside whatever had been thought about Photius in Rome: such a disclaimer would have cast a slur on the memory of a great Pope, and the Pontifical Chancellery is not in the habit of overriding previous declarations. Better to leave certain things severely alone, the more so as the aggrieved party had not insisted on such abjuration.

Pope John's letter to the Emperor Basil reveals why the Pope went as far as he did and why he agreed to all that had been done at the Photian Council for the Patriarch's reinstatement. After thanking Basil and his sons Leo and Alexander for their keenness on the restoration of peace in the Byzantine Church, he goes on:[1]

Now, after God, we thank your Serenity for having displayed such sincerity and devotion to the Church of St Peter and our own paternity not only in words but in striking deeds; we thank you for having sent your fleet and placed it at our service for the defence of the land of St Peter; second, because filled with divine inspiration and reverence for the Prince of the Apostles you have restored to our jurisdiction the monastery of St Sergius which was founded in your royal city and formerly belonged by right to the Holy Roman Church; third, we thank you profoundly for having for the love of us, though it was only fair, allowed St Peter to re-enter into possession of the Bulgarian diocese. Hence, we urge you for your own comfort in every way to help and to defend the Holy Roman Church in these critical days, so that your imperial glory may increasingly shine over the world with the help of our apostolic prayers and receive a great reward from the Almighty.

We also urge you to persevere in the feelings of good will and piety which for the love of God you have for the Church of Christ, for it is with the love of a father that we hold your Exalted Highness in our arms, venerate you with due honour and by constant prayers poured out near the sacred bodies of the Blessed Apostles Peter and Paul try to ask the Almighty, for all the great services you are rendering to St Peter, ever in this world to keep your holy Empire in increasing prosperity, to bless it with glorious victories and give you eternal glory and happiness with His saints and elect in the Heavenly Kingdom. We also approve what has been mercifully done in Constantinople by the synodal decree of the very reverend Patriarch Photius' reinstatement and if perchance at the same synod our legates have acted against apostolic instructions, neither do we approve their action nor do we attribute any value to it.

These words are significant, and disclose the great joy the Pope felt over the reconciliation with Byzantium and his sincere gratitude to the Emperor. And he had excellent reasons for being thankful to Basil, for the military aid which the Emperor had sent him was substantial and

[1] *M.G.H.* Ep. VII, pp. 229, 230.

well-timed, and the Pope knew better than anyone in Rome or in Italy that without Byzantium's assistance it would have been impossible to ward off or even to take the sting out of the Arab threat. The gift of the convent of St Sergius was a free donation on the part of the Emperor; but the permanent transfer of Bulgaria to the Roman patriarchate was the best part of the transaction. John VIII could now boast of having secured what the great Nicholas had had so much at heart and what for over twenty years had been the main bone of contention between East and West. After securing such concessions from Byzantium, could the Pope have refused to endorse the Constantinople settlement, and could anyone seriously believe that John VIII, after agreeing to all the Constantinople decisions, could in the same breath make such reservations as would unsay what he had said? The assumption is too absurd. A careful analysis of the Pope's letter to Basil drives us to the same conclusion: the Pope cancels the conditions he had laid down for Photius' rehabilitation; he agrees to the annulment of all the anti-Photian decrees issued by his predecessors and by the synod of 869–70, and he sanctions the Acts of the Photian Council brought to him by the legates in the version as we know it to-day.

The main objection to the above conclusion has been drawn from the fact that Bulgaria, after all that was said and done, remained as before under the jurisdiction of the Byzantine patriarchate; hence, it is contended that the concession made by Basil and Photius was only a blind and that the Pope was again duped by the astute Byzantines. As soon as he perceived the fraud, John VIII is alleged to have withdrawn his consent by falling back on the safety clause that qualified his two letters.

But the objection does not hold water. The Bulgarian concession was sincere and was actually carried into effect, for we find that from that time onward Bulgaria ceased to be listed among the dioceses belonging to Byzantium in the official catalogue or the ninth-century episcopal directory,[1] a fact significant enough to be taken into account. In this respect, the Byzantines were always punctilious.

But how was it that Photius and the Emperor could make such a concession to Rome in all seriousness, seeing how fiercely the government of Michael III and Bardas had fought for the conquest of that province and that Basil had followed his predecessors' policy to the very last? Did Bulgaria lose overnight its importance in Byzantine eyes? Certainly not. Then how can we explain the fact?

[1] Cf. J. Gay, *L'Italie Méridionale et l'Empire Byzantin* (Paris, 1904), p. 124.

Some light can be thrown on the problem by the terms of the compromise arrived at by the legates and the Emperor after the Council in Byzantium. Photius, in his speech at the second session of his synod,[1] clearly showed he was quite aware of the importance of the issue to John VIII; nor did he overlook the fact that reconciliation with Rome would be a hopeless proposition without some concession from his side on the Bulgarian issue. That is why he so pointedly stated that since his accession to the throne he had refrained from sending the pallium to Bulgaria and holding ordinations there, just to demonstrate to the legates his readiness to come to an agreement on that very issue.

What Photius stated may have been correct for, as a matter of fact, the Byzantine bishops in Bulgaria made their own provision for the spiritual needs of their flocks. If after Photius' accession to the patriarchal throne no change occurred among the higher clergy, Photius had in fact no opportunity for sending the pallium to anybody.

John VIII defined his own point of view best in his letter to Photius:[2]

Furthermore, as it is your duty to lend strength to your will, so it is our will that our Bulgarian diocese, which the Apostolic See received by the efforts of the blessed lord Pope Nicholas of apostolic memory and held at the time of blessed Pope Hadrian, be restored as soon as possible; and by apostolic authority we forbid any ecclesiastical ordinations to be performed in the same diocese by the heads of the Church of Constantinople. You will see that the bishops consecrated there and all lower clergy leave the country and refrain from entering our Bulgarian diocese. If you give them the pallium, perform any ordination or communicate with them, as long as they refuse to obey us, you will fall under the same excommunication as theirs.

The Pope, therefore, maintained the same general attitude to the Greek clergy operating in Bulgaria as he explained in April 878, in his letters to Ignatius, Basil and the Bulgarian bishops;[3] but it was less resolute. There is one particular sentence in the letter showing that the Pope leaves a door open to a compromise: 'Si tu...donec nobis obediant, cum eis communicaveris', a broad hint that a simple transfer from one patriarchate to the other would be acceptable in Rome and that agreement on the future of the Greek clergy working in Bulgaria would be possible.

This portion of the letter was completely suppressed in its Greek edition. The pontifical letter to Basil has a similar passage, only more

[1] Mansi, vol. XVII, cols. 417, 419.
[2] *M.G.H.* Ep. VII, pp. 185, 186.
[3] Loc. cit. pp. 62–5. See above, p. 157.

pointed, in which the Pope, after recalling Nicholas' efforts to gain the confidence of the Bulgarians, says:[1]

If the Patriarch...refrains from claiming or retaining possession of the Bulgarian diocese, performs there no ordination of any degree (there seem to be some bishops or priests there who were illicitly ordained by either the Patriarch or the archbishop) and does not send them the pallium which prelates wear at solemn Mass....

These words suggest possibilities of a compromise and Photius was quick to detect the Pope's drift. This is how he translates them in the Greek edition of the letter:

And yet, some people were bold enough to appropriate by force a province that did not belong to them, made ordinations there, consecrated churches and did, in short, what they had no right to do. Besides what we have said already, be warned also of this, that if we hear of any bishops over there damaging our interests and if we proceed against them with ecclesiastical penalties, let them not find sanctuary with you, but behave in a way apt to convince us that on this point you think as we do and agree with our opinion.[2]

This, then, was the basis of the compromise between Rome and Byzantium: as long as the Bulgarians were ministered to by Greek clergy and remained culturally dependent on Constantinople, the danger to Byzantium of a Bulgarian Empire rising at its very gates could easily be dealt with; but Byzantium could never tolerate the proximity of a Bulgaria drifting under the cultural influence of the Franks and the spiritual ministrations of a Latin and Frankish clergy: yet for all that, the Emperor could allow the Bulgarian archbishop to apply for his pallium to Rome instead of Byzantium.

This also goes to prove that the desire for a real and permanent *entente* was perfectly sincere on the part of both John VIII and Photius, since both made substantial sacrifices for the lasting peace of the Church.

The above reading of the facts has to this day escaped the experts, who have allowed themselves to be mystified by the fragment of a letter from John VIII to Boris, erroneously attributed to the year 882.[3] The following are the words of the fragment: 'Si ab his quos excommunicatos habebamus sacramenta quaecumque suscipitis, constat quia

---

[1] Loc. cit. pp. 173 seq.   [2] Mansi, vol. XVII, col. 405.
[3] *P.L.* vol. 126, col. 959. Zlatarski, in his *History of Bulgaria* (*Istoria na Blg. Drzhava*, Sofia, 1927), vol. II, pp. 200 seq. infers from the passage that the Pope had excommunicated not only Photius, after detecting his deceit, but also the Bulgarians. Cf. M. Jugie, *Theologia Dogmatica Christ. Orient.* vol. I, p. 145. See my study, 'Le Second Schisme de Photios', in *Byzantion* (1933), vol. VIII, p. 435.

idololatriam, non ut Catholici essetis, sed ut schismatici efficeremini, reliquisse videmini.' But this fragment does not belong to the period generally postulated; and in the new edition of the letters and register of John VIII brought out by E. Caspar,[1] it is placed where it belongs, at the end of a letter which the Pope dispatched in 874–5.

We possess two letters by John VIII belonging to the period that followed the Photian Council and addressed to Boris, both indirectly bearing out what was said above on the Bulgarian compromise between Byzantium and Rome. The first of them assumes the transfer of Bulgaria under the jurisdiction of Rome, as arranged between the Pope and the Patriarch, and even leads one to suspect that the Pope had made other attempts to obtain Boris' consent to the arrangement. John VIII had used as his go-between the Croat bishop of Nin, Theodosius, an individual specially equipped for such a mission. As head of the Roman party in Dalmatian Croatia, Theodosius had proved in 879 a valuable supporter of Duke Branimir in his revolt against his rival, Prince Zdeslav, the Byzantines' special *protégé*.[2] This revolution, besides restoring the Dalmatian Croats' independence, also checked the expansion of the Byzantine patriarchate in that region. In 880 Theodosius went to Rome for his consecration as a bishop, on which occasion the Pope charged him with a mission to Boris. Theodosius carried it out so well, that the Khagan promised to send his ambassadors to Rome; but as they never arrived, John VIII had to remind Boris of his promise by letter. The document bears no date, but must have been written in the latter half of the year 881. As the Pope's reminder fell on deaf ears, John sent another letter to Bulgaria the following year,[3] more impetuous in tone and bearing evident traces of exasperation at Boris' obstinate silence.

Neither of these two letters makes mention either of Photius or of the Greeks and the Pope has no complaint to make about Emperor or Patriarch: the correspondence clearly shows that if Bulgaria did stay under the influence of the Byzantine patriarchate, none but Boris must bear the responsibility, for in a second fit of obstinacy he refused even to hear of Rome, which had once refused to pander to his moods.

But this time, Boris' refusal to submit to the Pope was not inspired

---

[1] *M.G.H.* Ep. VII, p. 295.

[2] Cf. my book, *Les Slaves, Byzance et Rome au IXe siècle* (Paris, 1926), pp. 229 seq.

[3] See the text of these letters in Mansi, vol. XVII, cols. 211, 217; *P.L.* vol. 126, cols. 919, 938; *M.G.H.* Ep. VII, pp. 260, 266, 267.

by any caprice of his. Anxious to make his country as independent as possible, and weary of the endless bickerings between the two patriarchates, Michael-Boris saw his opportunity to take another step towards the realization of his old dream—a Bulgarian Patriarch; and by his refusal to bring his country directly under the patriarchate of Rome Boris actually laid the first foundation of the Bulgarian National Church. The work, thus started by the shrewd Boris, was to be completed by his son Simeon in 918 by the erection of an autonomous and independent Bulgarian patriarchate. In 927 the Bulgarian Patriarch was officially acknowledged by the Byzantine Church.[1]

It is interesting to note how circumstances helped Boris in his schemes. Death prevented John VIII from pursuing his Bulgarian designs with his customary doggedness and his successors followed each other too rapidly to gather up the threads of a policy initiated by their great predecessors, with the result that relations between Bulgaria and the Holy See came to be completely suspended. Even Formosus, though still remembered in Bulgaria, did not, on becoming Pope, renew contact with that country, which at that time was rapidly progressing towards the status of a great power.

And yet, the very reverse is often taken for granted, and it is believed as a matter of course that Formosus tried to wrest Bulgaria from the Byzantines. This would explain why they kept such unfriendly recollections of this Pope. There is in a letter from the Bulgarian Prince Caloyan, addressed to Pope Innocent III, a vague reference to Simeon as one of the Bulgarian Tsars who applied to Rome for the imperial crown, this being taken as evidence that relations between Rome and Bulgaria were renewed under Formosus, were continued by the Tsar Simeon and that Rome had agreed to the foundation of the Bulgarian Empire and the national patriarchate.[2]

But the reference to Simeon in Caloyan's correspondence with Innocent III is extremely vague and warrants no such conclusion.[3]

---

[1] Cf. Zlatarski, loc. cit. vol. II, pp. 399–401, 529 seq. Also idem, 'Blgarski Arkhiep.-Patriarsi Pryez prvoto Tsarstvo', in *Izv. Istor. Druzhestvo* (1924), kn. VI, pp. 1–22; Gelzer, 'Der Patriarchat von Achrida', in *Abh. d. kgl. Sächs. Akad.* (Phil.-Hist. Kl. 1902), Bd 20, p. 3.

[2] D. Farlati, J. Coletti, *Illyricum Sacrum* (Venetiis, 1751–1819), vol. VIII, p. 194; Hergenröther, *Photius*, vol. II, p. 694.

[3] The following are the passages under discussion: In his first letter to the Pope, Caloyan writes (*P.L.* vol. 214, col. 1113): 'Imprimis petimus ab ecclesia Romana matre nostra coronam et honorem, tamquam dilectus filius, secundum quod imperatores nostri veteres habuerunt. Unus fuit Petrus, alius fuit Samuel et alii qui eos in imperio praecesserunt, sicut in libris nostris invenimus esse scriptum.' No

Simeon, moreover, felt in no need of permissions, for he adopted in 918, long after Formosus' death, the title of Emperor and founded the Bulgarian patriarchate.

Bulgaria's surrender by Constantinople, of which Rome could not take advantage, only stimulated, as we have stated, Bulgaria's dreams of independence, and from that time onward we can watch Boris acting as a sovereign, even in the country's religious problems, asking leave from neither Rome nor Byzantium, and after the expulsion of the disciples of St Methodius from Moravia (884) offering them sanctuary in his country and adopting the Slavonic liturgy, which Pope Stephen V had banished from Moravia. Thus there gradually arose in Bulgaria a Slav National Church, which soon displaced all Greek elements. Happily for Boris, Bulgaria was possessed about the year 880 of a fairly numerous native clergy: a letter from Pope John VIII to Boris, dated 878,[1] mentions a Slav priest, Sergius, appointed bishop of Belgrade; and Photius' letter to Arsenius[2] makes reference to many young Bulgars who had joined the monastic life and received their theological and ascetical training in Byzantium. Such foresight certainly helped the slow, but well-directed, formation of a Bulgarian National Church; though one is left to wonder whether such a transformation would have taken place if Bulgaria had remained under the direct jurisdiction of Byzantium, or if, by the terms of the compromise between Photius and John VIII, the Popes had secured a footing in Bulgaria. It thus happened by a strange whim of destiny that this very compromise facilitated the creation of a Bulgarian National Church and thereby saved the Slav liturgy.

It is therefore evident that the charge against Photius of having prevented by his intrigues the implementing of his solemn undertaking is false: Photius had nothing whatever to do with the astute Boris's flat and obstinate refusal to place his country under the direct jurisdiction of Rome. Again, after the Photian synod John VIII has no complaint to make against Photius, and Photius has no fault to find with John VIII after their reconciliation—only matter for praise. So, whatever has been said about Photius' second condemnation by John VIII is sheer perversion, and in any case, the Bulgarian incident had nothing to do with it.

conclusion can be drawn from this text. In his second letter (*P.L.* vol. 215, col. 290) Caloyan seems more definite, but even this passage warrants no such conclusion: '...ut impleret desiderium imperii mei sanctitas tua, secundum consuetudinem praedecessorum meorum, imperatorum Bulgarorum et Blachorum, Simeonis, Petri et Samuelis progenitorum meorum et caeterorum omnium imperatorum Bulgarorum.'

[1] *M.G.H.* Ep. VII, p. 60.   [2] *P.G.* vol. 102, cols. 904, 905. See p. 160.

The assertion that John VIII had repudiated his legates' stewardship and again condemned Photius, and that this condemnation was reiterated by his successors Marinus, Stephen V and Formosus, is based on data found in some documents included in the anti-Photian Collection and added in some Greek manuscripts to the Acts of the Eighth Council.[1]

This Collection is divided into three parts. The first includes the encyclical letter of the Eighth Oecumenical Council and the letter addressed by the Fathers of the Council to Pope Hadrian II, together with an extract from a letter from Hadrian to Ignatius on the Bulgarian issue, and a lengthy correspondence by the Ignatian Metropolitan Metrophanes, explaining to the Logothete Manuel how Photius had been condemned. The second part is important. It has a letter from Pope Stephen to the Emperor Basil on the legality of Pope Marinus' tenure; a short historical commentary on Photius' second deposition; a long letter from archbishop Stylianos of Neocaesarea to Stephen anent the recognition of Photian ordinations; a reply from the Pope to this letter, as also to that of the Emperor Leo the Wise; a second letter from Stylianos; then a letter from Pope Formosus announcing the rigorous proceedings he would take against the Photianists. The third part contains several writings on the Photian case; a short supplement on the *stauropatai*, i.e. the Photianists who, by frequently violating their promises, had discredited the cross which by common usage preceded their signatures; a document under the pompous heading—'Collection of the Synodical Letters of the Roman Pontiffs Nicholas, Hadrian, John, Marinus, Stephen and Formosus against the Prevaricator Photius'; the copy of an inscription placed at the entrance of St Sophia and recalling the decrees of the Council against Photius; a long explanation by the compiler to prove that Photius, after repeated condemnations, could no longer be absolved, followed by a note on the Eighth Oecumenical Council borrowed from a small hand-book on the Councils, and, finally, a letter from Pope John IX to Stylianos, with a free commentary.

The Collection was compiled at the end of the ninth century, in the reign of Pope Formosus (891–6).[2] This is beyond dispute. The anonymous compiler was therefore contemporary with Photius and was one of his bitterest enemies. In its original form, the work ended with a 'synodicon', or short list of the oecumenical councils; but the copyist who transcribed it in the last years of the ninth century or the first of the tenth, omitted the passage bearing on the first seven councils, only copying what was said about the eighth. He added, however, the

---

[1] Mansi, vol. XVI, cols. 409–57.   [2] See pp. 271 seq.

remark about the 'apostasy' of Stylianos, who had ended by acknowledging Photius' ordinations—and the letter with commentaries of Pope
John IX to Stylianos. It is mainly the latter part of the Collection which
supplies information about the fate of the compilation and about the
date when it was made and copied.

Now it is from this anti-Photian Collection, as already stated, that
the main arguments have to this day been assembled to prove Photius'
second condemnation by John VIII and his successors and to make out
a case for the serious deterioration in the relations between Byzantium
and Rome under the pontificates of Stephen V and Formosus. I have
shown elsewhere[1] that the arguments covering the period 880–5 are
valueless. I have also examined the whole problem in all its details
in another study[2] and all I intend to do here is to go over the main
points of my argument and draw attention to the compiler's methods
in building up his case. This should help us to understand the attitude
of John's successors, from Marinus I to Stephen V, to Photius and his
followers, and to realize to what extent the die-hards made use of the
Collection for their campaign of misrepresentation against Photius.

The compiler of the Collection treats of the relations between Photius
and John VIII in a special chapter under the comprehensive title[3] of
'Collection of synodical letters by the Popes who condemned Photius'.
What does he produce as a synodical letter from John VIII? After
quoting a passage from a letter by Nicholas I and an extract from the
Acts of the Roman synod of 869, the compiler gives the declaration by
the archdeacon John, introduced as spokesman to the Fathers of that
same synod, whose truculent philippic ends: 'May the sharpness of your
sentence tear his memory to tatters and let those who follow or protect
him be bound by the fetters of an anathema. Should they fail to anathematize him either in speech or in writing, let them be excluded from lay
communion.' The compiler then goes on:

When John, who had uttered these words, mounted the throne after
Hadrian, he also anathematized Photius for outwitting Eugenius and the
messengers accompanying him to Bulgaria. Seizing the Gospels, he [the
Pope] went up into the pulpit and declared to all present: 'Let him be
anathematized who refuses to admit that Photius was lawfully struck by the
judgement of God, and was moreover condemned by my predecessors, the
very saintly Popes Nicholas and Hadrian.'

[1] *Les Légendes de Constantin et de Méthode*, pp. 317 seq.
[2] 'Le Second Schisme de Photios—Une Mystification historique', in *Byzantion*
(1933), vol. VIII, pp. 42 seq.   [3] Mansi, vol. XVI, cols. 448, 449.

The compiler then quotes the inscription recalling the decrees of the Eighth Council, enumerates the Pontiffs who condemned Photius and adds:

None of Nicholas' successors has absolved them.[1] They had not even the power to do so. When in the Patriarch Ignatius' lifetime John sent Eugenius and his companions on the Bulgarian mission, Photius had them seized to induce them by various methods of pressure to communicate with him and thereby deceive the world. But on their return to Rome, they were reprimanded by John, who excommunicated them from the ambo.[2]

This is all the writer has to say as evidence for Photius' condemnation by John VIII, and it is very little. The bombastic heading promised better. Instead of John VIII's synodical letter condemning Photius, the compiler produces a long statement made, so he pretends, at the Roman synod of 869 under Hadrian's chairmanship. The declaration is pure invention. We have seen that the Acts of this synod were read at the end of the seventh session of the Council of 869–70 and they make it evident that the spokesman of the synod was not John, then Roman archdeacon, but Gauderich, bishop of Velletri. Naturally, archdeacon John, as head of the Roman deacons, signed the Acts, but only after the bishops, the archpriest George and the priests attached to the churches of Rome.[3] On the strength of this, the compiler invented a long anti-Photian statement which he put into the mouth of John, the future Pope, and passed off as a synodical letter against Photius by Pope John VIII.

The same Pope's alleged condemnation of his legates is likewise the compiler's invention and it is easy to imagine on what grounds the legend was framed. The Ignatians of course knew that the legates' instructions brought from Rome did not go as far as the decisions of the Photian Council, nor was there any secret about it in 879–80. Some die-hards then sought comfort in the thought that the legates would meet the same fate as had befallen Zachary and Radoald after the synod of 861. But no message to that effect came from Rome (the collection of Pope John's letters seems to be complete for the period it covers and there is no trace of any such communication to Constantinople), and the die-hards made up the story that the Pope had condemned both his legates and Photius from the ambo of St Peter's.

---

[1] Photius and Gregory Asbestas.　　　　　　　　[2] Mansi, vol. XVI, col. 452.
[3] Ibid. col. 131. The signatures are introduced as follows: 'his sententiis a nobis promulgatis, sicut superius legitur, consensi et propria manu subscripsi.'

The compiler seems to be conscious of the weakness of his argument, for he covers his tracks with theological and canonical disquisitions and then tries to prove that the Pope had no powers to absolve a man condemned by the other Patriarchs and by the Council.[1] Why such insistence, if the Pope went back on his first decision and excommunicated Photius a second time? The compiler is not even aware that such a statement smacks of heresy and contradicts his emphasis in other places on the sacredness of pontifical decrees.

On the other hand, the treatise on the 'stauropats' in the same Collection lists also the Romans among those prelates who violated their signatures; for after signing the Acts of the Roman synods of Nicholas and Hadrian for Photius' condemnation, they ended by acknowledging the Patriarch. The same Acts were 'also signed by archdeacon John, who became Pope after him [Hadrian]'.[2] The inconsistency is obvious.

Another document reproduced by the compiler, the letter of archbishop Stylianos to Pope Stephen V, gives the direct lie to his tale about John's condemnation of his legates and Photius. Though the writer insists in his letter[3] on the legates' responsibility for Photius' recognition by John VIII by repeating the conventional fable, not only has he nothing to say about the new verdict attributed to John VIII, but he dare not even repeat to the Pope the story of the legates' castigation so solemnly administered from the ambo. And yet, it was actually his purpose to induce the Pope to indict Photius and his partisans. He recalls with much relish the Acts of Nicholas and Hadrian II together with the decisions of the Council of 869–70, but is completely silent about John VIII, though he could not have produced a more striking illustration than John's outburst. It is therefore evident that in this particular matter the anti-Photian Collection deserves no credit and that John VIII never fell out with Photius.

To prove that the successor of John VIII, Marinus I, was unfriendly to Photius, the compiler proceeds again in the same way. Here also he promises to produce Marinus' synodical letter and again omits to do so, quoting instead the inscription placed at the entrance of the Great Church to commemorate the sessions of the Eighth Council, with a summary of the conciliar decrees against Photius, and a list of the names of the apostolic legates present at the meeting, including those of

---

[1] Mansi, vol. XVI, cols. 452, 453.
[2] Ibid. col. 444.   [3] Ibid. col. 432.

bishops Donatus and Stephen and of deacon Marinus. The last name is enough for the compiler to record with triumph that Photius was condemned by all the Popes from Leo IV to Formosus, including Marinus. When he uses the same argument in the manual of the Councils, of which the copyist preserved only the reference to the Eighth Council, he cites, as representing the Holy See, Marinus, 'who was destined to become Pope'. Bishops Donatus and Stephen, who in the first official document were placed before Marinus in accordance with protocol, now disappear before the future Pontiff, a clear indication of the compiler's purpose: Since Marinus had, together with the other Fathers, condemned Photius at the Council of 869–70, he of course condemned him for ever after, and could not, even as a Pope, go back on his pre-papal verdict. After this direct argument—the only one we are given—the compiler offers as indirect argument the letter from Pope Stephen V to the Emperor Basil, in which the Pope defends the memory of Marinus, unfairly attacked by the Emperor in a letter to Hadrian III. But Stephen V attributed these attacks to Photius' intrigues and towards the end of his letter referred enigmatically to an embassy of Marinus to Constantinople, which ended in his imprisonment:

Because he felt and thought as our predecessor and teacher, the very holy Pope Nicholas, felt and thought, whose decision he wished to carry out to the letter, the godly Marinus fell into your utter disfavour; because he refused, as reported, to admit those who thought differently and to declare null and void what had been decided at a synod in the presence of your Majesty, Marinus was imprisoned for thirty days.

The above extract has been commonly quoted to prove that John VIII, after discovering the deception of his legates and of Photius, sent to Constantinople an embassy headed by Marinus, who thereby incurred the anger of Photius and the Emperor, and was imprisoned. The general drift of the letter has also been advanced as evidence of Marinus' hostility to Photius.

The deduction is unwarranted, for nothing in the letter justifies the inference that Pope Marinus was in open conflict with the Patriarch. Stephen V does not refer to it in the letter included in the Collection, and had there been anything in the letter to prove that Marinus, on becoming Pope, openly broke with John VIII's policy, the compiler would certainly not have omitted it.

Historians who, in order to make a breach between John VIII and Photius more likely, invented a second embassy of Marinus to Constantinople in 880 and dated the incident of his imprisonment from that year, made a serious mistake. Stephen V explicitly states that Marinus incurred the Emperor's displeasure because 'he refused...to admit those who thought differently and to declare null and void what had been decided at a synod in the presence of Your Majesty'. Now these words could not refer to an embassy whose purpose was, not to refuse to declare, but to declare null and void the decisions of the Council of 879–80 taken in the presence of His Imperial Majesty. The words should not be severed from the context. In the first part of the passage, Stephen V writes that Marinus 'fell into the Emperor's disfavour' because he 'felt and thought as did our predecessor and teacher, the very holy Pope Nicholas, whose decisions he wished to carry out to the letter'. These words can only refer to Marinus' presence in Constantinople at the Eighth Council in 869–70, when he refused categorically to depart from the instruction he had received from Hadrian II. These reflected the true spirit of Nicholas' Eastern policy, though the Emperor tried hard to bring the legates to a frame of mind more sympathetic to the Photian clergy. It follows then that the second part of Stephen's reference to Marinus' relations with the Emperor should also refer to the same Council, and it would besides fit in with the incident in connection with the 'Libelli'. The Emperor disliked the condition (pressed by the legates) to admit to the Council only those prelates who had signed the 'Libellus', and when the prelates urged him to take the 'Libelli' away from the legates lest they should be used as evidence of Byzantium's submission to Rome, the legates refused to hand them over, arguing that such were the Pope's orders, to which the Emperor had agreed at the opening of the Council.

This incident should be placed within the interval of three months that came between the eighth and the ninth sessions of the Council. By that time the 'Libelli' must have been duly signed by the prelates and it is possible that the Emperor, infuriated by the incident, confined the legates to their quarters.[1] Nor should it be forgotten that Basil's letter had not been addressed to Marinus but to his successor, Hadrian III, and that the Emperor's criticism was meant for a dead Pope. This and the fact that the anti-Photian Collection knows nothing of a

[1] It is also possible that Stephen V confused the 'Libelli' incident with what befell Marinus at the Bulgaro-Byzantine frontier in 866, when the papal embassy may have been in some sort of confinement for a month whilst the Byzantine frontier authorities awaited instructions from the capital upon what to do with the papal legates. Marinus had thus quite a number of unpleasant experiences with the Byzantines. Cf. above, p. 117.

correspondence exchanged between Marinus and the Byzantines is evidence sufficient that the alleged embassy of 880 was never sent.[1]

And yet, it has been asserted[2] that if Marinus did not actually sever relations with Photius, acknowledged as he had been by John VIII, it was very much against his better feelings; that at heart he regretted this recognition by his predecessor; that he deliberately refrained from corresponding with the Patriarch and that he continued to hate him openly, in spite of the letter which Photius sent after the Council of 879–80 with offers of pardon and friendship. The differences that existed between Marinus and Photius under the latter's first patriarchate are appealed to as evidence that such was also Marinus' attitude during his enemy's second patriarchate.

It seems, however, that the extent of those differences is apt to be exaggerated. It is true that Marinus was prominent at the Council of 869–70. It is, however, good to remember that much the same happened to the future Pope John VIII, who as archdeacon to Hadrian II signed the Acts of the Roman synod that preceded the Council of Constantinople and gave to Marinus and his colleagues, representing the Holy See at the Eastern Council, the very instructions which Marinus carried out so literally and with such fervent conviction. At that time John certainly also approved the decisions of that Council, which did not prevent him forgetting later the part he had played in Photius' condemnation and making friends with him. Why then should Marinus, once Pope, be assumed to harbour such resentment?

It is also true that Marinus' signature is missing from the Acts of the Roman synod of 879, which was prior to the Photian Council summoned to rehabilitate Photius. But can a mountain really be made of such a mole-hill? Was Marinus in Rome at the time? For it seems possible that he was still acting as the bishop of Cere and, as we shall see presently, he was not to officiate as archdeacon in Rome until 880.

Such conclusions might be admissible, if it could be proved that Marinus entirely reprobated his predecessor's policy.

This has been attempted with two main arguments: first, it is well

[1] Hergenröther's allegation (*Photius*, vol. II, p. 578) that the Emperor and the Patriarch kept Marinus' embassy of 880 a secret cannot be taken seriously. The same author states that the Ignatians were alone in Byzantium to remain in communion with Rome. In that case, how can he explain that they did not learn anything more definite about Rome's altered attitude to Photius? He cannot have it both ways.

[2] Cf. Grumel, 'La Liquidation de la Querelle Photienne', in *Échos d'Orient* (1934), vol. XXXIII, pp. 258 seq. For details, see my reply, 'Études sur Photios', in *Byzantion* (1936), vol. XI, pp. 2 seq. Here I only summarize the main drift of my study.

known that John VIII had dealt rather severely with Formosus, the distinguished prelate whose mission to Bulgaria had been such a success. As it provoked jealousies in Rome, he had been recalled by Nicholas, and Boris' request to place the prelate at the head of the Bulgarian Church did not allay suspicions. Followed a dispute with John VIII, who then suspended and excommunicated him. But Marinus' first act on ascending the papal throne was to rehabilitate Formosus, and it was this move that has served as evidence that Marinus disowned John's policy.

It has been further suggested that John VIII was on bad terms with Marinus and made him bishop of Cere in order to remove him from Rome and wreck his chances as a candidate for the next papal election,[1] since it was not customary in those days to transfer bishops from one see to another. For this reason, so it is alleged, Marinus resigned his see after the death of John VIII on the pretext that he had been forced to accept the episcopal appointment, but in reality to canvass for the papal throne. Once there, he settled accounts with his predecessor by reversing the whole of his Eastern policy.

But this is a misreading of the facts. If John made Marinus a bishop to spoil his chances of promotion, he stultified his own principles, for at a Roman synod which met between 811 and 818, i.e. at the time of Marinus' consecration, John VIII reminded the bishops of the prohibition to follow similar proceedings in the case of their own deacons and archdeacons.[2]

Contrary to what has been said, John seems to have availed himself later of Marinus' services, as we learn from his correspondence that he sent a certain bishop Marinus, whom he calls 'arcarius sedis nostrae'— a function in the Roman Curia usually performed by the archdeacon— on two important embassies, one to Charles III in March 880 and another in 882 to Athanasius, bishop of Naples.[3] This may have been the bishop of Cere whom John asked to resign his see for that purpose. It was rather John's confidence in Marinus that helped his candidature to the Papacy in December 882, and he was elected just because he was the archdeacon and had ceased to exercise episcopal functions.[4]

---

[1] See the latest publication on Marinus I by J. Duhr, 'Le Pape Marin I', in *Recherches des Sciences Religieuses* (1934), vol. XXIV, pp. 200–6.

[2] F. Maassen, *Eine Römische Synode* (Wien, 1878), ch. XVII, p. 20.

[3] *M.G.H.* Ep. VII, pp. 200, 265.

[4] This explains why one of the Continuators of the Fulda Annals was shocked to see Marinus, bishop of Cere, changing sees in defiance of canonical rules, whereas the other only designates Marinus at the time of his election by the title of archdeacon (*M.G.H.* Ss. I, pp. 397, 398).

Another item of especially strong evidence may be quoted: Marinus, once on the throne, kept as librarian Zachary of Anagni,[1] who had occupied the same post under John VIII; and it was precisely this Zachary who, as Photius' faithful friend, was the strongest supporter in the Roman Curia of a Graecophil policy. Now it is inconceivable, if Marinus had nursed his old resentment against Photius and disapproved his predecessor's Graecophil policy, that he would have kept Zachary in his office. And it was the same Zachary who must have wielded a certain influence at the pontifical court under Pope Stephen V, his former pupil, until his death in 891. If this conjecture by Lapôtre is correct,[2] one can understand how the pontifical policy towards the East remained so favourable under the three successors of John VIII.

If such is the case, we can no longer adduce Marinus' omission to send a synodical letter to the Patriarch of Constantinople as evidence that he had abandoned John's policy and continued to hold Photius in detestation; for we have better reasons to account for the omission. Marinus' reign was a short one (December 882–April 884). Then Formosus' rehabilitation[3] in the first months of Marinus' pontificate must have caused some unrest, and these troubles forced the Pope to give his full attention to Roman affairs. As Marinus' death presumably followed a period of illness, which prevented the execution of several of the Pope's projects, his successor Hadrian III hurriedly dispatched his synodical letter to Constantinople in the first days of his pontificate, for fear the long delay should create an unfavourable impression in that city. Since Basil makes reference to Marinus in his reply to Hadrian III, his name must have been mentioned, probably in connection with his failure to send the synodical letter.

All this had to be said in defence of this Pope's memory, there being no evidence to show that the Roman Pope was any less noble and generous than the Patriarch of Constantinople or that he lacked the moral strength to sacrifice his personal feelings to the needs of the Church he governed.

[1] It was Zachary who wrote Marinus' letter 'pro monasterio Saviniensi' (*P.L.* vol. 126, col. 970).

[2] 'Le Souper de Jean le Diacre', in *Mélanges d'Archéologie et d'Histoire* (1901), vol. XXI, pp. 333 seq. D. Amelli published in the *Spicilegium Casinense*, vol. I, p. 381, a letter attributed to Stephen V which hints that Zachary participated in the activities of the Church even under the pontificate of Stephen V.

[3] It is possible that Marinus hoped to use Formosus' services in Bulgaria to induce Boris to return to the Roman obedience.

To return to our main source, the anti-Photian Collection which has provided the materials for the argument that Marinus had severed relations with Photius, we may conclude that here again the compiler mainly relies on the Patriarch's first condemnation, to which Marinus had naturally subscribed, and adduces in support of the second condemnation only scraps of evidence, which have led historians to conjectural conclusions.

Now let us see how he treats the relations between Photius and Hadrian III. In this case, he can scarcely hide his embarrassment, for not only does he lack a single statement by Hadrian III with reference to any Roman Council or to the Eighth Oecumenical Council, but he must have heard and known about the resumption of friendly relations between Photius and the new Pope, as attested by the Patriarch himself.[1] So he prefers to skip lightly over this period and coolly omits the name of Hadrian III from the list of Popes, whose anti-Photian synodical letters he intends to publish.[2]

The copyist of the Collection, to whom we owe the present edition of the compilation, and who was a fiercer Ignatian even than the compiler himself, thought he had discovered evidence in support of Photius' condemnation by Hadrian III in the letter from Pope John IX to Stylianos, which he duly included in the anti-Photian Collection.[3]

The Pope says there among other things: 'We therefore wish the decrees of the very saintly Pontiffs who preceded us to remain intact and to be held in the same esteem as before. We also admit Ignatius, Photius, Stephen and Anthony to the same rank to which they have been admitted by the very saintly Popes Nicholas, John, Stephen V and the whole Roman Church to this day.' Having explained this letter after his own fashion and enumerated all the Popes from Nicholas to John IX, the copyist goes on: 'When he therefore said "as the whole Church has admitted him to this day", he included all the Patriarchs who preceded him[4] and succeeded him and whose decrees he [John IX] also wishes to observe.'

This, it must be confessed, is an extremely weak argument and its weakness will be more evident when we examine the bearing of John IX's letter. The Ignatians had to be satisfied with it for want of a better; but it is surprising that historians should have taken it seriously.

---

[1] *P.G.* vol. 102, col. 381.

[2] Mansi, vol. XVI, col. 445. [3] Loc. cit. cols. 456, 457.

[4] He means either Stephen V or Formosus. Formosus is not mentioned in this, though the copyist may be responsible for the omission.

What then are we to think of the relations existing between Photius and Stephen? At a first glance, the position looks quite different. As Stephen appears on the scene, the schism seems to have recurred, and Rome to have repeated her old anathemas against Photius. The compiler has given us in the second part of his Collection two letters from the Pope, one addressed to the Emperor Basil and the other to archbishop Stylianos;[1] and the form in which they have come down to us apparently justifies the assumption, universally accepted for several centuries, that Pope Stephen did break off relations with Photius.

What of the documents that look so irreconcilable with friendly relations between the two Churches? In his letter to the Emperor Stephen begins by registering surprise at the unfriendly references to Marinus contained in Basil's letter. He then proceeds to trace the dividing line between the priestly and the imperial powers and to urge the Emperor to confine himself within the limits laid down by divine power. He denounces the man who had slandered Marinus in the Basileus' eyes. Then, taking his predecessor's defence in general terms, Stephen again urges the Emperor to stay within the limits of his power, scorns the slanderous denial that Marinus was a bishop at all, and quotes numerous instances from history of transfers from one see to another:

Where is the sin of that Roman Church [he adds] against which wicked people have urged you to turn and use your tongue? Did she not send her legates to Constantinople under your reign according to ancient synodal usage? Did she not spend infinite care on that synod? And are you asking to whom the Roman Church sent her legates? To none but Photius, the layman; for if you had a Patriarch, our Church would visit him more frequently. For it has been that city's misfortune, for all her fame and God's protection, that she has no pastors and that her only light comes from Your Imperial Majesty. If love for you did not restrain us, and help us to put up with the insult flung at our Church, we should most certainly consider ourselves obliged to order against Photius, the transgressor, who used such defamatory words against us, penalties more severe than any imposed by our predecessors. But whatever we say here is not meant to offend you, for we bear witness that you are God's beloved, but only in self-defence and to Photius' utter shame.

After thus unburdening himself, the Pope recalls Marinus' adventure in Constantinople at the time of the Eighth Oecumenical Council and once more urges the Emperor to follow the example of Constantine the Great, who used to cast into the fire any accusations brought against

[1] Mansi, vol. XVI, cols. 420–5, 436, 437.

226

priests, declaring himself unworthy to sit in judgement over the servants of God. He then goes on to express his joy on hearing that Basil had given one of his children to the Church and implores him to send to Italy further subsidies for the campaign against the Saracens, whose incursions were so severe that Rome ran short even of oil for her sanctuary lamps.

More important still is the Pope's second letter in reply to another request by Stylianos that the Pope should dispense the Photianists and ratify under certain conditions their ordinations. As this is a document of the greatest importance, we quote it in full:

Stephen, servant of the servants of God, to all the bishops of the whole world and other clergy. Our Catholic Church of God, founded on the firm rock of Peter's confession, though shaken by storms and gales, is steadily consolidating herself and growing apace. It was only to be expected that the Evil One should attack and tempt the members of the Church, since he did not hesitate in tempting the Head of the Church, Our Lord Jesus Christ; and it is no surprise to us that you should have banished from the Church the execrable Photius, for deriding Our Lord's life-giving Cross, the venerable symbol that inspires all the charisms of the priestly ministry and sanctifies our baptismal fonts. If only the said layman had followed the royal road and kept the regulations laid down by the Fathers, he would not have stumbled into such folly. For this reason, those who mocked Christ's humility, i.e. His venerable Cross, were stricken like the Egyptian first-born, whereas those among the Israelites who bore the mark were spared. What else did the blood of the Lamb on the Israelites' doors signify but the Cross of Christ's suffering, which marks the Christians' foreheads? Whoever then despises the salutary Cross will be slain by the sword of the Gospel.

This is how you wrote about Photius, but on reading the Emperor's letter we find it substantially[1] differing from yours. For it was written there that Photius had joined the monastic life and resigned the patriarchal throne, preferring, as his private life proved, humility to pride. But this caused us to hesitate, as there is a difference between voluntary abdication and expulsion. So, being unable to pass sentence without serious examination, we reserved judgement. It will be necessary to send trustworthy bishops from both sides, so that we may clear up doubts, discover the truth, and make such pronouncement as God may inspire us to make. For the Holy Roman Church is held up as a pattern to other Churches and what she decides holds for centuries. Hence the necessity for an inquiry before passing sentence.

Now these two documents have so far been used as evidence to prove that Pope Stephen did not consider Photius to be the legitimate

[1] πλεῖστον.

Patriarch; and there was something to be said for the contention, as long as a rupture between the two Churches was assumed to exist and this rupture was attributed to Stephen's predecessors. But it has already been established that their relations remained friendly till 885, so that, if the documents we have quoted really corroborate the assumption, the rupture should be attributed to Stephen V.

But their evidential value is highly suspect, for neither of the two texts contains any direct stricture on Photius. The few derogatory remarks on the Patriarch, provided they be reported in their original version (which is doubtful, as we shall see presently), can be read as relieving the resentment left in Roman hearts, reconciliation notwithstanding, by the old disputes about Photius' first pontificate. But even if reported in their genuine version, they are no proof that Stephen V had broken with the policy of his three predecessors—sanctioned as it was by a Council whose authority was recognized by Rome as well as by Byzantium—and excommunicated Photius. An act of such importance should have been communicated to the Church of Constantinople in unmistakable terms, as was the practice at the Pontifical Chancellery. The fact that the compiler knows nothing about such a pontifical declaration is a sign that the Church of Constantinople never received it.

To find out whether any radical change in the Popes' Eastern policy occurred at the beginning of Stephen's reign, we must search Stephen's register for any letter that might reveal the Pope's attitude to Byzantium and we find a significant one that was dispatched to the bishop of Oria, Theodosius, immediately after the Pope's accession, and from which we quote the following:[1]

We have learned from the reports of the faithful how our predecessor Hadrian sent you once to Constantinople as ambassador to the pious Emperor and received from him not only the pension that was due to your merits, but also other gifts which he sent to our Church and to others of the faithful. We wish to thank your Holiness for carrying out your mission so loyally.

Now we know that Pope Hadrian III, in the course of his short pontificate (April or May 884–August or September 885) did send, as attested by Photius, an embassy to the Patriarch of Constantinople for the usual exchange of synodal letters. We may take it for granted that the embassy was headed by the bishop of Oria, Theodosius, and considering that Hadrian's reign was so short, it must have been the only one he undertook. Imagine then a Pope, who is supposed to have

[1] *M.G.H.* Ep. VII, p. 334.

severed relations with the Byzantine Church, sending a message of praise and thanks to an ambassador for having presented the Holy See's homage to the Emperor as well as for having assured the Patriarch that the Church of Rome desired to remain on good terms with him. It is true that Stephen only mentions the mission to the Emperor, but the letter implies approval of whatever Theodosius did in Byzantium. We must conclude then from this letter that relations between Byzantium and Rome were of the best at the outset of Stephen's reign.

From letters on the affairs of southern Italy we gather the impression that Stephen V, far from departing from his predecessors' policy of friendship, actually co-operated with the Byzantines against the Arab danger. When the Arabs recaptured the ancient stronghold of Agropolis and Garigliano and repeated their incursions into the Principality of Salerno and pontifical territory, the Pope asked Byzantium for assistance, his request reaching the city a few months before the arrival of Guaimar, Prince of Salerno, who appealed to Leo VI, Basil's successor, for the same object.[1]

Again, Stephen's action taken against Athanasius II, bishop of Naples, at the time of his request addressed to the Emperor, contributed not a little to the Duke-bishop's improved behaviour. He had been severely blamed by John VIII for secret dealings with the Arabs.[2] Stephen's resolute stand must have impressed the bishop, for we find him turning to Byzantium for auxiliaries. He obtained 300 soldiers and probably acknowledged Byzantium's supremacy in return.[3]

These are serious indications of Stephen's friendly policy. A weightier document in Stephen's register proves up to the hilt that the Pope was on excellent terms with the Church of Byzantium about the years 887-8, the period in which the Pope's letter to Stylianos, since used as counter-evidence, was written. It was addressed to the Patricius George, commander of Calabria, the province recently wrested from the Arabs. The change of masters in Calabria inevitably brought many changes in its ecclesiastical organization. It was only natural that many Greeks were eager to spread their liturgy and their own institutions in the newly conquered land. This led to a conflict in Tarento, where the people, Latin by a good majority, promptly elected a new bishop to be

[1] For particulars, see Gay, *L'Italie Méridionale et l'Empire Byzantin* (Paris, 1904), pp. 129, 137 seq. Cf. my study, 'Le Second Schisme de Photios', in *Byzantion*, vol. VIII, p. 448.

[2] See John's letters in *M.G.H.* Ep. VII, pp. 204, 217, 246, 264. On Stephen's intervention, ibid. p. 337.

[3] Erchemperti Historia Langob. *M.G.H.* Ss. III, pp. 258 seq., cap. 56 seq.

consecrated by the Pope; but the Byzantine commander expelled him and in his stead had another priest elected for consecration by the Byzantine Patriarch. Stephen V at once addressed a strongly-worded remonstrance to George. In claiming the right to consecrate the bishop of Tarento, he used a phrase which is pertinent to our inquiry:[1]

By expelling the same [priest] after his election and, in defiance of canonical rules, electing one who belonged to another Church, you aimed at having him consecrated by the Church of Constantinople. This body, on learning that he should be consecrated by the Holy Church over which, by the grace of God, we preside, postponed the consecration.

This protest must have struck home, for in another letter[2] written about the same date, the Pope informs the Tarentans of his refusal to consecrate the priest Deusdona who had presented himself for consecration, claiming to be the elected bishop of Tarento, but without a single testimonial in support of his statement. Further, Tarento was not listed among the Byzantine dioceses of the period, so that we may conclude that this time the Byzantine Church really did acknowledge the Roman patriarchate's rights and withdrew its claims.

This is important. Here we have clear evidence that the two Churches were at peace and that Stephen V acknowledged Photius' successor Stephen, the same man who had been raised to the diaconate by Photius and was for this reason refused obedience by the die-hard Ignatians. But this is not all. The reign of Leo VI, brother of the Patriarch Stephen, coincided with the Byzantines' political and ecclesiastical reorganization of their Italian possessions, and the list they drew up of their dioceses shows what importance they attached to them and what trouble they took over their reorganization.[3]

All the more surprising that Greek influence in the south of Italy did not spread as far and as rapidly as one would have expected: Oria, Bari and Tarento remained Latin and Roman sees.[4] The Acts of the local synod of Oria held by Theodosius in 887–8,[5] which gives a vivid picture of the distressing religious conditions of those regions, show that the bishop, though a loyal subject of the Byzantine Empire, remained like the rest of his clergy Latin and Roman. Even in northern

---

[1] *M.G.H.* Ep. VII, p. 343. [2] Ibid. p. 344.
[3] See the list in H. Gelzer, *Georgii Cyprii Descriptio Orbis Romani* (Leipzig, 1890), pp. 59, 77, 82.
[4] Gay, loc. cit. pp. 184 seq.
[5] *Spicilegium Casinense* (1888), vol. I, pp. 377–81. Cf. D. G. Morin, 'Un Concile Inédit', in *Revue Bénédictine* (1900), pp. 143–51.

Calabria, where Byzantine claims seem to have been pressed more forcibly, it was mutually agreed that the bishops of Cosenza and Bisignano should be Latins elected from the local clergy, but consecrated by the Byzantine Metropolitan of Reggio.[1] Now such an arrangement can only be explained by the reasonable desire not to use force in the subjugation of the Lombards or to Hellenize them against their will. Had the two Churches been at loggerheads at that time, such political scruples would never have been considered for a moment and the opportunity of getting on even terms with a Pontiff who could be so unpleasant to the Byzantine patriarchate would never have been missed.

But all this does not accord with the implication attributed to the two letters of Pope Stephen. If our findings about the relations between the two Churches under Stephen's pontificate are correct, then it follows that the Pope's two letters have not been handed down in their original form and must in some way have been doctored by the compiler of the anti-Photian Collection. Two passages in the first letter addressed to Basil corroborate the inference.

First of all, Constantinople is called 'most famous city' and 'protected by God', a most unusual designation in a document issued by the Roman Chancellery, though common in Byzantine documents. And it significantly appears in the passage dealing with Photius, which therefore betrays a Byzantine hand and must be held to be suspect. Suspicion grows stronger when we consider that in the same passage Photius is designated as 'layman'. This appellation would be quite in its place in any Ignatian writing, as such was the interpretation put upon the declarations of Popes Nicholas I and Hadrian II and upon the decisions of the Eighth Council against Photius by the die-hard Ignatians. The letter addressed to Manuel[2] by Metrophanes may serve as an illustration.

Again, though, as stated before, Nicholas I was induced by Theognostos to use many of the 'epithets' which the die-hard Ignatians were fastening on Photius, he seems to have refrained from adopting that of layman.[3] No doubt, the two notions of the invalidity and the unlaw-

---

[1] Cf. Gay, loc. cit. pp. 188–92. This famous scholar, who also believes in a quarrel between the two Churches, feels embarrassed in trying to square the facts with the alleged enmity between the Churches.

[2] Mansi, vol. XVI, col. 416: 'but the godly Pontiff [Nicholas]...after summoning a Council of Western bishops, condemned him...calling him a "layman".'

[3] For evidence, see my study 'Le Second Schisme de Photios', in *Byzantion*, vol. VIII, pp. 452 seq.

fulness of ordinations uncanonically performed were often confused even in Rome in those days, but I have the impression that the Pontifical Chancellery unconsciously refrained from using the 'title' layman, in order to preclude a misunderstanding of a more serious character. It is also admitted that Photius' own ordination and the ordinations performed by him were regarded as valid, once the Patriarch was reconciled with the Roman See.

Now it was the specific purpose of the anti-Photian Collection, which rescued from oblivion the papal letter under discussion, to make out a case for the invalidity of Photius' ordination and for the absolute prohibition to hold communion with the bishops and clerics ordained by the Patriarch. This makes me think that the passage on Photius was doctored and that the offensive names given to Photius were added by the compiler.

I do not suggest that Photius was not mentioned in the Pope's letter. Stephen V apparently answered a letter which Basil had sent to Hadrian III in reply to a letter of his brought to Constantinople by the bishop of Oria. The Emperor presumably had taken exception to Marinus omitting to pay homage to him. In spite of explanations offered by Hadrian III, Marinus' successor, the Emperor took the omission as evidence of ill-feeling and resentment for incidents that occurred during Marinus' stay in Constantinople. He also took exception to such a person being raised to supreme honours in defiance of the canons forbidding a bishop's transfer from one see to another.

This objection to Marinus' elevation must have galled the Romans. Translations were forbidden by the first canon of the synod of Sardica, the same which forbade the precipitate elevation of laymen to the episcopate. Now the neglect of that canon had been one of the main reasons for Nicholas I to contest the legitimacy of Photius' elevation. Photius defended himself on the ground that the canons of Sardica had not been accepted by the Church of Constantinople, so that the Byzantines could retort with some satisfaction that the Roman Church did not observe them either, though she had accepted them and adopted them as part of her routine. The Byzantines could take a serious view of it, since the Photian Synod had decided that each Church should observe its own ancient customs and traditions.[1] By transferring Marinus to another see, the Roman Church had broken with her own customs:

[1] Mansi, vol. XVII, col. 489, canon 2. The point was made very forcibly by M. Jugie in one of his best studies on the subject ('Les Actes du Synode Photien de Ste Sophie', in Échos d'Orient (1938), vol. XXXVII, p. 90).

how could she then object to Photius' elevation, which at least had been in accordance with the old tradition of the Byzantine Church? Marinus' elevation was therefore uncanonical and illegitimate, and we may well imagine that the Emperor's representations did not please the Romans.

The Pope in his letter politely suggested that such calumnies against a Roman Pontiff could not have come from the pious Emperor, but must have been prompted to him by somebody else. It should be observed here that there is nothing in the first part of the letter to suggest that the 'somebody else' was Photius. The Emperor, in presuming to give a lesson to the Church of Rome—the Pope went on—was overreaching himself; there was nothing unusual about Marinus' election, since the Roman Church had more than once approved the transfer of bishops from one see to another. Basil had no reason to complain of the Roman Church, which had always complied with his wishes. Did she not send her legates to a synod (the so-called Eighth Council) at the Emperor's request and spend infinite care on it? She even sent legates to Photius (the Pope here has in mind the Photian synod of 879–80), and given the opportunity, would have done more. You have therefore no grounds for complaint, and were it not for the love we bear you restraining us and helping us to put up with such insults flung at our Church, we should most certainly consider ourselves obliged to impose on the slanderer penalties more severe than any inflicted on Photius by our predecessors. It is not in a spirit of aggressiveness, but in pure self-defence that we are writing this.

Such in all probability must have been the passage in the letter on Photius in its original form and nothing in it could possibly be construed into a second censure on Photius. The Pope on the contrary mentioned, besides the Eighth Council, the council which rehabilitated Photius, a sign that he subscribed to it. That such was the case and that the incriminating words must have been added by the indiscreet compiler will be seen from an analysis of the second document, the Pope's letter to Stylianos.

This letter, in the form in which it has been preserved, is still more enigmatic than the first and contains glaring discrepancies between the first and second parts. In the first, the Pope accuses the Patriarch of blasphemy against the Cross, whereas in the second, he defends him in the matter of deposition or abdication under compulsion. At the end of his letter the Pope quotes from the imperial letter the compliments in praise of Photius, in flat contradiction of what he had written in the first part of his letter. The only possible conclusion is that here again the letter has been tampered with.

The designation of 'layman' is also repeated, and it should be noted that a legend circulated in ultra-Ignatian circles to the effect that Photius had committed blasphemy against the symbol of salvation.[1] It makes one look instinctively in the Pope's letter for some mention of the word 'cross' which the compiler could have twisted into the sense of the legend. In fact, we read in the fragment of the pontifical register, in a letter by Stephen V:[2] 'To Stylianos, Anastasius, Eusebius, John and Paul, archbishops and their clergy.—Are not all the charisms of the priestly ministry operated by the sign of the Cross? Does baptismal water not remit sin on the one condition that one be sanctified by the Cross? And, omitting the rest, can anyone ascend the steps of the priesthood without the sign of the Cross?' *Item*: 'If therefore the Roman Church, which we govern by the will of Christ, is held to all as a mirror and a pattern, whatever she decides must be at all times unequivocally observed.'

Another document included in the anti-Photian Collection, Stylianos' reply to the Pope's letter, will show in what connection the Pope mentioned the Holy Cross. This is the text of the letter:[3]

Our lowliness has received the godly and saintly letters of your most saintly and excellent pontifical honour and they have filled us with great joy. After the introduction, which lavishes high praise on the Apostolic See, we read the following: 'It was stated in the letter of your venerable pontifical majesty that the letters of our serenest Emperors [Leo and Alexander] did not agree with ours'; but this is the reason of the discrepancy: Whereas those who wrote that Photius had resigned, acknowledged him as a priest, how could we, who, in keeping with the legitimate and canonical decision of the most venerable Pontiffs Nicholas and Hadrian and in conformity with the holy and oecumenical Synod held in Constantinople by the representatives of the Holy See and the three Oriental thrones, refuse to attribute to Photius any degree of priesthood, have written that one who had been condemned had resigned? We were also surprised to note that you say at the end of your letter that he should be judged as a legitimate archbishop, after stating at the beginning that he had been severed from the solid rock of Christ: how can he be judged, who has been severed? Is this the way the decrees of your holy predecessors are emasculated? But I believe that if any one wished to recon-

---

[1] For particulars, see my study 'Le Second Schisme de Photios', in *Byzantion*, vol. VIII, p. 456. See the anecdotes in Pseudo-Simeon (Bonn), pp. 669–71.

[2] *M.G.H.* Ep. VII, p. 348.

[3] Mansi, vol. XVI, cols. 437, 439; *M.G.H.* Ep. VII, pp. 381, 382.

sider Photius' case, he would only aggravate the condemnation. But omitting all the rest, what do you think of his misrepresentation of Pope Marinus? The letter you wrote to Basil, our glorious Emperor, shows that you are not ignorant of them.[1] But again, we take refuge in prayer, interceding for those who were forced to submit to Photius, and we ask you to be good enough to send encyclical letters to the Eastern Patriarchs, that they also may receive, acknowledge and confirm our dispensation, the more so as the Emperor, who drew us from the darkness and shadows of death into the light of day, desires it.

The letter makes it clear that Stylianos only took notice of the sentences passed on Photius by Nicholas I, Hadrian II and the Eighth Council and read into them the meaning that Photius had been stripped of every degree of the priesthood. On this point he was at variance with Stephen V, who in his letter referred to Photius as the legitimate Patriarch. Stylianos tried to bring the Pope round to his own opinion and induce him to give a special dispensation to all those who had under Photius' patriarchate acknowledged him as the legitimate pastor. It is in this light that we must now study the Pope's letter to Stylianos.

It seems to have followed this train of thought:

I am not surprised that you should have disowned Photius, since he did come under canonical strictures; but regarding your request to dispense the clergy who held communion with Photius, I do not see the necessity, since Photius, though condemned, was validly ordained. The validity of the sacraments is not dependent on the worthiness or otherwise of the person administering them; and the grace of the sacraments does not come from men, but from the virtue of Our Lord's Cross. Are not all the charisms of the priestly ministry operated by the sign of the Cross? Does baptismal water not remit sin on condition only that one be sanctified by the Cross? And to omit the rest, can anyone ascend the steps of the priesthood without the sign of the Cross?[2]

The Pope then returned to the discrepancy between the Emperor's letter and that of Stylianos concerning Photius' resignation, repeating finally his injunction addressed to Stylianos and his friends always to obey the orders of the Roman Church.

[1] It is not here implied that Stephen V accused Photius of slandering Marinus. It may be Stylianos' own interpretation of the Pope's charitable excuse that the words might have been prompted to the Emperor by somebody else.

[2] I readily accept the suggestion offered by V. Grumel (*Échos d'Orient*, 1934, vol. XXXIII, p. 263): his interpretation harmonizes better with the drift of the fragment of this letter, and confirms among other things the fact that even under Nicholas I the Pontifical Chancellery made the necessary distinction between the validity and the illicit nature of Photius' ordination.

It was in this sense, I believe, that the Pope was led to speak of the Lord's Cross, and one can understand why Stephen V insisted so forcibly on Photius' first condemnation.[1] Having no wish to treat the Ignatians too roughly, as they had addressed themselves to him with such reverence for the Holy See, he acknowledged that their attitude was justified at first, since Photius had really been condemned by the Holy See; but ended by gently chiding them and observing that what the Church has decided must hold good for ever: and what she had decided was not only the first condemnation, but also Photius' rehabilitation.

It will thus be seen that the compiler made considerable modifications in the text of the letter: he betrayed himself by referring to Photius as 'layman' and by his characteristic distortion of the Pope's reference to the Cross; the sentence is given an 'Ignatian' twist and there is a clumsy gap in the join of the two parts of the letter.

Stylianos' reply proves moreover that the Ignatians had understood the Pope's idea perfectly well; that they were aware of his persistence in holding Photius to be the legitimate Patriarch and his ordinations to be valid, and that they rightly assessed the interest he took, being in possession of the conflicting evidence, in the change that came over the patriarchal throne.

Here again the compiler took his materials from the Pope's utterance on Photius' first condemnation, but gave it a wider connotation than was really justified. Now that we have seen through the device, we can confidently state that Pope Stephen V, whatever may to this day have been said about him, did not break with Photius, but like his predecessors continued to treat him as the legitimate Patriarch. It may now be stated that the same Pope, who was always believed to be Photius' particularly venomous enemy, will in fact champion his cause on the occasion of his second deposition by the Emperor. There is only one possible conclusion: Photius' second schism, assumed so far to have been particularly fatal to the friendly relations between the two Churches, belongs to the realm of legend.

---

[1] The forceful terms which the compiler puts into the Pope's mouth on the subject of this condemnation are, however, in all probability the compiler's own concoction.

CHAPTER VIII

PHOTIUS, LEO VI AND THE HEALING OF THE EXTREMISTS' SCHISM

Photius acknowledged by the Moderate Ignatians—Leo VI's change of policy and Photius' resignation—Leo, the 'Little Church' and the Moderates—Was there a schism under Formosus?—The 'Little Church's' liquidation—A reunion synod in 899?—Authorship of the anti-Photian Collection and date of composition of the *Vita Ignatii*—The Extremists and the Moderates in the tetragamy conflict.

In our examination of the relations between Stephen V, the Emperor Leo VI and Photius, the problem of the so-called second Photian schism made it necessary to reverse the chronological sequence of events and temporarily to abandon the historical method previously followed. We may now return to the Patriarch's story.

The Council, after rehabilitating Photius, voted severe penalties against those who refused to acknowledge Photius as the legitimate Patriarch. But it took more than a Council to crush the ultra-Ignatian opposition. The reader will remember that part of the clergy attached to the church of St Sophia completely ignored the new Patriarch and, the moment he took possession of his throne, suspended the celebration of the sacred mysteries and left the church, affecting to be deeply shocked by the 'invasion' of the 'intruder'. Photius himself had to confess in the course of the Council that two bishops had been banished by the Emperor for exceptional refractoriness.

So the opposition persisted; but it is difficult to state anything more definite about its extent or about the number of bishops and clergy who remained obdurate even after Rome had declared in favour of Photius. Stylianos addressed his letters to the Pope not merely in his own name, but also in the name of Eusebius, bishop of Nazianzus, John of Comana, John of Leontopolis, in the name 'of all the bishops, priests and deacons of the most holy Church of Constantinople, of the abbots in West and East, priests, monks and anachorets'.[1] We also know that Metrophanes of Smyrna refused to make peace with Photius, and the more intractable bishops were banished, in company presumably with the prelates mentioned in Stylianos' letters. Yet, everything seems to indicate that the

---

[1] Mansi, vol. XVI, cols. 425, 437. Pope Stephen V, as we saw previously, addressed his letter 'to the archbishops Stylianos, Anastasius, Eusebius, John and Paul and their clergy' (*M.G.H.* Ep. VII, p. 348).

bishops who refused to compound with Photius were not many, the most recalcitrant elements being mainly to be found in the monasteries. The smaller the number, the more bitter their fanaticism.

The more moderate elements among the episcopacy and the clergy rallied to Photius, and among the outstanding members of Ignatius' party was St Joseph the Hymnographer. Joseph, at first, belonged to the die-hards. He also suffered persecution under the last iconoclastic Emperor Theophilus, and though recalled by Theodora refused to leave his place of banishment, preferring 'to enjoy his exile for the sake of Christ as though it were paradise', says his biographer, John the Deacon.[1] This particular portion of his biography definitely suggests that Joseph refused to return to Constantinople because he did not approve the election of Methodius and his religious policy. Not until the patriarchate of Ignatius did he go back to the capital,[2] where he soon won the new Patriarch's confidence and received from him an appointment as synkellos. Now it is remarkable that the same Joseph unhesitatingly rallied to Photius, and his biographer even extolled the intimacy between the two men: yet, Joseph was one of those who were banished after the fall of Ignatius.[3]

The case of Metrophanes of Smyrna is not so clear. We possess a letter addressed to Metrophanes[4] by Photius, whose cordial and light-hearted tone would at first lead one to believe that the metropolitan of Smyrna had made peace with Photius; but a closer study of the text of the letter—and certainly the Patriarch's Greek is of such finesse and subtlety as to embarrass any translator, however familiar with Byzantine Greek—shows that things happened somewhat differently.

The letter was apparently written after Photius' accession to the patriarchal throne after Ignatius' death, but before the Council of

[1] Vita S. Josephi Hymnographi, *P.G.* vol. 105, col. 968.

[2] Note that Ignatius the Deacon, biographer of St Tarasius and St Nicephorus, never mentions Joseph the Hymnographer in his biography of St Gregory the Decapolite, though these two men were intimately united in their lifetime. Ignatius the Deacon belonged to the Moderate party. Did he omit to mention Joseph because the latter disliked Methodius' religious policy and was an enthusiastic follower of Ignatius? Cf. my book, *La Vie de St Grégoire le Décapolite et les Slaves Macédoniens au IXe siècle* (Paris, 1926), p. 19.

[3] *P.G.* vol. 105, cols. 968, 969. Cf. the Life, written by Theophanes and published by Papadopoulos-Kerameus, *Monumenta Graeca et Latina ad Historiam Photii pertinentia* (Petropoli, 1901), vol. II, pp. 1–14. Cf. Van de Vorst, 'Note sur St Joseph l'Hymnographe', in *Analecta Bollandiana* (1920), vol. XXXVIII, pp. 148–54.

[4] A. Papadopoulos-Kerameus, *Ss. Patris Photii...Epistolae XLV* (Petropoli, 1896), pp. 18, 19.

879–80, for the purpose of bringing Metrophanes round to his cause. But Photius had previously addressed a letter to him offering him peace and reconciliation, the letter being accompanied with a gift, whose nature is not revealed. Metrophanes returned the present to Photius on the plea that the state of his health did not permit him to make use of it; at the same time he conveyed to him the indignation of one of his intimate friends, who was living with him at the time (was it Stylianos?) and had taken offence at Photius' omission to make the same overtures to him.

In his reply, of which the text has been preserved, Photius apologizes for not having selected a better present, being ignorant of Metrophanes' state of health. If he overlooked his friend, it was because he was busy and quite unaware that they were living together; but he apologizes for the omission and regrets that his good will has not been appreciated.

This reveals a new trait in Photius' character: evidently, the Patriarch was doing his best to pacify the Church, never hesitating, though he had every reason to consider himself wronged by his old opponents, to meet them half-way. He failed, however, in his peace overtures to Metrophanes and had to replace him on the see of Smyrna by one of his own supporters, Nicetas; for the latter figured among the prelates who attended the Council of 879–80. As Metrophanes' case came up for consideration by the Fathers of the Council, this prelate, who was in Constantinople whilst the Council was in session, obstinately refused to take notice of the legates' pressing invitation to appear before the assembly; his plea was always that of ill-health, until finally the legates proposed, in obedience to the Pope's decision, to deal very severely with Metrophanes on grounds of contumacy. They themselves, however, did not pronounce excommunication, but left the decision to Photius, who had received powers from the Pope to that effect.[1]

Whether Photius did excommunicate him is not stated in the Acts of the Council. He apparently reserved sentence, perhaps in the hope of conciliating Metrophanes, but to no effect, and eventually the recalcitrant prelate had to pay the penalty imposed by the Fathers on all those who refused to accept Photius as the legitimate Patriarch. Photius must have been sorry for his failure in placating the most eminent among the Ignatians and one he esteemed so highly for his literary work.[2]

[1] Mansi, vol. XVII, cols. 496, 500, 501.
[2] It is very likely that Metrophanes recovered his see after Photius' second resignation in 886, for his disciple Arsenius calls him the Metropolitan of Smyrna

As we have seen, Photius did not remain idle and did what he could to pacify the Byzantine Church; but he did more. His short treatise dating from that period and quoted by the title 'Collationes Accurataeque Demonstrationes de Episcopis et Metropolitis',[1] had no other purpose than to ease the tension among the clergy and attenuate the bad impression which Rome's intervention against Photius had produced on certain minds in Byzantium. Historical instances of bishops being deposed and reinstated must have defeated the arguments of those diehards who remained obdurate and worked against Photius, for his efforts proved partly successful. For one thing, relief was felt in Byzantium at the final settlement of past differences and joy at the restoration of peace within the Church. The biographies of St Joseph the Hymnographer and of Nicholas the Studite[2] breathe an atmosphere of peace and the biographers, in writing about these two saints who once supported Ignatius, deliberately avoid any word that might disparage the memory of either Ignatius or Photius.

But in spite of all his efforts, a small extremist minority, under the leadership of Stylianos of Neocaesarea and Metrophanes of Smyrna, formed a sort of 'Little Church' which remained stubborn and shunned all contact with Photius and the bishops consecrated by him. The leaders were sent into exile and did not return to Constantinople till after Photius' second downfall.

To return now to the anti-Photian Collection, this is how the compiler reports Photius' reverse and the exiles' recall; after quoting the letter from Pope Stephen V to Basil, previously mentioned,[3] the compiler says:[4]

This letter had been addressed to Basil, but, the father being dead, was received by his son Leo. On realizing its importance and learning of Photius' wicked intrigues, he recalled all the priests who had served the truth and been so bitterly persecuted by the cursed Photius, expelled Photius the tyrant and usurper, and replaced him by Stephen, the same Leo's own brother. He then

in 912, in a panegyrical poem probably written after Metrophanes' death (S. G. Mercati, 'Inno anacreontico alla SS. Trinità di Metrofane Arcivescovo di Smirne', in *Byz. Zeitschrift* (1929–30), vol. XXX. Nicetas, however, may have succeeded him again. Two letters from Symeon Metaphrastes (*P.G.* vol. 114, cols. 228–9) are addressed to Nicetas, Metropolitan of Smyrna.

[1] Ed. F. Fontani, *Novae Eruditorum Deliciae* (Florentiae, 1786), vol. I, pt. 2, pp. 1–80; *P.G.* vol. 104, cols. 1220–32. Cf. Hergenröther, *Photius*, vol. II, pp. 558 seq. As I cannot enter into all the details of Photius' argumentation and Hergenröther's criticisms, I deem it sufficient to give the drift of the pamphlet.

[2] *P.G.* vol. 105, cols. 908, 913.

[3] P. 226.

[4] Mansi, vol. XVI, col. 425.

summoned Stylianos, called Mapas, the Metropolitan of Neocaesarea and all the bishops, abbots, priests and deacons who had stood by him in persecution, with all the other champions of justice, and said to them: 'Our godly majesty has examined the true state of things, dethroned the iniquitous man and put an end to your persecution. Unwilling to force any of you to hold communion against his will, I would rather appeal to your piety and invite you to join my brother so that the flock may at last be one. But if you object to holding communion with my brother because he was ordained by Photius without the consent of the Romans who had excommunicated him, well then, let us write and send a joint request to the Pope asking him to absolve from the sentence of excommunication all those who were ordained by Photius.' The Emperor and all those who supported Mapas, the Metropolitan of Neocaesarea, then wrote a letter to the Pope.

This is, indeed, an extraordinary and unexpected testimony. The way in which the die-hards of the 'Little Church' represented the facts and again succeeded in embroiling the See of Rome is truly remarkable. But did things actually happen as the compiler asserts? To verify the allegations made by the compiler of the anti-Photian Collection, it will be necessary to inquire into the circumstances of Photius' second downfall.

The problem offered for solution is not an easy one, as we unhappily possess little reliable information about the reign of Leo VI, and Photius tells us nothing in his vast correspondence about the circumstances that raised a quarrel between him and his former pupil. So the story of Photius' humiliation remains wrapped in mystery; but to understand as best we can the sequence of events at the outset of the reign of Leo VI, it will be necessary to go back to the last years of the reign of Basil I and examine the ties that linked the father to his son and successor.

It was no secret that Basil was not fond of his son Leo. All his love and fatherly affection had centred in his eldest son Constantine, whose loss was the worst trial of Basil's life. To him Basil had hoped to hand over his life's work, and when his hopes were dashed he had little heart left either to resign himself to his fate or to love his son Leo, designated to the succession in 879, although crowned co-emperor as early as 870.[1]

To make matters worse, Basil touched his son on the place where a young man of Leo's age would feel most sensitive: though he knew

---

[1] The fact that Leo was not Basil's legitimate son can no longer serve to explain the estrangement. This question has been definitely settled by M. N. Adontz, 'L'Oraison funèbre de Basile I', in *Byzantion*, vol. VIII, pp. 508 seq.

of his son's attachment to Zoe, daughter of his compatriot Zautzes, he gave Leo, against his will, in marriage to Theophano, of the Martiniakioi family, to which the Empress, Eudocia Ingerina, also belonged. The marriage, as is well known, was not a happy one. Theophano was her rival Zoe's exact opposite: equally passionate, she yet gave her passion a nobler object, too noble in fact to suit Leo's taste—the practice of virtue, prayer and works of mercy;[1] and as her practices were not such as to interest her husband, then in the full glow of youth and passion, he looked for consolation elsewhere and resumed his relationship with Zoe.

Here Theophano made a bad mistake, natural and comprehensible no doubt, but none the less fatal: instead of trying to draw him away from her rival and give him the satisfaction he was looking for, she complained to her father-in-law about her young husband's infidelity. The panegyrist of the future saint says nothing about this incident,[2] but we gather the details from another source, a reliable one, the Life of St Euthymios.[3] Basil lost his temper and decided to give his son a lesson that went further than mere verbal exhortation; but this time the young prince thought that Basil had abused his paternal authority and Leo gave an account of the stormy scene to his spiritual director, the monk Euthymios. To end it all, Basil gave Zoe in marriage, against her will, of course, to Theodore Guzuniates.

The incident only exasperated the young man, embittering him not only against his wife, but his father, and from that time he began to treat with the party which opposed his father's policy. The Extremists, disappointed in Basil, who at first had encouraged their hopes, were quick to take advantage of the quarrel between father and son and saw to it that Leo's wrath should not be allowed to cool.

There is no doubt that the party of the Extremists, ever active and watching their opportunity to seize the reins of government, relied on Leo's co-operation to attempt a political plot against Basil; but their conspiracy was quickly detected, for the other party, conscious that Basil's downfall would mean the end of its supremacy, was also on the alert. The chief representative of the Moderates who supported Basil's

---

[1] Cf. the panegyric of Nicephorus Gregoras: Hergenröther, *Monumenta Graeca ad Photium pertinentia* (Ratisbonnae, 1869), pp. 80–1.

[2] Nicephorus Gregoras, loc. cit., rather extols Theophano's patience in putting up with her husband's infidelity.

[3] Ed. C. de Boor, *Vita Euthymii* (Berlin, 1888), pp. 20 seq. This Life gives interesting details about the relations between Leo, Theophano and Zoe. See de Boor's commentary on pp. 156 seq.

rule happened to be the learned Theodore Santabarenos, former abbot of the monastery of Studion, metropolitan of Euchaita, whom Photius had introduced to Basil. He gradually took the place formerly occupied by Gregory Asbestas, and for all practical purposes became the leader of the Moderates' ecclesiastical wing.

It was Theodore who drew the sovereign's attention to the machinations of the opposition party and to the efforts made by the malcontents to win his son's support. Taking action again with his usual energy, Basil locked up his son in the triclinium of the Margarita, threatening in his rage to put his eyes out, and it was all that Photius and the Senate could do to save the boy from torture. According to the chroniclers,[1] all the men of Leo's circle were arrested, cross-examined, some of them tortured and banished, special mention being made of Andrew, Domestic of the *Scholae*, Stephen, the Magister and the protovestiarios Nicetas Helladicos.

It is in this way that the facts should be interpreted. The chroniclers are unanimous, and their unanimity arises from the mutual dependence of their reports, in accusing Santabarenos of having staged the whole fracas and instigated Leo's imprisonment. He is alleged to have advised the prince to remain armed—some say with a dagger, others, with a sword—to protect his father's life in case of assault. Leo would have taken the advice, but was immediately accused by Santabarenos of attempting his father's life and the seizure of his throne; to prove Leo's evil intention, he averred that the prince always carried a weapon to use against Basil at the first propitious moment. The weapon was found and Leo was imprisoned.

But the story does not deserve the credit it has been given. As the chroniclers state in the same breath that Leo detested and distrusted Theodore,[2] it is hard to believe that the young man fell into the trap so easily and armed himself on his enemy's advice. It is true, however, that Basil was enraged and that he took a serious view of the affair: in spite of repeated intervention by Photius and the Senate, Basil remained deaf to all protests and entreaties on his son's behalf; it was only after three months that he relented, setting his son free and

---

[1] Cf. Georg. Mon. Cont. (Bonn), pp. 846 seq.; Pseudo-Simeon, pp. 697 seq.; Leo Gram. pp. 259 seq.; Cedrenus (Bonn), vol. II, pp. 245 seq. An interesting repercussion of this wrangle between father and son is also found in the Life of S. Constantine the Jew, *A.S.* Nov. vol. IV, p. 648. The anonymous biographer makes Constantine prophesy the reconciliation at an early date of the Emperor and Leo. The Life was written in the reign of Leo the Wise.

[2] Pseudo-Simeon (Bonn), p. 697.

restoring him to his former honours. Clearly there was something more in all this than the vile calumny of a personal enemy; the future Emperor was in serious danger and was well aware of it; for the rest of his life he maintained a special devotion to the prophet Elias, his father's favourite saint, on whose feast day he was released from prison.[1]

The chroniclers also mention another plot against Basil's government, under the leadership of the Domestic of the *Scholae*, John Crocoa (Curcu), with the support of sixty-five senators and high court officials. Specifically mentioned among the conspirators are the Comes of the Foederati, Michael Catudares (Catudes), Myxaris (Myxiares) and Babutzicos; but this attempt was also nipped in the bud. The conspirators were publicly arraigned in the circus by the Emperor, scourged and banished. The chroniclers who mention the incident[2] put the responsibility for this revolt on a recluse of the church of Our Lady of Blachernae, who had prophesied the imperial crown to John Crocoa.

The significance of the chroniclers' report is obvious and enables one to lay these frustrated attempts against Basil's government at the door of the Extremist party, whose radical wing was always packed with fanatical monks. To judge by the number of arrests made among the high State officials,[3] the party must have been powerful and gave Basil every reason to be on the alert and even to suspect his own son of making common cause with his political opponents. It makes Leo's troubles only too comprehensible and the anecdote on Theodore Santabarenos may safely be consigned to the realm of chroniclers' fables.

It is also to be noted that archbishop Stylianos, Theodore's relentless enemy, does not quote this story in his letter to Pope Stephen,[4] though he accuses Theodore and Photius of intriguing against Leo and mainly vents his feelings on Theodore, who in his view had set Leo and

[1] Cf. the panegyric of S. Elias, delivered by Leo, ed. Akakios, Λέοντος τοῦ Σοφοῦ πανηγυρικοὶ Λόγοι (Athens, 1868), p. 260.

[2] Georg. Mon. Cont. (Bonn), pp. 847, 848; Pseudo-Simeon, p. 699; Leo Gram. p. 261.

[3] Theoph. Cont. (Bonn), ch. 45, p. 277, dates the conspiracy immediately after Photius' reinstatement by Basil, though the other chroniclers place it after Leo's reconciliation with Basil. The object of the plot could not be Leo's release from prison, as A. Vogt, *Basile Ier*, pp. 153 seq., seems to think, though even Vogt attributes the second conspiracy to the political party which backed Leo against Basil. In his study, 'La Jeunesse de Léon VI le Sage', in *Revue Historique*, vol. CLXXIV, pp. 417 seq., he repeats the incidents in detail but can scarcely conceal his embarrassment in trying to disentangle their complications. He is right, however, when he refers to the machinations of the two political parties.

[4] Mansi, vol. XVI, col. 433.

Basil against each other. And yet, if he wanted the Pope to see that 'monster' in his true colours, that was the right moment to release the tale, which is found in all later chronicles.[1] It all confirms our surmise that the anecdote was invented later by the historians of the Macedonian House to free Leo from all suspicion. The fact is that the incident was far more serious than gossip suggests.[2]

Again, no sooner was Leo on the throne than the same men who had been under suspicion for plotting against Basil, Andrew and Stephen, exercised considerable influence on Leo: they are the men, together with the father of the Emperor's mistress, Stylianos Zautzes, whose names are displayed on the very first page of the works of Leo's historians.

It is clear, then, that the party in opposition to Basil's government reared its head after Leo's accession; but Basil's unexpected death disheartened his supporters,[3] as they realized that it was now their opponents' turn to govern. As a matter of fact, Leo, at the beginning of his reign, distributed all his favours to the Extremist party, to which he had already shown his partiality in his father's reign, if not from personal conviction at any rate out of spite against his father and his father's policy. It would be impossible to explain the first act of his government—the solemn translation of the body of the Emperor Michael III—except as a display of the young sovereign's petulance; it could not be meant to flatter the feelings of the Extremists, who detested Michael's memory. The translation ceremony had the additional advantage of rallying round the young sovereign the old partisans of Michael III, who had refused to support Basil (for each party had its die-hards) but under the new regime had no excuse for detachment.

But Leo's gesture could not prevent every Byzantine from observing that things had completely altered at the imperial palace. The first victim of the Extremists was Theodore Santabarenos, who was arrested. It was proposed to intern him in the monastery of Studion, of which he had once been the abbot, but as the monks would not have him he was then interned in the monastery of Dalmata.[4] Photius was also in their

---

[1] The anecdote is not even mentioned by Nicephorus Gregoras, writer of the thirteenth and fourteenth centuries, in his panegyric of Theophano.

[2] Cf. Yared, *Khrist. Chtenie* (1872), vol. III, p. 683; N. Popov, *Imperator Lev VI Mudryi i ego Tsarstvovanie* (Moscow, 1892), pp. 6 seq.

[3] The first chapter of the biography of Euthymios (loc. cit. p. 2) gives a vivid impression of the gloom that seized the courtiers on learning that Basil's death was imminent.

[4] de Boor, loc. cit. p. 4.

black books. Andrew, the Domestic of the *Scholae*, and the Magister Stephen accused Santabarenos and the Patriarch of having attempted to usurp imperial power and to set up a relation of Photius' instead of Leo. This was a repetition of the way in which Bardas and Michael had proceeded against Ignatius, who also had been accused of conspiring against the government. Methods did not vary much in Byzantium.

There was no difficulty in convincing Leo of the danger he courted by keeping Photius at the patriarcheion. Photius had been Leo's preceptor, but only for two or three years when Leo was eleven or twelve years old, so that the Patriarch's influence over him could not count for much. There was, on the contrary, no love lost between them, as Photius must have often reproved his pupil about his private life and his behaviour to his father.[1] There was, moreover, his mistress' father, Stylianos Zautzes, to whose obvious benefit it was to make bad blood between master and pupil, the same Stylianos who could submit without question to the iron will of his compatriot Basil,[2] but hoped, after Basil's death, to see his daughter play a more profitable part than that to which he himself had been condemned by Basil's omnipotence. His influence was considerable at the time, for he had recently been appointed Magister and Logothete of the Course.[3] But he had, for all that, every reason to fear Photius, who could easily have foiled his plans. Euthymios' biographer makes Zautzes responsible for all the afflictions that befell Photius and his party, which is undoubtedly an exaggeration. As Zautzes was Euthymios' personal enemy, Euthymios' biographer makes Zautzes solely responsible for every intrigue, but even this indictment contains a modicum of truth.

Having once decided that Photius should vacate the patriarcheion, Leo could not use force, for fear of provoking a violent reaction among the Moderates; nor could he summon a synod, and have the Patriarch tried and convicted, for the Patriarch commanded the clergy's unswerving loyalty; the only way was to use judicious pressure to make the Patriarch resign. This, in fact, he did, on the candid pretext that he

---

[1] Vogt-Hausherr, 'Oraison funèbre de Basil Ier', in *Orientalia Christiania*, vol. LXXVI, p. 22, insist on discovering in Leo's homily on St Elias a hint of the remonstrances which Photius had often addressed to the young prince; but a closer study of the passage (Akakios, loc. cit. p. 260) would seem to indicate that the panegyrist is not referring to Photius at all, but only means to pay homage to St Elias and his intercession 'with the King of Heaven'.

[2] Cf. de Boor, loc. cit. p. 136.

[3] Georg. Mon. Cont. (Bonn), p. 849; Theoph. Cont. (Bonn), p. 354; Leo Gram. (Bonn), p. 263.

wished to bestow the patriarchal throne on his brother Stephen, already predestined to the honour by Basil. Photius' resignation has often been questioned, as the chroniclers say nothing about it;[1] yet its attestation by Euthymios' biographer leaves no room for doubt. Relating Photius' downfall, he writes: 'As regards Photius himself, he [Leo] immediately relieved him of his charge, and after ignominiously dismissing him called upon him for his resignation, which Photius gave under pressure and much against his will. He then ordered him to take up his residence on the outskirts of the city of Hieria as an exile.'[2]

Such was the act of abdication which Magister Andrew and the Logothete John Hagiopolites read to the faithful from the ambo of St Sophia.[3] It goes without saying that the chroniclers pictured them mounting the ambo to enumerate the Patriarch's misdeeds and proclaim his overthrow, though the procedure was most unlike the usual practice of the Byzantine Church.

Photius probably consented to sign the act of abdication to expose the futility of his adversaries' accusations and to prove his own unwillingness to stand in the way of his former pupil; but not satisfied with this, his enemies insisted on public proceedings against him and Santabarenos. The case was heard at the palace of the Source, the presiding judges being John Hagiopolites and the Patricius Gumer, with Andrew, the Magister, and Stephen, the Domestic of the *Scholae*, as plaintiffs and prosecuting counsel all in one;[4] with the result that the ex-Patriarch was banished to the monastery of Hieria,[5] and Santabarenos was exiled to Athens, where his enemies' hatred dogged his steps, for, as reported by Euthymios' biographer, he was later blinded at the instigation of Zautzes and banished to Asia Minor.

Leo Catacoilas, a relative of Photius, who had formerly been one of his most devoted supporters,[6] was also banished by the new government

---

[1] The only mention of Photius' abdication is to be found in the letter from Pope Stephen V to Stylianos (Mansi, vol. XVI, col. 436), but the truth of the information was questioned, after the example set by Hergenröther, *Photius*, vol. II, p. 691.

[2] de Boor, loc. cit. p. 5.

[3] Georg. Mon. Cont. (Bonn), p. 849; Theoph. Cont. (Bonn), p. 354; Leo Gram. (Bonn), p. 263; Cedrenus (Bonn), vol. II, p. 249.

[4] Georg. Mon. Cont. (Bonn), pp. 850, 851; Pseudo-Simeon (Bonn), pp. 700, 701; Theoph. Cont. (Bonn), p. 355; Leo Gram. (Bonn), pp. 264, 265.

[5] Chroniclers state that Photius was interned in the monastery of Gordon of Armeniakoi. The two traditions can be reconciled, if we admit with de Boor (loc. cit. p. 142) that Photius was first interned in Gordon and sent to Hieria after the trial.

[6] Nicetas, Vita Ignatii, *P.G.* vol. 105, col. 569.

and had all his property confiscated,[1] to be used later by the Emperor for the erection of the monastery of Psamathia. Young Nicholas, destined later to ascend the patriarchal throne, but fearing meanwhile similar proceedings against himself (he was Photius' nephew), fled to the monastery of St Tryphon in Chalcedon, and to make assurance doubly sure, adopted the monastic life.

Euthymios' biographer refers to other molestations, which were such that the father had to plead with the Basileus in favour of the victims, and this led to a heated argument on the subject with Zautzes.[2] From this account by a contemporary witness, one can see that the sole pretext for these annoyances was the fear of danger threatening the Emperor on the part of those who were so severely dealt with, and that undoubtedly these measures were prompted by political motives. With the new regime, influences and tendencies other than those that had found favour with Basil came into play. In other words, we are faced again with the old antagonism between the two politico-religious parties—the Extremists and the Moderates—that had striven for control over the political and religious affairs of the Empire. But this time the Extremists got the upper hand, and the change over brought with it, as a logical sequel, the recall from exile of the ultra-Ignatians.

That is the proper explanation of the events which occurred in Byzantium after the change on the imperial throne in 886; no other explanation can reconcile the chroniclers' reports, often mutually contradictory in important details, with accounts from other sources, and especially the narrative of Euthymios' biographer, that are closer to the events they deal with. If, then, we compare all this with the version of the compiler of the anti-Photian Collection, we realize more than ever the inaccuracy of this source. Rome's personal feelings in no way influenced the decisions taken by Leo VI: Photius' second humiliation was nothing but a matter of internal policy, of which the course had been altered by the new Basileus.

On this particular point, too, the compiler flatly contradicts the documents he quotes in the Collection. The papal letter which, in the compiler's opinion, had such a disastrous effect on Photius' fate, can have reached Byzantium only after Stylianos had dispatched his first letter to the Pope; in that letter Stylianos had no knowledge of Photius' attack on Marinus, which is believed to be mentioned in the letter referred to from the Pope Stephen to Basil, which was received by Leo: he mentions it only in his second letter to the Pope. Evidently

[1] de Boor, loc. cit. pp. 5, 6, 16.   [2] Ibid. pp. 6–8.

248

then the compiler's short 'historical' commentary, inserted between the Pope's letter to Basil and Stylianos' first letter to the Pope, is sheer misrepresentation.

The prominence in this affair attributed to Stylianos by the compiler of the anti-Photian Collection points to the probability of Metrophanes, with other Extremists, abandoning his die-hard attitude and accepting, on the Emperor's invitation, Leo's brother as a Patriarch, which left Stylianos as the sole leader of the 'Little Church'.

It was precisely the untenable position taken by Stylianos and his friends and the appeal they sent to Rome on their own authority which must have compromised their interests in the Emperor's eyes; for, shortly after, another change was noticeable in Leo's attitude to Photius and his friends: the exile, against whom the Emperor had immediately after his accession staged such a sensational arraignment for high treason, was quietly living in his retreat and devoting himself to scientific and literary pursuits. His treatise on the *Mystagogy* of the Holy Spirit was the fruit of that period, at least in its revised and enlarged edition.[1] And what is still more remarkable, Leo was reconciled with Photius' nephew, Nicholas, for Euthymios' biographer[2] reports that Leo recalled Nicholas from exile and gave him the important appointment of 'Mysticos' or private secretary. Even Santabarenos benefited by the alteration in Leo's feelings, as he was recalled from exile and pensioned out of the revenues of the New Basilica.[3]

An echo of the young ruler's new mood is found in the funeral oration he delivered in honour of his father, in which the praise he bestowed on his father and his father's reign was in strange contrast to his first acts as a sovereign; abandoning his attitude of petulance, he poured rhetorical approval on Basil's policy, from which he had openly and completely departed at his accession. This was evidently an attempt to establish among the public a good tradition of the dynasty and to make a hero of its founder. The passage dealing with Photius[4] is also at variance with Leo's treatment of him after his accession, for his words breathe peace and reconciliation, and sound as though they were meant to convince the Photianists and the Moderates of the Emperor's desire for more harmonious relations. In short, one notices in Leo VI the same change of mind as came over Basil I, who also courted the Extremists at the beginning of his reign, afterwards turning to the

---

[1] Cf. Hergenröther, *Photius*, vol. II, p. 714.   [2] de Boor, loc. cit. p. 6.
[3] Theoph. Cont. (Bonn), p. 356; Georg. Mon. Cont. (Bonn), pp. 851, 852; Leo Gram. (Bonn), p. 265; Cedrenus (Bonn), vol. II, p. 252.   [4] See p. 169.

Moderates, who gradually ousted their opponents from the palace and the patriarcheion.

The funeral oration also indicates the date of the turn, M. N. Adontz[1] having proved that Leo delivered his panegyric on the second anniversary of his father's death, i.e. in the month of August 888. In composing his oration, Leo took for his models the orations of St Gregory of Nazianzus, being true to pattern in the very date he chose for his speech. The date also serves to explain how the transformation had come about: two years had been enough to convince Leo that the support he had been expecting from the Extremists was not as solid as he had hoped; and what disappointed him most was the ecclesiastical wing of the party. Stylianos and his friends had actually refused to acknowledge his brother Stephen as the legitimate Patriarch, the reason of their refusal being, not the Patriarch's uncanonical promotion— Stephen was only eighteen years old when he became Patriarch[2]—but the fact that the prince had been ordained deacon by Photius. However, they declared their willingness to submit to him on the one condition that Rome and the other Patriarchs should grant dispensation by 'oeconomia' to those promoted by Photius. We have seen with what results they appealed to Rome.

In drawing up his memorandum, Stylianos committed a blunder which showed up the Ignatians' manœuvres and gave the lie to what the compiler says about the consequences of Photius' resignation. As his explanation of the change of Patriarchs differed from the Emperor's, he unwittingly, but neatly, exploded the legend which the compiler tried to circulate, namely, that the request for dispensing the ecclesiastics ordained by Photius had been made not only by the Ignatians, but by the Emperor as well. How is it, then, that before making an application of such importance the Ignatians and the Emperor had not taken concerted action? But the omission alone proves that the Ignatians acted on their own initiative. All that the Emperor had asked of them was recognition of his brother, but Stylianos' *faux pas*, which merely delayed the brother's recognition by Rome, at a time when the Pope was anxious to arbitrate between the Emperor's brother and the dethroned Photius, must have infuriated Leo. Luckily for him, he knew what he was doing, for he could produce the letter of abdication, whether free or not, and he certainly tried to expedite the settlement of a question in which he was personally interested. At any rate the

---

[1] 'L'Oraison funèbre de Basile Ier', in *Byzantion*, vol. VIII, pp. 507 seq.
[2] Cf. Adontz, loc. cit. p. 508.

incident must have effectively prejudiced the Emperor against the Extremists, on whom he had built such hopes immediately after his accession to power; but the fanaticism of these Extremists soon cooled his enthusiasm, and this cooling was accelerated by the Photianists' promptitude and unhesitating support of the new Patriarch.

Stylianos' second attempt with the Pope was made only three years[1] after he had received the disappointing reply from Stephen V, and the long delay showed the Ignatians' embarrassment at the Papacy's attitude. Stylianos' second effort may well have been provoked by the Emperor's impatient insistence and his vexation at the 'Little Church's' obstinacy, which did his brother no good.

It was not Stephen V, but his successor Formosus (891–6) who replied to archbishop Stylianos' letter. This reply is an important document as a piece of plausible evidence that this Pope at least condemned Photius, if not in his capacity as a Patriarch, at any rate on the ground of acts committed during his patriarchate; it therefore deserves careful examination. The following is the text of the letter as the compiler of the anti-Photian Collection has handed it down to us:[2]

Letter containing the reply to the preceding and written by the most holy Pope Formosus, successor to the blessed Stephen, to the same Stylianos; for it was Formosus who wrote, he [Stephen] being dead. We have received with joy the letter your Holiness addressed to the Holy See....And after many [other] things contained in the letter, there was also this: You ask for mercy, but you do not explain how and for whom, whether for a layman or a priest. If you mean a layman, he deserves pardon, as he received a dignity from a layman; but if you mean a priest, you overlook the fact that one who has no dignity cannot impart any to others. Photius could not give anything except the condemnation he incurred by the imposition of an impious hand [Gregory Asbestas], and this condemnation he gave. How could anybody come by a dignity by association with a condemned man? Take care: when you ask for mercy for one ordained, you seem to make common cause with the ordainer, according to the Lord's words: you are either a good tree whose

---

[1] de Boor, loc. cit. p. 147, disagrees with Hergenröther (*Photius*, vol. II, p. 692), who counts the three years from the time of Stylianos' first recourse to Rome. The compiler (Mansi, vol. XVI, col. 437) states that the Emperor had dispatched the explanations requested by the Pope concerning his brother's accession to the patriarchal throne at the same time as Stylianos. The statement is very questionable. It was the easiest thing for Leo to produce a copy of the letter of resignation signed by Photius, and it was in his interest and that of the new Patriarch that the incident should be closed as soon as possible.

[2] Mansi, vol. XVI, cols. 440, 441; *M.G.H.* Ep. VII, pp. 382 seq.

fruits will be good; or a bad tree whose fruits will be bad. Can a fig tree bear grapes, or a vine figs? This [our] Church, to which such things belong, should inflict the severest punishments, so that yours be thereby purged; but our goodness and clemency preclude such a course and prompt us to tolerate one thing, whilst completely uprooting another. For this purpose we sent from our side (a latere nostro) the most pious bishops Landulph of Capua and Romanus; we urge your Holiness to come to an understanding with them: also Theophylactus, Metropolitan of Ancyra, and Peter, our confidant. But take care above all that the sentence synodically passed on Photius, violator and transgressor of the law, by our predecessors, the œcumenical pontiffs, and besides confirmed by our humble self, remain for ever valid and unchanged. As for those ordained by Photius, this is our merciful verdict: they will have to present the *libelli* with the acknowledgement of their sin and to ask pardon by their penance, with the promise never to commit it again. This being done, your Holiness will see to the rest, in obedience to our orders and in agreement with the legates above mentioned, without any addition or alteration whatsoever. Once they have been received into the communion of the faithful as laymen by ourselves and by your Reverence, the scandal will be removed. This done, if any of them should refuse to hold communion with you, let him know that he would likewise be severed from our communion. Greetings in Christ.

It looks at first sight as though Formosus had repealed the decisions of all his predecessors, from John VIII to Stephen V, and adopted towards Photius and his friends the unfriendly and wooden attitude of Nicholas I and Hadrian II. If the document is authentic, it goes to prove that the Roman Church did condemn Photius and once again break off relations with the Church of Constantinople: the responsibility in that case would fall on Formosus.

But time after time it has been established that the anti-Photian Collection does not always deserve the implicit trust which, unfortunately, has too often been placed in it. We must therefore examine the document in detail before pronouncing on Formosus' line of conduct towards Photius.

Why has this feeling of dislike for the Byzantines been so commonly attributed to Formosus? First, because he is supposed to have disagreed with John VIII's Eastern policy and this on purely personal grounds, and to have been a fervent Nicholaite who found even Hadrian's policy too accommodating to his taste.[1] The second reason is that Formosus'

---

[1] Lapôtre ('Hadrien II et les Fausses Décrétales', in *Revue des Questions historiques* (1880), vol. XXVII, p. 410) attributes to Formosus the passionate 'Nicholaite plea' made at the Roman synod of 869.

interest in Bulgaria must have made him a political enemy of the Greeks. His name has even been associated with Simeon the Great's endeavour to set up an independent Bulgarian Church and to assume the imperial title.[1] Lastly, the criticisms of Roman activities in Bulgaria in Photius' letter to the Eastern Patriarchs[2] and his reference to the gruesome trial over Formosus' dead body in his *Mystagogy*[3] are quoted as evidence of Photius' antagonism to Formosus.

But all this is no proof of Formosus' anti-Greek feelings. Marinus and Stephen V also diverged from John's policy on many points— Stephen even wrecked that Pontiff's achievement in Moravia, the Slav liturgy—yet both remained faithful to his Eastern policy. It should also be remembered that it was Nicholas who recalled Formosus from Bulgaria.

In the preceding chapter,[4] I have shown that whatever has been said about Formosus' activities in Bulgaria after his recall is pure fabrication; so it is idle to seek there any grounds for his declaration of war on the Byzantine Church.

As to Photius' writings, nowhere does he even mention Formosus. In the first instance, he only refers to the Romans in general; and in the second, Photius never mentions any offence committed by the Pope against himself personally, but only against the Symbol. And the Pope whom he had in mind was not Formosus, but Nicholas.[5]

So the weather was after all not so stormy as is commonly imagined and one is left to wonder how a squall could suddenly burst over the Byzantine Church from a sky that was to all appearances fairly serene. Formosus, besides, had his hands full during his short reign (891–6) dealing with another menace—Guy of Spoleto, who had been crowned Emperor by Stephen V and was trying to carve out for himself an Italian kingdom. Formosus saw the danger and tried to prevail on Arnulf, King of Germany, to save the independence of the Roman Church. How could he, under such conditions, run the risk of another breach with the Byzantines and imperil the position of the Papacy in the south of the peninsula at the very moment when the Byzantines were occupying Benevento and preparing to march on Capua and Salerno?[6] Since nothing in Formosus' reign makes a departure from

[1] Hergenröther, *Photius*, vol. II, p. 694. Cf. de Boor, loc. cit. p. 153.
[2] *P.G.* vol. 102, cols. 724 seq.
[3] Lapôtre, *L'Europe et le Saint Siège* (Paris, 1895), p. 69.
[4] See pp. 214 seq.
[5] See the last short study on the problem by V. Grumel, 'Formose ou Nicolas Ier?', in *Échos d'Orient* (1934), vol. XXXIII, pp. 194 seq.
[6] For particulars, see Gay, *L'Italie Méridionale et l'Empire Byzantin*, p. 147.

his predecessors' policy at all likely and the compiler's fragment asserts it as a fact, the only possible conclusion is that the Pope's letter was not reproduced in its original form.

Again, there are in the fragment expressions that betray the ultra-Ignatian hand. Photius is again called a layman, who could only confer condemnation on those he ordained. The reference to Gregory Asbestas could not have been written in Rome, where the incident must have been long forgotten. The first part of the letter was certainly considerably altered, for the passage, as it stands, makes no sense and the compiler himself confesses that the letter contained other things, obviously left out because they did not suit his purpose.

The second part of the letter possibly reveals the Pope's real intention and the compiler's method. The words—'our goodness and clemency ...prompt us to tolerate one thing whilst uprooting another'—and 'take care above all that the sentences synodically passed on Photius remain for ever valid and unchanged'—give us perhaps the key to Formosus' policy. One may imagine that in his anxiety to give satisfaction to Stylianos for his deference to the Holy See and to settle the difficulties of the Byzantine Church, he proposed a compromise between the two parties, by letting Stylianos' partisans have their own way and by admitting justification for Photius' condemnation by Nicholas and Hadrian, yet at the same time by ordering the clergy ordained by Photius under his first patriarchate to apply for supplementary dispensation to the pontifical legates. If this be so, then Formosus must have used words with reference to the dispensation which the compiler, true to his method, stretched to suit his own views about the invalidity of Photius' ordinations.

At all events, Formosus upheld the legitimacy of Photius' rehabilitation by John VIII and by the Council of 879–80, so that the ordinations made by Photius under his second patriarchate were not only valid, but also licit and there was no reason for reconsidering them. The latter part of the compromise was of course meant to satisfy the Photianists. The legates Landulph of Capua and Romanus were commissioned, in the light of this suggestion, to conduct an inquiry on the spot and to settle the dispute in accordance with the instructions outlined in the letter. This reading of Formosus' letter seems in keeping with public opinion prevailing in Rome at the time about the Photian affair. We have seen that not even John VIII could make up his mind to throw over completely the opinion that the first condemnation of Photius by his predecessors was not justifiable; and yet, none was better placed to judge from the legates' report how things stood.

Furthermore, Photius was called upon to resign for the second time, and after his resignation Leo VI recalled the Ignatians from their exile, which was enough to convince any distant observer that all was not well in Photius' chequered career. Yet on the other hand, even Formosus had to admit the fact of the reconciliation with all its consequences, especially as the position of his patrimony imperatively demanded the maintenance of friendly relations with Byzantium.

But if Formosus actually made the proposal he made a mistake, as the compromise so ingeniously devised could please neither the Photianists nor the Ignatians. The Extremists could not for a moment consider Photius' ordinations, even those made under his second pontificate, to be valid; for in the Ignatian version of the Pope's letter which has come down to us, we find Formosus saying about these Photian ordinations: 'Whenever they are received by us and by your Reverence to communion with the faithful *as laymen.*' But this was exactly the interpretation which the Ignatians put on the verdicts of Nicholas and the Eighth Council, when they decided that the repentant Photianists could be admitted to lay communion. And yet, no Pope, after the reconciliation effected under John VIII, could have countenanced such a claim, for it would have meant the complete revocation of the decisions of the Photian Council which John had sanctioned.

Nor could the Photianists agree to the solution proposed by the Pope, for they would never admit that there was any justification for the judgement passed against Photius and themselves by Nicholas, Hadrian and the Eighth Council; and nothing but ignorance of the true state of things in Constantinople could excuse the Pope in the eyes of the majority of the Byzantines.

What happened then in Byzantium after the legates' arrival in 892? Did the legates carry out the sentence supposed to have been passed by the Pope? If they did, it would have meant that from that very year the two Churches were again in schism, for in no case could the Church of Constantinople submit to such a decision. To what conclusion can we come?

We find in the anti-Photian Collection clear evidence of one thing at least—that the Stylianites did not make their peace with the Photianists in 892, for the compiler states that Stylianos did not communicate with the Photianists until seven years after the receipt of Formosus' letter, i.e. in 899;[1] and the same document affirms that Stylianos again applied to the Pope in 899 for permission to communicate with the Photianists. This at any rate proves that Formosus' intervention failed to establish internal peace in the Byzantine Church.

Does this mean that the two Churches were in schism? If the legates did carry out the supposed sentence and excommunicate the clergy ordained by Photius during his first patriarchate for refusing to produce the penitential *libellus*, a schism should have followed automatically, since the official Church in Byzantium could not possibly accept such a verdict. Attempts have been made to prove that there was such a schism,[2] but I hold to my position[3] and repeat that things never came to such a pass. Formosus' efforts in Constantinople failed, no doubt, to restore peace in the Byzantine Church, but they did not provoke a new schism between Byzantium and Rome.

Had they done so, traces of it would have been left in contemporary literature. First of all, there are some contemporary writings by two Neapolitan ecclesiastics, Eugenius Vulgarius and Auxilius, who may enlighten us on Formosus' attitude to the East. Eugenius published about the year 907 a plea in defence of Formosus under the title *De Causa Formosana Libellus*, and another in the form of a dialogue.[4] Auxilius, who probably hailed from the Frankish Empire originally but was living in Naples, published about the year 908 two writings for the same purpose: *In Defensionem Sacrae Ordinationis Papae Formosi*, and *Libellus in Defensionem Stephani Episcopi*.[5] Two other publications followed towards 911 (*De Ordinationibus a Formoso Papa Factis*, and *Infensor et Defensor*).[6] This series of Formosian writings concluded with an anonymous pamphlet, *Invectiva in Romam pro Formoso Papa*,[7] probably published in 914.

Now we find in Auxilius' first treatise a passage referring to Formosus' recognition by the Church of Constantinople, which was recently adduced as evidence that Pope Formosus, however desirous he was of restoring peace in the Church of Constantinople, rent as it was by the 'Ignatian' schism, eventually brought it to another rupture

---

[1] Mansi, vol. xvi, col. 456.

[2] Grumel, 'La Liquidation', in *Échos d'Orient*, vol. xxxiii, pp. 280 seq.

[3] Cf. my 'Études sur Photios', in *Byzantion*, vol. xi, pp. 7 seq.

[4] E. Dümmler, *Auxilius und Vulgarius* (Leipzig, 1866), pp. 117–39; Mabillon, *Vetera Analecta* (1723), pp. 28–31.

[5] Dümmler, ibid. pp. 58 seq.

[6] *P.L.* vol. 129, cols. 1061–1102.

[7] E. Dümmler, *Gesta Berengarii* (Halle, 1871), pp. 137–54.

with Rome, and that this rupture persisted until the Council of Ravenna (898), which was summoned by John IX to sanction the ordinations made by Formosus. Here is the passage referred to:[1]

Personally, we have no doubt that the same ordination was valid and lawful, since, as was shown previously, it is known to be based on the writings and examples of the holy Fathers. It was besides publicly rectified by the authority of a venerable synod in the town of Ravenna at which were known to be present not only the heads of the Holy Roman Church, but also the archbishops, bishops, priests and deacons of the Franks. Likewise the Church of Constantinople, after approving this ordination, unfailingly remains united in the Lord's peace. ['Nihilominus autem et Constantinopolitana ecclesia hanc ordinationem complexa dominicae pacis concordiam regulariter fovet.']

As to the interpretation of this passage, it seems at least an exaggeration to find in it evidence that Constantinople acknowledged Formosus only after the Council of Ravenna. The word *nihilominus* in particular, on which the erroneous interpretation is meant to rest, does not, as I understand it, express time sequence.[2] The author only means to quote at the end of his argument another case in its support: 'Likewise the Church of Constantinople, after approving [complexa] this ordination, unfailingly remains united in the Lord's peace.'

For its exact bearing on the argument, the passage must be studied in its context, read in the spirit in which the whole work was written and compared with other writings in connection with the Formosus incident. These works were written by members of the clergy in southern Italy where Greek problems were a local interest and opinions in the Church of Constantinople carried weight.[3] The writers' casual remarks show that they were informed of all important happenings in Byzantium. And yet, they know nothing of a schism between the Churches under Formosus. They speak of the peaceful conditions in all the Churches with the exception of the Roman Church, where this con-

---

[1] V. Grumel, loc. cit. pp. 285, 286.
[2] As can be proved by many instances in the eleventh-century chronicler of Monte Cassino, Leo of Ostia, the meaning of the word was at this period and in southern Italy *etiam, perinde* (*M.G.H.* Ss. VII, l. I, chs. 9, 18, 25, 34, 36, 39, 52, 53; l. II, chs. 12, 13, 25, 32, 36, 43; l. III, chs. 6, 9, 10, 19, 32, 33). Cf. Du Cange, *Glossarium ad Scriptores Mediae et Infimae Latinitatis* (Niort, 1882–7), col. 740. No other meaning is admissible.
[3] For more details, see my study, 'Études sur Photios', in *Byzantion*, vol. XI, p. 9.

troversy had been causing trouble.[1] A pertinent passage is to be found in the *Invectiva in Romanam Ecclesiam*:[2]

Thus the whole world and all its Christian inhabitants raise their voices against thee (O Rome!), because thou hast deceived them and thou hast been deceived. Constantinople, Sicily, the whole of Italy, Gaul, Germany, on whose territories metropolitans who claim to have consecrated their episcopal suffragans are known to dwell, depose and argue against thee, because no metropolitan may consecrate unless he receives the pallium from the Apostolic See. Then from whom but Rome do Byzantium, called Constantinople, Ravenna, Frioul, Milan, Habrudunum, Arles, Lyons, Rheims, Cologne, Mainz and other metropolitan cities receive the pallium? If things are as you pretend them to be, nearly the whole world has for thirty years been on the brink of disaster to the damnation not only of their bodies, but what is worse, of their souls.

How could this writer, in this passionate apostrophe, contrast Constantinople with Rome, if that Church had cast the same doubts as Rome on the ordination of Formosus? As the writer estimates that this sorry state of affairs had lasted thirty years since the days of Marinus I,[3] the Pope who rehabilitated Formosus, we may infer from the context that unlike Rome the Churches enumerated acknowledged Formosus and his ordinations throughout that period. Well may the writer quote the great metropolitan sees of the West, since Formosus' case seems to have all but exclusively concerned Rome and the patrimony of St Peter, where nearly all those who had been ordained by Formosus were living; but frequent references to Constantinople in this and other writings of Formosus' champions make it plain that they knew about his intercourse with the Church of Constantinople, which had acknowledged him as Pope and never went back on that recognition.[4]

[1] *Auxilius und Vulgarius*, ch. I, p. 119: 'Patet enim ratio quia, dum omnis mundus in suo stet statu omnisque ecclesia sub Christi militet optentu, sola ecclesia Romana peragit, unde post omnium ecclesiarum ordinatio tabescit.' *Invectiva in Romanam Ecclesiam* (E. Dümmler, *Gesta Berengarii*, pp. 137–38): 'Mirum tamen et valde mirandum est, cum omnes ecclesiae tam cismarine quam transmarine in proprio statu permaneant, sola Romana ecclesia procellosis a fluctibus navitas suos morti proximos redundat.' Both authors are evidently thinking here also of the Church of Constantinople, but the reference would have no point, if Byzantium had impugned the ordination of Formosus and if a special move had been necessary to obtain recognition.   [2] Loc. cit. pp. 148–49.

[3] Cf. Dümmler, loc. cit. p. 67, on this computation and on the date of the writing.

[4] Note that the author (loc. cit. p. 151) refers not only to the condemnation, but also to the rehabilitation of Zachary, papal legate at the synod of 861. For details, cf. my study, 'Études sur Photios', in *Byzantion*, vol. XI, p. 11.

We possess another document of the same period, Flodoard's *History of the Church of Rheims*, which proves that Formosus did not, by his alleged method of settling the Ignatian schism, provoke another rupture between Byzantium and Rome. In reporting the correspondence between Formosus and Folco of Rheims, Flodoard says:[1]

In reply, the same Pope Formosus urges him [Folco] to sympathize with the Roman Church, to save it from imminent peril and not refuse it his help, adding that heresies and schisms are springing up everywhere with nobody to oppose them. He also states that pernicious heresies are harassing the East and that the Church of Constantinople is troubled with regrettable schisms; also, that envoys from Africa insist on instructions in connection with the schism that has long divided the bishops of those provinces. The delegations from the different parties all claim different answers. It was for this reason that he decided to summon a General Council on the 1st March of the XIIth Indiction, to which he urged him to hasten without delay to enable them to treat these matters in a general discussion and to give answers to each of the delegations.... He had also sent other letters about this same Council to our Metropolitan, stating that he had ordered it to be summoned for the middle of May of the Xth Indiction.... He admits in these letters that Italy had twice been devastated and all but ruined by disastrous wars and that he deplored the insane heresy of the East which was blaspheming Jesus Christ....

This document goes far to substantiate our contention that under Formosus peace between the two Churches endured and that his fruitless attempt to end the 'Ignatian' schism did not make the relations between Rome and Byzantium any worse than they were. The fact is that Formosus here refers only to a schism within the Byzantine Church, and it is hard to see how the evidence of such a witness could possibly be questioned.[2] In any case, Folco knew only of troubles inside the Roman Church,[3] probably provoked by Formosus' rehabilitation, and which the synod in question was designed to put an end to.[4]

---

[1] Flodoardi Historia Remensis Ecclesiae, lib. IV, *M.G.H.* Ss. XIII, p. 559.

[2] Cf. my study, 'Études sur Photios', in *Byzantion*, vol. XI, pp. 12 seq.

[3] Flodoardi Historia Rem. Eccl. *M.G.H.* Ss. XIII, p. 558: 'quod audierat a quibusdam sanctam Romanam Ecclesiam turbari, paratumque se totis viribus pro ipsius honore omnimodis decertare....' In the same letter to Formosus Folco complains that he received no answer to his last letter addressed to Pope Stephen V. The extract under investigation is taken from Formosus' answer to Folco's letter.

[4] Moreover, Formosus was not the first Pope desirous to see the Frankish episcopate joining in deliberations in Rome on Eastern as well as on Western affairs; twice did Nicholas summon a similar Council in Rome, but to little avail. See *M.G.H.* Ss. I, pp. 460, 466, 476. E. Perels, 'Ein Berufungsschreiben Papst Nikolaus' I. zur fränk. Reichssynode in Rom', in *Neues Archiv* (1906), vol. XXXII, pp. 135 seq.

Greek sources confirm our reading of the events. We read in the Life of St Euthymios[1] that 'Anthony [the Patriarch] died after the reconciliation between the Pope and Stylianos and after the unification of the whole Church'. The author therefore distinguishes between the two events, and the latter happened shortly before 898, the probable date of Anthony Cauleas' death. An allusion to the same event is found in Nicholas Mysticos' letter and in the Life of Anthony Cauleas, as we shall see in connection with the date of the unification.[2] It all goes to prove that Formosus did not break off relations with the Byzantine Church, and that he did not agree with Stylianos' views, since the latter needed a special reconciliation with Pope John IX. One of the later Greek treatises on the so-called Eastern schism, often quoted as evidence that Formosus was on bad terms with Byzantium,[3] states that on becoming Pope Formosus sent to the Patriarch of Constantinople an encyclical letter containing the Symbol without the *Filioque* formula, again another indication that Formosus was on friendly terms with the East.

Let me repeat here what I have already said elsewhere,[4] that the silence in this Collection on an excommunication of a number of Photianists is the best proof that such an excommunication was never uttered. And it is no answer to this to say that after all Formosus' decision meant a set-back for the Ignatians, whose demands had been only partially met; for all the papal decisions provoked by the Ignatians were a set-back for them and yet they carefully preserved copies of them, though with the usual distortion in their own favour. But such an event as the excommunication of some Photianists by Formosus would have played into the Ignatians' hands, and I fail to understand why the copyist should not have insisted on such an event, instead of drawing from the letter of John IX, whose general drift conflicted with his own views, a lame argument in support of his contention. We are thus forced back to our first conclusions. If it is true that Formosus made a futile attempt to end the schism within the Byzantine Church

[1] De Boor, loc. cit. p. 34.

[2] See p. 271. The problems raised by these writings are treated in my 'Études sur Photios', in *Byzantion*, vol. XI, pp. 13 seq. There I prove that the Church mentioned in these passages cannot be the Universal Church but the Church of Constantinople.

[3] Hergenröther, *Monumenta Graeca ad Photium pertinentia* (Ratisbonnae, 1869), pp. 160, 179. Greek ill-feeling for Formosus as expressed in the later treatises on the Schism is probably due to Formosus' activities in Bulgaria, which possibly started rumours about his heretical doctrine on the *Filioque* of which he is accused in those writings.

[4] 'Le Second Schisme de Photios', in *Byzantion*, vol. VIII, p. 468.

and to reconcile the Ignatians with the official Church of Byzantium, there is nothing to suggest a new breach between Byzantium and Rome as a result of a blunder or short-sightedness on the part of Formosus.

If then our reading of Formosus' letter is correct, in 892 there happened in Byzantium what had happened in 879; the legates, on arriving in Constantinople and discussing matters with the two parties, soon perceived the real state of affairs. Like the legates in 879 they saw that the 'Little Church' did not deserve the interest it claimed, that the Stylianists had misrepresented the facts and that a literal compliance with the Pope's orders and the papal scheme would only spell disaster for Christian peace. They took no action and referred the matter to the Pope.

But the evidence for friendly intercourse between Rome and Byzantium under Formosus is so overwhelming that I have my misgivings about the reading of Formosus' letter proposed above. What is so strange is that there is not a trace of his attempt to bring about peace by a compromise so little in line with the attitude of his predecessors John VIII and Stephen V. Moreover, the tone of the Formosian writings on the subject is too friendly to be compatible with an attempt that would have hurt official feelings in Constantinople. It makes one think that Formosus never went so far as the alleged compromise suggests and that the letter partly reproduced in the anti-Photian Collection was more seriously altered than we supposed at first. It is possible that the words about Photius only gave the sense of Stylianos' request, and summarized previous papal decisions, giving them an interpretation which the Pope could not make his own, and that the letter and the papal embassy simply aimed at inducing Stylianos and his followers to get reconciled with their Mother Church. The compiler's method and his confession that the letter 'contained many other things' make this supposition more plausible. Formosus only abode by the decisions of John VIII and tried to enforce Stephen V's injunctions upon the ultra-Ignatians.

Anyhow, in justice to Formosus' memory it should be said that he was not responsible for a second breach or that he was swayed by prejudice. Far from this being the case, this unfortunate Pope gave evidence of such good sense as to make it ungracious to lay at his door the failure to restore peace in the Church of Constantinople.

So the Ignatians' schism persisted after the legates' departure, to last until Formosus' death, as nothing more is heard of any other overture by Stylianos to that Pope. We stated that the copyist of the anti-Photian Collection mentioned in a lengthy postscript appended to the compilation a reunion under Pope John IX to which Stylianos had rallied. Other documents such as the Life of St Euthymios, of the Patriarch Cauleas and of Nicholas Mysticos, also refer to a reunion of the Ignatians with the official Church of Constantinople. When and under what circumstances did this reunion take place?

It seems strange that the Ignatians did not approach the official Church at the time of the legates' presence in Constantinople, although Photius' death should have been the right moment for such a reunion. Presumably, Photius had died before the legates' arrival, as the compiler of the anti-Photian Collection states that Photius had lain under a ban of excommunication for thirty years since his accession to the throne. On the strength of this statement, one arrives at the year 892; and he must have died in February, as the Synaxaria place his feast on the 6th or the 9th of that month.[1] The legates probably reached the capital in the spring of 892, as it is unlikely that Formosus sent them immediately after his accession, which probably took place in October 891. Preparations for a delegation took time and winter was near.

The date of the receipt of that letter may also serve as a starting-point to fix the date of Stylianos' reunion with the official Church, for the copyist of the Collection, in his postscript, dates the reunion from the seventh year after the receipt of Formosus' letter by Stylianos,[2] which would make it 899. Many have disputed the computations of both compiler and copyist, but as they were contemporary witnesses and deeply interested in the events, we have no reason to dispute their calculations.

This is how the copyist comments on the event:

It should also be known that Mapas [i.e. Stylianos], the Metropolitan of Neocaesarea, seven years after receipt of the letter quoted above, softened by his friends and relatives, strayed from the path of truth and, turning to the opposite doctrine, wrote to Rome asking for his ordination to be sent from there and for permission to communicate with them [the Photianists]. Pope John received and examined Mapas' request, but fearing that it was written in irony, to make the Romans look ridiculous if the request were granted, he refused the application and did not even send an autograph letter.[3] But

---

[1] Ed. Delehaye, *A.S.* Nov., Propylaeum, cols. 448, 453.

[2] Mansi, vol. XVI, col. 456.

[3] Loc. cit.: διὸ οὔτε ἐπέτρεψεν, οὔτε τὸ ἰδιόγραφον ἀπέστειλεν· ἀλλ' ἀντέγραψε πρὸς αὐτὸν γράμμα ἔχον οὕτως.

he let him have the following reply: 'We owe a deep gratitude to your love, honoured brother, as you never consented to leave your Mother, the Holy, Catholic and Apostolic Roman Church; neither persecution nor exile nor the machinations of evil-minded men[1] ever succeeded in severing you from your Mother. It is my fervent hope that the ardour of your prayers will soften the hearts of those who must be saved and bring back the peace we so much desire. Unmistakable signs are pointing that way and the schism which has lasted now for nearly forty years bids fair to give place to the peace of old. And what your Mother has condemned to this day, you also have condemned, as you have approved what she approved.

'That is why we wish the decisions of our most holy predecessors to be observed even now in the same spirit and without any alteration; for which reason we also receive and confirm Ignatius, Photius, Stephen and Anthony in the same spirit as they were received by the most holy Popes Nicholas, John, the seventh Stephen and the whole Roman Church to this very day. And to those of their ordination who are still alive we offer our hand in the same spirit of love, and exhort you to do the same as we do. And if they on their part will obey our orders, we offer them the grace of peace and communion.

'As to the document signed by yourself[2] and which you drew up for us, we have been, after a long search, unable to find it.

Now for the examination of this document. It is easy to see that it has been subjected to but slight doctoring at the copyist's hand; it deserves credit for its essentials and provides valuable information. There is in it one sentence that deserves noting: the copyist says that Stylianos had asked for the return of his ordination paper from Rome.[3] The passage puzzled J. S. Assemanus,[4] who interpreted it as a request 'to be confirmed in his orders', but thought that Stylianos was referring to the confirmation of the Patriarch Mysticos' consecration.

Hergenröther[5] has proved that the passage could only concern Stylianos himself, and in this respect he is right. In his interpretation of the word 'cheirotony' the Cardinal identifies it with the 'idiographon' mentioned in the copyist's comments and with the 'cheirographon' mentioned by the Pope in his reply and whose return Stylianos had applied for.

This reading is admissible, though it remains to be explained why the copyist used the word 'cheirotony'. But the passage is too short

---

[1] ἀπάται τῶν πορνοβοσκησάντων. These words were certainly not in the original papal letter. [2] τὸ δὲ σὸν χειρόγραφον.

[3] These are his words in Greek: Ἔγραψε πρὸς Ῥώμην, αἰτούμενος πεμφθῆναι ἐκεῖθεν χειροτονίαν αὐτοῦ, καὶ ἐπιτροπὴν ἐκεῖθεν λαβεῖν τοῦ συγκοινωνῆσαι αὐτοῖς.

[4] *Bibliotheca Juris Orientalis Canonici et Civilis* (Romae, 1762), p. 319.

[5] Loc. cit. vol. II, pp. 708 seq.

to allow for such an error as 'cheirotony' being used for 'cheiro-graphon'. The copyist, no doubt an ecclesiastic, must have known the real meaning of the word 'cheirotony', and if he read over what he had written, it was only too easy for him to make the necessary correction. And yet, it is also possible that the Pope's refusal mentioned by the copyist in his preliminary comments referred to the two requests which Stylianos had made in his letter—the dispatch of the cheirotony and permission to hold communion with the Photianists—the copyist adding that Stylianos failed to obtain from the Pope even the document he had signed with his own hand, whose dispatch he had also requested and which the Pope mentioned at the end of his reply. But even in this case it would be necessary to admit—and this is possible, but not certain —that the words 'idiographon' and 'cheirographon' are identical.

Should then the passage not rather be taken to mean that Stylianos had asked Rome for a second confirmation of his priestly character? If the words could be understood in this sense, they would bear out the fact that Stylianos had not yet made his peace with his Church in 892, when Formosus sent his legates to Constantinople, and that he was still under the Church's ban in 899. We know that the members of the clergy who had refused to submit to Photius and to communicate with the clerics ordained by him were excommunicated and deprived of all sacerdotal character. This sentence was of course as valid in Rome as it was in Constantinople, the Popes having no choice but to accept in these special matters all the decisions issued by the Patriarchs as though they had been issued by themselves. Stylianos had thus, in changing his attitude, to be reconciled with both Churches and since Stylianos and his followers had so often prided themselves upon having Rome on their side, it was the least he could do to explain his new attitude to the Pope and to become reconciled with him. The puzzling passage in the copyist's comment that Stylianos 'wrote to Rome asking for his ordination (*cheirotony*) to be sent from there' could then be interpreted in the sense that Stylianos asked the Pope to recognize him again as a legitimate bishop with all his rights restored.

With regard to the specific document which Stylianos was so anxious to recover, we may best suppose that he referred to some document which the last Roman embassy sent by Formosus had brought to Rome and which probably contained Stylianos' explanation why he could not enter into communion with the Photianists. Such a declaration was of course valueless once Stylianos had changed his mind and it was quite natural that the bishop should be anxious to recover its possession. It may of course have been a document which Stylianos sent to Rome on another occasion and we are probably not in possession of all the details that marked the endeavours made by the die-hards in Rome; but it would be difficult to imagine an opportunity more suitable than the one mentioned above.

It has been generally believed that Stylianos' reconciliation with the Patriarch and the Pope was enacted at a special synod held in Constantinople and attended by the representatives of the Pope and of all the Patriarchs. Let us see how far this opinion can still be defended, and begin by recapitulating once more the evidence of the chief witnesses who happen to speak of the liquidation of the schism.

There is first the important deposition by the anonymous biographer of St Euthymios. This is what he says: 'After the reconciliation between the Pope and Stylianos of Neocaesarea and the reunion of the whole Church, Anthony, whose happy and praiseworthy life was a credit to all, died the same year on February 12.' Now even this contemporary writer, who was acquainted with the religious events in Byzantium in his time, says nothing about the reunion synod.[1]

Nicholas Mysticos is another contemporary witness who describes the reunion in the same way as Euthymios' biographer:[2] 'And again, in the days of the Emperor Leo, you know that when Mapas and they

[1] V. Grumel, 'Chronique des Événements du Règne de Léon VI', in *Échos d'Orient* (1936), vol. XXXV, p. 18, is of opinion that even in this text Mapas should be read for Papas. In that case, the copyists of the Life of Euthymios made the same mistake as the copyists of the letter of the Patriarch Nicholas and one should read: ἰστέον δὲ ὅτι μετὰ τὴν τοῦ Μάπα ⟨τοῦ⟩ καὶ Στυλιανοῦ τοῦ Νεοκαισαρείας συνέλευσιν καὶ τῆς ἁπάσης ἐκκλησίας ἔνωσιν.... The suggestion is so attractive, because the editor of the Life observes that the first π in the word πάπας was written by another hand after deletion. The text, however, is perfectly clear even in the version adopted by the editor; this is not the case with the text of Nicholas Mysticos, which makes no sense unless the word πάπας be changed into Μάπας. Besides, according to the anti-Photian Collection, the Pope certainly had a hand in this συνέλευσις. On Grumel's supposition, one must also admit that there must have been in the original letter the article τοῦ and that this was also suppressed. One should be cautious about alterations in texts that are perfectly clear without them.

[2] Nicolai Mystici Epistolae, ep. 75, *P.G.* vol. III, col. 277: Πάλιν ἐν ταῖς ἡμέραις τοῦ κυροῦ Λέοντος γινώσκεις ὅτι ὁ Πάπας ⟨to be read Μάπας⟩ συνῆλθε καὶ οἱ μετὰ τούτου ὄντες, καὶ ἡνώθησαν τῇ Ἐκκλησίᾳ, καὶ εἰρήνης βαθείας οὔσης ἀπῆλθεν ἡ Θεσσαλονίκη καὶ τὸ Ταυρομένιον. V. Grumel ('La Liquidation de la Querelle Photienne', in *Échos d'Orient*, vol. XXXIII, pp. 266 seq.) has shown that Μάπας should be read instead of πάπας. The reading πάπας makes the text unintelligible. Nicholas has here in mind not the Church universal, but that of Constantinople, as should be evident to any careful reader of the whole letter.

who were with him made peace and were united with the Church, and when a profound peace was reigning, Salonica and Tauromenium were lost.' Nicholas knows nothing about a Council, though we need not overlook the fact that he does not mention any Councils at all in connection with other occasions recalled in the same letter.

The third witness who also mentions this reunion is Nicephorus the Philosopher in his biography of the Patriarch Cauleas: 'Thereby the flock of the Church felt persistently drawn to higher things and God was made merciful; the great Emperor rejoiced exceedingly, for he saw in him [Cauleas] the discretion of a pure mind that keeps its balance and is not deceived. By healing the old ulcer of the Church, i.e. the schism, he united East and West.'[1]

It has been the practice to find support in this passage for the assumption that the schism was wound up by a General Synod of the whole Church of East and West, but it must be confessed that the reference is anything but clear and may simply mean a certain collaboration between the Eastern Patriarchs and Rome in the winding up of the schism. This collaboration did indeed take place. The correspondence between Stylianos, the leader of the schismatics, and the Pope is an historical fact and it is more than likely that Stylianos addressed the other Patriarchs in much the same way, for in his second letter to the Pope Stylianos suggests it is advisable for other Patriarchs to be consulted in this matter and to give their dispensation to the clergy ordained by Photius.[2]

One may wonder whether the biographer is really thinking here, as is commonly assumed, of East and West, i.e. of the Eastern and Western Churches, for in the same biography he uses an expression nearly identical, but in quite a different sense. In comparing his hero, towards the end of his biography, with the Fathers of the Old Testament and halting at St John the Baptist, Nicephorus describes his life and work and says: 'Around him there crowded not only a town and a people, but innumerable multitudes from an over-crowded city, gathered there from various towns and nations, Eastern and Western,

---

[1] A.S. Febr., d. 12, vol. II, p. 626. Papadoulos-Kerameus, *Monumenta Graeca et Latina ad Historiam Photii pertinentia*, p. 4: Βασιλεύς...δι' αὐτοῦ τὸ παλαιὸν τῆς ἐκκλησίας ἕλκος ἤτοι σχίσμα, εἰς συνούλωσιν προθέμενος ἀγαγεῖν, εἰς ἓν συνάγει τὰ Ἑῷα καὶ τὰ Ἑσπέρια....

[2] Mansi, vol. XVI, col. 437: ἀλλ' ἡμεῖς πάλιν τῶν προτέρων δεήσεων ἐχόμεθα περὶ τῶν δεξαμένων τὸν Φώτιον κατὰ βίαν, καὶ παρακαλοῦμεν ἐγκυκλίους ἐπιστολὰς πέμψαι πρὸς τοὺς πατριαρχικοὺς τῆς ἀνατολῆς θρόνους, ὡς ἂν καὶ αὐτοὶ τὴν παρ' ἡμῶν οἰκονομίαν δεξάμενοι, συνασμενίσωσι καὶ ἐπισφραγίσωσι....

not to be baptized with water, but to be purified by the spiritual mystery.'[1] No one can pretend that the biographer is here thinking of the Eastern Churches and of Rome: all that he means is that people, including the Jews of the *diaspora*, flocked from every country.

In the same way, does he not simply mean in the first passage the totality of the Byzantine Church? The fact is that after the reconciliation of Stylianos by the combined efforts of St Anthony Cauleas and the Emperor Leo VI, peace reigned throughout the Byzantine Church from the West—the south of Italy, which also belonged to the Byzantine Church—to the East as far as the interior of Asia Minor, so that we are justified in holding that this piece of evidence in favour of a reunion synod is anything but conclusive.

There remains a witness, contemporary, or slightly posterior to the events—the *Kletorologion* of Philotheos, which clearly and pointedly refers to a reunion synod of the Church:[2] 'The legates who in the reign of the Emperor Leo had come from Rome for the union of the Churches, especially bishop Nicholas and Cardinal John, received honours that raised them above the rank of Magistri.' As the *Kletorologion* was drawn up on 3 September 899, the synod referred to must have taken place before that date.

But there is a difficulty. P. Maas[3] asserts that this passage is an interpolation dating from the beginning of the tenth century and that the synod referred to is that which took place in Constantinople in 906–7 for the purpose of settling the issue of Leo VI's fourth marriage.[4] I also believe that the text is an interpolation later than 899 and that it actually refers to the synod of 906–7. Let us review the principal objections to this interpretation. First of all, none but the Patriarchs

---

[1] Papadopoulos-Kerameus, loc. cit. vol. I, p. 24: καὶ συνέρρει πρὸς αὐτὸν οὐ μία πόλις, οὐδὲ ἓν ἔθνος, ἀλλ᾽ ὄχλοι παμπληθεῖς τῆς πολυανθρώπου πόλεως, ἐθνῶν καὶ πόλεων συνειλεγμένοι παντοδαπῶν, Ἑῷοί τε καὶ Ἑσπερίοι, οὐχ ὕδατι βαπτισθησό-μενοι, ἀλλὰ πνευματικῇ καθαρθησόμενοι τελευτῇ....

[2] Constantinus Porphyrogennetos, *De Ceremoniis*... (Bonn), p. 739; Bury, *The Imperial Administrative System in the Ninth Century* (London, 1911), p. 155: ἐτιμήθησαν δὲ οἱ ἀπὸ Ῥώμης ἐλθόντες διὰ τὴν ἕνωσιν τῆς ἐκκλησίας ἐπὶ Λέοντος τοῦ φιλοχρίστου δεσπότου, οἷον ὁ ἐπίσκοπος Νικόλαος καὶ ⟨ὁ⟩ καρδινάλιος Ἰωάννης, ἐπάνω πάσης τῆς τάξεως τῶν μαγίστρων.

[3] 'Der Interpolator des Philotheos', in *Byz. Zeitschrift* (1934), vol. XXXIV, pp. 258 seq.

[4] V. Grumel, in the study ('Notes d'Histoire et de Litt. Byz.') he wrote for the *Échos d'Orient* (1930), vol. XXIX, pp. 337 seq. was of the same opinion. But as his arguments were inconclusive he altered it in his 'Chronique des Événements du Règne de Léon VI', loc. cit. pp. 23 seq., to return to the theory that the passage refers to the Synod of 899.

of Antioch and Jerusalem are mentioned in the *Kletorologion*, though it is a well-known fact that the Annals of the Patriarch Eutychius of Alexandria,[1] which give a long account of the synod of 906–7, not only mention the Patriarchs of Antioch and Jerusalem, but also the Patriarch of Alexandria. Let us examine this difficulty.

The imperial ambassador to the Oriental sees in 906 was Leo Choerosphactes and we possess a letter of his addressed to the Emperor Leo in which he quotes this very embassy as a deed that deserved well of His Majesty. After mentioning his embassies to the Bulgarians and to the Arabs, he boasts with some relish that he succeeded in taking to Constantinople even the representatives of the patriarchates of Antioch and of Theopolis.[2] Theopolis undoubtedly stands for Jerusalem. It is known that Justinian had conferred this name on Antioch, but in this particular place the ambassador can only mean the Holy City, the City of God.[3] Leo says nothing about the representative of Alexandria, though this should have been the right moment for mentioning him to impress the Basileus, considering that the letter was an urgent plea for the recovery of imperial honours which Leo had lost.

Euthymios' biographer corroborates the fact that the imperial ambassador to the Eastern Patriarchs was Magister Leo, while Simeon had gone to Rome in the same capacity, and he relates that before returning to Constantinople, Leo informed the Emperor that he was taking with him legates 'bringing *libelli* from the Patriarchs of Antioch, Alexandria and Jerusalem'.[4] But he omits to give the legates' names[5] and nothing is said about the legate of Alexandria in the rest of Leo's correspondence.[6]

---

[1] *P.G.* vol. III, col. 1144: 'Scripsit ergo Leo imperator ad Patriarcham Romanum, Michaelem, Patriarcham Alexandrinum, Eliam Mansuri filium Patriarcham Hierosolymitanum, et Simeon Zaruaki filium, Antiochenum, rogans ut ad ipsum accederent....'

[2] J. Sakkelion, Λέοντος Μαγίστρου ἀνθυπάτου πατρικίου, Συμεὼν ἄρχοντος Βουλγαρίας καὶ τινῶν ἄλλων ἐπιστολαί, in Δελτίον τῆς ἱστορικῆς καὶ ἐθνολογικῆς ἑταιρίας τῆς Ἑλλάδος, I (1883), p. 396: ναὶ μὴν καὶ τοὺς ἱερεῖς Ἀντιοχέων καὶ τοὺς ἐκ τῆς Θεουπόλεως οὓς διὰ τὴν ἐπὶ σοὶ σύνοδον ἠγαγόμην συνοιδοπόρους, ἄρας μέχρι τῆς πόλεως. Cf. the new edition of Leo's letters with a French translation by G. Kolias, 'Léon Choerosphactès', *Texte und Forschungen zur Byzant.-Neugriech. Philologie*, no. 31 (Athens, 1939), p. 113.

[3] Mansi, vol. XVI, col. 190. Helias, who represented the Patriarch of Jerusalem at the Eighth Council, signed the Acts as follows: 'Hierosolymorum, sanctae Christi Dei civitatis.'

[4] *Vita Euthymii*, loc. cit. p. 46.   [5] Cf. loc. cit. pp. 42, 54.

[6] In his letter to the Patrician Genesios, Leo states, but only in general terms (Sakkelion, loc. cit. p. 406): καὶ τὸ κρεῖττον τοὺς ἀρχιερεῖς αὐτοὺς ὡς βασιλέα ἀνάξομεν (Kolias, loc. cit. p. 91). Another mention of this embassy occurs in a letter from the spathar Procopius to Leo and is also couched in general terms.

It is therefore quite possible that the Patriarch of Alexandria only sent a *libellus* or a written declaration, and that he was himself represented by the other Patriarchs' legates. It is none the less extraordinary that the name of this Patriarch should not be mentioned either in the *Kletorologion* or in Leo's report, though the omission is not absolute proof that the reference is to any synod other than that of 906–7.

Another difficulty may arise from the fact that according to the *Kletorologion* this meeting had been summoned for the purpose of bringing about the reunion of the Church, whereas the actual result of the synod of 906–7 was another schism in the Byzantine Church, since the Patriarch Nicholas Mysticos refused to accept the synod's decision on the legality of a fourth marriage.

But this difficulty can also be explained. P. Maas is right in saying[1] that the purpose of the synod in the matter of the tetragamy was precisely to forestall the schism that was then threatening the Church, so that the synod did actually aim at its pacification. At the same time, it was inconceivable that the Byzantines should quote in this connection the names either of the Emperor or of the Empress, especially in the book of ceremonies—which made it imperative to find for the synod some euphemistic designation to disguise the true purpose of the meeting.

It also appears that this synod actually received the name of 'reunion synod', as hinted in a letter written by the spathar Procopius to Leo Choerosphactes, when the latter was away on an embassy to Bagdad. The writer extols Leo's character and the success of his embassies, particularly his successful mission to the Arabs and to the Eastern Patriarchs, so much so that he brought with him the prelates whose task it was to restore peace to the Church.[2] Restoring peace to the Church is not very much different from reuniting the Churches.

Unluckily, the names of the Eastern legates who attended this synod have been lost, and the *Kletorologion* only mentions the Roman legates, bishop Nicholas and Cardinal John. In 921 the Patriarch Nicholas asked John X to send legates to Constantinople and in his letter expressed the desire to see again on this occasion in Byzantium bishop John, who had been there as a legate before. What he had said in Constantinople 'was worthy of the Roman Church'.[3]

---

[1] Loc. cit. p. 260.

[2] Sakkelion, loc. cit. p. 409; G. Kolias, loc. cit. p. 97: ...καὶ πρὸ πάντων τοὺς τὴν ἐκκλησιαστικὴν εἰρήνην οἰκονομήσαντας ἀρχιερέας ἔρχῃ φέρων μετὰ ταυτοῦ.

[3] *P.G.* vol. III, col. 252; Baronius, *Annales*, ad annum 916.

Would the John mentioned by Nicholas be the same as Cardinal John of the *Kletorologion*? We know that the manuscript used for the publication of the Patriarch's letters and edited by Migne calls this legate by the name of Jacob, which makes the identification of this personage rather doubtful; but theoretically, on the supposition that the legate was really called John, he might be identified with the Cardinal John of the *Kletorologion*. It is true that the Patriarch Nicholas had no clear recollection of the Roman legates of 906–7, but this may be the very reason why he wished to see the same individual in Constantinople in 921, just for the satisfaction of making him witness his triumph. Photius also would have preferred to have Marinus in Constantinople in 879; it was he who in 869–70 had been foremost in humiliating the deposed Patriarch and his disciples.

On the whole then it is not at all certain that the *Kletorologion* offers any evidence for the assumption that the reunion of the Church in 899 was brought about by a special synod attended by the representatives of all the Patriarchs. One thing should be noted: neither Stylianos nor the Emperor Leo had asked for the convocation of a synod to end the ultra-Ignatian schism. Stylianos had contented himself with a request for dispensation, which could easily be given in writing, and in 892 Formosus sent legates 'ex privata industria', there being no question of summoning a synod.

We have also seen that this schism was not of such importance as to call for the convocation of a quasi-general synod, which for one thing would have done far too much honour to Stylianos and his 'Little Church'. Both court and city were aware of this. The Emperor, no doubt, wished to see the end of the dissensions in the Church and for this reason insisted, through the good offices of Cauleas, that Stylianos should definitely make peace with the official Church; but a synod— that was quite another matter. It was certainly not in the best interests of the Empire, nor even of the Church of Constantinople, to draw too much attention to such petty quarrels and to give Rome another chance to meddle with a small domestic matter that could be settled by a procedure more in keeping with the prestige of Byzantium.

Again, in comparing and weighing all the evidence on the settlement of this schism, we note that it was Stylianos himself who took the first step in the direction of reunion and that he gave his followers the lead towards reconciliation with the official Church. It is true that even after the reconciliation there were some dissidents left—the commentator of the letter of John IX was one of them—but one cannot assume, after collating the documents, that Stylianos only asked for peace after the majority of his followers had rallied to the official Church. I once put forward this theory,[1] feeling unable to explain how the reunion synod took place before 899 while Stylianos had written to the Pope only seven years after receipt of Formosus' letter, i.e. in 899. But everything is satisfactorily explained once we assume that the Council in question never took place and that reunion was put into effect at a local synod of Constantinople.

The commentator on the letter of John IX has it that Stylianos had decided to take the plunge 'softened by his friends and relations'.[2] Among these friends there certainly was the Patriarch Anthony Cauleas, for it is to him that some sources give the credit of having contrived the reunion: he was of Methodius' ordination, a qualification that must have carried weight in the negotiations. Since the reunion must be dated from 899, we must assume that Anthony was still alive in that year and discard the notion that he died in February 898.[3] I feel inclined to accept the alternative date of his death, namely, 12 February 901.[4]

The letter from Pope John IX is an interesting document, very cleverly worded and reflecting the Roman policy to Photius as it had prevailed since Nicholas I. The Pope pays a tribute to Stylianos for his constant obedience to the orders of the See of Rome, tested by persecution under Nicholas I and again by his recent submission to the decisions of John VIII. It is evident that not even Pope John IX could completely shake himself free from the notion, common in Rome, that Photius' first condemnation was justifiable. Such would appear to be the best explanation of the reunion of the extremist Ignatians with the official Church of Byzantium and with Rome.

The anti-Photian Collection which has preserved the letter of John IX is therefore, in spite of its tendentious character, a very valuable piece of documentary evidence, and may well have been compiled after the legates' failure in 892. One can understand that as the ultra-Ignatians' intransigent refusal to compromise, in spite of the legates' expostula-

---

[1] 'Le Second Schisme de Photios', in *Byzantion*, vol. VIII, p. 471.
[2] Raderus' translation (Mansi, vol. XVI, col. 455) is again at fault here. χυνωθεὶς ὑπὸ τῶν φίλων καὶ συγγενῶν does not mean, as Raderus would have it, 'stolida per amicos et cognatos superbia elatus'.
[3] H. Grégoire, 'Études sur le IXe siècle', *Byzantion* (1933), vol. VIII, pp. 540 seq.
[4] As proposed by V. Grumel, 'Chronique des Événements du Règne de Léon VI', in *Échos d'Orient*, vol. XXXIX, pp. 6 seq.

tions, provoked much criticism in Byzantium, the Ignatians felt themselves obliged to prove that their attitude to Photius and his ordinations was both fair and consistent with the decisions of the Holy See. We have already studied the passage in which the compiler indicates the length of time that Photius remained under the ban of excommunication, which provides the clue for fixing the date of his compilation, i.e. 892, the year of the failure of Formosus' negotiations. The compiler's desperate efforts to prove that Photius could not possibly be absolved by any Pope should help us to appraise the criticisms levelled at the die-hard Ignatians.

The Life of the Patriarch Ignatius, which forms the third part of the Collection, was also written at the same period, and one passage in the Life shows clearly that it was written soon after Photius' death. Nicetas admits that he would never have spoken of Photius' misdeeds, had he not seen how 'those who did such things and their friends, far from being conscious of any feeling of shame, boasted of them and conferred on him [Photius] an aureole of sanctity which he did not deserve'.[1] These words speak for themselves; they illustrate the Byzantines' feelings towards Photius after his death and provide the first evidence of the cult of Photius. The admission is all the more welcome, as it comes from a bitter enemy of the late Patriarch's, and shows that the author of the Life of Ignatius is taking the offensive against this spurious saint and that his 'biography' of the Patriarch Ignatius is meant to be a counter-blast showing the Byzantines who was the true and only saint of the time, the Patriarch Ignatius, the victim of Photius' pride.

Another passage in the Life clearly denotes that it was written during the first years of the reign of Leo, for the writer recalls the disasters that had afflicted the Empire ever since Photius' restoration to the patriarchal throne. He mentions the loss of Syracuse (21 May 878): 'The whole island,' the writer goes on, 'the whole city and the province were pillaged and the population decimated by the enemy, because the prayers of those who make a pretence of administering sacred things can never incline God to mercy.'[2]

These words show that at the time the Life was written people were

---

[1] *P.G.* vol. 105, col. 541: καὶ διὰ τοῦτο παντάπασιν εὖ ἴστε, κατησίγησα ἄν, εἰ μὴ ἑώρων τοὺς ταῦτα καταπραξαμένους, καὶ τοὺς αὐτῶν οἰκείους, οὐ μόνον ἐν τούτοις οὐκ ἐγκαλυπτομένους, ἀλλὰ καὶ ἐγκαλλωπιζωμένους καὶ δόξαν ἁγιωσύνης ἐπιψευδομένους αὐτῷ.

[2] Ibid. col. 573: καὶ πᾶσα νῆσος, καὶ πᾶσα πόλις καὶ χώρα προνομεύεται καὶ καταφθείσεται μεχρὶ καὶ τήμερον τοῖς ἐχθροῖς, οὐδεμίας ἐκ τῶν ἱερᾶσθαι δοκούντων ἱλουμένης τὸν Θεὸν προσευχῆς.

still under the recent impression of the great loss sustained by the Empire by the Arab occupation of Syracuse and that desperate efforts— one of them ending in the disastrous defeat of the Byzantine fleet at Mylae (Milazzo) in 888—were being made to retrieve the remnants of Byzantine possessions in Sicily, the last important town, Taormina, being taken by the Arabs in August 902. The first fourteen years of the reign of Leo VI proved generally disastrous to the Empire, and the wars with the Bulgarians and the Arabs brought more than one humiliation on the Byzantines.[1]

The same passage also makes it clear that the reigning Patriarch at the time the book was written was not reckoned to be the legitimate Patriarch by the author, who found nothing better to say than that the man was only a make-believe Patriarch. The taunt fits Stephen best, the Emperor's brother who ruled the Byzantine Church till 893. His successor Anthony Cauleas must have been ordained by Methodius, or at least by Ignatius, so that the sneer could hardly be applicable to him.

We also find in the Life of St Ignatius passages suggesting a certain similarity between the author and the writer of the treatise on the Stauropats, as also between the Life and other documents collected by the compiler of the book. The violent abuse hurled at the Photianists by the author of the treatise against the Stauropats reveals a similar truculence. Nicetas-David Paphlago took the same line, severely reproving the Council of 869–70 for letting off the priests ordained by Photius too lightly, and so repeating the mistake made by their predecessors of the Seventh Council[2] in relation to the repentant iconoclasts. The Fathers should have proscribed the Photianists without mercy and refused communion even to those who had been ordained by Methodius or Ignatius.

Nicetas is also violent against the bishops who had rallied again to Photius after his rehabilitation and calls them Stauropats, i.e. people who disowned their own signatures, and we know that the author of the treatise on the Stauropats similarly abuses the bishops who had 'apostatized'. Nicetas also indulges in an angry outburst against Photius in his account of the ex-Patriarch's recovery of Basil's favour.[3] Photius, of course, is called a Stauropat for having forced the bishops to violate their signatures, and at the end of his work Nicetas[4] calls Photius the leader of all Stauromachs and hypocrites. This final outburst forms a

---

[1] Cf. *Cambridge Medieval History*, vol. IV, *The Eastern Roman Empire* (1927), pp. 140 seq. (A. A. Vasiliev, 'The Struggle with the Saracens', pp. 867–1057).
[2] *P.G.* vol. 105, cols. 545–9   [3] Ibid. cols. 569 seq.   [4] Ibid. col. 573.

suitable pendant to the abuse poured at the beginning of the pamphlet on all the followers of Photius for their many sins: but the greatest of these is the sin of *stauropaty*.[1]

The comparison suggests that the author of the Life of Ignatius might well be the same man as the compiler of the whole Collection. Nicetas' frequent appeals to various signs such as earthquakes, etc., as irrefutable evidence of the truth of his own lucubrations betray the pseudo-pious die-hard and the uncompromising fanatic and are equally characteristic of the author of the whole compilation.

The Life of St Ignatius is therefore little better than a 'political tract'[2] and its veracity is highly questionable. It should, however, be said to the credit of the Byzantines that they seem to have been aware of the partisan character of this 'biography'. Cedrenus, for instance (or rather Skylitzes whom Cedrenus is copying), in the introduction to his *Compendium Historiarum*,[3] speaks of writers who had their own axe to grind, 'one to extol an Emperor, another to calumniate a Patriarch, a third to advertise a friend', and among the writers who perpetrated such books he mentions Nicetas the Paphlagonian.

This passage is important, as it may help towards the definite solution of the problem of the authorship of the anti-Photian Collection. Skylitzes, who wrote his work at the end of the eleventh century, possibly had in mind the writings against Photius; for it is difficult to think of any Patriarch before Skylitzes' time whose memory was so deliberately besmirched as that of Photius. Does the fact that he mentions amongst the authors of the calumny Nicetas the Paphlagonian indicate that in Skylitzes' days the writings against Photius were attributed to him?[4]

I am on the whole inclined to attribute the entire Collection to the author of the *Vita Ignatii* and this is attributed to Nicetas-David of Paphlagonia,[5] though of course not all the documents were written

---

[1] *P.G.* vol. 105, col. 508.

[2] Cf. A. Vogt, 'Deux Discours inédits de Nicétas de Paphlagonie', in *Orientalia Christiana* (Rome), vol. LXXV, 1, p. 10.   [3] (Bonn), pp. 4, 5.

[4] This is by no means certain. We shall presently learn that a certain Nicetas of Paphlagonia wrote a pamphlet against the Patriarch Euthymios, and it is quite possible that Skylitzes has this incident in mind, as it came nearer to his period and was perhaps better remembered by Skylitzes' and Cedrenus' contemporaries than the anti-Photianist campaign. In this case, could Nicetas be taken to be the author of the writings against both Patriarchs? Cf. what I write on this on p. 277.

[5] There is, however, still some doubt about the identity of Nicetas-David, to whom the Life of Ignatius is ascribed, with Nicetas of Paphlagonia, the author of some theological and philosophical writings, only a few of which have so far been

by him. It is possible that under the second patriarchate of Ignatius there circulated among the Ignatians an extract from the Acts of the Eighth Council which Nicetas simply annexed to his Collection, and the same might be said about the treatise on the Councils of which Nicetas quotes only the lines on the Eighth Council.[1]

It follows, then, that Assemanus[2] was well inspired in attributing the anti-Photian Collection to Nicetas-David. But the reference to Mapas and the letter of Pope John IX, with its commentary, were added to the Collection after 899, probably by another copyist, one even more stubborn than Nicetas-David. It is clear then that the Collection, which was to do duty for a justificatory plea in favour of the Stylianists in extenuation of their refusal to reunite in 892, also served some followers even more obdurate than Stylianos in justification of their refusal in 899 to follow the majority of their own kind.

Did the author of the compilation—Nicetas-David—follow Stylianos, or was he the man who added the notorious postscript to his Collection? It is hard to say. Nor do we know when, or how, the last traces of the schism faded out. These ultra die-hards were apparently not many, and besides, the Byzantines' attention was soon to be diverted to another

published. On the two Nicetases, cf. Chr. Loparev, 'Zhitie sv. Evdokima', in *Izvestiya Russkago Arkh. Instituta*, vol. XIII (1908), pp. 164 seq. (reprinted in *Vizantijskiy Vremennik* (1912), pp. 143 seq.) and A. Vogt, loc. cit. p. 6. It seems doubtful, if not impossible, that one man should be the author of the Collection and of the works mentioned. The writer of the so-called Life of St Ignatius was not to all appearances a man of high intellectual attainment and could hardly be supposed to be the author of works of any theological or philosophical value. I think that the authorship of the Collection will never be elucidated without a thorough study of the manuscript text of the anti-Photianist Collection. It had been my original intention to collate all the MSS. of the Acts and documents connected with the Ignatian and Photian Councils, when recent events upset my plans and I was only able to examine the principal MSS. of the Acts of the Photian Council. It seems now established that all the MSS. of the anti-Photian Collection are derived from the Venetus Marcus Graecus 167, the result of researches made by K. Schweinburg, as we read in the preface to the edition of some extracts from this Collection published by G. Laehr in the *M.G.H. Ep.* VII, p. 371. According to K. Schweinburg, this MS., from which all others are derived, dates from the fourteenth century. As the study of the original manuscript Collection which K. Schweinburg promised to publish in the *Byz. Zeitschrift* has not yet appeared, the difficult verdict on this problem must be held over till after the publication of K. Schweinburg's researches. In the meantime, we may assume, until the problem is definitely settled, the author of St Ignatius' Life and of the Collection to be Nicetas-David of Paphlagonia, as the MSS. have it.

[1] Mansi, vol. XVI, col. 453.
[2] Loc. cit. vol. II, pp. 322–4. Hergenröther's objections (loc. cit. vol. II, pp. 73 seq.) against this attribution are anything but convincing.

controversy, the tetragamy, before which the old issue faded into oblivion.

After all, the controversy provoked by the refusal of the Patriarch Nicholas Mysticos, successor to Cauleas, to allow the Emperor Leo VI to marry a fourth time was merely a continuation of the struggle between the Extremists and the Moderates, or partisans of the policy of oeconomia. The new contest brought about a certain redistribution in the ranks of the old antagonists; for instance, Nicholas Mysticos, a student and relation of Photius, became the leader of the Extremists on the issue of the tetragamy and was destined to organize a vicious campaign against Euthymios, to replace him on the patriarchal throne in 906; whilst Euthymios, formerly a Moderate Ignatian who acknowledged Photius under his second patriarchate and was likewise in communion with Stephen,[1] became after 906 the head of the Moderates, the partisans of the policy of oeconomia, with old Photianists, like Arethas of Caesarea, fighting by his side.

It is even more surprising that Nicetas-David appears to have joined Nicholas and with his usual venom to have attacked Euthymios. In the Life of this Patriarch we find a lengthy paragraph[2] on a certain monk Nicetas the Paphlagonian, surnamed the Philosopher, who was suspected of acting in collusion with the Bulgarians, a nation that was at the moment at war with the Byzantines. From the passage we learn that Nicetas fell foul not only of Euthymios, but also of the Metropolitan who supported him, that he wrote a pamphlet against Euthymios and uttered words offensive to the Emperor. Only the intervention of the aggrieved Patriarch saved Nicetas from the heavy punishment which by the Emperor's orders awaited him. The publication mentioned was a pamphlet of the Extremist party, then the party of Nicholas, against the Moderate party which supported Euthymios and the Emperor. It would be interesting to know more about this Nicetas the Paphlagonian. Was he the author of the philosophical and theological works and thereby sufficiently known in Byzantium to attract the attention of Euthymios' biographer? Or was he the author of the Life of Ignatius and of the anti-Photian Collection?

De Boor,[3] the editor of the Life, expressed doubts about Nicetas' identification with the author of the Life of Ignatius on the score that such a passionate partisan of Ignatius would on that supposition have

---

[1] *Vita Euthymii* (ed. de Boor), pp. 17 seq. Euthymios had his monastery consecrated by Stephen.

[2] Loc. cit. pp. 56–8.   [3] Loc. cit. pp. 194–6.

become a protagonist of the Photianist party. De Boor is right in questioning the identity of this Nicetas with the author of the Life of Ignatius, for the fact is questionable and the passage in Euthymios' Life is too short to establish even the identity of this Nicetas with his name-sake, the author of the philosophical and theological writings; but the reason for de Boor's hesitation is not compelling. Nicetas, the Igna-tianist, in turning against Euthymios never became a Photianist; he only followed his bent for reactionary tenets and his instinctive aversion to the application of the famous principle of oeconomia to religious matters. All that happened was that the Photianist and Ignatian parties were transmuted into Nicholaite and Euthymian parties. Nicholas Mysticos, relative and pupil of Photius though he was, remained by nature an Extremist.

From this point of view we are in a position to assess the issue that again divided the parties in Byzantium. It is also quite admissible that Nicetas-David, intransigent by instinct, by character and by experience, offered his services to Nicholas, who had become the leader of those who believed in uncompromising rigour in the settlement of eccle-siastical questions.[1] But even this problem cannot be finally solved until the identity of Nicetas-David and the authorship of *Vita Ignatii* can be definitely settled.

We cannot pursue any further the detailed story of this conflict and all its incidents. Once again, there were between 907 and 920 exiles in both camps; again, the Byzantine Church found itself split into two factions, the faithful in many dioceses being given the choice, according to personal tastes, between a Nicholaite, or Extremist bishop, and an Euthymian bishop, that is, a Moderate and partisan of oeconomia; again, Rome intervened at the request of the Emperor and the ecclesiastical authorities of Byzantium, and the synod of 907 ended in a Nicholaite schism, which lasted till the death of Leo VI in 911. Nicholas' reinstate-ment was the signal for a persecution of the Euthymians like that at the time of the Photianist and Ignatian dispute, and again the Emperor's death brought about the Patriarch's dismissal, as the new Emperor relied for his support on the opposition party, all in accordance with long-established custom. Lastly, like the feud between Ignatius and Photius, so the breach between the Nicholaites and the Euthymians ended in a concordat between the leaders of the opposite camps[2] and

[1] Cf. Kurganov, *K izsledovaniyu o Patr. Fotiye*, pp. 218, 219, as against Ivantsov-Platonov, *Sv. Patriarkh Fotii*, pp. 11, 12.

[2] *Vita Euthymii* (ed. de Boor), pp. 73 seq.

a Council, this time the real reunion Council, held in Byzantium in 920. A *tomos* of the reunion [1] was passed unanimously and the acclamations addressed to the late Patriarchs, from Germanus to Tarasius, promulgated to the whole Empire and to the Church that the old divisions were healed for ever.

But the Fathers were gravely deluded, if they really believed this. Dissensions were to revive again, as occasions arose, because Byzantium was never without its partisans of rigidity and its partisans of adaptation, its extreme conservatives and its Moderates: only the issues varied. Even the final death-struggle of the Byzantine Church for and against union with the West was at bottom but a revival of the old antagonisms between Moderates and Extremists; this time the die-hards carried the day, despite the desperate efforts of the last Byzantine Emperor, who met his heroic death on the walls of the city, 'protected by God'. And the struggle is not yet ended, and will never be ended, as long as the two tendencies compete for the mastery within the human heart and degenerate into passions when religious issues are involved.

And yet it is in the very clash of these two tendencies that we shall find the key to the understanding of many a problem of Byzantine history, and in particular, of the history of the Photian Schism.

[1] Mansi, vol. XVIII, cols. 336 seq.

II. *The Legend*

CHAPTER I

THE PHOTIAN CASE IN LATIN LITERATURE TILL THE TWELFTH CENTURY

Contemporary repercussions—The *Anselmo Dedicata*—Tenth-century writers—
Unpublished canonical Collections of the tenth century—Historians of the eleventh
century—The Photian case in the 'Gregorians'' canonical Collections—The Latin
Acts of the Photian Council in the writings of Deusdedit and Ivo of Chartres.

FROM the examination of the history of Photius, it should now be
clear that one account of the growth and the importance of the Photian
Schism, as based on contemporary evidence, differs in many respects,
some of them fundamental, from the accounts that have been accepted
through the centuries down to our own time. It is evident, then, that
if our argument is sound the true historical picture of the Photian
Schism has been blurred in the distant past and that there has gradually
grown up a Photian Legend which was finally adopted as canonical
truth. We shall now follow the growth of this legend in Western, and
even Eastern, tradition from the ninth century to our present era,
noting the different phases of its evolution and the men responsible
for the conversion of legend into accepted truth.

As regards Western tradition,[1] we have had occasion to point out
some of the factors that facilitated the birth of the Photian legend, and
the most telling of these was the enormous prestige enjoyed by the great
Pope Nicholas I in the ninth century and throughout the Middle Ages:
his reputation was so universally established as to make it next to
impossible for anybody to question his well-known attitude to
Photius. Anti-Greek animosity, which for the first time broke out
in its more violent form in the reign of Nicholas and gained strength
in medieval centuries, also militated against the memory of a
Patriarch who was daring enough to 'rebel' against the great Nicholas,
the first great precursor of Gregory VII, the man whose opinions

---

[1] This chapter is a re-edition, with additions, of my study 'L'affaire de Photios
dans la Littérature Latine du Moyen Age', in *Annales de l'Institut Kondakov*
(Prague, 1938).

on pontifical primacy became the leading axioms of the Latin Middle Ages.

To turn first to the repercussions of the Photian case among his contemporaries in Latin countries, it was between 863 and 870 that the Western world began to take an interest in the bold Patriarch of Constantinople, whose conflict with Pope Nicholas I all but set the whole Western Church at odds with the Eastern Church.

Nicholas I, the gallant champion of papal rights, of which he entertained such a lofty notion, endeavoured to mobilize his whole Church against the Emperor Michael III and his Patriarch, and the Pope's letter of 23 October 867[1] was meant to organize the movement in Gaul and Germany; Hincmar of Rheims was personally commissioned to set up the common front of the Frankish Church against the Greeks.

The Frankish Church, indeed, took its mission very seriously. The bishops of the Rheims metropolis charged Odo, bishop of Beauvais, with the task of refuting the Greek calumnies in writing; whereas the mouthpiece of the Sens metropolis was to be Aeneas, bishop of Paris. Odo's work has been lost, but the bishop of Paris did not exert himself in carrying out his honourable mission; his production is extremely feeble.[2] But Ratramnus, abbot of Corbie, who probably had also been requested to place his learning at the service of the common cause, wrote a reply,[3] which is a credit to the theological learning of the Frankish clergy of the time, and must have deeply impressed his contemporaries in Gaul, and possibly in Italy, too.

Hincmar has given us in his writings a version of these events, to which he refers in his letter to Odo of Beauvais;[4] and we also find in his polemical writings against his namesake of Laon[5] a spirited attack on the Greeks, in which the archbishop takes the Patriarchs of Constantinople to task for pretensions that had already been made by the Council of Chalcedon, and takes exception to their use of the title 'oecumenical'—the whole passage being probably a hint at the Photian Affair.

But a more detailed account of the facts is found in the Bertinian Annals, in which Hincmar mentions the embassy of Radoald and Zachary to Constantinople in 860–1, refers to the Pope's intention to condemn them and to his scheme of summoning a Council in 864, with the Frankish bishops in attendance and even with the Patriarch Ignatius'

---

[1] M.G.H. Ep. VI, pp. 169 seq. [2] P.L. vol. 121, cols. 685 seq.
[3] P.L. vol. 121, cols. 225–346. [4] P.L. vol. 126, Ep. XIV, cols. 93, 94.
[5] Loc. cit. ch. XX, cols. 345–50.

case on its agenda;[1] he then describes the moral and physical depression in which his legates found the Pope in August 867, as also the vigour of his appeal to the Western bishops, in particular, the archbishop of Rheims.[2] Hincmar's main sources are the Pope's letters, which he often copies textually, and his information is confirmed and completed by the historiographer of the church of Rheims, Flodoard.[3]

The Bertinian Annals also contain a report on the dispatch by Pope Hadrian II of the legates to Constantinople to sanction Ignatius' reinstatement and on the convocation of a Council in this connection.[4] And there ends the information supplied by the archbishop of Rheims.

The account of the Annals takes us as far as the year 882, without giving any further details on subsequent developments in the Photian affair—which seems surprising. If, however, one brings together Hincmar's various references to Photius, it becomes evident that the issue interests him only in so far as it concerns his Church and his own person, since he had been charged by the Pope to enlist public feeling in Gaul against the Greek pretensions. That is why Hincmar often prefers to quote word for word the letters Nicholas had addressed to him.

Weaker still is the reaction of the Photian case in Germany. Nicholas I had requested the archbishop of Mainz, Liutbert,[5] to summon a council of Germanic bishops to formulate a common reply to the Greek calumnies: the Germanic bishops did meet at Worms, but committed themselves to nothing more exciting than a short synodic reply.[6]

Except for the mention of this Council, there is only one reference to the Photian case in German contemporary literature and we have it from the *Annals* of Fulda; but here again, the annalist confines himself to a laconic commentary. This is what he says:[7] 'Nicholas, the Roman Pontiff, addressed two letters to the bishops of Germany, one on the

---

[1] Cf. E. Perels, 'Ein Berufungsschreiben Papst Nikolaus' I. zur fränkischen Reichssynode in Rom', in *Neues Archiv d. Ges. f. ält. deutsche Gesch.* (1906), vol. XXXII, pp. 135 seq.

[2] *M.G.H.* Ss. I, pp. 466, 475. Cf. above, p. 124.

[3] Flodoardi Hist. Rem. Eccl., *M.G.H.* Ss. XIII, lib. III, ch. 17, p. 508; ch. 21, pp. 516 seq.

[4] *M.G.H.* Ss. I, p. 494.

[5] Cf. Nicholas' letter to Louis the German of 23 October 867, *M.G.H.* Ep. VI, p. 610.

[6] Cf. A. Weringhoff, 'Verzeichnis der Akten fränk. Synoden', in *Neues Archiv* (1901), vol. XXVI, p. 639; *P.L.* vol. 119, cols. 1201–12. Cf. above, p. 123.

[7] Ad a. 868, *M.G.H.* Ss. I, p. 380.

Greek divisions, the other on the deposition of the bishops Theotgand and Gunthar.... A synod was held in the month of May in Worms... where the bishops... gave answers apposite to the Greek futilities.' We might expect to find more in contemporary literature of Roman and Italian origin; but while information on the first stage of the Photian quarrel is extremely abundant—the letters of Popes Nicholas I, Hadrian II, John VIII, the writings of Anastasius the Librarian—accounts of the second stage of the conflict are, as a result of the concurrence of several unfortunate circumstances, very scanty. First, Anastasius vanished from the scene about 878; his death is untimely, as in the last years of his life he gave signs of a modified attitude to Photius. He was the writer, as I have shown elsewhere,[1] who settled the preliminaries of a rapprochement between John VIII and Photius as well as of a new departure in the Holy See's Eastern policy; Anastasius was not a man of fastidious temperament and would certainly not have hesitated to say exactly the reverse of what he had written in the preface to the translation of the Acts of the Eighth Council and in his biographies of Nicholas and Hadrian, if there had been any such need in the interests of the new policy of the master he was then serving. Unluckily, death prevented him from giving the last touches to his 'conversion', though it seemed to have been well on the way.

More light would have been thrown on the revision of John VIII's policy towards Photius, had that Pope been blessed with a biographer; but unfortunately the *Liber Pontificalis* breaks down at this very place. Hadrian II was the last Pope to be favoured in this respect, but his biography does not cover the last years of his pontificate. About John VIII, Marinus and Hadrian III there is complete silence. The biography of Stephen V, which concludes the *Liber Pontificalis*, deals apparently only with the first year of his reign.[2]

Lastly, it is much to be regretted that John the Deacon, an intimate associate of John VIII, failed to fulfil his intention of publishing an ecclesiastical history and devoting special attention to Greek affairs, for, judging by the biography he wrote of St Gregory the Great,[3] his work would have been of the highest value.

We are thus reduced to one single source of information, which makes a brief, but important, reference to Photius' rehabilitation, the history of the Benevento Lombards, written by the monk Erchempertus. This

---

[1] *Les Légendes de Constantin et de Méthode*, pp. 314 seq.
[2] L. Duchesne, *Liber Pontificalis*, vol. II, pp. vii, viii.
[3] *P.L.* vol. 75, cols. 60–242.

is what he has to say about the ascent of Leo and Alexander to the imperial throne:[1]

At the death of Serene and August Basil, his two sons were elected to the throne, namely, Leo the eldest and Alexander, his younger brother; the third, called Stephen, took charge of the archiepiscopal see of that city, after the expulsion of Photius, who had come under the perpetual anathema of Nicholas, the Pontiff of the first See, for usurping the see of Ignatius in his lifetime and had been reinstated in his previous dignity by Pope John, who, so to speak, acted in ignorance.

Brief as it is, this testimony is of capital importance, for not only does Erchempertus bear witness to Photius' rehabilitation, but he also indirectly certifies that the Holy See never went back on its decision. We are of course aware that Erchempertus was no friend of the Greeks, at whose hands he experienced some rough handling as a prisoner in his younger days, and that for the rest of his life he never forgave them. As a zealous patriot, he frankly detested the Greeks as his country's worst enemies; and pious monk as he was, he readily forgave even the prince of Capua, Atenolf, for his ruthless treatment of the sons of Benedict in that city and—what is more remarkable—of himself, in consideration of the victory the prince had won over the combined Neapolitans, Saracens and Greeks. He warmly applauded this victory,[2] and his account contains bitter asides addressed to the Greeks, whom he describes as 'akin to animals in feelings, Christians by name, but for morals worse than Agarenes'.[3]

Erchempertus also relieves his feelings against the Greeks in his reference to Photius, making it quite clear that he did not approve John VIII's conduct and excusing the Pope's 'weakness' on the ground of his ignorance of the true state of affairs.

It is easy to imagine with what relish he would have recorded on this occasion that the Pope had realized the cunning of those people 'who were Christians but in name', revoked his decision, and again excommunicated Photius. The fact that Erchempertus says nothing about the second excommunication of the Patriarch of Constantinople by John, clearly indicates that it never took place.

[1] Erchemperti Historia Langobard. Benevent., ch. 52, M.G.H. Ss. Rer. Lang. p. 256: '...eiecto Focio, qui olim a Nicolao primae sedis pontifice ob invasionem episcopatus Ignatii adhuc superstitis perpetuo anathemate fuerat multatus, et a Ioanne papa, ut ita dicam ignaro, ad pristinum gradum resuscitatus....'

[2] Ibid. ch. 73 seq. p. 262. Cf. Waitz's Introduction to this edition, p. 232 and Pertz's remark in his edition in the M.G.H. Ss. III, p. 240.

[3] Ibid. ch. 81, p. 264.

Erchempertus' silence is a sign that not even John's successors broke off relations with the Greeks. He was in personal contact with Stephen V for instance, who at Erchempertus' request had intervened against Atenolf and sanctioned the privileges of the Brothers of St Benedict in Capua.[1] Had Stephen V severed relations with the Greeks, the action would have been commended by this enthusiastic patriot as a meritorious deed, and Erchempertus, who thought highly of Stephen for intervening in favour of his confrères, would never have lost the chance of emphasizing the Pope's unbending attitude towards the Greeks.

For lack of other contemporary historical documents, we may seek some indications of John VIII's dealings with the Greeks in another class of literature which is still little known and has not so far been utilized by historians—the Collections of canon law. It happens that the period we are studying—that of Nicholas I, Hadrian II and John VIII —is marked by a revival of canonical activity,[2] and canon law Collections invariably reflect with faithful precision the spirit of the policy of the Popes who inspired them.

Now there exists a canonical Collection of the period of John VIII which goes by the name of *Anselmo Dedicata*, and was composed by a cleric of Lombardy, devoted to the policy of John VIII, probably towards the end of that Pontiff's reign, about 882.[3] The author dedicated his Collection to Anselm, archbishop of Milan (882–96), who had been the Pope's faithful lieutenant in an acrimonious campaign which John had fought against Anspertus, Anselm's predecessor in the see of Milan, who tenaciously championed the rights of his see even at the risk of falling foul of the Pope.

This Collection is relevant to our investigation, as it seems to reflect the Pope's political opinions. The author has the same lofty notion as John VIII of the Papacy's mission in the Church. According to the description given by P. Fournier[4] of this unpublished Collection, the author aims at assembling the greatest possible number of texts on the

[1] Historia Langobard. Benevent., loc. cit. ch. 69, p. 261.
[2] Cf. Giesebrecht, 'Die Gesetzgebung der Römischen Kirche zur Zeit Gregor VII' (München), *Historisches Jahrbuch für das Jahr 1866*, pp. 93 seq.
[3] P. Fournier-G. Le Bras, *Histoire des Collections Canoniques en Occident* (Paris, 1931), vol. I, pp. 239 seq.
[4] Loc. cit., P. Fournier, 'L'Origine de la Collection Anselmo Dedicata', in *Mélanges P. F. Girard* (Paris, 1912), vol. I, pp. 475–98; P. Fournier-G. Le Bras, *Histoire des Collections Canoniques en Occident*, vol. I, pp. 235 seq. Cf. F. Maassen, *Geschichte der Quellen der Litteratur des can. Rechtes im Abendlande* (Gratz, 1870), pp. 717 seq.

primacy of the bishop of Rome, both authentic and spurious, the latter being drawn from the False Decretals. On the other hand, he neglects anything that is not Roman and does not quote a single text of Frankish, Irish or Anglo-Saxon origin. P. Fournier rightly discovers traces of the Roman spirit animating John VIII, but the author's bias in favour of Rome does not prevent him from being polite to the Greeks. Evidence of this is to be found in the first book of the Collection. In canon 128 the author copies the decision of the Council of Constantinople conferring second rank on the Patriarch of that city. The next canon is taken from one of Justinian's *Novels*[1] and defines the rights of the Patriarchs in Constantinople in the following terms: 'Be the Pope first of all bishops and patriarchs, and after him the bishop of the city of Constantinople.'[2] As this composition appears to belong to the last reign of John VIII's pontificate, such partiality to a Graeco-Roman entente may be taken as indirect evidence that John VIII had not swerved from his Graecophil policy. How then could a writer so loyal to his master's opinions have inserted in his Collection these two canons, so favourable to the Patriarchs of Constantinople, if John VIII had in that year, or in the previous year, excommunicated Photius for the second time, after discovering, as has so often been asserted to this day, that he had been disgracefully duped by the astute Greek? Such a demonstration would have provoked in Rome, and throughout Italy, a reaction very different from that revealed in the *Anselmo Dedicata*.[3] It should be enough to recall the agitation that arose in the West at the first declaration of hostilities between Photius and Nicholas I. In the writings of Ratramnus of Corbie,[4] and of Aeneas, bishop of

---

[1] Codex Justinianus, lib. III, tit. 3, novella 130: '...Sancimus...Senioris Romae papam primum esse omnium sacerdotum; beatissimum autem archiepiscopum Constantinopoleos Novae Romae secundum habere locum post sanctam apostolicam Senioris Romae sedem: aliis autem omnibus sedibus praeponitur.' The author of the *Anselmo Dedicata* quotes Justinian's *Novels* mostly from the Epitome made by Julianus (ed. G. Haenel, 1873).

[2] 'Papa Romanus prior omnibus episcopis et patriarchis, et post illum Constantinopolitanae civitatis episcopus.'

[3] An extract from the *Anselmo Dedicata* will be found in a Latin manuscript of the Prague National Library, Codex Lobkovicz, no. 496 (13th c. parch.), fols. 85a–102, under the title: 'Incipiunt Excerpta sanctorum pontificum', where the copyist has transcribed 87 chapters of the famous Collection, but without the slightest reference to the Pope and the Patriarchs. The extracts date from the end of the ninth or the beginning of the tenth century. Cf. Schulte, 'Über Drei in Prager Hs. enthaltenen Canonen-Sammlungen', in *Sitzungsberichte d. Akad. Wiss. Wien, Phil.-Hist. Kl.* (1867), pp. 171–5.

[4] Contra Graecorum Opposita, L. d'Achery, *Spicilegium* (Paris, 1723), pp. 107 seq., chiefly p. 111. *P.L.* vol. 121, cols. 223 seq.

Paris,[1] we find that these two writers, who were thoroughly cognizant of Pope Nicholas' ideas, emphasized that the Patriarch of Constantinople was subject to the Pope, and did all they could to minimize Justinian's *Novel* on the right of the Patriarch. Remembering the vicious castigation, which only a few years previously Hincmar had administered to the Greeks for calling their Patriarch 'oecumenical', and to the Council of Chalcedon for deciding in favour of Byzantium, we can readily appreciate how far the spirit of those invectives was removed from that which inspired the author of the Collection *Anselmo Dedicata*—to conclude that the Holy See's Oriental policy under John VIII had turned a full circle.

Thus the echoes of the Photian Affair in the Latin literature of the ninth century are feeble enough, but what little evidence they offer contains no reference to a second Photian schism.

In any examination of the literary documents of the period, it must be remembered that the tenth century is characterized by the complete collapse of the Carolingian Empire. As a result of external dangers, especially the Hungarian invasions, and of internal trouble, historiography was barren for several decades and no relevant description of the period survived. Decadence was worst in Rome, at the very centre of Western Christianity, where Anastasius the Librarian and John the Deacon were the last surviving historians. Nor was the position any better in Gaul and Germany, as there other problems, more absorbing and topical than Greek controversies, occupied the few writers who were at work.

So we search in vain through the Germanic writings of the period for the barest reference to Photius. The works published in Gaul are equally unsatisfactory, and when we turn to Italy, the only reference to the incident is to be found in the Chronicle of Salerno written about the year 978,[2] in which the chronicler merely copies the extract from Erchempertus verbatim.

But not even in Rome was the memory of Photius quite obliterated. In a letter addressed to the Frankish episcopate, Pope Sergius III seems to make him responsible for the campaign against the Latin *Filioque* and mention of it is made in the Acts of the Frankish synod of Trosley

---

[1] Liber adversus Graecos, ibid. pp. 143 seq. *P.L.* vol. 121, cols. 683 seq.

[2] *M.G.H.* Ss. III, p. 538. A MS. of the Chronicle of Monte Cassino, written by Leo (eleventh century), also copies this extract from Erchempertus. Ibid. vol. VII, p. 609, ad ann. 880.

in the Soissonnais, summoned in 909 by Hérivée, archbishop of Rheims;[1] but to judge from what Hérivée has to say about it, remembrance of Photius is extremely faint among the Frankish episcopate:

As the Holy Apostolic See has brought to our knowledge that the errors and blasphemies in the East against the Holy Spirit by a certain Photius are still rife, asserting that He proceeds, not from the Son, but from the Father alone, we exhort you, brethren, each of you, to join me in obedience to the warnings of the Lord of the Roman See and after studying the opinions of the Catholic Fathers, in drawing from the quiver of divine Scripture the pointed arrows that will crush the head of the wicked serpent.

I expected to meet Photius' name again in some Formosian writings early in the tenth century, but the references there proved to be insignificant. But as I hope I have demonstrated elsewhere, it is a mistake to look in these writings for any evidence of schism between the two Churches, provoked by Pope Formosus' obstinate attitude to the Photian ordinations.[2] On the contrary, we may infer from a careful examination of these writings that even Pope Formosus remained on good terms with the Byzantine Church and that the issue of the Photian ordinations had ceased to disturb peaceful relations between the two Churches.

Another document of the end of the tenth century recalls the energetic measures taken by Nicholas I against Photius: it is a letter by Leo, abbot of St Bonifacius in Rome and legate of Pope John XV to Kings Hugh and Robert in connection with the case concerning Arnulf, archbishop of Rheims, and his successor Gerbert. Leo's letter is in reply to the charges made by the Rheims synod against Arnulf and against the Pope, the synod disputing the Pope's right to meddle with what is the business of the church of Rheims. After a virulent attack on the Popes of the tenth century, the Council quotes in support of its contention a letter from Hincmar to Pope Nicholas.[3] The legate replied:[4] 'So you draw Pope Nicholas to your side on the ground of his silence in face of the bishops' deposition against the Roman Church. Yet, you will find in his letters how severely he dealt with Photius, the usurper of the Church of Constantinople, till the day he recalled Ignatius to his own see.'

[1] Mansi, vol. XVIII, cols. 304, 305.
[2] 'Études sur Photios', in *Byzantion* (1936), vol. XI, pp. 1–19. See pp. 251–65.
[3] *P.L.* vol. 139, cols. 312–18.
[4] Loc. cit. col. 342; *M.G.H.* Ss. III, p. 689. In this connection cf. J. Havet, *Lettres de Gerbert* (Paris, 1889), pp. xxiii seq.

Leo does not here touch on any other problems raised by the Photian incident, as it would have been a clumsy move on his part to mention Photius' rehabilitation. The fact is that the King had applied to Pope John XV for an identical act, i.e. the recognition of Gerbert in the see of Rheims. It would have served his purpose better to point in this connection to Photius' second condemnation by John VIII, if it had in fact taken place.

We may also note that the decree by Nicholas I against Photius and the clergy ordained by him is cited in a letter from the clergy of Verona to the Holy See.[1] It was written by the bishop of Verona, Ratherius, and the metropolitan appeals there to a number of pontifical documents in his own defence, and for the invalidity of the ordinations made in Verona by his rival, the illegal bishop Milo. That he should pass over Photius' rehabilitation by John VIII in silence is natural enough, since it would only have harmed his cause.

And that is all there is about Photius in the Latin literary output of the tenth century, and it is very little. It is disappointing to find that the only Latin writer who at that time specially dealt with Greek affairs did not make the slightest reference to the Photian case: this is Liudprand the Lombard, deacon of the church of Pavia (Ticino) and later bishop of Cremona, who between 948 and 950 made a long stay in Constantinople as the ambassador of King Berengar. He speaks, however, on two occasions of the Emperor Michael III and of Basil I in his *Antapodosis*.[2] His malevolence against the Greeks should have induced him to quote an excellent illustration of Greek astuteness, of which he complains so often, if the history of Photius had in fact been what modern historians have made it.

There remain the canonical Collections of the period, though here again we must not expect any sensational finds, as the canonists of the time contented themselves with out-of-date documentation which went no further than the ninth century. This is noticeable, for instance, in the *Libri de Synodalibus Causis*, by Regino of Prüm of the beginning

[1] Loc. cit. vol. 136, col. 480. Cf. ibid. cols. 97 seq., for remarks on this move by the Veronese clergy. Ratherius lived between 890 or 891 and 974. Cf. *M.G.H.* Ep. VI, p. 519; A. Vogel, *Ratherius von Verona* (Jena, 1854), vol. I, pp. 316 seq.; vol. II, pp. 206 seq.; C. Pevani, *Un Vescovo Belga in Italia nel secolo X* (Torino, 1920).

[2] Lib. I, chs. 9, 10, lib. III, chs. 32–4; *M.G.H.* Ss. III, pp. 276, 277, 309, 310. Cf. English translation by F. A. Wright, *The Works of Liudprand of Cremona* (Broadway Medieval Library; London, 1930), pp. 36 seq., 124 seq.

of the tenth century:[1] all he adds to the documents taken from existing Collections are the canons of the Gallo-Roman or Merovingian Councils with a few extracts from the Frankish kings' capitularies or Collections of *Decreta*. Some of these new documents, it is true, belong to the second half of the ninth century, but one would seek there in vain for any decisions by the Popes and Councils of the period bearing on general topics, except for some fragments from Nicholas' letters about Frankish affairs.

Fragments of letters from John VIII have here and there found their way into the Germanic Collections from the end of the ninth to the beginning of the tenth century, but hardly any of them bear on the subject under discussion.[2]

Similarly one looks in vain for any light on our problem in the famous compilation of the beginning of the eleventh century, Burchard's *Decretum*, which for all the success it had in the ecclesiastical world of the time, makes only fragmentary use of the conciliar and pontifical documents of the ninth century;[3] and the same may be said of Lanfranc's canonical Collection, which in its day had a great vogue in England.[4]

The canonical Collections of southern Italy, though primarily of local interest, belong to a country which lies at the cross-roads of papal and Byzantine currents of influence and faithfully reflect the general lines of pontifical policy towards the Greeks.

The first of this class is the Collection preserved in the Manuscript T XVIII of the Vallicellania.[5] The author is, of course, a Latin, probably a native of southern Italy, who wrote his Collection between

---

[1] *P.L.* vol. 132, cols. 175 seq.; cf. P. Fournier-G. Le Bras, loc. cit. pp. 244–67.

[2] Chiefly the collection in four volumes of the Chapter of Cologne (Fournier-Le Bras, loc. cit. p. 285: Letter from Nicholas to the Emperor or Michael III); the collection of St Emeran of Ratisbon (ibid. p. 294); the collections of the Manuscript of St Peter of Salzburg (ibid. p. 306).

[3] *P.L.* vol. 140, cols. 537–1053; cf. Fournier-Le Bras, loc. cit. pp. 364–414.

[4] MS. of the British Museum Cotton. Claud. D. IX: Decreta Romanorum Pontificum, Canones Apostolorum et Conciliorum. The MS. dates from the eleventh or the beginning of the twelfth century. It has two decrees by Nicholas, fols. 125 *a*, 126, but they are irrelevant to our subject. The author of the Collection only makes use of the first seven Councils and local synods (chiefly fols. 128–59).

[5] See detailed description of the manuscript in Patetta, 'Contributi alla Storia del Diritto Romano nel Medio Evo', in *Bullettino dell' Istituto di Diritto Romano* (Rome, 1890), vol. III, pp. 273–94; P. Fournier, 'Un Groupe de Recueils canoniques Italiens', in *Mémoires de l'Institut, Acad. des Inscriptions et Belles-Lettres* (1915), vol. XL, pp. 96 seq.

912 and 930; he is a very outspoken partisan of pontifical primacy, yet none the less favourable to the Greeks. In the first part, we find the same canon as in the *Anselmo Dedicata*, which gives the archbishop of Constantinople precedence over all the other Eastern Patriarchs and first place after the Pope.[1] Besides this canon, the Collection includes some canons one would never expect to find in a Western production of the kind. For instance, the author gives five texts on the question, so much discussed in the East, of image worship (fol. 145 of the manuscript). One of these texts (no. 13, as reckoned by Patetta and Fournier) is an extract from the Second Council of Nicaea, very little known in the West. He also gives (under no. 432) a list not only of the Popes, but of the Patriarchs of Jerusalem, Antioch, Alexandria and Constantinople (fol. 143 of the manuscript), and the compiler includes in his Collection texts taken from Justinian's *Novels* purporting to regulate the relations of the higher clergy with the imperial court and the Byzantine Patriarch, as well as texts concerning the archimandrites;[2] but no indication on the Photian affair, except perhaps an allusion to no. 451, which is a rule prohibiting the raising of laymen to the episcopacy. It is, however, not clear whether the text is taken from the Council of 869–70 or not. The manuscript is very incomplete; the last part is missing and from fol. 143 onwards—the portion which would be of the greatest interest—there is merely a list of chapters.

Although the Collection provides nothing relevant to our subject, it nevertheless has some interest, since it throws light on the relations between the two Churches in the first years of the tenth century, when the Latin clergy of southern Italy, in obedience to the Roman Pontiff, showed the sincerest deference to the distinctive institutions of the Church of Byzantium. Such mutual regard would be inexplicable, had the two Churches been at enmity till about 890, the date of their so-called reunion. Had this been the position, one might have looked in a canonical Collection of the beginning of the tenth century for some traces of a contest fought under the author's eyes in a general atmosphere of discomfort; and the first to feel its consequences would have been the clergy of southern Italy, where the rival interests of the two Churches would be the first to be engaged in any general clash.

A similar impression is conveyed by another canonical Collection of the same period, unpublished, but preserved in MS. 1349 of the Vatican

[1] Vol. I, p. 129 of the *Anselmo Dedicata* and no. 28 of the Collection as numbered by Patetta and P. Fournier.
[2] Cf. Fournier, loc. cit. pp. 120, 121; Patetta, loc. cit. pp. 281, 282.

Latin MSS. section,[1] called the Collection in Nine Books. It is later than the Vallicellania Collection which served the compiler as one of his sources and manifests the same partiality to Byzantium. The author includes the canon on the precedence of the Patriarchs of Constantinople over the other Eastern Patriarchs and unhesitatingly enters a canon (canon 29 of Book IX, folio of MS. 200a–201)[2] with its definite bias in favour of the Greek clergy for treating third and fourth marriages as illicit. Even in penitential questions, the author is influenced by the practices of the Greek Church, without prejudice to his own loyalty as a son of the Roman Church.

Another work on canon law, the Collection in Five Books, dates from the beginning of the eleventh century.[3] Apparently published in Italy, somewhere between Naples, Monte Cassino and Benevento, about 1020, it clearly shows Byzantinophil feelings. The three manuscripts that have preserved it date from the eleventh century. In the Vatican MS. (Latin section, no. 1339) several miniatures picture the Assumption of the Blessed Virgin and the six oecumenical Councils (fols. 7–14a),[4] showing in the midst of the assemblies the Byzantine Emperors presiding over the Councils, as well as the principal authors of the canons quoted in the Collection. Byzantine influence is undoubtedly traceable in the miniatures of the general Councils, and there is in this Collection the same spirit of repugnance to third and fourth marriages as in the Collection in Nine Books.[5] We must remember that we are on the eve of the final rupture between the two Churches, which makes the Byzantinophil bias of this Collection all the more striking.

The Collection in Five Books enjoyed great popularity in Italy and was widespread throughout the eleventh and twelfth centuries. P. Fournier[6] lists a whole series of Collections produced in Italy under the inspiration of the Collection in Five Books, most of them being simply extracts from it and offering nothing particularly relevant to the Oriental Church.

The Italian canon Collections of this period therefore deserve special attention, chiefly from those who are bent on finding evidence to prove

---

[1] The MS. is described by Patetta, loc. cit. pp. 286 seq., and by P. Fournier, loc. cit. pp. 124 seq. The bibliography of this Collection is also to be found there.

[2] Cf. P. Fournier, loc. cit. p. 153.

[3] P. Fournier, loc. cit. pp. 159–89 (Vatic. Lat. 1339, Vallicellan B, 11, Monte Cassino no. cxxv).

[4] Cf. P. Fournier, loc. cit. pp. 160, 187.

[5] Cf. the chapter 'De Legitimis Conjugiis et de Raptibus', fols. 253 seq.

[6] P. Fournier, loc. cit. pp. 190 seq.

that the two Churches were in schism long before 1054: the spirit that animates this class of writing will give little encouragement to their prejudice.

We should note particularly that Justinian's *Novel* summarizing the famous 28th canon of the Council of Chalcedon and determining that the Patriarch of Constantinople should occupy second rank among the Patriarchs immediately after the Pope of Rome found its place in the *Anselmo Dedicata* and in other Italian Collections as early as the tenth century. This important finding has so far escaped the attention of Church historians, who assumed that Rome did not accord such a prerogative to Constantinople before 1215, i.e. at the Lateran Council, when Constantinople and its patriarchate were in Latin hands and Rome no longer felt in any danger. This general opinion is thus shown to be incorrect.

The second half of the eleventh century was of paramount importance to the internal growth of the Western Church—the period of the great reforming Popes, of the gigantic struggle led by the noble figure of Gregory VII against lay Investiture and for the freedom of the Church.

Naturally, one notes a renewal of activity in the literary field, and the Papacy's reforming ideas had a good deal to do with it, since it was thought necessary to school contemporary minds in the loyal acceptance of the lofty notions of the sovereign Pontiff's supremacy, to stabilize the ascendancy of the spiritual power over lay power and to popularize the schemes for reforming clergy and laity. The historical and juridical documents available up to that time soon proved inadequate and others had to be sought; the need for them was all the more urgent, in that the reformers' leading ideas on the plenitude of pontifical power in matters spiritual and temporal were provoking vigorous opposition; the champions of lay power declared them to run counter to the spirit and the true evolution of the Church.

In the arguments of the eleventh-century reformers, the writings of Nicholas I naturally had a prominent place. Had their ideals not been at least partially formulated by this great Pope of the ninth century? Was he not the Pontiff who so gallantly resisted refractory princes and their attempts to violate the laws of the Church? His brave attitude to Lothar, his refusal to 'yield to the whims of Michael III' had not been forgotten. And what a test was provided by the Photian case to put in their place rebellious and haughty bishops who refused to obey the Pope's commands! How could the reformers have overlooked the

Council of 869–70, which helped them with the detailed story of a Patriarch's solemn condemnation, and best of all with canon XXII, forbidding the laity to meddle with episcopal elections?

It was, then, only natural at this period that special attention should be given to the Photian incident in the reformers' writings, though even in these one notes some sort of progression. The supporters of Leo IX for instance still contented themselves with stale documentation, to the neglect of the Photian case. Peter Damian does not even mention it. Cardinal Humbertus, for all the dominant part he played in the contest with Michael Cerularius, is surprisingly discreet about our Patriarch, making no reference to him either in his writings against the simoniacs,[1] or in his report on the embassy to Constantinople,[2] or in the excommunication bull that was certainly drawn up by him, or in his *Rationes de S. Spiritu a Patre et Filio*.[3] There is but one allusion to the Photian affair in the letter of Pope Leo IX, written for the benefit of Michael Cerularius, perhaps by Humbertus. After mentioning the decrees of the iconoclastic synod and the intrigues of the enemies of image-worship, the text goes on:

Though the authority of the Roman Pontiff, and above all, the independence, so universally praised, of the saintly Pope Nicholas, always opposed them, he closed the church of St Sophia through his legates in defence of the sacred images and on account of the deposition of the saintly bishop Ignatius and the substitution of the neophyte Photius, until the decrees of the Apostolic See should be obeyed.[4]

This question is suggestive, showing that the Pope's entourage was still ill-informed about the whole affair; that reformers were too easily carried away by their zeal and that they loved to exaggerate the importance of the pontifical intervention in Constantinople.

A bolder position is adopted by Bonizo of Sutri, Gregory VII's devoted henchman. The conflict had become more venomous than under Leo IX: Gregory VII's partisans were called upon to defend a daring move by the Pope—the excommunication of the Emperor Henry IV—which led Bonizo to search into history to prove that Gregory's proceeding was not an isolated case, since the Popes always

---

[1] *P.L.* vol. 143, cols. 1005 seq.; *M.G.H.* Lib. de Lite, vol. I, pp. 100–253.

[2] Will, *Acta et Scripta quae de controversiis eccl. Gr. et Lat. s. XI extant* (Leipzig, 1861), pp. 150 seq.

[3] *P.L.* vol. 143, cols. 1002–4; A. Michel, *Humbert und Kerullarios* (Paderborn, 1925), vol. I, pp. 77 seq.

[4] *P.L.* vol. 143, col. 760. This passage is also quoted by Ivo of Chartres in his *Decretum*, IV, ch. 147; *P.L.* vol. 161, col. 299.

possessed the right to excommunicate kings and emperors. Of the 'historical' instances he quotes in the *Liber ad Amicum*, written in 1085 or 1086, several would carry little weight with historians. Nicholas I is given pride of place as a matter of course,[1] but even here Bonizo exaggerates, claiming that both Michael III and Lothar had been excommunicated by Nicholas I. It is well known, of course, that this is untrue.[2] But Bonizo had inaugurated a tradition which the Middle Ages readily accepted and Bonizo's fiction obtained a surprising currency in later literature.

The first to copy this passage was Rangerius (1112), the biographer of St Anselm of Lucca.[3] Archbishop Romuald (1181), author of the Salerno Chronicle,[4] also quotes it in his work, which contains no other reference to the subject. The same passage occurs in the *Chronica Pontificum et Imperatorum Tiburtina*, begun about 1145.[5] The *Liber de Temporibus* of Albert Miliolus, written about 1281, quotes it too,[6] but without giving any reason why Michael was excommunicated. Sicard, bishop of Cremona, is more explicit in his chronicle, written at the beginning of the thirteenth century,[7] but does not name either Ignatius or Photius. Bonizo's report is then textually repeated in the *Chronica Apostolicorum et Imperatorum Basileensia*,[8] written about 1215, and in an abbreviated form in the Chronicle of John of God,[9] of the first half of the thirteenth century. Martinus Polonus has similarly come under Bonizo's influence.[10]

The credit given to Bonizo is all the more impressive, as those of his contemporaries who could not yet quote him, however devoted they were to the reformers' cause and eager to find instances to bolster up the Popes' power over princes, never refer to the alleged excommunication of Michael III.

[1] Liber ad Amicum, *M.G.H.* Lib. de Lite, vol. I, pp. 607–9: '...Et quid dicam de Nicolao qui duos imperatores uno eodemque tempore excommunicavit, orientalem scilicet Michaelem propter Ignatium Constantinopolitanum episcopum sine iudicio papae a sede pulsum, occidentalem vero nomine Lotharium propter Gualradae suae pelicis societatem.'

[2] With regard to Lotharius, cf. E. Perels, 'Ein Berufungsschreiben Papst Nikolaus' I zur fränkischen Reichssynode in Rom', in *Neues Archiv* (1906), vol. XXXII, pp. 143 seq.

[3] *M.G.H.* Ss. XXX, pp. 1210, 1222.

[4] Muratori, *S.R.I.* vol. VII, pars I, p. 161 (new ed.).

[5] *M.G.H.* Ss. XXXI, p. 254.

[6] Ibid. p. 420.   [7] Ibid. p. 155.

[8] Ibid. p. 287.   [9] Ibid. p. 318.

[10] Ibid. vol. XXII, p. 429; cf. also Chronica Minora auctore Minorita Erphordiensi, loc. cit. vol. XXIV, p. 183.

Berthold, author of the Annals bearing his name and an emphatic 'Gregorian', only cites the excommunication of Lothar in his plea for supreme papal power.[1] He probably began writing his chronicle in 1076. The chronicler Bernold, who started his work about 1073, likewise only knows of Lothar's excommunication.[2] Marianus Scottus[3] gets nearer the mark, when he mentions the excommunication of Waldrada only, and, in his *libelli*, Bernold only refers to that of Lothar.[4]

More characteristic still is the prominence lent to the Photian affair in the chronicle of Hugh of Verdun. Hugh knows of the Eighth Council and even quotes canon XXII, a document very popular with the reformers of that period.[5] He also endeavours to collect the greatest possible number of precedents, more or less authentic, to prove that the Pope had the right to judge and depose Emperors and that the temporal power must remain in subordination to the spiritual power. Among the precedents he quotes one so absurd as to raise a smile on the face of the most solemn Byzantinist; he pretends that the Emperor Michael II was deposed by the Patriarch Nicephorus[6] for nothing more serious than professional incapacity. Of Michael III Hugh knows nothing; probably he had no knowledge of Bonizo's writing, though he started his chronicle about 1090.

These examples are not without value, since they illustrate the mentality of the reformers of the time of Gregory VII, who were carried away by a zeal that made them distort historical facts to suit their polemics. The examples also explain how and why advantage was so unexpectedly taken of the Photian incident in the writings of this and the following period.[7]

---

[1] *M.G.H.* Ss. v, p. 296.

[2] Ibid. p. 420.   [3] Ibid. p. 551.

[4] Libelli Bernaldi Presbyteri monachi (ed. F. Thaner), *M.G.H.* Lib. de Lite, vol. II, pp. 1 seq. (written between 1084 and 1100). P. 148: 'Item beatus Nicolaus papa primus Lotharium regem pro quadam concubina excommunicavit. Item beatus Adrianus papa generaliter omnes reges anathematizavit, quicumque statuta violare presumpserint.' This last statement was probably inspired by canon XXII of the Eighth Council. Bernald is identical with the chronicler Bernold.

[5] Loc. cit. vol. VIII, pp. 355, 412.

[6] Ibid. p. 438.

[7] Note also how the monk Placidus comments on canon XXII of the Eighth Council, without mentioning Photius. Placidi monachi Nonantulani Liber de Honore Ecclesiae, *M.G.H.* Lib. de Lite, vol. II, pp. 566 seq. The treatise written in defence of Pope Paschalis II, p. 618: 'Quomodo Adrianus papa anathematizavit principes electioni praesulum se inserentes. Non debere se inserere imperatores vel principes electioni pontificum sanctus Adrianus papa VIII synodo praesidens ait: Promotiones etc....'

But controversialists and chroniclers only partly represented the literary activity that stirred the Church in the second half of the eleventh century: more important was the contribution by the canonists. Research in this field was inspired by Gregory VII, whose anxiety to give his reforming ideas a solid juridical basis prompted him to guide his collaborators' work in this direction.

Gregory's first care was to enlarge his canonical documentation by throwing open the registers and archives of the Lateran, where numerous copyists and compilers at once proceeded to hunt for documents that might be of interest to the canonists. Though the mass of this intermediate work must have been enormous, it is difficult to-day to conceive the size of it, as most of the work done by anonymous collaborators has been lost. Only one specimen of this class has come down to us, the *Collectio Britannica*, preserved in one single manuscript at the British Museum (Additional MS. No. 8873) and very probably belonging to the end of the eleventh century.[1]

These were the intermediate Collections, extracted from official documents that have remained unknown to this day, which the great canonists of the Gregorian period turned to such good account. One of the first big canonical Collections to be adapted to the new needs was put together about the year 1083 by Gregory VII's most loyal associate, St Anselm of Lucca.[2] Obviously, documentation is attaining considerable proportions. It is chiefly the letters of Pope Nicholas I that are pressed into service;[3] this is but natural, since the reformers of the Gregorian period only aimed at carrying on the work begun by Nicholas; and most often quoted is the letter in which Nicholas rebutted Michael III's accusations.[4] But letters by John VIII are also reproduced, though none of them bears on the Photian incident. The Collection has but three references to the Eighth Council in connection with canons XXI, XVIII and XXII.[5] The first, or canon XXI, forbids rash judgements about Popes and Patriarchs, and Photius is compared with Dioscorus—the only direct reference to Photius in the whole Col-

---

[1] Cf. P. Fournier on the canonists' activities at this period. Fournier-Le Bras, loc. cit. vol. II, pp. 7 seq. On the *Collectio Britannica* see Paul Ewald, 'Die Papstbriefe der Britischen Sammlung', in *Neues Archiv* (1880), vol. v.

[2] See Fournier-Le Bras, loc. cit. vol. II, pp. 25 seq. F. Thaner, *Anselmi, episcopi Lucensis, collectio canonum* (Oeniponte, 1906).

[3] I, 63, 72; II, 64, 65, 66, 67, 70; IV, 44; V, 39; VII, 135; X, 21.

[4] I, 79; II, 73; IV, 31, 46; V, 42; VI, 89; X, 30.

[5] II, 72 = Mansi, vol. XVI, col. 174; IV, 30 = Mansi, vol. XVI, col. 172; VI, 20 = Mansi, vol. XVI, col. 174.

lection. Canon XVIII concerns the privileges of the Church and the third is the famous canon XXII, so often appealed to by the reformers that its quotation here is not surprising.

On the whole, therefore, the choice of texts bearing on the Photian incident seems to me remarkably restrained; none of the violent passages that abound in Nicholas' letters and in the Acts of the Council of 869 are even mentioned.

Much the same restraint is to be found in the canonico-moral Collection under the title of *Liber de Vita Christiana*, written between 1089 and 1095 by another propagandist of Gregorian ideas, Bonizo of Sutri.[1] Bonizo, as stated before, even omits to mention Photius in the famous passage (also quoted in his *Liber ad Amicum*) about the excommunication of Michael III by Nicholas,[2] and only once, in canon XXI of the Eighth Council, does the name of Photius appear;[3] this is in the same passage as is found in the Collection of St Anselm of Lucca. Besides this canon, Bonizo also quotes, as a matter of course, canon XXII.[4]

Of the letters of Nicholas, only one refers to the Photian incident: it is an extract from this Pope's famous reply to the letter of Michael III.[5] Most of the letters by John VIII only concern the rights of the Papacy over Bulgaria and Pannonia.[6] And this is all that interests us in the Collection.

However remarkable the discretion of these reformers in dealing with the Photian case, more revealing still is the study of the masterpiece of the Gregorian reform, the canonical Collection of Cardinal Deusdedit, who wrote his work between 1083 and 1087.[7] His subject-matter was not quite the same as Anselm's, for whereas the bishop of Lucca aimed at collecting the documents concerning every possible article of canonical legislation, Deusdedit's main object was to illustrate the Roman Church's privileged position and the reasons why the primacy was part and parcel of it. His aim was 'to raise a monument to the glory of the Roman

---

[1] Cf. Fournier-Le Bras, loc. cit. vol. II, pp. 139 seq.; E. Perels, 'Bonizo, Liber de Vita Christiana' (*Texte zur Geschichte des Röm. und Kanon. Rechtes im Mittelalter*, vol. I, Berlin, 1930).

[2] E. Perels, loc. cit. p. 131; cf. *M.G.H.* Lib. de Lite, vol. I, pp. 607–9.

[3] IV, 95 (ed. Perels), p. 159.   [4] II, 17 (ed. Perels), p. 42.

[5] Especially IV, 86*a* = *M.G.H.* Ep. VI, p. 456.

[6] IV, 91–94 (ed. Perels), pp. 158, 159 = *M.G.H.* Ep. VII, pp. 281 (letter to Carloman), 282 (letter to Kocel of Pannonia), 284 (Commonitorium to legates).

[7] Cf. Fournier-Le Bras, loc. cit. vol. II, pp. 37 seq. Edition of Wolf von Glanvell, *Die Kanonensammlung des Kardinals Deusdedit* (Paderborn, 1905). Cf. also the judicious comments on this edition in W. M. Peitz, S.J., 'Das Originalregister Gregors VII', in *Sitzungsberichte d. Ak. Wiss. Wien, Phil.-Hist. Kl.* (1911), vol. 165.

Pontiff's supreme power, so necessary and indispensable an instrument of ecclesiastical reform'.[1]

It is important to stress this leading tendency in the cardinal's Collection, since it governs the choice of his texts. He first made generous use of the numerous letters of Nicholas I and John VIII; most of these extracts had been utilized by Anselm of Lucca in his Collection,[2] but Deusdedit's quotations are usually longer. The cardinal also draws freely upon the Acts of the Eighth Council,[3] but it is to his credit that he shows the utmost restraint with regard to the Photian case. It is true that the passages borrowed from the Acts of the Eighth Council several times mention the fallen Patriarch, but they suggest no ill will towards the alleged author of the alleged schism and relentless opponent of the papal claims. And yet, should he not have treated Photius as such, if contemporary opinion had deserved to be taken seriously? An associate of Gregory VII must have been particularly sensitive on the point.

His discretion is all the more unexpected, since the Photian case provided a ready-made argument for the propositions outlined on the first pages of the work by Deusdedit, who meant to deal with the following topics:[4]

1. De ecclesia Constantinopolitana.

2. De episcopis Constantinopolitanis damnatis a R[omana] sede.

3. De excommunicatione eiusdem civitatis episcopi, qui se universalem nominavit.

4. De interdictu apostolicae sedis pro eodem vocabulo.

5. Quod Constantinopolitani episcopi anathematizaverint se et successores suos, si quicquam praesumerent contra alicuius episcopi sedem.

---

[1] Fournier-Le Bras, loc. cit. vol. II, pp. 41, 51.

[2] Here is the list, for documentary purposes, of the different passages with their reference to St Anselm's work: Nicholas' letters: I, 152=A. II, 64; I, 153=A. II, 66; I, 154=A. II, 67; I, 155=A. V, 44; I, 157=A. V, 65; I, 158; I, 159, 160=A. II, 65; I, 161=A. IV, 43; I, 162=A. II, 65; I, 163=A. II, 70; I, 164=A. II, 69; I, 259; II, 62=A. VII, 154; IV, 159–73, a long passage from the letter of the Pope to the Emperor Michael=A. I, 74; IV, 174; IV, 175=A. XII, 35; IV, 176=A. III, 66. Letters of John VIII: I, 166=A. VI, 92; I, 238=A. VI, 92 (98); I, 239; I, 240=A. IV, 45; I, 241; I, 242; I, 243=A. II, 73; II, 90; III, 53=A. V, 50; III, 54; III, 55=A. IV, 31; III, 56, 57=A. IV, 32; III, 142; III, 143; III, 144; IV, 91=A. III, 107; IV, 92=A. I, 81; IV, 178; IV, 182=A. I, 82; IV, 382.

[3] I, 47=canon 21 of the Council, Mansi, vol. XVI, col. 174=A. II, 72; I, 48=an extract from Session VI, Mansi, vol. XVI, col. 86; I, 48a=an extract from Session VII, Mansi, vol. XVI, cols. 97–99; III, 10=canon 15, Mansi, vol. XVI, cols. 168, 169=A. VI, 171; III, 1=canon 18, Mansi, vol. XVI, col. 172=A. IV, 20; III, 12=canon 20, Mansi, vol. XVI, cols. 173, 174; IV, 17=an extract from Session IX, Mansi, vol. XVI, cols. 152, 153=A. XI, 151; IV, 18=canon 22, Mansi, vol. XVI, cols. 174, 175=A. VI, 23.

[4] Ed. Wolf von Glanvell, loc. cit. p. 13.

Thus Deusdedit proposes a thorough examination of the relations between Constantinople and Rome: now let us see which documents he uses and what he thinks of the Photian case. As an argument in support of his first proposition, the cardinal quotes a passage from the letter of Pope Gregory the Great[1] to John, bishop of Syracuse, in which he asserts that the Church of Constantinople is subordinate to the Church of Rome; in support of the second proposition, he quotes the condemnation of the Patriarch Nestorius by the Council of Ephesus,[2] followed by a long extract from the letter of Pope Nicholas I[3] to the Emperor Michael III, dated November 865, about Ignatius' deposition. This excerpt is significant, for the cardinal is satisfied with pointing to the condemnation—recalled in this letter by Nicholas—of the Patriarchs Maximus, Nestorius, Acacius, Anthemius, Sergius, Pyrrhus, Paul and Peter—without a word about Photius. On the whole of the Photian incident, he quotes from the Pope's letter only the following: 'Cum ergo ita sit, cur in solo Ignatio beati Petri memoriam despicere ac oblivioni tradere studuistis? nisi quia pro uoto cuncta facere uoluistis constituentes synodum Ephesinae secundae crudelitati consimilem.'

And yet, there was in Nicholas' correspondence a whole series of letters with particularly pointed statements about Photius' condemnation. Is it not extraordinary then that the learned cardinal, who was acquainted with the correspondence of this great Pope, should have omitted them?

Under propositions III and IV Deusdedit quotes an apocryphal letter by Pelagius II[4] against the Patriarch John of Constantinople and a letter by Gregory the Great[5] anent the same John, the apocryphal letter also doing duty as evidence for what he says under V.

This discretion suggests that the compiler's view of the history of Photius differed from that current in the Western Church of the modern period: not only did he know that Photius had been indicted by the Holy See, but he knew of the reinstatement by the same supreme authority.

I have deemed it necessary to examine the spirit of this canonical Collection before coming to the study of the last documents that conclude it, and which are quite favourable to Photius: there is, first,

---

[1] I, 188, after the edition of Wolf von Glanvell (p. 115). *M.G.H.* Ep. II, p. 60.
[2] I, 32, Actio V, Mansi, vol. IV, col. 1239.
[3] IV, 164, *M.G.H.* Ep. VI, p. 469.
[4] I, 141, p. 95.
[5] I, 142, p. 96. *M.G.H.* Gregorii Reg. II, p. 157.

the extract from the Acts of the synod that met in Constantinople in 861 [1] under the chairmanship of Photius and in the presence of Nicholas' legates, Radoald of Porto and Zachary of Anagni. The insertion of a document of this kind in a canonical Collection of Gregory VII's period is, at least, noteworthy, and raises some doubt whether the extract in fact appeared in Deusdedit's original work.[2] Yet, if what has been said about the spirit in which the whole of this Collection was put together by the Cardinal be remembered, few will feel inclined to be sceptical, for if the Cardinal really knew that Photius had been rehabilitated by the Holy See and that the Papacy did not revise its judgement, the Acts of the 861 synod against Ignatius must have sounded less odious to him than they did to the refractory Ignatians in Byzantium and to Nicholas' contemporaries in Rome in the ninth century.

The last exhibit also completes the documentation on the judicial procedure and on the manner of taking the oath, given by the learned compiler at the end of his book; for the Acts of that Council aptly illustrate the supreme judicial power of the Bishops of Rome, when appealed to in the last instance of any 'major cause' by the Church of Constantinople. The procedure to be adopted in a suit against a bishop is more clearly explained there than, for instance, in the Acts of the Council of 869–70.

There are also many striking signs of deference to the Bishops of Rome. Nicholas' legates openly declare that the Pope has the right to revise the case of any bishop:[3] 'Credite fratres quoniam sancti patres decreverunt in Sardiniensi concilio, ut habeat potestatem Romanus pontifex renovare causam cuiuslibet episcopi, propterea nos, per auctoritatem, quam diximus, eius [i.e. Ignatii] volumus investigare negotium.' And the bishop of Laodicea, Theodore, replies in the name of the Church of Constantinople: 'Et Ecclesia nostra gaudet in hoc et nullam habet contradictionem et tristitiam.' The Pope, so the legates declare at the fourth session, has the care of all the Churches;[4] and far from protesting, the synod spontaneously accepts the authority of the Roman See. The 'adiutores Ignatii' enthusiastically exclaimed:[5] 'Qui hoc [i.e. iudicium vestrum] non recipit, nec apostolos recipit.'

---

[1] IV, 428–31, pp. 603–10: 'Sinodus habita in Constantinopoli sub Nicolao papa de Ignatio Patriarcha.' See pp. 78 seq.

[2] W. von Glanvell, p. xiii, casts doubts at any rate on what concerns the extract from the Acts of the Photian Synod that follows this document. Fournier-Le Bras, loc. cit. vol. II, p. 48 are of opinion that the two documents may have been added to the Collection later.

[3] Loc. cit. p. 605.   [4] Loc. cit. p. 609.   [5] Loc. cit. p. 604.

As such declarations must have filled 'Gregorian' hearts with supreme satisfaction and joy, it is only natural that such a text should have found its way into a canonical collection of that period.

Further, the authenticity of the exhibit is above suspicion and its form is in the best style as used on similar occasions by the Chancellery of Constantinople. Deusdedit, or else the copyist who entered it into the Collection, took it from the Latin translation of the Acts of the 861 synod, brought to Rome by Zachary and Radoald and deposited in the *scrinium Lateranense*; they are, moreover, the same Acts as are mentioned by the author of the *Liber Pontificalis*,[1] which he must have consulted. The question whether the document was entered into the Collection by Deusdedit or by the copyist in transcribing his book is immaterial, though everything seems to suggest that we owe its preservation to Deusdedit himself. W. M. Peitz, S.J.,[2] was struck by the great number of oath formularies in the Collection under consideration and ingeniously inferred that Deusdedit had perhaps occupied the post of *cancellarius*, in which capacity he would have had opportunities for administering the oath to bishops and other notabilities. We should also remember that as the only complete manuscript which preserved this compilation was written under Paschal II (1099–1118), it was roughly contemporary with Deusdedit.[3] That such a document should have been preserved only in this Collection is not surprising, since the same applies to other writings reproduced there and not to be found elsewhere, at any rate in their oldest and most reliable form.[4]

It is, however, possible that another document, which closes this Collection, was added by the copyist of Deusdedit's work, the famous summary of the Photian Council of 879–80: as a matter of fact, it seems not to fit into the scheme of the original Collection, nor is it mentioned in the Index, which was drawn up by the Cardinal.[5]

---

[1] Ed. Duchesne, vol. II, p. 158: 'convocata generali synodo, eundem virum Ignatium patriarcham denuo deposuerunt, *sicut in gestis Constantinopolim ab illis compilatis facile reperitur* et per legatos, Leonem scilicet a secreto et alios, necnon per epistolam predicti imperatoris [Michaelis] veraciter mansit compertum.'

[2] 'Das Originalregister Gregors VII', in *Sitzungsberichte...Phil.-Hist. Kl.* (Wien, 1911), vol. 165, p. 144.

[3] About this MS. cf. the study by E. Stevenson, 'Osservazioni sulla Collectio Canonum di Deusdedit', in *Archivio della R. Storia Patria* (1885), vol. VIII, pp. 304–98; cf. also W. M. Peitz, loc. cit. pp. 133–47.

[4] For instance the famous extracts from the Lateran Archives (ed. W. von Glanvell, lib. III, 191–207, pp. 353–63) and one extract from the Frankish Annals (ibid. lib. IV, 195, pp. 496, 497).

[5] Cf. W. von Glanvell, loc. cit. p. xiii.

But this trifle does not impair the value of the work. Deusdedit knew the Photian case and notably his rehabilitation by John VIII, since he pointedly alludes to it in his *Libellus contra Invasores et Simoniacos*,[1] a paragraph strangely reminiscent of John VIII's letter to the Emperor Basil which was read at the second session of the Photian Council and is also summarized in the extracts from these Acts preserved in Deusdedit's Collection.[2]

This document also originates from the Pontifical Archives and it matters little whether it appeared in the original collection or was added by contemporary copyists. It at least illustrates the mentality of the eleventh-century reformers and proves that their view of this Council and of Photius' rehabilitation was not that which has been accepted by modern historians; otherwise, how could the Acts of a Council, which it is the fashion to-day to call 'pseudo-synodus', have been admitted into a Collection of such importance?

Furthermore, the Acts of the Photian Council must, through a number of extracts, have circulated among the canonists of the time, to be utilized not only by Deusdedit and his copyists, but also by another great canonist of the period, Ivo of Chartres.[3] To establish the accuracy of this statement, we must collate the extracts from the Acts as handed down by the two canonists.

In the famous prologue, which was probably to serve as a preface to his *Decretum*, written about 1094, Ivo proves among other things that the Pope has the right to annul a sentence passed on a defendant, and quotes in support several cases gathered from history, including that of Photius:[4] 'Sic Joannes papa VIII Photium neophytam a papa Nicolao depositum Augustorum interventu Basilii, Leonis, Alexandri, in patriarchatu Constantinopolitano restituit, scribens praedictis Augustis

---

[1] Cf. the passage on the admission of Simoniacs and Schismatics to the priesthood and on those ordained by them. *M.G.H.* Lib. de Lite, vol. II, chs. 9, 10, p. 327: '...Sed et Alexander primus et Celestinus et Joannes VIII simili sententia decernunt, ut id, quod invenitur pro summa necessitate toleratum nullatenus assumatur in legem....'

[2] W. von Glanvell, loc. cit. pp. 612–14; cf. the letter in Mansi, vol. XVII, col. 397; Jaffé, no. 3271.

[3] On Ivo of Chartres and his writings, see P. Fournier, 'Les Collections canoniques attribuées à Yves de Chartres et le Droit Canonique', in *Bibl. de l'École des Chartes* (1897), vol. LVIII; idem, 'Yves de Chartres et le Droit Canonique', in *Revue des Questions historiques* (1898), vol. LXIII, pp. 51 seq.; Fournier-Le Bras, loc. cit. vol. II, pp. 55 seq. Ivo's writings, *P.L.* vol. 161.

[4] *P.L.* vol. 161, col. 56.

in haec verba: Scripsistis nobis dilectissimi filii....' There follows a long extract from the letter of John VIII to Basil I.[1] The context reveals that the Photian case provides in the opinion of Ivo the leading argument of his thesis. The bishop of Chartres only mentions in this place Photius' reinstatement and not any second excommunication either by John VIII or by any of his successors, although this was the right place to quote the Pope's second verdict, since it would have provided the canonist with the most typical instance for his demonstration. And yet, the canonists of the period and their co-workers must have delved into the pontifical archives with some care, noting every single text that could, in one way or another, corroborate their doctrines on the plenitude of papal powers.

How could a document of such importance as the fulmination of a second excommunication have escaped their attention? The compilation called *Collectio Britannica* contains long extracts from the registers of John VIII and Stephen V, which are lost to-day—a sure sign that all the documents relative to their pontificate were duly scrutinized by the canonists; but this complete silence about a second excommunication and condemnation of Photius can point to only one conclusion— that they never took place.

The study of the long fragment from the letter of John VIII to Basil I, quoted by Ivo, brings out another remarkable point. It is identical with the text of the letter read out to the Council at the second session and we are given the same version in the Cardinal's Collection[2]—an excellent testimony to the authenticity of Deusdedit's extract.

Nor is it the only excerpt from the Acts of the Photian Council, common to Ivo and Deusdedit. Ivo included in his *Decretum* (*Decr.* VII, 149) a declaration by the pontifical legates ordering bishops who become monks to relinquish their episcopal charge for good; this is followed by the declaration of the second canon of the Council taking similar action and passed by the assembly at its fifth session: now, the same prohibition is mentioned at the end of the extract from the Acts in Deusdedit's Collection;[3] and yet, the passage quoted by Ivo of Chartres is considerably longer than the quotation by Deusdedit, and

---

[1] As far as the sentence: 'si quis vero tale quid amodo facere praesumpserit, sine venia erit.' Mansi, vol. XVI, col. 487; vol. XVII, cols. 141, 395; Jaffé, vol. I, no. 3271; *M.G.H.* Ep. VI, pp. 168 seq.

[2] Ed. W. von Glanvell, lib. IV, 434, pp. 612 (l. 16)–614 (l. 20).

[3] Loc. cit. p. 617.

does not quite tally with the account given in the Acts of the Photian Council.[1]

This shows that Ivo was not copying from Deusdedit, but derived his information from elsewhere, perhaps from the Acts themselves which he summarized at this place, or more probably from an intermediary compilation made from the original documents of the Pontifical Archives, which gave a longer extract from the Acts of the Photian Council.

This is the more plausible as Ivo's *Decretum* completes Deusdedit's extracts on three points. In the fourth part, where he writes 'de observandis festivitatibus et jejuniis legitimis, de Scripturis canonicis et consuetudinibus et celebratione concilii', Ivo quotes two important passages, which raise the problem of the condemnation of the Oecumenical Council of 869–70 by John VIII. He says (*Decr.* IV, 76):

That the synod of Constantinople against Photius is not to be accepted. John VIII to the Patriarch Photius.—We annul and absolutely abrogate the synod against Photius held in Constantinople as much for other reasons as because Pope Hadrian did not sanction it. ('Constantinopolitanum synodum eam quae contra Photium est non esse recipiendam. Joannes VIII patriarchae Photio.'—'Illam quae contra Photium facta est Constantinopoli synodum irritam facimus et omnino delevimus, tam propter alia, tam quoniam Adrianus papa non subscripsit in ea.')

The first part of this passage tallies with the canon IV voted by the Photian Council at its fourth session.[2] The sentence, 'because Pope Hadrian did not sanction it [the synod of 869–70]', is an extract from the Greek edition of John VIII's letter to Basil I. Photius gives there a curious interpretation to John's words contained in the Latin edition of the letter to Basil, to the effect that the legates had signed the Acts of the Ignatian Synod with the saving clause 'usque ad voluntatem sui pontificis'.[3]

---

[1] See the comparison of the texts in my study 'L'Affaire de Photios dans la Littérature Latine', in *Annales de l'Institut Kondakov* (1938), vol. x, p. 89.

[2] Mansi, vol. XVII, col. 490 (Latin translation): 'Synodum Romae factam contra Photium sanctissimum patriarcham, sub Hadriano beatissimo papa, et factam Constantinopoli synodum contra eundem sanctissimum Photium, definimus omnino damnatam et abrogatam esse, neque eam sanctis synodis adnumerandam esse aut recensendam, neque synodum omnino appellandam aut vocandam esse. Absit.'

[3] Mansi, vol. XVII, col. 416 (Greek edition of John's letter to Basil I); *M.G.H.* Ep. VII, p. 181 (Latin and Greek edition of the letter). For more details, see *infra*, part II, ch. II, p. 329.

This passage and canon IV of the Photian Council are not mentioned in the extract from the Acts of Deusdedit's Collection;[1] nor does the extract even quote another passage of equal importance in the Commonitorium which John VIII handed to his legates. It is well known that these instructions only survived in the Greek Acts of the Photian Council. In the Cardinal's Collection the extract from the Acts is a summary of eight chapters of the Commonitorium, with the omission of chapter VI, which lays down for the legates' benefit the procedure to be followed at the opening of the Council—and of chapter X, which is about the Council of 869–70. But this chapter is inserted by Ivo of Chartres in his *Decretum* IV, 77:

About the same, John VIII to his legates. You will tell them that we annul those synods held against Photius under Pope Hadrian either in Rome or in Constantinople and that we take them off the list of Holy Synods. ('De eodem Joannes VIII apocrisiariis suis. Dicetis quod illas synodus quae contra Photium sub Adriano papa Romae vel Constantinopoli sunt factae, cassamus et de numero sanctarum synodorum delemus.')

If the Latin translation[2] of chapter X of the Commonitorium be compared with Ivo's quotation, it will be evident that here also the canonist takes his excerpt from the Photian Council.

That some of the quotations from the Acts preserved by Deusdedit should be almost identical with Ivo's extracts seems to indicate that both canonists had at their disposal copies of the same intermediary Collection which reproduced extracts from the Acts of the Photian Council. It is also possible that Ivo's copy contained longer extracts from the Acts than the copy used by Deusdedit or by the copyist of the Cardinal's Collection.

There must have been a considerable number of those intermediary compilations circulating in the West from the end of the eleventh century. As they were only meant to provide the canonists with juridical materials to bolster up the reformist ideals of the Gregorian period, the choice of extracts from papal letters and conciliar decisions was left to the copyists' discretion.

On the other hand, in comparing the Latin of Deusdedit's extract from the Acts of the anti-Ignatian Synod of 861 with that of the one he

---

[1] Loc. cit. pp. 615, 616.

[2] Mansi, vol. XVII, col. 471: 'Volumus coram praesente synodo promulgari, ut synodus quae facta est contra praedictum patriarcham Photium sub Hadriano sanctissimo papa in urbe Roma et Constantinopoli ex nunc sit rejecta, irrita et sine robore; neque connumeretur cum altera sancta synodo.'

quotes from the Photian Synod, it is obvious that the two extracts could hardly have been written by the same copyist. The Latin of the first extract is clumsy, whereas the copyist of the second extract not only wrote better Latin, but he had evidently read the Acts of the Photian Council intelligently and with an open mind. I have explained[1] how he grasped the meaning of his Greek original and its Latin translation; here he even completes the information supplied by the Acts in his extract from the second session with reference to Photius' reply to the Pope's request not to make any new ordinations for Bulgaria, for he writes: 'We have occupied this priestly throne for three years, but have neither sent a pallium nor made any ordinations there.'[2] Here the Acts are not so circumstantial, as Photius only speaks in general terms ('having been Patriarch so long').[3] Without using any other copy of the Acts than the one we know, the copyist may have got his information from a careful reading and from other documents which he found in the Archives.[4]

It is therefore possible that the copy used by Ivo contained only the extracts of the Photian Council and that Deusdedit or his copyist disposed of conciliar materials gathered from the Archives by two different copyists. Since all these intermediary compilations have been lost, with the exception of the *Britannica*, it is difficult to imagine what they were like. We shall have occasion to show[5] that even the *Britannica*, in spite of the mass of new materials it contains, was probably in many places only an extract from longer compilations. Its concluding portion gives an extract from Deusdedit's Collection.

A comparison of the *Britannica* materials with Deusdedit's conciliar extracts shows the working method of the copyists, who on the invitation of Gregory VII searched the Lateran Archives for canonical documentation. Some of them searched the Registers of the Popes and copied whatever they considered to be useful to canonists. The *Britannica* has many such excerpts from the Pontifical Register—letters of Popes Gelasius I, Pelagius I, Pelagius II, Leo IV, John VIII, Stephen V, Alexander II and Urban II—together with extracts from the correspondence of Boniface, the Patron Saint of Germany. The letters of Nicholas I are not found among them: as they were of special value to Gregorian canonists, they must have circulated in a special copy.

---

[1] See pp. 186 seq. [2] W. von Glanvell, IV, 334, p. 615.
[3] Mansi, vol. XVII, col. 417.
[4] It is also possible that this precision was due to the translator of the Acts.
[5] See pp. 325 seq.

Other copyists made extracts from the conciliar Acts and their work can be traced in Deusdedit's documentation. But the method was the same in either case: the copyists and the anonymous compilers of the intermediary Collections were only interested in such passages as would prove useful to canonists, especially those that justified the privileges of the Holy See. They were of course not always able to quote literally and had to summarize the longer texts, as was the case with the Acts of the Councils, but the documents were always faithful to the originals.

No other explanation will account for the inclusion of the extracts from the two Councils in the Western canonical Collections of the eleventh century and for the form in which they are preserved. The copyists omitted for instance the lengthy discourses addressed to Photius, since they did not meet their purpose, and what that purpose was we can infer from Deusdedit's extracts—to take from the Acts only such passages as could serve to document the privileges of the Roman Pontiffs.

It is therefore futile to seek in those documents evidence for the theory that the legates brought from Constantinople only an extract from the Acts, as though the Byzantines feared to send to Rome a full account of what had happened in Constantinople at the Photian Council, or as though John VIII had only seen the Acts in the abbreviated form we know.[1] It was never the custom to send to Rome only summaries of conciliar Acts. John VIII knew exactly what had happened. A copy of the Acts brought from Constantinople by the legates was kept in translation in the Lateran Archives, where the document hunters found it towards the end of the eleventh century.

Because the Acts offered materials that served the copyists' purpose, they summarized them or extracted their most telling passages. Two of the most eminent canonists of the Gregorian and post-Gregorian periods—Cardinal Deusdedit, or his copyist, and St Ivo of Chartres—saw the value of this material for the privileges of the Holy See and used them independently in their canonical Collections.

By a curious irony of fate, the same Acts which in the eleventh century were regarded as favourable to the Papacy were discarded by historians and canonists of later periods as damaging to the same Gregorian claims. Even their authenticity was questioned. What I have said, however,

[1] This is M. Jugie's suggestion ('Les Actes du Synode Photien', in *Échos d'Orient*, vol. XXXVII, pp. 89–99; *Le Schisme Byzantin*, loc. cit. pp. 129 seq.). Cf. also V. Grumel, 'Lettres de Jean VIII pour le Rétablissement de Photius', in *Échos d'Orient* (1940), vol. XXXIX, pp. 138–55.

establishes the conclusion that the doubts cast by the West on the Greek Acts of the Photian Council are no longer justified. To repeat it once more, the extracts used by Deusdedit and Ivo of Chartres prove that the Latin translation, the only one known till their time, and which provided their information, faithfully rendered the Greek text of the Acts; indeed, the source of the intermediary compilation used by Deusdedit and Ivo actually was the official copy brought from Constantinople by the legates.[1] The Greek Acts of the Photian Council must therefore be considered absolutely authentic, at least in regard to the five sessions, since it is at the fifth session that the extract of Deusdedit and the quotations by Ivo come to an end.[2]

The examination, now concluded, of the Latin literature on the subject of the Photian incident between the ninth and the twelfth centuries has provided some interesting results: the view held, at that period at any rate, of the Photian case was not the same as the view current in the modern period; Photius' litigation with the Papacy occupied a very restricted place in the writings of the time; above all, to our great surprise, absolutely nothing was known of what to-day goes by the name of the second schism of Photius; whereas against this, the Patriarch's rehabilitation by John VIII was common knowledge and the 'Gregorian' canonists unreservedly accepted the decisions of the Photian Council of 869–70.

[1] Hergenröther, *Photius*, vol. II, p. 573, ftn. 25, is right, as against Hefele, *Konziliengeschichte*, vol. IV, p. 483, in stating that the translation of the Acts was made from the copy brought home by the legates (ed. Leclercq, vol. IV, 1, p. 605).

[2] Cf. pp. 383 seq. on the authenticity of the sixth and seventh sessions.

CHAPTER II

OECUMENICITY OF THE EIGHTH COUNCIL IN MEDIEVAL WESTERN TRADITION

Number of councils acknowledged by the Gallic, Germanic, English and Lombard Churches until the twelfth century—Rome and the seven councils—The Popes' profession of faith and the number of councils—Eleventh-century canonists and the Eighth Council—Was there any other edition of the Popes' *Professio fidei* covering the eight councils?

THE solution so far reached now raises another weighty problem. If it be true that the Council of 869–70 was cancelled by the Council of 879–80, a decision that was ratified by Pope John VIII, how was it possible for the Western Church to persist in numbering this Council among the oecumenical synods? It is inconceivable that no trace of Pope John's decision should be found in the tradition of the Western Church: the Pontifical Chancellery had inherited from the Roman Empire its sense of logic, its respect for tradition and its spirit of continuity, and the offices of the Holy See remained true to the tradition. If then we should fail to discover in the documents that issued from the Chancellery and in the tradition of the Western Church any traces of John's ratification, there would be ample justification for repudiating our conclusions about the Eighth Council.[1]

To find what position the Eighth Council occupied in the Western tradition of the Middle Ages, we must retrace our steps to the ninth century and see how Christendom reacted to that Council. Our first informant is Hincmar, archbishop of Rheims, who in his Bertinian Annals[2] wrote as follows on the dispatch by Hadrian II of legates to Constantinople in connection with the Ignatian incident:

Et synodo congregata, *quam octavam universalem synodum illuc convenientes appellaverunt*, exortum schisma de Ignatii depositione et Photii ordinatione sedaverunt, Photium anathematizantes et Ignatium restituentes. In qua synodo de imaginibus adorandis aliter quam orthodoxi doctores antea diffinierant, et pro favore Romani Pontificis, qui eorum votis de imaginibus

---

[1] I here go again over the ground of my study, 'L'Oecuménicité du VIIIe Concile dans la tradition occidentale du M.A.', published in the *Bulletin de la Classe des Lettres de l'Académie Royale de Belgique* (1938), vol. XXIV, pp. 445 seq.

[2] *M.G.H.* Ss. I, p. 494.

adorandis annuit, et quaedam contra antiquos canones, sed et contra suam ipsam synodum constituerunt, sicut qui eamdem synodum legerit, patenter inveniet.

Whilst concurring with Photius' condemnation, the representative of the Frankish Church none the less definitely refuses to admit the oecumenicity of the Eighth Council and his attitude, however unexpected, is perfectly consistent with Hincmar's point of view; for in his writings concerning his nephew and namesake, this eminent prelate forcibly rejected the Seventh Oecumenical Council and acknowledged only six universal synods.[1] He thus shared the Frankish Church's distrust of the Second Council of Nicaea, and had no option but to repudiate the oecumenicity of the Fourth Council of Constantinople as well.

The Frankish Church must have unanimously inherited this mistrust from its great representative of the ninth century. A century after Hincmar's death, another metropolitan of Rheims, the famous Gerbert, the future Pope Sylvester II, made in 991, before taking possession of his see, a profession of faith in which he expressly said:[2] 'Sanctas sinodos sex, quas universalis mater ecclesia confirmat, confirmo.' In his letter to Wilderode, bishop of Strasbourg, Gerbert mainly insists on the first four councils,[3] as true in this to an old tradition of the whole Church, stressed particularly by Gelasius, as Hincmar's special veneration for the same councils.[4]

This profession of faith was apparently not Gerbert's own composition, for it is found repeated word for word in the biography of Gauzlin, abbot of Fleury and archbishop of Bourges, who died in 1029, written by André de Fleury (d. 1056) who as a matter of course attributed it to Gauzlin.[5] J. Havet asserts that this profession was issued to combat the doctrines of the Cathari:[6] the biographer, so he states, assigns it to Gauzlin, who is alleged to have written it in opposition to the doctrines of other heretics, who were at that time gaining a foothold in his diocese.[7] But it seems more likely that the profession came from a formulary

---

[1] *P.L.* vol. 126, col. 359.

[2] J. Havet, *Lettres de Gerbert (Collection de Textes pour servir à l'Étude et à l'Enseignement de l'Histoire* (Paris, 1889), p. 162, pièce no. 180).

[3] Havet, loc. cit. pp. 208 seq., pièce no. 217.

[4] *P.L.* vol. 126, cols. 384–6.

[5] L. Delisle, 'Vie de Gauzlin, Abbé de Fleury et Archevêque de Bourges, par André de Fleury', in *Mém. de la Soc. Archéol. de l'Orléanais* (1853), vol. II, pp. 256–322.

[6] Havet, loc. cit. p. 161.

[7] Delisle, loc. cit. p. 303.

used by the Frankish Church in the tenth and eleventh centuries.[1] In any case, it all goes to show that as late as the eleventh century the Frankish Church officially acknowledged only six oecumenical councils.

The Frankish formularies contain very few references to the oecumenical councils. Formula 1024 of the Collection published by E. Rozières has an archbishop's profession of faith,[2] which mentions the first four councils, whereas another formula mentions only two councils.[3]

It is also noteworthy that this ancient tradition remained long in force in the Western Church. Throughout the historical works published between the end of the ninth century and the second half of the eleventh century, the writers pay little attention to the number of oecumenical councils, and if they do happen to mention them, most of them go no further than the Sixth or, at most, the Seventh Oecumenical Council. Here are a few instances.

The Annals of Hildesheim, which copy textually the *Annales Laurissienses Minores* down to the year 814, stop short at the Sixth Oecumenical Council. The Annals of Quedlinburg, which rely on the Annals of Hildesheim as their principal source until the year 1100, mention no council after the Sixth.[4] The same holds good for the *Annales Lambertinienses*,[5] which take us as far as 1077, and the *Annales S. Jacobi Leodiensis*,[6] which stop in 1055. John the Deacon follows the same tradition in his *Chronicon*, where he gives us the history of Venice till 1088.[7] There also ends the *Chronicon Herimanni Augiensis*,[8] which carries events till 1054. Marianus Scotus (born in 1028, died about 1087) knows nothing of the councils after that of the year 680–1.[9] Bernold, monk of St Blasius (born about 1054, died in 1100), who follows the Chronicle of Herimannus Augiensis Contractus till 1055, also enumerates only six councils in his Chronicle.[10]

---

[1] Cf. Jules Lair, *Études critiques sur divers Textes des Xe et XIe siècles* (Paris, 1899), vol. I, p. 334.

[2] E. Rozière, *Recueil Général des Formules Usitées dans l'Empire des Francs du Ve au Xe siècles* (Paris, 1859), vol. II, pp. 644–5: 'Praeterea constitutiones quatuor principalium conciliorum, Nicaeni, Constantinopolitani, Ephesini et Chalcedonensis, canones quoque synodorum et decreta quae orthodoxa fides suscipit et complectitur, me suscipere, tenere et praedicare velle confiteor.'

[3] E. Rozière, loc. cit. pp. 1133–4, form. no. 1387.

[4] *M.G.H.* Ss. III, p. 32.

[5] *M.G.H.* Ss. III, p. 29.

[6] *M.G.H.* Ss. IV, p. 12.

[7] *M.G.H.* Ss. VII, p. 10.

[8] *M.G.H.* Ss. V, p. 96.

[9] *M.G.H.* Ss. V, p. 544.

[10] *M.G.H.* Ss. V, p. 416.

Most of these writers use as their source the *Ecclesiastical History* of Bede and close their list of the oecumenical councils exactly where it is concluded by that great medieval authority. We should also remember the Frankish Church's emphatic refusal at the time of Charlemagne to accept the authority of the Seventh Council, a disclaimer that must have persisted very long in the West, and at least some of these writers must have shared it.[1]

Few also are the chroniclers who add the Seventh Council to their list. The *Gesta Episcoporum Neapolitanorum*,[2] an important authority of the eleventh century, mention the Second Council of Nicaea, but say nothing of the Fourth of Constantinople. The Chronicle of Sigebertus Gemblacensis[3] also mentions the Eighth Council, and so do the *Annales Laubienses*.[4]

We naturally omit the works of Frankish origin which, as is well known, simply deny the oecumenicity of this Council.

Much the same is found in the other writings of the period. Burchard of Worms, whose canonical work on the rule of the Catholic faith enjoyed great authority in the West, quotes the decree of Pope Gelasius I on the sacred books and on the councils, where only the first four oecumenical councils are mentioned.[5] The decree goes on: 'Sed si qua sunt concilia a sanctis patribus hactenus instituta, praeter istorum quatuor auctoritatem, et custodienda et recipienda decrevimus.'

Atto Vercellensis, enumerating in his Capitulary of 954 the sacred books which constitute the canon of the faith, mentions only the Councils of Nicaea, Ephesus and Chalcedon,[6] whereas St Udalrich, in his Instruction on the Duties of Religious Practice, mentions no council at all.[7]

St Alfric, archbishop of Canterbury, who died in 1006, only insists

---

[1] We come across a curious instance of this mistrust at the outset of the thirteenth century in the *Chronicon Helinandi Frigidi Montis monachi* (*P.L.* vol. 212, col. 840): 'Ad a. 794 Pseudosynodus Graecorum, quam falso septimam vocant, pro adorandis imaginibus, rejecta est a pontificibus.' About the Eighth Council Helinandus says nothing.

[2] *M.G.H.* Ss. Rer. Lang. p. 427.

[3] *M.G.H.* Ss. VI, p. 335. Sigebert died in 1112.

[4] *M.G.H.* Ss. IV, p. 13.

[5] *Decretorum Libri XX*, Lib. III, cap. 220; *P.L.* vol. 140, col. 717.

[6] *P.L.* vol. 134, cols. 49–52.

[7] *P.L.* vol. 135, cols. 1069–74, ann. 1009. Cf. Ratherius, *Praeloquiorum Libri Sex* (*P.L.* vol. 136, col. 248) for a similar Instruction; also his *Itinerarium* (loc. cit. cols. 581, 592). St Odilo does not, in his profession of faith, mention the councils either (*P.L.* vol. 142, cols. 1035–6).

on the first four councils;[1] and the priest and monk Bernald, born about 1054 and who died in 1100, follows the old tradition by listing only six oecumenical councils.[2]

Textbooks on the councils scarcely exist in the Latin literature of this period, while the Greek Church, as is well known, could boast of a profusion of writings on the subject. All I have found is one single short Latin textbook, anonymous and unpublished, in a MS. of the tenth century and preserved in the Latin MS. section of the Paris National Library (No. 1451), which enumerates only six councils. This is the original text:

De sex prioribus conciliis. Primum concilium Nicaenum factum est temporibus Constantini imperatoris Magni sub Silvestro papa urbis Romae antiquae, ubi fuerunt episcopi sanctissimi CCCXVIII. Secundum concilium fuit temporibus Theodosii Maioris sub Damaso apostolico antiquae Romae senioris, ubi fuerunt episcopi CL. Tertium concilium fuit Ephesinum sub tempore Theodosii iunioris sub Caelestino apostolico urbis Romae antiquae, ubi fuerunt episcopi CC. Quartum concilium Chalcedonense fuit temporibus Martiani imperatoris sub Leone apostolico urbis Romae antiquae senioris, ubi fuerunt episcopi CCXXX. Quintum concilium item Constantinopolitanum fuit temporibus Justiniani imperatoris sub Vigilo papa urbis Romae antiquae, ubi fuerunt episcopi CLXV. Sextum concilium item Constantinopolitanum fuit temporibus Constantini iunioris, sub Aagata (sic) papa urbis Romae, ubi fuerunt episcopi CCC.

The manuscript then takes stock of the heretics who were condemned by the different councils, beginning: 'In Nicaenum concilium (sic) fuerunt damnati Arrius et Photinus et Sabellius....' Note that Pope Honorius is not included among the condemned. This little treatise reminds one of the numerous Greek handbooks and textbooks on the councils and one may justifiably assume that it followed the Greek pattern.[3]

In another Latin manuscript of the Paris National Library (No. 1340), dating from the eleventh century, we find a short anonymous history, which is 'ex sancti Leonis et sancti Gregorii epistolis, et Gelasii papae

---

[1] S. Alferici ad Wulfinum ep. Canones, canon XXXIII (P.L. vol. 139, cols. 1475–6: 'Quatuor istae synodi adeo observandae sunt a Christi ecclesia ut quatuor Christi codices.'

[2] Apologeticus (M.G.H. Lib. de Lite, II, p. 61); De excom. vitandis (M.G.H. Lib. de lite, II, pp. 126, 129, 130–5).

[3] Cf. also a small treatise on the six first councils found in the Introduction to the Vita Methodii. See my translation in Les Légendes de Constantin et de Méthode, pp. 383, 384.

tomulo concinnata', a short compilation on the first four councils, which may be quoted to illustrate that the old tradition of the Church, started by Leo the Great, St Gregory and Gelasius, was readily followed in the West as late as the eleventh century.

On the whole, down to the middle of the eleventh century, no single contemporary writing, of all those I have been able to consult, provides any evidence of the oecumenicity of the Eighth Council. But weighty as the indication is, it is not adequate. The few writers who do mention the oecumenical councils in their books follow, as was stated, the old tradition of the Church as based on Gregory the Great's synodical letter and Bede's *Ecclesiastical History*. For the Westerners of that period, councils had not the same significance as for the Greeks;[1] and what matters is not so much the tradition that prevailed in Gaul, Germany, England, or even Italy, but the practice observed in Rome.

What then was the attitude in Rome to the Eighth Council? Documents on this precise question are few, but the few that survive are suggestive.

Pope Marinus II (942–6) addressed to Sicus, bishop of Capua, a letter[2] blaming him for his unclerical principles and conduct, taking particular exception to his violation of the church attached to the monastery of St Agnalius de Monte and threatening the bishop with excommunication, unless he atoned for the damage he had wrought:

Therefore, by the authority of Almighty God, of the Blessed Apostles Peter and Paul, of all the saints and of the seven universal canons [general councils], we send you this threat of excommunication, so that you may seriously endeavour to be on your guard against the above-mentioned [sins] and to amend yourself.... But if you disobey... this our warning, you will

---

[1] A classical instance illustrating the mentality will be found in the Legatio of Liudprand (*M.G.H.* Ss. III, p. 351). The Patriarch of Constantinople had asked Liudprand which councils were acknowledged by the West and Liudprand replied with the list of the four first oecumenical councils and of the ancient synods of Antioch, Carthage and Ancyra. The answer tickled the Greeks immensely: 'Ha! Ha! Ha! ait [patriarcha], Saxonicam dicere es oblitus, quam si rogas, cur nostri codices non habent, rudem esse, et ad nos necdum venire posse, respondeo.'

[2] *P.L.* vol. 133, cols. 874–5: 'Quapropter Dei omnipotentis et beatorum principum Petri et Pauli, et omnium sanctorum, et septem universalium canonum te excommunicando, mittimus, ut ab omnibus his supra memoratis praecavere te, atque emendare summopere studeas.... Si vero huic nostrae exhortationi... inobediens fueris, sis Dei omnipotentis et beatorum Petri et Pauli et omnium simul sanctorum, atque venerabilium septem universalium conciliorum auctoritate necnon et Spiritus sancti iudicio omni sacerdotali honore alienus....'

be deprived of all sacerdotal dignity by the authority of Almighty God, of the Blessed Peter and Paul, of all the saints and of the venerable seven general councils, as also by the judgment of the Holy Spirit....

The passage is clear enough: Pope Marinus II acknowledges no more than seven oecumenical councils. Nor can there be any question of a slip, since the formula used by the Pope is couched in solemn terms and repeated twice; and Marinus had no special reason for omitting the Eighth Council in this particular place, if he believed in its oecumenicity.

The other document on the same issue is better known: it is the famous synodical letter of Leo IX, sent in 1055 to Peter, Patriarch of Antioch.[1] After enumerating the first four councils, the Pope writes:

In the same way, I accept and venerate the other three Councils, i.e. the second of Constantinople, held under Pope Vigilius and the Emperor Justinian; then, the third of Constantinople against the Monothelites, under Pope Agatho and Constantine, nephew of Heraclius; and lastly, the second of Nicaea, under Pope Hadrian and Constantine, son of Irene, for the preservation of the images of Our Lord Jesus Christ and the saints. Whatever the afore-mentioned seven holy and universal Councils decreed and praised, I believe and praise, and I anathematize whomsoever they anathematized.

The words leave no room for doubt. C. Will, in his collection of documents bearing on the schism of 1054,[2] tried to evade the difficulty raised by the specific reference to seven councils by suggesting that the Pope omitted the Eighth Council for fear of offending the Greeks who did not acknowledge it: the suggestion seems to us preposterous, if not offensive to the supreme head of the Church. Could anyone seriously imagine a Pope deliberately disregarding an oecumenical council to oblige anyone, even the Greeks? The ruse would amount to a thinly veiled capitulation, a concession made to save himself trouble. Think of the consequences of the deception—for such it would be—had the issue been a council like that of Chalcedon: it would have spread joy

---

[1] *P.L.* vol. 143, cols. 772–3, letter 101: 'Pari modo recipio et veneror reliqua tria concilia, id est, secundum Constantinopolitanum, sub Vigilio papa et Justiniano Augusto; deinde tertium Constantinopolitanum contra Monothelitas, sub Agathone papa et Constantino nepote Heraclii; ultimum secundum Nicaenum, sub Adriano papa et Constantino Irenae filio, pro servandis Domini nostri Jesu Christi et sanctorum imaginibus. Quidquid supra dicta septem sancta et universalia concilia senserunt et collaudaverunt, sentio et collaudo: et quoscumque anathematizaverunt, anathematizo.'

[2] *Acta et Scripta quae de controversiis eccl. Graecae et Latinae saec. XI composita extant* (Leipzig, 1861), p. 171.

and jubilation among Armenians and all the Monophysites and opened the gates to heresy.

There is no eluding the force of the argument by pretending that in the eleventh century the number of oecumenical councils was not yet definitely fixed.[1] The evasion could pass muster in the case of annalists, or even of the canonical Collections published between the ninth and eleventh centuries, but is inadmissible in the case of an important pontifical document. The letter is an official statement, purporting to teach the Church of Antioch the faith of the Roman Church—a matter of some moment—and at least we must credit the supreme pontiff with knowing the standards of the faith of his own Church. The Pontifical Chancellery of the eleventh century was not so incompetent as to be uncertain about the number of oecumenical councils. The truth is that Marinus II and Leo IX, in speaking of only seven oecumenical councils, were true to the tradition of the Roman Church.

There are two more documents of the same kind belonging to the period of Leo IX and his immediate successors, both endorsing the Pope's attestation of the number of councils as officially acknowledged in Rome.

The first of these witnesses is Leo IX's faithful associate, Cardinal Humbert de Silva Candida. After the definite rupture with Michael Cerularius, Humbert pronounced excommunication in the name of the Fathers of the seven councils: 'auctoritate...patrum ex conciliis septem....'[2]

It has often been wondered why Humbert did not, at that particular moment, mention the Eighth Council: was it a slip or diplomatic caution? It was neither. Humbert no longer felt it necessary to consider the feelings of the Greek spiritual leaders. He had many other grievances against them and never minced his words: why should he suddenly exercise restraint in the matter of the councils? Humbert was not prone to compromise on such matters. A man of his stature, perfectly at home in the procedure of the Pontifical Chancellery, a good jurist and a conscientious theologian, he would have been the last to omit an oecumenical council in a document of such fundamental importance, in which he spoke in the name of the Pope and of the whole Western Church. Humbert may be blamed for many things, but not for overlooking an oecumenical council, whose authority would have added weight to his passionate anathema. The truth is that in quoting only seven oecumenical councils, Humbert faithfully rendered the

[1] A. Michel, *Humbert und Kerullarios* (Paderborn, 1930), vol. II, p. 425.
[2] *P.L.* vol. 143, col. 1004.

doctrine of his Church, which at that time officially knew no more than seven councils. On this point, Humbert was at one with his master, Pope Leo IX.[1]

The other testimony is later than the Cardinal's by a few years, dating from the time of Nicholas II. At the beginning of 1059, this Pope sent St Peter Damian as a legate to Milan on a mission to reform a concubinary and simoniacal clergy, and Peter Damian duly reported on his mission to Hildebrand, then promoted archdeacon of the Roman Church.[2] Among the documents appended to this interesting report, we find a copy of the oath which Peter Damian administered to those clergy who wished to repent. The following is what we read in this formula with reference to the number of councils:[3]

> I Arialdus, called deacon of the Chapel of the archbishop of Milan, profess to hold the same faith as the seven sacred Councils have by evangelical authority decreed and as the blessed Roman Pontiffs have explained to various people in their brilliant expositions of the truth.

Are we also to accuse St Peter Damian, doctor of the Church, of an unfortunate slip of memory or of misplaced diplomatic caution? The pontifical legate surely had nothing to hide in Milan; the formula must have been drawn up at the office of the Pontifical Chancellery, and Peter and his companion St Anselm of Lucca, the future Pope Alexander II, must have been given definite instructions in Rome, before starting on their official mission. Did the parties concerned forget to remind them of the number of oecumenical councils then officially recognized by the Church? It would be a poor compliment to the Roman theologians of the time.

Here again Peter Damian and his companion Anselm of Lucca bear witness to the fact that the Church of Rome in those days knew only seven oecumenical councils and therefore upheld the decision of John VIII who suppressed the Council of 869–70: there lies the true solution of all these puzzles, a solution perfectly consistent and straightforward.

---

[1] Humbert refers to the number of councils in another place, namely, in his writing against Nicetas (*P.L.* vol. 143, col. 992), but there he only mentions six councils.

[2] Actus Mediolani, de Privilegio Romanae Ecclesiae, Opuscul. v (*P.L.* vol. 145, cols. 89–98): 'Ego Arialdus dictus diaconus de capella Mediolanensis archiepiscopi ...profiteor me eam fidem tenere, quam sacrosancta septem concilia evangelica auctoritate firmarunt et quam beatissimi pontifices Romani ad diversos data praedicatione lucidissimae veritatis exposuerunt.'   [3] *P.L.* vol. 145, col. 97.

There remains a document which confirms that such was indeed the tradition of the Church of Rome in the eleventh century, the profession of faith which, according to century-old usage, each Pope had to read and sign before his enthronement. It was then laid on the tomb of St Peter and subsequently kept in the Pontifical Archives. The formula of this profession was to be found in the *Liber Diurnus*, the oldest known formulary of the Roman Chancellery.[1] It has been lost, but we get an idea of what it was from a school-book intended for the training of notaries, also called *Liber Diurnus*, as it contained copies of most of the formulae of the official formulary. It has survived in three Manuscripts, those of the Vatican Library, of Clermont and of Milan, representing three slightly different versions. All of them give an idea of what the *Liber Diurnus* must have looked like in the eighth century and at the beginning of the ninth.

Among the formulae bearing on the election and the consecration of Popes, we are here mainly interested in their profession of faith. It is a venerable document whose importance to the history of the Papacy and the evolution of dogmas our specialists have not yet fully realized.[2]

The formula preserved by the school-book *Liber Diurnus* enumerates the six oecumenical councils to be accepted by the Popes as the norm of the Catholic faith, but it is clear from the text that the original number

---

[1] I am only summarizing here the results of my researches. See the detailed discussion in Appendix I.

[2] So far, only the Jesuit W. M. Peitz has tried to show the connection of the profession of faith with the development of Catholic doctrine (see details in Appendix I, p. 442). I have not seen his latest studies on this subject ('Das Vorephesinische Symbol der Papstkanzlei', in *Miscellanea Historiae Pontificiae edita a Fac. Hist. Eccl. in Pont. Universitate Gregoriana*, no. 1 (Rome, 1939), nor 'Methodisches zur Diurnusforschung', ibid. no. 3 (Rome, 1940), but the review of the two studies published by E. Hermann in *Orientalia Christiana Periodica* (1940), vol. VI, pp. 270–4 stresses the importance of Peitz's researches and the necessity for proceeding carefully in this delicate matter. Peitz's conclusions may sound bold to many, but they follow the right direction. The reviews of Peitz's studies by B. Altaner and C. Mohlberg in the *Theologische Revue* (1939), vol. XXXVIII, were also unobtainable. L. Santifaller's study, 'Zur Liber Diurnus-Forschung', in *Hist. Zeitschrift* (1940), vol. CLXI, pp. 532–8, summarizing the latest contributions to the problem, is too short and the author has failed to convince me that the *Liber Diurnus* was not a school-book used in the Pontifical Chancellery, but merely a valuable document of canon law. He should have stuck to his previous conclusions. This controversy has no immediate bearing on the profession of faith formula of the *Liber Diurnus*. Even if it was only a collection of canon law formulae or the oldest formulary of the Papal Chancellery, it remains established that it was repeatedly revised, the last known revision having been made in the eleventh century. It was this last edition that was used by Cardinal Deusdedit.

was four, the other two being added when they were officially adopted by the Roman Church. This number was considered to meet the needs till the end of the ninth century. As will be explained elsewhere,[1] the Seventh Council was officially included only after 880.

It may be taken for granted then that the official formulary of the *Liber Diurnus* was altered from time to time, as some formulae needed to be brought up to date. But another formulary came into use, and there are traces of a different edition of the *Liber Diurnus*, published in the ninth century with alterations that are not registered in the school-book. This edition may have been in use till the middle of the eleventh century, when another revision of the *Liber Diurnus* was made. This was used by the famous canonist of the Gregorian period, Cardinal Deusdedit, who copied a number of formulae from the revised *Liber Diurnus* for his canonical documentation. The profession of faith for newly elected Popes is one of them. This formula, when compared with formula 83 of the school-book, will give an idea of the profession as used in Rome till the ninth century and of the radical revisions to which the book was subjected in the eleventh century, probably in the reign of Leo IX. Even so, the new profession gives only seven oecumenical councils, without a word about the Eighth. It is the same with the formula called *Cautio Episcopi*, or the profession form used by bishops after their election, in which the passage on the oecumenical councils was also brought up to date and 'modernized' in the eleventh century, yet without a reference to the Eighth Council. Only one explanation is possible: the Church of Rome knew only seven, and not eight, oecumenical councils in the first half of the eleventh century. And this tallies with the facts as I have tried to establish them in the first part of this book. In the eleventh century, John VIII's verdict on the so-called Eighth Council and on Photius' rehabilitation was still in force and that Council was not numbered among the oecumenical synods.

If this is so, how is it that the Council of 869–70 is regarded to-day as an oecumenical council by the Western Church? How and when was it added to the list?

Everything points to the conclusion that this change of attitude to the Eighth Council in the West and in Rome occurred at the end of the eleventh century and was contrived by the canonists and reformists of the period. It was they who really 'discovered' this Council, together

[1] See Appendix I, p. 444.

with some canons extremely useful for their documentation, chiefly canon XXII prohibiting interference by lay power in episcopal elections, a discovery that was of considerable importance in the struggle against lay investiture.[1]

But the acceptance of the oecumenicity of the Eighth Council was gradual and the first great canonist of the period, St Anselm of Lucca, still seems to follow the old tradition in computing the number of oecumenical councils. In book VI, ch. 49, of his Collection, he mentions the Popes' ancient practice of sending to the Eastern Patriarchs synodical letters with a profession of faith, and he quotes a fragment from the Life of St Gregory the Great, written by John the Deacon.[2] In chapter 50 Anselm appeals to the authority of the first four councils, and quotes the synodical letter of St Gregory the Great mentioning the five councils.

But again, it was St Anselm who introduced canon XXII, since grown so famous, into canonical legislation. He also quotes canon XVIII, which prohibits all violation of ecclesiastical privileges, and canon XXI on the honours due to Pope and Patriarchs,[3] and in quoting the latter gives it the title, which the Council had arrogated to itself, of 'universalis octava synodus'.

Anselm's example is followed by another reformer of the time, Bonizo, who quotes canons XXI and XXII in his *Liber ad Amicum*[4] and in his *Liber de Vita Christiana*.[5] Gerhohus of Reichersberg (1132–69) also draws an argument from canon XXII against the champions of lay investiture.[6] The same canon is appealed

---

[1] See my study, 'L'Affaire de Photios dans la Littérature Latine du Moyen Âge', in *Annales de l'Institut Kondakov* (1938), vol. X, pp. 82 seq. and pp. 293 seq.

[2] He also quotes John the Deacon's comments on this practice and mentions there the Eighth Council: 'Quam videlicet consuetudinem, sicut nostri quoque, qui ante biennium ab Adriano papa *in sancta octava synodo* testantur, ita Orientales praecipue retinent usque hactenus sedes, ut in suis dypticis nullius pontificis nomen describunt, quo usque ipsius synodicum suscipiant....' When John was writing, this council was still in force in the West.

[3] F. Thaner, *Anselmi, episcopi Lucensis, collectio canonum*, loc. cit. II, 72, p. 109; IV, 30, p. 205; VI, 20, p. 276.

[4] *M.G.H.* Lib. de Lite, I, p. 607.

[5] E. Perels, 'Bonizo, Liber de Vita Christiana', loc. cit. I, 1; IV, 95; II, 17.

[6] Opusculum de Edificio Dei (*M.G.H.* Lib. de Lite, III, p. 151, cap. 19). The passage is very suggestive: 'Hinc est quod octava synodus electionem laicali potestate fieri sub anathemate interdicit: quae synodus, petente et presente Basilio magno imperatore, habita fuit. Neque tamen vel ipse Basilius vel ceteri catholici imperatores questi sunt hoc ad sui contemptum fieri, ut nichil de pontificum electione eorum referretur potestati: immo potius leguntur sanctorum patrum insti-

to by the monk Placidus[1] and in the pleading in favour of Pope Paschal II.[2]

As for Deusdedit, he naturally makes frequent use of the Acts of the Eighth Council in his Collection and in his other writings, but it is generally the same canons that interest him,[3] although he betrays some hesitation about the oecumenicity of this Council. Knowing that the number of officially acknowledged oecumenical councils amounted to no more than seven—the very reason why he dared not touch the profession of faith which he copied from his *Liber Diurnus*—he also noticed that the Eighth Council had conferred on itself the title 'oecumenical'. It was also bestowed on it by Anastasius[4] and by John VIII[5] —and that before 879. Though it offered canons of great value to the reformers, Deusdedit, being a conscientious canonist, hesitated, at least in some places, to give it the title 'oecumenical'.

In his *Libellus Contra Invasores et Simoniacos*, he writes: 'Synodus vero pro Ignatio, quae a quibusdam octava dicitur....' 'In synodo universali CCXL (!) patrum habita pro Ignatio patriarcha, quae a quibusdam VIII. dicitur.' 'In octava synodo universali habita pro Ignatio.' 'In synodo universali patrum CCXL (!) habita pro Ignatio patriarcha, quae a suis conditoribus octava dicitur....'[6]

The words clearly reveal Deusdedit's misgivings about describing the Eighth Council as oecumenical; he simply gave it the title which its authors had claimed for it. The *Libellus* was composed in 1097:[7] we should therefore interpret what he says about it in his canonical Collection, completed in 1087, in the same sense.

tutiones amplexati fuisse easque quidam eorum post quinque patriarcharum subscriptiones suis quoque subscriptionibus roborasse.' Cf. also ibid. p. 451 (Commentarius in psalmum 64). Gerhohus here follows Deusdedit's argumentation, 'Libellus contra Invas.' (*M.G.H.* Lib. de Lite II, p. 307).

[1] Liber de Honore Ecclesiae (*M.G.H.* Lib. de Lite II, p. 618).

[2] Disputatio vel Defensio Paschalis papae (*M.G.H.* Lib. de Lite II, p. 662).

[3] Lib. I, 47, can. XXI; Lib. I, 48, extract from the *Actio VII*, Mansi, vol. XVI, col. 86; Lib. I, 48a, extract from the *Actio VIII*, Mansi, vol. XVI, cols. 97–9; Lib. III, 10, can. XV; Lib. III, 11, can. XVIII; Lib. III, 12, can. XX; Lib. LV, 17, extract from the *Actio IX*, Mansi, vol. XVI, cols. 152, 153; Lib. IV, 18, can. XXII. *Libellus contra Invas.* (*M.G.H.* Lib. de Lite II, p. 305) also mentions can. XXII.

[4] Mansi, vol. XVI, cols. 8 seq.

[5] *M.G.H.* Ep. VII, p. 307, letter 53, written in 875. Cf. the passage in the Life of Saint Gregory the Great, written by John the Deacon, mentioned previously, p. 320.

[6] *M.G.H.* Lib. de Lite II, pp. 327, 346, 349, 356; pp. 307 and 313, though the Council is simply called 'octava synodus universalis'.

[7] *M.G.H.* Lib. de Lite II, p. 294; preface by M. E. Sackur, the editor.

For he writes in his prologue:[1] 'Itaque primum defloravi neque optima de quibusdam universalibus sinodis idest Nicena, Ephesina prima, Calcedonensi et VI et VII et VIII, quae partim a IV sive a V patriarchis, ab eorum partim vicariis sub diversis temporibus universaliter celebratae fuisse noscuntur.' Then, to endorse his notion 'quod legati eius [papae] in omnibus sinodis primi damnationis sententiam inferunt et primi subscribunt', he also quotes part of the seventh session of the Eighth Council,[2] containing Photius' condemnation as pronounced by the pontifical legates, without, however, expressly designating the Council. In support of another proposition, 'Quod necessitate exigente ab universalibus sinodis ad Romanam sedem appellatur', he also cites canon XXI of the same Council,[3] whilst the passage from the seventh session mentioned above is appealed to in support of the phrase: 'Quod eius auctoritate iam VIII universales sinodi celebratae sunt.'

But, since the synod of 869–70 was actually held 'auctoritate papae', and the rules governing the organization of ecclesiastical synods had been observed and the Council was for some time considered oecumenical by the two Churches, the Cardinal could with some show of reason and for the benefit of his thesis add it to the seven preceding councils, even though certain decisions were later annulled by the same authority.

Pope Gregory VII also called this Council 'octava synodus' in his correspondence, when quoting canon XXII against lay Investiture,[4] though it would be difficult to infer from the statement anything in favour of its oecumenicity.

The important point in all this is to gain a clear view of the attitude adopted towards this Council by the reformers of the Gregorian and post-Gregorian periods, for whom the temptation to include it among the oecumenical councils was irresistible. Why the first generation of canonists did not yield to the temptation is easily explained, since their case rested directly on the original texts found in Rome, and Deusdedit was too conscientious a scholar to tamper with his sources.

But as the second generation strayed further from the original texts, they gradually receded from the old tradition of the Church; and since

---

[1] See Glanvell ed. p. 3.
[2] Lib. I, cap. 48, Glanvell ed. pp. 7, 57; Mansi, vol. XVI, cols. 97–9.
[3] Lib. I, cap. 47, Glanvell ed. pp. 7, 56.
[4] E. Caspar, 'Das Register Gregors VII' (*M.G.H.* Ep. sel. II, I, p. 333): letter to Hugh, bishop of Die.

relations with the Greek Church had been severed, and the West felt no longer under any obligation to respect its traditions and the Photian incident had been quite forgotten, the only remembrance left of the whole affair was that of Nicholas I excommunicating a disobedient emperor.[1] As against this, the struggle against lay Investiture and in defence of the rights of the papacy had reached a climax of unprecedented virulence, and since the canons of the Council of 869–70 provided such an efficient weapon in the hands of the Roman canonists, it was natural that they should give the Council the oecumenical title which it had claimed for itself.

What is remarkable is that this was done by the canonist who laid least stress on this Council, Ivo of Chartres, who quotes only one canon, the eleventh.[2] In the Collection called *Tripartita*, so far unpublished, and in Book IV of his *Decretum*, chapter 132, we nevertheless read the following:

De octo universalibus conciliis. Ex libro diurno professio Romani pontificis. Sancta VIII universalia concilia, id est I Nicenum, II Constantinopolitanum, III Ephesinum, IV Chalcedonense, item V Constantinopolitanum et VI. Item Nicenum VII. Octavum quoque Constantinopolitanum, usque ad unum apicem immutilata servare, et pari honore et veneratione digna habere, et quae praedicaverunt et statuerunt omnimodis sequi et praedicare, quaeque condemnaverunt ore et corde condemnare profiteor.[3]

Thus it happened that the Council of 869–70 made its semi-official appearance among the oecumenical synods at the end of the eleventh century and the beginning of the twelfth. Ivo's testimony is all the more impressive, as he relies on the famous *Liber Diurnus* of the Pontifical Chancellery and once again the profession of faith of the newly elected Popes is put forward in a recension different from that of Deusdedit.

[1] See my study, 'L'Affaire de Photios', loc. cit. pp. 79 seq.; also, pp. 294 seq. in this text.

[2] *Decr.* V, 122; *Pan.* III, 8.

[3] One notes, besides, at this place a certain confusedness on the part of Ivo. In *Decr.* IV, 132, he says for instance: 'De secunda Nicaena synodo inter universalia octava (?).' *Decr.* IV, 131: 'Item de eodem....' After the historical information about the Second Council of Nicaea, he writes: '...In Nicaenam civitatem et celebrata est sancta octava universalis synodus.' But we need not make much of this. It is quite possible that the confusion is to a great extent due to the copyists of the *Decretum*. In the MS. of the *Decretum* at the National Library of Paris (*Latin* 3874), for instance, fol. 68, the parts *Decr.* IV, 129–31, are gathered into one, and the inscription of *Decr.* IV, 130, 'De secunda Nicaena synodo inter universalia octava' is missing.

The *Liber Diurnus* is also quoted by Ivo in two different places, first in the *Decretum* (IV, 19) and again in his letter to archbishop Hugh,[1] and in both places the issue concerns the extract from the profession of faith. Even this passage, including a variant of smaller moment, corresponds to the version of the profession copied by Deusdedit. In another letter, Ivo also refers to the profession of faith taken from the *Liber Diurnus*.[2]

The question then is whether Ivo was able to consult the original *Liber Diurnus* or whether he borrowed the two passages from another Collection. Everything seems to point to the conclusion that the saintly bishop of Chartres did not see the original copy of the *Liber Diurnus*, since it was difficult, if not impossible, to consult it anywhere but in Rome;[3] and even in Rome, it was to be found only at the Pontifical Chancellery, for whose exclusive use it had been composed.

On the other hand, Ivo does not seem to have used Deusdedit's Collection;[4] presumably he copied the fragment from Deusdedit's version and simply added the Eighth Council. As P. Fournier[5] has proved, Ivo of Chartres used one of those Collections called 'intermediary', which abounded at the time; and the Collection or Collections he disposed of had some affinities with the Collection called *Britannica*, the only one of its kind to survive. It is possible, on a first examination, that this Collection served Ivo and his associates as one of their sources. The *Britannica*, according to Fournier,[6] was composed about 1090 or 1091, and a palaeographic examination of this unique manuscript (British Museum 8873 Addit.) supports this assumption.

---

[1] *P.L.* vol. 162, ep. 60, cols. 70–5: '...In libro quoque pontificum, qui dicitur Diurnus, ita continetur de professione Romani Pontificis: Nihil de traditione...' as far as the words 'observare ac venerari profiteor.' The last word is added by Ivo.

[2] *P.L.* vol. 162, ep. 73, cols. 92–5: '...Bernardo majoris monasterii abbati.' Col. 94: 'Ipse enim summus pontifex, antequam consecrationis gratiam consequatur, consuetudines Romanae Ecclesiae et decreta praedecessorum suorum se inviolabiliter servaturum profitetur. Sic reliqui pontifices ante consecrationem examinantur.'

[3] Even the three MSS. of the edition of this school-book, *Liber Diurnus*, we possess show reliable affiliation to Rome. Cf. Sickel, loc. cit., in the Introduction to his edition, pp. viii–xxxiii, Peitz, loc. cit. p. 29: 'Trotzdem dürfte Ivo nicht auf den Diurnus selbst zurückgehen, sondern ihn nur durch Deusdedit oder eine von diesem abhängige kanonische Quelle kennen, wie *Decr.* IV, 197, als Quelle ähnlich wie Deusdedit II, 109 angibt: Ex libro pontificum qui dicitur Diurnus.'

[4] P. Fournier, 'Les Collections canoniques attribuées à Yves de Chartres', in *Bibl. de l'École des Chartes*, vols. LVII, LVIII, does not quote this Collection among Ivo's sources.

[5] P. Fournier, loc. cit. vol. LVII, p. 661; vol. LVIII, pp. 53 seq.

[6] P. Fournier, loc. cit. vol. LVIII, p. 53.

The handwriting of the manuscript is certainly that of the end of the eleventh century.

The minute analysis of the *Britannica* carried out by Ewald[1] shows that the concluding part of the Collection, which Ewald calls *Varia* II (fols. 171–210*a*), is simply an extract from Deusdedit's canonical Collection. Even the sequence of the texts is scrupulously observed.

Now it happens that we find there a copy of two extracts from the *Liber Diurnus* made by Deusdedit—the protocol regulating the announcement of a new Pope's election[2] and the profession of faith of the elected Pope (Lib. II, 110), which is identical with the text given by the Cardinal; except that, instead of the seven councils, it enumerates eight,[3] with the addition of the Fourth Council of Constantinople.

As it is unlikely that the author of this compilation was able to consult the *Liber Diurnus*, it may be assumed that he introduced the alteration into the profession of faith on his own initiative; and one can quite understand why he considered the addition justifiable. At another place he quotes, again in Deusdedit's version, three passages of the Eighth Council in which it gives itself the title of oecumenical.[4] Surprised to find that this Council should not be numbered, in the Pope's profession, among the oecumenicals, he joined its name with the others.

And yet, Ewald, Conrat and Fournier[5] agree in pointing out that the subject-matter of the *Britannica* does not exactly correspond to the source which Ivo used for his *Decretum*. The *Tripartita* also implies a source similar to the *Britannica* but more extended in scope. Conrat indicated the true solution of the difficulty when, at the end of his book,

---

[1] Loc. cit. *Neues Archiv*, vol. v, p. 282.

[2] *Britannica*, fols. 204, 204*a*.

[3] *Britannica*, fols. 205, 206: 'Sancta quoque octo concilia...et VIII Constantinopolitanum....' Besides this alteration there are only two insignificant variants that differ from Deusdedit's text; towards the end of the profession: 'et vicem intercessionibus *tuis* [*om.* Britannica] adimpleo'; and at the end: 'indictione quibus *ut* [*add.* Britannica] supra.'

[4] *Varia* II, 21; II, 81; II, 107. These passages correspond to Deusdedit, I, 47 (38); III, 10 (9); IV, 17 (15). The copyist of the *Britannica*, however, erroneously attributes the first passage (fol. 148) to the Eighth Council. In fact the passage is from the Seventh Council, as Deusdedit had rightly pointed out. It only shows that the copyist is not quite accurate in the transcription of the Cardinal's work. This is important and needs emphasizing.

[5] Cf. Ewald, loc. cit. (*Neues Archiv*, vol. v, chiefly pp. 294, 323, 350); M. Conrat (Cohn), *Der Pandekten und Institutionenauszug der Brit. Dekretalensammlung, Quelle des Ivo* (Berlin, 1887); M. Conrat (Cohn), *Geschichte der Quellen und Litteratur des Röm. Rechts im früheren Mittelalter* (1891), vol. I, p. 372; Fournier, loc. cit. vol. LVIII, p. 53; Fournier-Le Bras, loc. cit. vol. II, pp. 72 seq.

after comparing the extract of the *Pandects* in the *Britannica* with the extract of the *Pandects* included in Ivo's work, and noting that Ivo's extract is more lengthy than that of the alleged source, he writes: 'Man mag sich dies damit erklären, dass Yvo neben unserem Auszug noch eine zweite Quelle excerpiert hat oder, was ich für wahrscheinlicher halte, der letztere in der britischen Sammlung in einer unvollständigen Gestalt vorliegt.' A comparison of the extracts from the pontifical registers preserved in the *Britannica* and in Ivo's work clearly points to the same conclusion.

Ivo therefore used a canonical Collection belonging to the class of 'intermediary collections', probably written in Italy, perhaps in Rome. The *Britannica* Collection gives us a fair idea of the character of Ivo's source, since it is simply a long extract from that original, anonymous Collection, now lost. This original Collection also contained an extract of Deusdedit's, which seems to have been copied by the scribe of the *Britannica*, and it was from this portion of their source that Ivo and his collaborators derived the Pontiff's profession of faith.

Thus the alteration in the number of councils in the Sovereign Pontiff's profession of faith was probably the work of the copyists of Deusdedit's Collection. Not being endowed either with the acumen or the accuracy of the Cardinal, they failed to understand why the Eighth Council, which claimed to be oecumenical and supplied a good weapon against lay Investiture and was called 'oecumenical' even by Deusdedit in his quoted canons, did not figure among the oecumenical councils in the Pope's profession of faith. Accordingly, they added it to the list on their own account. It was not Ivo, but one of his sources, now untraceable, that was responsible for the addition.

There remains, however, an alternative. The author of that original Collection, the source of the *Britannica* and of Ivo, must apparently be sought in Italy, perhaps in Rome. Had he been able to verify the text of the profession of faith by the original, we should have to assume that the Eighth Council was worked into the profession about 1090, and at first sight this may seem quite possible. But let us look more closely.

If the profession was still in use,[1] it would in all likelihood not have been altered till the advent of a new Pope. Pope Victor III died on

---

[1] We note in this connection that Deusdedit himself calls the rules of the Pope's election and consecration, whose extracts he publishes, 'ordo antiquus'. Traces of the usage in the *Liber Diurnus* can be followed up only as far as Gregory's pontificate. See pp. 328, 440.

16 September 1087 and Urban II could not be consecrated and enthroned in Rome till 9 May 1088. Now for that period we possess the evidence of Deusdedit, who knew nothing of a new edition of the profession, and it was about this time that his own Collection was completed. Had the profession been altered, Deusdedit would have been the first to take note of it in his Collection and in other writings: and yet, as late as 1097, he seems still to be in doubt about the oecumenicity of this council.

Urban II reigned till 1099, but the canonical Collection which Ivo used had apparently been published before that date. In fact, the *Britannica* presupposes its existence. The *Britannica* must have been issued in either 1090 or 1091, when Deusdedit was still alive, so that any official alteration in the Pope's profession of faith at this period would be out of the question.

Another query: Was the Eighth Council, when its popularity was already widespread in the Western Church, officially added to the other oecumenical councils by a special decree of the Pontifical Chancellery? Of such a decree we know absolutely nothing, though one thing is certain—if the profession of faith was still imposed on the newly elected pontiffs in the twelfth century, then the Fourth Council of Constantinople was certainly included in it. This addition would in any case, as stated before, have been prepared by the works of the canonists of the eleventh century. But we know nothing about the persistence of this custom in Rome in the twelfth century and it could be established only by the discovery of a new official edition of the said profession giving the list of eight oecumenical councils.

So far, there is only one known MS. copy of a profession of faith for the use of Sovereign Pontiffs (Cod. Bibl. Vaticanae, Latin 7160), posterior to the profession used by Deusdedit, which enumerates eight councils and could be offered as evidence that the Popes of the twelfth century were asked to subscribe to eight councils. But on closer examination, this profession[1] is discovered to be but another version of the notorious profession of Boniface VIII which, as is well known, is a fourteenth-century forgery.

Everything considered, it is impossible to trace the existence of a new edition of this profession of the Sovereign Pontiffs after that of the eleventh century as it survives in Deusdedit's Collection, nor is there any satisfactory evidence that this profession was still imposed on the Popes in the twelfth century. As some faint traces have brought us as far as Gregory VII's reign, it would not be surprising if it marked

[1] See Appendix II, pp. 448 seq.

the *terminus ad quem* in the practice of this venerable custom. Indeed, this Pope's conception of the plenitude of papal power, as outlined in his *Dictatus Papae*, though not at variance with the usage, is hardly compatible with it.

If, as I am explaining elsewhere,[1] we admit that in Deusdedit's time, in the eleventh century, the *Liber Diurnus* was already to some extent differentiated from the handbook as used at the Chancellery and that the title came to be attached to what was left of the primitive hand-book, which for the importance of its contents was still held in great honour at the Chancellery, it becomes easy to understand how this part of the regulations fell into desuetude under Gregory VII without creating something of a sensation at the Chancellery. As the notaries had much more to do with the modernized handbook, the disappearance of the old-fashioned *Liber Diurnus* from circulation could easily escape their notice. In Gregory's time there were many canonical documents that fell out of fashion and lost their importance in Rome, to be replaced by others that better represented the Pontiff's opinions on supremacy. If then we take into consideration the progress in canonical documenta-tion made under Gregory's inspiration, we shall find it easier to assume that Gregory VII discontinued the procedure of the ascent to the throne as laid down in the old *Liber Diurnus* and that the first thing to be suppressed was the profession of faith. If it may be assumed that this pious practice was dropped by Gregory VII, we shall find here a new illustration of how the notion of papal supremacy developed between Leo IX, who merely modernized the formula, and Gregory VII.[2]

To return now to the question of the number of councils in this profession, Baronius quoted in his *Annals* as evidence of the oecumenicity of the Eighth Council[3] the profession of faith I have demonstrated to be a forgery of the fourteenth century: therefore, Baronius' only argument in favour of that oecumenicity is valueless. From all that has been said we must conclude that the said Eighth Council was listed among the oecumenical councils by an extraordinary error committed by the canonists at the end of the eleventh century.

---

[1] See Appendix I, pp. 437 seq.

[2] On the subsequent growth of the same notion and its influence over the usage at the Papal Chancellery, cf. J. B. Sägmüller, 'Die Idee Gregors VII vom Primat in der päpstlichen Kanzlei', in *Theologische Quartalschrift* (Tübingen, 1896), vol. LXXVIII, pp. 577–613—and the same author's booklet, *Zur Geschichte der Ent-wicklung des päpstlichen Gesetzgebungsrechtes* (Rottenburg a. N. 1937), pp. 16 seq.

[3] Even Hefele followed Baronius. Cf. Hefele-Leclercq, loc. cit. vol. VI, p. 544; Buschbell, 'Professiones Fidei', in *Röm. Quartalschrift* (1896), vol. X, p. 279.

Yet those canonists can hardly be blamed. In their heroic campaign for the freedom of the Western Church, they had a perfect right to use canons voted by a council where all the representatives of the patriarchates were assembled; they were considered faithfully to express the feelings of the Church and could therefore be quoted, notwithstanding the decision by Pope John VIII, who sanctioned the annulment voted by the synod of Photius in 879–80. Whereas this condemnation fell upon the particular decision of the Eighth Council against Photius, the canons voted by the assembly were not expressly repudiated either by the Photian Council or by John VIII's letter sanctioning the Photian Council.[1]

It must, however, be admitted that the revival of the Eighth Council by the Western Church would never have taken effect, had it not been for the severance of the Roman and the Byzantine Churches, as contact with the Greeks, so sensitive on this very point, would certainly have acted as a powerful brake on the zeal of the canonists of the eleventh and twelfth centuries. This control gone, they found it only too easy to proceed unhindered.

Thus, at the end of our investigations on the oecumenicity of the Eighth Council, we have arrived at results that may at first seem startling. The Eighth Council was not included among the oecumenical councils by the Roman Church from 880 till the beginning of the twelfth century, and until that time the two Churches were in perfect agreement on this important point. It was only as a result of the canonists' extraordinary oversight at the end of the eleventh century that this Council

---

[1] This can be ascertained from the Pope's letter to Photius (*M.G.H.* Ep. VII, p. 185), where he insists on the observance of the canon which forbids the elevation of laymen to the episcopacy and had been voted at the Council of 869–70 (Mansi, vol. XVI, col. 162): 'iuxta kapitulum, quod super hac re in venerabili synodo tempore scilicet decessoris nostri Hadriani iunioris papae Constantinopoli habita est congruentissime promulgatum.' It should, however, be noted that the Pope does not here call this Council 'Eighth Oecumenical' as he did in another letter written in 875 (*M.G.H.* Ep. VII, p. 307), when the Council was still accepted in Rome as authentic. Note also that this reference to the Council of 869–70 found in the Latin edition of the letter is, in the Greek edition, made to the Seventh Council under Hadrian I. This is followed by the statement that Hadrian II is said to have refused to sign the Acts of the Council of 869–70 (Mansi, vol. XVII, col. 416). This bold assertion was based on a passage contained in the Latin edition of John's letter to Basil I (*M.G.H.* Ep. VII, p. 171), where the Pope writes that Hadrian II's legates had signed the Acts with the saving clause 'usque ad voluntatem sui pontificis'. This Greek emendation had the good fortune to be copied by Ivo of Chartres from the extract of the Photian Council he was using (*Decr.* IV, 76; *P.L.* vol. 161, col. 285) and thus to be assigned an important place in pre-Gratian canonical documentation. See *supra*, Part II, ch. I, p. 304.

reappeared on the list of the oecumenical councils. Canon XXII, forbidding laymen to interfere in episcopal elections, 'discovered' by the canonists of the Gregorian period, mainly contributed to the popularity of the Council in the West and facilitated the canonists' misrepresentation. Until the twelfth century at the earliest, no declaration had ever been issued by the Holy See including this Council among the oecumenical synods.[1] That it should have figured as one of the venerable oecumenical councils must necessarily have influenced the Western verdict on the Photian Affair and supplied an important factor in the growth of what we call 'the Photian Legend' in the Western world.

[1] Proof is supplied by Ivo of Chartres. As a conscientious canonist, he tries to find authentic texts in support of the oecumenicity of the eight councils listed in the profession of faith of the *Liber Diurnus*, and having found them, presents them in Book IV of his *Decretum*. And yet he cannot, to support the oecumenicity of the Eighth Council, quote a better document than (*Decr*. IV, cap. 133; *P.L.* vol. 161, col. 296) the letter addressed by John VIII to the Salernitans and the Amalfitans, in which he recommends the legates Eugene and bishop Donatus 'cuius laus est in sancta synodo octava' (*M.G.H.* Ep. VII, p. 307). Yes, but this letter was written in 875, therefore at the time when the Council still possessed all its validity. Ivo of Chartres overlooked this. It was perhaps that passage which helped to prompt Ivo to number this Council among the oecumenicals, despite the Pope's decision annulling it which the canonist had quoted before.

CHAPTER III

WESTERN TRADITION FROM THE TWELFTH TO THE FIFTEENTH CENTURY

The Eighth Council in pre-Gratian law Collections, influenced by Gregorian canonists—Collections dependent on Deusdedit and Ivo—Gratian's Decretum and the Photian Legend—From Gratian to the fifteenth century: Canonists—Theological writers and Historians.

SUCH then is the result of our research into the period when the Eighth Council was given unmerited pride of place among the oecumenical councils in the West. At the same time we have been able to establish —be it repeated once more—that the responsibility falls on the canonists of the eleventh and twelfth centuries, not on the Pontifical Chancellery. We must now extend our inquiry further and examine the remaining canonical Collections of the period. What attitude to the Eighth Council and to the Council of Photius did their authors adopt? And did any of them follow the lead of Deusdedit and Ivo of Chartres in their estimate of the anti-Photian and Photian Councils? Clearly our thesis will rest on more solid foundations, if we can throw more light on the place this problem held in the minds of the other canonists of the period.

Certainly, we are venturing on a difficult and perilous undertaking. For one thing, it is well known that many problems relative to the evolution of canonical legislation in the Middle Ages still await an adequate solution and that few of the canonical works of that period have yet been published. P. Fournier and his collaborator Le Bras have drawn up a long list of them in their excellent work on the canonical Collections anterior to Gratian, but even their lengthy catalogue is not exhaustive, though it may serve as a reliable basis, since it seems unlikely that any Collection surpassing in importance the great Collections of that period remains to be discovered.

The canonical Collections of the end of the eleventh century down to Gratian can be divided into two distinct groups: the first included those compilations which show the influence of the first handbooks of canon law revised and completed by the canonists of the period of Gregory VII, namely, the author of the Collection under 74 Titles,[1]

---

[1] On this Collection, which offers nothing important on our subject, cf. P. Fournier, 'Le premier manuel canonique de la Réforme Grégorienne', in *Mélanges d'Archéologie et d'Histoire* (Paris, 1894), vol. XIV, pp. 223, 285-90.

St Anselm of Lucca and Burchard of Worms. The other group includes the Collections that were influenced by Ivo of Chartres.

Let us now rapidly survey the principal Collections of the first group, with special emphasis on those we have been able to study at first hand.

The influence of Anselm, of Burchard and of the Collection under 74 Titles is particularly pronounced in the Collection in Two Books contained in MS. 3832 of the Latin MS. section of the Vatican Library.[1] It dates from the end of the eleventh, or from the beginning of the twelfth century, and the compiler has made good use of the letters of Nicholas I, including a few on the Photian case, notably the Pope's famous reply to Michael III,[2] his reply *ad consulta Bulgarorum*[3] and an extract from his letter to Photius.[4] The famous canon XXII of the Eighth Council is quoted, too, as a matter of course.[5]

Though there is no definite statement about the number of oecumenical councils recognized by the Roman Church the compiler quotes the profession of faith which an elected archbishop (fol. 120) had to make before his consecration, with its reference to the first four great councils; but the formula is the same as that published by E. Rozière.[6] At the end of the Collection (fols. 188–190) is found a copy of Cardinal Humbert's bull of excommunication against Cerularius, with its enumeration of seven oecumenical councils, but added to the Collection in a different handwriting, so that it was not part of the original Collection.

The Collection in Five Books, contained in MS. 1348 of the Vatican Library, was studied by V. Wolf von Glanvell.[7]

Though the compiler is indebted to the work of Anselm, among others, he omits nearly all the documents of the ninth century, once so highly appreciated by the archbishop of Lucca, only canon XXII of the Eighth Council being quoted (lib. I, cap. III, 5).[8]

The most important Collection of the group is the 'Polycarpus',

---

[1] See Fournier-Le Bras, op. cit. vol. II, pp. 127–31.
[2] Fols. 34–45.　　　　　　　　　　　　　　　[3] Fols. 116a, 118a.
[4] Fol. 117a.　　　　　　　　　　　　　　　　[5] Fol. 88.
[6] *Recueil Général des Formules Usitées dans l'Empire des Francs du Ve au Xe siècles* (3 vols.; Paris, 1859–71), vol. II, form. 1024, pp. 644, 645; and K. Zeumer, *Formulae Merovingici et Karolini Aevi*, M.G.H., *Legum Sectio V*, *Formulae* (Hanover, 1886), pp. 555, 556.
[7] 'Die Kanonensammlung des Cod. Vatican. Lat. 1348', in *Sitzungsberichte der Ak. Wiss. Wien, Phil.-Hist. Kl.* (1897), vol. CXXXVI.
[8] Fol. 13a.

made by Cardinal Gregory between the years 1104 and 1106,[1] but even in this Collection texts referring to the Photian case are few. We can read there an extract from Nicholas' letter[2] to Michael and two canons of the Council of 869–70,[3] but nothing on the number of oecumenical councils.

Nor is anything relevant to our thesis or to the number of councils to be found in the second recension of 'Polycarpus', included in MS. 3882 of the Latin MS. section of the Paris National Library.

Much the same may be said of some other Collections of canon law which borrow from 'Polycarpus'. The Collection in Seven Books of the Latin MS. 1346 of the Vatican Library, which dates from the year 1112,[4] has, besides the extracts from the letter to the Emperor Michael,[5] three canons of the Eighth Council.[6]

The Collection in Three Books of the beginning of the twelfth century quotes only canon XXII.[7] Even the Prague Collection,[8] of the middle of the twelfth century, offers nothing of interest here, apart from a few quotations from letters of Nicholas I,[9] and none of these concerns the Photian case, whilst the conciliar decisions did not attract the compiler's attention.[10]

The same applies to the other local canonical Collections studied by P. Fournier-Le Bras: the Collection in Seventeen Books of the Poitiers and Rheims MSS., the Collection in Four Books of the Tarragona and the Bordeaux Collections, the Collection in Thirteen Books of the

[1] On this collection cf. P. Fournier, 'Les deux recensions de la Collection Canonique Romaine dite le Polycarpus', in *Mélanges d'Archéologie et d'Histoire* (1918–19), vol. XXXVII, pp. 55–101; ibid. pp. 58–60, where is to be found the list of MSS. of this unpublished Collection. Cf. also P. Fournier-Le Bras, loc. cit. vol. II, pp. 169–85.

[2] I have examined MS. 1354 of the Vatican Library, fol. 22 (lib. I, c. 22).

[3] Ibid. fol. 31 (lib. III) = canon XXII and fol. 63a (lib. III) = canon XVIII.

[4] P. Fournier-Le Bras, op. cit. vol. II, pp. 185–92. The same Collection has moreover been preserved in MS. 1346 of the Vienna National Library and in MS. 43 of Cortona.

[5] Vat. Lib. Lat. 1346, fols. 25a, 26a.

[6] Fol. 32a (lib. I, c. 33) = canon XXI, fol. 37 (lib. II, c. 4) = canon XXII, fol. 53 = canon XVIII. Nicholas' letter to Michael III is quoted twice = fol. 25a (lib. I, c. 11) and fol. 26a (lib. I, c. 14).

[7] Vatic. Latin. 3831, fol. 19. The letter to Michael III is quoted, fol. 60.

[8] Codex Membran. VIII H. 7. Cf. Schulte, 'Über drei in Prager Handschriften enthaltenen Canonensammlungen', in *Sitzungsberichte der Ak. Wiss. Wien, Phil.-Hist. Kl.* (1867), vol. LVII, pp. 175–221.

[9] Fols. 27a, 28, 29a, 55, 56.

[10] Fols. 15, 15a make a vague reference to the first five councils and fol. 37a to the seventh.

Arras MS. 425, the Collection in Nine Books of Saint-Victor.[1] So far I have been in a position to study only the Collections of Tarragona,[2] of Saint-Victor[3] and of Bordeaux,[4] but they offer nothing remarkable.

A certain number of Collections of the same class have unhappily remained inaccessible to me: the Collection of Lord Ashburnham's MS.,[5] the Palermo Collection of Santa Maria Novella, the Turin Collection in Seven Books, the Assisi Collection, the St Peter's Collection in Nine Books, the Gaddiana Collection, the Vatican Collection 3829 and the Turin MS. E.V. 44 (903),[6] but it appears that these Collections are of the same order as those we have been able to examine, and it is very doubtful that they would provide anything fresh, since the sources of all of them are practically the same.

Examination of the canonical Collections belonging to the first group has therefore yielded nothing new and at least we have been able to ascertain that no new element has found its way into these compilers' canonical documentation. With regard to the Photian case, we noticed also that they attributed to it no special importance and that the scant information they produce invariably derives from the same sources, namely, the canon law Collections of the first period of the Gregorian reform and, chiefly, the work of St Anselm of Lucca.

Now let us turn to the second group. The Collections of this category are more interesting, as their compilers had access to more extensive documentation. Of these Collections, the most important from our point of view is the one called *Caesaraugustana*,[7] originating, as the

---

[1] See Fournier-Le Bras, loc. cit. vol. II, pp. 230–61.

[2] Paris, Lat. 4281 B, lib. I, 47, fol. 18 *a* = canon XXII of the Council of 869–70, lib. I, 85, fol. 22 *a*, Nicholas' letter to Michael III. Fol. 187, *Incipit praefatio: canones generalium conciliorum*, enumerates the first four councils. The passage was inspired by Gregory the Great's famous letter (cf. also lib. I, ch. 173: 'de professione archiep.'—four councils).

[3] MS. 721 of the Bibliothèque de l'Arsenal. This Collection is especially disappointing for our study.

[4] MS. 11 of the Bibliothèque Municipale de Bordeaux.

[5] MS. 1554, the Laurentiana, Florence. According to Fournier-Le Bras, loc. cit. vol. II, p. 136, Ivo's famous prologue was later added to the Collection by another hand.

[6] See description of these unpublished Collections, with their bibliographical information: Fournier-Le Bras, loc. cit. vol. II, pp. 150–218.

[7] Cf. Fournier, 'Les Collections canoniques attribuées à Yves de Chartres', loc. cit. vol. LVIII, pp. 416 seq.; Fournier-Le Bras, loc. cit. vol. II, pp. 269–84, and chiefly Fournier, 'La Collection Canonique dite *Caesaraugustana*', in *Nouvelle Revue Historique de Droit Français et Étranger* (1921), vol. XLV, pp. 53 seq.

name implies, from Saragossa. Two recensions of it are known: the first dates from 1110–20, whereas the second must be anterior to 1143. In both versions of this Collection[1] it is surprising to find the extract from Ivo, condemning the Eighth Council.[2] Further on, we also find a canon of the Photian Council, which is even designated here as 'quinta synodus Constantinopolitana CCCLXXXIII patrum sub Johanne papa: "Apocrisiarii papae dixerunt...".'[3] The author of the *Caesaraugustana* has also borrowed from the Acts of the Eighth Council, quoting three canons of it,[4] where the Chartres canonist quotes only one.[5]

What is extraordinary is that the author of the *Caesaraugustana* does not reproduce in his Collection the Sovereign Pontiff's profession of faith listing the eight oecumenical Councils; all the more so, as in the first book of his Collection he treats of 'the councils to be admitted'.[6] He quotes Gelasius' letter, that of St Gregory the Great on the first four councils, some texts on the confirmation of the Sixth Council, Bede's passage on the six oecumenical councils and a few texts on the Seventh Oecumenical Council, a number of them being copied from the fourth part of Ivo's *Decretum* and showing that in preparing his compilation the author had this writing of Ivo lying on his desk. Strange, then, that he should have omitted the pontifical profession with its eight councils as well as Ivo's paragraphs purporting to prove the oecumenicity of the Eighth Council. How is this to be explained?

P. Fournier[7] once drew attention to the fact that the editor of the *Caesaraugustana* repeatedly corrected the texts produced by Ivo and rectified his quotations and references, justifying the inference that he was very judicious in his choice of texts from the *Decretum* and that he many times referred back to the originals, some of which had been inaccessible to Ivo.

The *Caesaraugustana*'s most important source is Deusdedit's Collection; here the author of the *Caesaraugustana* could find material for comparisons with certain texts of the *Decretum*, his second principal

---

[1] I have studied MS. 3875 of the Latin MS. section of the National Library containing the first recension and MS. 3876 of the same Library containing the second recension.

[2] MS. 3875, fol. 9 and MS. 3876, fol. 6a: 'Damnatio synodi Constantinopolitanae cui papa non subscripsit.'

[3] MS. 3875, fol. 70a, MS. 3876, fol. 62.

[4] Canon XXII, MS. 3875, fol. 17a, MS. 3876, fol. 14; canon XXI, MS. 3876, fol. 30; canon XV, MS. 3875, fol. 51, MS. 3876, fol. 47.

[5] *Decr.* V, 122; *Pan.* III, 8.

[6] MS. 3875, fols. 5–8, MS. 3876, fols. 2a–5a.

[7] 'Les Collections canoniques attribuées à Yves de Chartres', loc. cit. pp. 416–26.

source, and also a profession of faith of the Sovereign Pontiffs substantially differing from the one he found in Ivo.

On the strength of all we know about the working methods of the
author of the *Caesaraugustana*, we must admit that he was not without
some critical sense, and so perceived that Deusdedit's text came nearer
to the original than the fragment quoted by Ivo. Did the difference
arouse any suspicions in the author's mind about the passage concerning
the number of councils, prompting him to omit Ivo's text from his
Collection and mention only the seven councils, without probing the
puzzle any further? What makes it difficult to conjecture what the
comparison of the two texts suggested to the author is that he also
quotes three canons of the Eighth Council. Certainly he did not do
what was done by most canonists who relied on Ivo and knew nothing
of Deusdedit's Collection—he did not include the impressive passage
of the *Decretum*.

One may surmise that Ivo himself would have done the same as the
author of the *Caesaraugustana*, had he been able to lay his hand on
Deusdedit's work and to compare the text of the profession handed
down by the Cardinal with the text of the only source he knew. For
the bishop of Chartres was also possessed of some critical acumen and
would never have perpetrated the paradoxical blunder of classing this
Council among the oecumenicals, whilst copying on another page the
pontifical decision declaring the same Council null and void.

The Collection called the *Caesaraugustana* served as a model for
another canonical Collection kept in a MS. of the Naples National
Library (XII, A, 27), but unfortunately I have not seen it, and
A. Theiner's[1] description of it is too scanty to be of any value for our
purpose.

The Collection of the Saint-Germain-des-Prés Manuscript, which
to-day is to be found in Wolfenbüttel (Gud. Lat. 212) and was written
about 1120 in the region of Rheims, also bears traces of Ivo of Chartres'
influence; but Sdralek's[2] description of it is not satisfactorily complete,
except for the information that the MS. quotes a fragment of the Pope's
profession (fol. 376),[3] which agrees with the text of the *Panormia*, III, 4.
The author also copied an extract from the letter of John VIII to Basil,
announcing his intention to reinstate Photius in deference to the

---

[1] *Disquisitiones Criticae in praecipuas canonum et decretalium collectiones* (Romae,
1836), p. 76.
[2] 'Wolfenbüttler Fragmente', *Kirchengeschichtliche Studien* I, II (Münster in
Westphalia, 1891).   [3] Sdralek, loc. cit. p. 28.

Emperor's wish—a paragraph which Ivo entered in his famous prologue. There is also, in the Saint-Germain Collection, Anastasius' comment on the Eighth Council (fol. 53 a) and canon XXII of the same synod, which shows that the writer of the collection certainly knew of Photius' reinstatement.

The same may be said of another canonical Collection, called the Collection in Ten Parts, still unpublished, which is in MS. 10743 of the Paris National Library;[1] where the compiler copied the whole of Ivo of Chartres' introduction to the *Decretum* with the paragraph on Photius' reinstatement under the heading: *Tractatus de Concordantia Canonum*. It has three excerpts from the pontifical profession quoted by Ivo in the *Decretum* and in the *Panormia*, with the passage relative to the recognition of the eight councils;[2] but only its canon XXII is mentioned.[3] There are many letters of Nicholas I in the Collection, but they do not relate to the Photian case. Of the four texts attributed to John VIII, one runs as follows:[4] *Johannes papa VIII: privilegia paucorum communem legem non faciunt*. The quotation is from John's letter to Basil, as found in Ivo's preface,[5] and directly bears on Photius' rehabilitation.

The Collection in Ten Parts found its summarist and his contribution (*Summa Decretorum Haimonis*) has survived in several manuscripts.[6] It was made between 1130 and 1135. The preface has a summary of the doctrine on the interpretation of the canons mentioned in Ivo's long prologue,[7] but the passage about Photius is not quoted, though the compiler borrowed the text from the famous letter of John VIII as we find it in the prologue.[8] It contains no reference to the list of eight councils quoted in the *Liber Diurnus*.[9]

---

[1] On this MS. of the Collection see P. Fournier, 'Les Collections canoniques attribuées à Yves de Chartres', loc. cit. pp. 433 seq.; Fournier-Le Bras, loc. cit. vol. II, pp. 296 seq.

[2] L. II, d. 49, fol. 104 of MS. 10743 = *Decr.* IV, 132 (eight councils); l. III, c. 2, nn. 1, 2, fol. 134: 'Profiteor diligenter...et abdicare' = *Pan.* III, 3; 'Nihil de traditione...profiteor' = *Decr.* IV, 197.

[3] L. III, c. 7, n. 8, fol. 139 (MS. 10743). [4] L. V, c. 1, n. 9, fol. 261.

[5] *P.L.* vol. 161, col. 58: 'quoniam...Photium fratrem nostrum recipimus, sicut et Adrianus papa Tarasium, nullus computet canonicum usum. Privilegia enim paucorum communem legem non faciunt.'

[6] P. Fournier, 'Les Collections canoniques attribuées à Yves de Chartres', loc. cit. pp. 442–4; Fournier-Le Bras, loc. cit. vol. II, pp. 306–8.

[7] Bibl. Nat. Lat. 4377, fols. 3–4a; Bibl. Nat. Lat. 4286, fols. 2–3a.

[8] Bibl. Nat. Lat. 4377, fol. 37; Bibl. Nat. Lat. 4286, fol. 82.

[9] Bibl. Nat. Lat. 4286, fol. 24a, where only the extract from the *Liber Diurnus*, identical to *Pan.* III, 3, is to be found. The two MSS. (MS. 4377, fol. 23a, MS. 4286, fol. 25a) summarize canon XXII of the Eighth Council.

We should also mention another summary of the Collection in Ten Parts found in MS. 14145 of the Latin MS. section of the Paris National Library,[1] though it is no more than a fragment (fols. 9–15) containing Ivo's prologue. Whatever may come after the reference to Marcellus' case is summarized on one page (fol. 12). There is a suggestion of the Photian case in the words quoted verbatim and placed by Ivo after the extract from John VIII's letter to Basil: 'sic aliae dispensationes salubri deliberatione admissae, cessante necessitate, debent cessare.'[2]

More explicit is the author of the Collection in Sixteen Parts which I found in a MS. of the British Museum (B.M. Harleian 3090), also dating from the twelfth century. Ivo's prologue which appears on the first folios of the MS. is abbreviated, but the main points relating to the Patriarch's reinstatement are duly quoted.[3]

The Collection contains many references to the letters of Nicholas I, and even of John VIII, but none of them touches on Photius. The *Liber Diurnus* is also omitted.

I have been able to consult the unpublished Collection preserved in MS. 1361 of the Vatican Library, dating from 1133–7, which merely combines Anselm's Collection and the *Panormia*, and contains Ivo's famous prologue.[4] An examination of the Collection of Sainte-Geneviève in MS. 166 of the Paris Sainte-Geneviève Library,[5] a Collection inspired by Ivo's work, was disappointing, as it contained not a single relevant text. More interesting is the Collection of MS. 47 of the Châlons Municipal Library, in which we read (fol. 20a) the famous extract from the *Liber Diurnus* on the eight councils, canon XXII of the Eighth Council (fol. 43a), and immediately after this the canon of the Photian Council about bishops who returned to monastic life:

Ex actione quinta synodi Constantinopolitanae 383 patrum sub octavo Joanne papa cui praesiderunt Petrus presbyter cardinalis et Paulus antiochenitanus episcopus et Eugenius episcopus: Ut quicumque de pontificatu ad monachorum descenderit vitam numquam ad pontificatum resurgat.... Item praecepit sancta synodus.

[1] L. Delisle, *Inventaire des manuscrits Latins* (Paris, 1863–71), vol. I, p. 129. This part of the MS. dates from the twelfth century.

[2] Cf. *P.L.* vol. 161, col. 58.

[3] Fol. 3a: 'Sic Johannes papa octavus...et honorem patriarchatus restituamus', *P.L.* vol. 161, col. 56. The extract from the prologue ends on the same words.

[4] Cf. P. Fournier, 'Les Collections canoniques attribuées à Yves de Chartres', loc. cit. pp. 430–3; Fournier-Le Bras, loc. cit. vol. II, pp. 225 seq.

[5] P. Fournier, loc. cit.; Fournier-Le Bras, loc. cit. vol. II, pp. 265–8.

The same passages are also quoted in another Collection kept in the same library (MS. No. 75) and also dating from the twelfth century. Though the *Liber Diurnus* is not quoted, the Collection opens with Ivo's prologue and gives the whole extract on Photius' reinstatement (fols. 8, 9 *a*). In the third part of the Collection, which treats of bishops' rights, there is also the famous canon about the Patriarch of Constantinople (fol. 51): 'De honore Constantinopolitani episcopi. De synodo Constantinopolitana: Constantinopolitanae civitatis episcopum habere oportet primatus honorem post romanum episcopum propter quod sit nova Roma.'[1]

I have not yet found it possible to consult the Collection of the Chapter of St Ambrose in Milan, composed after 1100.[2]

An examination of the second group of canonical Collections, extending from the end of the eleventh to the middle of the twelfth century, led to the conclusion that the compilers of these Collections had not discovered a single new source on the Photian case and that their knowledge of the case and of the Eighth Council was derived from the same source as the information provided by the compilers of the first group; but their documentation has a wider range, since they could draw on the Collections posterior to the reform period and chiefly on the Collections attributed to Ivo of Chartres. The author of the *Caesaraugustana* also makes use of Deusdedit's work. We have thus been able to ascertain that the surprising ideas of Ivo and his circle on the Photian case, far from being the private opinions of a single man and his circle, so successfully survived the famous canonist that they came to be adopted by a great number of jurists and even, as we shall have occasion to see later, by some historians as well.

We now come to the greatest canonist of the twelfth century, Gratian. It is unnecessary to repeat here what every canonist knows: it will be enough to note that his work does not, on the whole, represent anything very new in the history of canon law. Not only did Gratian fail to discover any new sources of information, he did not even take the trouble to verify those of the canonical works which he pressed into service for his own compilation, merely contenting himself with comparing the texts, often divergent, of those Collections and placing them in order. And yet his work, known by its pompous title *Concordantia*

---

[1] P. Fournier, 'Les Collections canoniques attribuées à Yves de Chartres', loc. cit. vol. LVIII, pp. 624 seq.; Fournier-Le Bras, loc. cit. vol. II, pp. 308–13.

[2] Fournier-Le Bras, loc. cit. vol. II, pp. 222–4.

22-2

Discordantium Canonum,[1] after its publication about the year 1150 succeeded, for all its shortcomings, in driving all previous canonical Collections, including those of Anselm of Lucca, Deusdedit and Ivo, into the background. Gratian's work, to the exclusion of all others, remained in the hands of canonists, historians and theologians for the remainder of the Middle Ages down to modern times.

It is not our concern here to examine to what extent Gratian's work deserved the reputation it enjoyed throughout the Middle Ages: suffice it to state that from the second half of the twelfth century onward, Gratian's *Decretum* must be considered to have been the main source from which the Middle Ages gathered their knowledge about the councils, the Popes' decrees and even the writings of the Fathers. It will therefore further our inquiry to know what Gratian thought about the controverted councils of the ninth century and about the Photian case.

In this respect, Gratian was implicitly dependent on his predecessors, since, not being able to consult the original documents, he merely copied what Anselm of Lucca and Ivo of Chartres had chosen to leave him. It is important to remember that he did not take advantage of Deusdedit's Collection, which was only used by his correctors, so that he did not know of the complete version of the Popes' profession as handed down by the Cardinal. In fact, Gratian considered it enough to copy the fragment of the text as Ivo of Chartres had it, with its list of eight oecumenical councils.[2] As Ivo's canonical works were forced into the background by Gratian's *Decretum*, it was Gratian—not Ivo—who was primarily responsible for the fact that this fragment of the profession has ever since been considered absolutely authentic and that it has served for most theologians as the stock argument in support of the oecumenicity of the Eighth Council in the Western Church.

In Gratian's view, the extract from the Popes' profession provided the main argument in favour of the oecumenicity of the Eighth Council, so popular among the canonists of the period for its famous canon XXII, and he considered it superfluous to quote the extract from the letter of John VIII, which in Ivo's opinion served as 'evidence' that a papal

---

[1] I quote from the edition of E. Friedberg, *Corpus Juris Canonici* (Lipsiae, 1879). See also *P.G.* vol. 187.

[2] D. xvi, c. 8. Here is the correctors' remark: 'Item ex Diurno: integram professionem fidei, quando quis in Romanum Pontificem promovebatur, refert Deusdedit Cardinalis in collatione canonum, quae servatur in bibliotheca Vaticana.' They therefore omitted to state that Deusdedit mentioned no more than seven councils.

decision had classed that synod among the oecumenical councils. Faithful to his principle of 'reconciling the discordant canons', Gratian calmly suppressed Ivo's text, according to which the Eighth Council should have been considered annulled by the same Pope. From his point of view this was simply a piece of elementary logic. Consequently, Gratian extracted as much as he could from the texts of the Eighth Council,[1] which he knew only at second hand from quotations. And yet, he does not for all that esteem the Photian Council any the less, for he copies in his *Decretum* the canon of this synod (the one utilized by Ivo) on the bishops' return to monastic life.[2] In quoting this canon, he also calls the Photian Council 'the Council of Constantinople of the 383 Fathers', and elsewhere 'nona synodus'. We are here referring to the two texts of the twentieth *causa* of the *Decretum*, and both, as is well known, are misquotations. The first (C. xx, 9, 1, c. 1) is really a quotation from the rules of St Basil, chapter xv, and the second (C. xx, 9, 11, c. 4) comes from chapter viii of the same work by Basil.

But the references are doubtful and Gratian's correctors even remarked that some MSS. had 'synodus octava' instead of 'synodus nona'.[3] Whether the confusion was or was not a mistake due to slovenliness, the fact remains that the Photian Council did somehow impress Gratian.

Gratian's *Decretum* represents therefore a very important stage in the evolution of what I call 'the Photian Legend'. As he dispelled the very last lingering doubts about the oecumenicity and the authority of the Eighth Council, the hesitations we noted in Deusdedit and Ivo yielded to absolute certainty and the Popes' profession closed the debate for ever. At the same time, Gratian still shared his predecessors' opinion on the Photian case, the Photian Council being in his view a great Council, whose authority was incontestable: this makes it clear that like Ivo, his principal authority, he knew of Photius' rehabilitation by this Council.

By omitting the text quoted by Ivo on the suppression of the anti-Photian Council, Gratian did indeed 'reconcile the discordant canon'.

[1] C. XII, qu. 2, c. 13 = canon XV of the Eighth Council; C. XVI, qu. 3, c. 8 = canon XVIII; D. 22, c. 7 = canon XXI; D. 63, c. 1 = canon XX; D. 63, c. 2 = Ivo's *Decr.* V, 122; *Pan.* III, 8.

[2] C. VII, qu. 1, c. 44: 'Unde in quinta actione Constantinopolitanae sinodi 383 Patrum, sub VIII. Joanne Papa, cui praefuit Petrus presbiter cardinalis, et Paulus Anchonitanus episcopus et Eugenius Hostiensis episcopus, apocrisiarii Papae dixerunt: (C. VII, qu. 1, c. 45) "Hoc nequaquam apud nos habetur..."'; Mansi, vol. XVII, col. 504. 'Item praecepit sancta synodus' = canon II.

[3] Cf. Antonii Augustini *De Emendatione Gratiani* (*Opera omnia*, Lucae, 1767, vol. III), pp. 127 seq.

Viewing events in a better perspective than those canonists who had the Acts themselves, or long extracts from the Acts of this Council, under their very eyes, he cut the Gordian knot after his own fashion: only, by so doing, he unwittingly opened the way to a misrepresentation of the Photian case: from his time onwards the anti-Photian synod has usurped a place among the oecumenical councils, whose authority is a law unto the whole of Christendom, and this has made it only too easy to assume that whatever that Council had said against Photius must be true and that the Papacy never went back on the anathemas hurled against him by the Fathers and endorsed by Rome. The Photian Council could then be allowed quietly to slip into oblivion. The only canon of this synod quoted in the *Decretum* is of minor importance and has been seldom appealed to, since during the Middle Ages few Western bishops who returned to monastic life had any wish to resume their discarded dignity.

But it is a pity that the Photian Council did not vote some other canons of a more practical and useful nature, as this would have secured it a prominent place in the canonical legislation of the Western Middle Ages and made it difficult for the 'Photian Legend' ever to see the light.

But let us pursue our investigations and inquire how the old tradition concerning the Photian case, a tradition which Gratian still knew and respected, ever came to be forgotten in the West. First of all, to remain within the limits of canon law, we shall confine ourselves to Gratian's most important commentators of the second half of the twelfth century: Pancapalea, Rolandus, Rufinus and Stephen of Tournay, whose *Summae* provide all canonical activity for the rest of the Middle Ages with its main basis and authority. As Gratian's *Decretum* was destined to become the common starting-point, it will suffice to examine how those canonists commented on the passages of the *Decretum* that bear on our subject-matter.

Pancapalea's *Summa* reveals nothing interesting,[1] and the short commentaries that accompany the passages of the *Decretum* we are considering are totally irrelevant. The same is true of Master Rolandus' *Summa*.[2] In the introduction to his book, Stephen of Tournay writes

[1] J. F. v. Schulte, *Die Summa des Pancapalea über das Decretum Gratiani* (Giessen, 1890; written between 1144 and 1150), pp. 18, 19, 21, 39, 74, 80, 87.
[2] F. Thaner, *Die Summa Magistri Rolandi, nachmals Papstes Alexander III* (Innsbruck, 1874), pp. 6, 9, 23, 46, 47.

about the oecumenical councils and insists on the first four of them, but his comments on Gratian's dicta that are of interest to us have no historical value.[1] The same criticism holds for Rufinus' *Summa*.[2] It is the commentaries which those jurists offer, for instance, on the *Liber Diurnus*, that make it clear how hopelessly unfamiliar they were with the original sources and how they gradually lost all insight into the historical implications of the documents they handled. Here is Pancapalea's misinterpretation of the *Liber Diurnus*:[3] 'Item ex libro diurno, prof. R. potest intelligi beati Gregorii registro.' Stephen writes:[4] 'Liber Diurnus dicitur, qui vel una die factus est vel una die totus legi potest.' More curious still is Rufinus' comment:[5]

Ex L.D., i.e. illo historico libro, in quo de unius diei tantum gestis agitur. Ut enim ait Isidorus in libro etimilogiarum: triplex historiarum genus est, annales, kalendaria et ephemeria. Annales, ubi agitur de rebus singulorum annorum; kalendaria appellantur, quae in menses singulos digeruntur; ephemeris dicitur de unius diei gestis. Hoc apud nos diarium sive diurnum vocatur. Namque latini diurnum, graeci ephemerida dicunt.

It is evidently hopeless to seek in these 'definitions' any remnants of a critical and historical sense.

Useless also to look for anything more definite in John Faventinus, who published a *Summa* on the *Decretum* after the year 1171. His work rests entirely on the *Summae* of Rufinus and Stephen of Tournay,[6] though it is well known that John's performance obtained a wider circulation than, and even supplanted, the works of his forerunners.

As for the canonists of the thirteenth century, their writings offer nothing interesting on the subject; it is, moreover, common knowledge that after the publication of the Gregorian Decretals the canonists' interest shifted mainly to this new source of canon law,[7] and that the study of the *Decretum* was consequently abandoned. Among the canonists who continued to study the *Decretum*, we must cite John Semeca, *alias* Joannes Teutonicus, who wrote his glosses about 1220;[8]

---

[1] J. F. v. Schulte, *Die Summa des Stephanus Tornacensis* (Giessen, 1891), pp. 2, 25, 26 (eight councils), 32, 89, 205, 206, 214–16, 222–9.

[2] H. Singer, *Die Summa Decretorum des Magister Rufinus* (Paderborn, 1902), pp. 37, 38, 49, 154, 155, 285–95, 325, 363.

[3] Loc. cit. p. 19.   [4] Loc. cit. p. 26.

[5] Loc. cit. (ed. Singer), pp. 37, 38.

[6] J. F. v. Schulte, *Die Geschichte der Quellen u. Litt. d. can. Rechts* (Stuttgart, 1875), vol. I, pp. 137 seq.

[7] Cf. A. Tardif, *Histoire des Sources du Droit Canon.* (Paris, 1887), p. 186.

[8] Schulte, loc. cit. vol. I, pp. 172 seq.

Bartholomaeus Brixensis, a professor in Bologna, who died in 1258,[1] and Guido de Baysio, also called Archidiaconus, belonging to the end of the thirteenth and the beginning of the fourteenth century.[2] While John Teutonicus, in commenting on the passages that concern us, generally limits himself to the notes of his forerunners, Bartholomew somewhat expands his commentary on Ignatius' deposition and on Photinus' (sic) elevation—one of many indications that the Photian Legend is gradually taking root among the scholars of the period.[3]

In reading the meagre comments on canon II of the Photian Council (C. VII, qu. I, c. 45), it does not take one long to perceive that the canonists have by this time completely lost sight of the history of the Council, being at a loss where to place it and how it came to be summoned. A striking illustration of their embarrassment is afforded by the greatest Pope of that time, Innocent III, who in his letter written in 1208 to bishop Hubaldus, newly elected archbishop of Ravenna, actually said:[4]

Verum postulationi hujusmodi videbatur concilii Constantinopolitani capitulum prima facie obviare, in quo statutum esse dignoscitur ut quicumque de pontificali dignitate ad monachorum vitam et poenitentiae locum descenderit, nequaquam ulterius ad pontificatum resurgat. Unde *contra dictum concilium, cum sit unum ex quatuor principalibus, quae sicut quatuor evangelia catholica Ecclesia veneratur*, nullatenus videbatur eadem postulatio admittenda....

---

[1] Schulte, loc. cit. vol. II, pp. 83–6.

[2] Ibid. vol. II, pp. 186 seq.: 'Rosarium super Decreto.'

[3] I have used the 1772 edition of John Fenton and the Venice edition of 1495 of the Archdeacon. We may quote here, according to the Venice edition (1514) of the *Decretum Gratiani*, which includes all the glosses of our three authors, some comments by Bartholomew on Ignatius: 'P. 105 (Ad. D. LXIII, c. 1) Ignatius patr. Const. injuste fuit depositus et Fotinus [!] loco eius substitutus. Quam prohibitionem Nicolaus voluit removere sed morte preventus non potuit. Sed Hadrianus, successor eius, misit nuntios tres in C/polim ad Basilium imperatorem et filios eius, cum quibus fuit cancellarius romanae sedis. Et ibi octava syn. congregata duo fecit: primo Fotinum [!] deposuit et Ignatium restituit. Secundo constituit ut clericorum sit electio....P. 155a (Ad. D. XCVI, c. 7 = letter from Nicholas to Michael III): Ostendit hic Nicolas quod Ignatius ratione Michaelis imperatoris deponi non potuit et hoc probat duobus exemplis....P. 201a (Ad. C. IV, qu. 1, c. 2): Ignatius patriarcha Const. anathematizavit quosdam subditos suos qui eumdem Ignatium postea accusaverunt ad quorum accusationem depositus fuit. Sed Nicolas probat, quod anathematizati eum accusare non potuerunt. Et hoc ostendit auctoritate concilii C/politani in quo statuit quod heretici a sacris electi, etc....'

[4] *P.L.* vol. 215, ep. 249, col. 1553, cf. col. 1592.

Innocent III evidently had only the vaguest notion about the Photian case, and his opinion on this Council was probably shared by several of his contemporaries.

With regard to the canonists of the fourteenth century, it is almost useless to look in their works for anything pertaining to our topic, although the Western Schism let loose a flood of polemico-juridical writings for and against Urban; but their authors drew most of their arguments from recent legislation and neglected the *Decretum* and the decisions of the oecumenical councils, as these did not provide suitable material for their controversies. The same is true of other writings of the same class at that time, when we only find a few vague references to the eight councils in Gulielmus Durandus junior,[1] but nothing in Nicholas de Clémanges,[2] John Carlerius de Gerson,[3] John of Paris,[4] Marsilius of Padua,[5] Augustinus Triumphus of Ancona,[6] to mention only such writers as one might expect to yield such information. William of Ockham[7] alone has a few references, insignificant though they be, to Gratian's *Decretum*.

It is curious to observe that in the controversies between Greeks and Latins during the twelfth and thirteenth centuries, very little was said about Photius and the number of councils. Thus, for instance, Anselm of Havelberg,[8] in his 'disputatio' with Nechites (Nicetas) in Constantinople in 1135, does not even mention Photius, though he argues about the procession of the Holy Ghost, the primacy and the Azymes, in fact about every problem that was once raised by Photius. Nor does his opponent father these differences on the unfortunate Patriarch, but rather presents them as topics of controversy that had always existed.

[1] *Tractatus de Modo Generalis Concilii Celebrandi* (Paris, 1671), pars I, tit. II, p. 8.

[2] *De corrupto Ecclesiae statu*, ibid.

[3] *Tractatus de Potestate Ecclesiastica*, M. Goldast, *Monarchia S.R.I.* (Harroviae, 1611–14), vol. II, pp. 1384–1404 and the other writings by the same author, ibid. pp. 1425–1526. See also Gerson, *Opera Omnia*, Paris (1606), vol. I, pp. 110–45.

[4] *Tractatus de Potestate Regia et Papali*, ibid. vol. II, pp. 108–47.

[5] *Tractatus de Translatione Imperii*, ibid. pp. 147–53; *Defensor Pacis*, ibid. pp. 154–312.

[6] *Summa de Ecclesiastica Potestate* (Coloniae Agrip. 1475).

[7] *Octo Quaestionum Decisiones super Potestate Summi Pontificis*, Goldast, loc. cit. vol. II, pp. 313–46 (nothing); *Dialogus de Potestate Imperatoris*, ibid. pp. 469, 645, 936. Cf. L. Baudry, *Guillelmi de Occam Breviloquium de potestate Papae* (Paris, 1937). At the end of this treatise Occam expresses doubts concerning the authenticity of the *Donatio Constantini*.

[8] Dialogi, *P.L.* vol. 188, cols. 1139–1248. The dialogues were written fourteen years after the controversy had subsided. Cf. J. Dräseke, 'Bischof Anselm von Havelberg', in *Zeitschrift für Kirchengeschichte*, vol. XXI, pp. 160–85.

In regard to the number of councils, Anselm still follows the old Western tradition and mentions only six councils.[1]

Another theological work that might be relevant to our problem is the treatise of Brother Bonacursius of Bologna, found, with a Greek translation, in a MS. of the Paris National Library:[2] but it is a scholastic treatise, which totally disregards the historical evolution of the schism, never mentions Photius and never raises the question of the number of councils.

Only one ecclesiastical and canonical writer of this period treats of the councils with more freedom—Humbertus de Romanis, who in 1273 issued a memoir for the use of the second Council of Lyons. In the second part of his *Opusculum Tripartitum*, Humbert devotes several chapters to the Greek schism, yet refers to the councils only once.[3] In reviewing the Greeks' objection against the supreme power of Rome, he states among other things that, according to the Greeks, the very fact that the first seven councils met in the East proves that in the earlier days of the Church the supreme power belonged to the Orientals. The curious thing is that Humbert is in no way alarmed by the mention of seven councils and does not feel tempted to add the eighth. Elsewhere, Humbert recapitulates certain causes of the schism as well as the liturgical and disciplinary differences between the two Churches, but nowhere does he mention Photius, though he had some knowledge of a misunderstanding in the ninth century; but in his opinion it was over nothing but the Bulgarians' baptism.[4]

Hugo Etherianus, another Latin controversialist, is far more provocative. In 1177 Hugo sent to Pope Alexander III a book on the Greek errors, in which he already fathers the Greek doctrine about the Holy Ghost on Photius and apostrophizes him in one place in a passionate plea.[5] More significant still is another work against the Greeks, which may, it appears, be attributed to Hugh, or better still, to his brother

---

[1] Dialogi, *P.L.* vol. 188, cols. 1225–8.

[2] Cod. Paris. Gr. 1251, fourteenth-century on parchment, fol. 145. Cf. B. Altaner, 'Kenntnisse des Griechischen in den Missionsorden während des 13 u. 14 Jh.', in *Zeitschrift für Kirchengeschichte* (1934), vol. LIII, pp. 457, 471.

[3] Ed. Crabbe, *Concilia Omnia...* (Coloniae, 1551), vol. II, pp. 990, 991, c. 3.

[4] Ibid. c. 12, 18, pp. 993, 998. About Humbert, see F. Heintke, 'Humbert von Romans, der fünfte Ordensmeister der Dominikaner', in *Histor. Studien*, Heft 222 (Berlin, 1933). Cf. also Karl Michel, *Das Opus Tripartitum d. Humbertus des Romans*, 2. umgearb. Aufl. (Graz, 1926). Cf. B. Altaner, 'Kenntnisse des Griechischen...', loc. cit. p. 446.

[5] De Haeresibus Graecorum, *P.L.* vol. 202, lib. II, cc. 15–18, cols. 322–6; c. 19, cols. 328, 334, lib. III, c. 15, col. 370.

Leo Tuscus.[1] It has a reference to the general councils as admitted by the Greeks. After enumerating the seven councils, the writer adds:[2]

It should also be stated that besides these seven universal Councils there was another, universal indeed, but as it did not deal with any articles of faith, it is not numbered by the ancient Greeks among the universal Councils, but only among those called Local. But the modern Greeks, being schismatics, have excluded it from all Councils and refuse to hear of it, because it was at that synod that their Patriarch Photius, the heresiarch, was once deprived of his patriarchal dignity which he had illegally usurped....[3]

That is how a Western scholar of the twelfth century tried to reconcile the Greek and Latin attitudes on the number of councils. Leo Tuscus, the probable author of this extract (or his brother Hugh), was well aware that according to Gratian, whose authority he, like everyone else, accepted, there were eight oecumenical councils. But in Constantinople, where the brothers arrived under Manuel Comnenus, no more than seven councils were admitted. As the Emperor's interpreter, Leo had many opportunities for getting entry into the city's libraries, and Hugh himself writes in his book that he devoted all his leisure hours in Constantinople to a search for Greek and Latin theological books.[4]

That was how they succeeded in discovering the notorious anti-Photianist Collection, which gave them the clue they were seeking, the summary of the Acts of the Eighth Council, prefaced by the life of Ignatius and written by the Paphlagonian. Armed with this document, they erected to their own satisfaction the hypothesis that the Greeks once acknowledged the Eighth Council, although their canonists did not class it among the oecumenical councils, numbering it instead

[1] R. Lechat, 'La patristique Grecque chez un théologien Latin du XIIe siècle, Hugues Ethérien', in *Mélanges d'Histoire offerts à Ch. Moeller* (Louvain, 1914; Recueil de Travaux de l'Université de Louvain, V, 40), pp. 492 seq. Cf. Hergenröther, *Photius*, vol. III, pp. 175 seq.

[2] J. Basnage, *Thesaurus Monumentorum Ecclesiast. et Hist. sive Henrici Canisii Lectiones Antiquae* (Antverpiae, 1725), vol. IV, p. 1. Cf. *P.G.* vol. 140, cols. 487 seq.: *Tractatus Contra Errores Graecorum*, composed by Dominicans in Constantinople (1252), attributed wrongly to Pantelemon and followed, cols. 541 seq., by extracts from Etherianus. The passage in question, col. 557.

[3] 'Dicendum quoque, praeter istas septem universales synodos, fuit et una alia, universalis quidem: sed quia non agit de articulis fidei, non ponitur in numero universalium synodorum ab antiquis Graecis, sed inter alias quae locales nominantur. Moderni vero Graeci, schismatici cum sint, ab omni numero illam excluserunt, et nomen eius audire subticuerunt, eo quod eorum patriarcha Photius, Heresiarcha, fuit in ipsa dignitate patriarchali, quam sibi injuste usurpaverat, nuper destitutus.'

[4] Loc. cit. *P.L.* vol. 202, col. 230.

among their local councils, as it had issued no dogmatic decision. But since the time the Greeks had become schismatics, they had decided to discard this council altogether, since Photius' condemnation was contained in its Acts.

This is the first time we come across Nicetas' notorious pamphlet about Photius in the Latin tradition. Its discovery produced on the Westerners the impression one might have expected and naturally affected their attitude to the authenticity of the Photian Council, for we read farther down in the same book, after the list of the local synods endorsed by the Greeks:[1]

But the Patriarch Photius, who was a heresiarch, held two Councils in succession in the City of Constantinople. The first in the church of the Holy Apostles, and the other, which was sanctioned by Pope John, as they assert, in the church of St Sophia....But the synod of Photius, which, as they insist, Pope John approved, made 17 canons, the last of which seems to be very favourable to the Latins.

To any reader of Nicetas' pamphlet, which could only confirm a twelfth-century Westerner in his conviction that the Eighth Council was really oecumenical, it must have been evident that the author could scarcely admit the Photian Council to have been sanctioned by a Pope, as the Greeks pretended.

The chief interest of the production lies in its being merely a translation of a Greek treatise on the councils. The Greek original seems to have been related to the group represented by the treatises of the Paris. Graec. 1335, Paris. Graec. 425.[2] The translation is literal, only a few passages having been added; but the seventeen canons mentioned were not voted, as the translator asserts, by the Council of 879–80, but by the Photianist Council of 861.[3]

The treatise against the Greeks,[4] written in 1252 in Constantinople by the Dominican Brothers, also discovers in Photius the principal author of the schism and (it is alleged) Michael Cerularius—the treatise calls him Circularios!—only follows his example in his revolt against the Pope.

The treatise supports the Pope's primacy with many arguments and the spurious *Donatio Constantini* is given pride of place—and no wonder, since no one in the West was in the least doubt about the authenticity

[1] Loc. cit. p. 73. Cf. *P.G.* vol. 140, col. 559.

[2] See Appendix III, pp. 452 seq.

[3] Mansi, vol. XVI, col. 548. Canon XVII forbids the election of a layman to the episcopacy.

[4] Basnage, loc. cit. vol. IV, pp. 50, 60–2. Cf. *P.G.* vol. 140, col. 540.

of this document. This sort of 'argument' must, however, have made a curious impression on the Greeks. The Dominicans certainly knew of the writings of Hugh in their Latin, and perhaps also in their Greek, edition, so that they may have felt his influence, although we find no other instance of Hugh's (or his brother's) writings exercising such fascination on his contemporaries.

We should also mention the controversies between Cardinal Benedict, legate of the Pope Innocent III, and the Greeks in 1205 in Thessalonica, Athens and Constantinople. Nicholas of Otranto, who acted as his interpreter, summarized the discussions and published them in Greek and in Latin; unfortunately, I have been unable to gain access to the edition of the three discussions made by the Metropolitan Arsenii after a Greek MS. of the Moscow Synodal Library. But I found in the Paris National Library a MS. written in Greek and in Latin, which has the discussions as they were reported by Nicholas of Otranto. This interesting MS. (Paris. Graec. Suppl. 1232) is mainly a palimpsest, but partly written on parchment and bombycine material (165 fols.); it is, moreover, contemporary, being written in the thirteenth century. It certainly looks more interesting than the copies of Moscow and Florence, as described by Baudinus in his *Catalogus Codic. Manuscript. Biblioth. Laur.* (vol. 1, pp. 60 seq.).

Fols. 1–12 have a dialogue on the procession of the Holy Ghost; fols. 12–14, an 'Opusculum de Barbis'; fols. 15–165, a synopsis of discussions on the Holy Ghost, the Azymes and some other controversial points that divided the Greeks and the Latins, and fols. 25 a, 26, a history of these discussions, which deserve a study to themselves. Arguments are freely drawn from conciliar decrees (chiefly fols. 28 a– 38 a), and it is surprising to read the cardinal's emphatic declaration (fol. 38): 'facta est tunc et septima synodus, quae a nobis Latinis non tenetur'; a sure sign that the Franks' disbelief in the Seventh Council prevailed among some people as late as the thirteenth century. Photius is mentioned, as his arguments against the *Filioque* were turned to account by the Greeks (fol. 64), but there is no reference to the Eighth Council. The discussion certainly makes it evident that the Greeks of the time admitted no more than seven oecumenical councils.[1]

The theological writings between the twelfth and fourteenth centuries I have been able to consult tell us nothing definite about either councils or Photius. Thus, for instance, Petrus Abelardus[2] does not

[1] Cf. about Nicholas and Cardinal Benedict, W. Norden, *Das Papsttum und Byzanz* (Berlin, 1903), pp. 182 seq. [2] *P.L.* vol. 178, cols. 105–8, 375, 376.

even mention the councils in his *Confession*, nor does St Bruno;[1] St Bruno de Segui, in his reply to abbot Leo of St Mary's in Byzantium on the affair of the Azymes, written between 1107 and 1111, mentions neither councils nor Photius;[2] St Bernard[3] only speaks of the four councils and his example is followed by Hugh de Saint Victor;[4] all these authors dealt with Greek errors and in their controversies with the Greeks never referred to Photius as the author of that heresy.

The same may be said about the conciliar documents. Paschal II,[5] in his profession of faith at the Council of the Lateran (1112), only mentions the first four Councils, in accordance with the old and fast-declining usage; and the Acts of the Council of Lyons of 1274 have nothing to say about the Photian incident.

There is no mention of Photius either in the letters of Pope John XIV to the Emperor and to the Patriarch, or in the Emperor's reply to the Pope;[6] and the Emperor's profession refers to the councils only in general terms.[7] The oath taken in the Emperor's name by the Logothete George Acropolites has no reference to the councils, nor has the profession of faith imposed on the Greek Metropolitans.[8] Nothing in the letter from the Patriarch John Beccos to the Pope, though it has the Patriarch's profession of faith;[9] and nothing in the Acts of the Synod of Constantinople held about 1280,[10] in which John Beccos proved that the opponents of the Union had tampered with Gregory of Nyssa's text on the Procession of the Holy Ghost. The Council of the Armenians for union with Rome says nothing about the number of oecumenical councils and mainly emphasizes the Council of Chalcedon, which is only natural;[11] but the point is interesting, as the Greeks acted quite differently on a similar occasion, when one of the conditions they imposed on the Armenians who wished to unite with them was the recognition of the Fifth, Sixth and Seventh Councils. Such lack of veneration—if we may put it so—for ecclesiastical tradition, observed at least to some extent in the Acts of the Council, was characteristic of the new theological method in the West, where scholasticism favoured

---

[1] *P.L.* vol. 153, cols. 571–2.   [2] *P.L.* vol. 165, cols. 1087–90.

[3] Epist. 194, Rescriptum D. Innoc. papae contra Haereses Petri Abel., *P.L.* vol. 182, col. 360.

[4] Eruditiones Didascalicae Libri Septem, *P.L.* vol. 176, cols. 785 seq.

[5] *P.L.* vol. 163, cols. 471 seq.   [6] Mansi, vol. XXIV, cols. 37–136.

[7] Loc. cit. col. 72.   [8] Loc. cit. cols. 73–7.

[9] Loc. cit. cols. 183–90.   [10] Ibid. cols. 365–74.

[11] Mansi, vol. XXV, cols. 1185–1270. Cf. also the decisions of the synod of Melfi (1284) (Mansi, vol. XXIV, cols. 569 seq.) purporting to regulate relations between Greeks and Latins in Sicily. There the question of councils is not even hinted at.

theological speculation rather than the historic method. Scholastic theologians also concentrated their efforts on the definition of the Catholic doctrine of the sacraments,[1] a section of Catholic dogma to which the first councils had given least attention. Even the prince of scholastic theologians, St Thomas Aquinas, disregards the historic method and in discussing the Procession of the Holy Spirit and the Greek errors limits himself to theological speculation[2] and ignores the origin of the errors he desires to confute.

One document, issued by the Papal Chancellery, reflects the vague notions that were current in the thirteenth century on Photius' responsibility for the Oriental schism. In his letter of 14 September 1267, to the deans, chapters and suffragans of Sens, Pope Clement IV writes:[3]

> Ancient and authentic writings attribute this schism to a certain incumbent of the see of Constantinople. Stripped of his patriarchal dignity by a fair sentence of the Holy See, he gave so many signs of sorrow, devotion and reform after the death of his substitute that the Holy See graciously restored him to favour, or rather allowed him to resume his patriarchal functions. Eventually he proved ungrateful for the favour, regarded as injustice the justice of his deposition, raised heresies that had been condemned and provoked schisms, seduced the emperor of Constantinople and thus was the cause of the schism.

It shows what hazy notions about the history of Photius were current in the West in the thirteenth century and what little importance was attached to his person, since the Pope did not even know his name. The Photian Legend, making Photius responsible for the Eastern schism, was growing. However, the Pope apparently knew nothing about a second condemnation of Photius by Rome, or at least, says nothing about it.

The examination of the main theological writings, which could have been expected to deal with our problem, has shown that remembrance of Photius' rehabilitation was gradually receding into the background

---

[1] A classical instance of the method, as used by local synods, too, is found in the Acts of the Council of Lavaur (in the Tarn), summoned in 1368 by the archbishop of Narbonne. We read there (Mansi, vol. XXVI, cols. 484–93) a lengthy exposition of the Catholic faith—the Blessed Trinity, the sacraments, the theological virtues, sin, etc.—made with full array of scholastic erudition, yet not a word about the general councils and their number.

[2] *Summa Theol.* qu. XXXVI, art. I–IV (Rome ed. 1888), vol. IV, pp. 375–86. Cf. 'Contra Errores Graecorum' and F. Reusch, 'Die Fälschungen in dem Tractat des Thomas von Aquin gegen die Griechen', in *Abh. Hist. Kl. bayr. Akad.* (1889), Bd XVIII.

[3] E. Jordan, 'Les Régistres de Clément IV', in *Bibl. des Écoles Franç. d'Athènes et de Rome* (Paris, 1893), série II, vol. XI, p. 203.

with the Western theologians of the twelfth, thirteenth and fourteenth centuries and that the authority of the Photian Council, which was still respected in Gratian's time, was almost forgotten. Still, this does not mean that the tradition so carefully fostered by Ivo and his jurists till Gratian's days was completely lost. Ivo's writings, chiefly his introduction to the *Decretum*, though supplanted by Gratian, never lost credit entirely.[1]

It was saved at this period by some historians who were gifted with a finer flair than Gratian's interpreters. The first was the Dominican Martinus Opaviensis (1278), mistakenly called—for he was really of Czech origin—Polonus. Martin of Opava was at the same time a good canonist and in his *Margarita Decreti*, which proved so popular in the Middle Ages, he included—of course with Gratian—the Eight Councils.[2] In his Chronicle he also came, as stated before, under Bonizo's influence, but in another place he speaks of the Fifth Council of Constantinople of the 383 Fathers.[3] It is true he does not specifically mention Photius' rehabilitation, but on the other hand he does not refer to his excommunication by Nicholas.

Martinus Polonus' example is followed by Ptolemaeus Lucensis (1327) in his *Historia Ecclesiastica*.[4]

Another important reference to the Photian case is found in the interpolation of the Chronicle of the monk Albrich (d. after 1252),[5]

[1] An indirect hint of his introduction is found in an anonymous writing of about 1111, in the course of the struggle against lay Investiture (Sdralek, 'Wolfenbüttler Fragmente', in *Kirchengeschichtl. Studien*, 1, 2 (Münster i. W. 1891), p. 5; Abschnitt, p. 151). In order to prove to the 'Nicholaites' that they could not appeal to the fact that the Pope had sometimes granted dispensation from celibacy, the author quotes the same case as Ivo, Pope Gregory I's dispensation to the English clergy, using terms reminiscent of Ivo (*P.L.* vol. 161, col. 58). The illustration is, however, not convincing.

[2] *Decr.* XVI. '*Margarita Decreti*' *seu Tabula Martiniana, edita per fratrem Martinum* (ed. Peter Drach, Spire, 1490 (?)), p. 10.

[3] *M.G.H.* Ss. XXII, p. 429: 'Sub hoc [Johannes VIII] celebrata fuit V. synodus C/poli 383 patrum, cui praefuit Petrus presbiter cardinalis et Paulus Antiochenus episcopus et Eugenius Hostiensis episcopus, apocrisiarii papae.'

[4] *Historia Ecclesiastica*, Muratori, Ss. R. I., vol. XI, p. 1019 (c. XXI): 'Sub hoc etiam Johanne papa, ut Martinus scribit, celebrata est Synodus in C/poli 383 patrum, cui praefuit Petrus presbyter cardinalis, et Paulus Antiochenus episcopus et Eugenius Ostiensis episcopus, et apocrisiarius Domini Papae.'

[5] Chronica Albrici monachi Trium Fontium a monacho Hoiensi interpolata, *M.G.H.* Ss. XXIII, p. 740. 'Ad. ann. 870: Secundum quosdam octava synodus celebrata est hoc anno. Vide in Gratiano dist. 63. Sine dubio ista octava synodus congregata fuit in urbe C/poli et in auctoritatem recipitur, sed post istam nulla Greca sinodus a Latinis recipitur.' The first clause is from the Chronicle of the monk Helinandus (d. 1277), *P.L.* vol. 212, col. 868.

where the writer treats first of the Council of 869 and quotes Gratian's *Decretum* as his source. About the Photian Council he writes:[1]

Idem papa Joannes patriarcham Constantinopolitanum nomine Photium neophitum a papa Nicolao quondam depositum in sede sua restituit, interventu Basilii imperatoris et filiorum ejus Leonis et Alexandri, sicut in libro qui Canones inscribitur plenius continetur. Idem Joannes papa regi Bulgarorum Michaeli nomine scripsisse in eodem codice invenitur.

Mention of the Fifth Council of Constantinople also occurs in *Flores Temporum*,[2] again under Martinus' inspiration.

Lastly, in the fourteenth century, we obtain from Dandolo[3] fuller information on the excommunication of Michael III (!) as a result of Ignatius' deposition, and about the Councils of 869–70 and 879–80, the same writer being also the first to point out the disagreement on this subject between the Latins and the Greeks. Writers living far away from regions like Venice, where Greek and Latin interests crossed and clashed, were not aware of this difference.

Writing about the Eighth Council, Dandolo adds: 'Hanc synodum Graeci inter generales non accipiunt quia in ea de articulis fidei non est actum, et etiam propter Photii depositionem.' This is what he writes about the Photian Council: 'Sub isto [Joanne VIII] celebrata est synodus Constantinopoli 383 patrum, cui praefuit Petrus, et Paulus Antiochensis episcopus et Eugenius episcopus Ostiensis, papae apocrisiarius. Photius enim patriarcha prius ibi duo concilia celebraverat.'

Thus we reach the conclusion that between the twelfth and the fourteenth centuries any just estimate of the Photian incident was beginning to disappear, although there are some historians who have a modicum of knowledge not only of the existence, but also of the validity of the Fifth Council of Constantinople. It goes without saying that even at this period absolutely nothing was known of Photius' second excommunication.

---

[1] Ibid. p. 742 ad ann. 881.

[2] *Flores Temporum. Pontifices. M.G.H.* Ss. XXIV, p. 244: 'Johannes VIII sedit annos 10. Constituit ut nullus iudex secularis placita secularia tractet in edibus consecratis. Item quod ibi non hospitentur nisi ex Grecia. Sub isto fuit quinta synodus C/politana.' The author of the Chronicle was a Minorite of Suabia who wrote between 1292 and 1294.

[3] Muratori, Ss. R. I., vol. XII, l. VIII, c. IV, pars XL, col. 181, c. V, part. XI, XVI, cols. 184, 185. On Dandolo's sources, see H. Simonsfeld, *Andreas Dandolo u. seine Geschichtswerke* (München, 1876), pp. 54 seq.

CHAPTER IV

FIFTEENTH CENTURY TILL THE MODERN PERIOD

The Eighth Council among opponents and supporters—Sixteenth-century writers—The *Centuriae*—Baronius' *Annals*—Catholic and Protestant writers of the eighteenth century—Hergenröther and his school.

THE fifteenth century ushered in a new period of conciliar tradition: it was the century of the great Western Schism, which was responsible for the 'conciliar notion' or the primacy of the councils over the Popes. It was natural that in this century a new fashion for the first councils, including the Eighth Oecumenical Synod, should be introduced.

To turn first to the Acts of the Councils of Constance and Basle, it is well known that the Council of Constance again, and this time officially, fixed the number of oecumenical councils, when the conciliar commission charged with the task of formulating reforms rediscovered the notorious profession of faith of Bonifice VIII and advised the revival of this pious custom in the ceremonial of papal elections.[1] The Council agreed to the proposal, and in its thirty-ninth session the Fathers drew up a new profession of faith for the Pope, after the pattern of the so-called profession of Boniface VIII.[2] For the first time since the end of the

---

[1] Mansi, vol. XXVIII, document 31, cols. 268–70: 'Avisamenta per XXXV cardinales, praelatos et doctores, in loco reformatorii Constantiensis.' Cf. Finke, *Acta Concilii Constantiensis* (Münster i. W. 1923), vol. II, pp. 616, 618, 621.

[2] Mansi, vol. XXVII, col. 1161: 'Forma de professione Papae facienda. Quanto Romanus Pontifex eminentiori inter mortales fungitur potestate, tanto clarioribus ipsum decet fulciri fidei vinculis, et Sacramentorum ecclesiasticorum observandis ritibus illigari: Eapropter, ut in futurum Romanis Pontificibus in suae creationis primordiis et singulari splendore luceat plena fides, statuimus et ordinamus, quod deinceps quilibet in Romanum Pontificem eligendus, antequam sua electio publicetur, coram suis electoribus publice confessionem et professionem faciat infrascriptam: In nomine sanctae et individuae Trinitatis, Patris et Filii et Spiritus Sancti, Amen. Anno a nativitate Domini millesimo etc. ego N. electus in Papam, omnipotenti Deo, cuius Ecclesiam suo praesidio regendam suscipio, et beato Petro Apostolorum Principi corde et ore profiteor, quamdiu in hac fragili vita constitutus fuero, me firmiter credere, et tenere sanctam fidem catholicam, secundum traditionem Apostolorum, generalium Conciliorum et aliorum sanctorum patrum, maxime autem sanctorum octo Conciliorum universalium, videlicet primi Nicaeae, secundi Constantinopolitani, tertii Ephesini, quarti Chalcedonensis, quinti et sexti Constantinopolitanorum, septimi item Nicaeni, octavi quoque Constantinopolitani, nec non Lateranensis, Lugdunensis et Viennensis generalium etiam Conciliorum. Et illam fidem usque ad unum apicem immutilatam servare et usque ad animam

ninth century the number of oecumenical councils was officially determined, those of the Lateran, Lyons and Vienne being added to the first eight councils; but the fathers of Constance did not take their inspiration from the original formula of the Popes' profession of faith, but from the spurious profession of Boniface.

That is how the famous Popes' profession reappeared, this time with 'an anti-papal flavour', illustrating the manner in which the Fathers of Constance revived the custom. This tendency took shape at the Council of Basle, which in its second stage is known to have bodily joined the opposition, the profession of faith which it imposed on its Pope Felix V being inspired by the conciliar notion of the council being above the Pope.[1]

One would have expected this Council to rehearse the arguments in support of its opinions[2] by taking fuller advantage of the Acts of the first councils, instead of leaving it to some jurists and theologians, sectarian partisans of the conciliar notion, to do it on their own account. A few of these may be quoted. Peter d'Ailly, to prove that the Pope's supreme power may be restricted by the authority of the oecumenical council 'ad excludendum abusum', quotes, among other things, the ancient usage of exacting from the Pope a profession of orthodox faith. He writes:[3] 'Ideo antiquo iure institutum est, quod papa professionem faceret...et eiusmodi professio per lapsum temporis ampliata est, ut patet ex professione Bonifacii VIII....' And later,[4] he quotes in support of his contention such phrases used by the councils as 'Placuit sacro concilio; concilium deffinit', etc.

Pope Gregory VII then clearly scented the danger which this practice

et sanguinem confirmare, defensare et praedicare, ritum quoque pariter Sacramentorum ecclesiasticorum Catholicae Ecclesiae traditum, omnimode prosequi et observare. Hanc autem professionem et confessionem S.R.E. me jubente scriptam, propria manu subscripsi, et tibi omnipotenti Deo pura mente et devota conscientia super tali altari etc. sinceriter offero in praesentia talium, etc. Datum, etc.'

[1] Mansi, vol. XXIX, sessions 29, 32, cols. 112, 113, 189; session 40, cols. 202, 203. Cf. the footnote below.

[2] Only a few references to the Councils of Nicaea and Chalcedon are found in the Acts (J. Haller, *Concilium Basiliense* (Basel, 1896), vol. I, p. 185; (1900), vol. III, pp. 500 seq.; (1903), vol. IV, p. 299; (1914, G. Beckmann, R. Wackernagel), vol. V, p. 232; (1926, G. Beckmann), vol. VI, p. 366. The Pope's profession (1910, H. Herre), vol. VII, pp. 220, 221. Cf. also J. Döllinger, *Beiträge zur pol., kirchl. u. Culturgesch. der letzten 6 Jh.* (Regensburg, 1863), vol. II: 'Informationes Pilei archiep. Januensis super reformatione Ecclesiae', p. 304.

[3] Petrus de Alliaco, 'De Ecclesiae et Cardinalium Auctoritate', in *Gersonis Opera* (Paris, 1606), vol. V, pars II, c. 3, p. 918.

[4] Ibid. pars III, 2, p. 925.

spelt for his idea of the plenitude of papal power and it was he who, as mentioned before, very probably suppressed this venerable custom.[1]

The *Aureum Speculum Papae*[2] also quotes the famous saying of St Gregory on the first councils, 'which must be as highly esteemed as the four Gospels', to prove that the Pope's power is limited by the councils. Nicolaus Siculus Panormitanus[3] (d. 1453) was still more explicit in the long speech he addressed to the Fathers[4] and inferred from the Pope's profession which mentions the eight councils 'quod papa non possit de aliquo mutilare, violare, seu mutare statuta universalium conciliorum'. Jacobatius, Cardinal of the titular church of St Clement[5] (d. 1527), and chiefly John de Torquemada[6] (d. 1468), outstanding champion of the Pope's supreme power and of the opinions of the Roman Curia, show us how the followers of the conciliar school made capital of the Acts of the Eighth Council to strengthen their views; and as we know from their writings, from the fact that Photius had been condemned by the Eighth Council they inferred that the council was above the Pope.[7] In their view, the speech of the Metropolitan of Tyre, Thomas (actio I), was evidence that a council could be summoned by the Emperor without pontifical intervention.[8]

Canon XXI is appealed to as proof that a council has the right to pass sentence even on the Popes,[9] and the case of Photius is made to prove that a Pope's judgement is subject to revision by a council, which shall decide in the last instance.[10] Sayings by Zachary, Photius' champion, at the sixth session are also quoted in support of the conciliar view.[11]

All these objections are met by Cardinal John de Torquemada, who counters them by quoting other extracts from the Acts of the same

---

[1] See pp. 327 seq., 440.

[2] Ed. E. G. Brown, *Fasciculus Rerum Expetendarum et Fugiendarum* (London, 1690), vol. II, Appendix, p. 83.

[3] Cf. Schulte, *Die Geschichte der Quellen...d. can. Rechts*, vol. II, pp. 312, 313.

[4] 'Pro Honore et Conservatione Concilii Basiliensis', Mansi, vol. XXX, cols. 1123 seq., and chiefly col. 1169. In his speech, he makes many false or erroneous claims for the councils.

[5] Schulte, loc. cit. vol. II, pp. 342, 343.

[6] Ibid. vol. II, pp. 322 seq.

[7] Joannes de Turrecremata, *Summa de Ecclesia* (ed. Card. Vitellius; Venetiis, 1561), l. III, c. 29, p. 306. Cf. c. 35, p. 315.

[8] Ibid. c. 30, pp. 314a, 315. Cf. Mansi, vol. XVI, cols. 30, 31.

[9] Loc. cit. l. III, c. 45, p. 325a. Cf. *Jacobatii card. Tractatus de Concilio Domini*. Ed. Tractatus Univ. Jur., loc. cit. vol. XIII, pars I, p. 389.

[10] Joannes de Turrecremata, loc. cit. p. 326. Jacobatius, loc. cit. p. 363.

[11] J. de Turrecremata, loc. cit. p. 327; Jacobatius, loc. cit. p. 363.

Council,[1] where he also finds constructive arguments in favour of his own views on the plenitude of pontifical power,[2] and makes it evident that he was not content with quoting from Gratian's *Decretum*, as had been done by the writers of the fourteenth century and many of his contemporaries. The Cardinal knew the Acts themselves in their translation by Anastasius, and some objections made against the curial thesis suggest that the partisans of the conciliar notion had also direct access to the Acts of the Council, this being the first time since the eleventh century that this source was directly used and that scholars were no longer content with copying extracts from Gratian.

Torquemada's comments on Gratian's *Decretum* yield nothing of importance to our subject.[3] To our surprise, he omits to quote the Eighth Council in another treatise of his on the power of Pope and councils,[4] and neglects to turn the Photian case to profit.[5] In his *Summa de Ecclesia*, published in 1450, the great canonist of this period devotes, however, some space to the Greek doctrines and draws his inspiration from Manuel Calecas, whose *Libri IV adversus Errores Graecorum* had been translated into Latin in 1421. In this passage (l. II, p. 93) Torquemada also writes on the Photian Council of 879–80, but merely reflects the ideas of Calecas, whose grave doubts he shares concerning the authenticity of the Council's Acts.

Nicholas de Cusa also knows the Eighth Council well[6] and at the end of his book *De Concordantia* even makes the Emperor Sigismund the 'successor of Basil I' and compares Sigismund's energetic action at the Council of Constance with Basil's performance at the Eighth Council. In his treatise *De Auctoritate Presidendi in Concilio Generali*,

---

[1] Loc. cit. l. III, c. 31, pp. 309 seq.; c. 36, pp. 316 seq.

[2] Loc. cit. l. II, c. 110, p. 255; l. III, c. 9, p. 284; c. 22, p. 298 a; c. 25, pp. 300 a, 301; c. 32, pp. 310 a, 311; c. 33, pp. 311 a, 312; c. 34, pp. 312 a seq. (note that Turrecremata, in adducing arguments to prove that all councils need confirmation by the Pope, knows nothing of the confirmation of the Eighth Council); c. 37, pp. 318 seq.; c. 38, pp. 319 seq.; c. 44, pp. 324 seq.; c. 45, pp. 325 seq.; c. 62, pp. 349–51; c. 63, pp. 351 seq.

[3] *Commentaria...in Decretum* (ed. de Bohier; Lugduni, 1519).

[4] *De Potestate Papae et Concilio Generali Tractatus Notabilis* (ed. J. Friedrich; Oeniponti, 1871).

[5] There is also a reference to the Eighth Council in his 'Responsio in blasphemantem et sacrilegam invectivam congreg. Basileensium' (Mansi, vol. XXXI, col. 95). About Turrecremata, see Schulte, loc. cit. vol. II, pp. 322 seq. and S. Lederer, *Der Spanische Kardinal Johann von Torquemada* (Freiburg i. B. 1879).

[6] *De Concordantia Catholica*, libri III, S. Schardius, *Syntagma Tractatuum de Imp. Iurisdict., auct. et praeeminentia ac potest. Cath.* (Argentorati, 1609), pp. 306, 311, 322, 325, 329–31, 333, 343, 377, 378.

Nicholas de Cusa frequently quotes passages from the Acts of the Eighth Council in support of his own thesis. He knows, however, no argument in favour of the oecumenicity of this Council other than the famous passage in Gratian's *Decretum*.[1]

The right to summon councils is discussed, among other writers, by Petrus de Monte Brixiensis, but in the treatise he devoted to this subject, written after 1447,[2] he never once mentioned the Eighth Council.

Now for a rapid survey of the other works, whose subject-matter holds promise of interesting discoveries.

For instance, Cardinal Alexandrinus (d. 1509) wrote a commentary on the *Decretum*,[3] and he is as disappointing as James de Paradiso[4] and John F. Poggio of Florence.[5] John Capistranus (d. 1456) reveals himself in his treatise on Pope and councils as a third-rate historian: his account of the transfer of the Empire from Greece to Rome is confused; he knows Gratian only for his authority and alludes to the councils in very general terms.[6] Nor does the Spanish bishop Andrew give evidence of any deep knowledge of the history of the councils in his *Gubernaculum Conciliorum*, written in Basle in 1435 and dedicated by the author to Cardinal Julian Cesarini.[7] He offers nothing of interest and refers to the Eighth Council in terms too vague to be useful.

Neither Peter d'Ailly's work on the authority of Church and Cardinals,[8] nor the main juridico-religious writings of J. Gerson yielded any results.[9] And yet, the problems raised by the Eighth Council deeply interested the scholars of that period, as is shown by a letter

[1] G. Kallen, 'Cusanus-Texte II, Tractate 1: De Auctoritate Praesidendi in Concilio Generali', in *Sitzungsberichte der Akad. in Heidelberg, Phil.-Hist. Kl.* (1935), pp. 10, 14, 22, 24, 26, 30.

[2] *Monarchia, sive Tractatus Conciliorum Generalium*. I consulted the Lyons ed. 1512. In the *Tractatus*, vol. XIII, I, pp. 144–54.

[3] *Commentarius super Decreto* (Mediolani, 1494).

[4] Jacobus de Paradiso, *De Septem Statibus Ecclesiae* (ed. E. G. Brown), *Fasciculus Rerum Expetendarum et Fugiendarum* (London, 1690), vol. II, Appendix, pp. 102–12.

[5] Johannis Francisci Poggii Florentini *De Potestate Papae et Concilii Liber* (J. Beplin: Rome, 1517 (?)).

[6] *Tractatus de Papae et Concilii S. Ecclesiae Auctoritate, Tractatus*, loc. cit. (1584), XIII, I, pp. 32–66.

[7] Ed. H. von der Hardt, *Const. Concilii Acta et Decreta* (Frankfurt and Leipzig, 1699), vol. I, cols. 139–334.

[8] Petri de Alliaco card. *De Ecclesiae et Cardinalium Auctoritate, Joannis Gersonii Opera* (Paris, 1606), vol. I, cols. 895–934.

[9] *De Potestate Ecclesiastica, De Auferibilitate Papae ab Ecclesia, De Modo se Habendi Tempore Schismatis, Tractatus de Schismate, De Unitate Ecclesiastica, De Concilio Unius Obedientiae, Trilogus in Materia Schismatis*, ibid. vol. I, pp. 110–315.

addressed by Nicholas de Clémanges to a Paris professor, asking him for explanations on the first four councils.[1]

What has now become of the Council of Photius? Was its existence completely forgotten in the fifteenth century? The writers just mentioned say nothing about this, with the sole exception of Cardinal Jacobatius, titular of St Clement,[2] who after referring to the eight councils writes:

It should be noted [he quotes Gratian, c. VII, g. I, c. 45] . . . that a synod was held in Constantinople under Pope John VIII with 383 Fathers present and presided over by. . . . Of this I find no mention in his Life; only of the Council held in Troyes; which makes one seriously doubt, as he [John] succeeded Hadrian II who held the last Council of Constantinople. But it might be answered that this same eighth synod of Constantinople was begun in the time of Hadrian II and concluded under John VIII.

This is some explanation; but Jacobatius proceeds: 'And some say that at this Council of John Photius was reinstated and that therefore it is recorded that whatever had been written or said against the saintly Patriarchs Ignatius and Photius be anathema.'

This is a curious afterthought on the Photian affair and, unfortunately, the only one, at least in canonical literature, though I should draw attention to the Latin MS. no. 12264 of the Paris National Library, which has a long study on the councils. It was copied at the request of Thomas Basin, bishop of Lisieux, later archbishop of Caesarea in Palestine, in 1459, as suggested by a remark on the last page of the volume. The MS. is on parchment, in a neat handwriting, and it contains a 'Liber Sententiarum Beati Gregorii, auctore Taione, Leonis Aretini Liber de Sapientia' (fol. 129a), 'Liber de Sectis Hereticorum' (fol. 158) and a study 'de XXII Conciliis cum suis Expositionibus' (fols. 172a–219).

After a list of the twenty-two synods mentioned by the Greek canonical books (fol. 172a), we read: 'Huc usque Graecorum concilia. Constantinopolitanum tercium et Nicaenum secundum hic non ponitur. Quidam putant quartum fuisse Constantinopolitanum concilium.' And this is all the treatise has to say about the Eighth Council, after which it deals with the local synods of Africa, Gaul and Spain. On fol. 174a the writer returns to the first seven councils and the chief local synods, insists, after the Historia Tripartita, on the authority of the first

---

[1] H. von der Hardt, loc. cit. vol. I, p. 1, col. 53.
[2] Loc. cit. p. 194a.

Council of Nicaea and gives us a translation of a Greek treatise on the Councils:

There exists a treatise in Greek on the seven Greek General Councils, which I recently caused to be translated into Latin. In this treatise this is what is said about the Nicene Synod. From the treatise on the Seven Synods. Every Christian ought to know that there have been held seven general synods. The first was held in Nicaea under Constantine, who is now among the saints, the great King, and under Sylvester, the Pope of Rome, under Mitrophanes and Alexander, the Patriarch of Constantinople.... ('Exstat tractatus graecus editus de septem conciliis generalibus graecis, quem ego nuper in latinum transferri feci. In eo autem tractatu de nicena sinodo sic habetur. Ex tractatu septem sinodorum. Oportet scire omnem christianum quod septem et generales factae sunt synodi. Prima quidem facta est in Nicea sub Constantino, in sanctis, magno rege et Silvestro papa Romae et Mitrophane et Alexandro patriarcha Constantinopolis....')

Evidently, the Greek original was a treatise akin to that published by Ch. Justellus,[1] with the addition of a summary of the Seventh Council.

After the translation of the summary of each council, the MS. gives a long explanation, of some importance in the history of dogma, of the dogmas defined by the various synods—a valuable document witnessing to the influence of Greek mentality on the Latin theologians of the fifteenth century. It should be noted that except for the short reference quoted above, the treatise has absolutely nothing to say about the Eighth Council.

Besides this important Latin treatise on councils, I have found two dissertations of the same class, probably belonging to the fifteenth or sixteenth century, in the Paris National Library. At least one of them is a translation from the Greek. The first MS., no. 2448 (sixteenth century, on paper, 103 folios), is of unusual interest. It contains a translation of the Greek essay on the councils which Photius included in his letter to Boris-Michael (fols. 1–16), followed by an 'Epitome Celeberrimorum et Clarissimorum Conciliorum' (fols. 17–48), which is a summary of the first four councils. On fols. 48–83 there is a memoir on the Councils of Constantinople, Basle and Ferrara, and lastly, on fols. 101–3: 'Psellus de Septem Sacris Synodis...usque ad Michaelem Imperatorem Constantinopolitanum.' It is known that Psellos wrote a short poem on the orthodox faith and on the seven councils that defined it. It is dedicated to the Emperor Michael Ducas.[2] It has often been

[1] At the end of his book, *Nomocanon Photii* (Paris, 1615).
[2] *P.G.* vol. 122, cols. 812 seq.

copied independently and I found it in the Paris. Graec. 1277 (thirteenth-century, bombycine, 309 folios), fol. 196.

The translator may have misunderstood the dedication, for even when the poem was made into a separate copy, the dedication to Michael Ducas used to be copied as well. The MS. I consulted also dedicates the poem to Michael, but a reader of the MS., who was a little more familiar with Byzantine history, thought that the poet meant the Emperor Michael III, as he noted in the margin, probably to correct the original: 'Octava universalis synodus sub Basilio Macedone eiusque filio Leone Sapiente fuit peracta, teste Nicephoro Calisto in sua chronologica historia.' We know that Nicephorus Callistus here meant the Photian Council of 879–80,[1] and the writer of the marginal note probably thought of the Council of 869–70, which at that time was mistaken in the West for the Eighth Oecumenical Council.

The same monograph by Psellus is also found in the Latin MS. 10. 589 (seventeenth-century, on paper, 243 fols.), fols. 208–12, where the copyist has also copied the reader's note in MS. 2448: 'Octava universalis sub Basilio Macedone eiusque filio libris [sic! instead of Leone] Sapientiae [sic! instead of Sapiente] fuit peracta teste Nicephoro Calisto in sua dialectica historia.' On pp. 213–43 the copyist has also transcribed the Latin translation of the extract from Photius' letter to Boris-Michael on the councils.

Among the historians, the little to be found is not without interest. The most popular textbook on ecclesiastical history at that period was the *Lives of the Popes*, written by B. Platina, where we read the edifying story of Pope Joan,[2] whose name is placed before that of Nicholas I; also the history of the Eighth Council under Hadrian II, but with the Photian Council left out, as Platina merged it with the Eighth Council, which he credits with a considerable number of attending prelates, borrowed in reality from the Council of Photius. About a second excommunication of Photius there is of course nothing.

But it is curious that H. Schedel (1440–1514), who in his Chronicle frequently plagiarized Platina, appears to have more knowledge. Of the Eighth Council he writes:[3] 'Hadrian...also allowed a synod to meet in Constantinople at which the rebel Photius was dethroned, and

---

[1] *P.G.* vol. 145, col. 620.

[2] B. Platinae *Historia de Vitis Pontificum Rom. a D.N.J. Christo usque ad Paulum II* (Venice ed. 1511), pp. 94–8.

[3] Hart. Schedel, *Registrum hujus operis libri cronicarum cum figuris et ymaginibus de Initio Mundi* (Nuremberg, 1493), Sexta aetas mundi, fo. clxx.

Ignatius, who had been unfairly dethroned, was reinstated.' He then credits John VIII, whose reign is related in Platina's terms, with the conversion of the Bulgars, but unlike Platina attributes to John VIII the Latin translation of the Acts of the Eighth Council. On the Photian Council we read: [1]

Fifth synod of Constantinople. John VIII, Roman Pontiff, sanctioned the fifth synod of Constantinople. He brought about the union of the Greeks with the Latins, which seemed the best way to defeat the Saracens. Over 380 delegates attended the Council. To gather what good work it did in defining articles of the Christian faith, read the canons. Since, as far as we know, no alliance between the Greeks and the Latins followed by which resistance could be offered to the Saracens....

This version of the Photian Council suggests that the writer had some vague knowledge of a reconciliation between the Pope and the Greeks for no other purpose than a combined struggle against the Saracens. The truth, however, is that John VIII was apprehensive about the Arab menace and that there was at the back of his kindly treatment of Photius a desire to secure Basil's naval assistance in protecting southern and central Italy against the raids of the Arab pirates.

Whilst all these fifteenth-century documents belong to a purely Latin environment, in which a faint influence of Greek tradition is scarcely discernible, there occurred at this time an event which forced Greek and Latin traditions to come to grips on the very point we are dealing with: that was the Council of Florence.

At its fifth session, use was made of the Acts of the first councils [2] to elucidate the true doctrine of the *Filioque*, and at the opening of the sixth session, Cardinal Julian Cesarini again begged the Greeks to lend him the book containing the Acts of the Eighth Council. To this the metropolitan of Ephesus replied:

As regards this book, we find it difficult to lend it to you; but even were it in our possession, we could on no account be asked to number among the oecumenical councils a synod which not only was never approved, but was even condemned. For the synod mentioned by Your Holiness drew up Acts against Photius in the days of Popes John and Hadrian, but another synod was subsequently held which reinstated Photius and abrogated the first synod.

---

[1] Ibid. fol. clxxi. On H. Schedel see R. Stauber and O. Hartig, 'Die Schedelsche Bibliothek' (*Studien u. Darstellungen aus dem Gebiete der Geschichte*, Bd VI, H. 2, 3; Freiburg i. B. 1908).

[2] Mansi, vol. XXXI, cols. 528–51.

This Council, also called the Eighth, met under Pope John and we even possess letters addressed by the same Pope John to Photius. It also dealt with the question of additions [additamentum] to the Symbol, deciding that nothing should be added. We are convinced that you are not ignorant either of this Council or of Pope John's letters. Since then the Acts of that Council were annulled, it is not these, but rather the Acts of the subsequent Council, that should be looked for. Since that time to this day the great Church of Constantinople has held that whatever was said and written against the saintly Patriarchs Photius and Ignatius be anathema.

The poor Cardinal must have been staggered by this Greek impromptu, which suddenly raised a new difficulty that might wreck all the efforts made towards an understanding with the Greeks; but he quickly rallied, made up his mind and, beating a hasty retreat, said: 'I will relieve your anxiety. Never fear; nothing will be read from the Eighth Council....'[1]

But this did not close the incident. Five days later (25 October), in the course of the seventh session, the archbishop of Rhodes, spokesman for the Latins, returned to the attack. He too had obviously been shocked by what the Greek had said, for though he rose to speak immediately after the Cardinal at the sixth session, he said nothing at that moment about the objection so forcibly presented by the Metropolitan of Ephesus. But he must have made some researches in the meanwhile with the following result:[2]

As at the last session you mentioned the Eighth Council, we shall say a few words about the objections you made on that subject. As to the first point, we maintain that Photius, who was an enemy of the Roman Church and wrote many unfriendly things about Nicholas and Hadrian, yet never accused them of having made additions to the Symbol, though it was the very thing he should have done.... Also, in the course of the Eighth Council, they passed sentence on Photius and in favour of Ignatius.... As to what you recently affirmed, namely, that a synod was summoned later and condemned the Eighth Council, I say that this seems very unlikely. It will not do to come forward with any doubtful argument to prove the contrary, [i.e.] that the synod did pass such a condemnation, for neither the Pope nor his representative were present. If things happened as you say, some remembrance of it would have survived among the Latins; for it would be surprising that the Roman Church, which in other matters displays such accuracy and care in the recording of past events, should have overlooked an occurrence of such gravity and importance...therefore, the council you mentioned never took place; and if it did take place, it never mentioned it [the *Filioque*]....

[1] Mansi, vol. XXXI, cols. 551, 553.
[2] Ibid. cols. 596, 597.

This shows that the archbishop of Rhodes anticipated in 1438 the famous Allatius, who also tried to argue that the Photian Council never took place. Yet the Fathers of Florence refused to make of this controversy about the Eighth Council a 'matter to haggle about'; despite contradictory premisses, the question was left open; the Greeks continued to reckon only seven councils[1] and in the drafting of the Council's definition every reference to the Eighth Council was scrupulously omitted,[2] none but dogmatic issues, which so far had kept the two Churches apart, being mentioned, particularly the *Filioque*, the primacy and Purgatory. Even the proposals for reunion with the Armenians referred to the number of councils in purely general terms.[3]

On the whole, then, it may be said that the fifteenth century had not wholly forgotten the Photian Council and that the writers who happen to touch on the subject invariably betray a feeling of embarrassment.

This brings us to the sixteenth century, a period full of feverish activity in every theological domain, when humanism invaded all centres of religious studies that had been the strongholds of the scholastic method and the progress of modern philology made itself felt even in the field of theology. Gradually, the writings of the Greek Fathers come into prominence; minds grow more critical, more keenly interested in the purity and the origin of their sources; Christian antiquities provoke a curiosity that is further roused by the lively discussions between Catholic theologians and rising Protestantism. In 1523 James Merlin publishes his book on the councils in Paris, and in 1538 Crabbe in Cologne leads us to expect a new stage in the growth of Western tradition on the Photian incident.

The discussions around the Council of Florence and the problem of the Eighth Council continued unabated and caused some excitement among specialists of this and the following period, the impulse being given by the Latin translation of the Acts of the Florentine Synod. Though the Council had its official Latin and Greek scribes or secretaries, charged to take down the Acts of the Council, the Latin Acts were lost and only a Greek version was preserved. At the invitation of the archbishop of Ravenna, the Greek bishop Bartholomew Abraham of Crete then translated the Greek Acts in an abridged form, as he explained in a preface addressed to the archbishop.[4]

---

[1] Cf. session xxv, ibid. col. 893 and Emperor's declaration.
[2] Ibid. cols. 1026–34. [3] Ibid. col. 1054.
[4] Reprinted in Mansi, vol. XXXI, cols. 1796 seq.

But in this preface the Greek calls the Council of Florence the Eighth Oecumenical Council, incidentally showing that the Greek Uniates continued, as before, to number only seven councils. The confusion which this categorical attitude created among the Latins is apparent from the fact that when Abraham of Crete asked Pope Clement VII (1523–34) for permission to proceed with the publication of his work, the Papal Chancellery approved also the designation[1] of Eighth Oecumenical Council conferred by the translator on the Council of Florence.

When in 1567 Laurence Surius published in Cologne his edition in four volumes of the Councils (*Concilia Omnia tam Generalia quam Particularia*), he left the designation of Eighth Council given to the Florentine Synod and contented himself with the brief remark:

Learned men are puzzled by what possessed the Greeks [quid Graecis in mentem venerit] to call this Florentine synod the Eighth Council. We could have suppressed the figure, but to avoid a charge of rashness [ne id temeritati tribueretur] we have preferred to leave it and considered it enough to warn the reader that this synod is not rightly called the eighth, as some important General Councils followed the second of Nicaea, which is called the seventh.[2]

Another editor of the Councils, S. Bini (*Concilia Generalia et Provincialia*, 5 vols., Cologne, 1st ed. in 1606), considered such discretion to be completely out of place. This is his commentary on the subject:

Though Laurentius Surius refused, for fear of I do not know what rashness, to suppress and discard in his short preface addressed to the reader, as quoted below, the spurious title of Eighth Council which Bartholomew Abraham of Crete prefaces to the Acts of the Council, I, urged by the encouragement of some men whom I quoted previously in my notes of the Eighth Council, have come to the conclusion that the designation 'Sixteenth' [Council] should be substituted for 'Eighth', not only in the title but in the Acts of the Council themselves.[3]

Naturally, Bini's correction became law for all editors of the Acts and when I. Simond published his edition of the Conciliar Acts (*Concilia Generalia*, 4 vols., Rome, 1608–12), called *Collectio Romana* and published by order of Pope Paul V, the 'error' committed by the

---

[1] Cf. the interesting remarks by Pagi in his commentary on Baronius' *Annals*, ann. 809, c. LIX, ed. of Lucca, 1744, vol. XV, p. 180. Pagi copies the commentary of Alexandre Noël (Alexander Natalis) on the subject.

[2] Reprinted by Mansi, vol. XXXI, col. 1798.

[3] Ibid. col. 1796. Cf. also the remark in Janus (J. Döllinger), *The Pope and the Council* (London, 1869), p. 324.

translator and first editor of the Florentine Conciliar Acts was duly corrected and the designation of Eighth Council given to the Ignatian Council of 869–70. This closed the incident and the other editors of the Conciliar Acts—Ph. Labbe and G. Cossart (Paris, 1671–2), I. Hardouin (Paris, 1715), Coletti (Venice, 1728–33), D. Mansi (Florence, Venice, 1759–98)—had but to follow in the wake of the Western tradition set once for all by the canonists of the eleventh and twelfth centuries and by the Council of Constance.

An interesting echo of the incident is found in Alexandre Noël's (Alexander Natalis) *Historia Ecclesiastica Veteris et Novi Testamenti*, published for the first time in Paris, 1660. This learned historian considered it necessary to devote a special paragraph to the problem of the Ignatian Council's oecumenicity. The erudite Dominican was well acquainted with all the documents related to the problem and accessible in his days, but he was very hard on Bartholomew Abraham of Crete. The passage is worth reproducing as it stands:[1]

Abraham of Crete, interpreter and first editor of the Florentine Council, gave it the title of Eighth Council, the same being accorded to it in the *Privilegium Editionis* or permission to publish, which Clement VII Medici granted, as John Launoi states in the 8th Part of his Letters, i.e. in the letter addressed to Claudius Amelius. But the Cretans were always liars: nor is Abraham truthful in this or commendable, since neither the Acts and Decrees of the Florentine Synod nor the *Diplomata* of Pope Eugene IV ever gave it the name of Eighth Council. The permission to publish granted by the Pontiff, whose name is given, was non-committal, the title as supplied by the editor being simply copied by the person who granted permission to publish. Furthermore, that in this matter the Sovereign Pontiff was taken off his guard may be inferred not only from the old profession of faith which recently elected Pontiffs used to make in the ninth century, but also from the profession of faith which the General Council of Constance in its 39th session laid down for Pontiffs to be elected in the future.... Clement VII would certainly have observed this tradition, if he had seriously considered the privilege he gave to the edition of the Florentine Council published by Abraham of Crete. But it was obtained by surprise, and in the Roman edition of the Council published under Paul V the designation was withdrawn.

[1] Vol. VI, Saeculum IX–X, pars II, Dissertatio II, par. 24 (ed. of 1660), p. 267. The tradition started by Abraham of Crete was followed by Cardinal Pole in his *Reformatio Angliae*, where the Council of Florence is put down as the eighth oecumenical (ed. Rome, 1562, fol. 184) and by Cardinal Contarini in his treatise on the most celebrated councils, which he dedicated to Paul III in 1553 (published in 1562, *Opera Omnia* (Paris, 1571), p. 563). Cf. A. H. Rees, *The Catholic Church and Corporate Union* (London, 1940), p. 19.

On turning to the canonists of the period, we shall find them less interesting. Jacobus Almainus, for instance[1] (d. 1515), in his reply to Thomas Caietanus de Vio, brings out the old arguments dear to the partisans of the conciliar notion and allots the councils a very limited, though more generous, space than his antagonist.[2] Silvester de Prierio (d. 1523) does not seem to know more about our subject than Gratian[3] and Thomas Stapleton[4] (d. 1598) has not yet shaken himself free from scholastic dialectics.

Thomas Campegius Bononiensis (d. 1564) is more interesting, as his knowledge of the Acts of the Eighth Council is more extensive, though he gets no further than Torquemada.[5] Much the same may be said of Laelius Jordanus (d. 1583).[6] Cardinal Stanislas Hosius makes only a slight reference to the Eighth Council[7] and Joannes Hieronymus Albani is not more explicit.[8] But F. Bartholomew Carranza Mirandevius, in his *Summa Conciliorum et Pontificum a Petro usque ad Paulum Tertium*, gives a minute account of the Eighth Council and all its sessions;[9] before summarizing its canons, however, he complains that the manuscript he is using is in a very bad state of preservation and regrets that he has looked in vain for a Greek MS. to collate with the Latin. We of course know the reason why he did not find his Greek MS., but his summary of the Eighth Council was destined to be a favourite with subsequent writers. It naturally makes no reference to the Photian Council.

[1] De Auctoritate Ecclesiae et Concilii contra Thomam de Vio, *Gersonis Opera* (Paris, 1606), I, cols. 707–49.

[2] De Auctoritate Papae et Concilii, *Bibliotheca* (Romae, 1699), vol. XIX, pp. 445 seq. Idem, *De Divina Institutione Pontificatus Romani Pontif.* (1521), *Corpus Catholicorum* (Münster i. W. 1925), vol. X, ed. F. Lauchert.

[3] De Irrefragabili Veritate Rom. Eccl., *Bibliotheca* (Romae, 1699), vol. XIX, pp. 265, 269, 272.

[4] De Conciliis, ibid. vol. XX, pp. 107–23.

[5] *De Auctoritate et Potestate Romani Pont.* (Venice, 1555), pp. 36a, 43, 55, 81a, 88, 110a, 115. In his Tractatus de Auctoritate Conciliorum (*Tractatus*, loc. cit. vol. XIII, I, pp. 398a–474) Thomas Campegius often refers also to the Eighth Council (chs. III, IX, X, XXIII, XXXV, pp. 401, 404a, 405, 410a, 412). In ch. X (p. 405) he alludes to the Photian Council, but the passage, quoted after Gratian, is confused and presents a good illustration of the embarrassment felt by the canonists at Gratian treating the Photian Council as a genuine and authentic synod.

[6] De Romanae Sedis Origine et Auctoritate, *Tractatus*, vol. XIII, p. 1 (Venice, 1584), a long account on Photius, pp. 6 seq.

[7] De Loco et Auctoritate Rom. Pont. in Eccl., *Bibliotheca* (Romae, 1699), vol. XIX, pp. 385 seq., and chiefly p. 415.

[8] De Potestate Papae, *Tractatus*, vol. XIII, I, pp. 79 seq.

[9] (Salmanticae, 1549), pp. 537–53. Cf. also idem, Quatuor Controversiarum de Auctoritate Pontificis et Conciliorum Explicatio, published in *Ad Sacros. Concilia a Ph. Labbeo et G. Cossartio edita apparatus alter* (Paris, 1672), pp. ci seq.

Far more interesting is Antonio Agustin (1517–86),[1] archbishop of Tarragona, the greatest canonist of his day and one who undoubtedly deserves a place of honour in the history of canon law. On several occasions he dealt with the Eighth Council and that of Photius: first, in his corrected edition of Gratian's *Decretum*, on which he began working in 1543 and whose first edition appeared in Tarragona in 1557. He several times refers there to the Photian Council and some of his observations are worth noting. After commenting on the famous D. XVI, c. 8 (on the eight oecumenical councils) Agustin goes on to discuss[2] 'de duplici octava synodo' and states that whereas some anti-Latin Greeks called the Photian Council the eighth, others numbered neither the Ignatian nor the Photian Council among the oecumenicals, but made the Council of Florence the Eighth. When asked by his interlocutor—the work is written in the form of a dialogue—which council should be listed as oecumenical, he replies:

In a Greek book that once was brought to me from Italy I find many things that the Roman Pontiffs did against Photius after these two Eighth Councils, and they easily convince me that John did not approve the synod held in Constantinople by his legates. B: But John states that the first synod was not approved by Hadrian. A: And what if this is untrue and was invented by Photius, who was convicted by the synod of forging signatures and reports on the Patriarchs? Add to this that if we repudiate the whole synod of Hadrian, we shall seem to approve whatever Photius did against Pope Nicholas and the Patriarch Ignatius. There is more consistency and likelihood in what previous Popes such as Nicholas and Hadrian, Leo IV and Benedict III did and wrote against Photius and Gregory of Syracuse, the bishop who consecrated Photius; and the acts and writings were approved by John VIII, Marinus, Hadrian III and Stephen VI, as I found recorded in Greek in the very words used by those Pontiffs. To this, add again the letters of John IX to Stylianos of Neocaesarea, who wrote many things against Photius to Pope Stephen VI, though afterwards he apparently changed his mind in other letters addressed to the same John. In the letters he wrote to Stephen he stated that bishops Paul and Eugene, who were sent by John to Ignatius, had been deceived. . . .

The above passage amply demonstrates that the great canonist had found in the Vatican Library the anti-Photian Collection, which convinced him that the Ignatian Council was 'the genuine Eighth Council',

[1] Schulte, loc. cit. vol. III, pp. 723 seq.
[2] *De Emendatione Gratiani Dialogus*, *Ant. Agustini Opera Omnia* (Lucae, 1767), vol. III, pp. 122 seq.

that the Photian Council had not been confirmed by John VIII and that all the excommunications of Photius attributed by the writer of the Collection to the various Popes were genuine and authentic.

Agustin often quotes the Acts of the Photian Council, a copy of which, he states somewhere,[1] was found in the Vatican Library. In other writings of his, particularly in his book on ancient pontifical law,[2] he frequently designates the Photian Council as 'synodus nona',[3] though he points out in one place that 'this synod was condemned by the Roman Pontiff'; and lastly, he mentions in his excellent handbook on the synods the Eighth Council as well as other councils held in connection with the Ignatian and Photian case.[4]

It is only fair to state that the famous canonist never gives his opinion on Photius in very categorical terms and it is hard to resist the impression of considerable hesitation on his part in passing an adverse judgement on the Photian Council; but in the end he did give an unfavourable verdict, completely misled as he was by the anti-Photianist Collection. It is interesting to note that whenever a Western scholar came upon this document, he went through the same process.

The Lateran Council (1514), although its Acts refer to older councils more frequently than did the Acts of councils immediately preceding, provides nothing new about the Eighth Council.[5] But in the Acts of the Council of Trent we find a well-known retrospective survey of our subject in the speech of Paul Quidellus,[6] though he does not seem to be very familiar with the history of that period. Another disappointment comes from the Bull of Pius IV 'super forma juramenti professionis fidei',[7] which gives no definite decision about the number of councils.

However, everything is changed when we turn to ecclesiastical history. This period must, of course, be regarded as the starting-point

---

[1] Loc. cit. p. 129.

[2] *Juris Pontificii Veteris Epitome, Opera Omnia* (Lucae, 1770), vol. v. It is a posthumous work, and Baronius consulted the MS. in the Vatican Library to borrow from it the Popes' profession of faith.

[3] Loc. cit., pars I, lib. I, tit. xx, c. x, p. 63; lib. II, tit. II, c. IX, p. 72; lib. II, tit. XXIII, cc. II, III, p. 89; lib. IV, tit. VI, c. I, p. 110; lib. IV, tit. LXXXVII, c. IV, p. 197; lib. v, tit. x, cc. VII, XVIII, pp. 209, 210; lib. v, tit. XXVI, c. LIV, p. 212 (Popes' profession of faith); lib. v, tit. XLIII, p. 255 ('de synodis damnatis'); lib. VI, tit. VII, c. I, p. 268; lib. IX, tit. XXX, c. I, p. 386; lib. XI, tit. XX, c. XIX, p. 469; lib. XII, tit. XXIV, c. I, p. 524; vol. VI, pars II, lib. XIV, tit. XXVI, c. I, p. 287.

[4] *De Synodis et Pseudosynodis, Opera Omnia*, loc. cit. vol. v, pp. xxix, lxxix, lxxx.

[5] Mansi, vol. XXXII, cols. 891, 967, 968.

[6] Mansi, vol. XXXIII, col. 516.   [7] Ibid. cols. 220–2.

for modern ecclesiastical historiography, of which the *Centuriae Magdeburgenses* and Cardinal Baronius' *Annals* are notable examples.

Flacius, with his collaborators, began publishing the *Centuriae* in 1559 and the whole work (thirteen volumes folio), for all its shortcomings an epoch-making achievement, was completed in 1574. Leaving on one side all other problems raised by the *Centuriae*, we have only to examine how the first Protestant historians presented the Photian case.

It should be borne in mind that this was the first time since the ninth century that the Photian case was studied in Western literature in all its bearings. No longer content with copying their predecessors' opinions, the writers of the *Centuriae* went to the original sources, as far as they were accessible, and with regard to the Photian incident, these sources were first the *Liber Pontificalis* (Life of Nicholas and Hadrian II), the letters of Nicholas and the history of Zonaras. The writers do not quote the Acts of the Eighth Council among their primary sources, but apparently rely on the work of B. Carranza; but among the historians, they quote Martin of Opava, the *Flores Temporum*, John de Oppido, Platina, Schedelius, sources that help us to forecast what view they will take of the Photian case.

The origin of the quarrel between Ignatius and the Government is attributed to Bardas, who had repudiated his wife, lived in incestuous concubinage with his daughter-in-law and deposed Ignatius for criticizing his immoral life. Thereupon, the legates of the Roman Pope summoned a council in Constantinople—the Council of 861—which ruthlessly (!) condemned the iconoclasts. Bardas was punished by Basil for the murder of Theoktistos and for persecuting the just, i.e. the iconoclasts, and the same punishment overtook Michael, for restoring the impious worship of images.[1]

The chapter on the government of the Church,[2] following the *Liber Pontificalis*, refers to Photius' outbreak against Nicholas' misdeeds, the convocation of his Council (867) and the reluctance of the bishops attending the Council of 869 to sign the *Libellus*. Strange to say, in trying to explain the origin of the schism under Michael III in chapter VIII[3] the authors father the divorce and the incest with a daughter-in-law on Michael and state in two different places[4] that Photius forbade Basil, after he committed his murder, entry into the church.

---

[1] M. Flacius, *Nona Centuria Historiae Ecclesiasticae* (Basileae, 1565), cap. III, *De Persecutione et Tranquil. eccl.* col. 25.

[2] Ch. VII, cols. 340 seq.   [3] Col. 353.   [4] Cols. 353, 425, 426.

The councils of the ninth century are reported in the chapter 'De synodis'[1] and the Photian synod is placed first on the list, contrary to chronological order:

Tempore Ioannis VIII, Constantinopoli synodus habita est ad quam 383 episcopi convenerunt. Romani pontificis vicem ibi sustinuerunt Petrus presbiter cardinalis, Paulus Antiochenus episcopus et Eugenius Hostiensis. Actum est de coniunctione ecclesiarum Orientis et Occidentis, quo animis et viribus associati, ad Saracenorum impetus sustinendos et propulsandos paratiores essent.

They then mention the two synods of Photius of 859 and 861, and the Roman synod of Nicholas I which condemned Zachary, Radoald and Photius. Photius, it is stated, then wrote a book against the Pope's tyranny and had it signed by a number of bishops as though it were a conciliar decree; a synod of Constantinople, summoned by Basil, deposed Photius, when the Roman synod of Hadrian II decided to summon a new council. There follows a description of the Eighth Oecumenical Council with an analysis of its various sessions.

The *Centuriae* writers evidently lacked accurate information on the Photian Council, whose Acts they naturally did not know, and they had at their disposal only those sources which were derogatory to Photius; yet, in spite of this handicap, the history of Photius began to improve in clarity and order under their treatment, and had they but known the Acts of the Photian synod, might have carried conviction.

The *Annals* of Cardinal Baronius (1588–1601), which were meant to provide the Catholic answer to the *Centuriae*, are no doubt a remarkable work, superior in many respects to that of Flacius and his associates. As Baronius' sources were far more numerous and the Cardinal made the best of the treasures of the Vatican Library, his documentation on the Photian incident and the Eighth Council is strikingly rich—a decided advance on the *Centuriae*. Over and above the sources at the disposal of the Magdeburg writers, Baronius consulted the history of John Curopalates, Cedrenus, and Glycas and had access not only to the letters of Nicholas, the *Liber Pontificalis* and the Acts of the Eighth Council, but also to Photius' letters; he even discovered the 'Greek equivalent' of these sources, the anti-Photian Collection, with its biography of Ignatius by Nicetas, the Greek summary of the Acts and the appended documents; he also found the Greek Acts of the Photian Council, which

[1] Ch. IX, cols. 413 seq.

for the first time since the eleventh century were turned to profit by a Western writer.

Of these sources, the most important find was of course the anti-Photianist Collection, in which, without a suspicion of its true character, Baronius and his followers saw a number of valuable and independent sources, chiefly the so-called biography of St Ignatius, considered to be of special value, since it confirmed and even went beyond anything the Eighth Council had said against Photius. Till then, Hugh Etherianus, Leo Tuscus and Antonio Agustin had been the only Western writers to know of the existence of this notorious Collection and we know what an impression it made on them: but it staggered Baronius.

In his account of Photius, Baronius exclusively follows Nicetas and the data of the Collection as completed by Anastasius' story, long extracts from Nicetas' pamphlet adorning the narrative and giving it a picturesque touch. Here are some of Baronius' reflections on Photius' misdeeds: after telling the story, according to Nicetas, of Photius' accession to the throne and of his persecution of Ignatius, the good Cardinal exclaims:[1]

You have heard what butchery this eunuch was preparing for the destruction of the Church, making his persecution stand comparison with any of those that schismatics, heretics, or even pagans ever raised against the Church.... In my opinion, no persecutor worse than Photius so effectively struck down the Eastern Church, since besides those cruelties he moved heaven and earth to tear her away from communion with the Church of Rome, with disastrous results that have afflicted the unhappy Orientals with ever-increasing gravity to this day.

He also follows Nicetas in describing the Photian synod and the legates' despatch to Rome, quotes Photius' letter to Nicholas and the Pope's letter to Michael III, then lets Nicetas tell the events of 861 in Constantinople. Theognostos' letter is also exhibited for the first time and Nicholas' letters, long extracts from which are cited to illustrate the events of the year 863, announce the final and harsh verdict against the legates and Photius. Even Photius' letters to Bardas are published and the responsibility for the offensive letter of Michael (ad ann. 865) is naturally put on Photius. There follows, also for the first time, a detailed account of the Bulgarian issue based on original sources and of the sensation created in the West by the Photian affair and Nicholas'

[1] *Annales Ecclesiastici, auctore Caesare Baronio Sorano...una cum critica historico-chronologica P. Antonii Pagii* (Lucae, 1743), vol. XIV, ad ann. 858, capp. 49–54, pp. 492–6.

alarmist letters. Photius is of course the author of the Procession of the Holy Ghost from the Father only: 'The unhappy Photius was the first (let this sculptured pillar of ignominy serve him in lieu of glory), he was the first, I say, to use this pretext to sever connection and cut himself adrift from the Roman Church....' Proceeding with the story of Photius, Baronius also produces reports from Greek historians: 'but the best of all is Nicetas who recorded the doings of Ignatius; as a contemporary he wrote what he had seen with his own eyes and explained how it was divulged, so that events of such importance should have the support of every possible proof and witness.'

Baronius vigorously attacks Zonaras who alleged that Photius, after the murder of Michael,[1] refused to let Basil into the church:

Such is the report by Zonaras, a schismatic and the supporter of a schismatic, out to trump up a new and unheard-of reason for Photius' expulsion. But there is no proof for his assertion that Photius was expelled for upbraiding the Emperor for the murder; rather was he dethroned because he had been condemned three times by Pope Nicholas. This is attested by the pontifical letters, by the Acts of the Eighth Council, by Nicetas and lastly by all the other ancient Greek historians, leaving no room for any possible doubt. Zonaras lived long after the events, and being himself a schismatic he favoured Photius, the promoter of a schism, praising him and concealing his crimes, patent though they were to the whole world....

Notwithstanding his crime, Basil is according to him 'God's chosen instrument...having been called by Him to exalt the humble and put down the proud'. Photius is nothing but a eunuch swollen with pride and temerity,[2] which Baronius proves by quoting the alleged letter of the Patricius John to Photius; the Acts of the Eighth Council are naturally emphasized, and the oecumenicity of the Council is established by the famous profession of faith published by Antonius Augustinus,[3] after which Baronius viciously turns on those who would refuse to range this council among the oecumenicals. Mark of Ephesus, who at the Council of Florence had denied its oecumenicity, is severely taken to task, while Cardinal Julian is roundly scolded for failing to correct 'the lie of that Greek slanderer', but Andrew of Rhodes is 'vir doctissimus aeque ac maxime pius...qui omnino negavit per Ioannem VIII abolitam esse octavam synodum oecumenicam....'.[4]

---

[1] Ann. 867, c. 101, pp. 110, 118 (loc. cit. vol. xv).
[2] Loc. cit. ann. 868, n. 46, p. 153.
[3] Loc. cit. ann. 869, n. 59, p. 180.
[4] Loc. cit. ann. 869, nn. 51–63, pp. 180–3.

All that followed the Council of 870 is told in the light of the documents of the anti-Photian Collection, so that Baronius was the first to introduce into history the garbling by Photius[1] of the Acts of the Council of 879–80, Marinus' second legation, and the second excommunication of Photius by John VIII.[2] Marinus was elected Pope, Baronius alleges, because he was Photius' bitter enemy;[3] all the condemnations of Photius catalogued by the *Breviarium* are maintained and the story of Stylianos is told in the version best known.[4]

At last we have now discovered, after long search, who was responsible for the final shaping of the Photian Legend: no other than Baronius. And yet, we need not be too hard on the Cardinal, for it will be remembered that he had some forerunners. Since the Eighth Council had been, thanks mainly to the canonists of the eleventh and twelfth centuries, replaced in the West among the oecumenical councils and gained popularity, the ground was ready for the Photian Legend to arise at any time, and as the medieval climate favoured this kind of growth, it gradually began to take root and to break to the surface. At a time when the power and weight of the Papacy were steadily rising, a man known to have once withstood the Pope could expect little sympathy; for the Council by which his condemnation had been made absolute was regarded as oecumenical and its canons had rendered signal service to the Western Church. Moreover, Baronius must have felt more strongly about it than his forerunners, since it was his duty to defend the authority of the Sovereign Pontiff against the scornful attacks of the Protestants. His critical sense was crushed under the avalanche of hitherto unknown documents, the bulk of which seemed to authenticate the severe condemnations of the Eighth Council. Only the Acts of the Photian Council had a good word to say for Photius, but these were discredited by the discrepant version of the pontifical letters which they reproduced.

Thus the seed sown by the eleventh century in the fertile soil steadily irrigated by the canonists flourished only too well: after five centuries the plant reached maturity and bore fruit under Baronius.

The verdict of Baronius, apparently based on a formidable array of documents, must have made a deep impression on his contemporaries.

---

[1] Loc. cit. ann. 879, nn. 53, 61–72, pp. 356–60.
[2] Loc. cit. ann. 880, nn. 10–13, pp. 366.
[3] Loc. cit. ann. 882, n. 10, p. 384.
[4] Loc. cit. ann. 886, nn. 5 seq., pp. 451 seq.; ann. 905, nn. 9–12, pp. 339–541.

He made, of course, many mistakes, some of them glaring, as was inevitable at a time when historical criticism was still in its infancy, and many of his errors have been corrected; but with regard to Photius' history, his opinion has held the field in the Catholic world to this day. Baronius' most important editor, A. Pagi, not only substantiated what the Cardinal had written about Photius, but on several occasions improved upon his account of the whole incident. Having access to a larger documentation, and being able to draw on the famous Ignatian Synodicon, the books of Leo the Grammarian, Simeon the Logothete, George the Monk, the Porphyrogennetos and a certain number of Greek canonists, and to complete the quotations from the sources which Baronius had used, it is small wonder that Pagi gave the Photian Legend a new lease of life.[1]

When in 1604 the Jesuit M. Raderus published the anti-Photian Collection with the Greek Acts of the Ignatian Council, it was natural that on the authority of Baronius he should adopt the opinion of the entire Middle Age and regard the Council as one of the most important and those documents as reliable; but when the Acts of the Photian Council were published by Hardouin, it was described as 'pseudo-synodus' and this designation has survived in Catholic circles to our own day. The treatise by F. Richerius[2] on the councils was of course written entirely under the influence of Baronius, the learned author going even so far as to copy in the introduction to his work the Popes' notorious profession of faith as Baronius had it.

Henceforth, the story of Photius and of the Eighth Council is treated even in canonical writings after Baronius' pattern. Dominic of the Blessed Trinity (d. 1687), for instance, in his treatise on the Papacy, repeatedly argues from the Eighth Council and the Photian case, quoting the Cardinal's work;[3] and the same is true of Eugene the Lombard (d. 1684).[4] Laurentius Bracatus de Laurea speaks of the suppression not only of the Acts of the 'synodus prima et secunda', but also of the

---

[1] For instance, he adds (loc. cit. ann. 857, vol. XIV, p. 473) that Photius had taught the doctrine of the two souls, completes the account of Ignatius' deposition (ibid. ann. 859, p. 491), the Cardinal's attack on Zonaras (ibid. ann. 868, vol. XV, p. 116) and his criticism of Mark of Ephesus (ibid. ann. 869, p. 180).

[2] *Historia Conciliorum Generalium* (Coloniae, 1683), ch. XII, pp. 666–752, 'History of the Eighth Council'.

[3] Dominicus a Ssa Trinitate, *De Summo Pontifice, de Sacris Conciliis,* in *Bibliotheca,* vol. X, pp. 364–77, 512–34, 575.

[4] Eugenius Lombardus, *Regale Sacerdotium, Bibliotheca,* vol. XI, pp. 409–13, 420, 457, 481.

Photian Council of 879–80.[1] Don Rodrigo da Cunha, archbishop of Lisbon (d. 1643), comments on various passages in Gratian's *Decretum* bearing on the Eighth Council, but confuses the Photian Council with the Eighth.[2]

The same notions also filter into various histories of ecclesiastical literature, like those of L. Ellies du Pin,[3] Robert Bellarmine,[4] Phil. Labbe,[5] and Trithemius as enlarged by Miraeus.[6]

From all these authors one important passage concerning the Eighth and the Photian Councils should be quoted: it is written by Cardinal Bellarmine in his book *De Conciliis et Ecclesia*, which has been used as a classical handbook of the Catholic doctrine on councils until the modern period. In the first book[7] the Cardinal writes:

The eighth synod is the fourth of Constantinople, held under the pontificate of Hadrian II and under the Emperor Basil, in the third year of his reign. The first session, as it was understood in the synod itself, was held in A.D. 870. It was attended by 383 bishops, one of whom was Photius and the other Ignatius of Constantinople, the others being represented by their delegates.

It should be noted here that three synods were held in Constantinople on the Photian case. One met at the time of Pope Nicholas I and the Emperor Michael, when Ignatius was deposed and Photius was consecrated. It is recorded by Zonaras in his Life of Michael and, as is evident from the letters of Nicholas I and Alexander II, the profane character of this synod is beyond all doubt.

The second synod is the one we have called the Eighth Council, which is recorded, however imperfectly, in books on the councils—when Photius was deposed and Ignatius was reinstated. This synod is mentioned by Zonaras in his Life of the Emperor Basil.

The third is the one which was held in the reign of the same Basil by the successor of Hadrian, John VIII, represented by his legates, when again,

---

[1] Laurentius Bracatus de Laurea, *De Decretis Ecclesiae, Bibliotheca* (1698), vol. xv, pp. 20, 40.

[2] *Commentarii in Primam Partem Decreti Gratiani* (Bracharae Augustae, 1629), pp. 112–14, 141, 154 seq., 847. Cf. also the Protestant jurist Gerhard von Mastricht, *Historia Iuris Ecclesiastici et Pontificii* (Halae, 1705), pars. 238, 239, 405 ('octo concilia'), who naturally is more discreet, though influenced by Baronius and Bellarmine.

[3] *Nouvelle Bibliothèque des Auteurs Ecclésiastiques* (Paris, 1698), vol. iii, ch. ix, pp. 80–103, 109–12.

[4] Rob. Card. Bellarmino, *De Scriptoribus Ecclesiasticis* (Coloniae, 1684), p. 156.

[5] *Dissertationes Philosophicae de Scriptoribus Ecclesiasticis quos attigit Em. S. R. E. Card. Bellarminus* (Parisiis, 1660), vol. ii, pp. 221–4.

[6] Trithemius, *De Scriptoribus Ecclesiasticis* (ed. Fabricius, *Bibliotheca Ecclesiastica*, Hamburg, 1718), *Auberti Miraei Auctarium*, pp. 46, 47.

[7] Ch. v, *Opera omnia* (Coloniae Agrippinae, 1619), tom. ii, pp. 8, 9.

after Ignatius' death, Photius was reinstated and, if the statement of the Greeks at the 6th session of the Council of Florence and the record of Francis Turrianus in his book on Acts 6, 7 and 8 of that Synod are true, all the Acts of the preceding Council under Hadrian were rescinded and it was even decreed that that word [*Filioque*] was to be taken out of the Symbol, which is altogether unlikely.

Hence I am very much inclined to think either that whatever is said about John VIII is pure fabrication, as St Antoninus teaches in his historical Summa, p. 3, title 22, ch. 13, para. 10; or that it is certain that Photius was reinstated on the throne of Constantinople after Ignatius' death by John VIII through his legates; or that the whole story is uncertain, untrue, fictitious and was invented by the Greeks, as Turrianus shows on the authority of Manuel Callecas in the book quoted above. What confirms me in my opinion is that Zonaras did record Photius' reinstatement, but had not a word to say about the abrogation of the Eighth Council and the removal of the word [*Filioque*] from the Symbol; and also, that at the 6th session of the Florentine Council the Greeks did not regard the Council held under John VIII as an Oecumenical Synod, though it would have greatly helped them, had that Council been legitimate and genuine.

Some Catholic historians went even further than the Cardinal, for instance, the celebrated Greek Leo Allacci, whose life and work would claim a special study. He certainly deserved credit for his encouragement of Greek studies in the Western Church, but his keen desire to see the Greek Church reunited with the Latin Church led him astray in the study of the Photian case. Through Baronius' eyes, he naturally saw in Photius the principal mischief-maker in the schism and considered it his duty to expose the guilt of the prominent culprit whose villainy did so much harm to the whole of Christendom in general, and to Greece in particular. That is how he speaks of him in his scholarly work on the union between the two Churches in matters dogmatic,[1] but he goes much further in his work on the Photian Council, where he tries to prove that the Acts of this council were forged from beginning to end by Photius and that this council never took place.[2] The book on the schism written by L. Maimbourg[3] is less scholarly, but in some places more violent than anything ever written on this subject in the West.

[1] Leo Allatius, *De Ecclesiae Occidentalis atque Orientalis Perpetua Consensione* (Coloniae Agrippinae, 1648), lib. II, chs. IV, V, VI, VII, pp. 544, 552 seq., 566 seq., 577, 587 seq., 591 seq., 600 seq. Cf. also idem, *De Libris et Rebus Eccl. Graecorum* (Parisiis, 1646), pp. 147 seq.

[2] *De Octava Synodo Photiana* (Rome, 1662).

[3] *Histoire du Schisme des Grecs* (Paris, 1680).

Writings so unfair to Photius, and all from Catholic writers, necessarily provoked reactions among Protestant historians. J. H. Höttinger[1] undertook Photius' defence by trying to put his case in a more conciliatory light, supporting Zonaras' assertion that Photius had banned Basil from the church in punishment for a murder—for which Allatius viciously attacked him in his reply.[2] The same treatment was meted out to R. Creighton, who also dared to defend Photius in his edition of the Council of Florence.[3] Another attempt in the same direction was made by W. Beveridge.[4]

But the most substantial study of Photius of that period which marks a decided advance on Baronius came from M. Hanke, who was able to refute Baronius on many points, for instance: Hanke affirmed that even Metrophanes of Smyrna submitted to Photius after his election to the patriarchate;[5] he makes short work of the assertion that Photius was a eunuch;[6] he shows that Asbestas was excommunicated neither by Benedict nor by Gregory;[7] he believes that Photius had really no desire for patriarchal honours, as he stated in his letter to Bardas;[8] he repeatedly charges Nicetas with partiality and maintains that Photius did keep Basil outside the church;[9] he also places the incidents that accompanied the Eighth Council in a different light, as the Patriarchs' representatives were only Arab ambassadors on a visit to the Emperor;[10] he puts another complexion on the relations between Basil and Photius after his fall, when Basil acknowledged his mistake;[11] he defends the authenticity of the Photian Council against Allatius,[12] but he believes in Photius'

---

[1] J. H. Höttinger, *Historiae Ecclesiasticae Novi Testamenti Enneas I* (Tiguri, 1651), p. 673.

[2] Leo Allatius, *De Octava Synodo*, loc. cit. pp. 244 seq.

[3] Leo Allatius, *De Octava Synodo*, pp. 274 seq. and his answer to R. Creighton's translation of the Acts of the Florentine Council. (Leonis Allatii *In Roberti Creyghtoni Apparatum, Versionem et Notas ad historiam Concilii Florentini Scriptum a Silvestro Syropulo, de Unione inter Graecos et Latinos Exercitationes* (Romae, 1665), Exerc. XIII–XVIII.)

[4] W. Beveridge, Συνόδικον *sive Pandectae Canonum SS. Apost. et Conciliorum* (Oxonii, 1672), vol. I, pp. xxiii, 331 seq.

[5] M. Hankius, *De Byzantinarum Rerum Scriptoribus Graecis* (Lipsiae, 1677), p. 264.

[6] Loc. cit. pp. 270, 272. This alleged disablement of Photius also plays a curious part in the controversy about Pope Joan: S. Maresius, *Joanna Papissa Restituta* (Groningae Frisiorum, 1658), p. 47; N. Serarius, *Moguntiacarum Rerum ab Initio usque ad...hodiernum Archiepiscopum...libri V* (Moguntiae, 1604), pp. 213–18.

[7] Loc. cit. pp. 277 seq.

[8] Loc. cit. pp. 284–8.

[9] Loc. cit. pp. 336 seq.

[10] Loc. cit. pp. 344 seq.

[11] Loc. cit. pp. 334–58.

[12] Loc. cit. pp. 378 seq.

second excommunication by John VIII and accepts Baronius' statement about the second Photian schism.

Another Protestant ecclesiastical historian, J. Basnage,[1] followed the same line as Hanke; and with regard to the letters from John VIII to Photius, he was of the opinion that they had been tampered with by the Latins after the Council. Basnage was not alone in being embarrassed by the existence of two different versions of the same letters.

F. Spanheim was also strongly influenced by Baronius, though he concurs with Hanke and Basnage on a few points, as for instance when he defends the authenticity of the Photian Council and denies the falsification of the Commonitorium which John VIII gave his legates.[2]

The two conflicting tendencies in the accounts of the Photian incident which we had noted in the seventeenth century survived in the eighteenth, though Baronius' influence remained paramount; indeed, Photius' name has degenerated into a sort of shibboleth dividing Catholics and Protestants, the Catholics vilifying him as the historical enemy of the Papacy, and the Protestants glorifying him for his opposition to Rome.

Thus, for instance, J. M. Heinecke[3] and Gottfried Arnold[4] both adopt Nicetas' account as the starting-point for their history of Photius, merely trying to attenuate it in some details. L. T. Spittler[5] shares their opinion in thinking that in Photius' case the Papacy had stepped beyond its rights. J. G. Walch[6] even upholds the authenticity of John's letter to Photius on the *Filioque*. Chr. E. Weismann[7] seems to have been influenced by Hanke's balanced judgement, but believes that the letters of Pope John VIII to Photius were doctored by the Latins. Ch. W. F. Walch,[8] in his historical essay on the councils, also tries his best to be

---

[1] *Histoire de l'Église* (Rotterdam, 1699), vol. I, livre IX, ch. IX, pp. 572 seq.

[2] F. Spanheim, *Opera* (Lugd. Batav. 1701), vol. I: *Historiae Christianae s. IX*, c. XI, par. 4 (*De Schismate Photiano*), pp. 1387–93.

[3] J. M. Heineccius, *Eigentliche und Wahrhaftige Abbildung der Alten und Neuen Griechischen Kirche* (Leipzig, 1711), vol. I, cap. 3, part. 17–27, pp. 147–67.

[4] *Unparteyische Kirchen und Ketzer Historien...* (Schaffhausen, 1740), Th. I, Buch IX, c. IV, pp. 329 seq.

[5] Cf. his summary in the *Grundriss der Geschichte der Christl. Kirche* (Göttingen, 1785), pp. 201 seq.

[6] *Historia Controversiae Graecorum Latinorumque de Processione Spiritus S.* (Jennae, 1751), pp. 32 seq., 40–4.

[7] *Introductio in Memorabilia Ecclesiastica Historiae Sacrae Novi Testamenti* (Halae Magdeburgicae, 1745), vol. I, pp. 788–803.

[8] *Entwurf einer Vollständigen Historie der Kirchenversammlungen* (Leipzig, 1759), vol. IV, pp. 552–83.

fair to the Patriarch. J. M. Schröckh[1] occasionally displays a very shrewd critical sense, as when he persistently points out the obvious partiality of Nicetas and other Ignatian sources and refuses to repeat Baronius' assertion that the Patriarch Sisinnios had re-edited Photius' famous encyclical, though in this, he only followed the monks of Saint Maur.[2] W. Cave[3] is very restrained in his judgement on Photius, but to this English scholar's way of thinking the vehemence of the Popes' intervention against the Patriarch was uncalled for ('in Photium ad ravim usque debacchantes...').

One of the first monographs to deal with Photius from the Catholic side was written by Ch. Faucher,[4] and the solemn and impassioned preface shows in what spirit the monograph is written: the writer is entirely dominated by Baronius, whose severe verdict he can only repeat and endorse. Nor does the first history of the Greek schism written at this time by Laur. Cozza[5] mark any progress on Baronius. One detail deserves noting: in trying to explain how a canon of the Photian Synod found its way into Gratian's *Decretum* and was even quoted by Innocent III, Cozza writes: 'Evidently, Gratian was in the habit of quoting many apocryphal documents.' As to Innocent III, he merely made a mistake.

M. Le Quien[6] was mainly concerned to deny the authenticity of the letter from John VIII to Photius and in the *Panoplia* dwells at length on the Photian case, but always with Baronius as his guide. Among ecclesiastical historians we should mention first Alexander Natalis (Alexandre Noël),[7] L. Ellies du Pin,[8] and Claude Fleury;[9] the last-named dealt fully with the history of Photius and had the advantage of using a copy of the Acts of the Photian Council lent to him by Baluze, but even Fleury, like the rest, had to borrow from Baronius.

---

[1] *Historia Religionis et Ecclesiae Christianae* (ed. P. Marheineke; Berlin, 1828), p. 178. Idem, *Christliche Kirchengeschichte* (Leipzig, 1797), vol. XXIV, p. 160.

[2] *L'Art de Vérifier les Dates* (1783), p. 288.

[3] W. Cave, *Scriptorum Ecclesiasticorum Historia Literaria* (Oxonii, 1743), vol. II, pp. 1, 2, 47 seq., 79 seq.

[4] *Histoire de Photius, Patriarche Schismatique de Constantinople* (Paris, 1772).

[5] *Historia Polemica de Graecorum Schismate* (Rome, 1719), vol. II, pp. 1–162, chiefly p. 147.

[6] *Panoplia Contra Schisma Graecorum* (Paris, 1718), cent. IX, cap. I, pp. 159–85; *De Processione Spiritus S.* (Venetiis, 1762), pp. 302 seq.

[7] *Historia Ecclesiastica Veteris et Novi Testamenti* (Paris, 1699). Cf. his Dissertations in *Thesaurus Theol.* (Venice, 1762), vol. III and M. Sesavniczky, *Ex Hist. Eccles. P. Nat. Alex. De Schismate Graecorum* (Vienna, 1780).

[8] *Histoire de l'Église en Abrégé* (3rd ed. Paris, 1719), vol. III, pp. 12 seq.

[9] *Histoire du Christianisme*, Livre 50 (ed. Paris, 1836), vol. III, pp. 378 seq.

Though his Gallican tendencies sometimes break through his account of Photius' history, he yet gives evidence of critical sense and his study is far more moderate in tone than that of Baronius. He admits among other things the authenticity of the letter of John VIII to Photius on the *Filioque*.

So, thanks to the authority of Baronius and that of his followers, the fate of Photius seemed to be sealed for ever and Baronius' account of him was accepted as strictly accurate. Even the Ruthenes, who wished, in 1720, to unite with the Roman Church, were handed a special oath proclaiming among other things: 'Suscipio... Constantinopolitanam [synodum] quartam, octavam in ordine, ac profiteor in ea Photium merito fuisse damnatum, et sanctum Ignatium patriarcham restitutum.'[1]

Having now reached the modern period, we might close our examination of Western writers on Photius and refer the reader to a summary of Western Catholic opinion of Photius from the sixteenth century to the middle of the nineteenth, which is to be found in the works of Photius' second Catholic biographer, the Abbé J. N. Jager;[2] but we must do justice to another courageous writer who made a valiant attempt to deal more fairly with the Patriarch—A. Pichler.[3] Though his effort was not made altogether in vain, he found very few followers. His opinions did not invariably tally with those of Photius' great historian, Cardinal Hergenröther, but one cannot read without a feeling of sorrow Pichler's self-defence[4] against the severe, and sometimes exaggerated criticisms of the great scholar, however much his authority towered above that of all other historians of the Church in the second

---

[1] Mansi, vol. XXXV, pp. 1437 seq.

[2] *Histoire de Photius et du Schisme des Grecs d'après les Monuments Originaux, la plupart encore inconnus* (Paris, 1844). Some efforts, not always successful, to discover a position that was fairer to Photius were made by V. Gutté, *Histoire de l'Église* (Paris, 1889), vol. VI, ch. IV, pp. 238–50.

[3] *Geschichte der Kirchlichen Trennung* (München, 1865).

[4] *An meine Kritiker* (München, 1865). We may mention a few more ecclesiastical historians of the nineteenth century who preceded Hergenröther and wrote the history of Photius more or less in imitation of Baronius: H. J. Schmitt, *Die Morgenländische Griechisch-Russische Kirche* (Mainz, 1826), pp. 378–419; E. B. Swalue, *Disputatio Academica Inauguralis de Dissidio Ecclesiae Christianae in Graecam et Latinam Photii Auctoritate Maturato* (Lugduni Batavorum, 1829), chs. I–III; A. Neander, *Allgem. Geschichte der Christl. Religion u. Kirche* (Hamburg, 1836), vol. IV, pp. 590–633; A. F. Gfrörer, *Allgemeine Kirchengeschichte* (Stuttgart, 1844), vol. III, pt I, pp. 234–304; J. G. Pitzpius Bey, *Die Orientalische Kirche, übersetzt bei H. Schiel* (Wien, 1857), pp. 24–36; J. P. Bojarski, *Historya Focyusza...* (Lwów, 1895). About Hergenröther's work, see W. Drammer, 'Der Werdegang Hergenröther's *Photius*', in *Orientalia Christiana Periodica* (1941), vol. VII, pp. 36–90.

half of the nineteenth and the beginning of the twentieth centuries. Hergenröther certainly did revive interest in the history of the Greek Patriarch and his work will never lose its value as an indispensable introduction to Photian studies. He also, like his great predecessor Cardinal Baronius, was inspired by the honourable motive of defending the pontifical primacy against the Protestant and rationalist attacks of his day, but he also went too far, and, strangely enough, failed to discover in the history of his subject such materials as would have served his purpose much better. His great contemporary Hefele was similarly misled.

Before the revival of Byzantine studies in recent times, the Western history of Photius and the Eighth Council remained in the blind alley into which Baronius had driven it. Faced with the high walls of controversy, students were tempted to conclude that the path of research had come to a dead end. A few clear-sighted men could have shown the Westerners the mistake they were making—a few critics of Hergenröther in Russia, chiefly the Hieromachos Yared: but did Cardinal Hergenröther ever suspect that an obscure Syrian had been daring enough to answer him?

CHAPTER V

PHOTIUS AND THE EIGHTH COUNCIL IN THE EASTERN TRADITION TILL THE TWELFTH CENTURY

Unpublished treatise on the Councils by the Patriarch Euthymios—Other contemporaries—Photius' canonization—Historians of Constantine Porphyrogennetos' school—Polemists of the eleventh and twelfth centuries—Michael of Anchialos—Twelfth-century chroniclers.

AFTER our analysis of Western tradition on the subject of Photius and the Eighth Council, we must now extend our inquiry to Eastern literature, since it is important to know the Greeks' verdict at different periods on their great Patriarch. Did the Greeks always look upon Photius as the principal agent of the severance of their Church from Rome, as it was the general tendency in the West to assume? Was Photius always regarded as the author of the Latin heresy on the *Filioque*? What tradition was preserved in the long history of the conflicts between Latins and Greeks throughout the Middle Ages of his personality and his work? We must also take into account the Greek tradition on the controverted Councils of the ninth century and verify at what particular time the Greeks began to number the Photian Council among the oecumenical synods.

Attestations on Photius are not wholly lacking in the ninth and tenth centuries but they are not as many as might be expected. Some of those bearing on the adjustment of the Photian schism have already been mentioned; and we have now to consider the short treatise on the councils attributed to the Patriarch Euthymios (907–12), which I discovered in a Greek MS. of the British Museum. The Manuscript (Arundel 528) offers a curious collection of thirty-eight short patristic writings, polemical and otherwise, including a homily by St Basil and two fragments in old Slav, all copied out in different hands. The MS. is on parchment, size 18 (in quarto minori); it contains 192 leaves and the writing is of the second half of the fifteenth century. On pp. 111–17 we find a short tract entitled[1] *Treatise written at the patriarcheion of St Sophia by the saintly patriarch Euthymios of blessed memory.* On

---

[1] τοῦ τῆς μακαρίας λήξεως Εὐθυμίου τοῦ ἁγιωτάτου πατριάρχου ἅτινα ἐγράφησε ἐν τῷ πατριαρχείῳ τῆς ἁγίας Σοφίας.

closer examination, we find that it resembles the work on the councils attributed to Neilos, Metropolitan of Rhodes,[1] anti-Latin controversialist of the fourteenth century, and edited by Justellus,[2] though there are some fundamental differences between the two tracts.

Neilos' tract records nine oecumenical councils, the Eighth being that of Photius, and the Ninth the synod against Barlaam under the Emperor Andronicus. After a summary of the proceedings of the Photian Council, Neilos inserts an extract from the famous letter of John VIII to Photius in connection with the *Filioque* incident, whilst Euthymios' tract only mentions seven oecumenical councils and merely designates the Photian Council as 'the Union Synod'. On the face of it, Euthymios' work represents a much older tradition than that of Neilos, a supposition borne out by one further detail: Euthymios' tract includes, together with a summary of the proceedings of each synod, the definition of the faith of the five first and the seventh councils with the addition of a *homologia tôn paterôn*, or the Fathers' approval of the dogmatic definitions, of the first four synods. Collation of the two texts suggests that Neilos' pamphlet is only a later edition of Euthymios' tract, revised, abbreviated and adapted to the needs of the fourteenth century.

What bears out this deduction is that the Greek MS. no. 968 of the Paris National Library (fifteenth-c., 395 fols., on paper) contains a similar dissertation (fols. 392–5 a) which on careful examination is found to represent an intermediate tradition in the growth of the tractate. First of all, it is anonymous; indeed, this time it could not be attributed to Euthymios, a writer of the tenth century, since its new editor, though following a tradition different from that of Neilos' pamphlet, has added a summary of the Council of Barlaam. It is curious that the new editor remains loyal to the old tradition, so well established by Euthymios, in conferring the title of oecumenical on the first seven councils only. The Councils of Photius and of Barlaam are therefore not reckoned as the Eighth and the Ninth.

Moreover, the treatise of the Paris MS. copies the profession of faith of the first five councils and of the seventh of Euthymios' tract, but omits the Fathers' approval of these definitions. Even in other minor details it bears a greater similarity to Euthymios' work and the comparison of the three productions supports the conclusion that the tractate attributed to Neilos of Rhodes is merely a third edition, adapted to the

[1] Krumbacher, loc. cit. pp. 109, 205, 560.
[2] Chr. Justellus, *Nomocanon Photii* (Paris, 1615), pp. 175–79.

mentality of the fourteenth century, of a short study on the Councils by the Patriarch Euthymios of the tenth century.

The treatise under discussion could in fact have been written by Euthymios, though the MS. which attributes it to him is the only one of its kind and dates from the fifteenth century. Euthymios' biographer [1] himself assures us that the Patriarch had left to his disciples several of his writings, and we know three homilies of his composition in honour of St Anne and another on the Virgin's holy girdle.[2] Now the opening words of the homily in honour of St Anne's conception [3] are only a short dogmatic excursus on the Trinity and the Incarnation, strangely recalling in style and sometimes in words the definitions of the first oecumenical councils, as summarized in Euthymios' book and also by the anonymous Greek dissertations on the councils. Nothing then precludes the possibility of the Patriarch being the author of this treatise, which was later copied by an anonymous scribe of the fourteenth century and again circulated in a new edition over the name of Neilos of Rhodes.[4]

Two inferences of some importance can be drawn from this short study: first, that the Patriarch Euthymios knew the Acts of the Photian Council in the version that has come down to us and that the Acts he may have consulted had the protocol of the sixth and seventh sessions as we know it, so that these versions must be absolutely authentic. Since Euthymios quoted them some ten years after the Council, they could not possibly have been falsified, as some would have us believe, in the fourteenth century. Second, this short study provides evidence that the Byzantine Church did not officially confer on the Photian Council the title of Eighth Oecumenical Council. Even when the memory of that Council was still fresh, the Greeks continued to number only seven oecumenical councils, the Photian Council being ranked immediately after the first seven great councils. St Euthymios even gives it the designation which the Council itself had claimed, of 'holy and oecumenical synod'; but it is not termed the Eighth—it merely remains the 'Union Synod'.

Corroboration of this is found in another document, also unpublished, the profession of faith of a disciple of Photius, Nicholas Mysticos, which

---

[1] De Boor, *Vita Euthymii*, p. 30.

[2] M. Jugie, 'Homélies Mariales Byzantines', in *Patrologia Orientalis* (Paris, 1922, 1926), vol. XVI, pp. 499–514; vol. XIX, pp. 441–55.

[3] Loc. cit. vol. XVI, pp. 499–502.

[4] See Appendix III, pp. 456, 457, the edition of an extract from Euthymios' treatise concerning the Photian Synod.

he made after his elevation to the patriarchate and is preserved in the Vatican MS. Ottob. n. 147.[1] The new Patriarch there declares (fol. 440) that he accepts the decisions of the seven oecumenical councils, which he enumerates by name, an attestation which, coming from a disciple of Photius, is especially valuable, since he must have felt inclined more than anybody else to add the Photian Council to the oecumenical councils; and yet, he too clung to the old tradition of his Church.

As regards the person of Photius, we should in the first place note what was said about him by John, author of a biography of St Joseph the Hymnographer, a work of special value, since it accurately reflects the feelings towards Ignatius and Photius prevailing at the end of the ninth century. Writing of Ignatius and of how much he thought of the Patriarch Photius, John calls him[2] 'the godly Ignatius, distinguished by many virtues and full of zeal for Christ, mounted not long ago to the helm of the patriarchate'. Of Photius he writes: '[after him] the patriarchal throne fell to Photius, who was president of the Supreme Council [senate?][3] and excelled by his gift of eloquence, his knowledge and the rectitude of his character. For his skill in organization and administration,[4] he reached the primacy of the priesthood; into other things concerning him we need not enter, nor allow calumnies to distract us.' Here one is made to feel the changed atmosphere that prevailed in Byzantium after the settlement of the quarrel between Ignatius and Photius. The other biographer of the Hymnographer, Theophanes, is not so explicit in his references to the two rival Patriarchs, but he is true to the same feeling when he describes Photius as 'ever-remembered' Patriarch.[5] Arethas of Caesarea, a disciple of Photius, goes still further in his veneration for his master, when he places him in paradise next to St Chrysostom and St Nicephorus.[6] On another occa-

---

[1] Mentioned by A. Mai, *Spicilegium Romanum* (Rome, 1839–44), vol. x, p. ix.

[2] S. Josephi Hymnographi Vita, auctore Joanne Diacono, *P.G.* vol. 105, cols. 968–9.

[3] τῆς συγκλήτου βουλῆς.

[4] πρὸς τὸ συνθεῖναι καὶ σκευάσαι πράγματα ἐπιτήδειον.

[5] A. Papadopoulos-Kerameus, *Monumenta Graeca et Latina ad Photii Hist. pertinentia* (Petropoli, 1901), vol. II, p. 10: Ἰγνατίου δηλαδὴ τοῦ θείου ἀρχιερέως ὁσίως πατριαρχοῦντος.... Photius...ἀείμνητος πατριάρχης.

[6] Epitaphius in Euthymium Patr. republished by M. Jugie, *Patr. Orient.* of Graffin-Nau, vol. XVI, p. 498: μετὰ τοῦ χρυσοῦ Ἰωάννου ἐν ἐξορίᾳ συνθανατούμενε, μετὰ Νικηφόρου καὶ Φωτίου τῶν ἀοιδίμων τοῖς διωγμοῖς καὶ θανάτοις συνδοξαζόμενε.

sion, Arethas replies in unrestrained terms to the Armenians:[1] 'Among them there was recently found one holy by his family ties and holier still for his wisdom, both human and divine. Who is he? Photius, the one raised to-day to the highest in heaven.' This is frank canonization, and another disciple of the Patriarch, Nicholas Mysticos, goes still further in his letter to the Emir of Crete: 'The most eminent of God's high priests and the most famous, Photius, my father in the Holy Ghost, has likewise written to Your Excellency's father....'[2] In another letter, this time addressed to a Christian king, the ruler of Armenia, Nicholas calls Photius 'the very saintly patriarch'.[3]

To these attestations should be added a saying by the biographer of St Euthymios, Basil, archbishop of Thessalonica, whom I have quoted elsewhere.[4] The leading passage is worth quoting:

> It was the blessed Photius who, as his name suggests, enlightened the whole world with the fulness of his wisdom; who from his infancy had been devoted to Christ, suffered confiscation and exile for venerating His image and was from the outset associated with his father in struggles for the faith. Hence his life was wonderful and his death agreeable to God and sealed by miracles.

This at any rate is how I render the passage; but even if the last words refer not to Photius but to his father St Sergius, the main idea of the sentence would stand, since Photius is here 'associated' with a saint whose holiness was sealed by his miracles, and therefore is likewise looked upon as a saint. Besides, as Photius is the subject of the sentence and his father is mentioned only casually in a subordinate clause, it would only be logical to apply the concluding words to Photius.

There is another point in favour of the above reading. Photius' father has his commemorative notice in the Greek Synaxarion of 13 March,[5] but while he is recorded as confessor (*homologetes*), without any miracle being attached to his name, Photius is called the thaumaturgos[6] in a

---

[1] Preserved in the Synodal Library of Moscow, cod. 441, fols. 43a–4, quoted by A. Papadopoulos-Kerameus: Ὁ πατριάρχης Φώτιος ὡς Πατὴρ ἅγιος τῆς ὀρθ. Ἐκκλησίας, *Byz. Zeitschr.* vol. VIII, 1889, p. 662: μεθ' ὧν καὶ ὁ χθές τε καὶ πρώην ἱερὸς μὲν τὸ γένος, ἱερώτερος δὲ τὴν σοφίαν, ὅση τε θεία καὶ ὅση τῆς κατ' ἀνθρώπους λογίζεται· τίς οὗτος; ὁ τοῖς οὐρανίοις ἀδύτοις τανῦν ἐγκατοικιζόμενος Φώτιος.

[2] *P.G.* vol. III, cols. 36, 37: Ὁ ἐν ἀρχιερεῦσι θεοῦ μέγιστος καὶ ἀοίδιμος Φώτιος ὁ ἐμὸς ἐν Πνεύματι ἁγίῳ Πατὴρ πρὸς τὸν πατέρα τῆς ὑμῶν εὐγενείας....

[3] Loc. cit. col. 365.

[4] Cf. my *Les Légendes de Constantin et de Méthode*, p. 144.

[5] H. Delehaye, *Synaxarium Constantinopolitanum* (Brussels, 1902), A.S. Nov., col. 682. [6] Cod. Paris. Gr. 1594.

Synaxarion of the twelfth century. A miracle, remarkable enough in the eyes of posterity, signalized his life, namely the defeat of the Russians in their attack on Constantinople in 860. Whatever one may think about the miracle,[1] it remains none the less true that the Byzantines considered the event as such and the Continuator of Theophanes endorsed their opinion.[2] It is true that the account by Simeon the Logothete[3] assumes the miracle to have been performed by the Virgin, but still through the intercession of Photius. All these attestations point to the fact that Photius was venerated shortly after his death, at least by a section of the people. It is true that the depositions come from the circle of his students and admirers, but is the cult of any hero ever inaugurated otherwise?[4]

It remains to inquire whether and at what period the cult of Photius was approved by the Byzantine Church. In this inquiry, we need not attach too much importance to the evidence of Papadopoulos-Kerameus, as his zeal for his hero's glorification was somewhat extravagant and he apparently did not succeed in proving that Photius was canonized soon after his death. Similarly I refuse to accept his statement, until further evidence be forthcoming, that the Athos MS. containing the Patriarch's 'replies to Amphilochus' and representing Photius with a halo dates from the tenth century;[5] though it would be more difficult to dismiss his assertion that the Patriarch's name figures in the Synaxarion (Cod. 40) of the Holy Cross monastery of Jerusalem, which dates from the tenth to the eleventh century.[6] It is stated there that his feast was celebrated in the monastery of John the Baptist of the Eremia District, while similar references appear in eight other manuscripts whose dates range between the twelfth and fifteenth centuries.[7] It is true that his

---

[1] Cf. what I said about the Russian danger in my book, *Les Légendes de Constantin et de Méthode*, pp. 176 seq.

[2] (Bonn), p. 196.   [3] Loc. cit. p. 674.

[4] See p. 272 on what Nicetas the Paphlagonian says about the cultus of Photius after his death.

[5] Papadopoulos-Kerameus, loc. cit. p. 664.   [6] Idem, loc. cit. p. 662.

[7] Cod. 219 of the Berlin Royal Library (12th–13th c.); Cod. Paris. Gr. 1594 (12th c.); Cod. Ambrosianus C. 101 (12th c.); Cod. 227 of the Petrograd Imperial Libr. (12th c.); Cod. 354 of the Syn. Libr. of Moscow (13th c.); Cod. 163 of the Messina Univ. (12th c.); Cod. 239 of the Imp. Libr. of Moscow (14th c.); Cod. A. III, 16 of the Basle Libr. (15th c.). Papadopoulos-Kerameus (*Byz. Zeitschr.* pp. 668 seq.) adds two more MS. of eleventh- and twelfth-century pericopes containing readings for the feast of Photius. Cod. 266 of the monastic library of St John the Evangelist of Patmos (10th c.); Vatican Menologion Gr. 1613 (11th c.); Cod. Mediceo-Laurent. San Marco 787 (11th c.); Cod. Paris. Gr. 1590 (11th c.); Cod. Paris. Gr. 1589 (12th c.).

name is missing in some very important MSS., for instance, in the
Menology of Basil II, yet it remains beyond dispute that Photius' name
began to appear in Byzantine Synaxaria as early as the end of the
tenth century and the beginning of the eleventh, so that Photius must
have been canonized in the second half of the tenth century at the latest.
We may then subscribe to the opinion of M. Jugie,[1] who thinks that
Photius' name was added by the usual process of acclamation to the
other names of saintly Patriarchs, to the *tomos tês Henôseôs*, under the
Patriarch Sisinnios (996–8), at a time when the last traces of the schism
provoked by the fourth marriage of Leo VI had been obliterated.[2] For
the present, we have no solid justification for moving the date back to
an earlier period.

Whatever views may be held of this canonization, it cannot be gain-
said that it did take place. Whether the cult of Photius was widespread
or not, or whether St Ignatius was a more popular saint than Photius,
is another question altogether, and this is no place for wearying the
reader with details. Photius' canonization was at least no more unusual
than that, say, of Constantine the Great, who was baptized by an Arian
bishop, or than the canonization of the Empress Irene, who certainly
could not be held up as a model for Christian mothers to copy. Now
two considerations should not be omitted: first, if all that we have said
about Photius' 'schism' is true, then the Byzantine Church was, at the
time that Photius was canonized, in normal communion with Rome;
and second, that in the tenth century canonizations were not yet reserved,
even in the Western Church, to the decision of the Pope alone, but
could be promulgated by an ordinary bishop.

We may then conclude that Photius' name was held in great esteem by
most Byzantines in the tenth century, and of this indirect signs can be
found in some historical works. About the middle of the tenth century
a certain number of historical writings, inspired by Constantine Porphyrogennetos, were published in Byzantium and we know the main
purpose that prompted all this literary output within the learned
Emperor's circle:[3] it was necessary, for the glorification of Basil I,
founder of the new dynasty, to disparage his predecessor Michael III

---

[1] 'Le Culte de Photius dans l'Église Byzantine', in *Revue de l'Orient Chrétien*
(1922–3), 3rd ser., tom. III, pp. 109 seq. Note that this study, though out of date,
has not lost its value.

[2] Cf. also A. Michel, *Humbert und Kerullarios* (Paderborn, 1930), vol. II, pp. 13–18.

[3] Cf. Rambaud, *L'Empire Grec du Xe siècle* (Paris), pp. 51 seq., 137 seq.;
Krumbacher, loc. cit. pp. 252 seq.

as much as plausible propaganda could bear. Hence arose the legend of Michael as a drunkard, an atheist, a mocker of the sacred liturgy, who cared for nothing but pleasure and sport and let his reign take care of itself and the Empire go to pieces; Basil, on the other hand, was the providential tool in God's hands for the chastisement of an impious unbeliever and the salvation of the Empire. By the same token, Ignatius was placed by the writers of the Porphyrogennetos school in a brighter and more sympathetic light than his rival, since Ignatius had made a stand against the blasphemies of Michael and Bardas, suffering persecution for his pains; but it was under Basil's reign and by Basil's orders that he was set free. All this political propaganda did no good to Photius' reputation.

And yet, what is surprising is that the best of these writers are very discreet with regard to Photius. Joseph Genesios, who wrote a history in four volumes of the Emperors reigning between the years 813 and 886, is, in fact, very partial to Ignatius, but he dare not speak ill of Photius. In his opinion, the misfortunes that befell Ignatius were brought on him by Michael and Bardas, as has been pointed out already, and only in one place does he directly refer to Photius in connection with Ignatius' deposition, when he writes:[1] 'Bardas put in his place Photius, who excelled in a certain number of good things, but was inferior in others.' This is not a very flattering compliment, but we should not forget that Joseph Genesios' father, Constantine, was a keen partisan of Ignatius, whom he visited even in prison, so that the family tradition of the Genesios was decidedly Ignatian. Under the circumstances, one would have expected Constantine's son to be more emphatic in his dislike of Photius, but even he had to reckon with the fact that Photius' reputation had considerably improved during his second patriarchate. More characteristic still is the way Porphyrogennetos deals with Photius. In his biography of Basil I[2] he of course transforms Ignatius' reinstatement into a meritorious deed of Basil's, who thereby restored peace in the Church and, as behoved an Emperor, repaired the damage done to a prelate. He had to give the fact a slight twist; otherwise it would have been difficult to glorify the blessed memory of the founder of the new dynasty. Again, in telling the story of Photius' reinstatement after Ignatius' death, he does his best to colour Basil's treatment of Photius in exile as flatteringly to Basil as public credulity could stand:[3]

[1] (Bonn), l. IV, p. 100.
[2] Theoph. Cont. c. 32 (Bonn), p. 262.   [3] Ibid. c. 44, p. 276.

He handed back the government of the Church in a regular manner to one who previously had wished to conduct it in an irregular manner. He gave the succession to the learned Photius...canonically and lawfully. But even before that, he never ceased to treat him generously and with honour, in deference to his great learning and virtue, and when he deprived him of his throne, wishing to do no more than justice demanded, omitted nothing that would soften the blow, placed apartments in the palace at his disposal and appointed him teacher and tutor of his children.

The Continuator of Theophanes, who wrote mainly under Genesios' inspiration, proceeds in the same way: all Ignatius' trials are attributed to Bardas; Photius is 'renowned for his learning'; it was Bardas who forced priests to rally to Photius; Photius' prayers are credited with the divine intervention against the Russians in 860. Now it is my conviction that the testimony of the Porphyrogennetos school of historians is of exceptional importance, since despite its tendentious character they dared not make a frontal attack on Photius, whose memory was cherished and venerated by the majority of their contemporaries; at the same time, their testimony was a contributory factor in the growth of the 'Photian Legend', since it further explained away the sober and laconic statements by the Continuator of George the Monk,[1] whose narrative can be called an expurgated edition of Pseudo-Simeon's 'history' of the unfortunate Patriarch.

The writings of the 'imperial historians' moreover predisposed posterity to place its confidence in the historical efforts of Pseudo-Simeon, Photius' bitterest critic, certain statements of whom strangely recall the tone of the anti-Photianist Collection. No matter what one may think of the character of this anonymous 'historian', one thing is certain: he belonged to the camp of the oft-mentioned die-hards, who, even after the reunion of most of the Ignatians with the official Church and after Stylianos' capitulation, obstinately persisted in their hatred of Photius, and it is quite possible that this faction survived till the beginning of the second half of the tenth century, the time when that chronicle was written. In fact, the record goes as far as 963, the year of Romanos' death,[2] so that the party possibly vanished for good at the end of the tenth century, at the final adjustment of the quarrels over the fourth marriage of Leo VI—which would explain better why Photius' name was then added by acclamation to the names of the other Patriarchs.

[1] (Bonn), pp. 826, 829, 831, 841.
[2] Krumbacher, loc. cit. pp. 358 seq.

One thing at least should not be overlooked: none of the historians of the tenth century see in Photius the main author of the schism or the champion of the national Byzantine Church against Roman authority. Pseudo-Simeon frankly detests him, it is true, but the dominant motives of his hatred were either personal or confused with Byzantine issues of a political nature. The historians do not even credit Photius with championing the Byzantine faith on the *Filioque* against the Latin 'heresy' and, what is worth noting, Nicholas Mysticos' profession of faith makes no reference to the issue.

One would at first have expected Photius to grow in popularity in the Greek literature of the eleventh century, chiefly after the schism of Michael Cerularius; but here again we shall be disappointed. One of the first anti-Latin controversialists, the Russian Metropolitan Leo, for instance, breaks off the controversy on the *Filioque* started by Photius to confine himself to the discussion on the Azymes. Nowhere does he quote Photius;[1] and when he attacks the Frankish bishops, Leo of Achrida never once appeals to Photius as the patron and leader of these practices.[2]

Nicetas Pectoratus, who had the distinction of rousing Cardinal Humbert to anger, battles against the Azymes, the celibacy of the clergy and chiefly the Saturday fast, but all on his own initiative; for, had he harked back to Photius in this matter, we should probably have found in the impetuous cardinal's writings some explosive outburst on the Patriarch of Constantinople; but Humbert apparently does not even know the name of Photius, and his silence in this respect speaks volumes.[3]

More curious still is Cerularius' procedure: he certainly borrows from Photius' writings, but nowhere does he credit him with having taken the lead in the anti-Latin campaign, though he mentions him in his homily on the restoration of images, when he quotes the acclamations in honour of the holy Patriarchs and places Photius next in rank to Ignatius.[4]

Nor is any mention of Photius to be found in the correspondence

---

[1] Ed. Pavlov, Πρὸς Ῥωμαίους ἤτοι πρὸς Λατίνους περὶ τῶν ἀζύμων, *Kriticheskie Opuitui po Ist. drev. Greko-Russkoi Polemiki* (St Petersburg, 1878), pp. 115–32.

[2] *Epistola de Azymis et Sabbatis*, *P.G.* vol. 120, cols. 836–44.

[3] *Contra Nicetam*, *P.G.* vol. 120, cols. 1011–21, 1021–38. Cf. A. Michel, *Humbert und Kerullarios*, vol. II, pp. 371 seq. Cf. K. Schweinburg, 'Die Textgeschichte des Gespräches mit den Franken von Nicetas Stethatos', in *Byz. Zeitschr.* (1934), vol. XXXIV, pp. 313 seq.

[4] *Homilia in festo Restitutionis Imaginum*, *P.G.* vol. 120, cols. 729, 732.

between Michael Cerularius and Peter, Patriarch of Antioch,[1] a feat of discretion that seems significant. And yet, Michael lays every possible blame at the Latins' door, and had there been at the time any disagreement between Greeks and Latins on the Photian question and the ninth-century councils which concerned Photius, Michael and his partisans would undoubtedly have referred to it. Michael knew all about the Photian Council and even quoted one of its decisions in his *Panoplia*, if we suppose that this work was really his. The passage is taken from the sixth session:[2]

In the Acts of the holy and oecumenical synod, presided over by Photius, the very saintly Patriarch of Constantinople, the following was written: 'If any one should, as stated before, venture so far in his madness as to propose another symbol and call it a definition, or dare to make additions to, or omissions from, the symbol as handed down to us, let him be anathema.'

Nor does the writer here call the council 'Eighth Oecumenical': it is 'the Council of Photius', the designation of 'Union Council' being reserved to the synod of 995–6.[3]

Theophylactus, archbishop of Bulgaria, does not mention Photius,[4] but in the Life of St Clement attributed to him he makes St Methodius a keen opponent of the *Filioque*.[5]

Much to the point also is the study on the Greek schism attributed to Nicetas, chartophylax of Nicaea, whose pamphlet has this reference to the Photian schism:

Under Photius, Patriarch of Constantinople, there was a great schism, when the Romans were charged with numerous transgressions, as stated in his encyclical letter. When union between the Churches had been restored, as evidenced by the synod which Photius summoned, and John of Rome had canonically recovered his most ancient privileges, no one thought of examining the Romans' transgressions which the Sixth Council and Photius himself, so we are told, had laid to their charge. 108 years elapsed between the Sixth and the Seventh Councils, when the Churches remained united and Roman errors were never once mentioned, with the exception of the iconoclastic heresy over which they separated again. But ever since the Seventh Council—even previous to it—till Photius, no one had a word to say about those Roman errors, which Photius and the Sixth Council had made so much of; and when after all these troubles and rumours Photius

---

[1] Ibid. cols. 781–816.
[2] A. Michel, loc. cit. p. 218.   [3] Michel, loc. cit. p. 242.
[4] Liber de iis quorum Latini incusantur, *P.G.* vol. 126, cols. 221–49.
[5] Ibid. cols. 1201, 1205.

reunited with the Romans without the slightest difficulty, peace reigned undisturbed between the Churches.

But under Sergius, who ruled at the time of the Bulgaroctonos, we are told that there arose a schism—for what reason I do not know, but the quarrel was apparently over some sees. Well, if the Romans' errors had so far remained unknown, nobody could put the blame on that communion this time; but since they were known at the Sixth Council, and better still under Photius, the responsibility should lie with the union, as it was then that what was considered to be amiss should have been discarded and corrected—at least in words, if the evil was beyond human strength. If the complaints were really serious—which seems incredible, as we are driven to infer from the fact that the bishops left them so long unheeded—then what did the Greeks blame the Romans for? Hence you see that the schisms mentioned were brought about by our own people. Photius, who had fallen out with Nicholas....[1]

This extract shows first of all that in the eleventh century part of the clergy were not in favour of the new rupture between Rome and Byzantium provoked by Michael Cerularius, Photius' complaints against the Latins, repeated by Michael, being considered insufficient ground for a schism. The Emperor's policy, which favoured an entente with Rome, could therefore depend on support in the ranks of the clergy. Furthermore, the writer of this study considered the rupture between Photius and Rome to be a purely personal matter, and therefore, although not particularly friendly, did not look upon Photius as the symbol of anti-Roman tendencies.

We may also indirectly conclude from the text that the writer did not rank the Photian Council among the first oecumenical councils, for it is because he marks the different periods by their councils that he happens to mention the sixth and the seventh; but when he reaches the period of Photius, he merely mentions the Patriarch's name. The text also warns us not to make too much of the misunderstanding that arose between Rome and Byzantium under the Patriarch Sergius, since the author, who wrote some ten years after the event, reports it from hearsay and confesses ignorance of its motives; a rather surprising admission.[2]

---

[1] κατὰ πόσον καιρὸν καὶ ποῖα αἰτιάματα ἐσχίσθη ἀφ' ἡμῶν ἡ Ῥωμαϊκὴ Ἐκκλησία. P.G. vol. 120, cols. 717 seq.

[2] Pavlov, Kriticheskie Opuitui (St Petersburg, 1878), pp. 132–7, has published a treatise almost identical, taken from a manuscript of the Synodal Library (no. 368, fols. 248 seq., no. 207, fols. 314 seq.), attributed to the Patriarch Photius. It omits the schism of Cerularius. The treatise attributed to Nicetas of Nicaea is apparently of older date. Writings of this class have so often been recopied and recast that they deserve little confidence. Cf. Grumel, Regestes, vol. II, pp. 241 seq., Échos d' Orient (1935), pp. 129–38, and Hergenröther, Photius, vol. III, pp. 843 seq.

We are also in possession of two other official documents proving that the Byzantine Church of the eleventh century did not number the Photian Council among the great oecumenical councils. The first is the letter written by the Russian Metropolitan John II (1080–9) to the anti-Pope Clement III (1080–1100); this is interesting, because it illustrates the Byzantine mentality of the period in matters concerning Rome. Before detailing for the Pope's benefit all the errors that were imputed to the Latins, John II outlined the foundations of the true Catholic faith, namely, the oecumenical councils. One passage is so typical that it deserves full quotation: [1]

All profess that there are seven holy and oecumenical Councils, and these are the seven pillars of the faith of the Divine Word on which He erected His holy mansion, the Catholic and Oecumenical Church. These seven venerable, holy and oecumenical Councils have been treated with equal respect by all the bishops and doctors of the See of Peter, the standard-bearers of the Holy and Blessed Apostles.

They even attended these councils and spoke there the same language, some being personally present, commendably identifying themselves with what was done and associating themselves with what was said; others delegated their most intimate friends with equal commendation, to offer their collaboration, and they confirmed all matters by the authority of your apostolic and divine See. The first holy and oecumenical Synod was attended by Sylvester; the second by Damasus, the third by Celestin. The blessed and renowned Pope Leo laid the foundation of the Fourth holy and oecumenical Synod and the saintly letter, so full of wisdom, which he wrote to Flavian was called the pillar of orthodoxy by all who graced the Synod by their presence. Vigilius was present at the Fifth Synod, while the Sixth was attended by Agathon, a venerable man, full of godly wisdom, and the Seventh by the very saintly Pope Hadrian, who spoke through the mouth of the saintly and God-fearing [*theoforôn*] men he delegated, Peter, archpriest of the very Holy Church of Rome, the priest Peter and the Abbot of the monastery of St Sabbas in Rome.

Important as this letter is, it never once alludes to Photius and his Council.

The second document is the report of the synod held in 1089 in Constantinople at the request of Alexis I Comnenus, who was then working for reunion with Rome; in this synod it was decided to request the Pope to send to Constantinople his profession of faith,

[1] Pavlov, loc. cit. pp. 58 seq.

which was to include his acceptance of the first seven oecumenical councils.[1]

The Latin embassy sent to Constantinople in 1112, of which the archbishop of Milan, John Grossolanus, was a member, became the occasion for lively discussions between Latins and Greeks on the subject of the dogmatic and disciplinary differences between the two Churches, and seven Greek theologians were asked to reply to their Latin opponent; unfortunately, not all their writings have so far been published,[2] but what little there is provides a fairly comprehensive view of the debate. The fragments of Grossolanus' speech,[3] the short studies by Eustratios of Nicaea[4] and the contribution by John Phournes[5] make no reference either to Photius or to his Council. The *Filioque*, however, was the main topic of the discussion, in the course of which Eustratios even quoted the councils, but always in general terms, without referring to them by name. He probably also made use of Photius' *Mystagogy*. As far as we are able to judge to-day, Euthymios Zigabenos, who possibly also took part in the debate, was the only one to show that Photius was not forgotten by the Greek theologians in those days. In fact, Euthymios embodied Photius' treatise on the Procession of the Holy Ghost in his *Panoplia* and added at the end of his work a fragment of Photius' letter to Boris-Michael, with the Patriarch's essay on the oecumenical councils.[6] One would not wish to overrate the implication of the compliment—some would discover there the promotion of Photius to the rank of a Doctor of the Church—but it is none the less significant.

I have had occasion to refer to another Graeco-Latin dispute in Constantinople in 1135 between Anselm of Havelberg and Nicetas of

---

[1] W. Holtzmann, 'Unionsverhandlungen zwischen Kaiser Alexis I und Papst Urban II im Jahre 1089', in *Byz. Zeitschr.* (1928), vol. XXVIII, pp. 50–62. One may add the profession of faith of the Russian prince Vladimir in the Russian *Lietopis*, which also gives the seven councils. Cf. A. Pavlov, loc. cit. pp. 5–26.

[2] See the list of these writings in V. Grumel's 'Autour du Voyage de Grossolanus à Constantinople', in *Échos d Orient* (1933), vol. XXXII, pp. 22–33.

[3] *P.G.* vol. 127, cols. 911–19; *Bibliotheca Cassinensis* (Monte Cassino, 1880), vol. IV, pp. 351–8.

[4] Published by A. Demetrakopoulos, Ἐκκλησιαστικὴ βιβλιοθήκη (Leipzig, 1866), pp. 47–71 (see p. 68, a fine chapter on Popes Damasus, Celestin, Leo, Vigilius, Agathon, Gregory the Great and Zachary), pp. 71–84, 84–99, 100–21, 151–60, 161–98.

[5] Ibid. pp. 36–47.

[6] *P.G.* vol. 130, tit. XIII, cols. 876, 1360 (appendix). Cf. tit. XXIV, col. 1189, an extract from Photius' writings against the Paulicians. Photius there is called ὁ μακαριώτατος πατριάρχης.

Nicomedia;[1] but it was not the only theological disputation in which this German bishop engaged in the East, for in the course of his second journey he arranged another debate on 2 and 3 October 1154 in Thessalonica, this time with Basil of Achrida,[2] the archbishop of that city. According to the *Dialogue* published by the latter, the name of Photius did not come up in the discussion at all.[3] We may note in passing that the letter this same Basil wrote to Pope Hadrian IV (1154–9) was very deferential to the bishop of Rome.[4]

Among other Greek controversialists we should first mention Nicholas of Methone, an outstanding theologian in his day, who in his books, most of them published by Demetrakopoulos,[5] gives evidence of a fair knowledge of Photius' writings, but nowhere quotes him by name. Only once does he quote a canon of the Photian Council of 861, canon XVI, in his plea for the Patriarch Nicholas IV Muzaton.[6] The case of this Patriarch presented a curious similarity to that of Pope Formosus. It is known that Nicholas had resigned his see of Cyprus and retired to a monastery; but his rivals pretended that Nicholas had in so doing renounced episcopal honours and had ceased to be a bishop. Thereupon the bishop of Methone, at a synod summoned to settle the dispute and in the presence of the Emperor, made a great speech in defence of the validity and legitimacy of the election, but to little effect, since Nicholas IV was called upon to resign in 1151. Hergenröther[7] registers surprise that Nicholas of Methone should on that occasion have failed to quote the canon of the Council of 879–80, forbidding prelates who reverted to monastic life to resume their episcopal functions; but there is nothing surprising about it, since by quoting it the bishop of Methone would have played into the hands of the opposition, the canon of the Council of 879–80 being far more explicit and emphatic than canon XVI of the Council of 861.

[1] See p. 345.
[2] Cf. V. Grumel on when the theological controversy between Basil of Achrida and Anselm of Havelberg in Salonica took place, *Échos d'Orient* (1930), vol. XXXIII, p. 336.
[3] Jos. Schmidt, *Des Basileus aus Achrida...unedierte Dialoge* (München, 1901).
[4] *P.G.* vol. 119, cols. 929–33.
[5] Νικολάου ἐπ. Μεθώνης λόγοι δύο, loc. cit. pp. 199–380. Cf. also the Latin edition of two of his writings: *Nicolai Methonae episcopi Orationes Duae contra Heresim Dicentium Sacrificium pro nobis Salutare non Trisypostatae Divinitati sed Patri soli allatum esse* (Lipsiae, 1865).
[6] Loc. cit. pp. 284, 285.
[7] *Photius*, loc. cit. vol. III, p. 805. Cf. also what he says (ibid. pp. 806 seq.) on the letter of Basil of Achrida to Hadrian IV.

No mention of Photius is made either by John of Jerusalem in the second half of the twelfth century[1] or by John of Claudiopolis,[2] the only polemists of this school whose writings have been published.

One polemical work by Michael of Anchialos, the bitterest enemy of the union between the two Churches that was then being prepared under Manuel Comnenus, deserves special attention. It is written in the form of a dialogue between the Patriarch Michael of Anchialos and the Emperor,[3] who after vainly trying various arguments to convince the obstinate Patriarch of the urgency of reunion finally appealed to the example of Photius, who also had made peace with the same Latins he had fought. To this the Patriarch retorted:[4]

Even granting that Photius sinned by this action, they [the Latins] were not thereby justified, for it is not transgressions that make good law, and it is not in evil but in good deeds that we should imitate and follow others.... The fact is, however, that no such fault is to be found in relation to the case we are dealing with in that very godly man,[5] whose life offers no example of greater strength than his behaviour in this case; strength, I say, to crush and refuse to have anything to do with those atheistic and impious Italians, although here as elsewhere calumny may have its own way and some people have not hesitated to call him 'a good divider and a bad uniter'. The reverse is the truth. As a matter of fact, this very saintly Photius, after his formidable attack, far from unconditionally readmitting those he had cast off to unite with him and the Church, first imposed proper guarantees that they would be orthodox in future and recant the blasphemies they should never have uttered. They then addressed to him their symbol of faith, which they worded in orthodox terms, whereby they agreed to remain steadfast in that faith, to add or to subtract nothing, to number among the enemies of truth and the champions of mendacious error any who should dare to do so; they then followed the same procedure with the three other Patriarchs, according to the ancient custom by which one honoured with patriarchal and supreme dignity should send to his brothers and co-Patriarchs his encyclical letters of appointment to inform the whole world of his personal orthodoxy and agreement in faith with the Fathers who preceded him and were orthodox.

This, to my way of thinking, was what was fully meant by the canon on

[1] Dositheos, Τόμος ἀγάπης (Jassy, 1698), pp. 504–38.
[2] Pavlov, loc. cit. pp. 189–91.
[3] Published by Chr. Loparev with a commentary in *Vizantiiskii Vremennik* (1907), vol. XIV, pp. 334–57.
[4] Cf. V. Grumel, 'Le Filioque au Concile Photien de 879–880', in *Échos d'Orient* (1930), vol. XXIX, pp. 252–64.
[5] τὸν θειότατον τοῦτον ἄνδρα.

whose terms he readmitted the Italians, for we find there the following: 'Let the Pope as well as ancient Rome and the communion under him hold as rejected and likewise reject whosoever is considered rejected by the very saintly Photius, and through him by our Church in fulfilment of their duty.' Now it is evident from this that this man acted like those wise doctors who skilfully forestall future diseases and administer preventive remedies to those suspected of being threatened with a possible affection, and in this sense deserved no blame but acted for motives of prudence, however changeable he may have seemed to be, when he meant and intended to obtain but one thing—that the Italians had no right to add in writing anything as truth to the Symbol, knowing full well that they were in duty bound never to do anything in disagreement with the feelings of the Greeks and their spiritual leaders in connection with the Divinity and what touches religion; and that if they should be so daring, they would, by their own previous admission, fall under the anathema.

Here is evidence that Michael of Anchialos knew the same version as is known to-day of the Acts of the Photian Council. He first mentions canon I of the Council, voted by the Fathers during the fifth session as 'the true guarantee that they [the Latins] would be orthodox in future and recant blasphemies which they should never have uttered'. Their worst blasphemy was, to his mind, the addition of *Filioque* to the Symbol. So, after accepting canon I, 'they addressed to him their symbol of faith, which they worded in orthodox terms, whereby they agreed to remain steadfast in that faith, to add or to subtract nothing, to number among the enemies of truth and the champions of mendacious error any who should dare to do so....' The last words recall the solemn declaration[1] read by the protonotary Peter after the recitation of the Symbol of Nicaea without the addition of the *Filioque*. This was the only occasion under Photius' patriarchate when Rome's delegates presented to Photius and to the other Patriarchs the Symbol of Nicaea without the *Filioque*. In the same passage, there seems also to be an open hint of Photius' disclosure in his *Mystagogia* that Hadrian III had sent him his synodical letter containing the Nicene Symbol without the *Filioque*. This also was the only known instance under the same patriarchate.

Canon I does not mention the addition to the Symbol and Michael is quite aware of it, since he states that the canon was really meant as a manœuvre to bind the Romans to the faith without the *Filioque* as laid down in the Nicene Symbol. He therefore does not appeal to the canon

[1] Mansi, vol. XVII, p. 516.

as conclusive demonstration;[1] it only embodied[2] the promise which the Latins were asked at the sixth session of the synod to keep. The passage in question can therefore be taken as additional evidence that the Acts of the Photian Synod were known to the Greeks of the twelfth century in the same version as we know them to-day.

We may in this connection recall the attitude of another contemporary of Michael Anchialos, Nicetas of Maronea, a partisan of the union, who in his *Dialogues*, only a few fragments of which were published by Hergenröther, defended the truth of the Latin doctrine of the Holy Ghost, but strongly demurred to the addition of the *Filioque* to the Symbol.[3] He also must have had the decision of the sixth session of the Photian Council before his eyes, for he seems on the whole to have shared the opinion of the pontifical legates who were present at that session.

There is nothing surprising[4] in the way Michael Glycas, another contemporary of Michael of Anchialos, deals with the General Councils, when in defence of the Greek position on the *Filioque*[5] he appeals to the authority of the Oecumenical Councils, insisting on the Popes' participation in those councils, but says nothing about the Photian synod. This is sufficiently explained by the fact that the Greeks did not rank the Photian Council among the great oecumenical councils, so that its decision had not the same authority for them as the decrees of the seven oecumenical Councils. Besides, in the twelfth century, Photius himself, as we have pointed out already, was not yet a topic of controversy: his case was closed and full agreement had been reached on the conflicting issues between Photius and Ignatius. This at least partly explains why his Council was not quoted as often as might have been expected.

Photius' popularity, however, was to grow in proportion to the gradual recrudescence of anti-Latin polemics, when all the great controversialists of the second half of the twelfth century borrowed most of their arguments from Photius' writings; for instance, Andronicus

---

[1] V. Grumel misunderstood it in this sense ('Le Filioque au Concile Photien de 879–880', in *Échos d'Orient* (1930), vol. XXIX, pp. 252–64. M. Jugie ('Les Actes du synode Photien', ibid. (1938), vol. XXXVII, pp. 96 seq.) rightly dissociates himself from that line of argument.

[2] Leo Allatius, in his *De Ecclesiae Occid. et Orient. Perpetua Consensione*, col. 557, correctly translates the passage as follows: 'Hoc enim acute satis *innuere* existimo, cum in Canone, quo Italos admisit, continetur.'

[3] *P.G.* vol. 139, cols. 165–221. Nicetas also appeals to the decision of oecumenical councils, but his reference is too brief.   [4] V. Grumel, loc. cit. p. 264.

[5] Κεφάλαια εἰς τὰς ἀπορίας τῆς Γραφῆς, edited by S. Eustratiades (Athens, 1906), pp. 341, 342, but I have not been able to come across the work.

Camateros[1] and Nicetas Acominatos,[2] to cite only the best. We should also note in particular that the Fathers of the Council of 1156, held in Constantinople, also borrowed texts from Photius' writings for their own purposes[3] and quoted him next to the Fathers of the Church: not that they ranked him among the Fathers, but their opinion of him illustrates at any rate the authority Photius' writings and personality wielded in Byzantium in the twelfth century.

We may also mention as belonging to the same period some treatises on the Azymes; two short productions of this class were recently published by Leib.[4] Their anonymous authors display unvaried deference to the Latins and a sincere desire for union, but completely ignore Photius and the Greek Councils of the ninth century.[5]

To turn now to the Chroniclers of the twelfth century, whose works also touched on the period concerned, only five can be quoted: John Skylitzes, George Cedrenus, John Zonaras, Constantine Manasses, and Michael Glycas. The sources used by John Skylitzes, Cedrenus and Zonaras were, for our period, the Continuators of Theophanes and George the Monk, but their references to Photius are brief, briefer still than their sources, and they dwell chiefly on Bardas' incest and on Michael's orgies. Zonaras is still more laconic than his two colleagues, but all of them make Bardas responsible for the persecution of Ignatius and none is favourable to Photius, though they acknowledge his renown. They also dwell at some length on the second deposition by Leo the Wise.[6]

[1] Cf. Hergenröther, *Photius*, vol. III, pp. 810–15, materials of his unpublished treatise; and *P.G.* vol. 141, cols. 396–613.

[2] Thesaurus, *P.G.* vol. 140, col. 173. For other borrowings, cf. col. 289.

[3] Mai, *Spicilegium Romanum*, vol. X, pp. 38 seq.

[4] 'Deux inédits Byzantins sur les azymes', in *Orientalia Christ.* (1924), no. 9, p. 3. Cf. what the writer says (ibid. p. 153) on the treatise attributed to Nicetas-David.

[5] Examination of a treatise on the Azymes by John of Claudiopolis which I found in a MS. of the British Museum (Harl. 5657, fols. 128a–36, on fifteenth-century paper) also yielded negative results. Nor was anything relevant to be found in two unpublished letters of John Camateros, Patriarch of Constantinople, addressed to Innocent III (Bibl. Nat. Cod. Paris. Graecus 1302, on parchment, thirteenth century, containing 296 fols., fols. 270a–5) and in two other short theological writings of the same class in the same MS. (Responsa Theologica, fols. 275–81; Orationes Catecheticae Duae, fols. 281–95), the latter MS. being unfortunately in a very bad condition and scarcely legible in places.

[6] Skylitzes-Cedrenus (Bonn), pp. 161, 172–3 (Photios ἀνὴρ ἐπὶ σοφίᾳ γνώριμος), 205, 213, 246 seq. Zonaras, *Epitome Histor.* (Bonn), lib. XVI, caps. 4–11, pp. 403 (Photios ἐν λόγοις ὀνομαστότατος), 404, 405, 418, 422, 438 seq.

Manasses and Glycas are the only chroniclers to father Ignatius' ill-treatment on both Bardas and Photius, Manasses [1] following Photius' bitterest enemy, the Pseudo-Simeon, and on two occasions giving Photius some very uncomplimentary titles. Michael Glycas [2] is the least independent and the shortest of all; he simply plagiarizes his immediate predecessors, Skylitzes, Zonaras and Manasses, and is the only one to make Photius responsible for Ignatius' trials. In conclusion, the writings of the chroniclers of that period bring out what harm was done to Photius' good name by the writers of the Porphyrogennetos school and chiefly by the Pseudo-Simeon.

[1] *Compendium Chronicum* (Bonn), pp. 218, 219, 220 (Photios κακοῦργος), 224, 226 (ὁ βαθυγνώμων Φώτιος ἀεὶ διψῶν τοῦ θρόνου). *P.G.* 127, cols. 412 seq.
[2] *Annales* (Bonn), pars IV, p. 544.

CHAPTER VI

FROM THE THIRTEENTH CENTURY TO THE MODERN PERIOD

Unionists of the thirteenth century: Beccos, Metochita—The Photian Council in writings of the thirteenth century—Calecas and the champions of the Catholic thesis—Anti-Latin polemists and theologians of the fourteenth century: the Photian Council promoted to oecumenicity—Treatment of Photius and his Council by supporters of the Council of Florence—Unpublished Greek treatises on the Councils and opponents of the Union—Greek and Russian literature from the sixteenth to the nineteenth century. Influence of Baronius and Hergenröther on the Orientals.

It will have been noted that while Photius' name came gradually to be quoted more frequently in the polemical writings of the twelfth century, it was not until the thirteenth century that his personality and his unfortunate anti-Latin venture became favourite topics of dispute between the partisans and the opponents of reunion. Sufficient evidence will be found in the debates that preceded and followed the Council of Lyons, when the friends of reunion opened fire by trying to convince their opponents that first Photius' example was not one to be followed, and second, that he had no serious excuse for causing a rupture and that in any event he disowned his anti-Roman campaign by his reconciliation with Rome.

The first Greek champion of the Catholic doctrine on the Procession of the Holy Ghost, Nicephorus Blemmydes,[1] restricted himself to dogmatic arguments, but the Patriarch John Beccos was not satisfied with the sort of reasoning that had all but exclusively prevailed until his time: he was the first to use the historic method by trying to establish that no attempt to create a schism ever had a truly dogmatic cause behind it. He also directly attacked the first Greek controversialists.

It was natural that Beccos should single out the Photian case for special attention and he made Photius responsible for the whole trouble. From the way he continually harped on this topic through all his writings, it was clear how much importance he attached to what Photius had to answer for, and as in Beccos' days Photius had become a hero to all who hated the Latins and a Father of the Church representative of Greek doctrine, and as his example and his writings were the object

[1] *P.G.* vol. 142, cols. 533–84.

of the highest praise, it was necessary to tackle the evil by striking at its roots.

Beccos[1] dealt more fully with the Photius incident in his works on the reunion of the Churches, in which he aimed at showing that it was not the *Filioque* or any other alleged abuse of the Roman Church that was the cause of the Photian schism, and that Photius' history proved that he did not fall out with Rome over these 'abuses', though he knew them well, as long as he remained uncertain whether his ascent to the patriarchal throne would receive Rome's approval or not. This contention was borne out by the facts in the conflict between Photius and the Popes.

When Ignatius[2]—'a man of so exalted a degree of sanctity that his memory has been venerated to this day by the Church, the reward of all those who please God'—was Patriarch, Photius, 'a man of great learning and wisdom, cast his eyes upon the See' and yearned for its possession. He dethroned Ignatius, who appealed to Rome. Pope Nicholas summoned Photius to return the See to the legitimate Patriarch, but Photius tried to bring the Pope over to his side, and in a lengthy letter pleaded on his own behalf and detailed the issues that divided the two Churches. This passage of the letter is quoted by Beccos at full length, which proves, so the Patriarch asserts, that Photius was perfectly aware of all the characteristic customs that differentiated the Roman from the Greek Church. But, as long as there remained any prospect of Nicholas deciding in his favour, Photius refrained from making a grievance of any of these customs, altering his tactics when he was excommunicated by Nicholas and his successor Hadrian; then only did he bitterly reproach Rome with various customs as though they were grave abuses. Beccos quotes the most striking passages from the letter, and as his two quotations must have caused surprise, he concludes: 'This makes it clear that the schism was not brought about by any eagerness for truth [true doctrine] but by Photius' own wilfulness.' As though this were not enough, Beccos goes on:

As Pope John, who followed Hadrian, Nicholas' successor, on the apostolic throne, did not feel the same aversion to Photius and received him with kindness after his reinstatement on the patriarchal throne, Photius summoned a synod of over three hundred bishops in Constantinople, promulgated some canons and anathematized whatever he had said at the time of his quarrel

[1] On his writings, see V. Laurent, 'Le Cas de Photius dans l'Apologétique du Patriarche Jean XI Beccos (1274–82) au Lendemain du Deuxième Concile de Lyon', in *Échos d'Orient* (1930), vol. XXIX, pp. 396–407.

[2] *P.G.* vol. 141, cols. 928–42 seq.

with the Roman Church. Then, at one of the sittings of the Reunion Synod, het hus addressed John, who then governed the Church which Photius had so violently abused in his previous speeches.

Here Beccos quotes a few extracts from the opening speech of welcome addressed to the papal legates and other similar passages, all in praise of the Pope. 'Photius also said some flattering things in the course of this Reunion Synod, making it obvious, as we have been trying to prove, that whatever Photius had said or done against the Roman Church was merely an outlet for his ill-feeling and petulance.' All this is perfectly clear, says the Patriarch, and no other document is needed to prove it: to make sure, however, he also quotes the letters which Photius sent after his reconciliation to Marinus, Gauderich and Zachary of Anagni.

In the third book of his treatise, dedicated to Theodore,[1] bishop of Sugdea, Beccos returns to the subject and repeats the same argument; he quotes some passages from the letters of Nicholas and Hadrian to Photius, refers to the latter's reply and concludes by repeating word for word the extract of the Reunion Synod; he then adds a quotation from the *Mystagogy*, which pays homage to Pope John and recalls the fact that he made his legates sign the Symbol of the Faith at the Reunion Synod. 'Our enemies'—so Beccos goes on—'would have it that Photius made peace with the Romans only because John had sanctioned the Symbol without the *Filioque*; but no one in his senses will ever believe that things happened this way, and this because no dogmatic decision was issued by a synod that had only been summoned to restore peace in the Church.' Photius, as soon as he found a Pope willing to sanction his appointment, merely wished to cover his true motives and screen himself behind soft and apologetic words to soothe those who might have criticized his sudden *volte-face*. Photius only wanted an excuse to make his peace with John and found his chance when John made his legates sign the Symbol without the *Filioque*.[2]

Beccos returned to this theme in his refutation of the *Mystagogy*, where he sharply criticizes Photius for his instability, so unworthy of a Prince of the Church, and insinuates that Photius had prepared some sort of an apology, pretending that John had appreciated the compliments addressed to him by the Patriarch. He then goes on: 'I refuse to admit that Photius shifted from hostility to peace just because Pope John had signed and approved the Symbol, since we profess the same without the addition.'[3] This is not all. The zealous champion of Catholic doctrine and reunion also mentions Photius in a sermon on

[1] Ibid. cols. 326 seq. [2] Ibid. cols. 852 seq. [3] Ibid. col. 853.

his deposition,[1] when Beccos recalls the demonstration he once published to the effect that Photius had been roused against the Church not by any breath of divine zeal, but by sheer perversity. However that may be, the scandal was short-lived, as the culprit himself removed it; he summoned 'a great and all but oecumenical synod',[2] when he healed the sore of the scandal by applying the remedy of correction. Then again, more than 160 years elapsed between Photius and Cerularius, when the Church lived in perfect peace.

Beccos' method of presenting the Photian Council is quoted[3] to justify the assertion that the Acts of that Council were falsified at the end of the thirteenth century or the beginning of the fourteenth, on the ground that Beccos knew a version of the Acts totally different from the version known to-day, Beccos' Acts containing a solemn anathema undoing all that Photius had said and written against the Roman Church, and a statement that he intended to meet John VIII's written recommendation to humble himself and apologize to the Council.

This is an overstatement of the case, as there is nothing to justify such an interpretation of Beccos' words. We only need to recall what he said in his book on the reunion of the Churches: to prove his allegation that Photius had anathematized whatever he had said and written against the Church of Rome, Beccos merely quotes the compliments which the Patriarch of Constantinople addressed to the legates of the Holy See and to Pope John. This—Beccos contends—is sufficient proof of his statement, and he quotes, as additional support to his argument, the three letters addressed by Photius to some Italian bishops.

Now these letters and compliments did show that Photius had completely veered round in his attitude to Rome, but not that Photius had uttered the anathemas attributed to him by Beccos. As Beccos is always looking for conclusive arguments and omits nothing that serves his purpose, he would have been only too delighted to quote the famous anathemas uttered in the presence of a council against all Photius' anti-Latin writings, if they had in fact been uttered. If he could not quote them, it was only because there were none to quote.

We are forced, then, to fall back upon canon I of the Reunion Council, since the anathemas which Beccos utilizes to the utmost are found nowhere else. Controversialists naturally make mountains of mole-hills and the Patriarch did find some justification for reading into

---

[1] *P.G.* vol. 141, Oratio II, col. 980.
[2] διὰ μεγάλης καὶ ἀντικρὺς οἰκουμενικῆς συνόδου.
[3] V. Laurent, 'Le Cas de Photius...,' loc. cit. pp. 407–15.

Photius' action the actual recantation of his words and deeds against Rome. Beccos also admits that the legates of John VIII signed the Symbol of the Faith. According to the Acts of the Photian Council, this was done during the sixth session, and as we know of no other suitable occasion, we must conclude that Beccos knew the same version of the Acts as we do.

Beccos' writings on the Photian schism are supplemented by the interpretation which his disciple George Metochita gives to the unionist Patriarch's opinion on Photius. Metochita dealt with the Photian schism in the first book of his history of dogma,[1] where he recalled, after the manner of his master and often using the same phrases as Beccos, the origin of the quarrel between Ignatius and Photius and Rome's intervention.

Such behaviour on the part of Photius [he writes later] might with some show of reason be called satanic; but since Photius controlled himself and displayed his better feelings, we need not attribute it to anything but common human aberration. For once the skilful pilot came to the helm of the Roman barque, he who was so gracious to Photius in word and deed, directed him to quieter waters and offered him the anchor of reconciliation, Photius took in sail and sang, as we say, the palinode,[2] as he followed the straight course indicated to him. After his rancour had subsided, he set to work as best he could for reconciliation. He ceased to act as carelessly as he had done during the conflict; nor was he alone this time as he was known to be when he worked for the schism, but followed a definite plan and on canonical lines. At a synodical conclave of more than three hundred bishops gathered from many places he set everything right, decided that the Pope should keep for ever his age-long privileges and applied to the evil a remedy so strong as to make people say rightly: Where hatred once abounded, the grace of peace has abounded more.

[Chapter VII] But let none be so perverse as to object that Photius and his synod settled nothing until the Symbol had been publicly read without its addition, as though implying that the Romans implicitly consented to its suppression. Granted that the Symbol was read in that form (I am not questioning that, for I know that the Romans, at some definite date, recited with or without us the Symbol minus the *Filioque* in accordance with ancient tradition); but what I ask is whether the Romans, as a result of dogmatic discussions or otherwise, acquiesced in its suppression, as though they had been reprimanded for the addition and confessed to their mistake. But I find

---

[1] *Georgii Metochitae Diaconi Historiae Dogmaticae Lib. I et II*; A. Mai, *Patrum Nova Bibliotheca* (Roma, 1854–1905), vol. VIII, lib. I, chs. VI–IX, pp. 9 seq.

[2] καὶ παλινῳδίαν ᾖσε κατὰ τὸν φάμενον.

no evidence of such a surrender and nobody after reading the books on the subject will dare to affirm such a thing, unless some recent writers have altered, or are trying to alter, the case, a common practice with those who are out to back up schism, as happened recently and in the more remote past.[1]

The truth is exactly the reverse. Anybody can see for himself that the oft-mentioned Photius consigned to fire and anathema, without any hesitation or discussion,[2] and in token of his clear and genuine reprobation, all he had said and written against the Roman Church in connection with the addition of words which he had considered to be wicked and absurd and which had prompted a series of blasphemies and charges against the Roman Church for the most horrible crimes. The Romans then did what I know they are still doing to-day: they approved, held dear and considered as orthodox all those who recite the Symbol as it has always been recited, and with them they wished to be at peace. For the Romans also, as I have stated before, openly recite the Symbol on certain days in the same manner, with full knowledge of the tradition of the Fathers.

[Chapter VIII] But...no one capable of judging these matters and reading the account of them would admit that the reading of the Symbol in full Council implied the Romans' consent to the suppression of the additional words...and it would surely be easy to find in the records of that time that whatever has been said and written against the Roman Church in connection with these words was disowned and wiped out....

Neither can it be said that the Romans consented to the suppression 'of those oft-repeated words', since 'they were weary of the protracted struggle', or 'because they showed themselves too obliging, since at that time the Greeks were anxious to conciliate the Roman Church'. Both assumptions are preposterous.

Photius knew all this [Metochita goes on] and he knew that he had to make up for his invectives against the Roman Church and against true peace, the results, as I said, of human weakness; and by thinking thus, he only did what was owing to the legates who had shown him such kindness and acquitted themselves of their mission so well. Their mutual affection was no more than one would expect.

They had brought him liturgical presents from the Holy See—a phelonion, an omophorion, with a sticharion and sandals, which he received with great joy, paying homage to the Pope who had sent the gifts and overwhelming the legates with praise: and that is how things happened, as far as Photius and the entente between the two Churches were concerned. The result was a greater stability, further guaranteed by a conciliar decree, which increased as time went on and the Patriarchs succeeded each other for many years.

---

[1] ὁποῖα πλεῖστα τοῖς τὸ σχίσμα κρατύνασι καὶ κρατύνουσι, καὶ νῦν καὶ πρότερον πέπρακται.   [2] δίχα πολυπραγμοσύνης τινός.

They numbered sixteen after Photius, all shedding lustre on their patriarchal dignity by the splendour of their many charismata, their eloquence and their wisdom, and all of them bent on keeping the laws of union and harmony with daily increasing diligence, and on persevering in concord.

Now what is one to make of these words of George Metochita?[1] They certainly do not warrant the conclusion that either Beccos himself or George Metochita knew any other edition of the Acts of the Photian Council than the one we possess to-day. Metochita first throws light on his master's words about the reading of the Symbol at the Council, when he states that the Symbol was read at the Council, but without the *Filioque*; but this can only refer to the sixth session. In mentioning the Roman custom of reciting the Symbol 'in accordance with ancient tradition', Metochita also follows his master, who on two occasions quotes such a custom in his works,[2] while taking Photius to task for exploiting the fact that Leo III had had the Symbol engraved on two tablets to be placed on the tomb of St Peter.

Metochita also makes reference to the anathema pronounced on all that Photius had said or written against the Roman Church in connection with the *Filioque*, but his words can only be explained in the same way as those of Beccos, since both embody an interpretation of canon I of the Photian Council. Metochita states that everything was 'consigned to fire and anathema without any hesitation, without discussion', but 'as implying a clear and unmistakable condemnation'.

These were, after all, the contents of the Acts as we know them, and if they are to be credited no notice was taken of what Photius had previously said or written; not a word was said about it: the implicit condemnation in the anathemas of canon I seemed to be all that mattered.

We also note that Metochita, exactly like his master, flatly denied that any dogmatic question was raised at the Photian Council:

What I should like to know [he exclaims] is whether the Romans, as a result of dogmatic discussions or otherwise, acquiesced in its [i.e. *Filioque*] suppression, as though they had been reprimanded for the addition and had confessed to their mistake. But I find no evidence of such a surrender and nobody after reading the books on the subject will dare to affirm such a thing.

---

[1] Metochita also mentions Photius in three other places of his long treatise: ibid. l. I, ch. XIII, p. 18, ch. XXXI, p. 44, and he tells of Beccos' efforts to get at the truth: *De Historia Dogmatica*, Sermo III, ch. 67–9; A. Mai, ibid. vol. x, Sermo III, p. 353, ch. 67–9; and in his treatise *Contra Manuelem Cretensem* (ed. L. Allatius), *Graecia Orthodoxa* (Rome, 1652, 1659), vol. II, pp. 1068 seq.

[2] *De Unione Ecclesiarum*, loc. cit., col. 112; *Refutatio Photiani Libri de Spir. S.* loc. cit., cols. 845 seq.

This is exactly what happened according to the Acts in our possession, and were we to think that Photius acknowledged the hollowness of his attacks and even apologized to the Council, we should have to assume a dogmatic discussion at the same Council, and contradict Beccos' and Metochita's emphatic assertion that in the course of the Council, according to the Acts they had in their possession, no such theological discussion ever took place.

At the end of his exposition, Metochita, like his master, offers no other argument in support of his contention, i.e. that Photius had anathematized and committed to the flames all his anti-Roman invectives, than the Patriarch's own kind words to the legates and to John VIII, but nothing of this proves that the Acts of the Photian Council had been tampered with at that time. Beccos and Metochita assert on the contrary that they knew of no other account of what took place at the Photian Council than the one we read in the Greek Acts we possess to-day, and in their examination of the Photian case they came to the same conclusion as Nicetas of Nicaea had reached in the eleventh century. He also discovered that Photius' schism was without any foundation in fact, and with the Acts of the Photian Council before his eyes noted that no mention whatever was made there of Roman errors, concluding, like Metochita, that if those errors were at all reprehensible, they should have been dealt with at that Council.

The writings of these two champions of the cause of unity also corroborate the fact that in their days the Photian Council, for all its great reputation, was not classed among the oecumenical councils. Metochita calls it 'almost oecumenical':[1] the first Graeco-Catholics therefore admitted the validity of this synod, whereas they did not admit the validity of the Ignatian Council of 869–70; logically enough, since it had been annulled by the Council of 879–80. For all the esteem they professed for St Ignatius, they shared in this respect the opinion of their opponents.

Note also that Nicetas of Nicaea had a vague remembrance of having heard of a quarrel between the two Churches under Patriarch Sergius, but Metochita knows nothing about it; on the contrary, he emphatically states, complementing his master's words, that from Photius to Cerularius the two Churches lived in perfect peace and even gives the number of Patriarchs who succeeded each other in the interval. Of any dis-

---

[1] *De Historia Dogmatica*, Sermo III, ch. 67; Mai, loc. cit. vol. x, p. 353: διὰ μεγάλης καὶ σχεδὸν οἰκουμενικῆς συνόδου, τὰ τῆς προτέρας ἑνοτικῆς....

agreement arising between the two Churches under Pope Formosus he knows nothing, and as the Photian incident should have been recalled in this connection, a champion of the Catholic side might at least have been expected to say a word about it. But he did not.

The verdict of these ardent Unionists on Photius and his relations with Ignatius is also interesting in other respects: the Byzantines were beginning to lose completely the true notion of what happened in Byzantium in 859; and no wonder, if we remember how the writers of the Porphyrogennetos school mishandled the facts. At the time when Beccos and Metochita were writing, it was scarcely possible for anybody to verify the facts as reported by nearly all the chroniclers—which may also explain why the name of Photius is missing from some Byzantine Synaxaria of this period. Evidently, the name of Photius had by this time become a symbol of division between the unionists and the orthodox,[1] the clash between the two affording the opportunity to hasten the growth of the Photian Legend, even in the Eastern world.

Confirmation of what we have said about Beccos and his disciple comes from a work—unpublished, unfortunately—by Job Jasites, though its most interesting passage has been made public by Cardinal Hergenröther.[2] In a book written against the Latins at the suggestion of the Patriarch Joseph, Job writes: 'The sixth session of the Council summoned at the time gives us clear evidence of the manner in which Photius received the Latins.' After quoting a long portion of the session, Job proceeds: 'Do not come and tell me that the Roman Church made no innovations later....' Now Job Jasites makes it evident that he knows exactly the same version of the Photian Council as that used by his opponents, for he uses the same argument as Metochita attempted to refute, namely, that the Romans, by signing the Symbol without the *Filioque*, had 'abjured' their heresy, and that therefore Photius was quite consistent in making peace with the Latins. In another Greek code of the Munich Library, again on Hergenröther's information,[3] there is another quotation from the sixth session made by the Bulgarian archbishop Gennadios.

[1] A curious parallel is found in the Synodicon of the Church of Rhodes (N. Cappuyns, 'Le Synodicon de l'Église de Rhodes au XIVe siècle', in *Échos d'Orient* (1934), vol. XXXIII, pp. 196–217). Photius' name appears in three different places of this document, is scored out and later replaced. Cappuyns (pp. 212, 213) is of opinion that the name figured in the original composition and was scored out perhaps at a time when the Church of Rhodes had moved towards Rome, i.e. about 1274. There is a good deal to be said for the conjecture.

[2] *Photius*, vol. II, pp. 525, 526, Cod. Monac. Gr. 68, fols. 45–52a.

[3] Loc. cit. vol. II, p. 536, Cod. Monac. Gr. 256, fol. 28.

In the present stage of research in this field, this is almost all we can find about Photius in the controversial writings of the thirteenth century. A rapid survey of the works I have been able to consult will facilitate the verification of our statements.

Nicholas Mesarites, one of the first polemists of that period,[1] Nicephorus Blemmydes,[2] George Acropolites[3] have nothing to say about either Photius or the councils; Manuel Moschopulos[4] and the other students of Beccos, Constantine the Meliteniot,[5] George of Cyprus,[6] John Chilas,[7] Theoleptos of Philadelphia,[8] the Patriarch Anastasius Makedon[9] and Maximos Planudes[10] are all silent on the subject.

Other writers discuss the oecumenical councils, but leave Photius out; the Patriarch Gregory of Alexandria, for instance, who in the profession of faith he submitted to John, Patriarch of Constantinople, declared his acceptance of the seven oecumenical councils.[11] A very

---

[1] A. Heisenberg, 'Die Unionsverhandlungen vom 30 August, 1206. Patriarchenwahl und Kaiserkrönung in Nikaia, 1208', in *Sitzungsber. d. bayr. Akad., Phil.-Hist. Kl.* (1923), pp. 15–25. Cf. J. Pargoire, 'Nicolas Mésaritès, Métropolite d'Éphèse', in *Échos d'Orient* (1904), vol. VII, pp. 219–26. I have not been able to consult the edition of Nicholas' three works by Arsenii (Novgorod, 1896). Cf. also Janin, 'Au lendemain de la conquête de Constantinople', in *Échos d'Orient* (1933), vol. XXXII, pp. 5–21, 195–202.

[2] De Process. S. Spir., *P.G.* vol. 142, cols. 533–84; Lämmer, *Graeciae Orth.* loc. cit. pp. 108–86.

[3] Λόγος περὶ τῆς Ἐκπορεύσεως, in Demetrakopulos, Ἐκκλ. βιβλ. pp. 395–411.

[4] Διάλεξις πρὸς Λατίνους, Cod. Parisinus Graecus 969 (14th c.), fols. 315–19.

[5] De Process. S. Spir., *P.G.* vol. 141, cols. 1032–1273.

[6] Scripta Apologetica, *P.G.* vol. 142, cols. 233–300. Beccos' reply to these writings, *P.G.* vol. 141, cols. 864 seq.

[7] Libellus de Process. S. Sp., *P.G.* vol. 135, cols. 505–8. A few of John's letters preserved in Cod. Paris. Graec. 2022 (14th c.), fols. 150–7 provide no information on the subject.

[8] Tractatus de Operatione in Christo, *P.G.* vol. 143, cols. 381–404 (only a fragment).

[9] *P.G.* vol. 142, cols. 480–513 (Letters to the Emperor, Cod. Paris. Graec. 137, fols. 16–113).

[10] Tria Capita, refuted by G. Metochita, *P.G.* vol. 141, cols. 1276–1308. Another work against the Latins, Cod. Vindob. Theol. 269, fol. 77, only I have not made a thorough study of it. M. Laurent, 'La Vie et les Œuvres de Georges Moschabar', in *Échos d'Orient* (1929), vol. XXVIII, p. 135 mentions a debate between the monk Hierotheus and the Latin bishop of Crotone, who had entered the service of Michael Palaeologus: preserved in the Marc. Gr. 153.

[11] *P.G.* vol. 152, cols. 1102, 1103: οὕτως ὁμολογῶ οὕτως κηρύττω, δεχόμενος καὶ στέργων καὶ ἀσπαζόμενος ἐκ μέσης ψυχῆς τὰς ἁγίας καὶ οἰκουμενικὰς ἑπτὰ συνόδους, ἔτι δὲ καὶ τόπους ὀρθοδόξως γεγενημένας.

curious and important reference to the councils is to be found in a work by the Emperor Theodore II Lascaris against the Latins and on the Procession of the Holy Ghost,[1] where the imperial writer proves his point with quotations from Holy Scripture and the Fathers, maintains that all the councils approved the Symbol as drawn up by the Councils of Nicaea and Constantinople, and finally enumerates the seven councils with a few particulars on each. It may be noted that while omitting most of the names of other Patriarchs, he always places the Pope or his representative at the head of each list. None but the Emperor has the right to summon councils; the Photian Council is not mentioned, as it was not classed with the oecumenical councils, but the Emperor's list of the councils is borrowed from one of those pamphlets on the councils which were very widespread at the time.[2]

But it is useless to prolong our search through the works of the historians and chroniclers of the period: George Acropolites and George Pachymerus, as we know, do not deal with the period we are concerned with; Joel's chronicle offers nothing interesting, as Photius and his case receive only scant treatment; and all he has to say is that the Patriarch Ignatius was forcibly dethroned and that Photius was expelled from the patriarchate for having reproved Basil for his crime. A single sentence, and very vague at that, summarizes Photius' second deposition.[3]

Equally scant and unimportant is the information to be found in the anonymous history published by Sathas,[4] a chronicle which lightly

---

[1] H. B. Swete, *Theodorus Lascaris Junior de Processione Spiritus Sancti* (London, 1875), Λόγος προλογητικὸς πρὸς ἐπίσκοπον Κοτρύνης κατὰ Λατίνων περὶ τοῦ Ἁγίου Πνεύματος, pp. 17–20. Note also the writings of an anonymous controversialist of the period published by C. Simoniades, Ὀρθοδ. Ἑλλήνων θεολογικαὶ γραφαὶ τέσσαρες (London, 1859), and attributed by him partly to Nicholas of Methone (cf. Krumbacher, loc. cit. p. 87). Reference is there found to the first six councils (pp. 36–8) but not to Photius. The same is true of a treatise by George Coressios, published in the same work (pp. 91–108).

[2] The Patriarch Germanos II (1222–40), in his second letter to the Cypriots, lists seven Oecumenical Councils (Epistola II ad Cyprios), J. B. Cotelerius, *Ecclesiae Graecae Monumenta* (Paris, 1681), vol. II, ch. VII, p. 479. So does the Patriarch Arsenios (1267) in his Testament (Testamentum Ss. Arsenii archiep. Const., ibid. vol. II, p. 169). Cf. ibid. vol. III, pp. 495 seq., Criminationes adversus Ecclesiam Latinam, written after the conquest of Constantinople; and Norden, *Das Papsttum und Byzanz*, loc. cit. pp. 204 seq., on the *pourparlers* between the Greeks and the Latins. On the same subject, A. Heisenberg, 'Neue Quellen zur Geschichte des Lat. Kaisertums und der Kirchenunion', in *Sitzungsber. d. bayr. Akad., Phil.-Hist. Kl.* (1923), part II: 'Die Unionsverhandlungen vom 30 August 1206.'

[3] (Bonn), pp. 55, 56.

[4] C. Sathas, *Bibliotheca Graeca Medii Aevi* (Paris, 1894), vol. VII, pp. 142–51.

runs over the principal events of Photius' history and also attributes to Bardas Ignatius' deposition and the unjust treatment meted out to him.

It should now be clear that it was the unionist writers and controversialists who in the thirteenth century began to make a more systematic use of Photius, while the orthodox copied their opponents' tactics by trying to turn to their own advantage the facts connected with Photius' schism and his reconciliation; and so the Photian Council came into prominence for the first time. The Photian litigation was also turned to controversial profit in the fourteenth century and there again, after the example of Beccos and his students, it was the Catholics who took the initiative. Of all the unionists, the writer who ventured farthest in this direction was Manuel Calecas, who more than any of his predecessors had been influenced by the Latin point of view and shared with the Western theologians of his day an exalted notion of the Papacy.

Take for instance the interesting passage on the Pope's power in the fourth book of his work against the Greeks,[1] where Calecas takes his cue from the notorious *Donatio Constantini* and faces the problem: Who has the right to summon councils?

We saw just now how the Emperor Theodore Lascaris claimed this right for the Emperors exclusively by quoting the precedent that all general councils had in fact been summoned by them. The notion was general among the Greeks, but the question was how to reconcile it with the rights of the Papacy. To the great relief of the unionists, Manuel Calecas set out to solve it, stoutly upholding the *Dictatus Papae* to prove that the right belonged to the Pope alone, endeavouring to explain the convocation of the first councils in this sense and supporting his position with many quotations from St Basil and St Gregory of Nazianzus.

Calecas betrays the debt he owes to the Latin theology of his time even in his references to Photian polemics,[2] when he re-echoes the Patriarch Beccos and Metochita and emphasizes the injustice done to Ignatius and throws the whole responsibility on Photius, who was craving for the patriarchal throne 'quem adipisci non poterat, nisi permittente Romano Pontifice; necesse enim erat, ex more, ab eo auctoritatem confirmationemque venire...'. Calecas, like his forerunners,

---

[1] Adversus Graecos Libri IV, *P.G.* vol. 152, cols. 243 seq.
[2] Ibid. lib. IV, cols. 205 seq.

then describes how Ignatius appealed to Rome and how Nicholas I and Hadrian II intervened; but his tone is far more aggressive than that of the Patriarch or Metochita. After describing the reconciliation made under John VIII, he attacks the claim that Photius was reconciled with the Latins because they had condemned the addition of the *Filioque* to the Symbol, though it is true, he adds, that there is a reference to the *Filioque* in the sixth session, but 'it should be known that this was later added by synodal decisions purporting to show that such additions are prohibited; it is evident, however, that this is not reasonable'. Calecas then recalls as his main argument the fact that the Commonitorium, in outlining a procedure for the legates to follow, said nothing about the *Filioque*. Since the main object of the Council was the recognition of Photius, there was no call for him to raise the *Filioque* scare, for he would have risked the Pope's recognition. No, he concludes, it was not the *Filioque* that caused the schism: only Photius' pride. Calecas also wrote a work on the Procession of the Holy Ghost which has long been erroneously attributed to Demetrios Cydones,[1] but it makes no reference to Photius.

Calecas' line of argument has of course its weaknesses, and given the Greeks' mentality at the time he could not expect to rally much sympathy among them towards the Pope's supreme power. It was only too easy to deny an inconvenient historical fact and it takes more than emphasis to make a denial convincing.

The other champions of the Catholic position do not appear to have gone the length of Calecas. Maximos Chrysoberges takes his cue from Beccos in telling the story of the origin of the schism,[2] but in his opinion Ignatius was not ill-treated by Photius, as Calecas asserts, but only by the Government. Unfairly raised to the patriarchal throne and unable to obtain Rome's recognition, Photius trumped up the Latin heresy of the *Filioque*; and this is all he has to say about the incident in his treatise, which is unfortunately too short.

A study by another unionist, Manuel Chrysoloras, still remains unpublished,[3] but I was able to consult it in a MS. of the Paris

---

[1] *P.G.* vol. 154, cols. 864–958. See G. Mercati, 'Notizie di Procore e Demetrio Cidone, Manuele Caleca e Teodoro Meliteniota ed altri appunti per la storia della teologia e della litteratura Bizantina del secolo XIV', in *Studi i Testi* (Città del Vaticano, 1931), vol. LVI, pp. 62 seq.

[2] De Process. S. Spir., *P.G.* vol. 154, cols. 1224 seq.

[3] Paris. Graecus 1300 of the sixteenth century on paper. Manuel contents himself with quoting Fathers of the Church who, he thinks, favour the *Filioque*, says very little of the councils and mentions neither Photius nor his synod.

National Library, only to find that it entirely neglects the historical problems under discussion. His published letters provide no information.[1] Demetrios Cydones[2] never once alludes to Photius in his long apology in which he explains to his countrymen how he was driven to the conviction that the Catholic doctrine is true and why he had translated some Latin theological works into Greek.

The anti-Latin controversialists and theologians have little to say about Photius: Barlaam[3] merely notes in his treatise against the Latins that the origin of the schism is connected with the name of Photius; Nilus of Thessalonica[4] has nothing about Photius in his published writings, though he wrote about the schism and about the Pope. Joseph Bryennios is more definite and refers in his work about the Trinity[5] to the sixth session of the Photian Council, which he interprets in an anti-Latin sense, quoting in support the letter of John VIII to Photius, the authenticity of which remains very doubtful—the first occurrence, as far as I know, of this document in the polemical writings about the *Filioque*. One may regret that Nicephorus Callistus Xanthopulos did not complete his Ecclesiastical History, as he announced in his introduction[6] that he would deal with the history of Ignatius and Photius in the twenty-second chapter, but the book stops short at the year 610.

In order to gather a clear idea of the place Photius and his Council occupied in the writings of the anti-Latin controversialists and theologians of the fourteenth century, I have consulted a number of treatises, some of them unpublished, but found to my surprise that

---

[1] *P.G.* vol. 156, cols. 24–60.

[2] G. Mercati, 'Notizie di Procore e Demetrio Cidone', loc. cit. pp. 359 seq. Cf. M. Jugie, 'Demetrius Cydonès et la Théologie Latine à Byzance aux XIVe et XVe siècle', in *Échos d'Orient* (1928), vol. XXXI, pp. 385–402. G. Mercati also discovered some letters by Demetrius Cydones, published by M. Cammelli, but I have not seen them. Cf. G. Mercati, 'Per l'Epistolario di Demetrio Cidone', in *Studi Bizantini e Neoellenici* (1930), vol. III, pp. 203–30; V. Laurent, 'La Correspondance de Demetrius Cydonès', in *Échos d'Orient* (1931), vol. XXXIV, pp. 338–54. Cf. G. Cammelli, 'Personnaggi Bizantini dei secoli XIV—XV attraverso le Epistole di Demetrio Cidonio,' in *Bessarione* (1920), vol. XXIV, pp. 77–108.

[3] Pro Latinis, *P.G.* vol. 151, col. 1266 (written when he became a partisan of the union). Few of his anti-Latin writings have been published.

[4] De Dissidio Ecclesiarum et de Papa, *P.G.* vol. 149, cols. 683–729.

[5] Περὶ τῆς ἁγίας Τριάδος Λόγος (8th ed. by E. Bulgaris; Leipzig, 1768), vol. I, pp. 138 seq.

[6] Ecclesiastica Historia, *P.G.* vol. 145, col. 617.

Photius' case is never mentioned.[1] On the other hand, Simeon, archbishop of Thessalonica, in his treatise Of Heresies,[2] refers several times to the Latin 'heresy' of the *Filioque*, as well as to other 'abuses', but without mentioning Photius by name. He only alludes to his Council.

More interesting is the observation on Photius found in the biography of Anthony Cauleas, attributed to Nicephorus Gregoras, where the author tells us that the troubles of which his hero was to remedy the consequences were the sequel of the iconoclastic struggles. He is full of praise for Photius, but in the same breath severely blames him for his pride and the lust for power that roused him against Ignatius. Photius is there alleged to have drawn the young Emperor Michael, or rather Bardas, into his scheme, the author here evidently taking his cue from the historians and chroniclers who since the tenth century had misrepresented Photius' accession in that manner. His appreciation is none the less worth considering.[3]

[1] Paris. Graecus 1303 (14th–15th c., on paper), fols. 176: Arsenii monachi Scholia in Sanctorum Patrum Loca, quae Latinorum Doctrinae Favent, ibid. fols. 35 seq.; Gregorii Cyprii Expositio fidei adversus Beccum, fols. 36a–49a; ejusdem Apologia, fols. 50–64; ejusdem confessionis excerptum, fols. 65a–69a; ejusdem ad Andronicum imp. epistola, fol. 70; Theodosii mon. tract. de process. Spiritus S., fols. 71a–77a; Arsenii mon. Nicolai Methonensis et Anonymi fragmenta de eodem, fols. 78–144a; only the Treatise of Nicephorus Blemmydes, fols. 145–62, makes mention of the Seventh Council (fols. 161a–162a); the pamphlet by the monk Philarges (Paris. Graecus 1295, 15th–16th c., on paper, fols. 85a–98); the short letters by Demetrius Chrysoloras (Paris. Graecus 1191, 15th c., on paper, fols. 39a–45). The letters are interesting for the personal information they supply on the Emperor Manuel II Palaeologus, whose trusted confidant Chrysoloras was; but his correspondence has nothing about Photius (Legrand, *Lettres de l'Empereur Manuel Paléologue*, Paris, 1893); nothing in the treatise by the hieromonachus Macarius Macres (Πρὸς Λατίνους, ed. Dositheos, Τόμος Καταλλαγῆς (Jassy, 1692), pp. 412–21). There is a treatise by another Macarius in the Paris. Graecus 1218 (15th c.), but I have not seen it. There is no mention of Photius in the short study by Isaias of Cyprus (*P.G.* vol. 158, cols. 971–6).

[2] *P.G.* vol. 155, cols. 33–176.

[3] This biography is found in the Munich MS. 10, fols. 87, 88 and is quoted by Hergenröther, *Photius*, vol. II, pp. 697, 719 and 720: σοφὸς μὲν γὰρ ἦν ὁ ἀνὴρ [Φώτιος] καὶ πολλὴν τὴν ἐν λόγοις ἐπλούτει σύνεσιν, καὶ μέντοι καὶ τῶν πραγμάτων τῶν γενομένων καὶ τῶν γινομένων πολλὴν αὐτῷ καὶ οὐκ ἀγενῆ τὴν ἐμπειρίαν ὁ χρόνος ἐχαρίσατο....Δόλοις κακομηχάνοις περιελθὼν τὴν τοῦ τηνικαῦτα βασιλεύοντος Μιχαὴλ νηπιώδη κουφότητα καὶ παιδικὴν ἀπειρίαν, ἢ μᾶλλον συμμάχῳ χρησάμενος τῇ τοῦ Βάρδα χειρί...καθεῖλεν ἐπ' οὐδεμιᾷ προφάσει τὸν πατριάρχην Ἰγνάτιον... καὶ παραχρῆμα καθάπερ λῃστὴς τὸν πατριαρχικὸν ἀδίκως ἐπέβη θρόνον, καὶ αὐτὸν μακραῖς καὶ ποικίλαις κολάσεσι περιέβαλε τὸν Ἰγνάτιον....M. R. Guilland, *Essai sur Nicéphore Gregoras* (Paris, 1926), vol. XXVI, pp. 174, 175, was unaware of this passage and attributes to Gregoras another biography of Cauleas (*P.G.* vol. 106, cols. 181–200) written by a certain Nicephorus. I must see the MS. before attempting a definite solution of this problem.

This is of course not all that was written on Photius in the fourteenth century and more than one interesting remark could be found in other works. Cardinal G. Mercati, for instance, in discussing the writings of Isaac Argyros,[1] gives two quotations very complimentary to our Patriarch. Unluckily, the works of many controversialists and theological writers of that age are still patiently waiting for publishers to rescue them from the dust of their libraries: so long is the list,[2] that it is still impossible to obtain a full picture of what the Byzantines of the fourteenth century thought about their great Patriarch; nevertheless the works that have come to light give us a fair notion of it.

We also possess fairly definite information on the growth of Byzantine opinion about the Photian Council in the fourteenth century, as the anti-Latin controversialists often quoted its sixth session in order to support their opinions and naturally tried to make the most of its authority. Manuel Calecas tells us, for instance, in the quotation on Photius, that some people were calling that synod the Eighth Council,[3] and Simeon of Thessalonica substantiates the report. After giving the names of the seven great oecumenical councils and commenting on their decisions regarding the Symbol, he adds in chapter XIX of his *Dialogue* against Heresies the following words:[4]

After the Seventh Council, no other oecumenical council was held with the exception of the one called the Eighth, of which even the Latins make mention. Its Acts are fairly well known and they tell us what innovations the Latins have made and how that Council anathematized those who would presume to say that the Divine Spirit proceeds from the Son.

Neilos of Thessalonica[5] also states that the Latins knew of that Council:

The oecumenical Synod that follows the Seventh Council, summoned by three hundred and eighty Fathers, as the Latins say in their canons, aimed at the restoration of peace between the two Churches, removed from the Symbol the additional article on the Spirit being from the Son and condemned it as a source of scandals. This oecumenical Synod was attended by the Pope's representatives, the bishops Paul and Eugenius, and the Cardinal-priest Peter, who led all the debates. Even Pope John, in whose reign all this happened,

---

[1] Loc. cit. pp. 231, 232: ὡς ὁ πολὺς ἐν σοφίᾳ καὶ συνέσει Φώτιος ἐν τῇ πονηθείσῃ παρ' αὐτοῦ βίβλῳ ἀπορίας καὶ λύσεις περιεχούσῃ τῶν ἐν τῇ θείᾳ ἐμφερομένων γραφῇ.... Vatic. Graec. 1102, p. 290, ibid. fol. 13: ὁ σοφώτατος ἐν πατριάρχαις Φώτιος.

[2] Cf. A. Demetrakopoulos, Ὀρθ. Ἑλλάς, loc. cit. pp. 91-8; Krumbacher, loc. cit. pp. 110, 114.

[3] *P.G.* vol. 152, col. 206.   [4] *P.G.* vol. 155, col. 97.

[5] Passage quoted from an unpublished work against the Latins by L. Allatius, *De Octava Synodo*, loc. cit. pp. 162, 163.

approved by letters and decrees whatever had been done, after due explanations. This is denied by the Latins, though I do not know why, but as they never revoked the decision, the matter remains authentic.

The passage is curious and may suggest that the Greek controversialists knew Gratian's *Decretum* and had found there the famous canon of the Photian Council. No other explanation would properly meet the case.

Nicholas Cabasilas, like his uncle and predecessor in the see of Thessalonica, Neilos, mentions the same Council, but goes a step further by calling it the Eighth Oecumenical Council.[1]

Joseph Bryennios also deals with this synod without, however, calling it the Eighth Oecumenical Council:

Seventy-five years elapsed after the Seventh Council when another council was summoned in the imperial city in the reign of Basil the Macedonian. The purpose of this convocation, due to the Pope's approval and the Emperor's effort, was as follows: to bring about Photius' restoration to the see of Byzantium, to condemn and to excommunicate those who would have the daring and the perfidy to state that the Spirit proceeds from the Son. This it accomplished satisfactorily, and the synod was approved through his representatives by the very saintly Pope John himself who then governed the Church of Rome. He anathematized whoever should in future add anything to, or subtract from, the Symbol, and the pontifical legates duly signed this declaration in their own Roman fashion, or rather, he himself signed it through his legates, whose signatures have been preserved to this day in the Great Church....[2]

The account by Neilos Damylas is very confused:

In the days of Photius, a synod of over three hundred Fathers, called the Holy and Oecumenical first and second Synod, was summoned in Constantinople by order of the pious Emperor Basil the Macedonian...for the purpose of excommunicating Nicholas who had been the first in his time to make the addition to the Symbol. But after a warning, he confessed his error for fear of being expelled, sang the palinode and denied through his legates present at the Synod having made the innovation, protesting that he thought and argued about the Procession of the Holy Ghost exactly as was thought

---

[1] *P.G.* vol. 149, col. 679: '....Ἀπὸ τῶν πρακτικῶν τῆς οἰκουμενικῆς ὀγδόης συνόδου· δι' ὧν φαίνεται κοινὴν γενέσθαι δόξαν τῆς Ἐκκλησίας ἁπάσης, τὸ Πνεῦμα τὸ ἅγιον ἐκ μόνου τοῦ Πατρὸς τὴν ὕπαρξιν ἔχειν. Ἐπὶ γὰρ βασιλείᾳ τοῦ Μακεδόνος, καὶ Φωτίου πατριάρχου, καὶ πάππα Ἰωάννου, οἰκουμενικῆς κατὰ τὴν Κωνσταντίνου πόλιν συγκροτηθείσης συνόδου, καὶ κοινῇ περὶ τῆς ἐκπορεύσεως τοῦ ἁγίου Πνεύματος σκεψαμένης ἀνεφάνη, τὴν προσθήκην τῶν Λατίνων ἄτοπον εἶναι, καὶ ἀναθέματος, καὶ τῶν τοιούτων ἀξίαν....'

[2] Loc. cit. pp. 140, 141. Bryennios only counts seven oecumenical councils in his Διάλεξις περὶ τοῦ ἁγ. Πνεύμ. (Ibid. pp. 420, 421.)

and professed by the first and second universal Synod and by the Holy Symbol which he had received from other oecumenical Synods. Such being the opinion of the Synod, he was not severed from communion.[1]

Damylas, not having taken the trouble to read his documents, evidently confused here the three synods that were held under Photius.

Unimpeachable evidence proving that the Photian Council was at that time beginning to be reckoned among the oecumenical synods by some anti-Latin controversialists has been handed down to us by Neilos of Rhodes,[2] probably the new editor of the short study on the councils written by St Euthymios. Not content with calling this synod the Eighth Oecumenical Council, he added the Council against Palamas to the list as the Ninth.

But this promotion of the Photian Council was, as has been demonstrated, neither official nor general and the Greek Church continued to reckon seven oecumenical councils only. Of this evidence is found, among other places, in the Acts of the synod of 1350 against Palamas, Barlaam and Akyndinos, as in the profession of faith administered to Palamas only seven oecumenical councils were named.[3] On the other hand, not all the works on the councils written at that time follow the example of Neilos of Rhodes, as is shown by the publication attributed to Matthew Blastares which he appended to his short pamphlet against the Latins and in which he gave the names of all the councils with the figures of their attendance.[4] After remarking on the Seventh Council, he merely adds a general observation.[5]

To proceed with our inquiry into the Greek writings of the fifteenth century, we may begin with the Catholic writers who championed the union and the Council of Florence; and foremost among them is Cardinal Bessarion,[6] who mentions Photius in his encyclical to the

[1] Fragment published by L. Allatius, loc. cit. pp. 166, 167. Cf. Paris. Graec. 1295 (15th–16th c., on paper, 342 fols.), fols. 62a–85.

[2] Ed. Justellus, *Nomocanon Photii*, loc. cit. p. 177.

[3] Mansi, vol. XXVII, cols. 203–6. The profession names the synods held against Barlaam but volunteers no information on Photius.

[4] Κατὰ Λατίνων (ed. Dositheos), Τόμος Καταλλαγῆς (Jassy, 1692), pp. 444–8.

[5] ὅτι γὰρ ὡς δυσσέβειαν τοὺς Λατίνους νοσοῦντας διὰ τὴν τῶν προειρημένων ἁπάντων ἀθέτησιν ἡ καθολικὴ καὶ ἁγία τοῦ Θεοῦ ἐκκλησία τῷ ἀναθέματι παραπέμπει, ἱκανῶς μὲν δὲ τὰ φθάσαντα μαρτυρεῖ, οὐχ ἧττόν γε μὴν δείξει καὶ τὰ ῥηθησόμενα. Ἡ γὰρ ἁγία καὶ οἰκουμενικὴ ζ' σύνοδος. Εἴ τις φησὶ πᾶσαν παράδοσιν ἐκκλησιαστικὴν ἔγγραφόν τε καὶ ἄγραφον ἀθετεῖ ἀνάθεμα.

[6] On the Cardinal, see L. Möhler, 'Kardinal Bessarion als Theologe, Humanist und Staatsmann', in *Quellen und Forschungen aus dem Gebiete der Geschichte* (Paderborn, 1923), vol. XX.

Greeks. In defending the Pope's sovereign power, Bessarion recalls the story of Photius in the following terms:

Then the Pope excommunicated Photius for usurping the See of Constantinople and for unjustifiably expelling the very saintly Ignatius, and him he reinstated; evidently, because he wields power over all. Later, when the godly Ignatius had migrated to God and the Emperors continued pleading in favour of Photius in numerous memorials, is it not a fact that John, who succeeded to the government of the Church after Nicholas and Hadrian, replaced him on the patriarchal throne by sending him the pallium (*sic*) through the good offices of bishop Paschasius (*sic*)? Now what does all this mean but one thing, that the great Roman Pontiff rules supreme over the whole Church?[1]

The learned Cardinal's lack of knowledge about Photius is indeed surprising.

The same line of argument in support of the Pope's supreme power is followed by Joseph, bishop of Methone, in his treatise in defence of the Council of Florence.[2] In chapter XIII, where he deals with the primacy, he states: 'Nicholas I, at the time of Photius, excommunicated even the Greeks, not one iota being missed out of the excommunication. But like the Jews, the Greeks, as he stated in his own words, are like captives among the nations....' Later, he writes:[3] 'Nicholas I himself went to Constantinople, there to put an end to a schism; and as they refused to receive him, he excommunicated them all.' Naturally, Joseph makes use of the *Donatio Constantini*.[4] In his refutation of the writings of Mark of Ephesus, he unhesitatingly attributes the authorship of the schism to Photius, and Mark of Ephesus, another agent of the schism,[5] is made to join the coryphaeus of schismatics. The unionist Patriarch of Constantinople, Gregory Mammas, specifically dealt with Photius, when he refuted Mark's profession of faith, and in his writings there is to be found the notorious passage in which he denies the canonization of Photius.[6] No matter how much Mark insisted that Photius had taught the Procession of the Holy Ghost, Gregory retorts:

Observe well that Photius was not numbered among the saints, although Photius and Ignatius were living at the same time: whereas the latter is honoured among the saints and has his place in the Synaxaria on October 23,

---

[1] Encyclica ad Graecos, *P.G.* vol. 161, cols. 477, 490.
[2] Pro Concilio Florentino, *P.G.* vol. 159, col. 1365; Mansi, vol. XXXI (supplem.), 1214.
[3] Ch. xv, col. 1376.   [4] Ch. IV, cols. 1321 seq.
[5] *P.G.* vol. 159, cols. 1040, 1092.
[6] Contra Ephesium, *P.G.* vol. 160, col. 76.

Photius has fallen far short of the ideal of sanctity. But we had better say no more about him, since whatever is written against St Ignatius and Photius falls under anathema from this ambo.

The above words of Mammas have often been quoted against the fact that Photius was the object of a cultus in Byzantium long before the fifteenth century; but they prove nothing more than that the Greek unionists had ceased to number Photius among the saints. Now we understand still better why the name of Photius is missing in a number of Greek Synaxaria; it is because the unionists made the Patriarch mainly responsible for the schism, an extraordinary development of the Photian Legend among the Greek unionists. We were able to observe that in the tenth century, when the canonization took place, the Photian Legend had not yet developed in this direction.

Later,[1] the unionist Patriarch dealt with the profession of faith itself, and whilst Mark had acknowledged the seven oecumenical councils, with the Photian Council added as the Eighth, Mammas makes the eighth synod that of the Ignatian Council. The verdict of this synod against Photius, he continues, was backed by Cedrenos, Manasses, Glycas, Skylitzes and the Life of St Ignatius written by Nicetas. And yet, strange to say, the author adds: 'But we accept even the Acts produced by Mark of Ephesus as those of the Eighth Council.' The letter of John VIII to Photius rouses his suspicions, but he accepts it nevertheless and proceeds to tell how the reconciliation between Photius and the Pope during the sitting of the Council came about, repeats that he accepts that Council as oecumenical and quotes a long extract from the letter of John VIII to the Emperor Basil I to prove to his opponent that a synod can revoke the decisions of another synod. All this is most interesting, but it is curious to find the ideas once expressed by Ivo of Chartres in his Prologue, in a Greek writing of the fifteenth century. Lastly, to meet Mark's objection to the Latins re-ordaining converted Greek priests, he states that the Latin bishops did so sometimes, but only conditionally, as was the case in Bulgaria with Photius' Greek priests, who had been excommunicated by the Latins for having been ordained by him.[2]

Mammas' opinion on the two Councils of Ignatius and Photius is quite unexpected. So far, we have been accustomed to see the Greek

---

[1] Contra Ephesium, *P.G.* vol. 160, cols. 86 seq.

[2] Loc. cit., col. 165. We should add that in another place, col. 157, Mammas, referring again to the Photian incident, proves that the addition to the Symbol was not the cause of the schism.

Catholics not only refusing to acknowledge the oecumenicity of the Photian Council, but sometimes even questioning its authenticity, or, at least, that of the sixth session (in fact I gave the names of a few writers who, in opposition to the schismatics, adopted the Council of Lyons as their eighth, and even Joseph of Methone[1] goes so far as to state that the Council of Lyons should be called 'the Eighth Oecumenical Council'), but never had we come across any Catholic Greek writer who admitted the oecumenicity of the anti-Photian Council of 869–70. It only proves, to my mind, that the Photian Synod, despite opposition, was held in the highest esteem among the Greeks: no one could gainsay the hard fact that this Council had rehabilitated Photius and that its verdict never lost its validity.

An anonymous and unpublished treatise on the councils well illustrates the confusion on this topic in Byzantium in the fourteenth and fifteenth centuries. The author is a unionist and his work occurs in a single MS. of the Paris National Library (Paris. Graec. 1712, 14th-c. on parchment, 430 fols.). On folios 4–6 there is a section on the ten oecumenical councils with a summary of the first seven councils, to which the writer adds the Councils of Lyons, ratified by the Council of Constantinople under the Patriarch Beccos, and the Council of Florence, these three synods being reckoned as the Eighth, Ninth and Tenth Councils.

There is another class of Greek theological literature that claims attention as setting the Greek tradition on the number of oecumenical councils accepted by the Byzantine Church in the right light—the treatises on the councils. On this subject, Greek works are many and would claim a study to themselves; they are also interesting in many other ways, as for instance on the tradition of Eastern Christianity with reference to the councils, the infallibility of the Church and the position attributed to the patriarchs, especially the Patriarch of Rome. Here I can only express the hope to see this class of writing evaluated by specialists interested in the evolution of Christian dogma. The MSS. I have been able to study[2] make it clear that officially the Byzantine Church counted only seven oecumenical councils and that neither the Ignatian Council of 869–70 nor the Photian Council of 879–80 were numbered among them.

[1] Disceptatio pro Concilio Florentino, *P.G.* vol. 159, col. 969.
[2] In Appendix III, pp. 452 seq. will be found a survey of the treatises on councils which the author was able to study in Paris, Brussels, Vienna and London.

To turn now to the opponents of the union, I have already quoted the speech by Mark of Ephesus at the Council of Florence in defence of the validity of the Photian Council and I also mentioned his writing on the Procession of the Holy Ghost with its refutation by the Patriarch Gregory Mammas. In other polemical writings, Mark is less profuse about the great Patriarch,[1] but he twice returns to the subject of his council and writes towards the end of his *Dialogue* on the Addition to the Symbol:[2] 'After the seventh Synod, another, summoned by Photius, the very saintly Patriarch, met in the reign of Basil, Emperor of the Romans: this synod is called the Eighth and was attended also by the legates of John, blessed Pope of ancient Rome....' After quoting the decree of this Council on the addition, he adds: 'Pope John, too, said the same in clear and unambiguous terms, when he wrote to the very saintly Photius on the said addition to the Symbol.' Mark says much the same in his profession of faith, calling the Photian Council the Eighth Oecumenical and also quoting the letter of John VIII to the Patriarch.[3] These passages leave no room for doubt upon Mark's opinion about Photius and his Council.

Mark's brother, John Eugenicos, wrote a pamphlet against the union decree, in which he severely reproves those who attribute to the Council of Florence the title of Eighth Oecumenical, there being another synod to claim that distinction, the Council summoned under Basil by Photius.[4] George Gemistos Plethon, on the other hand, in his short tractate (the only one published) says nothing about it.[5] George Scholarios finds some very hard things to say about Photius, blaming him for splitting the Church to serve his own conceit and ambition,[6] though on other occasions he refers to him with respect and appeals to his authority. Thus, for instance, in his second treatise on the Procession of the Holy Ghost, he quotes the decree of the Eighth Oecumenical Council—as

---

[1] Nothing is found in his encyclical epistle, published by A. Norov (Paris, 1859), pp. 27–43 and by Mgr Petit, *Patrol. Orientalis*, vol. XVII, pp. 449–59, nor in the other short tractates published by A. Norov (ibid. pp. 44–66). An examination of his Ἐπίλογος πρὸς Λατίνους, which I found in the British Museum MS. Add. 34,060, 15th-c., fols. 348 seq., has also been unproductive of results.

[2] Mgr Petit, 'Documents relatifs au Concile de Florence', in *Patrol. Orientalis*, vol. XVII, p. 421.

[3] Ibid. p. 440.

[4] Dositheos, Τόμος Καταλλαγῆς, loc. cit. pp. 210 seq., 256 seq.

[5] *P.G.* vol. 160, cols. 975–80.

[6] De Process. S. Spir., *Tractatus I*, c. 3 (ed. by M. Jugie), *Œuvres complètes de Gennadie Scholarios* (Paris, 1929–38), vol. II, pp. 11 seq. Cf. Hergenröther, *Photius*, vol. II, p. 526.

he describes the Synod of 879–80—and the letter of John VIII to Photius on the Procession;[1] he returns to the subject of the Synod in his short Apology of the Anti-Unionists[2] and in his polemical writings against the Union of Florence.[3]

Theodore Agalianus, in the three short writings which have seen the light,[4] avoids touching our topic. The history of the Council of Florence, written by Sylvester Syropulos, has nothing of interest regarding our inquiry;[5] and Macarios Macres[6] is also silent about Photius. The anonymous treatise published by Dositheos (probably belonging to the fifteenth century)[7] is interesting for revealing Greek feelings, in particular towards the Papacy; it contains a vague reference to the Synod of Photius, summoned under Basil the Macedonian, the author saying in effect that Photius had condemned Nicholas I at a synod of a thousand Fathers.[8] To these witnesses we may add the great rhetorician Manuel, who in his book on Mark of Ephesus and the Council of Florence unaccountably calls this council the eighth, as the unionists called it at the time.[9]

Finally, two more attestations from the Emperor John Palaeologus. In his letter to Martin V on the summoning of a council for union, the Emperor expressly says on two occasions that the new council should meet 'secundum ordinem et consuetudinem sanctorum septem universalium conciliorum'.[10] He thus admits that in his time only seven oecumenical councils were officially recognized. The second attestation from the same Emperor is more surprising. The MS. containing it belongs to the fifteenth century, and on fols. 73 a and 74 there is a copy

---

[1] Ed. by M. Jugie, vol. II, pp. 323 seq.

[2] Apologia syntomos (ed. by M. Jugie), vol. III, pp. 88, 89.

[3] Letter to Demetrius Palaeologus against the Union of Florence, loc. cit. p. 127.

[4] Refutatio Argyropuli, P.G. vol. 158, cols. 1011–52; Συλλογή published by Dositheos, Τόμ. Καταλ., loc. cit. pp. 432 seq.

[5] Vera Historia Unionis Non Verae (ed. by R. Creighton; Hagae-Comitis, 1660). Only in Sectio IX, cap. 4, p. 254 the Emperor John Paleologus' speech, quoted by Syropulos, makes it clear that the Emperor knew only seven oecumenical councils: 'Ego quidem arbitror hanc synodum generalem nullatenus infra dignitatem aliarum septem Generalium subsidere, quae eandem antevertunt. Quare volo ut haec illis par in omnibus succedat, nec aliud quidpiam ab illis diversum in hac gestum prodeat....'

[6] Dositheos, loc. cit. pp. 413 seq.

[7] Loc. cit. pp. 1–204.

[8] Loc. cit. p. 40.

[9] Manuelis Magni Rhetoris Liber de Marco Ephesio deque Rebus in Synodo Flor. Gestis (ed. by L. Petit), Patrol. Orientalis, vol. XVII, p. 491.

[10] Mansi, vol. XXVIII, col. 1069.

of a profession of faith,[1] recalling that of Pseudo-Anastasius, which the Emperor had read engraved on the doors of the church of St Peter in Rome. This profession, so far unpublished, enumerates the seven oecumenical councils.

From these investigations we may now draw some important conclusions. First of all, we have been enabled to see that Photius was not considered in Byzantium to be the principal actor in the schism till much later than has been generally believed; the Photian Legend arose in the thirteenth century and it was the partisans of the union who contributed most to its development, even in the East. But, while their account of Photius' advent to the patriarchal throne was not based on fact, they always professed a certain respect for his great erudition. Certainly, they never believed in Photius' second excommunication, nor have we found in the tradition of the Byzantine Church any trace of such a belief. On the contrary, it was generally held that the peace between the two Churches, once sealed by the Council of Photius, lasted without a single break till the patriarchate of Michael Cerularius. No hint of any quarrel between the two Churches did we find under Pope Formosus, though at least some traces of it should have been left in tradition, had the two Churches fallen into schism in his reign. The oldest treatise on the schism, attributed to the chartophylax of Nicaea and dating from the eleventh century, knows nothing of any split under Formosus, though he vaguely mentions some quarrels under Sergius III; and the unionists of the thirteenth century seem to be no wiser.

With regard to the Photian Council, we may take it that it was never officially classed among the oecumenical councils as the Eighth Council by the Church of Byzantium and that, officially, it never admitted more than seven oecumenical councils, the reason being that in the Byzantine conception of canon law the Council of Photius did not issue any doctrinal decisions and was only summoned for the restoration of peace in the Church.

Yet the Greeks always professed the highest veneration for that Council, and even the Greek Catholics, with the exception of Calecas, who as a Dominican could not emancipate himself from Western influence, never denied the validity and the importance of that synod

---

[1] Paris. Graec. (Bibliothèque Nationale) 1191. The MS. is on paper and contains 141 fols. Examination of an anonymous opuscule *De Azymis adv. Latinos*, found in the Paris. Graec. 1295 (15th–16th c., on paper, fol. 342), fols. 22–6, and of another pamphlet (Paris. Graec. 1286 16th c., on paper, 318 fols.), fols. 47–56a, has given no result. George Koresios in his Ἐγχειρίδιον περὶ τῆς Ἐκπορεύσεως (ed. by Dositheos), loc. cit. pp. 276–410, has nothing to say about Photius.

and continued to respect it even after the fourteenth and fifteenth centuries, when their opponents promoted it to the rank of eighth oecumenical council. They protested against the promotion, but they treated its Acts with respect. At the same time, the writings of the friends of the Union in the fourteenth and fifteenth centuries are evidence that even the unionists never classed the Ignatian Council among the oecumenicals. Having been annulled by the synod of 879–80, the Council that condemned Photius remained in the estimation of the whole Church non-existent. In the eyes even of the Greek Catholics, only the decisions of the Council of Photius kept their full legal value. A few of the unionists made the Council of Florence the Eighth Oecumenical Council, but none of them ever designated the Council of Ignatius oecumenical; this is clear evidence that in this respect the Eastern Church remained to the end faithful to the tradition of the universal Church, a tradition forgotten in the West at the beginning of the twelfth century for reasons I have explained.

We shall now close our review of Eastern literature between the sixteenth and the nineteenth centuries, dealing only with the output of the principal Eastern writers and drawing an appropriate parallel with the contemporaneous development of Western literature during the same period.

The first of the modern Eastern writers to stand comparison with his Latin brothers of the pen is the Patriarch of Jerusalem, Dositheos. We have had occasion to appreciate his erudition and his scholarly editions of Greek texts; he also wrote a more detailed history of Photius in his *Tomos Charas*, in which he published among other things the Acts of the Photian Council and several of Photius' letters for the definite purpose of defending the Patriarch's memory against Baronius and more particularly against Allatius, the writer who denied even the existence of the Photian Council. His book was not published till 1705, at Jassy, after his death, by the good offices of the Metropolitan Anthimos. Though the Patriarch, in his summary of the history of Photius, often contradicts Catholic historians, Baronius in particular, even he must have yielded to the Cardinal's fascination. Dositheos presents the story of Photius' elevation in a manner unlike that of Baronius and follows the old tradition of his Church, nearly forgotten, that Ignatius had duly resigned; he defends the authenticity of the Acts of the Photian Council and disproves the libel that Photius was a eunuch, but with regard to the second schism of Photius Dositheos completely capitulates to the Cardinal.

But he was not the only modern orthodox writer to allow himself to be led astray by the great Roman historian. Baronius' prestige left its mark on the East, and as a Russian translation, naturally expurgated, of his *Ecclesiastical Annals* was published in Moscow in 1719, his main findings found ready favour with the Orthodox East.

This is important, for it explains how Eastern scholars came to abandon the sound tradition of their Church, a tradition which, as we have seen, had maintained itself almost intact from the ninth century down to our modern era. Had they but taken the trouble to examine with some care the works of those Greek writers who dealt with the history of Photius, they would perhaps have withstood the rush of documents and new arguments that came upon them from the *Ecclesiastical Annals*. But Baronius triumphed in the orthodox Eastern world, to the lasting detriment of the memory and the history of Photius.

It is easy to trace the Cardinal's influence in nearly all the Eastern writers, whether Greek or Russian, from the seventeenth century onward; for instance, Elias Menates, a contemporary of Dositheos, and bishop of Cercyra (1679–1714). In his book, *The Stone of Scandal*, published in Leipzig in 1711, Menates frequently endeavours to correct Baronius, but at other places succumbs to the force of the Cardinal's dialectics, so that even in the opinion of this orthodox bishop Photius' case is taken to be one of the most important issues that divide the two Churches.[1]

The Photian case is also a leading topic in the polemical work of the Patriarch Nectarios of Jerusalem.[2]

Sophocles Oikonomos, who edited Photius' *Amphilochia*,[3] and

---

[1] Unable to consult the original of this rare work, I have used an unpublished Latin translation kept in the British Museum (Harl. 5729): 'Elias Menatas, Cephalonis, Cernicae et Calavritae in Peloponeso episcopus, Petra Offensionis, sive de origine causaque schismatis inter ecclesiam orientalem atque occidentalem deque quinque illis circa quos dissident sententiis, dilucida narratio. Edita a Rev. Do. Francisco Meniata archiepresb. Cephaloniae Athoo Patre, atque ad certiorem plenioremque rei notitiam, omnibus qui Vetera apost. et synodica sectantur dogmata, sive episcopi fuerint sive presbyteri, sive principes laici, sive orthodoxi christiani, ab eodem dedicata, rogatu atque hortatu splendidissimi doctissimique viri, Domini Jacobi Pilarini Cephalonii, Medicinae doctoris.'

[2] Περὶ τῆς ἀρχῆς τοῦ Πάπα (Jassy, 1672). Cf. the English translation by P. Allix, *Nectarii Patr. Hierosolymitani confutatio imperii Papae in Ecclesiam* (Londoni, 1702). Cf. the Catholics' replies to Patriarch Dositheos: A. Andruzzi, *Vetus Graecia de Sancta Sede Romana praeclare sentiens* (Venice, 1713); idem, *Consensus tum Graecorum tum Latinorum Patrum de Processione Sp. S. ex Filio* (Romae, 1716). On Le Quien's *Panoply* see p. 380.

[3] Athens, 1858; cf. Krumbacher, *Geschichte der Byzantinischen Litteratur*, p. 77.

J. Valetta,[1] the editor of his letters, also bear traces of Baronius' influence, though both try to rectify some of his mistakes, and the same is true of the *Greek Ecclesiastical History*, the first great work of its kind, published by Meletios, the Metropolitan of Athens.[2] Andron. K. Dimitrakopoulos[3] also adopts Baronius' opinions; and Filaret Vafeidos[4] mostly follows Neander and Schröckh in his account of Photius.

Equally marked is the influence of Dositheos, Meniates,[5] Baronius and the Protestant historians on the first modern Russian historians. The works dealing with our subject that I have been able to consult are the following: the Manual of Ecclesiastical History, by the archimandrite Innokentis (I. Smirnov),[6] the works of A. N. Muraviev,[7] of Filaret,[8] archbishop of Tchernigov, and of P. A. Lavrovskii[9] (on St Cyril and St Methodius).

Western scholars had since the sixteenth century monopolized the entire field of Photian studies and Eastern scholars could only follow their lead, at most contenting themselves with discarding some of their opinions; then in the middle of the nineteenth century another Roman scholar, Cardinal Hergenröther, came on the scene, bringing to light an imposing number of new or little-known documents in evidence of his theory on Photius, and the influence which he exerted upon orthodox scholars was similar to that of Baronius. N. I. Kostomarov,[10] the first Russian critic of Hergenröther's work, accepted nearly all the Cardinal's postulates and could scarcely disguise his embarrassment in some of his controversies with the German scholar. Golubkov's critique of the

---

[1] Φωτίου ἐπιστολαί (London, 1864), *Prolegomena*, pp. 1–98.

[2] Ἐκκλησιαστικὴ ἱστορία (Wien, 1783), 4 vols., vol. II, pp. 272–80, 299–302, 306–24.

[3] Ἱστορία τοῦ σχίσματος τῆς Λατινικῆς ἐκκλησίας ἀπὸ τῆς ὀρθοδόξου ἑλληνικῆς (Leipzig, 1867), pp. 1–21.

[4] Ἐκκλησιατικὴ ἱστορία (Constantinople, 1886), vol. II, pars. 110–13, pp. 48–64.

[5] His book was translated into Russian and published at St Petersburg in 1783 (*Kamen Soblazna*).

[6] *Nachertanie Tserkovnoi Istorii* (St Petersburg, 1817).

[7] *Pravda Vselenskoi Tserkvi o Rimskoi i Prochikh Patr. Kaf.* (St Petersburg, 1849), pp. 124–81.

[8] *Istoricheskoe Chtenie ob Ottsakh Tserkvi* (St Petersburg, 1859), vol. III, pars. 281–6, pp. 219–46.

[9] *Kiril i Mefodii* (Kharkov, 1863), pp. 39–182. For other works, scarcely accessible in the West, see bibliography of Ivantsov-Platonov, loc. cit. pp. 175–7.

[10] 'Patriarkh Fotii i Pervie Razdyelenie Tserkvei,' published in *Vyestnik Evropui* (1868), books I and II, pp. 120–68, 591–636.

Cardinal's first volume [1] displayed a minimum of originality; only A. P. Lebedev could summon more courage and critical sense.

To the credit, however, of Oriental scholars, it must be admitted that the great Catholic historian found among their ranks an antagonist worthy of his steel, an obscure Syrian hieromonachus, educated in Russia, Gerazim Yared. Reference has been made to some of his opinions and criticisms, and in spite of many reservations to be made, I must again insist that the work of this humble scholar was the real reply which Hergenröther deserved. It is a matter of regret that the Cardinal probably never knew that a hieromonachus had boldly answered him, and that Yared's deductions, often well founded and unanswerable, passed unnoticed in the West. Even so, Yared could not remain wholly immune from the influence of Baronius and Hergenröther, particularly with regard to Photius' second schism.

What is more extraordinary is that Yared's findings met with such a poor response, even in the East. He found his severest critic in the person of A.P. Lebedev, professor at the Moscow Theological Academy, and this famous scholar's [2] criticisms on the Syrian's conclusions were partly justified. Yet, on many points, the Syrian had a finer flair than his critic. A. P. Lebedev [3] was not so original in his inferences as appeared at first and though he often crossed swords with Hefele and Hergenröther, he was indebted to the latter more than he would have cared to confess; lacking a deeper knowledge, he succumbed to the superficial cogency of the Cardinal's logic. As Lebedev's ideas held the field in Russia and the Eastern world, their influence can be traced in the Russian literary output on Photius published about 1890 [4] to commemorate the millennium of Photius' death. It was then that a new period in Photian studies in Russia was inaugurated by Ivantsov-Platonov, in the speech he addressed on 12 January 1892 to the assembled Moscow University. His lecture, completed and enriched with numerous critical observations and discussions, is a masterpiece of original and well-balanced judgement; but, I regret to say, not even this study has so far come to the knowledge of our Western Byzantinist scholars. The

[1] 'Novuiya Izsledovaniya o Vremeni i Lichnosti Patr. Fotiya,' published in *Pravoslavnoe Oboʐryenie* (May 1868), pp. 54–89.

[2] *Chteniya Obshchestva Lyubitelei Dukhovn. Prosvyeshcheniya*, 1873, no. 1.

[3] Chiefly in his two works: *Rimskie Papui v Otnosheniakh k Tserkvi Viʐantiiskoi v IX–X. v.* (Moscow, 1875) and *Istoriya Konst. Soborov IX. v.* (Moscow, 1880).

[4] The list of these studies, most of which were published in Russian theological reviews and which Westerners would find it difficult to get at, is found in Ivantsov-Platonov, loc. cit. pp. 183 seq. I have only been able to consult Platonov's book.

upshot of it is that though the influence of the two cardinal-historians has not vanished altogether, it has certainly, in this particular study, come upon evil days. Some of Ivantsov-Platonov's conclusions were completed and corrected by Th. A. Kurganov.[1]

Rosseikin's book, published in 1913, merely marked time and failed to carry Ivantsov-Platonov's work further to any appreciable extent.

So much for the growth of what we call the 'Photian Legend' in the Eastern world. Its history has had its ups and downs in the East no less than in the West, though not to the same extremes; but even in the orthodox world the true notion of the history of the great Father of the Eastern Church has been sadly dimmed and blurred in the course of centuries. The remarkable thing is that the Eastern point of view of Greek and Russian scholars so affected the Photian incident that when the two traditions met on the threshold of the modern era in the sixteenth century, they found themselves in agreement on one important item of the Photian Legend, the so-called second schism of Photius.

[1] 'K Izsledovaniyu o Patr. Fotiye,' *Khrist. Chtenie*, 1895, vol. I, pp. 192 seq., 286 seq.

CONCLUSION

We have now reached the end of a long journey and have concluded our researches on the Photian Schism. Many additional details might have made the picture more attractive and the argument more convincing; nevertheless, it may be hoped that none of the essential aspects of the problem have been overlooked. If our inferences are right, we are justified in saying that the Photian problem is one of the most complex yet the most enthralling of the *causes célèbres* bequeathed to us by the Middle Ages. The way the whole case has been handled, clouded and misinterpreted in the West illustrates the less agreeable kind of medieval mentality and shows the prejudices and misunderstandings that may arise from a lack of critical sense and from historical misinterpretation.

From my researches it would appear that the person of Photius, the great Patriarch and Father of the Eastern Church, has for centuries been treated by the whole of the West with unmerited scorn and contempt; and it is the historian's task not merely to correct misinterpretation, but also to rehabilitate the historical figures who have suffered from it. Of this Photius is a notable example and history owes him reparation for the calumnies that have for centuries darkened his memory.

If I am right in my conclusions, we shall be free once more to recognize in Photius a great Churchman, a learned humanist and a genuine Christian, generous enough to forgive his enemies and to take the first step towards reconciliation. On the literary and scholastic side, Photius has always ranked fairly high amongst those scholars who have studied his writings; in this field his name always commanded respect, as his contemporaries, friend and foe alike, unanimously testified. Scholars familiar with his literary work were not inclined to believe all the stories brought up against him by his opponents; they were true to the scholar's instinct which prompted them to feel that a man who had spent his best days amongst books, in the company of the best representatives of the classical period and in daily contact with many devoted disciples, was not likely to descend to such meanness and petty ambition as were imputed to him by his enemies; and it was a right instinct which led them to honour a scholar who has been prominent in transmitting Hellenistic culture to posterity. At the same time, the firm conviction which prevailed among the simple orthodox that their Church could not be wrong in crowning its leader with the halo of sanctity for setting an example of Christian virtue was bound to find its justification.

My researches have also demonstrated that Photius had, like every human being, his weak moments. The worst mistake he made was his loss of self-control in 867, when instead of waiting for better days he went out of his way to launch a futile attack on the Patriarch of Old Rome. Events were to show that the lapse was inconsiderate, hasty and big with fatal consequences. It precipitated Basil's change of policy towards the Extremists and the Pope, whilst it strengthened the position of the anti-Byzantine party in Rome at a moment when it was losing its influence after the death of Nicholas. It not only contributed to Photius' downfall, but widened the gap between East and West. The excited clamours against the great Pope of the ninth century uttered by the Eastern bishops at the synod of 867 re-echoed over East and West for many years afterwards.

Did Photius ever realize his mistake? There are many signs to show that he did: his obvious endeavours to make peace with prominent Roman personalities, especially Marinus, his willingness to compromise on the Bulgarian issue which had been the occasion of his outburst in 867, his tardiness in pressing his case, his silent acceptance of Pope John's words in which he could read traces of bitterness even after the reconciliation. He evidently hoped that time would heal the wound and obliterate the past.

If he did so, events were to show that he was wrong. The cloud that hung over the synod of 867 was never dispelled from the minds of the Romans: it blinded them to the brighter aspects of Photius' history, affected all religious and cultural contacts between East and West and raised problems that were to poison the relations between the two Churches and influence the whole course of Christian development for centuries. We may well reflect how differently certain events would have shaped, if the Photian case had been judged from the beginning in the spirit we have outlined: both Western and Eastern Christianity would have run along different lines.

One may also regret that the Acts of the Photian Synods of 861 and 879–80 escaped the notice of the Western canonists and were completely obliterated by the Ignatian Synod of 869–70. At a time when the medieval West was framing its conception of universality and its political philosophy, it would have helped the framers to have before their eyes the solutions arrived at in the East when the Eastern Church was in communion with the West. As a result, her de facto acceptance of the right of recourse to the Patriarch of Rome as the highest court of appeal, even in disciplinary matters, as implied in the Acts of the

861 Synod, was overlooked by the Western canonists. The same happened to the stipulation of the other Photian Synod to the effect that each Church should follow its own practices. It was not in this broadminded spirit that East and West fought each other throughout the Middle Ages. And there lies the true significance of the history and legend of Photius.

The time has now come to reconsider in the light of history both the vital period of the ninth century and the trail of misconceptions it has left behind, and this in the best interests of Christianity; and if such a recension should lead to a better understanding between the two great Churches that have drifted apart for so many centuries to the obvious injury of the human race, the result should be widely beneficial.

It is therefore fitting at the end of this long and laborious research to evoke the conciliatory atmosphere that prevailed in Byzantium at the end of the tenth century, when the last echo of the struggles round Photius and Leo VI's tetragamy died down and was stilled by the decisions of the synods of 920 and 991. After reading the declaration of a final reconciliation between the parties in opposition—the famous *Tomus Unionis*[1]—the Fathers closed all previous dissensions and schisms by their acclamation and the dramatic scene of final pacification so impressed the faithful that the Orthodox Church commemorated for centuries, in the office of Orthodoxy,[2] the victory of the Eastern Church over the last heresy, iconoclasm and its aftermath. The walls of every cathedral church re-echoed the words, as they were repeated three times by the deacon and the faithful, recalling the struggles of the ninth century:[3] 'Eternal memory to Ignatius and Photius, the Orthodox and renowned Patriarchs! Whatever has been written or said against the holy Patriarchs Germanos, Tarasios, Nicephorus and Methodius, Ignatius, Photius, Stephen, Anthony and Nicholas, be for ever

ANATHEMA! ANATHEMA! ANATHEMA!'

[1] Mansi, vol. XVIII, cols. 341 seq. See Grumel, *Regestes*, loc. cit. pp. 169–71, 231.
[2] Th. J. Uspenski, 'Sinodik v nedelyu Pravoslaviya', in *Zapiski Imp. Novorossiiskago Universiteta* (Odessa, 1893), vol. LIX, pp. 407–502. On the date when the name of Photius was entered into the Synodica read on Orthodoxy Sunday, see A. Michel, *Humbert und Kerullarios*, loc. cit. vol. II, pp. 13 seq. Cf. also Hergenröther, *Photius*, vol. III, pp. 725 seq.
[3] Uspenski, loc. cit. pp. 415 seq.: Ἰγνατίου καὶ Φωτίου τῶν ὀρθοδόξων καὶ ἀοιδίμων πατριαρχῶν, αἰωνία ἡ μνήμη...."Ἅπαντα τὰ κατὰ τῶν ἁγίων πατριαρχῶν Γερμανοῦ, Ταρασίου, Νικηφόρου καὶ Μεθοδίου, Ἰγνατίου, Φωτίου, Στεφάνου, Ἀντωνίου καὶ Νικολάου γραφέντα ἢ λαληθέντα, ἀνάθεμα, ἀνάθεμα, ἀνάθεμα.

New Edition of the *Liber Diurnus* (eleventh century) and the Number of Councils listed as Oecumenical

THE problems raised by the Popes' profession of faith and contained in the *Liber Diurnus* call for a more thorough examination. Without attempting to trace the evolution of the *Liber Diurnus* or to quote the enormous bibliography bearing on the subject, I may refer to the study made by the late Pope Pius XI,[1] who as Librarian of the Milan Ambrosiana must have dealt with this document with exceptional care: indeed, of the three manuscripts that are known, one is preserved in Milan and was in course of publication under the supervision of Mgr Ratti.[2]

The *Liber Diurnus* in the edition of Th. E. von Sickel[3] is based on the Vatican manuscript and contains 99 formulas. Next to those regulating the composition of letters on various occasions, the presentation of the pallium and the granting of pontifical privileges, there are found seven formulas on the procedure to be followed at the election and the consecration of a new Pope (ff. 57–63); four other formulas deal with the announcement of the Pope's election and the routine prescribed for the new Pope on taking possession of the throne (f. 82 decretum pontificis, f. 83 indiculum pontificis

---

[1] A. Ratti, 'La Fine d'una Leggenda ed altere Spigolature intorno al *Liber Diurnus* Rom. Pont.' (*R. Istituto Lombardo di Scienze e Littere* (Milano, 1913), ser. II, vol. XLVI, pp. 238–52).

[2] Only a facsimile edition was published in 1921: L. Gramatica, G. Galbiati, 'Il Codice Ambrosiano del *Liber Diurnus* Roman. Pont.' (*Analecta Ambrosiana*, vol. VII, Milan-Rome, 1921). See the more recent bibliography, ibid. pp. 7–8. Cf. also the exhaustive article written on this subject by H. Leclercq in his *Dictionnaire d'Archéologie Chrétienne* (Paris, 1930), vol. IX, 1, cols. 243–344. The latest study on the *Liber Diurnus* was published by L. Santifaller, 'Die Verwendung des *Liber Diurnus* in den Privilegien der Päpste von den Anfängen bis zum Ende des II Jh.' (*Mitteilungen des Instit. f. Öster. Geschichtsf.* (1935), vol. XLIX, pp. 224–366, especially pp. 225–333). Idem, 'Neue Forschungen zur älteren Papstdiplomatik. Über den *Liber Diurnus*', *Forschungen und Fortschritte* (1938), vol. XIV, p. 41. Idem, 'Zur *Liber Diurnus*-Forschung', in *Hist. Zeitschr.* (1940), vol. CLXI, pp. 532–8. In the last study, Santifaller wrongly doubts the results of his own researches on the strength of some criticisms of Peitz's recent publications. See *supra*, p. 318.

[3] *Liber Diurnus Romanorum Pontificum* (Vindobonae, 1889). Cf. also Rozière's ed., *Liber Diurnus, ou Recueil des Formules Usitées par la Chancellerie Pontificale du Ve au XIe siècles* (Paris, 1869), which is based on Garnière's edition and reproduces the Clermont manuscript that was lost, but was recovered at the Dutch Abbey of Egmond-Binnen.

and formulas 84 and 85), formula 83 containing the profession of faith which the Pope is expected to read out and sign. It enumerates every one of the six oecumenical councils.[1]

Sickel[2] had already proved that the *Liber Diurnus*, as we know it, was the result of a lengthy evolution,[3] the three versions (in the Vatican, Clermont and Milan) representing the stage of its development at the time of Hadrian I, from the end of the eighth century to the beginning of the following, possibly also the period of Leo III, with the pontificate of Gregory the Great to represent a very important period of its growth.[4]

The Jesuit W. M. Peitz[5] went further, too far even, by alleging that many letters of Gregory the Great had been composed after certain formulas of the *Liber Diurnus*, thus making this book the oldest witness of the procedure of the Pontifical Chancellery.

It would be interesting to know whether this important handbook of the Pontifical Chancellery was still in use after the ninth or at the beginning of the tenth century. The existing manuscripts bear witness to its utilization by the Chancellery at that period, but we find traces of it in the centuries that followed, and the question is raised whether the formula of the Pope's profession of faith prior to his ascent to the throne was still used in the eleventh century. As we may reasonably assume that the handbook and its various formulas were subjected to such modifications as may have been dictated by changing practice at the Chancellery, new rules and regulations, and the modernization of pontifical office routine, it would be interesting to discover whether the formula of the Pope's oath underwent corresponding alterations and whether the computation of Councils was brought up to date.

The problem of later transformations of the *Liber Diurnus* has not yet been cleared up, but important progress has been made by scholars who have traced the use of some formulas in documents issued by the Pontifical

---

[1] Sickel, loc. cit. p. 91. Six councils are also enumerated in formula 84 (loc. cit. pp. 93–103), which contains the draft of the first pastoral letter a newly elected Pope is expected to send to his bishops and the faithful. This document is of particular interest to students of the evolution of dogma in the Church, and illustrates what the Roman Church thought of the councils and their convocation. Many sentences remind one of the old Greek treatises on the Oecumenical Councils, which the reader will find discussed in Part II, Chapter VI, and Appendix III.

[2] Sickel, loc. cit. pp. xvii seq.

[3] See the excellent summary of all the problems raised by the growth of the *Liber Diurnus*, in H. Breslau's *Handbuch der Urkundenlehre für Deutschland und Italien* (Berlin, 2nd ed. 1931), vol. II, pp. 241–7; and in E. Caspar, *Geschichte des Papsttums* (Tübingen, 1933), vol. II, pp. 782–5. Cf. also H. Steinacker, 'Zum *Liber Diurnus* und zur Frage nach dem Ursprung der Frühminuskel', in *Studi e Testi*, vol. XL (Miscellanea Francisco Ehrle, vol. IV, Rome, 1924), pp. 105–76.

[4] Cf. Breslau, loc. cit. vol. II, p. 243.

[5] 'Liber Diurnus', in *Sitzungsber. der Akad. Wiss. Wien, Phil.-Hist. Kl.* (1918), vol. 185, pp. 55–93. See the critique by M. Tangl, 'Gregor. Register und *Liber Diurnus*', in *Neues Archiv* (1919), vol. XLI, pp. 740–52.

Chancellery as far back as the reign of Gregory VII and Alexander V. A detailed study of the use of the *Liber Diurnus'* formulas in the papal privileges till the end of the eleventh century made by L. Santifaller[1] has brought some significant facts to light: for instance, that the handbook used by the papal notaries was given a form substantially different from that of the *Liber Diurnus* as we know it. From the second half of the ninth century to the second half of the eleventh, the handbook used by the Pontifical Chancellery contained only nineteen formulas on papal privileges out of all the formulas contained in the *Liber Diurnus*. Besides these, the handbook offered other formulas which were either new or variants of the *Liber Diurnus* formulas. This is of special importance to our subject, since it establishes the fact that the *Liber Diurnus*, or at least some portions of it, was used by the Chancellery in the eleventh century, whilst the existence of another handbook would also appear to be confirmed.

Interesting, too, are the conclusions which L. Santifaller[2] draws from his own and his predecessor's researches. According to him, the *Liber Diurnus*, as we know it from Sickel's edition, was not the handbook used by the Pontifical Chancellery, but only a school textbook for the training of future pontifical notaries, which included many formulas copied from the official handbook, together with some documents issued by other Chancelleries and addressed to the Popes. It would, of course, be helpful to the candidates for the Pontifical Chancellery to get acquainted with the style and the formulas of other Chancelleries, but these could scarcely be assumed to have their place in an official handbook designed to supply forms and regulations for the dispatch of letters from the Papal Chancellery.

This textbook was given the same title as the official handbook—*Liber Diurnus*—since it was only a selection of documents mainly copied from it. As it is unlikely that an educational book would remain in use long after much of it had become out of date and as on the other hand the Pontifical Chancellery must have adopted from the second half of the ninth century a handbook differing substantially from the old edition that served as the original for the school-book, it seems reasonable to infer that the latter was

---

[1] 'Über die Verwendung des *Liber Diurnus* in der päpstl. Kanzlei von der Mitte des 8. bis in die Mitte des 11. Jhs', in *Abhandlungen aus dem Gebiete der mittleren und neueren Geschichte und ihrer Hilfwissenschaften*, Eine Festgabe zum 70. Geburtstag Prof. H. Finke gewidmet (Münster, 1925), pp. 23–35. Idem, 'Die Verwendung des *Liber Diurnus* in den Privilegien der Päpste von den Anfängen bis zum Ende des 11. Jh.', loc. cit. pp. 225–366. In this study, see on pp. 231 seq. a brief but comprehensive summary of different studies dealing with the subject. Cf. M. Tangl, 'Die Fuldäer Privilegienfrage', in *Mitteil. d. Institut. f. Österr. Geschichtsforsch.* (1899), vol. XX, pp. 212 seq.; Breslau, loc. cit. vol. II, p. 245. It is to be regretted that death prevented Sickel from publishing the third part of his *Prolegomena*, where he intended to provide evidence for the use of the *Liber Diurnus'* formulas.

[2] Loc. cit. (1935), pp. 289 seq.

dispensed with by the tenth century: only up to the end of the ninth century, or the beginning of the tenth, would it have remained of any use.

It is admitted that the Pontifical Chancellery had been using special handbooks ever since the end of the sixth century, and that they were constantly being altered, new formulas being added and old ones suppressed, as the need arose. It was the oldest handbook that received the name of *Liber Diurnus* and, judging from the school-book bearing the same name and preserved in three MSS., it mainly contained important regulations on the appointment of bishops, papal elections and some diplomatic formulas. Thus it is quite possible that while the title *Liber Diurnus* was reserved for the oldest part of the handbook and the new formulary in circulation at the Chancellery was regarded as a separate handbook, the *Liber Diurnus* was treated with veneration as a valuable document of canon law.

This explanation, at the present stage of research, seems to be the most acceptable, and confirmation can be found in Deusdedit's collection of canon law; for as we have seen, the Cardinal often quotes from the *Liber Diurnus*, which he himself used at the Chancellery, and he always gives the correct title of his sources. In only one instance does he quote formula 115 of the *Liber Diurnus* as found in the MS. of Milan,[1] but in quoting it he does not give the *Liber Diurnus* as his reference, but the *Regesta* of Honorius I and Gregory II. As the formula was current at the Chancellery in the second half of the eleventh century, and, judging from Deusdedit's Collection, was not included in the copy of the *Liber Diurnus* he used, it seems fair to conclude that it came from another formulary in use at the Chancellery, but different from the old Collection of the *Liber Diurnus* (a reference-book now differentiated from the new *Kanzleibuch*).

Cardinal Deusdedit's Collection also provides other information of the greatest value on the ultimate fate of the *Liber Diurnus*. From it we learn not only that the original *Liber Diurnus* was doing service during the eleventh century, but that before the Cardinal's time it had been subjected to radical revision. As already mentioned, Deusdedit copied ten formulas out of the *Liber Diurnus*,[2] but used a version substantially different from those that survived in the three manuscripts. The alterations made in the old version of the *Liber Diurnus* are very thorough, several formulas of the old edition being welded into one,[3] besides numerous revisions in the text itself,[4]

---

[1] Lib. III, cap. 118, 119, Wolf v. Glanvell, loc. cit. p. 327.

[2] Wolf v. Glanvell, loc. cit., Lib. II, 109 = Sickel, f. 82; Lib. II, 110 = Sickel, f. 83; Lib. II, 111 = Sickel, f. 74; Lib. II, 112 = Sickel, f. 75; Lib. III, 146 = Sickel, f. 52; Lib. III, 147 = Sickel, f. 53; Lib. III, 148 = Sickel, f. 54; Lib. III, 149 = Sickel, f. 56; Lib. III, 150 = Sickel, f. 10; Lib. IV, 427 = Sickel, f. 76.

[3] Lib. II, 109 = Sickel, ff. 61–82–60; Lib. II, 111 = Sickel, ff. 83–73–4; Lib. III, 148 = Sickel, ff. 54–5.

[4] See detailed analysis of all these alterations in Peitz, 'Liber Diurnus', loc. cit. pp. 30–53.

though the older formulas, which even in the school *Liber Diurnus* that survives in the three MSS. have an antique flavour, were more substantially altered.

These alterations cannot, however, be credited to the ninth-century editors. There are unmistakable signs that this new edition was brought out in the eleventh century: first, the invocation 'in nomine sanctae et individuae Trinitatis', which in pontifical documents prevailed only at this period;[1] secondly, the dating is not after the indictions, but after the computation of years since the Lord's Incarnation, a practice, as is well known, which the Pontifical Chancellery did not adopt till the eleventh century.[2] Several formulas, instead of 'anno ill...' simply put 'anno milesimo ill...'. It is a well-known fact that the Cardinal was exceptionally meticulous in copying the texts he used for his collection,[3] faithfully quoting his sources, taking good care not to supply dates where the originals gave none and finally pointing out all the *lacunae* in the documents he utilized. We must therefore suppose that here also the Cardinal altered nothing, but scrupulously copied out the formulas as he found them in the new edition of the *Liber Diurnus*.[4]

It is difficult to assign any exact date to this edition, though everything points to the date of its issue as prior to 1059. As a matter of fact, that same year Nicholas II issued his famous rules on pontifical elections, investing Cardinal-bishops with preponderant influence in the elections, a privilege to which, as is well known, Cardinal-priests and deacons never assented, and as a result of their opposition, the Pope's decree was never enforced.[5] It was probably to this decree that Cardinal Deusdedit referred in his preface in justification of his extracts from the *Liber Diurnus*.[6] It all suggests the name

[1] Buschbell, 'Professiones Fidei der Päpste', in *Röm. Quartalschrift* (1896), vol. x, pp. 280 seq.

[2] Cf. A. L. Poole, *Studies in Chronology and History* (Oxford, 1934), p. 179.

[3] He says so himself in the preface of his work, Glanvell edition, p. 4: 'et omnimodis opera impendi, ut essent plenissima auctoritate quae hic congessi, quoniam sicut aliquos, quibus haec placerent, ita non defuturos quosdam, qui his inviderent, non ignoravi.'

[4] Cf. Sickel, loc. cit. pp. lii, liii. After noting that these changes could not have taken place till the eleventh century, he concludes: 'Negaverim vero hoc ipsum cardinalem Deusdedit novasse; aliis enim operis sui locis eam temporis significandi rationem quam eius exemplar propositum exhibuit, retinuit.' Peitz, 'Liber Diurnus', loc. cit. pp. 30–2, is still more explicit on the point.

[5] P. Scheffer-Boichorst, *Die Neuordnung der Papstwahl durch Nikolaus II* (Strassburg, 1879), pp. 14–18; I. B. Sägmüller, *Die Tätigkeit und Stellung der Kardinäle bis Papst Bonifaz VIII* (Freiburg i. B. 1896), pp. 128 seq.

[6] Glanvell, loc. cit. pp. 4–5: 'Praeterea antiquum ordinem electionis seu consecrationis Romani Pontificis et cleri eius huic operi inserere libuit. Nam quidam olim in Dei et sanctorum sanctionibus contemptum et ad sui scilicet ostentationem et adscribendam sibi ventosam auctoritatem, quae nullis canonicis legibus stare

of Leo IX, who displayed such remarkable activity in the reorganization of the Pontifical Chancellery.[1]

Having said thus much, let us examine the profession of faith as prescribed for the Sovereign Pontiff in the new edition of the *Liber Diurnus*. Though even this formula (Deusdedit, lib. II, 110) bears palpable traces of recent recasting, it is satisfactory to note that the new editor of the *Liber Diurnus* does not expect the Pope to acknowledge the Eighth Council, for the new Pontiff must swear, among other things, that he admits seven oecumenical councils:[2]

Sancta quoque VII universalia concilia, id est Nicenum, Constantinopolitanum, Ephesinum primum, Chalcedonense, V quoque et VI idem Constantinopolitanum et VII item Nicenum usque ad unum apicem inmutabilia servare et pari honore et veneratione digna habere et quae predicaverunt et statuerunt, omnimodis sequi et praedicare, quaeque condemnaverunt, ore et corde condemno.

The words are very plain and leave no room for doubt; and yet Buschbell, who specially dealt with the Popes' professions of faith, is reluctant to admit the significance of the fact, declaring that this profession of faith must have been drawn up in the first half of the ninth century; otherwise, he maintains, the Eighth Council would have been mentioned. In his opinion, this formula of the *Liber Diurnus* ceased to be used after 787.[3] But the same writer, curiously enough, demonstrates in his book, with full array of arguments, that this formula underwent a thorough transformation in the eleventh century, and makes Deusdedit responsible for it.

Buschbell's opinion on the use of the formula has been indirectly invalidated by the researches of other experts, proving that many formulas of the *Liber Diurnus* remained in use at least till the pontificate of Gregory VII.[4] In that

potest, scripserunt sibi novam ordinationem eiusdem Romani pontificis, in qua quam nefanda quam Deo inimica statuerunt, horreo scribere; qui legit intelligat.' In my hypothesis Deusdedit makes the Cardinal-bishops responsible for this prescription. Cf. Fournier-Le Bras, *Histoire des Collections Canoniques*, loc. cit. vol. II, p. 47.

[1] Cf. Peitz, loc. cit. p. 33. The learned Jesuit would also attribute to Leo IX a new edition of the *Ordo Romanus*, on the strength of one passage in the *Ordo* which makes a reference to Pope Leo. Mabillon and Germain, *Musei Italici tom. II, Complectens antiquos libros rituales S.R.E.* (Paris, 1724), pp. 89 seq.; *P.L.* vol. 78, cols. 1003 seq. On the activities of Leo IX in the reorganization of the Pontifical Chancellery see Poole, loc. cit. pp. 179, 181.

[2] Ed. v. Glanvell, loc. cit. vol. II, pp. 110, 236. The reader will find at the end of the appendix, pp. 445–7, the *Professio Fidei* of the *Liber Diurnus* as edited by Th. E. von Sickel and preserved in Deusdedit's Collection.

[3] Buschbell, loc. cit. p. 279.

[4] R. Zoepffel, *Die Papstwahlen und die mit ihnen im nächsten Zusammenhang stehenden Ceremonien in ihrer Entwicklung vom 11. bis zum 14. Jh.* (Göttingen, 1871), p. 228, cites some indications to the effect that the formula on the Pope's election was still in use in the eleventh century. Cf. chiefly Santifaller's study (in *Abhandlungen...*).

case, why should the papal profession alone make exception? Why should
it alone clash with the time? For if Deusdedit altered it to bring it into line
with certain usages in force at the Pontifical Chancellery of his day, why then
did he leave untouched the old version about the seven councils?[1] For if
he really meant thereby to lend the formula an archaic flavour in order to
support his view of the exclusive rights of Cardinal-deacons and priests in
the election of new Pontiffs, why did he not leave other archaic phrases
untouched, instead of modernizing them? If, in order to emasculate the
decision taken in 1059 by Nicholas II on the rights of Cardinal-bishops, he
wished to quote here 'the ancient work regulating the election and consecration of the Roman pontiff and of his clergy', as he himself puts it,[2] he
surely should give the correct text of it; for the slightest variation on his part
would have been detected and denounced by the Cardinal-bishops, who also
had access to official documents and could verify their colleague's quotations.

Unfortunately, Buschbell examined this document on its own merits,
without the least regard to other extracts borrowed by the Cardinal from the
same source; a detailed comparison of all the extracts with the edition of the
Liber Diurnus of the eighth and ninth centuries would certainly have made
him more cautious in his speculations. He had but to read the formula
(Lib. II, 111) that follows. This formula, which bears the title *Cautio Episcopi*,
was radically reversed. The new version is made after formulas 83, 73 and
74 of the old recension of the *Liber Diurnus* as published by Sickel, and it
is precisely the beginning of the formula that has been completely revised:[3]

In nomine Domini Dei et Salvatoris nostri Iesu Christi, anno incarnationis
eius ill. mense ill. die ill. indictione ill. Promitto ego ill' episcopus sanctae
Ecclesiae ill' vobis domino meo beatissimo ill' summo pontifici et universali papae
et per vos beatis apostolis Petro et Paulo et sanctae catholicae, apostolicae Ecclesiae
Romanae devota mentis integritate et pura conscientia, illam fidem et religionem
semper tenere et predicare atque defendere, quam ab apostolis traditam habemus
et ab eorum successoribus custoditam. Sancta quoque VII universalia concilia
immutilata servare et pari honore et veneratione habere, et quaeque predicaverunt
et statuerunt sequi et predicare....

Later, the bishop promises to invite the clergy to common life and to see
that sub-deacons, deacons and priests shall keep chastity. He promises also
to attend the synods that are summoned and to receive with honour the
legates of the Holy See. There is also found in this profession a reference to
simony, which the bishop promises to eschew. Now most of these passages
were missing in the old version of the formulas,[4] which suggests that they

---

[1] Even H. Breslau, loc. cit. vol. II, p. 246, rem. 2, is very sceptical about Buschbell's
deductions.

[2] Glanvell, loc. cit. p. 4. See p. 439.

[3] Glanvell, loc. cit. pp. 237–9; cf. Sickel, loc. cit. pp. 74–8.

[4] The formula 73 (Sickel, loc. cit. pp. 69 seq.) begins with these words: 'Promissio
fidei episcopi. In nomine domini et cetera.—Promitto ill. ego tal. episcopus sanctae

were inserted in the eleventh century, when notions of ecclesiastical reform had definitely prevailed at the pontifical court. One detects there at the first glance the reforming ideas that inspired the reign of Leo IX, who also extended the practice of sending pontifical legates to various dioceses to help in the reform of the clergy.

Now if Deusdedit were responsible for all these changes, it would be impossible to understand why he introduced the passage on the seven councils; for, having been completely modernized, the formula was in no way archaic, and it was the passage about the seven oecumenical councils that was most ruthlessly altered. The statement on the seven councils not being in the old formula, which only mentioned six, was therefore introduced in the eleventh century. Then why did the editor not proceed to add the Eighth Council?

But a more thorough examination of this profession of faith shows that the number of councils in the formula had been frequently altered, councils being added as they happened to be officially recognized by the Church of Rome. The Jesuit Peitz[1] claims to have discovered in this profession the key to the evolution of Catholic dogma from apostolic times, a theory which is perhaps too beautiful to be true. But those who refuse to follow him so far must at least admit that no more than four councils were mentioned in the original profession, others being added later, one after another, as their oecumenicity was admitted by the Holy See.[2] Moreover, the addition was not always made immediately after recognition; and it is understood that the original handbook *Liber Diurnus* was not always copied out at the advent of every new Pope: it could remain in use even after several formulas had grown out of date, a new edition being issued only when the number of

ecclesiae ill. vobis domino meo sanctissimo et ter beatissimo ill. summo pontifici seu universali papae et per vos sanctae vestrae catholicae ecclesiae et apostolicae sedis devota mentis integritate et pura conscientia (et iureiurando corporali ut.) oportet proposito, quae pro firmamento sive rectitudine catholicae fidei et ortho-doxae religioni conveniunt, me profiteri. Et ideo promitto atque spondeo vobis cui supra beatissimo domino meo papae et per vos beato Petro principi apostolorum eiusque sanctae ecclesiae illam fidem tenere predicare atque defendere quam ab apostolis traditam habemus et successores eorum custoditam, reverendam Nicenam sinodum trecentorum decem et octo patrum, sancto spiritu sibi revelante, suscipiens redegit in symbolum. . . .' The profession then enumerates all the six councils and their principal decisions in matters of faith.

Formula 74 (loc. cit. p.74) begins with the words: 'In nomine domini dei salva-toris nostri Iesu Christi, imperante et cetera.—Inter cetera salubris instituta doc-trinae quibus me ill. episcopum domine ille beatissime atque apostolice papa, ad accipiendum regendumque episcopatum ecclesiae ill. perducere atque informare dignatus es, hoc me quoque ammonuistis ut sacerdotium nullo premio concedi, excepto officiis quibus antiqua consuetudine dari solet, quia dignum est ut quod gratis accepi, gratis debeam, deo adiuvante, conferre. . . .'

[1] Loc. cit. p. 120. Cf. M. Tangl's critique, loc. cit. p. 752.
[2] Cf. H. Steinacker, loc. cit. pp. 116 seq.

antiquated formulas was considerable. On those occasions, the number of councils was brought up to date in the formulary.

We note, however, a curious point which at first would seem to contradict our contention: the Ambrosian manuscript of the *Liber Diurnus*, representing probably the more recent version of the formulary and dating from the second half of the ninth century, mentions only six oecumenical councils in the formula of the elected Pope's profession of faith. This sounds paradoxical, as the oecumenicity of the second Council of Nicaea seems to have been admitted in the Roman Church long before the new transcription of that formulary.

This is easily explained, if we remember what has been said about the origin and the nature of the *Liber Diurnus*. If the collection of formulas which has survived in three manuscripts and goes by the name of *Liber Diurnus* was only a school textbook for the use of would-be notaries, it is probable that since a school-book had not the official character of a handbook for the use of the Chancellery, the copyist, writing in the ninth century, contented himself with copying the old formula as he found it in his source. This would explain why the Ambrosian MS., though it dates from the end of the ninth century, enumerates only six councils in the *professio fidei*.

But such an explanation is not really necessary. Strange to say, even this version of the *Liber Diurnus* perfectly reflects the tradition of the Roman Church concerning the oecumenicity of the Seventh Council, which was not officially added to the other universal synods before 880. Here are the proofs.

In 863, Pope Nicholas I, together with the Fathers of the Roman Council, condemned Photius in the name of the six Councils,[1] and the Acts of the synod were appended to Nicholas' letters addressed to the Church of Constantinople and to the oriental Patriarchs,[2] and written in 866.[3] Hadrian II, his successor, still followed the same tradition in 872, as is shown in his letter to Charles the Bald.[4]

In June 880, ten years after the meeting of the Eighth Council and some

---

[1] Mansi, vol. xv, cols. 180, 661. Cf. Hergenröther, *Photius*, vol. i, p. 520, footnote 51. Cf. Hefele-Leclercq, *Histoire des Conciles*, vol. iv, p. 328. Cf. Baronius, *Annales*, ad ann. 863, ed. Pagi, vol. xiv, p. 581. Note the curious conjecture by J. F. Damberger, *Synchronistische Geschichte*, vol. iii: *Kritikheft* (Regensburg, 1850–63), pp. 206 seq., on the interpolation of this passage by Photius to enable him to accuse the Romans of refusing to acknowledge the Seventh Council.

[2] *M.G.H.* Ep. vi, pp. 520, 558.

[3] Cf. also the letter of Nicholas I to Ado of Vienne, in which the Pope asks the bishop to recognize the six Councils, though the authenticity of the letter is doubtful (*M.G.H.* Ep. vi, p. 669). Cf. C. A. Kneller, 'Papst und Konzil im ersten Jahrtausend', in *Zeitschrift für Kath. Theologie* (1904), vol. xxviii, p. 702.

[4] *M.G.H.* Ep. vi, p. 743: 'Sed de his nihil audemus iudicare quod possit Niceno concilio et quinque ceterorum conciliorum regulis vel decretis nostrorum antecessorum obviare.'

months after the Council of Photius, John VIII, in his letter to Svatopluk, the Moravian prince, approved the orthodoxy of St Methodius by assuring the prince that the Moravian archbishop's teaching was conformable to the doctrine of the six oecumenical councils;[1] which makes it plain that Photius' complaint about the recognition of the oecumenicity of the Seventh Council was well founded.

As far as the Church of Rome was concerned, it is certain that the Frankish Church's opposition to this Council did delay official and universal recognition of the oecumenicity of the Seventh Nicaean Council and a similar case might be quoted in connection with the *Filioque*, when to spare the feelings of the Greeks, Leo III energetically prohibited the addition of this formula to the Symbol, though the Roman Church did in practice profess the doctrine of the Procession of the Holy Ghost from the Father and the Son.[2]

The Seventh Council was therefore not officially added to the profession of faith till after 880. The new translation of the Acts of this Council, made by Anastasius the Librarian by order of John VIII, was at that time sufficiently known in the West to dissipate the last misgivings about the Council, whilst the complete reconciliation of John VIII with Photius and his Church certainly accelerated its acceptance. Thus there was nothing to prevent the demand formulated by Photius concerning that Council being met.

It was then, very probably, that the Seventh Council was added to the preceding ones, even in the newly elected Pontiffs' profession of faith. The new edition of the *Liber Diurnus* of the end of the ninth century, whose existence seems to have been established by Santifaller's research, probably included the list of the seven councils.

From the end of the ninth century to the middle of the eleventh, there were various opportunities for the completion of the list. Is it then not strange that the third edition of this valuable handbook of the Pontifical Chancellery, issued towards the middle of the eleventh century, should have listed no more than seven oecumenical councils?

But this is not so. No plausible explanation of the anomaly will ever be forthcoming unless it be frankly admitted that the Papacy did not, until the time of Deusdedit, number the Eighth Council among the oecumenical synods. And this was perfectly consistent, since the Pontifical Chancellery did nothing more than comply with the decision of John VIII, who annulled the anti-

---

[1] *M.G.H.* Ep. VII, p. 223. The author of the *Vita Methodii*, which was written at the end of the ninth century, probably in Moravia, follows this tradition, too, though he may have been influenced by the official tradition of the Western Church. See my translation of the *Vita* in my book, *Les Légendes de Constantin et de Méthode*, p. 384.

[2] A similar attitude is also found in John VIII, though on a less solemn occasion, one less 'official', he also speaks of 'sancta synodus octava' in his letter to the Neapolitans, Salernitans and Amalfitans (*M.G.H.* Ep. VII, p. 307). Note that this letter was written in 875, i.e. at the time when the Eighth Council was still considered valid by the two Churches.

Photian Council. By enumerating only seven oecumenical councils, Popes Marinus II and Leo IX only followed the tradition of the Church they ruled. For purposes of comparison, we may quote here the text of the profession of faith recorded in the *Liber Diurnus*, Sickel, loc. cit. pp. 90–3, formula 83:

Indiculum Pontificis.—In nomine domini dei salvatoris nostri Iesu Christi et cetera, indictione ill. mense ill. die ill.—Ill. misericordia dei diaconus et electus, futurusque per dei gratiam huius apostolicae sedis antistes tibi profiteor, beate Petre apostolorum princeps, cui claves regni coelorum ad ligandum atque solvendum in coelo et in terra creator atque redemptor omnium dominus Iesus Christus tradidit, inquiens: *quaecumque (ligaveris) super terram, erunt* // *ligata et in coelo, et quaecumque solveris super terram, erunt soluta et in coelis,* SANCTAEQUE TUAE ECCLESIAE QUAM HODIE tuo praesidio regendum suscepi, quod vere fidei rectitudine, Christo auctore tradente, per successores tuos atque discipulos usque ad exiguitatem meam perlatam in tua sancta ecclesia repperi, totis conatibus meis usque ad animam et sanguinem custodire temporum difficultate cum tuo adiutorio tolleranter sufferre; tam de sanctae et individuae trinitatis misterio quae unus est deus, quamque de dispensatione quae secundum carnem facta est, unigeniti filii dei domini nostri Iesu Christi et de ceteris ecclesiae dei dogmatibus, sicut universalibus conciliis et constitutis apostolicorum pontificum probatissimorumque doctorum ecclesiae scriptis sunt // commendata, id est queque ad rectitudinem vestrae nostraeque orthodoxe fidei a te traditae respiciunt, conservare; sancta quoque universalia concilia: Nicenum, Constantinopolitanum, Efesenum primum, Calcedonense et secundum Constantinopolitanum quod Iustiniani piae memoriae principis temporibus celebratum est, usque ad unum apicem inmutilata servare, et unam cum eis pari honore et veneratione sanctum sextum concilium quod nuper sub Constantino piae memoriae principe et Agathone apostolico praedecessore meo convenit, medullitus et plenius conservare, quaeque vero praedicaverunt, praedicare, queque condemnaverunt, ore et // corde condemnare; diligentius autem et vivacius omnia decreta predecessorum apostolicorum nostrorum pontificum, queque vel synodaliter vel specialiter statuerunt et probata sunt, confirmare et indiminute servare, et sicut ab eis statuta sunt, in sua vigoris stabilitate custodire, quaeque vel quosque condemnaverunt vel abdicaverunt, simili auctoritatis sententia condemnare; disciplinam et ritum ecclesiae, sicut inveni et a sanctis praedecessoribus meis traditum repperi, inlibatum custodire, et indiminutas res ecclesiae conservare et ut indiminute custodiantur operam dare; nihil de traditione quae a probatissimis predecessoribus meis // servatum repperi, diminuere vel mutare aut aliquam novitatem admittere, sed ferventer, ut vere eorum discipulus et sequipeda, totis (mentis) meae conatibus quae tradita comperio, conservare ac venerare; si qua vero emerserint contra disciplinam canonicam, emendare sacrosque canones et constituta pontificum nostrorum ut divina et celestia mandata custodire, utpote tibi redditurum me sciens de omnibus quae profiteor districtam in divino iudicio rationem, cuius locum divina dignatione perago et vicem intercessionibus tuis adiutus impleo. si preter haec aliquod agere presumpsero vel ut presumatur permisero, eris autem mihi in illa terribili die divini iudicii de//propitius. haec conanti et diligenter servare curanti adiutorium quoque ut prebeas obsecro in hac vita corruptibili constituto, ut inreprehensibilis appaream ante conspectum iudicis omnium domini nostri Iesu Christi, dum terribiliter de commissis advenerit iudicare, ut faciat me dextre partis compotem et inter fideles discipulos ac successores esse consortem. quam professionem meam, ut supra continet, per ill. notarium et scriniarium me mandante conscriptam propria manu subscripsi et tibi, beate Petre apostole et apostolorum omnium princeps, pura mente et conscientia devota corporali iureiurando sinceriter optuli.—Ego qui supra ill. indignus // diaconus et dei gratia electus huius apostolicae sedis Romanae ecclesiae hanc professionem meam, sicut supra continet, faciens et iusiurandum corporaliter offerens tibi, beate Petre apostolorum princeps, pura mente et conscientia optuli.

V. Wolf von Glanvell, *Die Kanonensammlung*, loc. cit., pp. 235 seq. (l. II, cap. 110): Ex *Libro Diurno*. Professio futuri pontificis, antequam consecretur.[1]

In nomine *sanctae et individuae trinitatis. Anno dominicae incarnationis* ill. die ill. mensis ill. indictione ill. *ego* ill. *sanctae Romanae ecclesiae* presbiter et electus, ut *fiam* per dei gratiam *humilis* huius *sanctae* apostolicae sedis antistes, profiteor tibi beate Petre apostolorum principi, cui claves regni coelorum ad ligandum atque solvendum in coelo et in terra creator atque redemptor omnium dominus *noster* Ihesus Christus tradidit inquiens: "quaecumque ligaveris s[uper] t[erram] erunt ligata et i[n] c[oelo], et quaecumque solveris s[uper] t[erram], erunt soluta et in coelis" sanctaeque tuae ecclesiae, quam hodie tuo praesidio regendam suscipio, quod verae fidei rectitudinem, quam Christo auctore tradente per *te et beatissimum coapostolum tuum Paulum, per quem discipulos et* successores vestros usque ad exiguitatem meam perlatam, in tua sancta ecclesia repperi, totis conatibus meis usque ad animam et sanguinem custodire tam de sanctae et individuae trinitatis misterio, quae unus est deus, quamque de dispensatione, quae secundum carnem facta est, unigeniti filii dei *unigeniti* domini nostri Ihesu Christi et de coeteris ecclesiae dei dogmatibus, sicut universalibus conciliis et constitutis apostolicorum pontificum probatissimorumque doctorum ecclesiae scriptis commendata. Idest, quaeque ad rectitudinem vestrae nostraeque orthodoxae fidei a te traditae respiciunt, conservare. Sancta quoque *VII* universalia concilia, *idest* Nicenum, Constantinopolitanum, Ephesinum primum, Chalcedonense V quoque et VI *item* Constantinopolitanum et *VII item Nicenum* usque ad unum apicem immutilata servare et pari honore et veneratione digna habere et quae praedicaverunt *et statuerunt, omnimodis sequi et* predicare, quaeque condemnaverunt, ore et corde condempnare. Diligentius autem et vivacius omnia decreta *canonica* precessorum apostolicorum nostrorum pontificum, quaeque vel sinodaliter statuerunt et probata sunt, confirmare et indiminuta servare et sicut ab eis statuta sunt, in sui vigoris stabilitate custodire; quaeque vel quosque condemnaverunt vel abdicaverunt, simili sententia condemnare *et abdicare*. Disciplinam et ritum ecclesiae, sicut inveni et a sanctis predecessoribus meis *canonice* traditum repperi, illibatum custodire et indiminutas res ecclesiae conservare et indiminute, ut custodiantur, operam dare. Nihil de traditione, quam a probatissimis predecessoribus meis *traditam* et servatam repperi, diminuere vel mutare aut aliquam novitatem admittere: sed ferventer, ut eorum vere discipulus et sequipeda, totis mentis meae conatibus, quae tradita *canonice* comperio, conservare et venerari. Si qua vero

[1] Changes in, and additions to, the profession of faith as published by Th. E. von Sickel are printed in italics.

emerserint contra canonicam disciplinam, filiorum meorum consilio emendare *aut patienter, excepta fidei aut christianae religionis gravi offensione, tua et beatissimi coapostoli tui P[auli] patrocinante intercessione tolerare* sacrosque canones et *canonica* constituta pontificum ut divina et celestia mandata, *deo auxiliante,* custodire, utpote *deo et* tibi redditurum me sciens de omnibus, quae profiteor districtam in divino iudicio rationem, cuius *sanctissimae* sedi divina dignatione *te patrocinante* presideo et vicem intercessionibus tuis adimpleo. Eris autem mihi in illa terribili divini iudicii die propitius haec conanti et diligenter servare curanti. Adiutorium quoque, ut prebeas, obsecro in hac corruptibili vita constituto, ut irreprehensibilis appaream ante conspectum iudicis omnium domini nostri Ihesu Christi, dum terribiliter de commissis advenerit iudicare, ut faciat me dextrae partis participem et inter fideles discipulos ac successores *tuos* esse consortem. Hanc *autem* professionem meam per ill. notarium et scriniarium *S[anctae] R[omanae] ecclesiae,* me iubente conscriptam propria manu conscripsi et tibi beate apostole P[etre] et apostolorum omnium princeps pura mente et devota conscientia *super sanctum corpus et altare tuum* sinceriter offero.

Actum Romae anno, mense die et indictione quibus supra.

Popes' Profession of Faith in Cod. Bibl. Vat. Lat. 7160 and the Profession of Boniface VIII

A MANUSCRIPT of the Vatican Library (Cod. Bibl. Vat., Lat. 7160) has rescued a profession of faith of the sovereign Pontiffs which differs in many respects from all the versions we have so far studied in this book. Comparing this formula with that of Deusdedit, we note the following discrepancies: at the beginning, we read after the words[1] 'ego diaconus vel presbyter': 'vel episcopus cardinalis.' After the clause 'quam hodie tuo praesidio suscipio', the new formula adds: 'quod quamdiu in hac misera vita constitutus fuero, ipsam non deseram, non relinquam, non abnegabo, non abdicabo aliquatenus, nec ex quacumque causa, cuiuscumque metus, vel periculi occasione dimittam, nec me segregabo ab ipsa, sed verae fidei....'

The number of councils listed is naturally the same as in the *Britannica*, and on two occasions emphasis is placed on the fact that the Pope may never abandon his See: after 'diligentius et vivacius' is added 'quamdiu vixero', and after 'traditum', 'quamdiu mihi vita in istis comes fuerit'. After the words 'res ecclesiae conservare', a new insertion is made: 'neque alienare seu in feudum, censum, vel emphyteusim dare quomodolibet ex quacumque causa, et ut indiminute.' Instead of 'filiorum meorum consilio emendare', we read: 'ex communicatione filiorum meorum S. R. E. Cardinalium, cum quorum consilio, directione et rememoratione ministerium meum geram et peragam, emendare....' Between 'quae profiteor...districtam' is inserted 'et quamdiu vixero, egero, vel obliviscar'.

This profession, such as we find it in the Vatican MS. no. 7160, was published by Antonius Augustinus in his *Iuris Pontificii Epitome*,[2] and reprinted by Baronius in his *Annals*.[3] How is this formula to be dated?

It could not have been composed before either 1159 or 1160,[4] for it was not until this period that the controversy between the Cardinal-deacons and priests on the one hand, and the Cardinal-bishops on the other, on their respective rights in the papal elections was definitely settled, and not until then that the word 'episcopus' cardinalis was added to the words 'Cardinal-deacons and priests' at the opening of the formula.

[1] Fol. 380. Cf. G. Buschbell, 'Die Römische Überlieferung der Professiones fidei der Päpste', in *Röm. Quartalschrift* (1900), vol. XIV, pp. 131–6.

[2] (Tarragona, 1587), pars I, lib. v, tit. X, cap. LIV, pp. 288, 289.

[3] *Annales*, ad ann. 869 (Pagi ed.), p. 181. Cf. Rozière, *Liber Diurnus* (loc. cit. cap. IV, form. 118, p. 265).

[4] See J. B. Sägmüller, *Die Tätigkeit und Stellung der Kardinäle bis Papst Bonifaz VIII* (Freiburg i. B. 1896), pp. 123–37.

But this new version of the profession could not in any event have been composed in Rome; one single argument, provided by William de Nogaret and his jurists in their *Rationes quibus probatur quod Bonifacius legitime ingredi non potuit Celestino vivente*, is decisive. This bitter opponent of Boniface VIII had collected and presented to his successor Clement V all the possible arguments calculated to prove that Celestinus could not abdicate and that the election of Boniface VIII was null and void.

To prove his contention that a Pope once elected is elected for life and that he may not abdicate Nogaret quotes, among other arguments, the elected Pope's profession of faith. How eagerly he would have quoted the solemn promise made by the Pope never to abdicate if the passage had been found in the profession that was in his collaborators' hands. Yet instead of quoting the passage as it stands Nogaret loses himself in general considerations, endeavouring to prove that the Pope's profession is comparable with a vow, tacitly made and binding.[1]

As Nogaret's *plaidoyer* was presented in 1303 the statement which so boldly precludes the possibility of a Pope's abdication could only have been forged after that date. Even the words 'quamdiu vivet' quoted by Nogaret must have been interpolated, since they were not in the profession which Nogaret had before him when his plea was written. It was but a slight exaggeration, a very natural one, and not the only one in his piece of writing. One might even explain the words 'totis conatibus meis usque ad animam et sanguinem custodire', found in Deusdedit's profession, in the sense of 'quamdiu vivet' as read in Nogaret's interpretation. His discretion at this

---

[1] P. Dupuy, *Histoire du Différend*... (Paris, 1655), Preuves, p. 459: 'Vigesimo quarto, quia annexa est statui Papatus professio, quae habetur in libro Diurno, cuius etiam professionis pars habetur in Canone, et in illa professione habetur expresse quod profitetur et promittit Deo et Principi Apostolorum Petro, quod quamdiu vivet curam gerit gregis Dominici sibi commissi, et gubernabit Ecclesiam secundum decreta et canones sanctorum conciliorum, et Patrum, et de consilio Cardinalium sanctae Romanae Ecclesiae: ergo obligatus est ad curam gerendam quamdiu vivit ex voto et professione astrictus. Illud autem notorie constat, quod votis et professionibus, et iis ad quae quis voto et obligatione obligatur, secundum omnes, nemine contradicente renunciari non potest, et sic nec Papa renunciare potest, obligatus quamdiu vivit ex voto et professione astrictus. Et sic dicatur quod ita profitebantur antiquitus Romani Pontifices, sed hodie non profitentur de facto verbaliter: responsio manifestissime patet, quia recipientes nunc Papatum tacite vovent et profitentur haec omnia: nam statui professio est annexa, et secundum omnes votum interpretativum ita obligat, sicut expresse emissum: quod est videre in sacris ordinibus, Subdiaconatu, Diaconatu, et Sacerdotio, ex quorum susceptione perinde interpretative in Occidentali Ecclesia obligantur, sicut si profitentur expresse castitatem: sic dicendum est hic in voto et professione summi pontificatus. Et sic patet manifestissime quod renunciare non potest. Vigesimo quinto, quia iis per quae quis Deo et homini, voto, professione, vel promissione, contractu vel quasi, obligatur secundum veritatem notoriam, quae per nullum negatur, renunciare non potest.'

particular place proves precisely that in the profession whose original he consulted the impossibility of a Pope's abdication was not expressly mentioned, otherwise Nogaret would have adopted a more confident and truculent tone. Hence it is quite unnecessary to assume the existence of a new edition of the profession, dating from the twelfth century, differing from Deusdedit's and from that of the Latin MS. no. 7160 of the Vatican Library and forbidding Popes to abdicate.

In this profession the clause on the Cardinals needs closer examination. Any interference by Cardinals in the administration of the Church, such as the profession assumes, would have been unthinkable in the Roman Church, at any rate before the twelfth century; but it would accord better with the mentality that prevailed in the Church in the fourteenth century.[1]

This new edition of the famous profession was therefore undoubtedly forged after 1303. Furthermore, it has survived only in one MS., where it is followed by the notorious profession of Boniface VIII,[2] with which it is nearly identical, and the profession of faith attributed to Boniface VIII is generally regarded as apocryphal:[3] this will be evident if we take into consideration what has been said about the interpolations found there.[4]

This consideration may have proved useful in the solution of some problems that have puzzled these scholars who have dealt with Boniface VIII's

---

[1] Souchon, *Die Papstwahlen von Bonifaz VIII bis Urban VI* (Braunschweig, 1888), p. 204, goes still further, asserting that such pretensions on the part of the cardinals in the administration of ecclesiastical affairs admit of no explanation before 1352.

[2] Fol. 385 of the MS.

[3] Cf. chiefly Buschbell, 'Professiones fidei der Päpste', in *Röm. Quartalschr.* vol. X, pp. 421 seq.; M. Souchon, loc. cit. pp. 192–205; H. Finke, *Aus den Tagen des Bonifaz VIII* (Münster i. W. 1902), pp. 54–65.

[4] One more detail may be quoted in support of this statement. Boniface's alleged profession adds after the word 'consilio' the phrase 'et consensu' (cardinalium, etc.). This claim by the Cardinals, so evidently limiting the Pope's supreme power in the Church, could never have been sanctioned by the Chancellery of the Holy See. Moreover, the interpolation could apparently not have been introduced into Boniface VIII's profession before 1303. In fact the Colonnas, who towards 1303 addressed a letter to Philip the Fair to complain about Boniface's persecution, seem to know nothing about such a privilege, though they try hard to define the Cardinals' rights and to give them as wide a connotation as possible. This is what they say (Dupuy, *Histoire du Différend...*, loc. cit., Preuves, p. 226): 'Cardinales instituti sunt ad assistendum Romanum Pontificem propter stilum veritatis. Item, cardinales positi sunt ad resistendum in faciem Romano Pontifici, cum reprehensibilis. Item, cardinales sunt coniudices Romani Pontificis et sunt membra, non tantum corporis Ecclesiae sed capitis.' Speaking of the Cardinals, whose advice the Pope promises in his profession to follow, Nogaret simply interprets—and very correctly, too—the words 'consilio filiorum meorum' as found in Deusdedit's profession. Cf. L. Möhler, 'Die Kardinäle Jakob und Peter Colonna' (Paderborn, 1914), in *Quellen und Forschungen aus dem Gebiete der Geschichte* (Görres-Gesellschaft, vol. XVII), especially pp. 125 seq.

alleged profession. It seems evident, first, that this forgery was not the work of William de Nogaret, as has been so far assumed too readily.[1] Then again we can better explain how Nogaret's fellow-workers came by a copy of the Pope's profession, without making it necessary to assume that they had found a copy of the *Liber Diurnus*, a very difficult proposition, considering the nature of this valuable document. I noted that this profession had been copied by several canonists after the edition preserved in Deusdedit's Collection, and we have only to remember the source of Ivo of Chartres and of the *Britannica*. As there was no difficulty in getting hold of a copy of this profession in the fourteenth century the appearance of this document in William de Nogaret's rejoinder should raise no serious difficulty.

One thing seems quite certain: Boniface's alleged profession was not forged before 1303; it was rather the mention of this notorious profession of the Popes made in Nogaret's rejoinder that suggested the idea to an anonymous enemy of Boniface VIII of interpolating it in the sense as we know it, for the purpose of discrediting the unfortunate Pope. This may have been done between 1303 and 1360. The profession contained in the Vatican Latin MS. no. 7160 is therefore only another version, nearly identical to the one falsely attributed to Boniface VIII, both versions being apocryphal.

[1] After re-examining the arguments of his pupil Buschbell, fathering the forgery on Nogaret, Finke, loc. cit. pp. 59 seq., already declared: 'Ich muss freilich zugeben, dass eine vollständig überzeugende positive Beweisführung für die Fälschung Nogaret nicht zu geben ist.'

APPENDIX III

Unpublished Anonymous Greek Treatises on the Councils

FOR the purpose of tracing the official tradition of the Eastern Church on
the number of oecumenical councils and its attitude with regard to the
Council of Photius, I have made some researches on a special class of
Byzantine theological literature—the Greek treatises on councils. These
treatises are many and scattered about all the great libraries of Europe.
Besides embodying the tradition on councils they also afford a clear illustration of the Orthodox doctrine on the infallibility of the Church, which
makes one regret that they should have remained a closed field to theologians
and historians. So far only one of the anonymous treatises has been published, edited by C. Justel.[1] It was my first intention to publish the best of
them, but recent events interfered with my plans and I have only been able
to study the MSS. of the National Libraries of Paris, London and Brussels
with a few of the Vienna Library. These were, however, sufficient for my
limited purpose—the Eastern tradition on the Photian Council—and a comparison of the catalogues of Greek MSS. in the possession of the leading
libraries of Paris, the Vatican, Moscow, Mount Athos and Vienna satisfied
me that the Paris MSS. are exceptionally complete and cover the Eastern
tradition in this matter.

I cannot give here the results, however useful, of my researches in full,
as they are not strictly relevant to the subject under discussion and the
prospect of pursuing these studies in the near future is but slight. I therefore limit myself to the enumeration of the MSS. I have studied and to a
few summary indications on their most important bearings.

ANONYMOUS GREEK TREATISES ON COUNCILS.
BIBLIOTHÈQUE NATIONALE, PARIS

1. MS. no. 11, fols. 320–7, twelfth century (written in 1186).
2. MS. no. 425, fols. 1–7, fifteenth to sixteenth centuries.
3. MS. no. 922, fols. 241–8 a, eleventh century.
4. MS. no. 947, fols. 110–15, written in 1574.
5. MS. no. 968, fols. 392–5, fifteenth century.
6. MS. no. 1084, fols. 199–205, eleventh century.
7. MS. no. 1123, fols. 166 a–72, fifteenth century.
8. MS. no. 1234, fol. 261, thirteenth century.
9. MS. no. 1259 a, fols. 25 a–8, fourteenth century.

[1] Ch. Justellus, *Nomocanon Photii...Accessere ejusdem Photii, Nili Metropolitae
Rhodi et Anonymi Tractatus de Synodis Oecumenicis ex Bibliotheca Sedanensi*
(Lutetiae Parisiorum, 1615).

10. MS. no. 1295, fols. 285 a–9, fifteenth to sixteenth century.
11. MS. no. 1302, fols. 21–4, thirteenth century.
12. MS. no. 1303, fol. 80, fourteenth century.
13. MS. no. 1319, fols. 1–9 a, thirteenth century.
14. MS. no. 1323, fols. 365–70, copied in 1598.
15. MS. no. 1335, fols. 12 a–14 a, fourteenth century.
16. MS. no. 1336, fols. 5–8 a, eleventh century.
17. MS. no. 1369, fols. 1–10, fourteenth century.
18. MS. no. 1370, fols. 123 a–25 a, written in 1297.
19. MS. no. 1371, fols. 24 a–33 a, thirteenth century.
20. MS. no. 1373, fol. 1 a, copied in 1525.
21. MS. no. 1375, fols. 9, 10 a, copied in 1540.
22. MS. no. 1381 a, fols. 113 a–14, fourteenth century.
23. MS. no. 1555 a, fols. 152 a–4, fourteenth century.
24. MS. no. 1605, fols. 285–6 a, twelfth century.
25. MS. no. 1630, fols. 64–9, fourteenth century.
26. MS. no. 1712, fols. 4–5 a, fourteenth century.
27. MS. no. 1788, fols. 199 a–200, written in 1440.
28. MS. no. 2403, fols. 172 a–3, thirteenth century.
29. MS. no. 2600, fols. 245 a, 246, fifteenth century.
30. MS. no. 2662, fols. 76–8, fourteenth century.
31. MS. no. 3041, fols. 131–2 a, fifteenth to sixteenth centuries.
32. MS. Coislin 34, fols. 23 a–6 a, twelfth century.
33. MS. Coislin 36, fols. 1–8, fourteenth century.
34. MS. Coislin 120, fols. 28–31, tenth century.
35. MS. Coislin 363, fols. 154–9, twelfth century.
36. MS. Coislin 364, fols. 204, 204 a, written in 1295.
37. MS. Coislin 374, fols. 315 a–20 a, eleventh century.
38. MS. Supplément 78, fols. 235 a, 236, seventeenth century.
39. MS. Supplément 482, fols. 111–20 a, written in 1105.
40. MS. Supplément 483, fols. 166 a–71, fourteenth century.
41. MS. Supplément 690, fols. 242 a–4, twelfth century.
42. MS. Supplément 1086, fols. 64–6, eleventh century.
43. MS. Supplément 1089, fols. 26–7, sixteenth century.

THE NATIONAL LIBRARY OF VIENNA

44. Codex Theologicus Graecus XIX, fols. 321, 321 a, written in 1097.
45. Cod. Theol. Graec. CCCVII, fols. 94 a–6 a, fourteenth century.
46. Cod. Theol. Graec. CCCXXV, fols. 163, 164 a, fifteenth century; fols. 228–35 a (profession of faith).
47. Cod. Historicus Graec. VII, fols. 184–7 a; fols. 193 a–4; fols. 194 a–6, eleventh century (?).
48. Cod. Theol. Graec. CCLIV, fols. 760 a–70, fourteenth century.
49. Cod. Juridicus Graec. XIII, fols. 38–71 a, fifteenth century.
50. Cod. Hist. Graec. XXXIV, fols. 359 a–61 a, fifteenth century.
51. Cod. Graec. Hist. Eccl. et Prof. LXX, fols. 83–6 a, eleventh century (?).

THE ROYAL LIBRARY OF BRUSSELS

52. MS. no. 11376, fols. 170a–3a, thirteenth century.
53. MSS. no. II, 4836, fols. 72a–6, thirteenth century.

BRITISH MUSEUM

54. Additional MS. 34060, fols. 218–81 (Canons of Greek Councils), fifteenth century.

It appears that treatises on Councils have been written since the fifth or sixth century, new Councils being simply added by later copyists. This can be inferred from some short summaries which list only five Councils, as for instance in the case of MS. no. 47, two of whose summaries (fols. 193a, 194 and 194a–6) mention only five Councils: the copyist relied on an old summary without taking the trouble of adding the other Councils. A longer treatise of the four first Councils is found in the MS. which I class as no. 27, though the MS. possibly contains only the first part of a treatise on six or more Councils.

What seems to be the oldest and most interesting treatise is found in MSS. nos. 3, 9 and 34 of our list, where the anonymous writer counts only six oecumenical councils and gives a summary of the local synods of Ancyra, Caesarea, Gangrae, Antioch, Laodicea and Carthage. By his definition no Council can be called oecumenical unless it be summoned by the Emperor, who must invite all the bishops of the Empire, and unless some dogmatic decision be arrived at. The Popes are placed at the head of the Patriarchs in the account of the first four Councils.

The treatise that seems to have had the widest circulation is the one published by Justellus. It originally contained, as far as I can see, only the summary of six councils, the seventh being added later, at least in some MSS. of the treatise. Justellus knew only the one MS., that was in the possession of the Sedan Library in his days; but the same treatise is found in the following MSS., several of which embody a more interesting tradition with many variants: MSS. nos. 6, 16 of my list (both mention only six councils), 11, 13 (the Popes' names are mentioned for each synod after the Emperor's name), 19, 28, 51, 52, 53.

MSS. nos. 2, 15 and 44, though very similar to Justellus' treatise, differ from it in many respects. For instance, the Popes are always named immediately after the Emperors and before the Patriarchs.

The Popes are also named first after the Emperors and accurate historical data are found in a treatise represented by the following MSS. of my list: nos. 1, 7, 32 (an abridged version) and 37.

An entirely different treatise is preserved in MSS. nos. 14 and 33. Again the Popes are placed after the Emperors and before the other Patriarchs as in other MSS. affiliated to this treatise (nos. 23 and 39).

Some similarities with Justellus' treatise are found in the following short works, which, however, are all of a different character: MSS. no. 4 (Popes presiding over the first and the fourth Councils, the Patriarch of Alexandria over the second and third, the Patriarchs of Antioch and Constantinople over the sixth, Tarasius over the seventh); no. 24 (Patriarchs of Constantinople are always named before the Popes); no. 45 (shorter than Justellus' treatise); no. 46.

Besides longer treatises on the Councils there exists a large number of short summaries and memoranda on the seven Councils, written probably for teaching purposes. Those I list here differ from each other in minor details and follow a common pattern: MSS. no. 9 (only six councils mentioned); no. 18 (the Popes are stated to have directed the first five councils; for the seventh the Pope is named before Tarasius); no. 20 (gives only the names of the Emperors and the Popes for each Council); nos. 21, 22, 28 (the Pope always named before the other Patriarchs); no. 29 (the Photian Councils of 859, 861, 879–80 are numbered among the local synods, but the so-called Eighth Oecumenical Council is omitted); nos. 36, 38 (analytical table of the seven Councils; the Popes come immediately after the Emperors); no. 47 (three summaries, one of them—fols. 193 a, 194—published by P. Lambecius in his *Commentarii de August. Bibl. Caesarea Vindobonensi* (2nd ed., A. Kollar, Vienna, 1782), vol. VIII, p. 930); no. 48.

The summary in MS. no. 31 of my list is of some interest for the way it mentions Popes and Patriarchs. It names the Popes first only in the case of the First and the Seventh Councils but, strange to say, it states that the First Council of Nicaea took place under Popes Sylvester and Julius, the Fifth under Mennas and Eutyches. It will be remembered that Photius, in his letter to Boris-Michael of Bulgaria, also writes that the Nicaean Council took place under the Popes Sylvester and Julius,[1] which has puzzled many; and I have pointed out that[2] the *Synodicon Vetus*—an Ignatian treatise on Councils—followed the same tradition. This new evidence makes it clear that the tradition must have been common in Constantinople and that it was not invented by Photius.

Some of the treatises must have been re-copied as professions of faith, as is the case with MS. no. 4 which is based on Justellus' treatise and contains such a profession.

Interesting also is the list of canons voted by the oecumenical and local synods acknowledged by the Eastern Church and preserved in MS. no. 54 of my list. The Ignatian Council of 869–70 is omitted, though it voted canons that became very popular in the West. But the canons voted by the Photian synods of 861 and of 879–80 are duly recorded.

---

[1] *P.G.* vol. 102, col. 632.
[2] See *supra*, p. 127. Also note that in the *Juridicus Graecus Viennensis XIII* (15th c., parchment, 347 fols.), fols. 38–71 a is found a version different from the *Synodicon Vetus* published by Pappe in the work mentioned, pp. 360 seq.

I may add in conclusion that MS. no. 46 contains in addition (fols. 228–35 a) a profession of faith addressed to an Emperor and drawn up in accordance with the decisions of the seven councils. Another profession of faith is found in MS. 47 (fols. 231, 231 a) and is the same as the Patriarch Photius used to tender to all candidates to the episcopacy, who naturally had to subscribe to seven councils.[1]

It goes without saying that what I have said here about the writings of this class is very incomplete; but I feel that what little I have been able to find on this matter amply confirms my contention that from the eighth to the seventeenth century the Greek Church officially knew only seven Oecumenical Councils.[2]

Euthymii Patriarchae Libellus de Definitionibus Fidei per Concilia Septem Oecumenica. British Museum Arundel 528 (15th c.). Extract on the Photian Council, fols. 116 seq., compared with the anonymous treatise of Parisinus Graecus 968 (fols. 392–5, 15th c.) and with the treatise of Neilos of Rhodes.[3]

I found in Vienna another Greek MS. containing an anonymous treatise,

---

[1] Ἔκδοσις Φωτίου τοῦ ἁγιωτάτου Πατριάρχου Κωνσταντινουπόλεως. Σύμβολον πίστεως πρὸς τοὺς μέλλοντας χειροτονεῖσθαι ἐπισκόπους. Πιστεύω εἰς ἕνα Θεόν.... Reference to the synods: τὰς ἁγίας καὶ οἰκουμενικὰς ἑπτὰ συνόδους ὑποδεχόμενος, ἅπαντα τὰ ὑπ' αὐτῶν....

[2] It would also be of great advantage to publish a new edition of the Greek treatises on the schism, and it is known that the first attempt of this kind is attributed to Nicetas of Nicaea. Three short works of this class have been published by Hergenröther, *Monumenta Graeca ad Photium...pertinentia* (Ratisbonnae, 1869), pp. 154 seq. In the Paris National Library I found several MSS. on the same topic and akin to the treatises that have been published, but offering a considerable number of interesting variants; for instance, the Paris. Graec. 1278 (15th c., on paper, 172 fols.), fols. 2–6 corresponds to Nicetas' treatise, but differs in many respects from the text so far known. The treatises of Paris. Graec. 1191 (15th c., on paper, 141 fols.), fols. 73, 80, 81, bear resemblance to treatises I and II published by the Cardinal, but with some curious variants. The treatises copied in the Paris. Graec. 1286 (16th c., on paper, 318 fols.), fols. 251–4 and Paris. Graec. 1295 (15th c.– 16th c., on paper, 342 fols.), fols. 98–101 a (not listed in the Omont Catalogue) also show affinity to treatises I and II of Hergenröther (ibid. fols. 26 seq., the treatise written by John of Jerusalem). But I have cautioned the reader against these later handbooks, as they often diverge widely from their common pattern, Nicetas' treatise, though they do give a good picture of fifteenth-century Byzantine mentality with regard to Rome. Note that Neilos Damylas (Paris. Graec. 1295, fols. 60a–85) volunteers explanations as nebulous as the treatises themselves. In the Cod. Theol. Graec. Viennensis CLXVIII (15th c., fol. 381), which contains anti-Latin writings, I found on fols. 375–6 a short treatise which seems to be identically the same as the first treatise published by Hergenröther, loc. cit. pp. 154–63 (Πῶς καὶ τίνα τρόπον ἐχωρίσθησαν ἡμῶν οἱ Λατῖνοι...ἣν ἐν τῇ ἑβδόμῃ συνόδῳ Ἀδριανὸς πάπας Ῥώμης). Circumstances prevented me from photographing the treatise and making a closer comparison.

[3] Ch. Justellus, *Nomocanon Photii...Accessere ejusdem Photii, Nili Metropolitae Rhodi et Anonymi Tractatus*, loc. cit. pp. 175–9.

all but identical to the treatise on the Paris MS. no. 968, in Historicus Graecus Viennensis xxxiv (chartaceus, 15th c., in folio, fol. 392), fols. 359a–61a. Unfortunately I have not been able to make a comparative study of the MS. and recent events have prevented me obtaining a photograph of it.

This is what Euthymios' treatise has to say about the Photian Council:

fol. 116: Συνόδου ἑνωτικῆς [om. Parisinus 968; ὀγδόη Neilos Rhod.]. Ἡ ἁγία καὶ οἰκουμενικὴ αὕτη σύνοδος [ὀγδόη τῶν τριακοσίων ὀγδοήκοντα ἁγίων πατέρων add. Neilos Rhod.] γέγονε ἐπὶ τῆς βασιλείας Βασιλίου τοῦ Μακεδόνος, καθ' ἣν σύνοδον γέγονεν ἡ εἰρήνη μεγάλη μεταξὺ τῆς δυτικῆς ἐκκλησίας καὶ τῶν ἄλλων πατριαρχείων, φανερῶς ὁμολογησάντων τῶν δυτικῶν, ὅτι οὕτως ἀναγινώσκομεν καὶ πιστεύομεν, ὡς καὶ ὑμεῖς [ἡμεῖς Paris. 968], χωρὶς προσθήκης τινὸς τὸ σύμβολον τὸ ἅγιον εἶναι τῆς ἀληθοῦς πίστεως [corrupted text in Neilos Rhod.: χωρὶς προσθήκης τινὸς τὸ σύμβολον τὸ ἅγιον ὡς οὕτως...ἔχον, ὄντως σύμβολον εἶναι τῆς ἀληθοῦς πίστεως], ἀλλὰ καὶ τοὺς προστιθέντας, ἢ ἐλλείποντας ἀναθεματίζομεν, ὄντος τηνικαῦτα Ἰωάννου πάπα Ῥώμης, Φωτίου πατριάρχου Κωνσταντινουπόλεως, καὶ τοποτηρητῶν τῆς Ῥωμαίων ἐκκλησίας, Παύλου καὶ Εὐγενίου ἐπισκόπου [ἐπισκόπων Paris. 968, Neilos Rhod.], καὶ Πέτρου πρεσβυτέρου καὶ καρδινάλου [καρδιναλίου Paris. 968, Neilos Rhod.], καὶ τῶν ἄλλων πατριαρχῶν διὰ τοποτηρητῶν, Κόσμα πρεσβυτέρου καὶ πρέσβεως Ἀλεξανδρείας / fol. 116a / καὶ Βασιλείου μητροπολίτου Μαρτυρουπόλεως τῆς Ἀντιοχείας καὶ Ἡλία πρεσβυτέρου Ἱεροσολύμων· [Κόσμα...Ἱεροσολύμων om. Paris. 968, om. Neilos Rhod.] ὧν συνελθόντων ὡς ἐν τοῖς πρακτικοῖς εὕρομεν μετὰ πολλὰ ἄλλα ὑπὲρ τῆς κοινῆς ὁμονοίας τῶν ἐκκλησιῶν γραφέντα καὶ ταῦτα ἐπὶ λέξεως· [ὡς ἐν τοῖς...λέξεως om. Neilos Rhod.] οἱ μὲν τοποτηρηταὶ τῆς Ῥώμης ἐβόησαν, πρέπον ἐστὶ μὴ ἕτερον ὅρον καινουργηθῆναι ἀλλ' αὐτὸν τὸν ἀρχαῖον [ὅρον add. Neilos Rhod.], καὶ κατὰ ἀνὰ [Neilos Rhod.] πᾶσαν τὴν οἰκουμένην κρατούμενόν τε καὶ δοξαζόμενον ἀναγνωσθῆναί τε καὶ ἐπιβεβαιωθῆναι· καὶ τοῦ ἱεροῦ συμβόλου ἀναγνωσθέντος [ἄνευ προσθήκης add. Neilos Rhod.] ὡς ἔχει, ἡ ἁγία σύνοδος ἐξεβόησεν· ἡμεῖς κατὰ τὴν τοῦ σωτῆρος διδασκαλίαν καὶ τὴν τῶν ἀποστόλων παράδοσιν [παράνεισιν Arund. 528], ἔτι δὲ καὶ τοὺς κανονικοὺς τύπους τῶν ἁγίων / fol. 117 / καὶ οἰκουμενικῶν [ἑπτά add. Paris. 968, Neilos Rhod.] συνόδων, τὸν ἄνωθεν ἐκ πατέρων καὶ μέχρι ἡμῶν κατεληλυθότα τῆς ἀκραιφνεστάτης τῶν χριστιανῶν πίστεως ὅρον, καὶ διανοίᾳ [ἐπινοίᾳ Neilos Rhod.] καὶ γλώσση στέργομέν τε καὶ πᾶσι τρόποις [om. Paris. 968, Neilos Rhod.] διαπρυσίως παραγγέλλομεν [περιαγγέλλομεν Paris. 968, Neilos Rhod.], οὐδὲν ἀφαιροῦντες, οὐδὲν προστιθέντες κατὰ διάνοιαν ἢ λέξιν, οὐδὲν ἀμείβοντες, οὐδὲν κιβδηλεύοντες· καὶ μετὰ τοῦτο οἵτε τοποτηρηταὶ τοῦ [om. Neilos Rhod.] Ῥώμης, καὶ ἡ σύνοδος ἅπασα ἐξεβόησεν· εἴτις τοίνυν εἰς τοῦτο ἀπονοίας ἐλάσας τολμήσει [εἴτις... τολμήσει om. Neilos Rhod.] ἕτερον ἐκθέσθαι σύμβολον καὶ ὅρον ὀνομάσαι [ἀνακινῆσαι Neilos Rhod.], ἢ προσθήκην ἢ ὑφαίρεσιν ποιῆσαι ἐν τῷ ἀναγνωσθέντι νῦν [om. Neilos Rhod.] ἱερῷ καὶ ἁγίῳ συμβόλῳ, ἀνάθεμα ἔστω.

LIST OF ABBREVIATIONS

Anal. Bol.   *Analecta Bollandiana.*

A.S.   *Acta Sanctorum of the Bollandists.*

Bibliotheca.   I. Th. de Rocaberti, *Bibliotheca Maxima Pontificia,* 21 vols. Romae, 1698, 1699.

Bonn.   *Corpus Scriptorum Historiae Byzantinae,* called the *Byzantine* of Bonn, 1826–97.

Byz. Zeitschr.   *Byzantinische Zeitschrift.* Leipzig, 1892–1939.

Mansi.   *Conciliorum Amplissima Collectio,* 31 vols. Florence, Venice, 1759 seq.

M.G.H.   *Monumenta Germaniae Historica.* Ep., Epistolae; Ss., Scriptores.

P.G.   *Patrologia Graeca,* ed. Abbé Migne, 140 vols. Paris, 1857–66.

P.L.   *Patrologia Latina,* ed. Abbé Migne, 221 vols. Paris, 1844–55.

Teubner.   *Bibliotheca Teubneriana.* Leipzig.

Tractatus.   *Tractatus illustrium in utraque tum Pontificii, tum Caesarei iuris facultate Iurisconsultorum,* 18 vols. Venetiis, 1584.

LIST OF MANUSCRIPTS QUOTED

GREEK MANUSCRIPTS

Anastasius Makedon. Litterae ad Imperatorem. Bibliothèque Nationale, Paris, MS. no. 137, fols. 16–113 (sixteenth century).

Anonymi Disputatio de Azymis. Bibl. Nat. Paris, MS. no. 1286, fols. 47–57 (sixteenth century).

Anonymi Fragmentum de Tempore quo Latini a Graecis dissidere coeperunt. Bibl. Nat. Paris, MS. no. 1286, fols. 251–4 (sixteenth century).

—— (similar treatise), Bibl. Nat. Paris, MS. no. 1295, fols. 98–101 a (fifteenth to sixteenth centuries).

—— (similar treatise), National Library of Vienna, Codex Theologicus Graecus CLXVIII, fols. 375–6 (fifteenth century).

Anonymi Operis Fragmentum de Italorum Doctrina. Bibl. Nat. Paris, MS. no. 1191, fols. 73–81 (fifteenth century).

Anonymi Opusculum de Origine Schismatis. Bibl. Nat. Paris, MS. no. 1278, fols. 2–6 (fifteenth century).

Anonymi Responsa Theologica. Bibl. Nat. Paris, MS. no. 1302, fols. 275–81 (thirteenth century).

Anonymous Treatises on Councils, 54 MSS.; see list in Appendix III, p. 452.

Arsenii Monachi Scholia. Bibl. Nat. Paris, MS. no. 1303, fols. 35–71 (fifteenth century).

—— De Spiritu Sancto. Ibid. fols. 78 seq.

Bonacursius of Bologna. Thesaurus Veritatis Fidei, Greek and Latin. Bibl. Nat. Paris, Greek MS. no. 1251, fols. 145 (fourteenth century).

Demetrius Chrysoloras. Epistolae ad Manuelem Pal. Bibl. Nat. Paris, MS. no. 1191, fols. 39 a–44 a (fifteenth century).

Elias Menatas...Petra Offensionis. Latin translation by the monk F. Meniata. British Museum, Harleian MS. 5729.

Euthymios Patriarch. Treatise on Councils. Brit. Mus. Arundel 528, fols. 111–17 (second half of the fifteenth century).

Joannes II Palaeologus. Symbolum Fidei, Romae in Foribus S. Petri ab. imp. Joanne II Palaeologo inventum. Bibl. Nat. Paris, MS. no. 1191, fols. 73 a–4 a (fifteenth century).

John Camateros. Letters to Innocent III. Bibl. Nat. Paris, Greek MS. no. 1302, fols. 270 a–5 (thirteenth century).

John Chilas. Letters. Bibl. Nat. Paris, MS. no. 2022, fols. 150–7 (fourteenth century).

John of Claudiopolis. Treatise on the Azymes. Brit. Mus. MS. Harl. 5657, fols. 128 a–36 (fifteenth century).

Joseph Philarges. Adversus Latinos de Processione Spiritus S. Bibl. Nat. Paris, MS. no. 1295, fols. 85–101 (fifteenth to sixteenth centuries).

Manuel Chrysoloras. Tractatus de Processione Spiritus S. Bibl. Nat. Paris, MS. no. 1300, 20 fols. (sixteenth century).

Manuel Moschopulos. Διάλεξις πρὸς Λατίνους. Bibl. Nat. Paris, MS. no. 969, fols. 315–19 (fourteenth century).

Mark of Ephesus. Ἐπίλογος πρὸς Λατίνους. Brit. Mus. Add. MS. no. 34060, fols. 348 seq. (fifteenth century).

Nicholas de Otranto. Disputationes. Bibl. Nat. Paris, MS. Graec. Supplém. no. 1232, 165 fols. (thirteenth century).

Nilus Damylas. Tractatus de Processione Spiritus S. Bibl. Nat. Paris, MS. no. 1295, fols. 60a–85 (fifteenth to sixteenth centuries).

Orationes Catecheticae Duae. Bibl. Nat. Paris, MS. no. 1302, fols. 281–95 (thirteenth century).

Photius. Ἔκδοσις...Συμβόλου Πίστεως. Nat. Lib. Vienna. Codex Historicus Graecus VII, fols. 231, 231a (eleventh century (?)).

Theodosius Monachus. De Processione Spiritus S. Bibl. Nat. Paris, MS. no. 1303, fols. 71–8 (fourteenth to fifteenth centuries).

LATIN MANUSCRIPTS

Caesaraugustana. First Recension. Bibl. Nat. Paris, Latin MS. no. 3876 (twelfth century).

—— Second Recension. Bibl. Nat. Paris, Latin MS. no. 3876 (twelfth century).

Collectio Britannica. Brit. Mus. Add. MS. no. 8873 (eleventh century).

Collection in Seven Books. Vatican Library. Latin MS. no. 1346 (written in 1112).

Collection in Ten Parts. Bibl. Nat. Paris, Latin MS. no. 10743 (first half of the twelfth century).

Collection in Two Books. Vatican Library, Latin MS. no. 3832 (end of the eleventh century).

Collection in Sixteen Parts. Brit. Mus. Harl. 3090 (twelfth century).

Collection of the Vatican Library, Latin MS. no. 1361 (beginning of the twelfth century).

Collection of Sainte Geneviève, Paris, MS. no. 166 (twelfth century).

Collection in Nine Books. MS. 1349 of the Vatican Library Latin MSS. (tenth century).

Collection in Five Books. MS. 1339 of the Vatican Library Latin MSS. (eleventh century).

Collection in Five Books. Vatican Library. Latin MS. no 1348 (twelfth century).

Collection of the Vallicellan Library, Rome, T. XVIII, 278 fols. (tenth century).

Collection in Three Books. Vatican Library, Latin MS. no. 3831 (beginning of the twelfth century).

Collection of Prague. University Library. Codex Membran. VIII H. 7 (beginning of the twelfth century).

Collection of Tarragona. Bibl. Nat. Paris, Latin MS. no. 4281 B (twelfth century).

Collection in Nine Books of S. Victor. Bibl. de l'Arsenal, Paris, MS. no. 721 (twelfth century).

Collection of Bordeaux. Bibl. Municipale de Bordeaux, MS. no. 11 (first half of the twelfth century).

De Conciliis cum suis Expositionibus. Bibl. Nat. Paris, Latin MS. no. 12264, fols. 172a–219 (written in 1459).

De Sex Prioribus Conciliis. Bibl. Nat. Paris, Latin MS. no. 1451 (tenth century).

Epitome Celeberrimorum Conciliorum. Bibl. Nat. Paris, MS. no. 2448, fols. 17–48 (sixteenth century).

Excerpta Sanctorum Pontificum (Collection of Canon Law). University Library, Prague, Codex Lobkovicz no. 496, fols. 85 a–102 (thirteenth century).

First Collection of Châlons. Bibl. Municipale de Châlons-sur-Marne, MS. no. 47 (first half of the twelfth century).

Second Collection of Châlons. Bibl. Mun. de Ch.-sur-M., MS. no. 75 (first half of the twelfth century).

Ivo of Chartres. Collectio Tripartita. Bibl. Nat. Paris, Latin MS. nos. 3858; 3858 A, B (twelfth century).

Lanfranc. Canonical Collection. MS. Brit. Mus. Cotton. Claudius D. IX: Decreta Romanorum Pontificum, Canones Apostolorum et Conciliorum (eleventh to twelfth centuries).

Notitia Historica de Conciliis. Bibl. Nat. Paris, Latin MS. no. 1340, fol. 17 v. (ninth to tenth centuries).

Photius ad Michaelem. De Conciliis. Bibl. Nat. Paris, MS. no. 2448, fols. 1–16 (sixteenth century).

Photius ad Michaelem. De Conciliis. Bibl. Nat. Paris, MS. no. 10589, fols. 213–43 (seventeenth century).

Polycarpus. First Recension. Vatican Library, Latin MS. no. 1354 (twelfth century).

—— Second Recension. Bibl. Nat. Paris, Latin MS. no. 3882 (end of the fourteenth century).

Psellus de Septem Conciliis. Bibl. Nat. Paris, MS. no. 2448, fols. 101–3 (sixteenth century).

Psellus de Septem Conciliis. Bibl. Nat. Paris, MS. no. 10589, fols. 208–12 (seventeenth century).

Summa Decretorum Haimonis. Bibl. Nat. Paris, Latin MS. no. 4377 (twelfth century) and no. 4286 (twelfth century).

Summary of the Collection in Ten Parts, Bibl. Nat. Paris, Latin MS. no. 14145, fols. 9–15 (twelfth century).

LIST OF SOURCES

Acta Concilii Sardicensis. Mansi, vol. III, cols. 1–83.

Acta Concilii Nicaeni II. Mansi, vol. XII, cols. 951–1154; vol. XIII, cols. 1–820.

Acta Concilii Primi et Secundi (859, 861). Deusdedit Card., *Collectio Canonum* (ed. W. von Glanvell), Paderborn, 1905, pp. 603–16; Mansi, vol. XVI, cols. 536–49 (canones).

Acta Synodi Romanae 863. *M.G.H.* Ep. VI, pp. 518–23.

Acta Concilii Constantinopolitani IV (869–870). Mansi, vol. XVI, cols. 1–208 (Versio Latina Anastasii Bibl.); Mansi, vol. XVI, cols. 300–413. (Versio Graeca.)

Acta Concilii Ravennensis (872). Mansi, vol. XVII, cols. 335–44.

Acta Concilii Constantinopolitani V (879–80). Mansi, vol. XVII, cols. 365–525. Deusdedit Card., *Collectio Canonum* (ed. von Glanvell), loc. cit. pp. 610–17 (extract from the first five sessions).

Acta Synodi Oriensis. *Spicilegium Cassinense*, 1888, vol. I.

Acta Concilii Lugdunensis II. Mansi, vol. XXIV, cols. 35–135.

Acta Concilii Constantinopolitani a. 1277 habiti. Mansi, vol. XXIV, cols. 185–90.

Acta Concilii Armenorum (1342). Mansi, vol. XXV, cols. 1185–1270.

Acta Concilii Constantinopolitani (1350). Mansi, vol. XXVI, cols. 127–212.

Acta Concilii Vaurensis (1368). Mansi, vol. XXVI, cols. 473–548.

Acta Concilii Pisani (1409). Mansi, vol. XXVII, cols. 1–502.

Acta Concilii Constantiensis (1414–15). Mansi, vol. XXVII, cols. 519–1240; vol. XXVIII, cols. 1–968. *See also* H. von der Hardt, *Constantiensis Concilii Acta et Decreta*, Frankfurt, Leipzig, 1696–1742; H. Finke, J. Holbisteiner, H. Heimpel, *Acta Concilii Constantiensis*, Münster i.W., 1896–1928, 4 vols.

Acta Concilii Basileensis (1431–42). Mansi, vols. XXIX, XXX; ed. J. Haller, *Conc. Bas.* Basel, vols. I–IV, 1896–1903; vols. V, VI (G. Beckmann, R. Wackernagel), 1904, 1926; vol. VIII (H. Herre), 1910.

Acta Concilii Florentini (1438). Mansi, vol. XXXI, cols. 463–1998.

Acta Concilii Lateranensis V (1512–16). Mansi, vol. XXXII, cols. 649–1002.

Acta Concilii Tridentini (1545–63). Mansi, vol. XXXIII, cols. 1–941.

Actus Mediolani. De Privilegio Romanae Ecclesiae. *See* Petrus S. Damianus.

Aeneas, Ep. Liber adversus Graecos. *P.L.* vol. 121, cols. 682–762.

Agalianus. *See* Theodorus Agalianus.

Albrich, Monachus. Chronica Trium Fontium a monacho Hoiensi interpolata. *M.G.H.* Ss. XXIII, pp. 631–950.

Alexandrinus, Cardinal. *Commentarius super Decreto*, Mediolani (G. A. de Sangiorgio), 1494.

Alferici S. ad Wulfinum ep. Canones. *P.L.* vol. 139, cols. 1470–6.

Anastasius Bibliothecarius. Epistolae. *M.G.H.* Ep. VII, pp. 395–412.

—— Acta Concilii Constant. IV. Mansi, vol. XVI, pp. 1–208.

—— Vita S. Nicolai I, Papae. *See* Liber Pontificalis.

Anastasius Makedon. Controversiae. *P.G.* vol. 142, cols. 480–513.

Andreas Ep. Mogorensis. Gubernaculum Conciliorum (ed. H. von der Hardt). *Constantiensis Conc. Acta* . . ., Franckfurt, 1690, t. VI, cols. 139–334.

Andronicus Camateros. J. Vecci Refutationes adversus A. Camateri. *P.G.* vol. 141, cols. 395–613.

Annales Bertiniani. *M.G.H.* Ss. I, pp. 423–515.

—— Fuldenses. *M.G.H.* Ss. I, pp. 343–415.

—— Hildesheimenses. *M.G.H.* Ss. III, pp. 22–116.

—— Lamperti. *M.G.H.* Ss. III, pp. 22–102.

—— Laubienses. *M.G.H.* Ss. IV, pp. 9–28.

—— Leodienses. *M.G.H.* Ss. IV, pp. 9–30.

—— Quedlinburgenses. *M.G.H.* Ss. III, pp. 22–90.

Anonymus Contra Latinos (ed. Dositheos). Τόμ. Καταλλαγῆς, Jassy, 1692, pp. 1–204.

Anonymus de Sex Synodis Oecum. (ed. Ch. Justellus), *Nomocanon Photii*, Paris, 1615; (ed. G. Voellus, H. Justellus), *Bibliotheca Iuris Canon. Vet.* Paris, 1661, pp. 1161–5.

Anselm of Havelberg. Dialogi. *P.L.* vol. 188, cols. 1139–1248.

Anselm of Lucca. Collectio Canonum (ed. F. Thaner). *Anselmi episcopi Lucensis Collectio Canonum.* Oeniponte, 1906.

Arethas of Caesarea. Epitaphius in Euthymium Patrem. M. Jugie, *Patr. Orient.* (ed. Graffin-Nau), vol. XVI, pp. 489–98.

Arsenius, Patriarch. Testamentum (ed. J. B. Cotelerius). *Eccl. Graecae Monumenta*, vol. II. Paris, 1681.

Assemanus, J. S. *Bibliotheca Iuris Orientalis Canonici et Civilis.* Romae, 1762.

Atto Vercellensis. Capitulare. *P.L.* vol. 134, cols. 27–52.

Aureum Speculum Papae (ed. G. Brown). *Fasciculus Rerum Expetendarum.* London, 1690.

Auxilius. De Ordinationibus a Formoso Papa factis. *P.L.* vol. 129, cols. 1061–74.

—— Libellus in Defensionem Stephani Epis. *P.L.* vol. 129, cols. 1101–12.

—— Infensor et Defensor. *P.L.* vol. 129, cols. 1073–6.

—— In defensionem Sacrae Ordin. Papae Formosi (ed. E. Dümmler). *Auxilius und Vulgarius.* Leipzig, 1866.

Balsamon, Th. Commentarii in Canones. *P.G.* vols. 137, 138.

Barlaam. Epistolae pro Latinis. *P.G.* vol. 151, cols. 1266–1330.

Bartolomaeus Brixiensis. Glossae. *See* Bibliography (Semeca, J.).

Basil of Achrida. Dialogi (ed. J. Schmidt). *Des Basileus aus Achrida, unedierte Dialoge.* München, 1901.

—— Letter to Hadrian IV. *P.G.* vol. 119, cols. 929–33.

Beccos, Joannes. De Unione Ecclesiarum. *P.G.* vol. 141, cols. 15–157, 925–41.

—— Refutatio Photiani Libri de Spir. S. Ibid. cols. 727–864.

—— In Tomum Cyprii. Ibid. cols. 864–926.

—— Ad Sugdaeae episcopum. Ibid. cols. 289–337.

—— De Depositione sua Oratio II. Ibid. cols. 969–1009.

Bernaldus. Apologeticus. *M.G.H.* Lib. de Lite, vol. II, pp. 58–88.

—— De Excommunicatis Vitandis. *M.G.H.* Lib. de Lite, vol. II, pp. 112–42.

Bernard, S. Epistolae. *P.L.* vol. 182, cols. 69–662.

Bernold. Chronicon. *M.G.H.* Ss. V, pp. 385–467.

Bertholdus. Annales. *M.G.H.* Ss. V, pp. 264–326.

Bessarion, Cardinal. Encyclica ad Graecos. *P.G.* vol. 161, cols. 449–90.

Bonizo de Sutri. Liber de Vita Christiana (ed. Perels). *Texte zur Geschichte des Röm. u. Kanon. Rechtes im M.A.* vol. I. Berlin, 1930.

—— Liber ad Amicum. *M.G.H.* Lib. de Lite, vol. I, pp. 568–620.

Bruno, S. Signiensis. De Sacrificio Azymo. Reply to Abbot Leo. *P.L.* vol. 165, cols. 1085–90.

Burchard of Worms. Decretorum Libri XX. *P.L.* vol. 140, cols. 537–1058.

Caloyan, Prince. Letters to Innocent III. *P.L.* vol. 214, cols. 1112 seq., and *P.L.* vol. 215, cols. 287–92.

Capistranus, J. Tractatus de Papae et Concilii S. Ecclesiae Auctoritate. *Tractatus*, vol. XIII, 1. Venetiis, 1584.

Carlerius (Charlier) de Gerson, J. *See* Gerson....

Cedrenus, G. (Skylitzes). Historiarum Compendium. *P.G.* vol. 121, cols. 23–1166 (Bonn, 1839).

Cerularius, M. Homilia in festo Restitutionis Imaginum. *P.G.* vol. 120, cols. 723–36.

—— Letters. *P.G.* vol. 120, cols. 751–820.

—— Edictum Synodale. Ibid. cols. 736–48.

Chronica Apostolorum et Imperatorum Basileensia. *M.G.H.* Ss. XXXI, pp. 266–300.

Chronica Pontificum et Imperatorum Tiburtina. *M.G.H.* Ss. XXXI, pp. 226–65.

Chronicon Salernitanum. *M.G.H.* Ss. III, pp. 467–561.

Chrysolanus, P. Oratio de Spir. S. *P.G.* vol. 127, cols. 911–20.

Clémanges, Nicolas de. In G. Durandus Junior, *Tractatus de Modo Gener. Concilii Celebrandi.*

Clement IV, Pope. E. Jordan, Les Régistres de Clément IV. *Bibl. des Écoles Fr. d'Athènes et de Rome*, série II, vol. XI. Paris, 1893.

Codinus. De Officiis. Bonn, 1839.

Coletus, N. *Sacrosancta Concilia...studio P. Labbe et G. Cossarti...curante N. Coleto*, 1728, etc.

Constantinus Melitaniota. De Ecclesiastica Unione et de Processione S. Spiritus. *P.G.* vol. 141, cols. 1032–1273.

Constantinus Porphyrogennetos. De Ceremoniis Aulae Byzantinae (ed. J. Reiske), Bonn, 1819; (ed. A. Vogt), *Le Livre des Cérémonies*, Paris, 1935.

—— De Administrando Imperio. Bonn, 1840.

—— *Vita Basilii.* Bonn, 1838 (Theoph. Contin.).

Crabbe, P. *Concilia omnia, tam generalia, quam particularia, ab Apost. temporibus in hunc diem celebrata*, Cologne, 1538.

Criminationes adversus Eccles. Latinam (ed. J. B. Cotelerius). *Eccl. Graecae Monum.* vol. III. Paris, 1681.

Dandolo. Chronicon Venetum. *Scriptores Rer. Ital.* (Muratori). Cf. H. Simonsfeld, *Andreas Dandolo u. seine Geschichtswerke.* München, 1876.

Demetrios Cydones. Letters published by G. Cammelli (*Correspondance*, Texte inédit et traduit). Paris, 1930. (*Collect. Byzant.*)

—— De Processione S. Spiritus. *P.G.* vol. 154, cols. 864–958 (written by Manuel Calecas).

Deusdedit, Cardinal. Canonical Collection (ed. V. Wolf von Glanvell), *Die Kanonensammlung des Kardinals Deusdedit.* Paderborn, 1905.

Deusdedit, Cardinal. Libellus contra Invasores et Simoniacos. *M.G.H.* Lib. de Lite, vol. II, pp. 292–365.

Disputatio vel Defensio Paschalis Papae. *M.G.H.* Lib., de Lite, vol. II, pp. 659–66.

Dominican Brothers. Tractatus Contra Errores Graecorum. *P.G.* vol. 140, cols. 487–541.

Durandus, G. Tractatus de Modo Generalis Concilii Celebrandi, Paris, 1671 (in *Tractatus*, vol. XIII, p. 1; Venice, 1583).

Erchempertus. Historia Langobardorum. *M.G.H.* Ss. III, and in *M.G.H.* Ss. Rerum Langobardorum (ed. G. Waitz).

Eustratios of Nicaea. Περὶ τοῦ ἁγίου Πνεύματος; Περὶ τῶν Ἀ3ύμων (ed. by Demetrakopulos), Ἐκκλησιαστικὴ βιβλιοθήκη. Leipzig, 1866.

Euthymios, Patriarcha. Encomium in Concept. S. Annae (ed. M. Jugie) in Graffin-Nau, *Patrol. Orient.* vol. XVI, pp. 499–505, 1921.

—— Encomium in Venerationem Zonae Deiparae. Ibid. pp. 505–14.

Euthymios Zigabenos. Panoplia. *P.G.* vol. 130.

Eutychius of Alexandria. Annales. *P.G.* vol. III, cols. 907–1156.

Faventius, Joannes. Summa Gratiani; Glossae. *See* Bibliography (Semeca, J., who quotes Faventius).

Flodoardus. Historia Remensis Ecclesiae. *M.G.H.* Ss. XIII, pp. 405–600.

Flores Temporum. Pontifices, by a Suabian Minorite. *M.G.H.* Ss. XXIV, pp. 228–50.

Formosus, Papa. Letters to Stylian. Mansi, vol. XVI, pp. 439, 456–8.

Formulae Merov. et Karolini Aevi. *M.G.H.* Leg. Sect. V, Form. (ed. K. Zeumer, 1886).

Gauzlin, Abbot of Fleury. The Life of Gauzlin, written by Andrew of Fleury. *See* Bibliography (L. Delisle).

Genesios, J. Regum Libri IV. Bonn, 1834.

Georgius Acropolita. Annales. *P.G.* vol. 140, cols. 969–1220.

—— Λόγος περὶ τῆς Ἐκπορεύσεως (ed. Demetrakopulos), Ἐκκλ. Βιβλ. pp. 395–411. Leipzig, 1866.

Georgius Cedrenus. *See* Cedrenus, G. (Skylitzes).

Georgius of Cyprus. Scripta Apologetica. *P.G.* vol. 142, cols. 233–70.

Georgius Gemistos Plethon. De Dogmate Latino. *P.G.* vol. 160, cols. 975–80.

Georgius Koresios. Ἐγχειρίδιον... (ed. Dositheos). Τόμος Καταλ. pp. 276–410. Jassy, 1692.

Georgius Metochita. Historiae Dogmaticae Lib. I et II (ed. A. Mai). *Patrum Nova Bibl.* vol. VIII. Roma, 1854–1905.

Georgius Monachus. *Chronicon* (ed. C. de Boor), Teubner, 1904, 2 vols.

—— Continuatus, *Vitae Imperatorum*. Bonn, 1838.

Georgius Pachymeres. *Historia Rerum a Michaele Paleologo...Gestarum.* Bonn, 1835.

Georgius Scholarios. De Processione S. Spiritus (ed. M. Jugie, Oeuvres complètes de Gen. Scholarius), vol. II. Paris, 1929–38.

—— *Apologia Syntomos* (ed. M. Jugie), vol. III.

—— Letter to Demetrius Palaeologus against the Union of Florence. Ibid. vol. III.

Georgius Syncellus. *Chronographia*, Bonn, 1829; ed. de Boor, vol. II (Teubner).

Gerbert of Rheims. Letters (ed. J. Havet). *Collect. de Textes pour servir à l'Étude et à l'Enseignement de l'Histoire.* Paris, 1889.

Gerhohus of Reichersberg. Opusculum de Edificio Dei. *M.G.H.* Lib. de Lite, vol. III, pp. 136 seq.

—— Libellus de Simoniacis. *M.G.H.* Lib. de Lite, vol. III, pp. 239–72.

Germanos II, Patriarch. Epistula ad Cyprios (ed. J. B. Cotelerius). *Ecclesiae Graecae Monumenta,* vol. II. Paris, 1681.

Gerson, Charlier de, J. *Opera Omnia.* 4 tom. Paris, 1606.

—— *De Potestae Ecclesiastica,* vol. I, pp. 110–45.

—— *De Auferibilitate Papae ab Ecclesia,* vol. I, pp. 154–71.

—— *De Modo se Habendi Tempore Schismatis,* vol. I, pp. 171–5.

—— *Tractatus de Schismate,* vol. I, pp. 210–20.

—— *De Unitate Ecclesiastica,* vol. I, pp. 178–86.

—— *De Concilio unius Obedientiae,* vol. I, pp. 221–30.

—— *Trilogus in Materia Schismatis,* vol. I, pp. 292–315.

—— Tractatus de Potestate Regia et Papali (ed. M. Goldast). *Monarchia S. Rom. Imp.* vol. II. Harroviae, 1611–14.

Gesta Episcoporum Neapolitanorum. *M.G.H.* Ss. Rer. Lang. pp. 398–436.

Gratianus. Concordantia Discordantium Canonum. 1772 edition by J. Fenton, and the Venice editions of 1495 and 1514; edition by Friedberg in *Corpus Juris Canonici* (Lipsiae, 1879). *See also P.L.* vol. 187.

Gregorius Abulpharagius. *Chronicon Syriacum* (ed. Bruns and Kirsch). Leipzig, 1789.

Gregorius Mammas. Contra Ephesium. *P.G.* vol. 160, cols. 13–205.

Gregory VII. Registrum (ed. E. Caspar), *Das Register Gregors VII; M.G.H.* Ep. Selectae, II, 1920, 1923, 2 vols.

Gregory of Alexandria. Profession of Faith. *P.G.* vol. 152, cols. 1102–3.

Guido de Baysio. Glossae in 'Decretum Gratiani'. Venice, 1495.

Habert, Isaac. Archieraticon. *Liber Pontificum Ecclesiae Graecae.* Paris, 1643.

Hadrianus II, Papa. Epistolae. *M.G.H.* Ep. VI, pp. 691–765.

Hardouin, J. *Conciliorum Collectio Regia Maxima....* 12 vols. Paris, 1715.

Helinandus Frigidi Montis. Chronicon. *P.L.* vol. 212, cols. 771–1082.

Herimannus Augiensis. Chronicon. *M.G.H.* Ss. V, pp. 74–133.

Hincmar. Annales. *M.G.H.* Ss. I, pp. 455–515.

—— Epistolae. *P.L.* vol. 126.

Hormisdas, Papa. Regula Fidei. Mansi, vol. VIII, col. 407.

Hosius, S. *De Loco et Auctoritate Rom. Pont. in Ecclesia, Bibliotheca,* vol. XIX. Romae, 1699.

Hugh of Verdun (Flaviniacensis). Chronicon Verdunense. *P.L.* vol. 154, cols. 112–403; *M.G.H.* Ss. VIII, pp. 280–503.

Hugo Etherianus. De Haeresibus Graecorum. *P.L.* vol. 202, cols. 231–396.

Hugo de Sancto Victore. Eruditiones Didascalicae Libri Septem. *P.L.* vol. 176, cols. 741–838.

Humbertus Cardinalis. Contra Simoniacos. *P.L.* vol. 143, cols. 1005–1210; *M.G.H.* Lib. de Lite, vol. I, pp. 100–253.

—— De Gestis Legatorum in Urbe CP. (ed. Will). *Acta et Scripta quae de Controversiis Eccl. Gr. et Lat. s. XI extant* (Leipzig, 1864); *P.L.* vol. 143, cols. 1002–4.

Humbertus Cardinalis. Adversus Graecorum Calumnias. *P.L.* vol. 143, cols. 930–74.

—— Rationes de S. Spiritu a Patre et Filio. A. Michel, *Humbert u. Kerullarios*, vol. I, pp. 77 seq. Paderborn, 1925.

—— Contra Nicetam. *P.G.* vol. 120, cols. 983–1000.

Humbertus de Romanis. Opusculum Tripartitum (ed. Crabbe). *Concilia Omnia*... vol. II (Coloniae, ed. 1551). *See also* Bibliography (F. Heintke and K. Michel).

Innocent III. Litterae. *P.L.* vol. 215.

Invectiva in Romam pro Formoso Papa (ed. E. Dümmler). *Gesta Berengarii.* Halle, 1871.

Isaias of Cyprus. Epistola de Processione S. Spiritus. *P.G.* vol. 158, cols. 971–6.

Ivo of Chartres. Decretum. *P.L.* vol. 161, cols. 59–1022. National Library, Paris, MS. Latin 3874.

—— Epistolae. *P.L.* vol. 162, cols. 11–288.

Jacobatius Ch., Cardinalis. De Concilio Domini, *Tractatus*, vol. XIII, p. 1. Venetiis, 1584.

Jacobus de Paradiso (de Clusa). De Septem Statibus Ecclesiae (ed. E. G. Brown). *Fasciculus Rerum Expetendarum et Fugiendarum.* London, 1690.

Joannes VIII, Papa. Epistolae. *P.L.* vol. 126, cols. 651–967; Mansi, vol. XVII, cols. 3–242; *M.G.H.* Ep. VII (ed. E. Caspar).

Joannes II, Russian Metropolitan. Letter to Clement III (ed. A. Pavlov). *Kriticheskie Opuitui.* St Petersburg, 1878.

Joannes Cantacuzenus. *Historiae*, 3 vols. Bonn, 1828–32.

Joannes Chilas. Libellus de Processione S. Spiritus. *P.G.* vol. 135, cols. 505–8.

Joannes Claudiopolitanus. Controversiae (ed. A. Pavlov). *Kriticheskie Opuitui.* St Petersburg, 1878.

Joannes de Deo. Cronica. *M.G.H.* Ss. XXXI, pp. 301–24.

Joannes Diaconus. Chronicon Venetum. *M.G.H.* Ss. VII, pp. 4–47.

Joannes Eugenicos. Treatise against the Council of Florence (ed. Dositheos). Τόμος Καταλλαγῆς, pp. 206–73. Jassy, 1692.

Joannes of Jerusalem. Περὶ τῶν Ἀζύμων (ed. Dositheos). Τόμος Ἀγάπης, pp. 504–38. Jassy, 1698.

Joannes VI Palaeologus. Letter to Martin V. Mansi, vol. XXVIII, col. 1069.

Joannes of Paris. Tractatus de Potestate Regia et Papali (ed. S. Schardius). *De Jurisdictione...Imperiali...scripta*, 1566.

Joannes Scholasticus. Syntagma 50 Titulorum (ed. V. Beneshevich). *S.B. bayr. Akad. Wiss.* (Philos.-Hist. Cl.), 1937.

Joannes Skylitzes. *See* Cedrenus.

Job Jasites. Contra Latinos (ed. J. Hergenröther), *Photius* (Regensburg, 1867–9), vol. II, pp. 526 seq.

Joel. *Chronographia.* Bonn, 1837.

Joseph Bryennios. Περὶ τῆς ἁγίας Τριάδος Λόγος (ed. E. Bulgaris). Leipzig, 1768.

—— Διάλεξις περὶ τῆς τοῦ ἁγίου Πνεύματος ἐκπορ. Ibid. pp. 407–78.

Joseph of Methone. Disceptatio pro Concilio Florentino. *P.G.* vol. 159, cols. 960–1394.

Justellus, H., Voellus, G. *Bibliotheca Juris Canonici Veteris....* Paris, 1661.

Justellus, Chr. *Nomocanon Photii....* Paris, 1615.

Justinianus. *Novellae* (ed. C. E. Zachariae von Lingenthal). Teubner, 1881.

Labbe, Ph., Cossart, G. *Sacrosancta Concilia ad Regiam Editionem Exacta,* 17 vols. Paris, 1672.

Laelius Jordanus. De Romanae Sedis Origine et Auctoritate. *Tractatus,* vol. XIII, p. 1. Venice, 1584.

Leo IV, Papa. Epistolae. *M.G.H.* Ep. V, pp. 585–612.

Leo IX, Papa. Epistolae et Decreta Pontificia. *P.L.* vol. 143, cols. 592–838.

Leo Achridanus. Epistola de Azymis et Sabbatis. *P.G.* vol. 120, cols. 835–44.

Leo Bardas. *Scriptor incertus de Leone Barda.* Bonn (1842), pp. 335–62.

Leo Choerosphactes. Letters to the Emperor Leo (ed. J. Sakkelion), in Δελτίον τῆς ἱστορ. καὶ ἐθνολ. ἑταιρίας, vol. I, 1883; (ed. G. Kolias), in *Texte u. Forschungen zur Byz.-Neugriech. Philologie,* no. 31. Athens, 1939.

Leo Diaconus. *Historia.* Bonn (1828).

Leo Grammaticus. Chronographia, *P.G.* vol. 108, cols. 1037–1164. Bonn (1842), pp. 3–331.

Leo Imperator. Panegyric of S. Elias (ed. Akakios). Λέοντος τοῦ Σοφοῦ πανηγυρικοὶ Λόγοι. Athens, 1868.

—— Panegyric of Basil I, A. Vogt, I. Hausherr, l'Oraison funèbre de Basile I. *Orientalia Christiana,* vol. 25. Rome, 1931.

Leo Metrop. of Russia. Πρὸς Ῥωμαίους...περὶ τῶν Ἀζύμων (ed. A. Pavlov). *Kriticheskie Opuitui,* pp. 115–32. St Petersburg, 1878.

Leo of Ostia. Chronicon Casinense. *M.G.H.* Ss. VII, pp. 514–727.

Leonis Abbatis et Legati Epistola ad Hugonem et Robertum Reges. *M.G.H.* Ss. III, p. 686; *P.L.* vol. 139, cols. 337–44.

Liber Diurnus. G. Galbiati, Il Codice Ambrosiano de Liber Diurnus. *Rom. Pont. Analecta Ambrosiana,* vol. VII. Milan-Rome, 1921; (ed. by Th. E. von Sickel), *Liber Diurnus.* Vindobonae, 1889.

Liber Pontificalis. (Ed. L. Duchesne), 2 vols. Paris, 1886, 1892.

Liudprandus. De Legatione Constant. *M.G.H.* Ss. III, pp. 347–63.

—— Antapodosis, *M.G.H.* Ss. III, pp. 273–339; Engl. transl. by F. A. Wright, *The Works of Liudprand of Cremona.* London, 1930.

Macarius Macres. Πρὸς Λατίνους (ed. Dositheos). Τόμος Καταλλαγῆς. Jassy, 1692.

Malalas, Jo. *Chronographia.* Bonn (1831).

Manasses, C. Compendium Chronicum. *P.G.* vol. 127, cols. 219–472. Bonn, 1837.

Manuel Calecas. Adversus Graecos Libri IV. *P.G.* vol. 152, cols. 17–258.

—— De Processione Spiritus S. *P.G.* vol. 154, cols. 864–958 (attributed to Demetrius Cydones).

Manuel II Palaeologus. *Lettres* (ed. E. Legrand). Paris, 1893.

Manuel Rhetor. De Marco Ephesio deque Rebus in Synodo Florentino Gestis (ed. L. Petit). *Patrologia Orientalis,* vol. XVII, pp. 491–522.

Marianus Scotus. Chronicon. *M.G.H.* Ss. V, pp. 481–568.

Marinus II, Papa. Litterae. *P.L.* vol. 133, cols. 863–80.

Mark of Ephesus. Dialogus de Additamento in Symbolo. *Patrol. Orient.* vol. XVII, pp. 415–21.

—— Epistola Encyclica. Ibid. pp. 449–59.

Marsilius of Padua (Menandrinus Patavinus). *Tractatus de Translatione Imperii* (ed. Schardius), 1566; (ed. M. Goldast), *Monarchia S.R.I.* vol. II, pp. 147 seq., Harroviae, 1611–14.

—— *Defensor Pacis* (ed. M. Goldast), vol. II, pp. 154–312. Franckfurt, 1592.

Martinus Opaviensis. 'Margarita Decreti', seu Tabula Martiniana (ed. P. Drach). Spire, 1490 (?).

—— Chronicon, *M.G.H.* Ss. XXII, pp. 377–475.

Matthaeus Blastares. Κατὰ Λατίνων (ed. Dositheos). Τόμος Καταλλαγῆς, pp. 441–55. Jassy, 1692.

Maximos Chrysoberges. De Process. S. Spiritus. *P.G.* vol. 154, cols. 1217–30.

Maximos Planudes. Tria Capita, refuted by George Metochita. *P.G.* vol. 141, cols. 1276–1308.

Merlin, J. *Conciliorum Quatuor Generalium Tomus Primus.* Paris, 1524.

Metrophanes of Smyrna. Letter to the Logothete Manuel. Mansi, vol. XVI, cols. 413–20.

Michael of Anchialos. Dialogue with Manuel Comnenos (ed. by Ch. Loparev), in *Viz. Vremennik,* vol. XIV, 1907.

Michael Cerularius. *See* Cerularius.

Michael Glycas. *Annales.* Bonn (1836).

—— Κεφάλαια εἰς τὰς ἀπορίας τῆς Γράφης (ed. Eustratiades). Athens, 1906.

Michael Syrus. *Chronicon* (ed. J. B. Chabot). Paris, 1899–1924.

Milliolus, A. Liber de Temporibus. *M.G.H.* Ss. XXXI, pp. 336–668.

Minorita Erphordiensis. Chronica Minor. *M.G.H.* Ss. XXIV, pp. 172–204.

Narratio de Beatis Patribus Tarasio et Nicephoro. *P.G.* vol. 99.

Nicephorus, Patriarcha. Epistola ad Leonem III. *P.G.* vol. 100, cols. 169–200.

Nicephorus Blemmydes. De Processione S. Spiritus. *P.G.* vol. 142, cols. 533–84.

Nicephorus Callistus Xanthopulos. Ecclesiastica Historia. *P.G.* vol. 145, cols. 603–1332.

Nicephorus Gregoras. *Byzantinae Historiae* (ed. Bekker), Bonn, 1855, vol. I, pp. 3–279; *P.G.* vol. 148, cols. 119–1450 and vol. 149, cols. 9–502.

—— Panegyric of Theophano. Hergenröther, *Monumenta Graeca ad Photium pertinentia.* Ratisbonnae, 1869.

Nicephorus Philosophus. *Vita Antonii Cauleae.* A.S. Febr., d. 12. *P.G.* vol. 106.

Nicephorus Phocas. *Novellae,* pp. 309–23. Bonn, 1828.

Nicetas Choniata. Thesaurus Orthodoxae Fidei. *P.G.* vol. 140, cols. 10–282.

Nicetas-David. Vita Ignatii. Mansi, vol. XVI, cols. 209–92; *P.G.* vol. 105, cols. 487–574.

Nicetas of Maronea. De Processione S. Spiritus. *P.G.* vol. 139, cols. 169–222.

Nicetas Nicenus. De Schismate Graecorum. *P.G.* vol. 120, cols. 713–20.

Nicetas Stethatos. Libellus contra Latinos. *P.G.* vol. 120, cols. 1011–22.

Nicholas I, Papa. Epistolae. *M.G.H.* Ep. VI, pp. 257–690.

Nicholas de Cusa. *See* Bibliography (Cusa, N. de).

Nicholas of Methone. Νικολάου ἐπ. Μεθώνης λόγοι δύο (ed. Demetrakopulos). Ἐκκλ. Βιβλιοθήκη. Leipzig, 1866. For the Latin edition see p. 397.

Nicholas Mysticos. Epistolae. *P.G.* vol. 111, cols. 27–392.

Nicolaus Siculus Panormitanus. Pro Honore et Conservatione Concilii Basiliensis. Mansi, vol. XXX, pp. 1123 seq.

Nilus (Neilos) Cabasilas of Thessalonica. De Dissidio Ecclesiarum; De Primatu. *P.G.* vol. 149, cols. 683–729.

Nilus (Neilos) of Rhodes. Treatise on the Councils (ed. Chr. Justellus), *Nomocanon Photii*, Paris, 1665; (ed. G. Voellus), H. Justellus, *Bibl. Juris Canonici Veteris*, vol. I, pp. 1155–60, Paris, 1661.

Nogaret, W. de. Rationes quibus probatur quod Bonifacius legitime ingredi non potuit Celestino vivente. P. Dupuy, *Histoire du Différend.* . . . Paris, 1655.

Ockham, William of. Octo Quaestionum Decisiones super Potestate Summi Pontificis (ed. Goldast). *Monarchia*, vol. II, pp. 313–91.

—— Dialogus de Potestate Imperatoris. Ibid. pp. 392–957.

—— *Breviloquium de Potestate Papae* (ed. L. Baudry). Paris, 1937.

Pancapalea. Summa. J. F. v. Schulte, *Die Summa des Pancapalea*. Giessen, 1890.

Pantaleo (Pantelemon) Diaconus. Contra Graecos. *P.G.* vol. 140, cols. 487–574.

Papadopoulos-Krameus, A. *See* Photius.

—— *Monumenta Graeca et Latina ad Historiam Photii Patriarchae Pertinentia*, 2 vols. Petropoli, 1901.

Paschalis II. Professio Fidei. *P.L.* vol. 163, cols. 471–2.

Patria Constantinopoleos (ed. Th. Preger). *Scriptores Originum Constantinopolitanarum*. Leipzig (Teubner), 1907.

Petrus Abelardus. Apologia. *P.L.* vol. 178, cols. 105–8.

Petrus de Alliaco Cardinalis. De Ecclesiae et Cardinalium Auctoritate, in *Gersonis Opera*. Paris, 1606.

Petrus S. Damianus. Actus Mediolani, Opusculum V. *P.L.* vol. 145, cols. 89–98.

Petrus Siculus. Historia Manichaeorum. *P.G.* vol. 104, cols. 1239–1304.

Philotheus. Cletorologion. Constantine Porphyrogennetos, De Ceremoniis (Bonn); J. B. Bury, *Imp. Admin. System in the Ninth Century*. London, 1911.

Photius. *Orationes et Homiliae* (ed. S. Aristarchos). Constantinople, 1900.

—— Ad Amphilochium, *P.G.* vol. 101 (ed. Sophocles Oikonomos), Athens, 1858.

—— Epistolae, Valetta, London, 1864; *P.G.* vol. 102, cols. 585–990.

—— Mystagogia. *P.G.* vol. 102, cols. 279–400.

—— Epistolae XLV (ed. Papadopoulos-Krameus). Petropoli, 1896.

—— Letter to Ashod, King of Armenia. A. Finck, Esnik Gjandschezian, Der Brief des Photius an Aschot u. dessen Antwort, in *Zeitschrift für Armenische Philologie*, vol. II, 1904; Papadopoulos-Krameus, *Palestinskii Sbornik*, vol. XI, 1892.

—— Collationes Accurataeque Demonstrationes de Episcopis et Metropolitis (ed. F. Fontani), Novae Eruditorum Deliciae, Florentiae, 1786, t. I; *P.G.* vol. 104, cols. 1220–32.

—— *Photiaca* (ed. Papadopoulos-Krameus). St. Petersburg, 1897.

Phournes, J. Graeco-Latin Discussions (ed. Demetrakopulos). Ἐκκλ. Βιβλιοθήκη. Leipzig, 1866.

Pius IV. *Bulla super forma Juramenti professionis fidei*. Mansi, vol. XXXIII, pp. 220–2.

Placidus Monachus. Liber de Honore Ecclesiae. *M.G.H.* Lib. de Lite, vol. II, pp. 566–639.

Poggio of Florence, Joannes. *De Potestate Papae et Concilii* (ed. J. Beplin). Rome, 1517 (?).

Prierio, Sylvester de (Mazzolini). De Irrefragabili Veritate Rom. Eccl. *Bibliotheca*, vol. XIX. Romae, 1699.

Psellos. Poem on the Orthodox Faith and on the Councils. *P.G.* vol. 122, cols. 816 seq.

Pseudo-Simeon. *See* Simeon Logothete.

Ptolemaeus Lucensis. Historia Ecclesiastica. Muratori, *Ss. Rerum Italic.* vol. XI.

Rangerius Lucensis. Vita S. Anselmi Lucensis Ep. *M.G.H.* Ss. XXX, pp. 1152–1307.

Ratherius. Praeloquiorum Libri Sex. *P.L.* vol. 136, cols. 145–344.

—— Itinerarium. Ibid. cols. 579–600.

—— Decreta et Libellus. Ibid. cols. 477–82.

Ratramnus Corbiensis. Contra Graecorum Opposita. *P.L.* vol. 121, cols. 225–346. L. d'Achery, *Spicilegium.* Paris, 1723.

Regino of Prüm. Libri Duo de Synodalibus Causis. *P.L.* vol. 132, cols. 185–400; (ed. F. G. A. Wasserschleben), Lipsiae, 1840.

Rolandus Magister. Summa. F. Thaner, *Die Summa M. Rolandi.* Innsbruck, 1874.

Romualdus (Guarna) Salernitanus. Chronicon. Muratori, *Ss. Rerum Italic.* vol. VII, pars I.

Rufinus. Summa Decretorum. H. Singer, *Die Summa Decr. des M. Rufinus.* Paderborn, 1902.

Sacchi de Platina, B. *Historia de Vitis Pontificum Rom.* Venice, 1511.

Sathas, C. Publisher of Anonym. Chronicle, *Bibl. Graeca Medii Aevi*, t. VII. Paris, 1894.

Semeca, J. (Joannes Teutonicus). Glossae in *Decr. Grat.* (ed. Venice, 1495). J. F. Schulte, Die Glosse zum Decret Gratians, in *Denkschr. Akad. Wiss. Wien* (Philos.-Hist. Cl.), 1872, Bd XXI, pp. 70 seq.

Sergius III. Letter to the Frankish Episcopate. (Synod of Trosley), Mansi, vol. XVIII, col. 304.

Sicardus Cremonensis. Chronica. *M.G.H.* Ss. XXXI, pp. 22–181.

Sigebertus Gemblacensis. Chronicon. *M.G.H.* Ss. VI, pp. 300–74.

Simeon Logothete (Pseudo-Simeon). *Chronicon.* Bonn, 1838 (Theoph. Cont.), pp. 603–760.

Sirmond, I. *Concilia Generalia*, 4 vols. Romae, 1608–12 (Collectio Romana).

Stephanus Tornacensis. Summa. J. v. Schulte, *Die Summa des Stephanus Torn.* Giessen, 1891.

Stephen V. Fragmenta et Epistolae. *M.G.H.* Ep. VII, pp. 334–65.

Stylianos of Neo-Caesarea. Letter to Pope Stephen V. Mansi, vol. XVI, pp. 426–35; *M.G.H.* Ep. VII, pp. 375–82.

Surius, L. *Concilia Omnia tam Generalia quam Particularia.* Cologne, 1567.

Symeon Magister. *See* Simeon Logothete.

Symeon of Thessalonica. Dialogus contra hereses. *P.G.* vol. 155, cols. 33–176.

Synaxarion. Synaxarium Constantinopolitanum. *A.S.* Nov. (ed. H. Delehaye). Brussels, 1902.

Synodicon Vetus, published by J. Pappe in J. A. Fabricius and G. C. Harles, *Bibliotheca Graeca*, vol. XII. Hamburg, 1809.

Σύνταγμα τῶν ἱερῶν κανόνων (ed. G. Rhalles and M. Potles), 6 vols. Athens, 1852–9.

Theodorus Agalianus. Refutatio Argyropuli. *P.G.* vol. 158, cols. 1011–52.

—— Συλλογή... (ed. Dositheos). Τόμος Καταλλαγῆς, pp. 432 seq. Jassy, 1692.

Theodorus II Lascaris. *De Processione S. Spiritus* (ed. H. B. Swete). London, 1875.

Theodorus Studita. Narratio de Beatis Patriarchis Tarasio et Nicephoro. *P.G.* vol. 99, cols. 1849–54.

—— Epistolae. *P.G.* vol. 99, cols. 904–1670.

—— Laudatio S. Platonis Hegumeni. Ibid. cols. 804–49.

Theognostos. *Libellus.* Mansi, vol. xvi, cols. 296–301.

Theoleptos of Philadelphia. Tractatus de Operatione in Christo. *P.G.* vol. 143, cols. 381–404.

Theophanes. *Chronographia* (ed. de Boor). Lipsiae, 1887 (Teubner). Bonn, 1839, 1841.

Theophanes Continuatus. Bonn, 1838.

Theophylactus of Ochrid. Liber de iis quorum Latini incusantur. *P.G.* vol. 126, cols. 221–49.

—— Vita S. Clementis. *P.G.* vol. 126, cols. 1193–1240.

Thomas S. Aquinas. Contra Errores Graecorum. *See* F. Reusch, Die Fälschungen in dem Tractat des Thomas von Aquin gegen die Griechen. *S.B. bayr. Akad. Wiss.* (Phil.-Hist. Kl.), 1889, vol. xviii.

—— *Summa Theologica* (Rome ed. 1888), vol. iv.

Torquemada (Turrecremata), Joannes de. *Summa de Ecclesia* (ed. Card. Vitellius). Venetiis, 1561.

—— *Commentaria in Decretum* (ed. de Bohier). Lugduni, 1519.

—— *De Potestate Papae et Concilio Generali* (ed. J. Friedrich). Oeniponti, 1871.

—— Responsio in...congregationem Basileensium. Mansi, vol. xxxi, cols. 63–127.

Triumphus, Augustus, of Ancona. *Summa de Eccl. Potestate.* Coloniae Agrip. 1475.

Udalrich, S. Sermo Synodalis. *P.L.* vol. 135, cols. 1069–74.

Vio, Th. de. De Auctoritate Papae et Concilii. *Bibliotheca*, Romae, t. xix.

—— De Divina Institutione Pontificatus Romani Pontificis. *Corpus Catholicorum* (ed. F. Lauchert), vol. x. Münster i.W. 1925.

Vita S. Anselmi Lucensis episcopi. *See* Rangerius.

—— Cauleae Patriarchae. *See* Nicephorus Philosophus.

—— S. Clementis, by Theophylactus. *P.G.* vol. 126, cols. 1193–1240.

—— S. Constantini Judaei. *A.S.* Nov. vol. iv.

—— Euthymii (ed. de Boor). Berlin, 1888.

—— Euthymii Junioris (ed. L. Petit). *Revue de l'Orient Chrétien*, 1903.

—— S. Evaristi (ed. C. van de Vorst). *Analecta Bollandiana*, vol. xli, 1923.

—— S. Gregorii Magni, a Joanne Diacono. *P.L.* vol. 75, cols. 63–242.

—— Ignatii, by Nicetas-David. *P.G.* vol. 105, cols. 487–573.

—— S. Joannicii, by Sabas and Peter. *A.S.* 4 November, pp. 311–435.

—— Josephi Hymnographi, by Theophanes (ed. Papadopoulos-Kerameus, in his *Monumenta Graeca et Latina*, Petropoli, vol. ii, 1901); by John the Deacon, *P.G.* vol. 105, cols. 926–76.

—— S. Methodii. *P.G.* vol. 100, cols. 1244–61.

Vita S. Nicephori, by Ignatius the Deacon (ed. C. de Boor). Lipsiae, 1880.

—— Nicetae Mediciensis, by Theosterictus Monachus. *A.S.* (3 Aprilis).

—— Nicolai Studitae, by John the Deacon. *P.G.* vol. 105, cols. 864–925.

—— S. Tarasii, by Ignatius the Deacon. *A.S.* (25 Februarii).

—— S. Theodorae (ed. Regel). *Analecta Byzantino-Russica.* Petropoli, 1891.

Vulgarius, Eugenius. De Causa Formosana Libellus (ed. E. Dümmler). *Auxilius und Vulgarius.* Leipzig, 1866.

Zonaras, J. *Annales.* Bonn, 1841; 2nd vol. 1844.

—— Commentaria in Canones. . . . *P.G.* vols. 137, 138.

BIBLIOGRAPHY

ADONTZ, M. N. L'Age et l'Origine de l'Empereur Basile I. *Byzantion* (1933), vol. VIII; (1934), vol. IX.

—— La Portée historique de l'Oraison funèbre de Basile I. *Byzantion* (1933), vol. VIII.

AGUSTIN, ANTONIO (ANTONIUS AUGUSTINUS). *Opera omnia*, 8 vols. Lucae, 1765–74.

—— *De Emendatione Gratiani dialogorum libri duo* (*Opera*, vol. III). Lucae, 1767.

—— *Juris Pontificii Veteris Epitome* (*Opera*, vol. V). Lucae, 1770.

—— *De Synodis et Pseudosynodis* (*Opera*, vol. V).

—— *Juris Pontificii Epitome*. Tarragona, 1587.

AILLY, P. D' (ALLIACO, PETRUS DE). De Ecclesiae et Cardinalium auctoritate (*Gersonis Opera*). Paris, 1606.

ALBANUS, J. H. De Potestate Papae, in *Tractatus*, t. XIII. Venice, 1584.

ALEXANDRE NOËL (ALEXANDER NATALIS). *Historia Ecclesiastica Veteris et Novi Testamenti*, 8 tom. Paris, 1660.

ALLACCI, L. (ALLATIUS). *De Ecclesiae Occid. atque Orient. Perpetua Consensione.* Coloniae Agrippinae, 1648.

—— *De Libris et Rebus Ecclesiae Graecorum*. Parisiis, 1646.

—— *De Octava Synodo Photiana*. Romae, 1662.

—— Diatriba de Methodiis. *P.G.* vol. 100, cols. 1231–40.

—— *In Roberti Creyghtoni Apparatum, Versionem et Notas ad historiam Concilii Florentini....* Romae, 1665.

—— *Graeciae Orthodoxae Tomus primus et secundus*. Romae, 1652, 1659.

ALLIX, P. *Nectarii Patriarchae Hierosolymitani confutatio imperii Papae in Ecclesiam* (Engl. transl.). London, 1702.

ALMAINUS, J. De Auctoritate Ecclesiae et Concilii contra Thomam de Vio (*Gersonis Opera*, ed. by Ellies du Pin, t. II). Parisiis, 1706 (ed. 1606, vol. I).

ALTANER, B. Kentnisse des Griechischen in den Missionsorden während des 13 u. 14 Jh. *Z. für Kirchengeschichte* (1934), vol. LIII.

AMANN, E. Photius. *Dict. de Théol. Cathol.* (1935), vol. XII, cols. 1536–1604.

—— Jean VIII. Ibid. (1924), vol. VIII, cols. 602–13.

—— L'Époque Carolingienne. *Histoire de l'Église* (ed. A. Fliche and V. Martin), vol. VI. Paris, 1937.

ANDREADES, A. Le recrutement des fonctionnaires et les Universités dans l'Empire Byzantin. *Mélanges de Droit dédiés a M. G. Cornil*. Paris, 1926.

ANDRUZZI, L. *Vetus Graecia de S. Sede Romana praeclare sentiens*. Venice, 1713.

—— *Consensus tum Graecorum tum Latinorum Patrum de Proc. Spir. S. ex Filio*. Romae, 1716.

ARISTARCHOS, S. Φωτίου λόγοι καὶ ὁμιλίαι. Constantinople, 1900.

ARNOLD, G. *Unparteyische Kirchen u. Ketzer Historien....* Schaffhausen, 1740–2.

ASSEMANUS, J. S. *Bibliotheca Juris Orientalis Canonici et Civilis*. Romae, 1762–4.

BARONIUS, C. *Annales Ecclesiastici,...una cum critica historico-chronologica P. Antonii Pagii*, 38 tom. Lucae, 1738–59.

BASNAGE, J. *Thesaurus Monumentorum Eccl. et Hist. sive Henrici Canisii Lectiones Antiquae.* Antverpiae, 1725.

—— *Histoire de l' Église.* Rotterdam, 1699.

BAUDRY, L. *Guillelmi de Occam Breviloquium de potestate Papae.* Paris, 1937.

BAYNES, N. *The Byzantine Empire.* London, 1925.

BEES, NICOS A. Un manuscrit des Météoris de l'an 861–2. *Revue des Études Grecques* (1913), t. XXVI.

BELLARMINE, R. *De Scriptoribus Ecclesiasticis.* Coloniae, 1684.

—— De Conciliis et Ecclesia, *Opera Omnia.* Coloniae Agrippinae, 1633.

BENESHEVICH, VL. Joannis Scholastici Synagoga L titulorum. *Abhandl. bayr. Akad. Wiss.* (Phil.-Hist. Kl.), 1937.

BEVERIDGE, W. Συνόδικον, *sive Pandectae Canonum SS. Apost. et Conciliorum,* 2 vols. Oxonii, 1672.

BÖHMER, A. Nikolaus I, *Realenzyklopädie f. prot. Theol.* (3rd ed.). Leipzig, 1904.

BOJARSKI, J. P. *Historya Focyusza....* Lwów, 1895.

BOOR, C. DE. *Excerpta hist. iussu Imp. Constantini Porphyrogeneti.* Berlin, 1903–6.

—— Nachträge zu den Notitiae. *Z. f. Kirchengeschichte* (1891), vol. XII.

BRACATUS DE LAUREA LAURENTIUS. De Decretis Ecclesiae. *Bibliotheca* (1698), vol. XV.

BRATIANU, G. I. Empire et Démocratie à Byzance. *Byz. Zeitschr.* (1937), vol. XXXVII.

BRÉHIER, L. L'Enseignement supérieur à Constantinople. *Byzantion* (1929), vol. IV.

BRESLAU, H. *Handb. der Urkundenlehre für Deutschland u. Italien* (2nd ed.). Berlin, 1931.

BROWN, E. G. *Fasciculus Rerum Expetendarum et Fugiendarum.* London, 1690.

BURY, J. B. The Relationship of Photius to the Empress Theodora. *English Historical Review* (1890), pp. 255–8.

—— *A History of the Later Roman Empire from Arcadius to Irene.* London, 1889.

—— *A History of the Eastern Roman Empire.* London, 1912.

—— *The Imperial Administrative System in the Ninth Century.* London, 1911.

—— *The Constitution of the Later Roman Empire.* Cambridge, 1910.

BUSCHBELL, G. Professiones Fidei der Päpste. *Röm. Quartalschr.* (1896), vol. X.

—— Die Römische Überlieferung der Professiones Fidei der Päpste. Ibid. (1900), vol. XIV, pp. 131–6.

CAMMELLI, G. Personnaggi Bizantini dei secoli XIV–XV.... *Bessarione* (1920), vol. XXIV.

CAMPEGIUS, T. BONONIENSIS. *De Auctoritate et Potestate Rom. Pont.* Venice, 1555.

—— Tractatus de Auctoritate Conciliorum. *Tractatus,* vol. XIII. Venice, 1584.

CAPISTRANUS, J. Tractatus de Papae et Concilii S. Ecclesiae Auctoritate. *Tractatus,* vol. XIII, Venice, 1584.

CAPPUYNS, N. Le Synodicon de l'Église de Rhodes au XIVe siècle. *Échos d'Orient* (1934), vol. XXXIII, pp. 196–217.

CARRANZA, BARTH. *See* Mirandevius.

CASPAR, E. *Geschichte des Papsttums.* Tübingen, 1930, 1933.

—— Studien zum Register Johanns VIII. *Neues Archiv* (1910), vol. XXXVI.

CAVE, W. *Scriptorum Ecclesiasticorum Historia Literaria.* Oxonii, 1740–3.

CLEMANGIIS, NICOLAS DE. De Corrupto Statu Ecclesiae (in G. Durandus Jr., *Tractatus de modo Gener. Concilii Celebr.* Paris, 1671).

COLETTI, J. *See* Farlati, D.

CONRAT, M. (COHN). Römisches Recht bei Papst Nikolaus I. *Neues Archiv* (1911), vol. XXXVI.

—— *Geschichte der Quellen und Litteratur des Röm. Rechts in früheren Mittelalter.* Leipzig, 1891.

—— *Der Pandekten und Institutionenauszug der Britischen Dekretalensammlung, Quelle des Ivo.* Berlin, 1887.

CONTARINI, CARDINAL G. *Opera* (ed. by L. Contarini). Paris, 1571.

COZZA, L. *Historia Polemica de Graecorum Schismate.* Romae, 1719–20.

CREIGHTON, R. *Vera Historia Unionis non Verae inter Graecos et Latinos.* Hagae-Comitis, 1660.

CUMONT, F. Anecdota Bruxellensia, Univers. de Gand. *Recueil de Travaux,* fasc. 10. Gand, 1894.

CUNHA, RODRIGO DA. *Commentarii in Primam Partem Decreti Gratiani.* Bracharae Augustae, 1629.

CUSA, N. DE. De Concordantia Catholica libri III, ed. S. Schardius, *Syntagma Tractatuum de Imp. Iurisdict.* pp. 285–390. Argentorati, 1609.

DAMBERGER, J. F. *Synchronistische Geschichte der Kirche im Mittelalter.* Regensburg, 1850–63.

DELEHAYE, H. Synaxarium Constantinopolitanum. *A.S.* Nov., Propylaeum. Brussels, 1902.

DELISLE, L. *Inventaire des manuscrits Latins à la Bibl. Impér.* Paris, 1863–71.

—— Vie de Gauzlin, Abbé de Fleury et Archev. de Bourges, par André de Fleury. *Mém. Soc. Archéol. Orléanais* (1853), vol. II, pp. 256–322.

DIEHL, CH. Le Sénat et le Peuple Byzantin aux VIIe et VIIIe siècles. *Byzantion* (1924), vol. I.

DIMITRAKOPULOS, A. K. Ἱστορία τοῦ σχίσματος.... Leipzig, 1867.

—— Ὀρθόδοξος Ἑλλάς. Leipzig, 1872.

—— Ἐκκλησιαστικὴ Βιβλιοθήκη. Leipzig, 1866.

DOBSCHÜTZ, E. VON. Methodios und die Studiten. *Byz. Zeitschr.* vol. XVIII (1909).

DÖLGER, F. Rom in der Gedankenwelt der Byzantiner. *Zeitschr. f. Kirchengeschichte* (1937), vol. LVI.

—— *Regesten der Kaiserurkunden.* München, 1924–32.

DÖLLINGER, J. *Beiträge zur pol., kirchl. u. Culturgesch. der letzten 6. Jh.* vol. II. Regensburg, 1863.

—— (JANUS). *The Pope and the Council.* London, 1869.

DOMINICUS A SS. TRINITATE. De Summo Pontifice, De Sacris Conciliis. *Bibliotheca* (1689), vol. X.

DOSITHEOS. Τόμος Καταλλαγῆς. Jassy, 1692. Τόμος Χαρᾶς, Jassy, 1705.

DRAMMER, W. Der Werdegang Hergenröther's *Photius. Orient. Christiana Period.* (1941), vol. VII.

DRÄSEKE, J. Bischof Anselm von Havelberg. *Zeitschr. für Kirchengeschichte,* vol. XXI (1902).

DU CANGE. *Glossarium ad Scriptores Mediae et Infimae Latinitatis.* Niort, 1882–7.

DUCHESNE, J. *Études sur le Liber Pontificalis.* Paris, 1877.

DUHR, J. Le Pape Marin I. *Recherches des Sciences Religieuses* (1934), t. XXIV.

DÜMMLER, E. *Auxilius und Vulgarius.* Leipzig, 1866.

—— *Gesta Berengarii.* Halle, 1871.

BIBLIOGRAPHY

DUPUY, P. *Histoire du Différend entre le Pape Boniface VIII et Philippe le Bel.* Paris, 1655.

DURANDUS, G. Tractatus de Modo Generalis Concilii Celebrandi, Paris, 1671 (in *Tractatus*, vol. XIII, 1; Venice, 1584).

DVORNIK, F. *Les Slaves, Byzance et Rome au IXe siècle.* Paris, 1926.

—— *Les Légendes de Constantin et de Méthode vues de Byzance.* Prague, 1933.

—— *La Vie de St Grégoire le Décapolite et les Slaves Macédoniens au IXe siècle.* Paris, 1926.

—— L'Affaire de Photios dans la Littérature Latine du Moyen Age. *Annales de l'Institut Kondakov*, vol. X. Prague, 1938.

—— Le Premier Schisme de Photios. *Bull. Inst. Archéol. Bulgare*, vol. IX. Sofia, 1935.

—— Le Second Schisme de Photios. *Byzantion* (1933), vol. VIII.

—— Études sur Photios. *Byzantion* (1936), vol. XI.

—— Lettre à M. H. Grégoire à propos de Michel III. *Byzantion* (1935), vol. X.

—— L'Oecuménicité du VIIIe Concile dans la tradition occidentale du Moyen Age. *Bull. Acad. Belg. Cl. des Lettres*, 5e série, vol. XXIV (1938).

—— De potestate civili in conciliis oecumenicis, Acta VI Congressus pro unione ecclesiarum. *Academia Velehradensis*, vol. X. Olomouc, 1930. (Engl. transl. in *Christian East* (1932), vol. XIV.)

—— Quomodo incrementum influxus orientalis in imperio Byzantino s. VII–IX dissensionem inter Ecclesiam Romanam et Orientalem promoverit. *Acta Conventus Pragensis pro studiis Orient. a. 1929 celebrati.* Olomouc, 1930.

—— Rome and Constantinople in the Ninth Century. *Eastern Churches Quarterly*, 1939.

—— The Patriarch Photius—Father of the Schism or Patron of Reunion. *Report of the Proceedings at the Church Unity Week.* Oxford, 1942.

—— East and West. The Schism of the Patriarch Photius, Restatements of Facts. *The Month* (1943), vol. CLXXIX.

—— *National Churches and the Church Universal.* London, 1944.

—— The Study of Church History and Church Reunion. *Eastern Churches Quarterly* (1945), vol. VI.

—— De S. Cyrillo et Methodio in Luce Hist. Byz. *Acta V. Conventus Unionistici Velehradensis.* Olomouc, 1927.

—— The Circus Parties in Byzantium. *Byzantina-Metabyzantina* (New York), vol. I.

ELLIES DU PIN, L. *Nouvelle Bibliothèque des Auteurs Ecclésiastiques*, vol. III. Paris, 1698–89–1711.

EUGENIUS LOMBARDUS. Regale Sacerdotium. *Bibliotheca* (1698), vol. XI.

EWALD, P. Die Papstbriefe der Britischen Sammlung. *Neues Arch. Ges. ältere dtsch. Geschichtskunde* (1880), vol. V.

FABRICIUS, J. A. and HARLES, G. C. *Bibliotheca Graeca*, 12 vols. Hamburg, 1790–1809.

FARLATI, D., COLETTI, J. *Illyricum Sacrum*, 8 vols. Venetiis, 1751–1819.

FAUCHER, CH. *Histoire de Photius.* Paris, 1772.

FILARET (D. G. GUMILEVSKI). *Istoricheskoe Chtenie ob Ottsakh Tserkvi*, 3 vols. St Petersburg, 1859.

FINCK, A. Esnik Gjandschezian, Der Brief des Photios an Aschot und dessen Antwort. *Zeitschr. für armenische Philol.* (1904), vol. II.

FINKE, H. *Aus den Tagen des Bonifaz VIII.* Münster i. W. 1902.

FINKE, H., HOLBISTEINER, J. and HEIMPEL, H. *Acta Concilii Constantiensis*, 4 vols. Münster i. W., 1896–1928.

FLACIUS, M. *Centuriae Magdeburgenses seu Eccles. Historia.* Basileae, 1561–74.

FLEURY, C. *Histoire du Christianisme*, 6 vols. Paris, 1836, 1837.

FONTANI, F. *Novae Eruditorum Deliciae.* Florentiae, 1785–93, 3 vols.

FOURNIER, P. L'origine de la Collection Anselmo Dedicata. *Mélanges P. F. Girard*, Paris, 1912.

—— Un Groupe de Recueils canoniques Italiens. *Mém. Inst. Acad. Inscript. Belles-Lettres* (1915), vol. XL.

—— Les deux recensions de la Collection Canonique Romaine dite le Polycarpus. *Mélanges d'Archéol. et d'Hist.* (1918–19), vol. XXXVII.

—— Les Collections canoniques attribuées à Yves de Chartres. *Bibl. de l'École des Chartes* (1897), vols. LVII, LVIII.

—— Yves de Chartres et le Droit Canonique. *Revue des Questions historiques* (1898), t. LXIII.

—— Le premier manuel canonique de la Réforme Grégorienne. *Mélanges d'Archéol. et d'Hist.* vol. XIV. Paris, 1894.

—— La Collection Canon. dite Caesaraugustana. *Nouv. Revue Hist. de Droit Franç. et Étranger* (1921), vol. XLV.

FOURNIER, P.-LE BRAS, G. *Histoire des Collections Canoniques en Occident*, 2 vols. Paris, 1931–2.

FRIEDBERG, E. A. *Corpus Juris Canonici*, 2 vols. Lipsiae, 1879, 1881.

FRIEDRICH, J. *Turrecremata, J. de. De potestate Papae et Concilio Generali tractatus notabilis.* Oeniponti, 1871.

GAY, J. L'Italie Méridionale et l'Empire Byzantin (867–1071). (*Bibliothèque des Écoles Françaises d'Athènes et de Rome*, fasc. 90.) Paris, 1904.

GELZER, H. Das Verhältnis von Staat und Kirche in Byzanz. *Ausgew. Kleine Schriften.* Leipzig, 1907.

—— Die Konzilien als Reichsparlamente. Ibid. Leipzig, 1907.

—— Der Patriarchat von Achrida. *Abh. sächs. Ges.* (*Akad.*) *Wiss.* (Phil.-Hist. Kl.), Bd XX, 1902.

—— *Byzantinische Kulturgeschichte.* Tübingen, 1909.

—— Die Genesis der Byzantinischen Themenverfassung (1899). *Abh. sächs. Ges.* (*Akad.*) *Wiss.* (Phil.-Hist. Kl.), vol. XVIII, 5.

—— Ungedruckte u. Ungenügend Veröffentliche Texte der Notitiae Episcopatuum.... *Abh. bayr. Akad. Wiss.* (Philos.-Phil. Kl.), Bd XXI, 1901.

—— *Georgii Cyprii Descriptio Orbis Romani* (Leipzig, 1890).

GERAZIM YARED. Otzuivui sovremennikov o sv. Fotiye Patr. Konst. *Khristyanskoe Chtenie*, 1872–3.

GERSON, J. CHARLIER DE. *See* List of Sources.

GFRÖRER, A. F. *Allgemeine Kirchengeschichte.* Stuttgart, 1841–6.

GIESEBRECHT, W. Die Gesetzgebung der Römischen Kirche zur Zeit Gregor VII, München. *Historisches Jahrbuch f. das Jahr 1866.*

GLANVELL, V. WOLF VON. *Die Kanonensammlung des Kardinals Deusdedit.* Paderborn, 1905.

GLANVELL, V. WOLF VON. Die Kanonensammlung des Cod. Vatic. Lat. 1348. *S.B. Akad. Wiss. Wien* (Phil.-Hist. Kl.), vol. CXXXVI, 1897.

GOLUBKOV, O. Novuiya Izsledovaniya o Vremeni i Lichnosti Patr. Fotiya. Published in *Pravoslavnoe Obozryenie*, 1868.

GORDILLO, M. Photius et Primatus Romanus. *Orientalia Christiana Periodica*, vol. VI. Rome, 1940.

GRAMATICA, L. and GALBIATI, G. Il Codice Ambrosiano del *Liber Diurnus* Rom. Pont. *Analecta Ambrosiana*, vol. VII. Milan-Rome, 1921.

GRATIUS, O. *Fasciculus Rer. expet. et fug.* See Brown, E. G.

GRÉGOIRE, H. Une Inscription datée au Nom du Roi Boris-Michel de Bulgarie. *Byzantion* (1939), vol. XIV.

—— L'Empereur Maurice s'appuyait-il sur les Verts ou les Bleus? *Ann. de l'Institut Kondakov*, 1938.

—— Maurice le Marcioniste, l'Empereur Arménien et Vert. *Byzantion* (1938), vol. XIII.

—— Une inscription au nom de Constantin III, ou la liquidation des Partis à Byzance. *Byzantion* (1938), vol. XIII.

—— Le Peuple de Constantinople (Manojlović' Carigradski Narod translated into Fernch). *Byzantion* (1936), vol. XI.

—— Études sur le IXe siècle. *Byzantion* (1933), vol. VIII.

—— Inscriptions historiques Byzantines. *Byzantion* (1927–8), vol. IV.

—— Michel III et Basile le Macédonien dans l'inscription d'Ancyre. *Byzantion* (1929–30), vol. V.

GREINACHER, A. *Die Anschauungen des Papstes Nikolaus I über das Verhältnis von Staat und Kirche.* Berlin, 1909.

GRUMEL, V. Autour du Voyage de Grossolanus à Constantinople. *Échos d'Orient* (1933), vol. XXXII.

—— La politique religieuse du Patriarche St Méthode. Ibid. (1935), vol. XXXIV.

—— *Les Regestes des Actes du Patriarcat de Constantinople*, vols. I and II. Istanbul, 1932, 1936.

—— Le Filioque au Concile Photien de 879–880. *Échos d'Orient* (1930), vol. XXIX.

—— 'Y eut-il un second Schisme de Photius?' *Revue des Sciences phil. et théol.* (1933), vol. XII.

—— 'L'encyclique de Photius aux Orientaux,' *Échos d'Orient* (1935), vol. XXXIV, pp. 129–38.

—— La Liquidation de la Querelle Photienne. Ibid. (1934), vol. XXXIII.

—— Chronique des Événements du Règne de Léon VI. Ibid. (1936), vol. XXXV.

—— La Genèse du Schisme Photien. *Studi Bizantini e Neo-Ellenici* (1939), vol. V.

—— Qui fut l'Envoyé de Photius auprès de Jean VIII? *Échos d'Orient* (1933), vol. XXXII.

—— Formose ou Nicolas Ier? Ibid. (1934), vol. XXXIII.

—— Le Décret du Synode Photien de 879–880 sur le Symbole de Foi. Ibid. (1938), vol. XXXVII.

—— Les Lettres de Jean VIII pour le Rétablissement de Photius. Ibid. (1940), vol. XXXIX.

GUILLAND, R. *Essai sur Nicéphore Grégoras.* Paris, 1926.

HABERT, I. *Archieraticon. Liber Pont. Ecclesiae Graecae.* Paris, 1643, 1676 (2nd ed.).

HALLER, J. *Das Papsttum, Idee und Wirklichkeit*. Stuttgart, 1934.

—— *Nikolaus I und Pseudo-Isidor*. Stuttgart, 1936.

—— *Concilium Basiliense*. Basel. Vols. I–IV, 1896–1903; vols. V, VI (G. Beck-mann, R. Wackernagel), 1914, 1926; vol. VII (H. Herre), 1910.

HANKIUS, M. *De Byzantinarum Rerum Scriptoribus Graecis*. Lipsiae, 1677.

HARDT, H. VON DER. *See* List of Sources, *Acta Concilii Constantiensis*.

HAUCK, A. *Der Gedanke der päpstlichen Weltherrschaft bis auf Bonifaz VIII*. Leipzig, 1904.

—— *Kirchengeschichte Deutschlands*, 5 vols. Leipzig, 1887–1920.

HAUSHERR, I. *See* A. Vogt.

HAVET, J. *Lettres de Gerbert—Collection de Textes pour servir à l'Étude et à l'Enseignement de l'Histoire*. Paris, 1889.

HEFELE, C. J. and LECLERCQ, H. *Histoire des Conciles*. Paris, 1907–14.

HEINECKE, J. M. (HEINECCIUS). *Eigentliche u. Wahrhaftige Abbildung der Alten u. Neuen Griechischen Kirche*. Leipzig, 1711.

HEINTKE, F. Humbert von Romans, der fünfte Ordensmeister der Dominikaner. *Hist. Studien*, Heft 222. Berlin, 1933.

HEISENBERG, A. Die Unionsverhandlungen vom 30 August, 1206. Patriarchen-wahl u. Kaiserkrönung in Nikaia, 1208. *S.B. bayr. Akad. Wiss.* München, 1923.

HENZE, W. Über den Brief Kaiser Ludwigs II an Kaiser Basilius I. *Neues Arch. Ges. ältere dtsch. Geschichtskunde* (1910), vol. XXXV.

HERGENRÖTHER, J. *Photius, Patriarch von Konstantinopel*, 3 vols. Regensburg, 1867–9.

—— *Monumenta Graeca ad Photium pertinentia*. Ratisbonnae, 1869.

HIRSCH, F. *Byzantinische Studien*. Leipzig, 1876.

HOLTZMANN, W. Unionsverhandlungen zwischen Kaiser Alexis I u. Papst Urban II im Jahre 1089. *Byz. Zeitschr.* (1928), vol. XXVIII.

HÖTTINGER, J. H. *Historiae Ecclesiasticae Novi Testamenti Enn. I*. Tiguri, 1651.

INNOKENTIS (ILARION SMIRNOV). *Nachertanie Tserkovnoi Istorii*. St Petersburg, 1817.

IVANTSOV-PLATONOV. *Sv. Patriarkh Fotii*. St Petersburg, 1892.

JACOBATIUS, CARDINALIS CH. De concilio, *Tractatus*, vol. XIII, 1. Venetiis, 1584.

JAFFÉ, PH. and EWALD, P. *Regesta Pontificum Romanorum*, 2 vols. Lipsiae, 1885–8.

JAGER, J. N. *Histoire de Photius et du Schisme des Grecs*. Paris, 1844.

JANIN, R. Au lendemain de la conquête de Constantinople. *Échos d'Orient* (1933), vol. XXXII.

JANSSENS, Y. Les Bleus et les Verts sous Maurice, Phocas et Heraclius. *Byzantion* (1936), vol. XI.

JUGIE, M. *Œuvres complètes de Gennadie Scholarios*. Paris, 1929–38.

—— *Theologia Dogmatica Christ. Orient*. Paris, 1926 seq.

—— Homélies Mariales Byzantines. *Patrologia Orientalis*, vol. XVI. Paris, 1922, 1926.

—— Le Culte de Photius dans l'Église Byzantine. *Revue de l'Orient Chrétien* (1922–3; 3rd ser.), t. III.

—— Demetrius Cydonès et la Théologie Latine à Byzance aux XIVe et XVe siècle. *Échos d'Orient* (1928), vol. XXXI.

—— Les Actes du Synode Photien de Ste Sophie. *Ibid*. (1938), vol. XXXVII.

JUGIE, M. Schisme. *Dict. de Théol. Cath.* (1939), t. XIV.

—— Le Schisme Byzantin. Paris, 1941.

JUSTELLUS, CHR. *See* List of Sources.

KALLEN, G. Cusanus-Texte. De Auctoritate Praesidendi in Concilio Generali. *S.B. heidelberg. Akad. Wiss.* (Phil.-Hist. Kl.), 1935.

KNELLER, C. A. Papst u. Konzil im ersten Jahrtausend. *Zeitschr. Kath. Theologie* (1904), vol. XXVIII.

KOSTOMAROV, N. I. Patriarkh Fotii i Pervoe Razdyelenie Tserkvei. Published in *Vyestnik Evropui*, 1868, books I and II.

KRUMBACHER, K. *Geschichte der Byzantinischen Litteratur.* München, 1897.

KURGANOV, TH. A. 'K izsledovaniyu o Patr. Fotiye', *Khrist. Chtenie*, 1895.

LABBE, P. *De Scriptoribus Ecclesiasticis quos attigit R. Bellarminus.* Parisiis, 1660.

LAEHR, G. Briefe und Prologe des Bibliothekars Anastasius. *Neues Arch. Ges. ältere dtsch. Geschichtskunde* (1927), vol. XLVII.

LAELIUS, J. De Romanae Sedis origine et auctoritate. *Tractatus*, vol. XIII, 2. Venice, 1584.

LAIR, J. A. *Études critiques sur divers Textes des Xe et XIe s.*, t. I. Paris, 1899.

LAMBECIUS, P. *Commentarii de August. Bibl. Caesarea Vindobonensi* (2nd ed., A. F. Kollar), vol. VIII. Vindobonae, 1782.

LÄMMER, H. *Papst Nikolaus I u. die byzantinische Staatskirche.* Berlin, 1857.

LANGEN, J. *Geschichte der Römischen Kirche von Gregor VII. bis zu Innozenz III.* Bonn, 1893.

LAPÔTRE, A. Hadrien II et les Fausses Décrétales. *Revue des Questions historiques* (1880), t. XXVII.

—— Le Souper de Jean le Diacre. *Mélanges d'Archéologie et d'Histoire* (1901), t. XXI.

—— *L'Europe et le Saint Siège.* Paris, 1895.

LAUREA, L. B. DE. De Decretis Ecclesiae. *Bibliotheca* (1698), vol. XV.

LAURENT, V. Le Cas de Photius dans l'Apologétique du Patriarche Jean XI Beccos au Lendemain du IIe Concile de Lyon. *Échos d'Orient* (1930), vol. XXIX.

—— Les Actes du Synode Photien et Georges le Métochite. Ibid. (1938), vol. XXXVII.

—— La Vie et les Œuvres de Georges Moschabar. Ibid. (1929), vol. XXVIII.

—— La Correspondance de Demetrius Cydonès. Ibid. (1931), vol. XXXIV.

LAVROVSKII, P. A. *Kiril i Mefodii.* Kharkov, 1863.

LEBEDEV, A. P. Chteniya Obshchestva Lyubitelei Dukhovn. Prosvyeshcheniya, 1873, No. I. (Review of Hergenröther's *Photius*.)

—— *Rimskie Papui v Otnosheniakh k Tserkvi Vizantiiskoi v IX–X. v.* Moscow, 1875.

—— *Istoriya Konst. Soborov IX. v.* Moscow, 1880.

LECHAT, R. La patristique Grecque chez un théologien Latin du XIIe siècle, Hugues Ethérien. *Mélanges d'Histoire offerts à Ch. Moeller.* Louvain, 1914.

LECLERCQ, H. Liber Diurnus. *Dict. d'Archéol. Chrét.* vol. IX, cols. 243–344. Paris, 1930.

LECRIVAIN, CH. Le Sénat Romain depuis Dioclétien à Rome et à Constantinople. *Bibl. des Écoles Franç. d'Athènes et de Rome*, vol. LII. Paris, 1888.

LEDERER, S. *Der Spanische Kardinal Johann von Torquemada.* Freiburg i. B. 1879.

LEGRAND, E. *Lettres de l'Empereur Manuel Paléologue.* Paris, 1893.

LEIB, B. Deux inédits Byzantins sur les azymes. *Orientalia Christiana*, No. 9. Rome, 1924.

LINGENTHAL, ZACHARIAE VON. *Geschichte des Griechischen-Römischen Rechtes* (3rd ed.). Berlin, 1892.

LOPAREV, CHR. Zhitie sv. Evdokima. *I*ʒ*vestiya Russkago Arkh. Inst.* (1908), vol. XIII.

MAAS, M. P. Der Interpolator des Philotheos. *By*ʒ. *Zeitschr.* (1934), vol. XXXIV.

MAASSEN, F. *Eine Römische Synode*. Wien, 1878.

—— *Geschichte der Quellen der Litteratur des can. Rechtes im Abendlande*. Gratz, 1870.

MABILLON, J. *Vetera Analecta*. Parisiis, 1723.

MABILLON, J. and GERMAIN, M. *Museum Italicum*, t. II. Lutetiae Parisiorum, 1724, 2 tom.

MACARIUS MACRES. *See* List of Sources.

MAI, CARDINAL A. *Nova Patrum Bibliotheca*, 10 vols. Roma, 1852–1905.

—— *Spicilegium Romanum*. Roma, 1839–44.

MAIMBOURG, L. *Histoire du Schisme des Grecs*, 2 vols. Paris, 1680.

MARESIUS, S. (DESMARETS). *Joanna Papissa Restituta*. Groningae Frisiorum, 1658.

MARTIN, E. J. *A History of the Iconoclastic Controversy*. London, 1932.

MASTRICHT, GERHARD VON. *Historia Juris Ecclesiastici et Pontificii*. Halae, 1705.

MELETIOS (OF JOANNINA). Ἐκκλησιαστικὴ ἱστορία, 4 vols. Wien, 1783–95.

MENIATES, ELIAS. *Der Stein des Anstosses*. Wien, 1787.

—— *Kamen Sobla*ʒ*na*. St Petersburg, 1783.

MERCATI, CARDINAL G. Per l'Epistolario di Demetrio Cidone. *Studi Bi*ʒ*antini e Neoellenici* (1930), vol. III.

—— Notizie di Procoro e Demetrio Cidone.... Città del Vaticano, 1931 (*Studi i Testi*, vol. LVI).

—— Inno anacreontico alla SS. Trinità di Metrofane Arcivescovo di Smirne. *By*ʒ. *Zeitschr.* (1929–30), vol. XXX.

MICHEL, A. Humbert und Kerullarios, I, II. Paderborn, 1924–30 (*Quellen u. Forschungen*, Bd XXI seq.), 2 vols.

MICHEL, K. *Das Opus Tripartitum d. Humbertus des Romans*, 2 umgearb. Aufl. Graz, 1926.

MIRANDEVIUS, B. CARRANZA. *Summa Conciliorum et Pontificum a Petro usque ad Paulum III*. Salmanticae, 1549.

—— Quatuor Controversiarum de Auctoritate Pontificis et Conciliorum Explicatio. Paris, 1672 (*Ad Concilia a Ph. Labbeo et G. Cossartio edita apparatus alter*, pp. ci seq.).

MÖHLER, L. Kardinal Bessarion als Theologe, Humanist und Staatsmann. Paderborn, 1923. (*Quellen u. Forschungen*..., Görres Gesellschaft, vol. XX etc.).

—— Die Kardinäle Jakob und Peter Colonna. Paderborn, 1914 (*Quellen u. Forschungen*..., Görres Gesellschaft, vol. XVII).

MONTE, P. DE (BRIXIENSIS). Monarchia, sive Tractatus Conciliorum Generalium (ed. N. Chalmot). Lyons, 1512 (in the *Tractatus*, vol. XIII, I).

MORIN, D. G. Un Concile Inédit. *Revue Bénédictine*, 1900.

MURAVIEV, A. N. *Pravda Vselenskoi Tserkvi o Rimskoi i Prochikh Patr. Kafedrakh*. St Petersburg, 1849.

NEANDER, J. A. W. *Allgem. Geschichte der Christl. Religion u. Kirche*, 6 vols. Hamburg, 1825–52.

Nectarios of Jerusalem. Περὶ τῆς ἀρχῆς τοῦ πάπα. Jassy, 1672. *See* Allix, P.

Nissen, W. *Die Regelung des Klosterwesens im Rhomäerreiche bis zum Ende des 9 Jhts.* Hamburg, 1897 (Programm Nr. 759 der Gelehrtenschule des Johanneums).

Norden, W. *Das Papsttum und Byzanz.* Berlin, 1903.

O'Brien Moore. The Roman Senate. Pauly's *Realenzycl. der Classischen Altertumswissenschaft.* Supplementband VI. Stuttgart, 1935.

Ostrogorskii, G. *Studien zur Geschichte des Byzant. Bilderstreites.* Breslau, 1929.

Papadopoulos-Kerameus, A. *Ss. Patris Photii...epistolae XLV.* Petropoli, 1896.

—— Φωτιακά. St Petersburg, 1897.

—— *Monumenta Graeca et Latina ad Historiam Photii pertinentia*, 2 vols. Petropoli, 1901.

—— Ὁ Πατριάρχης Φώτιος ὡς Πατὴρ ἅγιος. *Byz. Zeitschr.* (1889), vol. VIII.

Paradiso, J. de (Jacobus de Clusa). *De Septem Statibus Ecclesiae* (ed. O. Gratius and E. Brown). Fasciculus Rerum expetend., vol. II. London, 1690.

Pargoire, J. Nicolas Mésaritès, Métropolite d'Éphèse. *Échos d'Orient* (1904), vol. VII.

Patetta. Contributi alla Storia del Diritto Romano nel Medio Evo. *Bullettino dell' Istituto di Diritto Romano.* Rome, 1890.

Pavlov, A. *Kriticheskie Opuitui po Ist. drev. Greko-Russkoi Polemiki.* St Petersburg, 1878.

Peitz, W. M. Das Originalregister Gregors VII. *S.B. Akad. Wiss. Wien* (Phil.-Hist. Kl.) (1911), vol. 165.

—— Liber Diurnus. Wien, 1918. *S.B. Akad. Wiss. Wien* (Phil.-Hist. Kl., vol. 185). Cf. also above, p. 318.

—— Das Register Gregors I. Freiburg i. B. 1917 (*Stimmen der Zeit. Ergänzungshefte, Reihe 2. Heft 2*).

Perels, E. *Papst Nikolaus I und Anastasius Bibliothecarius.* Berlin, 1920.

—— Die Briefe Papst Nikolaus I. Die kanonische Überlieferung. *Neues Arch. d. Ges. f. ältere deutsche Geschichtskunde* (1914), vol. XXXIX.

—— Ein Berufungsschreiben Papst Nikolaus' I. zur fränk. Reichssynode in Rom. Ibid. (1906), vol. XXXII.

—— Bonizo, Liber de Vita Christiana. *Texte zur Geschichte des Röm. und Kanon. Rechtes im Mittelalter*, vol. I. Berlin, 1930.

Petit, L. Vie et Office de St Euthyme le Jeune. *Revue de l'Orient Chrétien*, 1903.

—— Documents relatifs au Concile de Florence. *Patrol. Orient.* vol. XVII, 1923.

Pevani, C. *Un Vescovo Belga in Italia nel secolo X.* Torino, 1920.

Pichler, A. *Geschichte der kirchlichen Trennung.* München, 1864-5.

—— *An meine Kritiker.* München, 1865.

Pin, L. E. du (Ellies-Dupin). *Histoire de l'Église en abrégé.* Paris (3e éd. 1719), 4 vols.

—— *Nouvelle Bibliothèque des Auteurs Ecclésiastiques.* Paris, 1690-1703 (2nd ed., 14 vols.).

Pitra, J. B. *Juris Ecclesiastici Graecorum Historia et Monumenta.* Romae, 1864-8, 2 tom.

BIBLIOGRAPHY

PITZPIUS BEY, J. G. *Die Orientalische Kirche*. Wien, 1857 (transl. by H. Schiel).

PLATINA, B. (SACCHI) DE. *See* Sacchi in List of Sources.

POGGIUS, J. F., FLORENTINUS. *De Potestate Papae et Concilii Liber*. J. Beplin, Rome, 1517 (?).

POLE, R. (CARDINAL). *Reformatio Angliae*. Romae, 1562.

POOLE, A. L. *Studies in Chronology and History*. Oxford, 1934.

POPOV, N. *Imperator Lev VI Mudryi i ego Tsarstvovanie*. Moscow, 1892.

PREGER, TH. *Scriptores Originum Constantinopolitan*. Leipzig, 1901–7 (Teubner).

PRIERIO, SILVESTER DA (MAZZOLINI). De Irrefragabili Veritate Rom. Eccl., *Bibliotheca*, vol. XIX. Romae, 1699.

QUIEN, M. LE. *Panoplia Contra Schisma Graecorum*. Paris, 1718.

—— De Processione Spiritus S. Venetiis, 1762 (ed. in *Thesaurus Theologicus . . .* vol. III). *P. G.* vol. 94, cols. 192 seq.

RAMBAUD, A. N. *De Byzantino Hippodromo et Circensibus factionibus*. Paris, 1870.

—— Le monde Byzantin. *Revue des Deux Mondes*, Aug. 15, 1871.

—— *L'Empire Grec du Xe siècle*. Paris, 1870.

RATTI, A. La Fine d' una Leggenda ed altere Spigolature intorno al *Liber Diurnus* Rom. Pont. (*R. Istituto Lombardo di Scienze e Littere*, serie II, vol. XLVI). Milano, 1913.

REES, A. H. *The Catholic Church and Corporate Union*. London, 1940.

RHALLES, G. and POTLES, M. Σύνταγμα τῶν ἱερῶν κανόνων, 6 vols. Athens, 1852–69.

RICHERIUS (RICHER), E. *Historia Conciliorum Generalium* (2nd ed., 4 pts). Coloniae, 1683.

ROCQUAIN, F. *La Papauté au Moyen Age*. Paris, 1881.

RODRIGO DA CUNHA. *See* Cunha.

ROSSEIKIN. *Pervoe Patriarshestvo Patriarkha Fotiya*. Sergiev Posad, 1915.

ROY, J. Principes du pape Nicolas I sur les rapports des deux puissances. *Études d'Histoire du Moyen Age* (dediées à G. Monod). Paris, 1896.

ROZIÈRE, E. DE. *Recueil Général des Formules Usitées dans l'Empire des Francs du Ve au Xe siècles*, 3 vols. Paris, 1859–71.

—— *Liber Diurnus, ou Recueil des Formules Usitées par la Chancellerie Pontificale du Ve au XIe siècles*. Paris, 1869.

RUNCIMAN, J. C. S. *A History of the First Bulgarian Empire*. London, 1930.

SÄGMÜLLER, J. B. *Die Tätigkeit und Stellung der Kardinäle bis Papst Bonifaz VIII*. Freiburg i. B. 1896.

—— Die Idee Gregors VII vom Primat in der päpstlichen Kanzlei. *Theol. Quartalschrift*, Tübingen, vol. LXXVIII, 1896.

—— *Zur Geschichte der Entwicklung des päpstlichen Gesetzgebungsrechtes*. Rottenburg a. N. 1937.

SAKKELION, J. Λέοντος Μαγίστρου . . . , Συμεὼν ἄρχ. Βουλγαρίας καὶ τινῶν ἄλλων ἐπιστολαί, in Δελτίον τῆς ἱστορ. καὶ ἐθνολ. ἑταιριάς τῆς Ἑλλάδος, vol. I, 1883.

SANTIFALLER, L. *Über die Verwendung des Liber Diurnus in der päpstl. Kanzlei . . . .* Münster i. W. 1925 (Festgabe H. Finke).

—— Die Verwendung des *Liber Diurnus* in den Privilegien der Päpste . . . . *Mitteilungen des Instituts f. Öster. Geschichtsforsch.* vol. XLIX, 1935.

—— Zur Liber Diurnus-Forschung. *Hist. Zeitschr.* (1940), vol. CLXI, pp. 532–8.

SANTIFALLER, L. Neue Forschungen zur ält. Papstdiplomatik.... *Forschungen und Fortschritte* (1938), vol. XIV.

SATHAS, C. *Bibliotheca Graeca Medii Aevi.* Venice, 1872–94 (7 vols.).

SCHARDIUS, S. *Syntagma Tractatuum de Imperiali Jurisdictione.* Argentorati, 1609.

SCHEDEL, H. *Registrum hujus operis libri cronicarum cum figuris et ymaginibus de Initio Mundi.* Nuremberg, 1493.

SCHEFFER-BOICHORST, P. *Die Neuordnung der Papstwahl durch Nikolaus II.* Strassburg, 1879.

SCHMIDT, J. *Des Basileus aus Achrida...unedierte Dialoge.* München, 1901.

SCHMITT, H. J. *Die Morgenländische Griechisch-Russische Kirche.* Mainz, 1826.

SCHRÖCKH, J. M. *Historia Religionis et Ecclesiae Christianae* (ed. by P. Marheineke; 7th ed.). Berlin, 1828.

SCHULTE, J. F. VON. Zur Geschichte der Literatur über das Dekret Gratians. *S.B. Akad. Wiss. Wien* (Phil.-Hist. Kl., vols. LXIII–LXV), 1870.

—— Die Glosse zum Dekret Gratians. *Denkschr. Akad. Wiss. Wien* (Phil.-Hist. Kl., vol. XXI), 1872.

—— *Die Summa des Pancapalea über das Decretum Gratiani.* Giessen, 1890.

—— *Die Summa des Stephanus Tornacensis.* Giessen, 1891.

—— *Die Geschichte der Quellen u. Litt. d. can. Rechts.* Stuttgart, 1875–80 (3 vols.).

—— Über drei in Prager Handschriften enthaltenen Canonensammlungen. *S.B. Akad. Wiss. Wien* (Phil.-Hist. Kl., vol. LVII), 1867.

SCHWEINBURG, K. Die Textgeschichte des Gespräches mit den Franken von Nicetas Stethatos. *Byz. Zeitschr.* (1934), vol. XXXIV.

SDRALEK, M. Wolfenbüttler Fragmente. *Kirchengeschichtliche Studien*, vols. I, II. Münster i. W. 1891.

SERARIUS, N. *Moguntiacarum Rerum ab Initio ad...hodiernum Archiepiscopum libri V.* Moguntiae, 1604.

SESAVNICZKY, M. *Ex Historia Eccl. P. Nat. Alex. De Schismate Graecorum.* Vienna, 1780.

SGOUROPULOS, SILVESTER. *See* Syropoulos.

SICKEL, TH. VON. Prolegomena zum Liber Diurnus. Vienna, 1889. *S.B. Akad. Wiss. Wien* (Phil.-hist. Kl., Bd CXVII).

—— *Liber Diurnus Roman. Pontificum.* Wien, 1889.

SIMONIADES, C. ᾽Ορθοδ. Ἑλλήνων θεολογικαὶ γραφαὶ τέσσαρες. London, 1859.

SINGER, H. *Die Summa Decretorum des Magister Rufinus.* Paderborn, 1902.

SOKOLOV, I. *Sostoyanie Monashestva v Viz. Tserkvi s polov. IX do nachala XIII v.* Kazan, 1894.

SOPHOCLES OIKONOMOS. *Photius ad Amphilochium.* Athens, 1858.

SOUCHON, M. *Die Papstwahlen von Bonifaz VIII bis Urban VI.* Braunschweig, 1888.

SPANHEIM, F. Historiae Christianae s. IX; De Schismate Photiano. *Opera*, vol. I. Lugd. Batav. 1701.

SPINKA, M. *A History of Christianity in the Balkans.* Chicago, 1933.

SPITTLER, L. T. *Grundriss der Geschichte der Christl. Kirche* (2nd ed.). Göttingen, 1785.

STAPLETON, T. De Conciliis. *Bibliotheca*, vol. XX. Romae, 1699.

STAUBER, R. and HARTIG, O. Die Schedelsche Bibliothek (*Studien u. Darstell. aus dem Gebiete der Geschichte*, Bd VI). Freiburg i. B. 1908.

BIBLIOGRAPHY

STEIN, E. *Geschichte des Spätrömischen Reiches*, vol. I. Wien, 1928.

STEINACKER, H. Zum *Liber Diurnus* und zur Frage nach dem Ursprung der Frühminuskel. *Studi e Testi*, vol. XL (Miscellanea F. Ehrle, vol. IV). Rome, 1924.

STEVENSON, E. Osservazioni sulla Collectio Canonum di Deusdedit. *Archivio della R. Storia Patria*, vol. VIII. 1885.

SWALUE, E. B. *Disputatio Academica Inauguralis de Dissidio Eccl. Christianae in Graecam et Latinam Photii Auctoritate Maturato*. Lugd. Batav. 1829.

SWETE, H. B. *Theodorus Lascaris Junior de Processione Spiritus S.* London, 1875.

SYROPOULOS, S. (SGOUROPOULOS). *Vera Historia unionis non verae* (ed. R. Creighton). Hagae-Comitis, 1660.

TANGL, M. Gregor. Register und *Liber Diurnus. Neues Arch. ältere dtsch. Geschichtskunde* (1919), vol. XLI.

—— Die Fuldäer Privilegienfrage. *Mitteil. Inst. Österr. Geschichtsforsch.* (1899), vol. XX.

TARDIF, A. *Histoire des Sources du Droit Canonique*. Paris, 1887.

TARDIF, I. Une Collection Canonique Poitevine. *Nouv. Rev. Hist. du Droit Franç. et Étranger* (1897), vol. XXI.

THANER, F. *Anselmi, episcopi Lucensis, collectio canonum una cum collectione minore*. Oeniponte, 1906.

—— *Die Summa Magistri Rolandi, nachmals Papstes Alexander III*. Innsbruck, 1874.

THEINER, A. *Disquisitiones Criticae in praecipuas canonum et decretalium collectiones*. Romae, 1836.

THIEL, A. *De Nicolao I papa commentationes duae historico-canonicae*. Brunsbergae, 1859.

TORQUEMADA, J. DE (TURRECREMATA). *See* List of Sources.

TRINITATE, DE S., S. DOMINICUS. De Summo Pontifice, de Sacris Conciliis. *Bibliotheca*, vol. X.

TRITHEMIUS, J. (TRITHEIM). *De Scriptoribus Ecclesiasticis* (ed. Fabricius, *Bibliotheca Ecclesiastica*). Hamburg, 1718.

USPENSKI, TH. J. *Ocherki po istorii Viz. obrazovannosti*. St Petersburg, 1892.

—— Partii tsirka i Demy v Konstantinopole, *Viz. Vremennik*, I, 1894.

—— Sinodik v nedyelyu Pravoslaviya. *Zapiski Imp. Novorossiiskago Universiteta* (Odessa, 1893), vol. LIX.

VAFEIDOS, FILARET. Ἐκκλησιαστικὴ ἱστορία. Constantinople, 1886.

VALETTA, J. Φωτίου ἐπιστολαί. London, 1864.

VASILIEV, A. A. *History of the Byzantine Empire*. (Univ. of Wisconsin Studies in the Soc. Sci. and Hist., nos. 13 etc.) Madison, 1928–9.

—— The Struggle with the Saracens. *Cambridge Medieval History*, vol. IV (1927).

VIO, THOMAS DE. *See* List of Sources.

VOGEL, A. *Ratherius von Verona*. Jena, 1854.

VOGT, A. *Basile Ier*. Paris, 1908.

—— Deux Discours inédits de Nicétas de Paphlagonie. *Orient. Christ.* no. LXXVI. Rome, 1931.

—— La Jeunesse de Léon VI le Sage. *Revue Historique* (1934), vol. CLXXIV.

VOGT, A. and HAUSHERR, I. L'Oraison funèbre de Basile I. *Orientalia Christiana*, no. XXVI, 1. Rome, 1932.

VORST, C. VAN DE. La Vie de Saint Évariste. *Analecta Boll.* (1923), vol. XLI.

—— Note sur St Joseph l'Hymnographe. Ibid. (1920), vol. XXXVIII.

WALCH, CH. W. F. *Entwurf einer Vollständigen Historie der Kirchenversammlungen.* Leipzig, 1759.

WALCH, J. G. *Historia Controversiae Graecorum Latinorumque de Proc. Spiritus S.* Jennae, 1751.

WEISMANN, C. E. *Introductio in Memorabilia Ecclesiastica Historiae Sacrae Novi Testamenti*, 2 vols. Halae Magdeburgicae, 1745.

WERINGHOFF, A. Verzeichnis der Akten fränk. Synoden. *Neues Arch. ältere deutsche Geschichtskunde* (1901), vol. XXVI.

WILKEN, F. Die Parteien der Rennbahn, vornehmlich im Byzantinischen Kaisertum. *Abh. preuss. Akad. Wiss.* (Phil.-Hist. Cl.), 1827.

WILL, C. *Acta et Scripta quae de controversiis eccl. Graecae et Latinae s. XI extant.* Leipzig, 1861.

WRIGHT, F. A. *The Works of Liudprand of Cremona.* London, 1930.

YARED. *See* GERAZIM Y.

ZACHARIAE V. LINGENTHAL. *See* Lingenthal.

ZEUMER, K. Formulae Merovingici et Karolini Aevi. *M.G.H.* Legum Sectio V, Formulae. Hanover, 1882–6.

ZLATARSKI, V. N. *Istoria na Blgarskata Drzhava*, vols. I, II. Sofia, 1918, 1927.

—— Blgarski Arkhiep.-Patriarsi Pryez prvoto Tsarstvo. *Izv. Istor. Druzhestvo*, kn. VI, 1924.

ZOEPFFEL, R. *Die Papstwahlen u. die mit ihnen im nächsten Zusammenhang stehenden Ceremonien in ihrer Entwicklung vom 11. bis zum 14. Jh.* Göttingen, 1871.

INDEX

INDEX

Habrudunum, 258
Hadrian I, Pope, 90, 174, 395, 436
Hadrian II, Pope, 30
  and anti-Photian Collection, 216–19,
    221, 222
  and Council of 869: 138–50, 153–8
  and Council of 879: 159–61, 164, 180,
    184, 186, 189, 193, 204, 211
  Roman synod of 867: 128–31
  varia, 231, 234, 235, 252, 254, 255,
    281, 282, 284, 304, 305, 309, 329,
    344, 359, 361, 362, 363, 370, 371,
    376, 377, 404, 405, 415, 421, 443
Hadrian III, Pope, 196, 220, 221, 224,
    225, 228, 232, 282, 368, 399
Hadrian IV, Pope, 397
Hagiopolites, John, 247
Haller, J., 97
Hanke, M., 378, 379
Hardouin, I., 366, 375
Havet, J., 310
Hefele, 430
Heinecke, J. M., 379
Helias, spathar and drungary, 163
Helinandi Chronicon, 312
Henry IV, Emperor, 293
Heraclea, 52
Heraclius, Emperor, 6, 7, 315
Hergenröther, J., Cardinal, 64, 72, 79,
    97, 125–7, 129, 137, 149, 188, 195,
    197, 204, 240, 251, 263, 381, 382,
    397, 400, 411, 429, 430
Herimannus Augiensis Contractus, 311
Hérivée, archbishop of Rheims, 287
Hexamilium, 64
Hiera, Isle of, 56, 247
Hildesheim, Annals of, 311
Hincmar, bishop of Laon, 280
Hincmar, chronicler, archbishop of
    Rheims, 115, 118, 119, 123, 124,
    280, 281, 286, 287, 309, 310
Hippodrome, 38, 132
Holy (Roman) See, 19, 24, 25, 27, 29,
    31, 32, 35, 48, 73, 74, 81, 82, 86,
    89, 90, 91, 93, 97, 98, 100, 101, 104,
    107, 108, 110, 112, 113, 124, 125,
    127, 128, 138, 143, 144, 146, 147,
    150, 153, 154, 156, 162, 171, 174,
    175, 177, 181, 188, 190, 193, 194,
    196, 199, 201, 208, 211, 214, 220,
    222, 229, 232, 234, 236, 241, 251,
    254, 258, 271, 272, 282, 283, 286–8,

293, 299, 300, 307, 309, 322, 330,
    351, 395, 408, 441, 442, 450
Honorius I, Pope, 438
Hormisdas, Pope, 90, 144
Höttinger, I. H., 378
Hubaldus, archbishop of Ravenna, 344
Hugh, archbishop of Lyons, 324
Hugh, King, 287
Hugh de Saint-Victor, 350
Hugh of Verdun, chronicler, 295
Hugo Etherianus, 346, 347, 349
Humbertus, Cardinal, 293, 316, 317,
    332, 392
Humbertus de Romanis, 346

Iconoclasm, 2, 3, 7–9, 12, 13, 67–70, 74,
    76, 98, 104, 273, 370, 393, 417
Ignatian schism, 259, 261. *See also*
    Church, the Little
Ignatians, 23, 31, 34, 35, 43, 46, 47, 49,
    50, 52, 54–6, 58, 59, 63, 65, 70, 75,
    87, 99, 100, 102, 169, 176, 178, 185,
    192, 193, 218, 225, 230, 231, 234,
    236, 237, 248, 250, 254, 255, 260–2,
    271, 272, 275–7, 300
Ignatius, St, Patriarch of Constanti-
    nople, 3, 4
  and anti-Photian revolt, 59, 61–5, 68
  and Basil's change of policy, 164–6
  and the Extremists' schism, 275–7
  and Nicholas I, 72–6
  and Nicholas' policy, 94–6
  and Photius' election, 49, 51–6
  and the Pope's legates, 88–91
  and Roman synod of 863: 97–101
  and synod of 861: 77–84
  and synod of 869: 142, 143, 145–7,
    150, 153–8
  and synod of 880: 178–81, 183, 187
  anti-Ignatian campaign, 32–4
  appeal of, 85–7
  Basil and Photius' downfall, 132, 136,
    137, 139, 140
  compromise of, 159–61
  enthronement of, 17, 18
  first difficulties with Asbestas, 21–3
  in Greek tradition, 368, 389, 391,
    400–2, 404, 407, 410, 411, 413–17,
    421, 422, 427, 434
  in Western tradition, 280, 281, 283,
    287, 293, 294, 300, 309, 321, 344,
    353, 368, 370–3, 375–7

494